Understanding Trauma

Integrating Biological, Clinical, and |

This book explores the individual and collective experiences of trauma from the perspectives of neuroscience, clinical science, and cultural anthropology. Each perspective presents critical and conceptual challenges for the development of an integrative model of the impact of trauma. The first section reviews the neurobiology of fear conditioning and extinction, and the effects of early life stress on the development of neural systems related to vulnerability to persistent effects of trauma. The second section of the book reviews a wide range of clinical approaches to the treatment of the effects of trauma in different populations, including refugees. The final section of the book presents cultural analyses of personal, social, and political responses to massive trauma and genocidal events in a variety of societies. This work goes well beyond neurobiological models of conditioned fear and the clinical syndrome of posttraumatic stress disorder to examine how massive traumatic events affect the whole fabric of a society, calling forth collective responses of resilence and moral transformation.

Laurence J. Kirmayer is James McGill Professor and Director, Division of Social and Transcultural Psychiatry in the Department of Psychiatry at McGill University. He is editor-in-chief of *Transcultural Psychiatry*, a quarterly scientific journal, and directs the Culture and Mental Health Research Unit at the Department of Psychiatry, Sir Mortimer B. Davis–Jewish General Hospital in Montreal, where he conducts research on mental health services for immigrants and refugees, the mental health of indigenous peoples, and the anthropology of psychiatry.

Robert Lemelson is currently a lecturer in the Departments of Anthropology and Psychology at the University of California, Los Angeles, and the president of the Foundation for Psychocultural Research (FPR). He is a psychological anthropologist with a specialty in culture and mental illness. He was a Fulbright scholar in Indonesia and is currently releasing several documentary films based on his research on culture and neuropsychiatric disorders. He has published in *Culture, Medicine and Psychiatry; Medical Anthropology Quarterly; Transcultural Psychiatry*; and other journals.

Mark Barad is Associate Professor of Psychiatry and Behavioral Sciences at the University of California, Los Angeles, and has been the Tennenbaum Scholar from the Department of Psychiatry. His current research and writing further explores the development of adjunctive treatments to accelerate and facilitate the behavioral psychotherapy of anxiety disorders. In addition to his research and teaching, Dr. Barad has supervised at the UCLA Anxiety Disorders Clinic and the UCLA General Outpatient Psychiatry Clinic. He also has a private practice as a psychiatrist.

Understanding Trauma

Integrating Biological, Clinical, and Cultural Perspectives

Edited by

LAURENCE J. KIRMAYER
McGill University

ROBERT LEMELSON
The Foundation for Psychocultural Research

MARK BARAD
University of California, Los Angeles

CAMBRIDGE
UNIVERSITY PRESS

CAMBRIDGE UNIVERSITY PRESS
Cambridge, New York, Melbourne, Madrid, Cape Town, Singapore, São Paulo, Delhi

Cambridge University Press
32 Avenue of the Americas, New York, NY 10013-2473, USA

www.cambridge.org
Information on this title: www.cambridge.org/9780521726993

First published 2007
First paperback edition 2008

Printed in the United States of America

A catalog record for this publication is available from the British Library.

Library of Congress Cataloging in Publication Data
Understanding trauma : integrating biological, clinical, and cultural
perspectives / edited by Laurence Kirmayer, Robert Lemelson, Mark Barad.
    p. ; cm.
Includes bibliographical references and index.
ISBN-13: 978-0-521-85428-3 (hardback)
ISBN-10: 0-521-85428-8 (hardback)
1. Post-traumatic stress disorder – Social aspects. 2. Post-traumatic stress
disorder – Physiological aspects. I. Kirmayer, Laurence J., 1952– .
II. Lemelson, Robert, 1952– . III. Barad, Mark, 1961– .
[DNLM: 1. Stress Disorders, Traumatic. 2. Cross-Cultural
Comparison. WM 172 U558 2007]
RA552.P67U53   2007
362.196'8521 – dc22   2006014725

ISBN 978-0-521-85428-3 hardback
ISBN 978-0-521-72699-3 paperback

In memory of Carl Gold and Bessie Blanshay, who fled pogroms to find a new life – LJK

Dedicated to Dorothy Lemelson and the memory of Jerome Lemelson: Without your love, assistance, and encouragement, this project and the ongoing work of the FPR would not have been possible – RL

For Ronnie Barad, my sister, who inspired my interest in psychiatry – MB

Contents

List of Figures

List of Tables

List of Contributors

Rosemary Bagot, B. Psych., Graduate student in neuroscience, McGill University, Montréal, Québec.

Mark Barad, M.D., Ph.D., Associate Professor, Department of Psychiatry and Biobehavioral Sciences, University of California, Los Angeles.

Gadi BenEzer, Ph.D., Senior Lecturer, Department of Behavioral Sciences, College of Management, Tel Aviv, Israel.

James K. Boehnlein, M.D., Professor, Department of Psychiatry; Assistant Dean, Oregon Health and Science University; Associate Director for Education, Department of Veterans Affairs Northwest Network, Mental Illness Research, Education, and Clinical Center (MIRECC); President, Society for the Study of Psychiatry and Culture.

Mark E. Bouton, Ph.D., Professor, Department of Psychology, University of Vermont.

Timothy W. Bredy, Ph.D., Postdoctoral Fellow, Department of Psychiatry and Biobehavioral Sciences and Brain Research Institute, University of California, Los Angeles.

J. Douglas Bremner, M.D., Director, Emory Center for Positron Emission Tomography (PET), Atlanta, GA.

Christopher K. Cain, Ph.D., Postdoctoral Fellow, Center for Neural Science, New York University.

Leslie Dwyer, Ph.D., Visiting Assistant Professor, Department of Anthropology; Coordinator, Peace and Conflict Studies Program, Haverford College, PA.

Michael S. Fanselow, Ph.D., Professor, Department of Psychology, University of California, Los Angeles.

Edna B. Foa, Ph.D., Professor, Department of Psychiatry; Director, Center for the Treatment and Study of Anxiety, University of Pennsylvania, Philadelphia.

Alain Gratton, Ph.D., Associate Professor, Department of Psychiatry, McGill University; Researcher, Douglas Hospital Research Centre, Montréal, Québec.

Alexander Hinton, Ph.D., Associate Professor, Department of Anthropology, Rutgers University, Newark, NJ.

J. D. Kinzie, M.D., Professor, Department of Psychiatry; Director, PTSD Clinic; Director, Torture Treatment Center, Oregon, at Oregon Health and Science University.

Laurence J. Kirmayer, M.D., James McGill Professor and Director, Division of Social and Transcultural Psychiatry, McGill University; Director, Culture and Mental Health Research Unit, Sir Mortimer B. Davis–Jewish General Hospital, Montréal, Québec.

Bessel A. van der Kolk, M.D., Professor, Department of Psychiatry, Boston University; Medical Director, HRI Trauma Center, Boston, MA.

Melvin Konner, M.D., Ph.D., Samuel Candler Dobbs Professor, Department of Anthropology and Program in Neuroscience and Behavioral Biology, Emory University, Atlanta, GA.

Kelimer Lebrón, Ph.D., Postdoctoral Fellow, Department of Psychiatry, Massachusetts General Hospital, Charlestown, MA.

Robert Lemelson, Ph.D., Lecturer, Departments of Anthropology and Psychology, University of California, Los Angeles; President, Foundation for Psychocultural Research (FPR); Co-director, Lemelson Foundation.

Emeran A. Mayer, M.D., Professor, Departments of Medicine, Physiology, Psychiatry, and Biobehavioral Sciences, University of California, Los Angeles; Director, Center for Neurovisceral Sciences and Women's Health; Co-director, CURE Digestive Diseases Research Center.

Michael J. Meaney, Ph.D., James McGill Professor of Medicine, Departments of Psychiatry and Neurology and Neurosurgery; Director, Program for the Study of Behaviour, Genes and Environment, McGill University; Associate Director of Research, Researcher, Douglas Hospital Research Centre, Montréal, Québec.

Toby Measham, M.D., M.Sc., Assistant Professor, Department of Psychiatry, McGill University; Transcultural Psychiatry Team, Montréal Children's Hospital, Québec.

Mohammed R. Milad, Ph.D., Instructor, Department of Psychiatry, Harvard Medical School; Assistant in Research, Department of Psychiatry, Massachusetts General Hospital.

Carine Parent, B.Sc., Graduate student, Neurological Sciences Program, McGill University, Montréal, Québec.

Gregory J. Quirk, Ph.D., Professor, Department of Physiology, Ponce School of Medicine, Puerto Rico.

Vinuta Rau, Ph.D., Postdoctoral Fellow, University of California, San Francisco.

Cécile Rousseau, M.D., M.Sc., Associate Professor, Department of Psychiatry, McGill University; Director, Immigrant and Refugee Child Mental Health Research Unit, Montréal Children's Hospital, Québec.

Degung Santikarma, M.A., Balinese anthropologist, Indonesian writer, activist.

Edwin Santini, Ph.D., Postdoctoral Fellow, Department of Pharmacology, Ponce School of Medicine, Puerto Rico.

Arieh Y. Shalev, M.D., Professor of Psychiatry, Hebrew University and Hadassah School of Medicine, Jerusalem, Israel; Chair, Department of Psychiatry and Director, Center for Traumatic Stress, Hadassah University Hospital.

Derrick Silove, M.B., Ch.B., M.D., FRANZCP, Professor, Department of Psychiatry, University of New South Wales; Director, Psychiatry Research and Teaching Unit, Sydney Southwest Area Health Service and Centre for Population Mental Health Research, Sydney, Australia.

Jaylyn Waddell, Ph.D., Postdoctoral associate, Department of Psychology, Rutgers University, NJ.

Elna Yadin, Ph.D., Research associate, Center for the Treatment and Study of Anxiety, University of Pennsylvania, Philadelphia.

Allan Young, Ph.D., Professor, Departments of Social Studies of Medicine, Anthropology, and Psychiatry, McGill University, Montréal, Québec.

Tieyuan Zhang, M.D., Ph.D., Postdoctoral Fellow, Program for the Study of Behaviour, Genes and Environment, McGill University, Montréal, Québec.

Foreword

Robert Jay Lifton, M.D.

As I write this in October 2005, the people of New Orleans and adjacent areas have been experiencing multiple levels of trauma, including the destruction of their homes by fierce winds and lethal flooding; deaths of family and friends, sometimes helplessly witnessed, and their own escape from that fate; loss of contact with family members; and a general breakdown of social order – all with a sense of having been abandoned by their government, which was only partly relieved when help finally arrived.

These forms of trauma were mainly a result of Hurricane Katrina but also of Hurricane Rita, which hit some of the same areas just ten days later. Both storms were extraordinary in their destructive power. Hundreds of thousands of people are undergoing dimensions of trauma that will affect their psyches, their bodies, and their overall sense of human viability. Though some will undoubtedly show impressive resilience in finding new life patterns, many will be left with permanent psychological pain and impairment.

Within just weeks following those hurricanes, a disaster of much greater magnitude occurred in the form of an earthquake in Pakistan, killing at least 40,000 people and leaving millions at profound risk.

This book seeks to explore the scope of human trauma, wherever it occurs. The diagnostic category of posttraumatic stress disorder becomes a baseline, a psychological indicator. Any such category will have its contradictions and confusions, but it does at least provide a structure for a very real and often neglected form of human suffering. In pursuing the ramifications of posttraumatic stress disorder, we are engaged not only in a scientific project but in an ethical one as well. Our challenge is to bring both compassion and intellectual rigor to the full array of suffering associated with trauma, from that of the individual person to the all-inclusive human community, and to seek understanding of interactions that occur at every level.

A dramatic example of these interlocking levels of trauma comes from my own study of Hiroshima survivors. At the individual-psychological level, I found that survivors who had been sufficiently close to the hypocenter of the bomb experienced a lifelong immersion in death: a sequence of exposure to a sea of death at the moment of the explosion; the witnessing or experiencing of acute radiation effects during the days and weeks that followed and of delayed effects in the form of leukemia and other cancers years later; and finally the acquisition of the death-haunted identity of the *hibakusha*, or atomic-bomb survivor. Some survivors experienced an overarching sense of the end of everything. A history professor described climbing a hill and then looking down in astonishment to see that "Hiroshima had disappeared. . . . Hiroshima didn't exist – that was mainly what I saw – Hiroshima just didn't exist." And a physicist told me of noting how black his body had become and that "everything seemed dark, dark all over. Then I thought, 'The world is ending.'" In a single sentence, he connected the burns on his body with an early sense of the danger that the new weapon posed for humankind.

Many survivors found meaning in conveying that danger by telling their stories, whether to others in Hiroshima or to people in various parts of the world. These energetic efforts to contribute to broader knowledge and wisdom could also enhance their own healing.

Here we encounter survivors' consuming struggle for meaning, for some kind of edifying narrative that can render their pain significant. No event, however traumatic, contains inherent meaning. Rather, such meaning is constructed by those exposed directly to it and by others more removed from it.

Meanings can vary enormously, as was impressed on me by two polarized responses to the Holocaust in the late 1960s. A group calling itself the Jewish Defense League, some of whose members came from survivor families, embraced the slogan "Never again!" and took on a quasifascist character, invoking the Holocaust to justify violence against designated enemies. At about the same time, a group of Auschwitz survivors asked me to join them in protesting the massacre by U.S. soldiers of 500 Vietnamese civilians in the village of My Lai, an atrocity which had just been reported in the American press. As one Auschwitz survivor put it, the My Lai massacre was "too close" to his own experience. However antithetical these two meanings, both were expressed with the searing emotion that an overwhelming immersion in death can evoke.

Our country has been undergoing what I call a war over meaning. Hurricanes Katrina and Rita occurred at a time of painful national conflict in relation to the Iraq war, when official assertions of its nobility and necessity were being questioned. Those doubts about Iraq have especially entered into responses to Katrina. With that hurricane, the lines between a natural disaster and a manmade disaster became completely blurred. There were decisive errors of human negligence – failure to take steps to protect a highly vulnerable city and, longer term, to control global warming, which scientists believe contributed greatly to the magnitude of destruction. We are led to ask whether every disaster is not in some measure manmade, whatever the natural forces at play.

No one can completely escape elements of responsibility for the traumatic events that bedevil our world, least of all those of us who are professionally concerned with what we call posttraumatic stress disorder. As a significant part of our professional responsibility, we do well to probe energetically not just the effects but the causes of trauma and to raise our voices publicly in contesting these destructive forces and in advocating more life-enhancing social policies.

Preface

The idea for an interdisciplinary book on trauma emerged from a series of workshops organized and funded by the nonprofit Foundation for Psychocultural Research (FPR). The FPR was founded in 2000 by Robert Lemelson to support interdisciplinary work in neuroscience, psychology, and anthropology. The FPR is dedicated to bringing researchers and clinicians together to think across disciplinary boundaries and address issues of fundamental clinical and social concern. This book is the first in what we expect will be a series of volumes on work at the intersection of culture, brain, and mind. Participants at the first FPR workshop, "New Research on Culture–Brain Interactions," which took place in Ojai, California, in June of 2001, agreed on psychological trauma as a three-year topical focus that could engage the various disciplines – anthropology, psychology, psychiatry, history, and neurobiology – in meaningful conversation. The incongruity and horror of 9/11 added a sense of urgency to the dialogue, and the second FPR workshop in June 2002 focused specifically on posttraumatic stress disorder as the future conference theme. However, at the urging of the anthropologists, the discussion opened onto a wider set of issues, considering how fear, threat, and danger are experienced across cultures and over time.

Most of the chapters in the present volume are based on papers presented at the first public FPR conference held in December 2002, entitled "Posttraumatic Stress Disorder: Biological, Clinical, and Cultural Approaches to Trauma's Effects," which was co-sponsored by the University of California, Los Angeles. Some of the participants in that conference were unable to contribute to this book and the chapters by Silove, Rousseau and Measham, and BenEzer were invited afterward. All of the contributors have had the chance to read each other's work and have tried to make links across disciplines and domains.

As editors, we have benefited from discussions with many colleagues and friends. Laurence J. Kirmayer thanks his colleagues Allan Young,

Cécile Rousseau, Jaswant Guzder, John Sigal, Eric Jarvis, Carol Kidron, and the participants in our seminar in the anthropology of psychiatry for many stimulating conversations about the cultural and clinical meanings of trauma and its treatment. Deepest thanks to Elizabeth Anthony for her intellectual and creative companionship and unfailing support throughout this project.

Robert Lemelson thanks the FPR board members for their wise stewardship and their provision of funding that enabled the writing of this volume, particularly Dr. Marvin Karno, for suggesting the idea of an interdisciplinary conference on PTSD, and Claudia Mitchell-Kernan and her staff, in particular Susan Townsley of the UCLA Graduate Division, for their invaluable support of our efforts and cosponsorship of the PTSD conference. Special thanks to Dr. Allan Tobin, former head of the Brain Research Institute at UCLA, who has served with such generosity of spirit as a mentor throughout the process. Lemelson also thanks the members of the Culture, Brain, and Development program and the Medicine, Mind, and Culture seminar, both at UCLA, where some of the ideas for this book were explored and discussed. Collaborative work with his Indonesian colleagues was also indispensable, and he wants to thank Dr. Luh Ketut Suryani, Dr. I. Gusti Putu Panteri, Dr. Made Nyandra, and especially Dr. Mahar Agusno and Dra. Ninik Supartini, whose friendship and support throughout his research he deeply appreciates. Finally, deep gratitude to the participants and patients who so generously gave their time to share the stories that provide the basis for the introduction and the concluding chapter.

Mark Barad thanks his generous neuroscience colleagues for their input into the issues surrounding the neuroscience of fear, and particularly Michael Fanselow, Mark Bouton, and Gregory Quirk. A special word of thanks to Marie-Françoise Chesselet for suggesting his participation in the mission of the FPR.

An undertaking of this scope involves many people behind the scenes. Dr. Constance Cummings has provided skillful editorial assistance and sage advice from the inception to the completion of this volume. Dr. Mamie Wong and other staff of the FPR have provided invaluable support. As director of the FPR, Irene Sukwandi skillfully managed the overall process of the conference and book writing project and ensured its smooth unfolding. Her hard work and dedication are reflected in every aspect of this book. We would also like to thank Philip Laughlin, formerly of Cambridge University Press and now at Springer, for guiding us through the proposal process; Eric Schwartz of Cambridge for his editorial guidance; and senior editorial assistant Armi Macaballug, who indefatigably responded to our questions.

Our special thanks to Susan Morse, whose painting graces the cover of this book. Finally, we would like to thank the outstanding scholars and clinicians who have contributed to this volume. It has been a pleasure and a privilege to take part in this colloquy, which we hope will stand as an inspiring example of the creative power of interdisciplinary work.

LJK
RL
MB
Los Angeles, December 2005

List of Abbreviations

β-NGF	nerve growth factor
ABN	arched-back nursing
ACR	acoustic startle response
ACTH	adrenocorticotropic hormone
ANS	autonomic nervous systems
APA	American Psychiatric Association
BDNF	brain-derived neurotrophic factor
bFGF	basic fibroblast growth factor
BNST	bed nucleus of the stria terminalis
BPD	borderline personality disorder
BZ	benzodiazepine
CBT	cognitive behavioral therapy
cDNA	complementary DNA
CE	central nucleus of the amygdala
ChAT	choline acetyltransferase
COMT	catechol-O-methyl transferase
CPP	2-carboxypiperazin-4-yl-propyl-1-phosphonic acid (NMDAr antagonist)
CR	conditioned response
CREB	cAMP-response-element–binding protein
CRF	corticotropin-releasing factor
CRH	corticotropin-releasing hormone
CRH-ir	CRH immunoreactivity
CRH-TG	CRH transgenic (mice)
CS	conditioned stimulus
DCS	D-cycloserine
DHEA	dihydroepiandosterone (DHEA)
DSM	*Diagnostic and Statistical Manual*
DST	dexamethasone suppression test

EMS	emotional motor system
FM	fibromyalgia
fMRI	functional magnetic resonance imaging
GABA	gamma-aminobutyric acid
GAD	glutamic acid decarboxylase
HPA	hypothalamic–pituitary–adrenal (axis)
Hz	hertz
IBS	irritable bowel syndrome
IL	infralimbic cortex
LVGCCs	L-type voltage-gated calcium channels
LDL	low-density lipoprotein
LG	licking and grooming (of rat pups)
LG-ABN	licking and grooming–arched-back nursing (of rat pups)
LTP	long-term potentiation
mPFC	ventral medial prefrontal cortex
N-CAM	neural-cell adhesion molecule
NMDA	N-methyl D-aspartate (receptors)
NR2B	NMDA receptor 2B
PET	positron emission tomography
PL	prelimbic cortex
PPI	prepulse inhibition
PVN(h)	paraventricular nucleus of the hypothalamus
SNS	sympathetic nervous system
SSDRAs	species-specific defense reactions
trkB (mRNA)	neurotrophic tyrosine kinase receptor (messenger RNA)
US	unconditioned stimulus

Introduction: Inscribing Trauma in Culture, Brain, and Body

Laurence J. Kirmayer, Robert Lemelson, and Mark Barad

INTRODUCTION

We live in a world torn and scarred by violence. Globalization has increased the speed and scale of conflicts and catastrophes, but violence has been integral to the human condition from our earliest origins. We should expect, therefore, to find its traces in the design of our brains and bodies no less than in the weave of our communities.

Trauma has become a keyword through which clinicians and scholars from many disciplines approach the experience of violence and its aftermath. The metaphor of trauma draws attention to the ways that extremes of violence break bodies and minds, leaving indelible marks even after healing and recovery. But the notion of trauma has been extended to cover a vast array of situations of extremity and equally varied individual and collective responses. Trauma can be seen at once as a sociopolitical event, a psychophysiological process, a physical and emotional experience, and a narrative theme in explanations of individual and social suffering.

Within psychiatry, much recent work on the psychological impact of trauma has focused on the diagnostic construct of posttraumatic stress disorder (PTSD). The diagnostic criteria for PTSD include a history of exposure to a traumatic event and symptoms from each of three groups: intrusive recollections of the trauma event, avoidance of reminders of the event and emotional numbing, and hyperarousal (American Psychiatric Association [APA], 2000). Although PTSD is just one of many clinically recognizable responses to trauma that often co-occur, it has come to occupy center stage in research, writing, and clinical intervention. This focus is partly because the construct overlaps with animal models of fear conditioning that have allowed experimental studies to begin to tease apart underlying biological mechanisms. Clinically, the emphasis on PTSD reflects the fact that specific treatment interventions based on learning theory are effective in helping some sufferers. Culturally, the diagnosis of PTSD has been an important move in the struggle to determine accountability for suffering and to seek restitution and redress. By connecting current symptoms and suffering to past events, the diagnosis of PTSD assigns causality and, to some degree, responsibility and blame.

Nevertheless, trauma covers a much larger and more ambiguous terrain than the construct of PTSD would suggest, contributing to individual and collective identities and the politics of memory. In this volume, we traverse some of this terrain to explore how different disciplines can contribute to deepening our understanding of the meaning, human consequences, and effective response to traumatic events.

TRAUMA IN THE SURVIVOR'S WORLD

The FPR-UCLA conference on cultural, clinical, and neurobiological perspectives on trauma, from which most of the chapters in this book were drawn, ended with a panel of survivors who gave accounts of their experiences in Congo, Afghanistan, and Laos. The first, a woman who endured the Taliban regime in Afghanistan, spoke eloquently about the oppression her people suffered under both the Soviet occupation and the Taliban, and her own struggles adapting to life in the United States:

We knew life would not be easy here because we were already aware of other Afghanis' living situation here. Still, to escape from a worse situation was not a bad idea. The new place had its own problems: no job, no income, getting new illnesses because of the new environment and living with...other people were stressful. The change of environment [and] an unknown future was just as bad as living in war in our country.... Coming to the United States of America we hoped to get relief. We did get a lot of relief – but it depends on each individual. We need time to melt into the new life and system. We need time to really forget what happened to us in the past. We need to overcome our past, our sorrows and sadness that have been observed in our mind and body, because we are not in a stable mental and physical situation and most of us are not yet able to forget everything easily. All these facts affected our lives here too, because we spend most of our lives in trouble [rather] than in comfort.

This woman had been in ongoing treatment for severe PTSD and associated depression. However, in her moving account, the clinical features of PTSD were not mentioned. Although there were veiled references to the violence she experienced and to continued suffering due to her inability to forget, her story was more about sadness, loss, and longing for her homeland.

The second speaker was a survivor of the civil conflict that swept over the Congo in the late 1990s. Her father, husband, and two children were killed by paramilitary gangs, and she was forced to flee to the United States. She too had symptoms of PTSD – intrusive memories of the massacres she had witnessed, recurrent nightmares in which she saw her murdered children – and depression over the losses she had suffered. Yet what she chose to emphasize in this public recounting was the powerlessness and shame she felt as a refugee needing assistance.

> And emotional problem, also.... I worry very much. I feel insecure. I get like, it was like I lost my self-confidence, you know. For a long time I was a leader. And now for the first time it was like I became a child. I became vulnerable, and I began just to cry for nothing, many times, in front of [the doctor]... it was too much for me. It was too much. For the first time, I have to ask for money, I have to ask for food. People... think that you are stupid because you have not skill... you have nothing and you have nobody... everybody just rejects you here.

The third speaker was from Laos, a highly educated man with a doctorate from the Sorbonne, who had been a member of the Lao government, and who then had been imprisoned by the Pathet Lao regime for many years. He endured torture and deprivation in several prison camps and finally immigrated to the United States. Again, while his clinical history centered around the core symptoms of PTSD – which as a counselor in the trauma clinic working with other Lao survivors, he knew well – his main concerns lay elsewhere:

> So now I want to talk about my illness in terms of PTSD, what I have learned.... Personally, I think I am not a superman. Perhaps I still have some PTSD, but I do not have nightmares, almost never. But of course, sometimes I dream of prison life.... I dream of some prison scene. In general, I think it's ok for me for PTSD. But the most PTSD trait I have is, I think, is I can be startled very quickly, you know. Suppose somebody call me, especially an authority call me, for example, I can be startled. I don't know, you call me for what? Because in prison life, if somebody calls me it's for execution, you know... so here after my release if somebody calls me I can be startled a little bit again.... Also, when I see a place where there is plenty of food, I think automatically [of] my former inmate, because really we did not have food.... Also, I do not feel very confident. And I have a tendency to want to be [in] my own world. I cannot say I am a very strong person, no. Sometimes I want to be alone, I don't want to be with other people, I like my place, my own world, my place, and I stay in my place, and I'm happy because I was in prison for seven years.... Still, I keep something like this... and also I cannot support, I cannot bear for somebody to talk loud... that is my story....

> And if you ask me how I could survive? I think, of course, I was physically strong, but... the physical factor has a limit, I think... you can stand for seven years but you cannot stand... for 30 years. So I think... the most essential thing for me... is psychology. It means you have to think positive in prison, you are what you are, what you think. Ok, this is what you think: "Keep alive.... I am not what you think about me. I am not a bad person."

> The second thing, I think, is my political education... because my background is political, and at that time because Communists told us our system, the social system, is the best in the world.... So I told myself, "Ok your system is good. But I do not agree with you. So I want to stay alive to see between your system and mine, which is the liberal system." ... I told myself, "I want to see – you said 'one

thousand years' – I want to see if your system can stand in our lifetime," I told myself.

A third thing is my character. . . . So, you want me to die, but I don't want to die in prison. So I had to keep alive. And the day I get out of the prison, that day I am the winner, I told myself. That is my character.

The fourth, I think, is love. My wife . . . suffered a lot for me so I want to leave her my love, so I had to keep alive for my wife.

The fifth reason that I can keep alive, I think, is the human rights struggle in the world also, because at the time they released me, 1988, at that time socialism began to change a little bit. But I am realist also, for this reason.

What is clear from all of these accounts is that although the symptoms of PTSD may be identifiable across disparate cultures and contexts, the diagnostic construct captures only part of the experience and concerns of sufferers and survivors. This does not mean that constructs like PTSD have no clinical or scientific utility, but rather that they represent only one strand in a complex reality with biological, personal, social, and political dimensions.

Trauma names a type of situation or outcome, not a discrete disorder or single pattern of injury and response. How then are we to approach the forms of human suffering collected under the notion of trauma? The emphasis on PTSD casts a long shadow in current discussions of trauma, organizing experience, simplifying causal explanations, and directing attention to symptoms in ways that may give a useful focus for treatment, but that may also distort a complex human and social predicament. In this volume, we examine broader notions of traumatic events, experiences, and responses relevant to the concerns of clinicians, neuroscientists, and social scientists.

A GENEALOGY OF TRAUMA

Despite the stark events it names, trauma is not a natural category but a culturally constructed way to mark out certain classes of experiences and events. The salient examples and cultural prototypes of trauma have changed over time, along with our ways of thinking about illness and suffering, our concepts of mind and personhood, and the moral politics of victimhood, blame, and accountability (Leys, 2000; Micale & Lerner, 2001). Trauma is a metaphor borrowed from the domain of medicine and extended to a wide range of experiences. Like any generative trope, the metaphor of trauma shapes our thinking in ways that are both explicit and hidden. The history of trauma, then, is not simply a story of the march of scientific, medical, and psychiatric progress toward greater clarity about a concept with fixed meaning, but a matter of changing social constructions of experience, in the context of particular clinical, cultural, and political ideologies.

The etymology of the word *trauma* goes back to the Greek word for wound. By the mid-1600s, *trauma* appears in medical literature to refer to bodily wounds, and this use of the term continues up to the present in medicine and surgery. Although trauma involves damage to tissue, the body has mechanisms of repair and healing that can restore its integrity and function, albeit often leaving scars. When physical trauma exceeds the body's capacity for repair, there may be lasting damage or death. Severe trauma can lead to a state of cardiovascular collapse, termed *shock*. This idea of shock as an overwhelming of the body's regulatory systems accompanies the notion of trauma throughout its medical history. Just as trauma to the body may result in a loss of physical function, trauma to the head or spinal cord, resulting in a shock to the nervous system, can lead to a loss of behavioral, psychological, or intellectual functioning. Throughout the medical history of trauma, the key concept is that a violent event can cause injury with structural damage to the body and its physiological systems, while also activating bodily systems dedicated to survival, recovery, and repair.

In the late 1800s, this notion of medical or surgical trauma was associated with new types of injury that emerged as unfortunate consequences of industrialization and the accelerating pace of modern life. Accidents in factories or on newfangled machinery and conveyances resulted in new kinds of trauma. The speed of travel itself was viewed as potentially traumatic, and individuals caught in railway accidents might suffer not only from physical injuries but also from a sort of physical shock to the nervous system that left them anxious and ill with "railway spine."

The application of the metaphor of trauma to psychic wounds dates from the late 1800s, and this extension of meaning is crucial for understanding contemporary uses of the term. The use of the term *trauma* for forms of violence associated with industrialization represented not only a social concern about the stresses and strains of modernity but also the beginnings of a shift toward a psychological notion of trauma. At the level of physical injury, while there was some debate about whether the sheer force of certain accidents could result in a new type of nervous shock, what was most obviously different was the person's experience of the nature of the accident.

Although trauma – in the sense of terrifying and violent events, fear, injury, and their aftermath – has been with us through human history and prehistory, current views of the ubiquity of trauma have been substantially shaped by three sets of events: (1) the wars of the twentieth century and the clinical and moral challenges they have raised, (2) the inclusion of PTSD in official psychiatric nosology, and (3) the increasing public and professional recognition of the prevalence and long-term effects of childhood abuse.

The social meaning of war has strongly influenced thinking about the nature of trauma and its impact (Shephard, 2001). Trauma has occurred in its greatest quantity and urgency in the context of wars and genocides.

Hence, the history of trauma is closely associated with the efforts to provide medical services to soldiers and civilians suffering in ever greater numbers as the technology and scale of war have expanded. With each war, new weapons have brought new types of injury and new things to fear. Each war has also left in its wake a cohort of veterans, who have struggled to rebuild lives shattered by injury and loss. However, some of the symptoms reported and viewed as central to war-related trauma have changed over time (Young, 1995, 2002).

In the American Civil War, the nervousness of veterans was conceived of as a physical disability termed "irritable heart" or "DaCosta's syndrome" (Hyams, Wignall, & Roswell, 1996). World War I brought the psychologized notion of "shell shock," which overlapped with previously identified syndromes of neurasthenia and hysteria. The favored construct in World War II was combat neurosis and treatments included hypnosis and emotional abreaction. The Vietnam War led to the introduction of the diagnosis of PTSD, which linked even greatly delayed symptoms to the horrors of war. The Gulf War brought a return to medical conceptions of the bodily effects of war in "Gulf War Syndrome," a collection of medically unexplained somatic symptoms that many psychiatrists believe are due to psychological stress or traumatic experiences, while some continue to search for toxic or infectious causes (Brown et al., 2001; Zavestoski et al., 2004).

Each genocide of the last one hundred years, from the slaughter of Armenians by Turkish forces, to the death camps of Nazi Germany, the killing fields of Pol Pot, and the massacres in Rwanda – the list is hellishly unending – has forced attention to the problem of massive social trauma (Hinton, 2002; Power, 2002). The initial impulse to turn away from distant horrors or to watch them through the controlled and controlling lens of mass media blunts our moral engagement (Dean, 2004; Kaplan, 2005; Sebald, 2003; Sontag, 2003). But clinicians, anthropologists, and those dedicated to advancing human rights and responding to the plight of refugees and displaced peoples insist we address both the immediate and enduring transgenerational impacts of massive trauma on individuals, communities, and whole nations (Agger & Jensen, 1996; Danieli, Rodley, Weisæth, & United Nations, 1996).

The psychiatric construct of PTSD must be understood in relation to the historical, political, and cultural contexts in which it emerged (Young, 1995, 1999). As originally introduced in *DSM–III*, PTSD was portrayed as a normal response to extreme circumstances (APA, 1980). The diagnosis served to link the suffering of Vietnam veterans to the terrible violence they witnessed and participated in.[1] By implying that the response was a direct effect of exposure to horrific violence, the diagnosis of PTSD served

---

[1] In fact, a substantial proportion of the patients with PTSD treated in the VA system and enrolled in research studies actually had no combat exposure (Frueh et al., 2005). This has

to simplify the complex causality and moral meaning of suffering and assign responsibility and blame. The diagnosis of PTSD supported veterans' claims for services and compensation for their war-related disabilities.

Over time, however, it has become evident that only some individuals exposed to extreme events develop symptoms of PTSD and that a variety of personal and social factors predict a poor outcome (Brewin, Andrews, & Valentine, 2000; Shalev, this volume; Yehuda & McFarlane, 1995). Hence, individual and collective vulnerability and resilience have emerged as crucial dimensions in any understanding of the impact of trauma. Clarifying these processes requires longitudinal studies in which a cohort of people is followed before and after exposure to traumatic events.

Trauma theory has moved on from the surgical metaphors of injury and healing to more precise, domain-specific models based on psychological and physiological processes. In popular discourse, however, although psychological notions of trauma have displaced its earlier physical meaning, the metaphor of physical trauma continues to hold sway: In contrast to the body's flexible adaptation to mild stress, severe stressors are thought to rupture, break, or shatter both body and mind.

What distinguishes PTSD from other psychiatric disorders is the attribution of causality and the role that memory plays in its symptomatology – as Allan Young (1995) has observed, memory is the linchpin that holds together trauma and disorder in the construct of PTSD. The dynamics of memory and of attributional processes are crucial for the diagnosis of PTSD because the criteria require that the person remember and attribute his or her symptoms to the traumatic event. Unfortunately, the fallibility of memory sometimes leads to ambiguity about what is veridical recall and what is reconstruction, embroidery, confabulation, or outright fabrication.[2] Add to this the high stakes of forensic settings where opponents try to determine culpability for past wrongs, and there are fertile grounds for conflict. What is at stake is not only psychological health but also moral legitimacy, legal credibility, economic benefits, and political power.[3]

In addition to symptoms related to fear and anxiety, the psychological consequences of trauma may include disturbances of memory, identity, and perception termed *dissociation* (Kihlstrom, 2005; Kirmayer, 1996).[4] The claim that individuals can forget, repress, or dissociate experiences

---

implications for understanding the nature of their distress and for the validity of conclusions drawn from the large amount of research based on this population.

[2] The classic study on the mutability of memory is Bartlett (1932). See also Schacter (1995).

[3] See Laney and Loftus (2005), McNally (1993), and Crews (1995). On the use of "false memory syndrome" to undermine the credibility of women in the courtroom, see Raitt and Zeedyk (2003).

[4] In fact, many types of dissociative experience occur commonly in the absence of trauma and are viewed positively, for example in religious ritual, healing practices, or creative fantasy (Kirmayer, 1994).

of trauma, only to have them cause distress later in time or reemerge in the form of symptoms, fantasies, or recovered memories caused enormous controversy in the 1980s and 90s as claims of "recovered memories" found their way into the courtroom (Appelbaum, Uyehara, & Elin, 1997).

Contrary to popular images and folk psychology, memory does not operate like a camera or videorecorder; that is, it does not record a continuous, accurate photographic copy of events or experiences (Schacter, 1995, 2003). Instead, we have a variety of learning and memory systems that extract details, meanings, and associations from the stream of experience according to specific needs, the ongoing deployment of attention, and cognitive and perceptual salience or relevance. Further, memories are changeable over time; that is to say, they are not fixed or perfect copies of experience but undergo repeated revision and transformation with each attempt at recollection. These basic facts about memory undermine claims about reexperiencing, flashbacks, and the like being the replaying of indelible records, suggesting that more complex processes of reconstruction must be going on (Laney & Loftus, 2005). Reflecting the cultural shaping of memory practices, reports of flashbacks have become more frequent in recent cohorts of British soldiers compared to those in earlier conflicts, who mainly suffered from somatic symptoms (Jones et al., 2003). Much of what gets labeled a flashback may reflect obsessional worry or vivid imagination rather than veridical recall (Frankel, 1994; Lipinski & Pope, 1994). Indeed, in many cases, apparent flashbacks are closer to imagined "worst case scenarios" about which the individual ruminates (Merckelbach, Muris, Horselenberg, & Rassin, 1998). However, it is certainly possible that trauma memories have unique characteristics that reflect the intensity of emotional arousal during their encoding and later retrieval (Brewin, 2005).

The notion that trauma involves a specific form of "body memory" remains contentious (Brewin, 2003; van der Kolk, 1994; van der Kolk, McFarlane, & Weisæth, 1996). Some accounts of body memory conflate two different types of learning: classical conditioning and verbal declarative memory. Declarative memory subserves our ability to describe past experiences and events – this is what is usually meant by memory in colloquial terms. Declarative memory may take episodic and semantic forms, which involve memory for specific scenes and events and memory of the meaning or significance of an event, respectively. Both forms of declarative memory involve reconstruction and usually interact in the process of recollection.

The body (more specifically, circuits involving subcortical and cortical areas of the brain not accessible to consciousness) acquires associations as conditioned emotional responses or habits (e.g., Pavlovian or classical conditioning as described in detail in Section I of this volume), but this does not yield declarative memory, and the origins of the learned association cannot be directly described unless the event was encoded in parallel as declarative memory in the first place. Body memories (conditioned learning and the like) cannot be directly converted into declarative memories. Indeed, in a way they are not memories at all in the colloquial sense of the term but rather learned dispositions to respond in particular ways.[5] Such patterns of conditioned response must be represented and interpreted to construct a declarative memory. Self-reflection or conversation with others may lead us to interpret our current experience in terms of past events and construct an account of how our patterns of response embody and express specific elements of our personal history. Hence, if a declarative memory of a trauma did not exist in the first place, what we end up with is a *post hoc* interpretation or attribution of experience, which – if we forget the way we constructed it – may form a pseudo-memory akin to many apparent childhood memories that are actually reconstructions based on incorporating family stories or photographs into one's own recollections.

The vividness and intensity of bodily experiences in response to conditioned cues is sometimes offered as evidence for the reality and durability of body memories. However, these reactions remain open to many possible attributions or interpretations. We do use the vividness of memories and images to judge whether they are fantasies or real memories, but this is an unreliable guide because vividness depends on imaginative processes and can be easily influenced by suggestions.[6] Further, emotional or psychophysiological reactivity does not confirm the veridicality of memories. McNally and his colleagues found that people who believed they were abducted by aliens showed greater physiological reactivity when recollecting their "memory" than did Vietnam veterans recalling their traumatic combat exposure (McNally & Clancy, 2005; McNally et al., 2004).

The reconstructions of memory always occur in social contexts that warrant certain types of story as more or less credible. The philosopher Ian Hacking has described how increasing recognition of the problem of domestic violence and child sexual abuse provided a setting in which the prevalence of posttraumatic symptoms, particularly dissociative disorders, came to be widely recognized (Hacking, 1991, 1995). This increased recognition was met with skepticism by some and eventually resulted in heated controversy, as dissociative disorders like multiple personality disorder,

---

[5] Indeed, most learning is of this type; that is to say, changes in dispositions to respond in specific contexts constitute our knowledge and skills. For example, we cannot describe the learning and memory that underlie our motor skills or linguistic ability. Most such learning involves what cognitive scientists have called *procedural knowledge*, ways of doing things given the right context and tools at hand. Perhaps declarative memory can also be understood in terms of the procedural learning required to produce a specific descriptive narrative given the requisite cultural and linguistic resources at hand.

[6] See Johnson and Kaye (2000). Ironically, some real memories may lack vividness and this may contribute to the tendency to disbelieve the events.

which were thought to be exceedingly rare, were reported with increasing frequency. Much of this "epidemic" was iatrogenic – due to the influence of clinicians determined to unearth repressed or dissociated memories of childhood abuse (Acocella, 1999). By their very nature, dissociative symptoms are culturally shaped and highly malleable (Kirmayer, 1994). But any attempt to challenge the traumatic origins of dissociative symptoms was viewed as tantamount to a denial of the abuse that had occurred. And such denial in the face of suffering may be experienced as a new betrayal, which constitutes its own trauma (Freyd, 1996).

In recent years, recognition has increased for the ways in which trauma can exert effects across the generations from parent to child to grandchild. This can occur both within families and in whole communities affected by collective trauma. Some have argued for the idea that PTSD itself can be transmitted across generations through secondary traumatization; however, most of these transmitted effects do not resemble PTSD, although some effects, like increased anxiety, might predispose individuals to develop PTSD when exposed to a traumatic event (Danieli, 1998; Newcomb & Locke, 2001; Sigal & Weinfeld, 1989).

Transgenerational transmission of the effects of trauma may include many processes at the level of parent–child interaction within the family: (1) The child may be frightened by the parent's story, a form of secondary traumatization through symbolic presentation of the original trauma, which may be narrated, nonverbally enacted, or obliquely referenced, evoked, and imagined by the child with an intensity that engenders anxiety symptoms. (2) The child may be frightened, worried, or depressed by the parent's symptomatic behavior, which in turn may or may not be attributed to the original parental experience of trauma. (3) The child may be rendered more anxious and vulnerable to trauma as a result of parental anxiety, impaired parenting (parental preoccupation, neglect, overinvolvement, overprotectiveness), abuse, or other patterns of child rearing. (4) Or people may simply learn to attribute their own symptoms of anxiety, depression, interpersonal difficulties, and other non–trauma-related psychiatric disorders to their parents' history of traumatic experiences.

The transgenerational effects of trauma visited on whole communities are still more complex, because massive trauma on a collective level disrupts the fabric of communal life, challenging core social institutions and cultural values. This points to the need to understand how interactions between individual and collective processes contribute to resilience and reconstruction in the aftermath of political violence (Alexander, 2004; Robben & Suárez-Orozco, 2000).

In the case of indigenous peoples, for example, transgenerational transmission at both individual and collective levels may link current social and mental health problems to the effects of colonization and policies of forced assimilation, in what has been called *historical trauma*

(Atkinson, 2002; Brave Heart & DeBruyn, 1998; Kirmayer, Brass, & Tait, 2000; Robin, Chester, & Goldman, 1996). However, framing the individual and collective responses to colonization and ongoing forms of oppression and marginalization as PTSD, "residential school syndrome," or other medicalized concepts of individual trauma undermines a social and historical analysis that would more appropriately lead to a collective political response (Chrisjohn, Young, & Maraun, 1997; Kenny, 1999). Viewing the predicaments of refugees, internally displaced peoples, and other survivors of organized violence through the lens of medicalized notions of trauma and mental health may also interfere with important political responses (see, for example, Ong, 1995; Summerfield, 1999).

Although trauma is always framed as the exceptional, even where violence is endemic, it has a curious relationship with modernity. Though violence has been a constant feature of human life, the industrial revolution and the accelerated pace of urban life that brought new forms of exhaustion, accident, and injury also held out the promise of new levels of wealth, comfort, and security (Rabinbach, 1990). While modernization and urbanization have brought greater levels of comfort and security to some, in many parts of the world, the politics and economics of development and globalization have given rise to forms of structural violence and inequality that result in profound stresses and a high prevalence of violent trauma. Trauma and its aftermath are not equally distributed even within the populations of developed countries,[7] and the inequities are far more dramatic across the globe (Desjarlais, Eisenberg, Good, & Kleinman, 1995; Kleinman & Desjarlais, 1995). The future of our understanding of and effective response to trauma is inextricably tied to our response to these inequalities and injustices, both globally and at home.

Clearly, trauma refers to very different sorts of events and one might question the usefulness of such a broad extension of the term. The justification for bringing these different events together under one rubric is threefold. First, this liberal use of the term *trauma* reflects the way in which it is has been deployed by mental health professionals to define their domain. Trauma is viewed as a coherent category or construct by health planners, practitioners, and researchers and used to orient mental health services offered in wealthy countries as well as by international organizations in developing countries (Atlani & Rousseau, 2000; Groopman, 2004; Summerfeld, 1999; van Ommeren, Saxena, & Saraceno, 2005; Weine et al., 2002). Given the potential social impact of such services and programs, trauma is worth studying for this reason alone. Second, as will be seen from the contributions to this volume, there are certainly common elements at play across the disparate situations called *traumatic*, such as the

---

[7] For example, inner city youth in the United States have very high lifetime rates of experiencing assault (Breslau, Wilcox, Storr, Lucia, & Anthony, 2004).

role of fear learning and extinction or the processes of collective remembering and forgetting. This has spurred the growth of the whole field of trauma studies, which extends the metaphor far beyond psychology to encompass the social and cultural ruptures and cataclysms that define our time (see, for example, Alexander, 2004; Kaplan, 2005). Finally, comparing the very different uses of the term *trauma* can throw into relief our hidden assumptions and unwarranted generalizations about health and illness. This comparative analysis has much to offer researchers and clinicians, as well as all who are concerned with the conceptual metaphors we use to reflect on the human prospect and predicament.

THE CHALLENGE OF INTERDISCIPLINARITY

What sets this book apart from the many other thoughtful works on trauma published in recent years is the effort to bring together researchers, practitioners, and scholars from very different – even distant – disciplines, including neuroscience, psychiatry, and anthropology, to build cross-disciplinary bridges. The contributors have responded to this challenge by identifying some salient examples, models, and metaphors that provide ways to integrate different levels of explanation. These integrative approaches include models drawn from evolutionary theory; cellular, behavioral, and systems neuroscience; the pragmatism of clinical pluralism; the notion of social suffering; and the cultural construction of our concepts of trauma itself.

Evolutionary biology suggests that trauma was an expected part of our environment of evolutionary adaptation; hence, we have adaptive mechanisms for coping with the threat of danger and the aftermath of violence. This evolutionary history justifies using animal models to study systems that have their analogues in the human brain. Fear learning, avoidance behavior, and extinction (learning not to fear) are part of an adaptive system for managing a dangerous environment. Systems that are normally adaptive can cause problems, however, when fear becomes inappropriate in its cues and intensity. From this perspective, the important questions include the following: What is the relationship between fear, stress, and trauma? What role do developmental factors play in the way individuals respond to stress? Specifically, how do genes and environment interact to shape the response to fearsome events? What neurophysiological processes underlie learning to fear and learning not to fear? What causes some people to continue to show a fearful response long after the threat has vanished? What constitutional or stress-related factors contribute to a failure to "get over" the experience of fear and lead to persistent symptoms of distress?

From clinical and psychological perspectives, however, animal models of stress and fear conditioning capture only a few important elements of the human experience of trauma. The great divide between humans and animals centers on our ability to think about, imagine, narrate, and converse with others about our experience to give it meaning. Indeed, much clinical work involves eliciting and transforming narratives of trauma. From the clinical perspective, crucial questions include the following: How do specific ways of thinking and talking about traumatic events generate distress or contribute to relief and healing? To what extent do such narratives function like the cue exposures that generate extinction? How do multiple or ongoing and traumatic experiences, such as chronic childhood abuse, differ in their effects from isolated traumatic events, such as car accidents or assault? Can interventions that help people who have suffered isolated, single traumatic events be useful for those who have suffered massive and repeated trauma? How do the effects of more socially pervasive forms of trauma that involve whole communities, like genocide, differ from the impact of violence inflicted on one or a few individuals? What role does social support play in mitigating the effects of trauma? Do social solidarity, peace, and security – rather than individual psychological interventions – provide the best therapy for acute traumatic stress reactions?

Cultural anthropology and the social sciences emphasize the historical contingency and particularity of events and experiences that make each story unique, irreducible to general principles, rooted in the specifics of a complex trajectory. The notion of social suffering, articulated by Arthur Kleinman and others, recognizes that the problems identified by psychiatry and psychology do not occur in isolation (Kleinman, Das, & Lock, 1997). Many seemingly unrelated problems co-occur because they arise from a common set of historical and social conditions. The same traumatic events that give rise to fear also involve loss, dislocation, and violations of trust and reciprocity with other people. Trauma is not evenly distributed economically or geographically, but occurs most commonly in the context of prevalent forms of structural violence rooted in power and prejudice (Farmer, 2003). Individuals' suffering must therefore be understood against the backdrop of these larger patterns and processes of collective or social suffering.

The questions raised by considering the social and cultural contexts of trauma include the following: Does the medicalization of trauma through PTSD undermine the need to address the social and political injustices that characterize large-scale traumas of war and genocide as well as the more local and personal traumas of childhood or domestic abuse? How do different cultural systems of meaning provide ways to understand and heal the ruptures of traumatic injury and loss? What are the trade-offs between individual and collective responses to trauma? In particular, when are repression, suppression, or forgetting of traumatic experiences adaptive for the individual, his or her family, and the community? What role does trauma play in the development and maintenance of collective memory and identity? What are the implications of different social responses to collective trauma, such as truth and reconciliation commissions, ceremonies of commemoration, or the actions of political regimes that seek to suppress or deny the historical facts of violence and genocide?

THIS VOLUME

Following these disciplinary questions and concerns, this book is divided into three sections: Section I explores biological perspectives on behavioral and physiological responses to trauma; Section II considers how trauma is expressed in clinical contexts and how developmental trajectories and clinical or social interventions can alter the impact and outcome of traumatic events; and Section III examines some cultural, historical, and political contexts of trauma and its social meaning. Each section begins with an introduction by the editors, which summarizes each chapter, highlights key issues and controversies, and identifies links to other sections. An epilogue discusses the lessons we have learned about the difficulties of and prospects for interdisciplinary integration. Here we highlight some of the important themes that emerged from this colloquy, which can be followed across the different sections and chapters.

The contributions to Section I recognize analogies or homologs to the human responses to trauma in the responses of animals to the threat or experience of pain and injury. The acute response to stress and trauma involves multiple systems with effects on physiology, experience, and social behavior. As Rau and Fanselow show, trauma activates systems involved with fear learning that organize avoidance behavior and defense against predators or other dangers. Trauma also activates other more general stress responses that have adaptive functions. Clinical symptoms of fear, intrusive recollection, and hyperarousal can be considered normal responses to a life-threatening event that may enhance learning how to evade such threats in the future – learning that must generalize across many different contexts.

The neurobiological research by Bouton, Quirk, Barad, and other contributors to Section I has made it clear that the extinction of fear and avoidance behavior involves a separate form of learning with its own dynamics, quite distinct from the learning of fear itself. Learned fears generalize more readily and widely than does learned security. A change in cues or context can reactivate fear and avoidance. This biology of fear is evident in patients' experiences of triggering or reactivating of posttraumatic symptoms by new threats, as described in the chapters by Kinzie, Lemelson, and others in later sections of this book. The psychology of fear learning and extinction provide the rationale for the treatment of symptoms of trauma and anxiety through prolonged exposure, as described by Yadin and Foa in Section II.

The response to potentially traumatic events depends on prior experiences with stress and trauma. Research by Michael Meaney and others has shown how infant rearing and developmental experiences, especially early exposure to stress or trauma, have a major impact on shaping the response to later exposures to stress and trauma. Genes and early environment interact to create vulnerability or resilience in the face of trauma. The importance of a developmental perspective on trauma experience is evident in many of the contributions to this volume. Early trauma can distort subsequent psychological development, as described by van der Kolk in his chapter, but many individuals weather these trials remarkably well, and in some circumstances, as described by Rousseau and Measham, trauma may lead to positive transformations and personal growth.

The contributions to Section II approach trauma from the perspective of clinicians, who focus on providing help for individuals with persistent symptoms and suffering. While acute stress responses reflect the normal operation of adaptive mechanisms, as Arieh Shalev argues, chronic symptoms and syndromes like PTSD emerge when the usual adaptive response is inadequate or incomplete. In Shalev's felicitous phrase, PTSD is a disorder of recovery. Bonds of social support, reconnection with loved ones, and communal solidarity are crucial to recovery from the ruptures created by trauma. This solidarity can be expressed nonverbally by presence, touch, and comfort but also through narratives told by the sufferer, which are witnessed and acknowledged by others. The community-based intervention program devised by Silove and his colleagues relies on this social solidarity as a crucial basis for healing and recovery at both individual and collective levels. Although exposure therapy can reduce the symptoms of anxiety and avoidance that follow trauma, as Kinzie argues in his chapter, individuals who have endured more massive or persistent trauma and loss may require other forms of intervention that address the larger issues of trust and meaning. The stories told by traumatized patients in psychotherapy do not involve the fixed replaying of events that gradually recede in significance but the construction of narratives that give new meaning to experience and situate it within a life trajectory and a larger social world. Studies of the construction, transformation, and stabilization of narratives form a bridge between the concerns of clinicians and the wider social, cultural, and political contexts that are the focus of Section III.

Many of the contributions provide evidence that the construct of PTSD covers only a small part of the complex response to trauma and that excessive focus on PTSD medicalizes social problems and predicaments that demand a more comprehensive social and political response. The personal and social meanings of traumatic events play a central role in their impact and in any subsequent process of integration and healing. The historical and social context in which traumatic experiences occur affects long-term psychosocial and psychiatric outcomes. The ways that individuals adapt to trauma reflect their personalities and psychological resilience and resources but also depend on the social, cultural, and political contexts in which they find themselves. Avoidance of stimuli and numbing may be socially acceptable or unremarkable when traditions (or political necessity) emphasize the value of detachment from the world and of contemplation rather than confrontation. This does not mean such quietism and acceptance are always optimal for the individual, but neither is well-being achieved by yielding to the desire to find someone to blame or ceaseless efforts to control uncontrollable events. The value of any mode or style of coping must be understood in terms of the tensions and trade-offs between individual adaptation and broader social concerns. This raises both moral and practical questions for clinicians and others who seek to intervene.

As the contributions to Section III make clear, trauma narratives have both personal and collective meanings at one and the same time. The individual's management of painful memories and scars of experience must be considered in the larger context of the collective significance of remembering and forgetting. Social and political forces may work to silence individuals who have dangerous stories to tell; in other circumstances, there may be strong sanctions that press people to narrate their suffering in ways that are "politically correct" even when this does not correspond to their experience. As Konner, Dwyer and Santikarma, Rousseau and Measham, and others in this volume show, the mental health professions also have their ideological versions of "correct" stories to tell about trauma and so work not simply to liberate or heal but to tame and domesticate the stories of sufferers and survivors.

The individual's desire to avoid reminders of pain and loss is mirrored by others' desire to avoid vicarious pain through listening. Yet, what is torment for the individual may spur the conscience of society. The tension between avoidance and confrontation experienced by traumatized individuals parallels a larger conflict between recounting, witnessing, or giving testimony and suppressing, forgetting, or even denying collective traumas and historical events.[8] These tensions seem irresolvable and pose unavoidable trade-offs. But the biological research reported in this volume shows that fear memory and extinction memory involve independent neural systems, with different temporal dynamics, and that both can be expressed after a terrifying experience. This tells us something significant about how remembering and forgetting can coexist and interact for individuals as well as whole societies. Understanding these dynamics of memory is important for efforts to reconstruct the social world in the wake of individual or collective trauma. Traumatic histories divide peoples, drawing sharp boundaries around the comfortable and familiar, making the other strange and fearsome. The intensity of pain, fear, and avoidance that follows from traumatic events must be assuaged so that feelings of anger and the desire for revenge can subside, while a sense of trust, safety, and confidence reemerges.

---

[8] Among recent discussions of these issues, see Margalit (2002) and Augé (2004).

At the same time, the memory of historical events must be maintained and enlarged to provide the collective awareness needed to rebuild a viable social and moral order and a hospitable community that protects the vulnerable and honors the stranger as our guest.

References

Acocella, J. (1999). *Creating hysteria: Women and multiple personality disorder*. San Francisco: Jossey-Bass.

Agger, I., & Jensen, S. B. (1996). *Trauma and healing under state terrorism*. London: Zed Books.

Alexander, J. C. (2004). *Cultural trauma and collective identity*. Berkeley: University of California Press.

American Psychiatric Association. (1980). *Diagnostic and statistical manual of mental disorders* (3rd ed.). Washington, DC: American Psychiatric Association.

American Psychiatric Association. (2000). *Diagnostic and statistical manual of mental disorders* (4th ed., text rev.). Washington, DC: American Psychiatric Association.

Appelbaum, P. S., Uyehara, L. A., & Elin, M. R. (Eds.). (1997). *Trauma and memory: Clinical and legal controversies*. New York: Oxford University Press.

Atkinson, J. (2002). *Trauma trails, recreating song lines: The transgenerational effects of trauma in indigenous Australia*. North Melbourne, Australia: Spinifex Press.

Atlani, L., & Rousseau, C. (2000). The politics of culture in humanitarian aid to refugees having experienced sexual violence. *Transcultural Psychiatry, 37*(3), 435–449.

Auge, M. (2004). *Oblivion*. Minneapolis: University of Minnesota Press.

Bartlett, F. C. (1932). *Remembering*. Cambridge: Cambridge University Press.

Brave Heart, M. Y., & DeBruyn, L. M. (1998). The American Indian Holocaust: Healing historical unresolved grief. *American Indian Alaska Native Mental Health Research, 8*(2), 56–78.

Breslau, N., Wilcox, H. C., Storr, C. L., Lucia, V. C., & Anthony, J. C. (2004). Trauma exposure and posttraumatic stress disorder: A study of youths in urban America. *Journal of Urban Health, 81*(4), 530–544.

Brewin, C. (2003). *Posttraumatic stress disorder: Malady or myth?* New Haven: Yale University Press.

Brewin, C. R. (2005). Encoding and retrieval of traumatic memories. In J. Vasterling & C. R. Brewin (Eds.), *Neuropsychology of PTSD* (pp. 131–150). New York: Guilford Press.

Brewin, C. R., Andrews, B., & Valentine, J. D. (2000). Meta-analysis of risk factors for posttraumatic stress disorder in trauma-exposed adults. *Journal of Consulting and Clinical Psychology, 68*(5), 748–766.

Brown, P., Zavestoski, S., McCormick, S., Linder, M., Mandelbaum, J., & Luebke, T. (2001). A gulf of difference: Disputes over Gulf War–related illnesses. *Journal of Health and Social Behavior, 42*(3), 235–257.

Chrisjohn, R., Young, S., & Maraun, N. (1997). *The circle game: Shadows and substance in the Indian residential school experience in Canada*. Penticton, BC: Theytus Books.

Crews, F. C. (1995). *The memory wars: Freud's legacy in dispute*. New York: New York Review of Books.

Danieli, Y. (Ed.). (1998). *International handbook of multigenerational legacies of trauma*. New York: Plenum Press.

Danieli, Y., Rodley, N. S., Weisæth, L., & United Nations. (1996). *International responses to traumatic stress: Humanitarian, human rights, justice, peace and development contributions, collaborative actions and future initiatives*. Amityville, NY: Baywood.

Dean, C. J. (2004). *The fragility of empathy after the Holocaust*. Ithaca, NY: Cornell University Press.

Desjarlais, R., Eisenberg, L., Good, B., & Kleinman, A. (1995). *World mental health: Problems and priorities in low-income countries*. New York: Oxford University Press.

Farmer, P. (2003). *Pathologies of power: Health, human rights, and the new war on the poor*. Berkeley: University of California Press.

Frankel, F. H. (1994). The concept of flashbacks in historical perspective. *International Journal of Clinical and Experimental Hypnosis, 42*(4), 321–336.

Freyd, J. J. (1996). *Betrayal trauma: The logic of forgetting childhood abuse*. Cambridge, MA: Harvard University Press.

Frueh, B. C., Elhai, J. D., Grubaugh, A. L., Monnier, J., Kashdan, T. B., Sauvageot, J. A. , et al. (2005). Documented combat exposure of US veterans seeking treatment for combat-related post-traumatic stress disorder. *British Journal of Psychiatry, 186*, 467–472.

Groopman, J. (2004, January 26). The grief industry. *New Yorker*, 30–38.

Hacking, I. (1991). The making and molding of child abuse. *Critical Inquiry, 17*, 253–288.

Hacking, I. (1995). *Rewriting the soul*. Princeton, NJ: Princeton University Press.

Hinton, A. L. (2002). *Annihilating difference: The anthropology of genocide*. Berkeley: University of California Press.

Hyams, K. C., Wignall, R. S., & Roswell, R. (1996). War syndromes and their evaluation: From the U.S. Civil War to the Persian Gulf War. *Annals of Internal Medicine, 125*(5), 398–405.

Johnson, M. K., & Kaye, C. L. (2000). Cognitive and brain mechanisms of false memories and beliefs. In D. L. Schacter & E. Scarry (Eds.), *Memory, brain, and belief* (pp. 35–86). Cambridge, MA: Harvard University Press.

Jones, E., Vermaas, R. H., McCartney, H., Beech, C., Palmer, I., Hyams, K., et al. (2003). Flashbacks and post-traumatic stress disorder: The genesis of a 20th-century diagnosis. *British Journal of Psychiatry, 182*, 158–163.

Kaplan, E. A. (2005). *Trauma culture: The politics of terror and loss in media and literature*. New Brunswick, NJ: Rutgers University Press.

Kenny, M. (1999). A place for memory: The interface between individual and collective memory. *Comparative Studies in Society and History, 41*(3), 420–437.

Kihlstrom, J. F. (2005). Dissociative disorders. *Annual Review of Clinical Psychology, 1*, 227–253.

Kirmayer, L. J. (1994). Pacing the void: Social and cultural dimensions of dissociation. In D. Spiegel (Ed.), *Dissociation: Culture, mind and body* (pp. 91–122). Washington, DC: American Psychiatric Press.

Kirmayer, L. J. (1996). Confusion of the senses: Implications of ethnocultural variations in somatoform and dissociative disorders for PTSD. In A. J. Marsella, M. J. Friedman, E. T. Gerrity, & R. M. Scurfield (Eds.), *Ethnocultural aspects of post-traumatic stress disorders: Issues, research and clinical applications* (pp. 131–164). Washington, DC: American Psychological Association.

Kirmayer, L. J., Brass, G. M., & Tait, C. L. (2000). The mental health of Aboriginal peoples: Transformations of identity and community. *Canadian Journal of Psychiatry, 45*(7), 607–616.

Kleinman, A., Das, V., & Lock, M. M. (1997). *Social suffering.* Berkeley: University of California Press.

Kleinman, A., & Desjarlais, R. (1995). Violence, culture and politics of trauma. In A. Kleinman, *Writing at the margins: Discourse between anthropology and medicine.* (pp. 172–189). Berkeley: University of California Press.

Laney, C., & Loftus, E. F. (2005). Traumatic memories are not necessarily accurate memories. *Canadian Journal of Psychiatry, 50*(13), 823–828.

Leys, R. (2000). *Trauma: A genealogy.* Chicago: University of Chicago Press.

Lipinski, J. F., Jr., & Pope, H. G., Jr. (1994). Do "flashbacks" represent obsessional imagery? *Comprehensive Psychiatry, 35*(4), 245–247.

Margalit, A. (2002). *The ethics of memory.* Cambridge, MA: Harvard University Press.

McNally, R. J. (2003). *Remembering trauma.* Cambridge, MA: Belknap Press, Harvard University Press.

McNally, R. J., & Clancy, S. A. (2005). Sleep paralysis, sexual abuse, and space alien abduction. *Transcultural Psychiatry, 42*(1), 113–122.

McNally, R. J., Lasko, N. B., Clancy, S. A., Macklin, M. L., Pitman, R. K., & Orr, S. P. (2004). Psychophysiological responding during script-driven imagery in people reporting abduction by space aliens. *Psychological Science, 15*(7), 493–497.

Merckelbach, H., Muris, P., Horselenberg, R., & Rassin, E. (1998). Traumatic intrusions as 'worse case scenarios.' *Behavior Research and Therapy, 36,* 1075–1079.

Micale, M. S., & Lerner, P. F. (2001). *Traumatic pasts: History, psychiatry, and trauma in the modern age, 1870–1930.* New York: Cambridge University Press.

Newcomb, M. D., & Locke, T. F. (2001). Intergenerational cycle of maltreatment: A popular concept obscured by methodological limitations. *Child Abuse and Neglect, 25*(9), 1219–1240.

Ong, A. (1995). Making the biopolitical subject: Cambodian immigrants, refugee medicine and cultural citizenship in California. *Social Science & Medicine, 40*(9), 1243–1257.

Power, S. (2002). *A problem from hell: America and the age of genocide.* New York: Basic Books.

Rabinbach, A. (1990). *The human motor: Energy, fatigue, and the origins of modernity.* New York: Basic Books.

Raitt, F. E., & Zeedyk, M. S. (2003). False memory syndrome: Undermining the credibility of complainants in sexual offences. *International Journal of Law and Psychiatry, 26*(5), 453–471.

Robben, A. C. G. M., & Suárez-Orozco, M. M. (2000). *Cultures under siege: Collective violence and trauma.* New York: Cambridge University Press.

Robin, R. W., Chester, B., & Goldman, D. (1996). Cumulative trauma and PTSD in American Indian communities. In A. J. Marsella, M. J. Friedman, E. T. Gerrity, & R. M. Scurfield (Eds.), *Ethnocultural aspects of post-traumatic stress disorders: Issues, research, and clinical applications* (pp. 239–254). Washington, DC: American Psychological Association.

Schacter, D. L. (Ed.). (1995). *Memory distortion: How minds, brains and societies reconstruct the past.* Cambridge, MA: Harvard University Press.

Schacter, D. L. (2003). *How the mind forgets and remembers: The seven sins of memory.* London: Souvenir.

Sebald, W. G. (2003). *On the natural history of destruction.* New York: Random House.

Shephard, B. (2001). *A war of nerves: Soldiers and psychiatrists in the twentieth century.* Cambridge, MA: Harvard University Press.

Sigal, J. J., & Weinfeld, M. (1989). *Trauma and rebirth: Intergenerational effects of the Holocaust.* New York: Praeger.

Sontag, S. (2003). *Regarding the pain of others.* New York: Farrar, Straus & Giroux.

Summerfield, D. (1999). A critique of seven assumptions behind psychological trauma programmes in war-affected areas. *Social Science & Medicine, 48*(10), 1449–1462.

van der Kolk, B. A. (1994). The body keeps the score: Memory and the evolving psychobiology of posttraumatic stress. *Harvard Review of Psychiatry, 1*(5), 253–265.

van der Kolk, B. A., McFarlane, A. C., & Weisæth, L. (1996). *Traumatic stress: The effects of overwhelming experience on mind, body, and society.* New York: Guilford Press.

van Ommeren, M., Saxena, S., & Saraceno, B. (2005). Mental and social health during and after acute emergencies: Emerging consensus? *Bulletin of the World Health Organization, 83*(1), 71–75; discussion 75–76.

Weine, S., Danieli, Y., Silove, D., van Ommeren, M., Fairbank, J. A., & Saul, J. (2002). Guidelines for international training in mental health and psychosocial interventions for trauma exposed populations in clinical and community settings. *Psychiatry, 65*(2), 156–164.

Yehuda, R., & McFarlane, A. C. (1995). Conflict between current knowledge about posttraumatic stress disorder and its original conceptual basis. *American Journal of Psychiatry, 152*(12), 1705–1713.

Young, A. (1995). *The harmony of illusions: Inventing post-traumatic stress disorder.* Princeton, NJ: Princeton University Press.

Young, A. (1999). An alternative history of traumatic stress. In A. Y. Shalev, R. Yehuda, & A. C. McFarlane (Eds.), *International handbook of human response to trauma* (pp. 51–66). New York: Kluwer Academic/Plenum.

Young, A. (2002). The self-traumatized perpetrator as a "transient mental illness." *Evolution Psychiatrique, 67*, 630–650.

Zavestoski, S., Brown, P., McCormick, S., Mayer, B., D'Ottavi, M., & Lucove, J. C. (2004). Patient activism and the struggle for diagnosis: Gulf War illnesses and other medically unexplained physical symptoms in the US. *Social Science & Medicine, 58*(1), 161–175.

NEUROBIOLOGICAL PERSPECTIVES ON TRAUMA

In recent years, neuroscience has gone a considerable distance toward unraveling some of the mechanisms of learning, memory, and emotion. Such research has also identified some of the processes that come into play in response to threat, fear, and injury. The contributors to this section present converging lines of research on behavioral, neurophysiological, and molecular mechanisms that may contribute to the response to trauma. These include studies of the neural mechanisms of fear learning and extinction, the role of gene–environment interactions in the development of normal and pathological stress responses, and the pathological effects of stress and trauma on brain and body. Recent progress in these fields has been nothing short of breathtaking, and this section presents only a sampling of the field, albeit a sample that captures findings of great relevance to the study of trauma and to the treatment of its psychological effects. The chapters in this section demonstrate both the power and the limitations of the scientific method as it approaches the complexity of human behavior.

Fear and defensive reactions serve obvious adaptive functions in all animals, and humans share this evolutionary heritage. Both normal and pathological responses to traumatic events can therefore be understood in part in terms of the functioning of these adaptive systems. Vinuta Rau and Michael Fanselow discuss how animals' responses to the threat of a predator provide a window on fear-related behavior. They explain the varieties of the fear response using a model of "predatory imminence." This model conceives of fear responses in balance with the need for foraging and other activities outside the safety of home territory. It explains different fear responses, such as vigilance, freezing, and fight or flight, as an escalating series of responses to threats that are becoming closer and more likely. Rau and Fanselow describe how preexposure to a traumatic stressor appears to sensitize rats to respond with inappropriately elevated fear to less intense stressors. They link these responses to specific anatomical locations within the brain, such as the amygdala, dorsal and ventral peri-aqueductal gray, and hippocampus. These areas modulate one important part of the mammalian stress response, the hypothalamic–pituitary–adrenal (HPA) axis, which controls the level of the stress hormone cortisol (or corticosterone in rats). Based on these ethological and neurobehavioral models, Rau and Fanselow suggest that posttraumatic stress disorder, as an anxiety disorder, may result from a sensitization of this stress response system.

Although the fear response to some triggers may be innate (Hebb, 1946), most fears are learned through a process called Pavlovian or classical conditioning. In this form of learning, an animal or person begins to fear an initially neutral cue (the conditioned stimulus, CS) when it is paired with an intrinsically frightening event like an unexpected electrical shock (the unconditioned stimulus, US). This simple paradigm has yielded a wealth of information on how fear is learned and controlled by the mammalian brain, using the same circuitry present in human beings. Conditioned fears last a lifetime, unless they are reduced by repeated presentations of the CS without any US, a procedure called *extinction*.

Experiments on extinction have had a long history as the basis for the development of behavior therapy for human anxiety disorders, which depends on repeated exposure to fear cues in a safe environment (Jones, 1924; Wolpe, 1969). Such exposure-based psychotherapies are very effective treatments for these disorders, including posttraumatic stress disorder (PTSD), as will be seen in the review of the evidence by Yadin and Foa in Section II of this volume.

There is now much evidence that the extinction of classically conditioned fear is not simply the weakening or erasure of a learned association, but rather the acquisition of new learning that inhibits the expression of the fear association, which remains intact. Fear conditioning and extinction learning are separate processes that display different patterns of acquisition and generalization, and are dependent on different brain pathways and molecular mechanisms. The next three chapters of this section explore these findings, which have important consequences for understanding and treating the human response to trauma.

Evidence for the independence of fear learning and extinction comes from observations that extinguished fears can be reinstated by changes in cues or contexts. Mark Bouton and Jaylyn Waddell present a series of behavioral experiments suggesting that these "return of fear" phenomena can be explained by the overarching idea that extinction learning is linked closely (more closely than fear learning itself) to the context in which it occurs. As Bouton and Waddell point out, that context can be a place, a time, or an internal state (including an anxious state). As the animal gets more distant from the original context of extinction, or is reminded of the context of fear conditioning by other cues or more generalized anxiety states, the extinction memory becomes weaker and the original fear returns. This process may help explain the recurrence of symptoms in people who appear to have recovered from traumatic fears through treatment or the passage of time, as described by Kinzie in this volume.

Gregory Quirk and his colleagues describe their discovery of an anatomical locus crucial to extinction learning. In an experimental *tour de force*, they demonstrate that lesions of the infralimbic prefrontal cortex impair extinction learning, that the firing of cells in that location tracks the consolidated memory for extinction, and that electrical stimulation of that area by experimenters can mimic extinction learning and reduce the expression of conditioned fear in rats.

Mark Barad and Chris Cain have used behavioral pharmacology to explore how extinction learning differs mechanistically from conditioning itself. They present experiments that describe an unusual molecular "switch" that initiates extinction learning. They also present a series of experiments identifying drugs that can block or facilitate extinction learning. Data showing that pharmacological strategies can accelerate or facilitate extinction suggest these same drugs may improve the speed and effectiveness of behavior therapy for anxiety disorders, including PTSD.

The brain systems involved with fear learning and extinction interact with neuroendocrine systems that respond to a wide range of stressors. A wealth of research shows that the sensitivity of these systems is influenced by developmental experiences. Michael Meaney and his colleagues summarize their studies showing how variations in maternal care contribute to individual differences in behavioral and neuroendocrine responses to stress. Normal variations in how a mother rat nurses, licks, and grooms her pup in the first week of life lead to stable differences in the reactivity of the neural systems that underlie the stress response. The maternal behaviors affect the expression of specific genes, and these "epigenetic" changes not only are expressed in the offspring when the pup has grown up, but also can be transmitted across generations. These studies underscore the importance of parental care as a mediator of the effects of environmental adversity on neural development and subsequent vulnerability or resilience in the face of stress.

The preceding chapters in this section have focused on the behavioral and brain mechanisms that underlie the biological response to trauma. The brain is not only the mediator of our experiences of stress and trauma but also a target itself. Douglas Bremner reviews the literature on the effects of stress on the brain. There is evidence that severe and prolonged stress has deleterious effects on several brain structures, particularly the hippocampus, with implications for learning and memory function. Bremner argues for the recognition of a spectrum of trauma-related disorders, within which he would include PTSD, depression, borderline personality disorder, and dissociative disorder.

In the final chapter of this section Emeran Mayer discusses some of the implications of traumatic stress for physical health, reviewing evidence that traumatic events can contribute to a wide range of symptoms and functional somatic syndromes including cardiovascular, gastrointestinal, and musculoskeletal disorders. Mayer focuses on irritable bowel syndrome and fibromyalgia, both of which are commonly reported by PTSD patients. Of course, not all individuals exposed to traumatic stressors develop functional somatic syndromes, nor do most patients with such symptoms report a history of traumatic events. However, trauma may contribute to the severity of somatic symptoms by increasing the sensitivity of systems involved in pain perception and regulation of the autonomic nervous system as well as the stress response.

Whereas the chapters on fear conditioning and extinction identify very specific mechanisms, the contributions by Mayer and Bremner take in a great variety of disparate conditions and group them together on the basis of trauma as a common causal factor. However, many of symptoms and conditions that Mayer and Bremner describe are associated not only with trauma or PTSD but also with a wide range of stressors of varying type and severity. And, as the studies of Meaney and others make clear, the impact of stress and trauma depends crucially on early developmental processes. As a result, no simple grouping in terms of trauma exposure or effects can capture the variegated patterns of interacting factors that account for illness.

The chapters in this section display the strengths of research in the basic sciences. There is consensus about a common body of established facts and a set of methods for resolving disputes. Compared to work in the social sciences, biological research advances rapidly, both because of the refined methodologies that are available to study simple systems and the large numbers of researchers at work today. As a result, some of the material presented in this section will no longer be cutting edge by the time this book appears in print.

Although the reductionist approach of using animal models to dissect the physiological and molecular mechanisms of behavior has many strengths, it also has important limitations. One limitation is the need for simplification and control. A good experiment demands that all factors that are not the direct object of the study remain constant. Only such control allows a definitive conclusion to be drawn about the variable in the study, say, the effect of a drug or of prefrontal cortex stimulation on extinction learning. But human life is not so controlled, and as the contributors to this book describe, most situations involve the interactions of many variables over time. The sheer numbers of these variables and the complexity of their interactions exceed the scope and explanatory power of current biological models and experimental paradigms.

Other limitations are the use of animal systems and relatively minor stressors to model human trauma. For example, the mild footshock given to rats or mice in extinction experiments to generate conditioned fear has little resemblance to the horrific events experienced by many PTSD patients and by many of the victims of genocidal war who may not show PTSD symptoms. Further, animal models cannot include factors that are clearly central to human experience: consciousness and self-reflection, speech and narrative, and the navigation of complex social relationships. This lack of cognitive and social complexity is particularly conspicuous because the therapy of PTSD, including the prolonged exposure therapy that is based on extinction, usually depends on the patient's narration of the story of the traumatic event, and on the relationship with an empathic and interested therapist.

Nevertheless, the power of neurobiological research is obvious, and some of these complexities may yield in the long run to scientific methods. More intense trauma, fear, and loss can be modeled (although this may raise ethical issues about the treatment of animals). The study of the functions of the prefrontal cortex in rodents may capture some aspects of the role of consciousness in human behavior. The importance of social interactions, albeit nonverbal, can also be modeled to some extent in animals, as is evident in the chapter from Meaney's group.

New technologies also will allow us to conduct more elaborate studies of human subjects. Although the human environment cannot be controlled, carefully matched samples allow comparative study of brain activity using imaging techniques. Cognitive neuropsychology has begun to explore the mechanisms of memory and emotion relevant to models of psychological trauma (Vasterling & Brewin, 2005). This work can be linked to studies of the role of narration and disclosure in coping with trauma (Pennebaker, 1995). The emerging field of social neuroscience holds the promise of allowing us to examine brain functioning in contexts that are culturally meaningful (Cacioppo & Berntson, 2004; Cacioppo, Visser, & Pickett, 2006). Such work will lead to models of the interactions of the neural mechanisms of emotional learning and memory with the processes of narration, social positioning, and collective remembering that are crucial elements of the human response to traumatic events.

References

Cacioppo, J. T., & Berntson, G. G. (Eds.). (2004). *Essays in social neuroscience.* Cambridge, MA: MIT Press.

Cacioppo, J. T., Visser, P. S., & Pickett, C. L. (Eds.). (2006). *Social neuroscience: People thinking about thinking people.* Cambridge, MA: MIT Press.

Hebb, D. O. (1946). On the nature of fear. *Psychological Review, 53,* 259–276.

Jones, M. C. (1924). A laboratory study of fear: The case of Peter. *Pedagogical Seminary, 31*, 308–315.

Pennebaker, J. W. (Ed.). (1995). *Emotion, disclosure, and health.* Washington, DC: American Psychological Association.

Vasterling, J. J., & Brewin, C. (Ed.). (2005). *Neuropsychology of PTSD: Biological, cognitive, and clinical perspectives.* New York: Guilford Press.

Wolpe, J. (1969). *The practice of behavior therapy* (1st ed.). New York: Pergamon Press.

1

Neurobiological and Neuroethological Perspectives on Fear and Anxiety

Vinuta Rau and Michael S. Fanselow

Predation is the most urgent threat to future reproductive success, and, as a result, powerful behavioral systems have evolved to enable animals to thwart their predators effectively. Viewed within this functional behavior systems perspective, fear evolved as a set of antipredator strategies designed to evaluate and respond to threat. The rapid learning of fear is a component of this system that usually facilitates an animal's ability to deal with the threats it may confront (Fanselow & Lester, 1988). Because failure to defend in the presence of life-threatening danger eliminates future reproductive success, fear evolved to dominate behavior in the face of threat. But the ability of fear to dominate behavior that is normally protective can also lead to devastating consequences if the system is not working adaptively. Inappropriate or excessive activiation of fear responses may lead to the development of psychopathology (Rosen & Schulkin, 1998). One clear example of this is posttraumatic stress disorder (PTSD). In this chapter, we outline the structure of antipredator behavior and then relate this structure to PTSD, which we view as an inappropriate activation of this normally adaptive system.

In response to a cue for danger, animals display unlearned behavior patterns that have a phylogenetic history of protecting that species from danger (Bolles & Fanselow, 1980). These innate behavior patterns have been termed *species-specific defense reactions*, or SSDRs (Bolles, 1970). Once an animal recognizes a stimulus that is predictive of threat, its range of behavior becomes restricted to a limited repertoire of SSDRs. The particular SSDR displayed is determined by the geographic–temporal and psychological distance of the animal from the threat, a relationship called the *predatory imminence continuum* (Fanselow & Lester, 1988). At one end of the continuum is the safest place for the prey, for example, its nest site. At the other end of the continuum is the ultimate cost to evolutionary fitness for the prey, being killed by a predator. Defensive behavior reflects (1) the physical distance between the predator and prey, or the geographic–temporal

relationship, and (2) how much of a threat the prey perceives the predator to be, or psychological distance. This relationship, called the predatory
imminence continuum, is shown in Figure 1.1.

During minimal predatory danger, the prey engages in nonaversively
motivated behaviors called the *preferred activity pattern*. These behaviors
include looking for food, feeding, exploring, mating, and nest upkeep.
An increase in predatory imminence causes the animal to deviate from
the preferred activity pattern and engage in defensive behavior. These
defensive behaviors serve to prevent further movement down the predatory imminence continuum. However, if further movement does occur, the
topography of defensive behaviors changes at different points along the
continuum.

When the preferred activity pattern puts an animal at risk of potential
predation, the activity pattern must be reorganized to protect the animal.
Such behaviors are called *pre-encounter* defense. Some examples of pre-
encounter defensive behaviors that may reduce an animal's risk of predation include meal pattern reorganization, protective nest maintenance, and
stretched approach (Fanselow, 1994).

Leaving the nest to seek food presents potential danger, and meal pattern
reorganization helps to reduce this danger. In an experiment designed
to study food-seeking behavior, rats were put in the dangerous situation
of receiving unpredictable shocks near their nesting area. These animals
reorganized their meal patterns to take less frequent larger meals, which
helped to minimize predatory risk yet maintain caloric balance (Fanselow,
Lester, & Helmstetter, 1988).

Defensive burying is one way for an animal to protect its nesting area.
This behavior enables the animal to remove unfamiliar or harmful objects
that may be near its nest site (De Boer & Koolhaas, 2003). For example,
animals will bury objects by which they have been shocked (Pinel & Treit,
1978), food coated with quinine (Poling, Cleary, & Monaghan, 1981), and
tubes delivering predator odors (Holmes & Galea, 2002), to ensure the
safety of the nesting site.

Stretched-approach behavior facilitates tentative and safe exploration
of an animal's environment (Pinel & Mana, 1989). Rats living in a habitat
made up of burrows connected to an open field by tunnels exhibit this
behavior when approaching the open field from the tunnel (Blanchard
& Blanchard, 1989). A rat typically extends its head from the tunnel and
scans the environment before either entering the open field or retreating
back into the tunnel (Blanchard & Blanchard, 1989). These pre-encounter
defense behaviors described are not a response to the immediate presence
of a predator itself, but instead occur when there is the likelihood of a
predatory encounter.

Post-encounter defensive behaviors occur when a predator is actually
present and has been detected by the prey. Post-encounter behaviors help

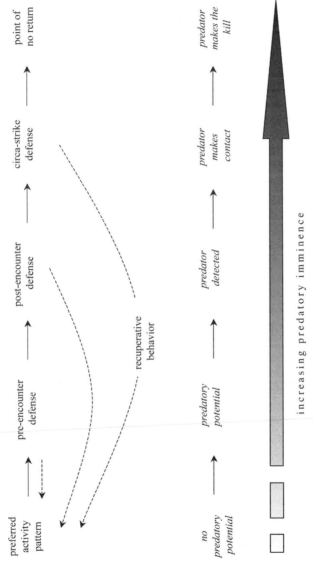

FIGURE 1.1. The predatory imminence continuum. (Adapted from Fanselow & Lester, 1988. Copyright 1988 by the Society for the Experimental Analysis of Behavior, Inc.)

the prey to avoid contact with the predator. In the rat, freezing is the dominant post-encounter defensive response, although flight may occur if an easily accessible and safe escape route is available (Fanselow & Lester, 1988). Freezing, defined as the absence of any movement except that needed for respiration (e.g., Fanselow, 1980), has the adaptive function of reducing the likelihood of detection and attack by a predator (Suarez & Gallup, 1981). Rats freeze when a predator is detected in the vicinity (Lester & Fanselow, 1985) and they will also freeze to stimuli paired with an aversive event, such as footshock (Bolles & Collier, 1976; Fanselow, 1980). If freezing provides insufficient defense, the freezing rat is ready to burst into action in response to a sudden change in the environment (Fanselow & Lester, 1988). This explosive burst of motor activity is a defensive behavior facilitated by freezing and is an example of *circa-strike* defensive behaviors, which aim to terminate contact with the predator. These behaviors occur prior to, during, and just after physical contact with the predator. They include jump attack, escape, upright posture, and vocalizations.

Endogenous analgesia occurs during the post-encounter stage to faciliate circa-strike behaviors (Fanselow, 1986). Endogenous analgesia is the release of endogenous opioid-like peptides that reduce nociception. This analgesia means that if potentially painful injury occurs during the encounter, defensive behaviors can continue (Bolles & Fanselow, 1980). If the animal survives the attack, there is usually a period of recuperation, especially if injury occurs during the circa-strike phase. Only after successful recuperation can the animal return to its preferred activity pattern.

Freezing is one defensive behavior that has lent itself to extensive study in the laboratory. As mentioned earlier, rats will freeze when they detect a predator in the vicinity. Rats can also learn to freeze in response to stimuli paired with an aversive event, such as footshock, a procedure called fear conditioning. In a typical fear-conditioning procedure (for review, see Fendt & Fanselow, 1999; LeDoux, 1995; Maren, 2001), a brief electrical current is delivered to an animal through the metal grid floor of a conditioning chamber. This aversive footshock, or unconditional stimulus (US), is usually paired with a conditional stimulus (CS), which can be the context or chamber in which the animal is shocked or an additional discrete cue such as a tone. Pairing the CS and US will eventually result in the CS eliciting a conditional response (CR), such as freezing, in the absence of the US. Freezing behavior has become a useful CR to assess an animal's fearfulness to a CS (Bolles & Collier, 1976; Fanselow, 1980).

In fear conditioning, the fear response is proportional to the level of threat. Specifically, the amount of freezing shown by an animal is directly related to the number and intensity of shocks it receives. Typically, as the number and intensity of shocks increase, so does the level of freezing (Fanselow & Bolles, 1979). However, if an animal is pre-exposed to a stressful event, it shows a disproportionate amount of fear and a response that is

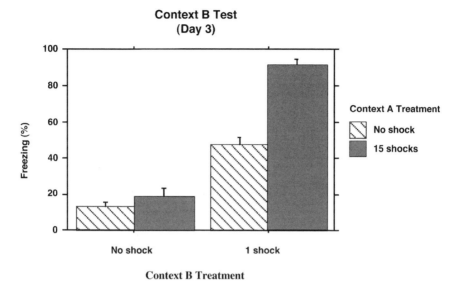

FIGURE 1.2. Effects of pre-exposure to shock on freezing behavior. Animals receiving 15 shocks during pre-exposure (in Context A) show higher levels of freezing to 1 shock in a second distinct context (Context B) compared to animals not given 15 shocks during pre-exposure, animals given just 1 shock without pre-exposure shock, and animals given no shock. Reprinted from Rau et al., 2005, Copyright 2005, with permission from Elsevier.

no longer appropriate for the level of threat. For example, rats receiving one brief mild shock show around 50% freezing during a test of contextual fear a day later. However, when animals are first given a series of 15 footshocks in a different context prior to the single shock, they show almost twice as much freezing when re-exposed to the single-shock context (Rau, DeCola, & Fanselow, 2005). The single shock now elicits a disproportionate level of fear, a level more appropriate to the original stressful event, the 15-shock session. The initial stressor, 15 shocks, appears to enhance or sensitize the reaction to a less intense similar stressor, 1 shock. This effect is shown in Figure 1.2.

Similarly, pre-exposure to a traumatic stressor may inappropriately activate fear in people, as seen in PTSD. Hallmark symptoms of PTSD include persistent reexperiencing of the traumatic event, avoiding stimuli associated with the traumatic event, and signs of increased arousal such as hypervigilance and exaggerated startle (American Psychiatric Association, 2000). These symptoms characteristic of PTSD can be adaptive in the face of severe trauma (Bonne, Grillon, Vythilingam, Neumeister, & Charney, 2004; Charney, 2004; Christopher, 2004; Eberly, Harkness, & Engdahl, 1991). Reexperiencing the traumatic event can help an individual learn from the event and develop more efficient ways of responding if the situation should happen again. Avoiding stimuli associated with the trauma decreases the likelihood of encountering similar threatening events. Heightened vigilance can increase the likelihood of detecting potential threats. However, when these symptoms impair normal functioning for a prolonged period of time, they become disabling to the affected individual. Reexperiencing the event may cause sleep disturbances, avoiding trauma-related stimuli may lead to a constricted lifestyle, and increased arousal can result in exhaustion (Eberly et al., 1991). This exemplifies how adaptive fear responses, when inappropriately regulated, may preclude normal functioning.

As with animals, fear has been described as hardwired and biological in humans, making it useful in protecting us from danger (Craske, 1999; Izard, 1992). People show true fear in the face of imminent threat, and what is experienced below this threshold can be described along a continuum akin to the predatory imminence continuum (Craske, 1999). According to Craske (1999), worry, fear, and panic are qualitatively different states that lie on a continuum, and their positions are dependent on a person's temporal, physical, and psychological proximity to a threat (Bouton, Mineka, & Barlow, 2001; Craske, 1999). In the absence of any threat, there is a preferred mode of safety and control, analogous to the preferred activity pattern. The potential for threat produces worry and elicits preparation and readiness, which can be compared to pre-encounter defensive behaviors. Worry may help prepare for threat by reducing the unexpectedness of an aversive event and by facilitating coping (Mathews, 1990). The detection of a threat produces anticipatory fear, and mobilization and vigilance occur, akin to post-encounter defensive behavior. And finally, imminent threat produces panic, resulting in fight or flight, which is similar to circa-strike behaviors observed in animals. In a nutshell, a low level of threat produces worry, increased threat produces anticipatory fear, and imminent threat results in panic. Future threatening events cause worry, then anticipatory fear as the event gets closer, and then panic when the threat becomes imminent (Craske, 1999). Here, threat imminence is defined by the individual's perception of risk and appraisal of danger (Craske, 1999).

The predatory imminence and threat imminence continuums organize behaviors such that normal activities and different types of defensive behaviors occur when they are most appropriate and adaptive (Fanselow & Lester, 1988). PTSD patients behave in a way to cope with an actual threat when only a perceived threat is present. This is analagous to an animal using circa-strike behavior when post-encounter defensive behaviors are appropriate. In PTSD, the threat imminence continuum may become distorted in such a way that normal adaptive behavior becomes constrained and defensive behavior is no longer appropriately coordinated to the threat imminence. Exposure to a trauma or severe stressor impairs the ability to judge threat imminence correctly and react accordingly, and a state of anxiety results. Worry, anticipatory fear, and panic-related behaviors occur in the absence of a threat. As pictured in Figure 1.3, instead of spending the majority of time in the preferred mode of safety and control, less time is spent here and continual activation of defensive behaviors occurs. Exposure to a previous trauma causes a sensitized reaction to a stimulus that is incongruent with its level of threat. Using animal models, it is possible to understand how this incongruency may develop.

In our rodent model of stress-induced enhancement of fear learning and in PTSD, behavioral sequalae result after exposure to a stressful traumatic event. Therefore, it seems likely that biological events that occur in response to stressors may be involved in mediating sensitized responses. During stress, the sympathetic nervous system and neuroendocrine stress cascade are activated. The activation of these systems causes the body to undergo a set of adaptive responses that enables it to deal with a challenge and restores homeostasis after the threat has passed. Adaptive stress responses include the mobilization of energy and resources to sustain the brain, heart, and muscles (like increased heart rate and blood pressure); preparation of the immune system; enhanced alertness and memory; and an inhibition of functions not immediately necessary such as feeding and sexual behavior (for review, see Johnson, Kamilaris, Chrousos, & Gold, 1992; Sapolsky, 2000).

The neuroendocrine stress response, mediated by the hypothalamic–pituitary–adrenal (HPA) axis, is initiated by the neuropeptide corticotropin-releasing hormone (CRH) (Antoni, 1986; Owens & Nemeroff, 1991; Vale, Spiess, Rivier, & Rivier, 1981). The paraventricular nucleus of the hypothalamus (PVN) has a high density of CRH neurons and receptors and coordinates activation of the axis (Chalmers, Lovenberg, & De Souza, 1995; Herman et al., 2003; Swanson, Sawchenko, Rivier, & Vale, 1983). CRH neurons in the amygdala contribute to modulating activation of the HPA axis. The inputs from the amygdala to the PVN play an important role in influencing the HPA axis because the amygdala is a key processor and integrator of information about environmental threats (Fanselow & Gale, 2003; Fanselow & LeDoux, 1999; Gray, 1993; Gray, Carney, & Magnuson, 1989; Maren, 2003; Maren & Fanselow, 1996; Sakanaka, Shibasaki, & Lederis, 1986). This amygdalar–PVN relay may quickly facilitate HPA axis activation after a threat has been detected by the amygdala (Herman et al., 2003).

Activation of CRH neurons in the PVN stimulates the release of adrenocorticotropic hormone (ACTH) from the anterior pituitary, which initiates glucocorticoid (primarily corticosterone in the rat, cortisol in humans) synthesis and release from the adrenal cortex (Antoni, 1986; Owens & Nemeroff, 1991; Vale et al., 1981). The release of glucocorticoids by the HPA axis during stress facilitates energy mobilization and helps to turn off

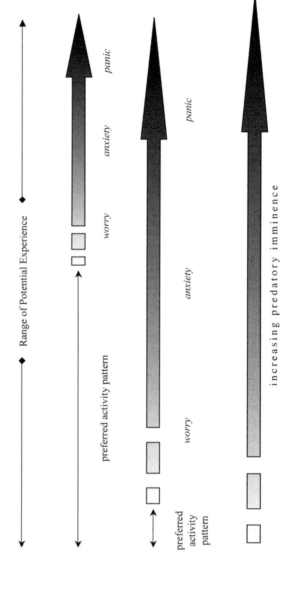

FIGURE 1.3. Shift of behavior in the predatory imminence continuum that may occur in PTSD.

34

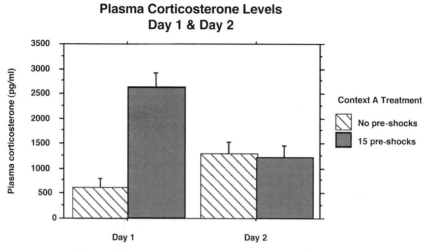

FIGURE 1.4. Effects of shock on corticosterone level. Animals given 15 shocks show an elevated level of corticosterone compared to animals not given shock.

the stress response after the threat has passed (Munck, Guyre, & Holbrook, 1984; Sapolsky, Romero, & Munck, 2000).

Previous experience with stress can alter the normal adaptive activity of the neuroendocrine stress response to future stressors. Rodents exposed to stressors or exogenous stress hormones show increased behavioral and HPA responsiveness to future stressful challenges (Bruijnzeel, Stam, Compaan, & Wiegant, 2001; Cordero, Venero, Kruyt, & Sandi, 2003; Plotsky & Meaney, 1993; Rau, Stenzel-Poore, Mayer, & Fanselow, 2004). This also appears to be the case for our model of stress-induced enhancement of fear learning. Preliminary observations from our laboratory indicate a role for stress hormones in mediating shock-induced enhancement or sensitization of fear learning. As mentioned previously, animals given 15 shocks in one context show enhanced conditional freezing to 1 shock in a second distinct context. Animals given 15 shocks show an elevation in plasma corticosterone, as shown in Figure 1.4 (Rau & Fanselow, 2005). Drugs that inhibit the neuroendocrine stress response attenuate the enhancement of freezing in the single-shock context. Animals given metyrapone, which blocks the synthesis and production of corticosterone, and animals given CP-154,526, which blocks CRH receptors, show attenuated contextual freezing in the single-shock context compared to animals given a vehicle (Rau & Fanselow, 2005). These data are shown in Figures 1.5 and 1.6. Blocking the rise in stress hormones that results from the 15 shocks attenuates the sensitized response to the less intense stressor, the single shock.

These findings are consistent with the hypothesis that altered HPA responsiveness may contribute to the sensitized responses PTSD patients

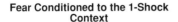

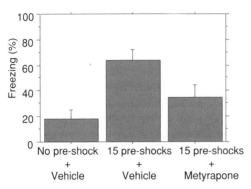

FIGURE 1.5. Effects of inhibiting corticosterone synthesis on freezing behavior. Animals given the corticosterone synthesis inhibitor metyrapone show a reduction in contextual freezing in both the 15-shock and 1-shock contexts.

experience to innocuous events that are perceived as threatening. It has been suggested that PTSD symptoms may develop by a sensitization process involving the HPA axis, which causes less-intense stressors to be perceived as more threatening (Rasmusson & Charney, 1997; Yehuda, 1997). The initial traumatic event activates the stress response. After reexperiencing aspects of the trauma or mild stressors similar to the trauma, the stress response reactivates. Repeated activation in turn modifies the HPA axis's negative feedback system and makes the stress response more

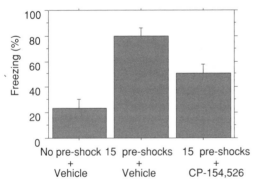

FIGURE 1.6. Effects of blocking CRH$_1$ receptors on freezing behavior. Animals given the CRH antagonist CP-154,526 show a reduction in contextual freezing in both the 15-shock and 1-shock contexts.

easily triggered. Sensitization may cause a lowered activation threshold for future stimuli, facilitating the perception of neutral stimuli as threatening (Hageman, Andersen, & Jorgensen, 2001; Rosen & Schulkin, 1998). Here, a system that is supposed to be adaptive in the face of a threat is instead producing maladaptive responses due to excessive and inappropriate activation. The distortion of the threat continuum shown in Figure 1.3 that may be responsible for some PTSD symptomotology may be the result of a dysregulated neuroendocrine stress system.

This chapter presents an evolutionary view of the role fear plays in protecting both animals and humans from danger. As exemplified by the predatory imminence continuum, fear is an adaptive response that has evolved to protect animals and humans from danger. Fear facilitates the use of defensive behaviors most appropriate to the threat, those that have the highest likelihood of a successful defense. Fear is only adaptive, however, when its level is appropriate to the level of the threat and when it is limited to situations in which an actual threat is present. When fear is inappropriately or excessively activated, negative consequences may result. Inappropriate or excessive activation of fear responses may occur after exposure to a severe stressor or trauma. Rats show enhanced fear responses to mild stressful events after pre-exposure to an intense stressor (Rau et al., 2005). Similarly, people exposed to a traumatic event may show sensitized reactions to neutral stimuli that may be related to the threatening experience. An alteration in the normal adaptive response of the stress system due to prolonged or excessive activation may ultimately decrease the threshold for response activation. In terms of the predatory and threat imminence continuums, less time is spent in the preferred activity pattern or preferred mode of safety and control and more time is spent preparing for attack or worrying about non-existent threats. There is now a decreased threshold for activation for continuum movement. Stress hormones may lower the activation threshold, and a better understanding of how this occurs will contribute to finding ways to return the fear system to its adaptive function.

References

American Psychiatric Association. (2000). *Diagnostic and statistical manual of mental disorders* [text revision] (4th ed.). Washington, DC: Author.

Antoni, F. A. (1986). Hypothalamic control of adrenocorticotropin secretion: Advances since the discovery of 41-residue corticotropin-releasing factor. *Endocrine Reviews, 7*(4), 351–378.

Blanchard, R. J., & Blanchard, D. C. (1989). Antipredator defensive behaviors in a visible burrow system. *Journal of Comparative Psychology, 103*(1), 70–82.

Bolles, R. C. (1970). Species specific defense reactions and avoidance learning. *Psychological Review, 77*, 32–48.

Bolles, R. C., & Collier, A. C. (1976). The effect of predictive cues on freezing in rats. *Animal Learning & Behavior, 41*(1A), 6–8.

Bolles, R. C., & Fanselow, M. S. (1980). A perceptual-defensive-recuperative model of fear and pain. *Behavioral & Brain Sciences, 3,* 291–301.

Bonne, O., Grillon, C., Vythilingam, M., Neumeister, A., & Charney, D. S. (2004). Adaptive and maladaptive psychobiological responses to severe psychological stress: Implications for the discovery of novel pharmacotherapy. *Neuroscience & Biobehavioral Reviews, 28*(1), 65–94.

Bouton, M. E., Mineka, S., & Barlow, D. H. (2001). A modern learning theory perspective on the etiology of panic disorder. *Psychological Reviews, 108*(1), 4–32.

Bruijnzeel, A. W., Stam, R., Compaan, J. C., & Wiegant, V. M. (2001). Stress-induced sensitization of CRH-ir but not P-CREB-ir responsivity in the rat central nervous system. *Brain Research, 908*(2), 187–196.

Chalmers, D. T., Lovenberg, T. W., & De Souza, E. B. (1995). Localization of novel corticotropin-releasing factor receptor (CRF2) mRNA expression to specific subcortical nuclei in rat brain: Comparison with CRF1 receptor mRNA expression. *Journal of Neuroscience, 15*(10), 6340–6350.

Charney, D. S. (2004). Psychobiological mechanisms of resilience and vulnerability: Implications for successful adaptation to extreme stress. *American Journal of Psychiatry, 161*(2), 195–216.

Christopher, M. (2004). A broader view of trauma: A biopsychosocial-evolutionary view of the role of the traumatic stress response in the emergence of pathology and/or growth. *Clinical Psychology Reviews, 24*(1), 75–98.

Cordero, M. I., Venero, C., Kruyt, N. D., & Sandi, C. (2003). Prior exposure to a single stress session facilitates subsequent contextual fear conditioning in rats. Evidence for a role of corticosterone. *Hormones and Behavior, 44*(4), 338–345.

Craske, M. G. (1999). *Anxiety disorders: Psychological approaches to theory and treatment.* Boulder, CO: Westview Press.

De Boer, S. F., & Koolhaas, J. M. (2003). Defensive burying in rodents: Ethology, neurobiology and psychopharmacology. *European Journal of Pharmacology, 463*(1–3), 145–161.

Eberly, R. E., Harkness, A. R., & Engdahl, B. E. (1991). An adaptational view of trauma response as illustrated by the prisoner of war experience. *Journal of Traumatic Stress, 4*(3), 363–380.

Fanselow, M. S. (1980). Conditioned and unconditional components of post-shock freezing. *Pavlovian Journal of Biological Sciences, 15*(4), 177–182.

Fanselow, M. S. (1986). Conditioned fear-induced opiate analgesia: A competing motivational state theory of stress-analgesia. *Annals of the New York Academy of Sciences, 467,* 40–54.

Fanselow, M. S. (1994). Neural organization of the defensive behavior system responsible for fear. *Psychonomic Bulletin & Review, 1*(4), 429–438.

Fanselow, M. S., & Bolles, R. C. (1979). Naloxone and shock-elicited freezing in the rat. *Journal of Comparative and Physiological Psychology, 93*(4), 736–744.

Fanselow, M. S., & Gale, G. D. (2003). The amygdala, fear, and memory. *Annals of the New York Academy of Sciences, 985,* 125–134.

Fanselow, M. S., & LeDoux, J. E. (1999). Why we think plasticity underlying Pavlovian fear conditioning occurs in the basolateral amygdala. *Neuron, 23*(2), 229–232.

Fanselow, M. S., & Lester, L. S. (1988). A functional behavioristic approach to aversively motivated behavior: Predatory imminence as a determinant of the topography of defensive behavior. In R. C. Bolles & M. D. Beecher (Eds.), *Evolution and learning* (pp. 185–211). Hillsdale, NJ: Erlbaum.

Fanselow, M. S., Lester, L. S., & Helmstetter, F. J. (1988). Changes in feeding and foraging patterns as an antipredator defensive strategy: A laboratory simulation using aversive stimulation in a closed economy. *Journal of the Experimental Analysis of Behavior, 50*(3), 361–374.

Fendt, M., & Fanselow, M. S. (1999). The neuroanatomical and neurochemical basis of conditioned fear. *Neuroscience & Biobehavioral Reviews, 23*(5), 743–760.

Gray, T. S. (1993). Amygdaloid CRF pathways. Role in autonomic, neuroendocrine, and behavioral responses to stress. *Annals of the New York Academy of Sciences, 697,* 53–60.

Gray, T. S., Carney, M. E., & Magnuson, D. J. (1989). Direct projections from the central amygdaloid nucleus to the hypothalamic paraventricular nucleus: Possible role in stress-induced adrenocorticotropin release. *Neuroendocrinology, 50*(4), 433–446.

Hageman, I., Andersen, H. S., & Jorgensen, M. B. (2001). Post-traumatic stress disorder: A review of psychobiology and pharmacotherapy. *Acta Psychiatrica Scandinavica, 104*(6), 411–422.

Herman, J. P., Figueiredo, H., Mueller, N. K., Ulrich-Lai, Y., Ostrander, M. M., Choi, D. C., et al. (2003). Central mechanisms of stress integration: Hierarchical circuitry controlling hypothalamo-pituitary-adrenocortical responsiveness. *Frontiers in Neuroendocrinology 24*(3), 151–180.

Holmes, M. M., & Galea, L. A. M. (2002). Defensive behavior and hippocampal cell proliferation: Differential modulation by naltrexone during stress. *Behavioral Neuroscience, 116*(1), 160–168.

Izard, C. E. (1992). Basic emotions, relations among emotions, and emotion-cognition relations. *Psychological Review, 99*(3), 561–565.

Johnson, E. O., Kamilaris, T. C., Chrousos, G. P., & Gold, P. W. (1992). Mechanisms of stress: A dynamic overview of hormonal and behavioral homeostasis. *Neuroscience & Biobehavioral Reviews, 16*(2), 115–130.

LeDoux, J. E. (1995). Emotion: Clues from the brain. *Annual Review of Psychology, 46,* 209–235.

Lester, L. S., & Fanselow, M. S. (1985). Exposure to a cat produces opioid analgesia in rats. *Behavioral Neuroscience, 99*(4), 756–759.

Maren, S. (2001). Neurobiology of Pavlovian fear conditioning. *Annual Review of Neuroscience, 24,* 897–931.

Maren, S. (2003). The amygdala, synaptic plasticity, and fear memory. *Annals of the New York Academy of Sciences, 985,* 106–113.

Maren, S., & Fanselow, M. S. (1996). The amygdala and fear conditioning: Has the nut been cracked? *Neuron, 16*(2), 237–240.

Mathews, A. (1990). Why worry? The cognitive function of anxiety. *Behaviour Research and Therapy, 28*(6), 455–468.

Munck, A., Guyre, P. M., & Holbrook, N. J. (1984). Physiological functions of glucocorticoids in stress and their relation to pharmacological actions. *Endocrine Reviews, 5*(1), 25–44.

Owens, M. J., & Nemeroff, C. B. (1991). Physiology and pharmacology of corticotropin-releasing factor. *Pharmacological Reviews, 43*(4), 425–473.

Pinel, J. P., & Mana, M. J. (Eds.). (1989). *Adaptive interactions of rats with dangerous inanimate objects: Support for a cognitive theory of defensive behavior.* New York: Kluwer Academic/Plenum.

Pinel, J. P., & Treit, D. (1978). Burying as a defensive response in rats. *Journal of Comparative and Physiological Psychology, 92*(4), 708–712.

Plotsky, P. M., & Meaney, M. J. (1993). Early, postnatal experience alters hypothalamic corticotropin-releasing factor (CRF) mRNA, median eminence CRF content and stress-induced release in adult rats. *Molecular Brain Research, 18*(3), 195–200.

Poling, A., Cleary, J., & Monaghan, M. (1981). Burying by rats in response to aversive and nonaversive stimuli. *Journal of Experimental Analysis of Behavior, 35*(1), 31–44.

Rasmussen, A. M., & Charney, D. S. (1997). Animal models of relevance to PTSD. *Annals of the New York Academy of Sciences, 821*, 332–351.

Rau, V., DeCola, J. P., & Fanselow, M. S. (2005). Stress-induced enhancement of fear learning: An animal model of posttraumatic stress disorder. *Neuroscience & Biobehavioral Reviews, 29*(8), 1207–1223.

Rau, V., & Fanselow, M. S. (2005). *The role of CRH$_1$ receptors in shock sensitization.* Paper presented at the Society for Neuroscience Conference, Washington, DC.

Rau, V., Stenzel-Poore, M., Mayer, E., & Fanselow, M. S. (2004). *Enhanced acquisition of contextual fear in CRH-overexpressing transgenic mice.* Paper presented at the Society for Neuroscience Conference, San Diego, CA.

Rosen, J. B., & Schulkin, J. (1998). From normal fear to pathological anxiety. *Psychological Reviews, 105*(2), 325–350.

Sakanaka, M., Shibasaki, T., & Lederis, K. (1986). Distribution and efferent projections of corticotropin-releasing factor-like immunoreactivity in the rat amygdaloid complex. *Brain Research, 382*(2), 213–238.

Sapolsky, R. M. (2000). Stress hormones: Good and bad. *Neurobiology of Disease, 7*(5), 540–542.

Sapolsky, R. M., Romero, L. M., & Munck, A. U. (2000). How do glucocorticoids influence stress responses? Integrating permissive, suppressive, stimulatory, and preparative actions. *Endocrine Reviews, 21*(1), 55–89.

Suarez, S. D., & Gallup, G. G. (1981). An ethological analysis of open-field testing in chickens. *Animal Learning & Behavior, 9*, 153–163.

Swanson, L. W., Sawchenko, P. E., Rivier, J., & Vale, W. W. (1983). Organization of ovine corticotropin-releasing factor immunoreactive cells and fibers in the rat brain: An immunohistochemical study. *Neuroendocrinology, 36*(3), 165–186.

Vale, W., Spiess, J., Rivier, C., & Rivier, J. (1981). Characterization of a 41-residue ovine hypothalamic peptide that stimulates secretion of corticotropin and beta-endorphin. *Science, 213*(4514), 1394–1397.

Yehuda, R. (1997). Sensitization of the hypothalamic-pituitary-adrenal axis in posttraumatic stress disorder. *Annals of the New York Academy of Sciences, 821*, 57–75.

2

Some Biobehavioral Insights into Persistent Effects of Emotional Trauma

Mark E. Bouton and Jaylyn Waddell

For many years, our laboratory has been interested in the biobehavioral mechanisms of classical conditioning and, in particular, the mechanisms behind the conditioning, extinction, and inhibition of fear (e.g., Bouton, 1993, 2002, 2004). In fear conditioning, an organism learns to associate environmental stimuli with a frightening event, and those stimuli consequently evoke fear. Fear can be defined as a loosely coordinated set of physiological, behavioral, and cognitive responses that are designed to get the organism ready for a future aversive event.

Fear conditioning has long been thought to play a role in many anxiety disorders (e.g., Barlow, 2002; Bouton, Mineka, & Barlow, 2001; Mineka & Zinbarg, 1996). It is not difficult to see its relevance when humans are exposed to the type of very intense emotional trauma that can lead to posttraumatic stress disorder, or PTSD (e.g., Pitman, Shalev, & Orr, 2000). Thus, a combat veteran might associate the sound of a helicopter with a horrific battle experience, or a person involved in a collision with a train might associate the blast of the horn and the flash of the headlight with the trauma of the crash. When any of these cues is later encountered or imagined, it might therefore trigger a number of physiological and cognitive responses, the so-called "reexperiencing criteria" used in diagnosing PTSD (e.g., Pitman et al., 2000). And further, the facts that fear elicited this way can motivate avoidance behavior (e.g., Rescorla & Solomon, 1967) and engage analgesic responses (e.g., Bolles & Fanselow, 1980) presumably contribute to the diagnostic "avoidance/numbing" criteria. There seems little doubt that conditioning can contribute to the understanding of disorders like PTSD.

As described by Barad and Quirk in later chapters, fear conditioning is often studied in the rat by presenting a tone conditional stimulus (CS) and pairing it with a footshock unconditional stimulus (US). After a few pairings, the tone evokes fear. We have been especially interested in *extinction*, the fear reversal process in which repeated exposure to the tone without shock eventually makes the fear go away. Extinction presumably plays a major role in exposure therapy, the method used by cognitive-behavioral therapists to reduce fear and anxiety by exposing patients to the feared stimulus. Yet it is also part of the natural world. That is, under normal circumstances, an organism that has been exposed to an emotional trauma might undergo extinction through natural exposure to associated events. Over the course of time, exposures to trigger stimuli without trauma will ensure a kind of recovery, assuming the source of the original trauma – the US – is gone. In this sense, extinction (and perhaps other similar retroactive interference processes) will be part of recovery from emotional trauma.

Our research on extinction, however, has consistently shown that it does not destroy the original fear learning. As we illustrate below, the tone–shock association can remain in memory, ready to return to performance and cause relapse (e.g., Bouton, 1988, 2002; Bouton & Swartzentruber, 1991). During the 2002 symposium that led to the present volume, Arieh Shalev referred to PTSD as a "disorder of recovery" (cf. Shalev, this volume; Shalev & Ursano, 2003), and J. D. Kinzie (this volume) described it as a "chronically relapsing syndrome." If extinction plays a part in the trauma recovery process, then understanding extinction and the factors that can undo it may help provide some additional insight into PTSD.

RELAPSE AND THE CONTEXT DEPENDENCE OF EXTINCTION

There is ample evidence from both behavioral experiments (e.g., Bouton, 2002, 2004) and behavioral neuroscience experiments (e.g., Barad & Cain, this volume; Quirk, Milad, Santini, & Lebrón, this volume) that extinction reflects new learning rather than the destruction of old learning. We have therefore suggested that after extinction the CS has two available meanings. Retrieval of the first one (formed during conditioning) causes fear, and retrieval of the second one (formed during extinction) causes recovery or "safety" performance. The availability of the two associations gives the CS the properties of an ambiguous word: The response it evokes (fear or safety) depends crucially on the current context (e.g., Bouton, 1984, 1988, 2002).

This idea is illustrated by the *renewal effect*. In the simplest example of renewal, a rat receives fear conditioning in which a tone is paired with shock in one context, Context A. Then she receives extinction training (tone without shock) in a second context, Context B, until the fear is gone. In most of this work, the contexts are operationally defined as the experimental chambers in which the rat receives its training. These differ in location in the lab, and in their visual, olfactory, and tactile aspects. (They are also always counterbalanced.) In a final test, the rat is returned to the original context (Context A) and presented merely with the tone. Invariably, even though fear of the tone had been eliminated in Context B, the tone evokes fear again – fear is renewed (e.g., Bouton & King, 1983). Extinction did not destroy the original learning; fear can return to behavior with the right manipulation of context.

The renewal effect can survive extended extinction training, and it occurs in virtually every conditioning preparation in which it has been studied (e.g., see Bouton, 2002). It can theoretically play a role whenever a recovered patient returns to the context of conditioning. For example, Solomon, Garb, Bleich, and Grupper (1987) noted a pattern in several Israeli veterans of the 1973 Yom Kippur War. In one especially compelling case, a serviceman acquired a combat stress reaction partly as a result of an incident in which his armored personnel carrier was bombed (he was the only survivor). He subsequently received treatment and went on to have a successful personal life – until he was called up to serve again in the 1982 Lebanon War. At first, he functioned "adequately." However, when his convoy was ambushed and his personnel carrier was hit, many of his earlier symptoms returned. As he put it, the event "aroused what was dormant inside of me for 9 whole years" (p. 52). Even old and well-extinguished fear reactions can be renewed on return to the original conditioning context.

It is not necessary to return the subject to the original fear context to observe renewal after extinction. In another variation of the experimental design, fear conditioning and extinction occur in Contexts A and B and then testing occurs in a third, neutral, context (Context C) (e.g., Bouton & Bolles, 1979a; Bouton & Brooks, 1993). Here again, extinguished responding is renewed. Alternatively, fear conditioning and extinction are both conducted in Context A and then the final test is conducted in a second context (Context B) (Bouton & Ricker, 1994). Although the strength of the renewal effect is smaller in these "ABC" and "AAB" designs than in the basic "ABA" design, renewal does still occur. Extinction learning is thus relatively context specific; testing the extinguished trigger stimulus in a context not associated with extinction can cause a lapse or relapse. To observe extinction performance, the best bet is to be in the context where extinction has been learned.

Notice that if fear is renewed when the animal is tested in a third, neutral, context, then the original fear learning must transfer to a new context better than extinction does. This is an important insight of our work on the renewal effect: Extinction learning is more specific to its context than the original fear learning is. This generalization is further confirmed by another result we have repeatedly observed in our experiments: Although extinction performance is disrupted by a context change after extinction, conditioning performance is much less disrupted when the context is changed after conditioning (e.g., Bouton & King, 1983). That is, fear elicited by a trigger cue, unlike fear extinction, generalizes easily across contexts. The observation has implications for recovery after trauma. If traumatic learning generalizes across contexts, but the subsequent safety learning (recovery) does so less, then the success of recovery might be an incremental affair in which safety needs to be connected with a wider and wider set of contexts. During the course of recovery, one might observe renewals of emotion as the trigger stimulus is encountered in each new context. Interestingly, this asymmetry between conditioning and extinction is not unique to fear. For example, we have observed the same pattern in appetitive conditioning, where the tone is associated with food rather than footshock (e.g., Bouton & Peck, 1989).

Research with animals further suggests that the "context" can be many different things. Most of the experiments have used physical apparatus cues, which are analogous to rooms and locations that influence human memory retrieval (e.g., Smith & Vela, 2001). However, recent events, deprivation state, hormonal state, and mood may also be part of the context; manipulations of each can produce the renewal effect (e.g., see Bouton, 2002). We also know that context can be provided by interoceptive cues, such as those created by ingestion of drugs. For instance, fear extinction produced while rats are under the influence of benzodiazepine tranquilizers (chlordiazepoxide, diazepam, and midazolam) is specific to the drug state: Testing the rat in the absence of the drug can cause a renewal of extinguished fear (e.g., Bouton, Kenney, & Rosengard, 1990). Similar results have been reported with other drugs, like alcohol (Cunningham, 1979). The implication is clear. If a drug generates an interoceptive context (consistent with the literature on state-dependent learning, e.g., Overton, 1985), then its short-term benefits (reducing fear) may give way to long-term costs (it enables a new renewal effect). We have also pointed out that state-dependent extinction suggests a mechanism for drug dependence. If a drug is taken to reduce fear, it will paradoxically shield the organism from the benefit of natural extinction, leaving the fear that motivated the drug use intact, initiating a vicious cycle in which fear in the absence of the drug will continue to motivate drug ingestion.

Another kind of context is the one provided by the passage of time. Just as extinction seems relatively specific to its physical context, so it is specific to its temporal one. This is our perspective on *spontaneous recovery*, first reported by Pavlov (1927), who found that an extinguished response returned at least partially if a retention interval is introduced between extinction and testing. Like the renewal effect, spontaneous recovery indicates that extinction does not destroy the original learning. The passage of time creates a gradually changing context. In principle, the relative sensitivity of extinction to its temporal and physical context could contribute to the delayed onset of PTSD symptoms. If recovery from a traumatic episode involves extinction, then spontaneous emergence of symptoms could occur.

Interestingly, like renewal in the analogous ABC or AAB renewal paradigms, spontaneous recovery again underscores the relative stability of conditioning across contexts. And, consistent with the idea that sponta-neous recovery and renewal are both produced by a failure to retrieve extinction outside the extinction context, a retrieval cue for extinction pre-sented just before the test abolishes both effects (e.g., Brooks, 2000; Brooks & Bouton, 1993, 1994). One implication is that successful recovery can be facilitated by providing ways for the patient to access or retrieve it in other contexts. Such an effect may be provided by cards or other props that remind clients of the therapy experience. Collins and Brandon (2002) recently demonstrated a renewal effect when social drinkers were given exposure to the sight and odor of beer in one room, and then extinction (of both salivation and an urge to drink) was tested in a second room. Although the responses were renewed, presentation of a distinctive cue from the extinction context retrieved extinction and attenuated the renewal effect.

Another context that might be relevant in humans is the mental one. Renewal effects have been produced in human associative learning tasks by simply manipulating the context through imagination. For example, Rosas, Vila, Lugo, and Lopez (2001) had participants learn about reac-tions to fictitious drugs over trials created by a series of medical cases. For instance, participants first learned that the drug "Batim" was asso-ciated with fever in a particular hospital ("Vanguardia Hospital"). Sub-sequently, Batim was associated with a different reaction (e.g., physical energy) in a different context ("the Central Clinic"). When the participants were asked what they believed Batim would do if it were presented in Vanguardia again, they expected it to cause fever – the first belief was renewed. Rosas et al. (2001) also reported a spontaneous recovery effect: When Batim had been associated with fever and then energy in the same hospital, if participants left the laboratory and then returned 48 hours later, they now believed the first association (fever) was in force again. This effect combined additively with the renewal effect; having temporal and men-tal context switches together produced more renewal than either alone. Additivity has also been observed in animal experiments that combined time and physical context change (e.g., Rosas & Bouton, 1997). Temporal, physical, and imaginary context changes combine in a way that suggests they operate similarly.

Mystkowski, Craske, Echiverri, and Labus (2006) have also reported an effect of manipulating contexts mentally. They found that a renewal of spider fear in humans that was induced by switching the context after an exposure treatment (see also Mystkowski, Craske, & Echiverri, 2002) can be attenuated by having the participant think about the context in which extinction had previously occurred. This effect is probably related to the effect of retrieval cues described above. Imagination and mental "set" might conceivably play interesting roles in promoting extinction and recovery across contexts.

Yet another relapse effect may be relevant in understanding the after-effects of trauma. In *reinstatement*, the extinguished response can return after extinction if the animal is merely reexposed to the US (e.g., Bouton, 1984; Pavlov, 1927; Rescorla & Heth, 1975). In a rat experiment, a few presentations of the original footshock can cause a return of fear when the CS is tested again. This phenomenon has implications for a chronically relapsing syndrome because it suggests that further trauma may undo the positive effects of extinction and recovery. However, reexposure to the US alone is not sufficient to cause reinstatement. Instead, when the shocks are presented after extinction, the organism associates them with the context. This creates a kind of *anticipation* of shock when the animal is next returned to that context. And this context-aroused anticipation needs to be present if reinstatement is to occur. For example, if the reinstating shocks are presented in an irrelevant context that is different from the one in which the CS is then tested, there is no reinstatement when the CS is tested again (e.g., Bouton, 1984; Bouton & Bolles, 1979b; Bouton & King, 1983; Frohardt, Guarraci, & Bouton, 2000; Wilson, Brooks, & Bouton, 1995). Or if the animal receives extensive extinction exposure to the context after the reinstatement shocks are presented, the effect may go away (Bouton & Bolles, 1979b). Mere reexposure to trauma is not sufficient to generate reinstatement. It is caused by anticipation of further harm when the CS is tested again.

Interestingly, Kinzie, Boehnlein, Riley, and Sparr (2002; Kinzie, this volume) have reported that the 9/11 disaster caused an analogous reinstatement of self-reported nightmares and flashbacks among PTSD patients. The patients were refugees who had experienced trauma in their home countries before emigrating to the United States. Kinzie et al. (2002) reported that the 9/11 disaster made their patients have a "sense of not being safe in America" (p. 438); in a sense, the current context had become dangerous. Toren, Wolmer, Weizman, Magal-Vardi, and Laor (2002) similarly found that the mere threat of Iraqi missile attacks in February 1998 among Israeli citizens whose homes had been damaged by Scud missiles during the 1991 Gulf War was correlated with increased intrusive thoughts, avoidance, and anger. In the study of Israeli combat veterans mentioned previously, Solomon et al. (1987) provided other evidence of a reinstatement effect. Some veterans of the 1973 war who had developed combat stress reaction eventually recovered, at least partially. But when they received the call to return to service for the 1982 war, this group experienced "high anticipatory anxiety," which led them to respond "with exacerbated stress to relatively minor events that reminded them of their earlier traumatic experiences. In many of these instances, reactivation of a residual or subthreshold posttraumatic stress disorder to full-blown posttraumatic stress disorder occurred without any substantial combat exposure" (p. 53).

To summarize, basic learning research is consistent with case studies in suggesting that the effects of fear learning can persist long after their behavioral manifestations have disappeared. Renewal, spontaneous recovery, and reinstatement all suggest that extinction does not create unlearning, and they are also consistent with the idea that performance after extinction is especially sensitive to the current context. Trauma learning is not necessarily erased during recovery but may be ready to reemerge in performance on return to the original context, in a new context, later in time, or in the presence of anticipatory anxiety. Extinction research may thus shed some light on PTSD as a chronically relapsing syndrome. For a more detailed review of these and additional phenomena, see Bouton (2002, 2004) or Bouton and Swartzentruber (1991).

EXTINCTION AND OTHER FORMS OF INHIBITION

Extinction is just one example of a situation in which new learning comes along to replace initial learning. There are a number of other paradigms in learning theory that involve such retroactive interference, and interestingly, all of them are similarly dependent on contextual and temporal factors (see Bouton, 1993). For instance, in counterconditioning, fear conditioning (pairings of tone and shock) is followed by appetitive conditioning (pairings of tone and food) instead of simple extinction (presentations of tone alone). Like extinction, new learning in the second phase also abolishes fear performance, and it is the theoretical basis for clinical treatments such as systematic desensitization (Wolpe, 1958). But it does not destroy the original learning; performance once again is sensitive to ambiguity and context. We have observed renewal (Peck & Bouton, 1990), spontaneous recovery (Bouton & Peck, 1992), and reinstatement (Brooks, Hale, Nelson, & Bouton, 1995) after counterconditioning. As we saw in extinction, counterconditioned performance is sensitive to context and time.

Another kind of renewal occurs with behavioral triggers that are being actively inhibited by other cues. For example, learning theorists have run many experiments with the so-called "conditioned inhibition" procedure (Pavlov, 1927). In this procedure, the experimenter mixes trials in which one CS (A) is paired with a US, and other trials in which A is combined with a second CS (X) and presented without the US: A+, AX−. The animal learns to discriminate between the two types of trial: Stimulus A triggers a response on its own, but X inhibits responding to A. We have asked whether this type of inhibition survives a change in context (Bouton & Nelson, 1994; Nelson & Bouton, 1997). Surprisingly, X's inhibition was not affected by the context switch; X could still inhibit responding to other CSs in a new context. But responding to A was more difficult to inhibit when it was tested in a new context. A PTSD parallel might be as follows. On her suburban college campus, a rape victim might learn to inhibit fear that is triggered by the sound of footsteps behind her (Stimulus A) by remembering the face of her therapist (Stimulus X). But in a different context, away from campus, the fear at the sound of sudden footsteps may be harder to suppress by Stimulus X. Although the image of the therapist might have pure inhibitory properties that transfer well across contexts, the fear evoked by sudden footsteps might be harder to inhibit in a different context. Although inhibition is not generally context specific, the inhibitability of trigger cues may be.

In recent unpublished work, we have discovered that another inhibitory process is also sensitive to context. Along with Russell Frohardt, Ceyhun Sunsay, and Richard W. Morris, we have given rats a series of sessions in which they receive repeated CS–shock pairings. Often, fear elicited by the CS reached a maximum after several conditioning sessions and then began to decline despite the fact that the CS and the shock were still being paired. Such "inhibition with reinforcement" is often observed in fear conditioning (e.g., Ayres, Berger-Gross, Kohler, Mahoney, & Stone, 1979; Overmier, Payne, Brackbill, Linder, & Lawry, 1979) and in other conditioning preparations (e.g., Pavlov, 1927). The rat gradually adapts and begins to exhibit less fear of the CS.

We do not have a full understanding of this process. Our own experiments indicate that it does not depend on "inhibition of delay," in which the animal learns the predictable timing of the shock presentation in the CS and extinguishes fear during the safer portions. It also is not due to recruitment of an endorphin response that makes the shocks less painful: Administration of the opiate antagonist naloxone does not abolish the effect (Vigorito & Ayres, 1987). Instead, our results suggest that it is due to the context-specific recruitment of some inhibitory process that allows the rat to adapt to conditioned fear. After adaptation has occurred, if we now test the CS in a different context, fear of the CS actually *increases* (see also Kaye & Mackintosh, 1990). This increase in fear is correlated with the degree to which the animal has otherwise adapted to fear (i.e., decreased its fear from the maximal point). Thus, we have tentatively identified a kind of inhibitory coping effect that is specific to the context in which it is learned.

We can only speculate about the relevance of such a process to PTSD. However, it might not be unreasonable to think that humans exposed to large-scale disasters (such as combat, genocide, or the 9/11 tragedy) are subjected to repeated emotional experiences that constitute an extended series of fear conditioning trials. If this were the case, a similar adaptation process might eventually develop. Our results suggest that the effectiveness of that adaptation would be reduced by contextual change, another potential contributor to a chronically relapsing syndrome. Bouton (2005) also noted that the increase in fear to trigger cues in new contexts might ultimately encourage patients to stay at home, a phenomenon that occurs in patients with panic disorder who develop agoraphobia. A stay-at-home strategy would be maladaptive in the long run if it interfered with the person's opportunities to go out and receive extinction.

It is also conceivable that organismic abnormalities (either organic or learned) may interfere with this inhibition process. Interestingly, there is a hint of evidence that it is compromised in PTSD patients. Such individuals show greater electrodermal conditioning than controls when a visual CS is paired over trials with shock (Orr et al., 2000). However, close inspection of the data suggests that over trials the controls (who had experienced similar trauma in their lives, but had not developed PTSD) reached a peak of electrodermal responding which then began to decline over additional CS–shock pairings. The heightened conditioning in the PTSD patients mainly took the form of a lack of such adaptation over trials.

FEAR, ANXIETY, AND EXTINCTION

Some of our recent research has investigated the effects of anxiety on fear extinction. Although fear and anxiety are conflated in many discussions of negative emotion, there is growing evidence that the two states may be elicited by different external stimuli and mediated by different brain substrates. According to Davis and his colleagues (e.g., Davis & Lee, 1998; Davis & Shi, 1999; Davis, Walker, & Lee, 1997), fear is mediated by the basolateral and central nuclei of the amygdala (for a recent review, see LeDoux, 2000), whereas anxiety relies on the integrity of the bed nucleus of the stria terminalis (BNST). The two systems appear to be doubly dissociated in the sense that manipulations of the amygdala affect fear and not anxiety, and manipulations of the BNST affect anxiety but not fear (Davis & Shi, 1999; Davis et al., 1997; Lee & Davis, 1997). At the behavioral level, fear is typically thought to be controlled by relatively brief CSs that are associated with shock. Anxiety, in contrast, is typically created by other manipulations, such as extended exposure to bright light (Davis et al., 1997) and by the administration of corticotropin-releasing factor (CRF) (Lee & Davis, 1997).

Davis and his colleagues have emphasized the idea that extended exposure to bright lights and CRF administration are unlearned means of evoking anxiety in rats (who are nocturnal animals). However, we believe that anxiety may also come under the control of learning through classical conditioning. Based on a functional, evolutionary perspective, we (Bouton, 2005; Bouton et al., 2001) suggested that fear is an emotion that is organized to deal with an aversive US that is highly imminent, whereas anxiety is an emotion that is designed to deal with an aversive US that is approaching more remotely in time (see also Rau & Fanselow, this volume). Based on the properties of other behavior systems (e.g., Domjan, 1994; Timberlake, 2001), we suggested that fear may therefore be elicited by short-duration cues that signal a US that is coming soon, whereas anxiety may be elicited by CSs that signal a US that is coming more remotely in time. We also suggested that a background of anxiety may potentiate fear elicited by a discrete CS. Temporal factors are known to influence the form of conditioned responses in many systems.[1]

Waddell, Morris, and Bouton (2006) tested whether a long CS paired with a footshock US would elicit a state of anxiety that depends on the BNST. Rats first received lesions of the BNST or a sham surgery. They then received conditioning in which a footshock US occurred at the end of either a 1-minute CS or a 10-minute CS. We used the conditioned suppression method, in which aversive conditioning is indexed by the degree to which the CS suppresses an ongoing operant lever-pressing baseline reinforced by food. Both the 1-min and the 10-min CSs suppressed the baseline as a function of repeated CS–US pairings. Consistent with previous work (e.g., Hitchcock & Davis, 1991; Lee & Davis, 1997), BNST lesions did not disrupt fear conditioning with the 1-min CS. In contrast, the lesions did attenuate fear to the 10-min CS. The result suggests that conditioning with a long signal for shock is affected by the brain area that controls anxiety. Long-duration cues may thus evoke anxiety rather than fear.

Another long-duration cue is the type of stimulus we discussed earlier: the background context. In the context experiments summarized above, the rat is typically placed in the experimental box (the context) for 90-min sessions in which several 1-min CSs may be presented. In a typical reinstatement experiment, four or eight 0.5-second shocks typically constitute the reinstatement treatment; these are sparsely distributed throughout the 90-min session. Interestingly, despite the clear evidence that contextual conditioning is necessary for reinstatement, the rat can show little fear of the context during the test. It does not usually freeze (perhaps the rat's dominant fear response, e.g., Fanselow & Lester, 1988; Rau & Fanselow, this volume) or show suppression of an operant baseline. When we were studying the role of context in reinstatement (Bouton, 1984; Bouton & King, 1983, 1986), we had to develop special measures of context conditioning to confirm its role. Specifically, we gave the rat the choice of sitting in a

---

[1] For example, in sexual conditioning in male Japanese quail, a short CS that predicts a copulatory experience within the next 60 s elicits approach behavior, whereas a longer CS that predicts copulation in 20 min elicits a very different pacing response that might function as a general search behavior (e.g., Akins, Domjan, & Gutierrez, 1994). Similarly, in rabbit aversive conditioning, a very brief (1-s) CS that signals shock near the eye will elicit an eyeblink response, whereas a longer (6.75-s) CS does not; the longer cue instead elicits a change in heart rate (e.g., suggesting fear; VanDerCar & Schneiderman, 1967). In these and other behavior systems, the conditioned response evoked by a CS of a given duration gets the organism ready for the US at the corresponding time scale (e.g., Timberlake, 2001). But long and short cues still interact; the presence of a long cue will potentiate responding to a short cue. Thus, fear aroused by the longer CS will potentiate eyeblink (Wagner & Brandon, 1989) and startle (Brown, Kalish, & Farber, 1951) responses, and the male quail's response to a short CS is potentiated when it is tested in the presence of a longer cue that gets the animal ready to respond more vigorously to the short CS (Akins et al., 1994).

safe side box or lever pressing for food reward in the main context, where US and CS were presented. Rats that had been shocked in the context the day before spent significant time in the side box, despite the absence of freezing. They did not usually exhibit many overt behaviors suggesting fear.

Perhaps the context was eliciting anxiety rather than fear. The BNST, the brain area thought to mediate anxiety, is involved when contexts are associated with shock. For example, lesions of the BNST may disrupt contextual conditioning but not CS conditioning (Sullivan et al., 2004). Even more to the point, Waddell et al. (2006) demonstrated that lesions of the BNST attenuated the reinstatement of extinguished fear. Rats received lesions of the BNST and then fear conditioning and extinction with our usual 1-min CS. The lesion again had no effect on fear conditioning. The rats then received eight shocks in a 90-min session. In controls, this was sufficient to reinstate extinguished fear when the CS was presented again. But animals with a lesioned BNST showed little reinstatement. The results suggest that context conditioning reinstates extinguished fear because the context evokes anxiety. Under normal conditions, anxiety conditioned to the context may reinstate extinguished fear.

The effects of the BNST are consistent with other research showing a similar role of the hippocampus (Frohardt et al., 2000; Wilson et al., 1995). It is widely thought that the hippocampus is involved in the integration of the various features of the context into one coherent neural representation (e.g., Fanselow, 2000). Consistent with this, the hippocampus is necessary for the acquisition of aversive contextual conditioning (Kim & Fanselow, 1992; Phillips & LeDoux, 1992). It is also involved in the reinstatement of fear: Disrupting hippocampal output with lesions of the fornix (Wilson et al., 1995) or neurotoxic lesions of the hippocampus proper (Frohardt et al., 2000) both abolish reinstatement. Whether there is a truly general role of the hippocampus in context learning is not clear. Both Frohardt et al. (2000) and Wilson et al. (1995) found that the hippocampal manipulations that abolished reinstatement had no effect on the renewal effect reviewed earlier (cf. Corcoran & Maren, 2004). But to date, there is little question that the hippocampus is involved in the fear-reinstatement effect.

The role of the hippocampus may be due to the fact that it (like the BNST) may be involved in anxiety. This similarity in function is supported by their anatomical relationship. The ventral hippocampus sends dense projections by way of the fimbria–fornix to the BNST, which also receives heavy inputs from the amygdala (Cullinan, Herman, & Watson, 1993; Sun, Roberts, & Cassell, 1991). In a dissociation that is reminiscent of that between the BNST and the amygdala, McHugh, Deacon, Rawlins, and Bannerman (2004) demonstrated that lesions of the ventral hippocampus have anxiolytic effects: They reduce the rat's latency to enter the bright side of a two-compartment box, reduce the latency to begin eating a novel food, and increase time spent in a bright compartment in a successive alleys test, a modified version of the elevated plus-maze (McHugh et al., 2004). Though amygdala lesions also reduced the latency to enter the brightly lit side of a two-compartment box, the lesion did not affect performance on the successive alleys test, and increased rather than reduced the latency to consume a novel food (McHugh et al., 2004). The absence of an effect of amygdala lesions on the modified elevated plus-maze agrees with previous investigations of amygdala lesions and this measure of anxiety (e.g., Treit, Pesold, & Rotzinger, 1993). The hippocampus may thus be part of a circuit that is sensitive to context and plays a role in producing anxiety.

The hippocampus, amygdala, and the BNST contain CRF receptors. As noted before, central administration of CRF arouses an anxiety in rats that is abolished by BNST lesions but not central amygdala lesions (Lee & Davis, 1997). We have therefore examined the role of CRF in reinstatement (Waddell, Falls, Bouton, & Lowe, 2006). Using a factorial design, different groups of rats were infused with the CRF antagonist α-helical CRF in the lateral ventricle either immediately before US exposure (contextual anxiety conditioning) or just before the final test (when the context should elicit anxiety). We found that α-helical CRF blocked reinstatement when it was administered before either testing or US exposure. A group that received the CRF antagonist before both context conditioning and testing also failed to exhibit reinstatement, suggesting that the drug was not merely causing state-dependent retention (Overton, 1985). Instead, CRF may play a role in both the conditioning and evocation of anxiety. We also found that local infusion of the CRF antagonist into either the BNST or the central nucleus of the amygdala during US exposure disrupted reinstatement. The results further implicate CRF and the circuitry involved in fear and anxiety in mediating the reinstatement effect.

The point, then, is that anxiety may play a role in causing a relapse of fear to an extinguished CS. (It is relevant to note that the same contextual conditioning that augments fear of an extinguished CS has no impact on fear of a CS that has not undergone extinction [e.g., Bouton, 1984; Bouton & King, 1986]). The presence of anxiety would make fear extinction difficult and thus interfere with recovery from trauma. There is evidence that anxiety does contribute to PTSD. We have already mentioned Solomon et al.'s (1987) suggestion that anxiety in combat veterans can cause trigger cues to evoke PTSD symptoms again. In addition, anxiety may be a more general vulnerability factor for the development of chronic PTSD (Breslau & Davis, 1992). Early emotional traumas, a family history of anxiety, or childhood physical abuse may be associated with higher rates of PTSD (Bremner, Southwick, Johnson, Yehuda, & Charney, 1993; Breslau & Davis, 1992; Yehuda, Schmeidler, Wainberg, Binder-Brynes, & Duvdevani, 1998). Based on the extinction mechanisms discussed previously, anxiety might make an individual more vulnerable to relapse.

This point represents a subtle change in emphasis. Anxiety is not only elicited by long-duration conditional stimuli; it may also be a more free-floating product of genetic predisposition or developmental challenges. Stressors early in life, such as childhood physical or sexual abuse (Bremner et al., 1993; see chapters by Bremner and van der Kolk, this volume) and separation from parents (Breslau & Davis, 1992) appear to increase the likelihood of the development of PTSD. Analysis of aversive events in early development of rats has implicated disruption of the HPA axis (Francis & Meaney, 1999). In rats, daily separation from the mother early in development can decrease adaptive behavioral and endocrine responses to stressful events experienced in adulthood. These early environmental manipulations modulate the development of CRF systems within the brain (Francis & Meaney, 1999). Interestingly, rats that received high levels of licking and grooming from the mother after isolation were less likely to exhibit exacerbated corticosterone responses to restraint stress in adulthood, probably caused by higher sensitivity to inhibitory feedback by stress hormones activated by the stressful event (Liu et al., 1997). The higher sensitivity appeared to be due to increased glucocorticoid receptors within the hippocampus, and a correlated decrease of CRF mRNA expression in the paraventricular nucleus of the hypothalamus (Liu et al., 1997). These results suggest that the hippocampus may play a role in the regulation of reactivity to aversive events by acting as a source of inhibition on central CRF systems. Equally important, early experience has long-lasting effects on the rat's reactivity to stress in adulthood.

Disruption of the HPA axis is associated with a number of pathological states, including both clinical depression and PTSD. While depression is consistently characterized by higher levels of cortisol, cortisol levels in PTSD patients may be higher or lower than controls (Bremner et al., 1997; Yehuda, Southwick, Nussbaum, Giller, & Mason, 1991). What is consistent across studies, however, is that the HPA axis is disregulated. Yehuda, Giller, Southwick, Lowy, and Mason (1991) suggested that anomalous cortisol levels in PTSD patients may reflect adaptation of the HPA axis to chronic stress. Individuals with PTSD do not exhibit normal negative feedback of the HPA axis. It appears that inhibition of the hypothalamus is lost in cases of PTSD, though results with this population are mixed (Yehuda, Golier, Halligan, Meaney, & Bierer, 2004).

Whether anxiety is elicited by anticipatory cues (e.g., long-duration contexts, as in reinstatement) or is chronically present, it might interfere with successful recovery after exposure to trauma in part by interfering with the normal response to stress and to the extinction process.

SUMMARY AND CONCLUSIONS

This brief review has uncovered several reasons why the effects of trauma may be persistent. Fear conditioning, which may be inevitably involved when organisms are exposed to traumatic events and experiences, seems remarkably durable and impervious to destruction by retroactive interference treatments. Extinction and other psychological recovery processes do not necessarily destroy the original fear learning. Instead, they leave it encoded in the brain, potentially available for retrieval and relapse.

We have discussed several phenomena from learning experiments that may provide some insight into relapse. The general rule of thumb is that extinction does not abolish the original learning, but instead gives the trigger cue a new meaning that is especially sensitive to the context. Thus, a return to the original context can cause a robust renewal of fear, as can presentation of extinguished trigger cues in a new context or at a later point in time. We also noted that other recovery effects (such as counterconditioning and the possible adaptation to fear that occurs during extended fear conditioning) are also context dependent. And we emphasized the possibility that anxiety, either elicited by conditioned long-duration contextual cues that signal aversive events relatively distant in the future or stimulated nonassociatively through other mechanisms, might cause a reinstatement of fear to extinguished trigger cues. Together, these phenomena help provide a framework for understanding some of the persistence of PTSD, a chronically relapsing syndrome, and perhaps for integrating many biological and psychological responses to trauma's effects.

ACKNOWLEDGMENTS

Preparation of this manuscript was supported by Grant RO1 MH64847 from the National Institute of Mental Health to Mark E. Bouton. We thank Karen Fondacaro, Laura Gibson, and Mark Barad for their comments. Send correspondence to Mark E. Bouton, Department of Psychology, University of Vermont, Burlington, VT 05405.

References

Akins, C. K., Domjan, M., & Gutierrez, G. (1994). Topography of sexually conditioned behavior in male Japanese quail (*Coturnix japonica*) depends on the CS-US interval. *Journal of Experimental Psychology: Animal Behavior Processes, 20*, 199–209.

Ayres, J. J. B., Berger-Gross, P., Kohler, E. A., Mahoney, W. J., & Stone, S. (1979). Some orderly nonmonotonicities in the trial-by-trial acquisition of conditioned suppression: Inhibition with reinforcement? *Animal Learning & Behavior, 7*, 174–180.

Barlow, D. H. (2002). *Anxiety and its disorders: The nature and treatment of anxiety and panic* (2nd ed.). New York: Guilford Press.

Bolles, R. C., & Fanselow, M. S. (1980). A perceptual-defensive-recuperative model of fear and pain. *Behavioral & Brain Sciences, 3*, 291–323.

Bouton, M. E. (1984). Differential control by context in the inflation and reinstatement paradigms. *Journal of Experimental Psychology: Animal Behavior Processes, 10*, 56–74.

Bouton, M. E. (1988). Context and ambiguity in the extinction of emotional learning: Implications for exposure therapy. *Behaviour Research and Therapy, 26*, 137–149.

Bouton, M. E. (1993). Context, time, and memory retrieval in the interference paradigms of Pavlovian learning. *Psychological Bulletin, 114*, 80–99.

Bouton, M. E. (2002). Context, ambiguity, and unlearning: Sources of relapse after behavioral extinction. *Biological Psychiatry, 52*, 976–986.

Bouton, M. E. (2004). Context and behavioral processes in extinction. *Learning & Memory, 11*, 485–494.

Bouton, M. E. (2005). Behavior systems and the contextual control of anxiety, fear and panic. In L. F. Barrett, P. Niedenthal, & P. Winkelman (Eds.), *Emotion: Conscious and unconscious* (pp. 205–227). New York: Guilford.

Bouton, M. E., & Bolles, R. C. (1979a). Contextual control of the extinction of conditioned fear. *Learning and Motivation, 10*, 445–466.

Bouton, M. E., & Bolles, R. C. (1979b). Role of conditioned contextual stimuli in reinstatement of extinguished fear. *Journal of Experimental Psychology: Animal Behavior Processes, 5*, 368–378.

Bouton, M. E., & Brooks, D. C. (1993). Time and context effects on performance in a Pavlovian discrimination reversal. *Journal of Experimental Psychology: Animal Behavior Processes, 19*, 165–179.

Bouton, M. E., Kenney, F. A., & Rosengard, C. (1990). State-dependent fear extinction with two benzodiazepine tranquilizers. *Behavioral Neuroscience, 104*, 44–55.

Bouton, M. E., & King, D. A. (1983). Contextual control of the extinction of conditioned fear: Tests for the associative value of the context. *Journal of Experimental Psychology: Animal Behavior Processes, 9*, 248–265.

Bouton, M. E., & King, D. A. (1986). Effect of context on performance to conditioned stimuli with mixed histories of reinforcement and nonreinforcement. *Journal of Experimental Psychology: Animal Behavior Processes, 12*, 4–15.

Bouton, M. E., Mineka, S., & Barlow, D. H. (2001). A modern learning theory perspective on the etiology of panic disorder. *Psychological Review, 108*, 4–32.

Bouton, M. E., & Nelson, J. B. (1994). Context-specificity of target versus feature inhibition in a feature-negative discrimination. *Journal of Experimental Psychology: Animal Behavior Processes, 20*, 51–65.

Bouton, M. E., & Peck, C. A. (1989). Context effects on conditioning, extinction, and reinstatement in an appetitive conditioning preparation. *Animal Learning & Behavior, 17*, 188–198.

Bouton, M. E., & Peck, C. A. (1992). Recovery in cross-motivational transfer (counterconditioning). *Animal Learning & Behavior, 20*, 313–321.

Bouton, M. E., & Ricker, S. T. (1994). Renewal of extinguished responding in a second context. *Animal Learning & Behavior, 22*, 317–324.

Bouton, M. E., & Swartzentruber, D. (1991). Sources of relapse after extinction in Pavlovian and instrumental learning. *Clinical Psychology Review, 11*, 123–140.

Bremner, J. D., Licinio, J., Darnell, A., Krystal, J. H., Owens, M., Southwick, S. M., et al. (1997). Elevated CSF corticotrophin-releasing factor concentrations in posttraumatic stress disorder. *American Journal of Psychiatry, 154*, 624–629.

Bremner, J. D., Southwick, S. M., Johnson, D. R., Yehuda, R., & Charney, D. S. (1993). Childhood physical abuse and combat-related posttraumatic stress disorder in Vietnam veterans. *American Journal of Psychiatry, 150*, 235–239.

Breslau, N., & Davis, G. C. (1992). Posttraumatic stress disorder in an urban population of young adults: Risk factors for chronicity. *American Journal of Psychiatry, 149*, 671–675.

Brooks, D. C. (2000). Recent and remote extinction cues reduce spontaneous recovery. *Quarterly Journal of Experimental Psychology, 53B*, 25–58.

Brooks, D. C., & Bouton, M. E. (1993). A retrieval cue for extinction attenuates spontaneous recovery. *Journal of Experimental Psychology: Animal Behavior Processes, 19*, 77–89.

Brooks, D. C., & Bouton, M. E. (1994). A retrieval cue for extinction attenuates response recovery (renewal) caused by a return to the conditioning context. *Journal of Experimental Psychology: Animal Behavior Processes, 20*, 366–379.

Brooks, D. C., Hale, B., Nelson, J. B., & Bouton, M. E. (1995). Reinstatement after counterconditioning. *Animal Learning & Behavior, 23*, 383–390.

Brown, J. S., Kalish, H. I., & Farber, I. E. (1951). Conditioned fear as revealed by magnitude of startle response to an auditory stimulus. *Journal of Experimental Psychology, 41*, 317–327.

Collins, B. N., & Brandon, T. H. (2002). Effects of extinction context and retrieval cues on alcohol cue reactivity among nonalcoholic drinkers. *Journal of Consulting and Clinical Psychology, 70*, 390–397.

Corcoran, K. A., & Maren, S. (2004). Factors regulating the effects of hippocampal inactivation on renewal of conditional fear after extinction. *Learning & Memory, 11*, 598–603.

Cullinan, W. E., Herman, J. P., & Watson, S. J. (1993). Ventral subicular interaction with the hypothalamic paraventricular nucleus: Evidence for a relay in the bed nucleus of the stria terminalis. *Journal of Comparative Neurology, 332*, 1–20.

Cunningham, C. L. (1979). Alcohol as a cue for extinction: State dependency produced by conditioned inhibition. *Animal Learning & Behavior, 7*, 45–52.

Davis, M., & Lee, Y. (1998). Fear and anxiety: Possible roles of the amygdala and bed nucleus of the stria terminalis. *Cognition and Emotion, 12*, 277–305.

Davis, M., & Shi, C. (1999). The extended amygdala: Are the central nucleus of the amygdala and the bed nucleus of the stria terminalis differentially involved in fear versus anxiety? *Annals of the New York Academy of Sciences, 877*, 281–291.

Davis, M., Walker, D. L., & Lee, Y. (1997). Roles for the amygdala and bed nucleus of the stria terminalis in fear and anxiety measured with the acoustic startle reflex. *Annals of the New York Academy of Sciences, 821*, 305–331.

Domjan, M. (1994). Formulation of a behavior system for sexual conditioning. *Psychonomic Bulletin & Review, 1*, 421–428.

Fanselow, M. S. (2000). Contextual fear, gestalt memories, and the hippocampus. *Behavioural Brain Research, 110*, 73–81.

Fanselow, M. S., & Lester, L. S. (1988). A functional behavioristic approach to aversively motivated behavior: Predatory imminence as a determinant of the topography of defensive behavior. In R. C. Bolles & M. D. Beecher (Eds.), *Evolution and learning* (pp. 185–212). Hillsdale, NJ: Lawrence Erlbaum Associates.

Francis, D. D., & Meaney, M. J. (1999). Maternal care and the development of stress response. *Current Opinion in Neurobiology, 9*, 128–134.

Frohardt, R. J., Guarraci, F. A., & Bouton, M. E. (2000). The effects of neurotoxic hippocampal lesions on two effects of context after fear extinction. *Behavioral Neuroscience, 114,* 227–240.

Hitchcock, J. M., & Davis, M. (1991). Efferent pathway of the amygdala involved in conditioned fear as measured with the fear-potentiated startle paradigm. *Behavioral Neuroscience, 105,* 826–842.

Kaye, H., & Mackintosh, N. J. (1990). A change of context can enhance performance of an aversive but not of an appetitive conditioned response. *Quarterly Journal of Experimental Psychology, 42B,* 113–134.

Kim, J. J., & Fanselow, M. S. (1992). Modality specific retrograde amnesia of fear. *Science, 256,* 675–677.

Kinzie, J. D., Boehnlein, M. D., Riley, M. A., & Sparr, L. (2002). The effects of September 11 on traumatized refugees: Reactivation of posttraumatic stress disorder. *Journal of Nervous and Mental Disease, 190,* 437–441.

LeDoux, J. E. (2000). Emotional circuits in the brain. *Annual Reviews in Neuroscience, 23,* 155–184.

Lee, Y., & Davis, M. (1997). Role of the hippocampus, the bed nucleus of the stria terminalis and the amygdala in the excitatory effect of corticotropin-releasing hormone on the acoustic startle reflex. *Journal of Neuroscience, 1,* 6434–6446.

Liu, D., Tannenbum, B., Caldji, C., Francis, D., Freedman, A., Sharma, S., et al. (1997). Maternal care, hippocampal glucocorticoid receptor gene expression and hypothalamic-pituitary-adrenal responses to stress. *Science, 277,* 1659–1662.

McHugh, S. B., Deacon, R. M. J., Rawlins, J. N. P., & Bannerman, D. M. (2004). Amygdala and ventral hippocampus contribute differentially to mechanisms of fear and anxiety. *Behavioral Neuroscience, 118,* 63–78.

Mineka, S., & Zinbarg, R. (1996). Conditioning and ethological models of anxiety disorders: Stress-in-dynamic-context anxiety models. In D. A. Hope (Ed.), *Current theory and research in motivation: Vol. 43. Perspectives on anxiety, panic, and fear* (pp. 135–210). Lincoln: University of Nebraska Press.

Mystkowski, J. L., Craske, M. G., & Echiverri, A. M. (2002). Treatment context and return of fear in spider phobia. *Behavior Therapy, 33,* 399–416.

Mystkowski, J. L., Craske, M. G., Echiverri, A. M., & Labus, J. S. (2006). Mental reinstatement of context and return of fear in spider-fearful participants. *Behavior Therapy, 37,* 49–60.

Nelson, J. B., & Bouton, M. E. (1997). The effects of a context switch following serial and simultaneous feature-negative discriminations. *Learning and Motivation, 28,* 56–84.

Orr, S. P., Metzger, L. J., Lasko, N. B., Macklin, M. L., Peri, T., & Pitman, R. K. (2000). De novo conditioning in trauma-exposed individuals with and without posttraumatic stress disorder. *Journal of Abnormal Psychology, 109,* 290–298.

Overmier, J. B., Payne, J., Brackbill, R. M., Linder, B., & Lawry, J. A. (1979). On the mechanism of the post-asymptotic CR decrement phenomenon. *Acta Neurobiologiae Experimentalis, 39,* 603–620.

Overton, D. A. (1985). Contextual stimulus effects of drugs and internal states. In P. D. Balsam & A. Tomie (Eds.), *Context and learning* (pp. 357–384). Hillsdale, NJ: Erlbaum.

Pavlov, I. P. (1927). *Conditioned reflexes.* London: Oxford University Press.

Peck, C. A., & Bouton, M. E. (1990). Context and performance in aversive-to-appetitive and appetitive-to-aversive transfer. *Learning and Motivation, 21*, 1–31.

Phillips, R. G., & LeDoux, J. E. (1992). Differential contribution of amygdala and hippocampus to cued and contextual fear conditioning. *Behavioral Neuroscience, 106*, 274–285.

Pitman, R. K., Shalev, A. Y., & Orr, S. P. (2000). Posttraumatic stress disorder: Emotion, conditioning and memory. In M. S. Gazzanig (Ed.), *The Cognitive Neurosciences* (pp. 1133–1147). Cambridge, MA: MIT Press.

Rescorla, R. A., & Heth, C. (1975). Reinstatement of fear to an extinguished conditioned stimulus. *Journal of Experimental Psychology: Animal Behavior Processes, 1*, 88–96.

Rescorla, R. A., & Solomon, R. L. (1967). Two-process learning theory: Relationships between Pavlovian conditioning and instrumental learning. *Psychological Review, 74*, 151–182.

Rosas, J. M., & Bouton, M. E. (1997). Renewal of a conditioned taste aversion upon return to the conditioning context after extinction in another one. *Learning and Motivation, 28*, 216–229.

Rosas, J. M., Vila, N. J., Lugo, M., & Lopez, L. (2001). Combined effect of context change and retention interval on interference in causality judgments. *Journal of Experimental Psychology: Animal Behavior Processes, 27*, 153–164.

Shalev, A. Y., & Ursano, R. (2003). Mapping the multidimensional picture of acute responses to traumatic stress. In R. Orner & V. Schnyder (Eds.), *Reconstructing early intervention after trauma: Innovations in the care of survivors* (pp. 118–129). New York: Oxford University Press.

Smith, S. M., & Vela, E. (2001). Environmental context–dependent memory: A review and meta-analysis. *Psychonomic Bulletin & Review, 8*, 203–220.

Solomon, A., Garb, R., Bleich, A., & Grupper, D. (1987). Reactivation of trauma-related posttraumatic stress disorder. *American Journal of Psychiatry, 144*, 51–55.

Sullivan, G. M., Apergis, J., Bush, D. E. A., Johnson, L. R., Hou, M., & LeDoux, J. E. (2004). Lesions in the bed nucleus of the stria terminalis disrupt corticosterone and freezing responses elicited by a contextual but not a specific cue-conditioned fear stimulus. *Neuroscience, 128*, 7–14.

Sun, N., Roberts, L., & Cassell, M. D. (1991). Rat central amygdaloid nucleus projections to the bed nucleus of the stria terminalis. *Brain Research Bulletin, 27*, 651–662.

Timberlake, W. (2001). Motivational modes in behavior systems. In R. R. Mowrer & S. B. Klein (Eds.), *Handbook of contemporary learning theories* (pp. 155–210). Mahwah, NJ: Erlbaum.

Toren, P., Wolmer, L., Weizman, R., Magal-Vardi, O., & Laor, N. (2002). Retraumatization of Israeli civilians during a reactivation of the Gulf War threat. *Journal of Nervous and Mental Disease, 190*, 43–45.

Treit, D., Pesold, C., & Rotzinger, S. (1993). Dissociating the anti-fear effects of septal and amygdaloid lesions using two pharmacologically validated models of rat anxiety. *Behavioral Neuroscience, 107*, 770–785.

VanDerCar, D. H., & Schneiderman, N. (1967). Interstimulus interval functions in different response systems during classical discrimination conditioning of rabbits. *Psychonomic Science, 9*, 9–10.

Vigorito, M., & Ayres, J. J. B. (1987). Effect of naloxone on conditioned suppression in rats. *Behavioral Neuroscience, 101*, 576–586.

Waddell, J., Falls, W. A., Bouton, M. E., & Lowe, H. B. (2006). *Central antagonism of central corticotropin-releasing factor blocks reinstatement of extinguished fear.* Manuscript in preparation.

Waddell, J., Morris, R., & Bouton, M. E. (2006). Effects of bed nucleus of the stria terminalis lesions on conditioned anxiety: Reinstatement and aversive conditioning with long-duration conditional stimuli. *Behavioral Neuroscience, 120*, 324–336.

Wagner, A. R., & Brandon, S. E. (1989). Evolution of a structured connectionist model of Pavlovian conditioning (AESOP). In S. B. Klein & R. R. Mowrer (Eds.), *Contemporary learning theories: Pavlovian conditioning and the states of traditional learning theory* (pp. 149–189). Hillsdale, NJ: Erlbaum.

Wilson, A., Brooks, D. C., & Bouton, M. E. (1995). The role of the rat hippocampal system in several effects of context in extinction. *Behavioral Neuroscience, 109*, 828–836.

Wolpe, J. (1958). *Psychotherapy by reciprocal inhibition.* Stanford, CA: Stanford University Press.

Yehuda, R., Giller, E. L., Southwick, S. M., Lowy, M. T., & Mason, J. W. (1991). Hypothalamic-pituitary-adrenal dysfunction in posttraumatic stress disorder. *Biological Psychiatry, 30*, 1031–1048.

Yehuda, R., Golier, J. A., Halligan, S. L., Meaney, M., & Bierer, L. M. (2004). The ACTH response to dexamethasone in PTSD. *American Journal of Psychiatry, 161*, 1397–1403.

Yehuda, R., Schmeidler, J., Wainberg, M., Binder-Brynes, K., & Duvdevani, T. (1998). Vulnerability to posttraumatic stress disorder in adult offspring of Holocaust survivors. *American Journal of Psychiatry, 155*, 1163–1171.

Yehuda, R., Southwick, S. M., Nussbaum, E. L., Giller, E. L., & Mason, J. W. (1991). Low urinary cortisol in PTSD. *Journal of Nervous and Mental Disease, 178*, 366–369.

3

Learning Not to Fear: A Neural Systems Approach

Gregory J. Quirk, Mohammed R. Milad, Edwin Santini, and Kelimer Lebrón

Most people who experience trauma do not develop posttraumatic stress disorder (PTSD). While 75% of adults have had a traumatic experience fulfilling current *DSM–IV* criteria as potential factors in the development of PTSD, only 12% actually developed PTSD (Breslau & Kessler, 2001). This suggests that the majority of persons are highly resilient in the face of trauma (Charney, 2004). What are the neural mechanisms that allow a person to recover from trauma without enduring effects? Recent work has focused on *extinction* of classically conditioned fear as a useful animal model of recovery after trauma. In cued fear conditioning, a tone is paired with a mild footshock. After several such pairings, rats learn that the tone predicts the shock and exhibit a range of species-specific fear responses, including freezing and potentiated startle responses (see Rau & Fanselow, this volume). In extinction, the conditioned tone is repeatedly presented without the shock, causing rats to learn that the tone is no longer dangerous. Understanding the neural mechanisms of extinction learning could lead to new treatments for PTSD, given that extinction underlies exposure-based therapies used to treat PTSD (Foa, 2000; Rothbaum & Schwartz, 2002).

EXTINCTION OF FEAR IS NEW LEARNING

While it may be tempting to think that extinction of conditioned fear simply erases the original tone–shock association, substantial behavioral evidence suggests that this is not the case. In his classic studies, Pavlov (1927) showed that conditioned responses of dogs trained to salivate in response to a bell paired with food would spontaneously recover after they were extinguished. Similar observations have been made for conditioned fear (Baum, 1988). Extinguished fear responses can be reinstated by presenting unsignaled shocks (Rescorla & Heth, 1975) or renewed by giving conditioned tones in a context other than the extinction context (Bouton & King, 1983; see Bouton & Waddell, this volume). We have observed that

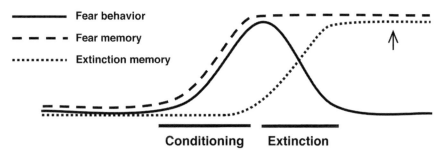

FIGURE 3.1. Memory for extinction and conditioning coexist in the extinguished brain. During acquisition of fear conditioning, rats learn a tone–shock association and display fear responses to the tone. The decline in fear responses seen in extinction occurs not because conditioning memory is dissipated, but because extinction (safety) memory is accumulated. This predicts that some structure or structures in the brain increase their activity after extinction (arrow), in order to inhibit the expression of the fear memory. (Reprinted from Milad, Rauch, Pitman, & Quirk, 2006, Copyright 2006, with permission from Elsevier.)

extinguished freezing can spontaneously recover to 100% of its original level after ten days (Quirk, 2002), indicating that extinction does not erase the original fear association.

If extinction forms a new memory, then both conditioning and extinction traces must exist at the same time in the postextinction brain. This relationship is diagrammed in Figure 3.1. The loss of conditioned responding is due to the accumulation of extinction memory, rather than the loss of conditioning memory. Therefore, extinction structures must be capable of inhibiting structures that generate conditioned responses (Konorski, 1967; Pavlov, 1927). This suggests that areas that encode extinction would increase their activity after extinction, in order to activate inhibitory interneurons and bring down fear. Indeed, the discovery of such structures would constitute strong support for Pavlov's original hypothesis that extinction is inhibition rather than erasure.

WHAT STRUCTURES LEARN AND STORE EXTINCTION?

Substantial evidence implicates the amygdala in acquisition, storage, and expression of fear associations in auditory fear conditioning (Davis, 2000; LeDoux, 2000; Maren, 2001; see Rau & Fanselow, this volume). Subcortical inputs communicate tone and shock information to the lateral amygdala, which is a critical site of plasticity in fear conditioning. The lateral amygdala projects (indirectly) to the central nucleus of the amygdala (CE), which is the main source of amygdala outputs to the periaqueductal gray and hypothalamic sites that produce behavioral and autonomic fear responses, respectively. Thus, the amygdala can be considered a "hub" of fear

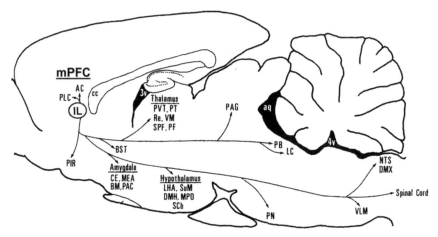

FIGURE 3.2. Outputs of the infralimbic (IL) subregion of medial prefrontal cortex (mPFC). Note that the IL projects to the amygdala, as well as to the amygdala's targets in the hypothalamus and midbrain periaqueductal gray (PAG), which mediate the expression of fear responses. Thus, the IL is in a good position to modulate the expression of fear after extinction. (Adapted from Hurley et al., 1991. Copyright 1991 by John Wiley & Sons, Inc.)

learning that controls the entire range of species-specific fear responses through diverging outputs. If the amygdala controls the learning and expression of fear associations, what controls the amygdala? LeDoux and coworkers were the first to suggest that cortical structures inhibit the amygdala in situations where the expression of fear responses is not appropriate (LeDoux, Xagoraris, & Romanski, 1989; Morgan, Romanski, & LeDoux, 1993; Morgan, Schulkin, & LeDoux, 2003). They observed that lesions of the ventral medial prefrontal cortex (mPFC) did not prevent rats from acquiring conditioned freezing responses, but greatly prolonged the number of days required to extinguish freezing (Morgan et al., 1993).

The most ventral part of the mPFC is the infralimbic cortex (IL). The IL projects to the amygdala as well as the amygdala's targets in the periaqueductal gray and hypothalamus (Hurley, Herbert, Moga, & Saper, 1991; McDonald, Mascagni, & Guo, 1996; Vertes, 2004) (see Figure 3.2). Thus, the IL is well situated to modulate the expression of conditioned fear. We observed that rats with greater than 70% destruction of the IL could extinguish freezing normally within a session. The next day, however, they were unable to recall extinction, showing high levels of freezing equivalent to a control group that did not receive extinction (Quirk, Russo, Barron, & Lebron, 2000) (see Figure 3.3A). This pattern of findings suggests that the IL is not involved in the initial learning of extinction but may be necessary for consolidation of extinction into a stable long-term memory. Extinction appears to be learned in *two stages*: an acquisition phase leading to short-term memory (mPFC-independent), and a consolidation phase

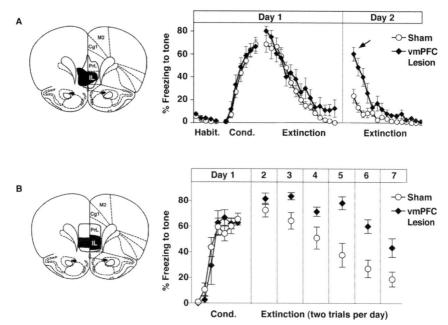

FIGURE 3.3. Lesions of the infralimbic (IL) subregion of medial prefrontal cortex (mPFC) impair recall of extinction. (A) Coronal sections through the prefrontal cortex showing the IL, prelimbic (PL), cingulate (Cg1), and motor (M2) cortices. Rats were given 30-s tones alone (habituation phase), paired with footshock (conditioning), and alone again (extinction phase). Electrolytic lesions of the ventral mPFC had no effect on a rat's ability to acquire and extinguish conditioned freezing on Day 1. The following day, however, lesioned rats are unable to recall extinction, showing high levels of freezing. This suggests that the IL is not necessary for the initial learning of extinction, but may be necessary for consolidation of extinction into a stabile long-term memory. (Adapted from Quirk et al., 2000. Copyright 2000 by the Society for Neuroscience.) (B) Consistent with this, IL-lesioned rats are deficient in across-day extinction, when just two extinction tones are given per day. Rats with lesions required 6 days of extinction trials to show significant decreases. (Adapted from Lebron, Milad, & Quirk, 2004. Copyright 2004 by Cold Spring Harbor Laboratory Press; atlas sections adapted from Paxinos & Watson, 1998, Copyright 1998, with permission from Elsevier.)

leading to long-term memory (mPFC-dependent). The plasticity in IL may be necessary for recalling extinction memory long after training, thereby keeping spontaneous recovery of fear at bay.

If the IL is necessary for remembering extinction from one day to the next, then across-day extinction in lesioned rats should be deficient. Replicating the finding of Morgan and coworkers (1993), we found that IL-lesioned rats were delayed in across-day extinction (Figure 3.3B). Lesioned rats required 6 days of extinction training to show a significant decrease in freezing, compared to only 3 days in controls (Lebron et al., 2004). Despite this delay, however, freezing levels in lesioned rats eventually declined. Thus, in addition to the IL, other structures are capable of consolidating and expressing extinction, albeit at a slower rate. Substantial evidence indicates that the amygdala itself is a site of plasticity in extinction of fear (Falls, Miserendino, & Davis, 1992; Lin, Yeh, Lu, & Gean, 2003; Lu, Walker, & Davis, 2001; Myers & Davis, 2002). It is also possible that other parts of the prefrontal cortex contribute to extinction of fear, as suggested by metabolic mapping (Barrett, Shumake, Jones, & Gonzalez-Lima, 2003; Nair, Berndt, Barrett, & Gonzalez-Lima, 2001). While other structures may be capable of learning extinction, the IL is necessary for rapid access to recently learned extinction memories. In this way, the IL facilitates the recall of extinction learning and maximizes the potential for behavioral flexibility (Delatour & Gisquet-Verrier, 2000; Lebron et al., 2004).

INFRALIMBIC NEURONS SIGNAL MEMORY FOR EXTINCTION

While the lesion approach is important for implicating a structure in a given behavior, it cannot tell us the type of information that is processed by the

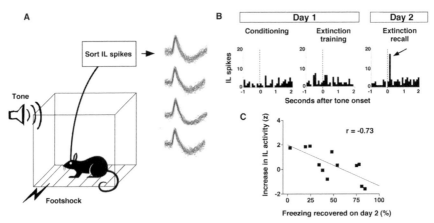

FIGURE 3.4. Infralimbic activity signals recall of extinction. (A) Rats were chronically implanted with fine-wire electrodes in order to monitor the firing rate of individual infralimbic (IL) neurons during conditioning and extinction. (B) Poststimulus-time histogram of a representative IL neuron showing the number of action potentials (spikes) fired in response to the tone (dashed line) at various points during training. IL neurons did not signal the tone during conditioning or extinction training but did signal the tone at the start of Day 2, when rats were recalling extinction. (C) Consistent with a role in inhibition of fear, IL potentiation was inversely correlated with the amount of freezing expressed on Day 2. Each point represents one rat. (B and C adapted with permission from Macmillian Publishers, LTD: *Nature*, Milad & Quirk, 2002, copyright 2002.)

structure. One way of doing this is by monitoring the activity of single neurons in awake rats undergoing learning (Figure 3.4A). The response of a typical IL neuron during all phases of training is shown in Figure 3.4B. IL cells showed no tone responses during conditioning or extinction phases, consistent with lesion data showing that the mPFC is not necessary during these times. The next day, however, IL cells exhibited robust tone responses as rats were recalling extinction (Milad & Quirk, 2002). This is just the time at which rats with IL lesions showed increased fear, suggesting that IL tone responses are responsible for inhibiting fear after extinction. In support of this, IL tone responses were inversely correlated with the amount of freezing on Day 2. Rats with the greatest IL activity showed the least freezing (Figure 3.4C). A similar inverse correlation between IL activity and expression of freezing after extinction has been observed with evoked potentials (Herry & Garcia, 2002) and metabolic mapping (Barrett et al., 2003).

INFRALIMBIC STIMULATION INHIBITS FEAR AND STRENGTHENS EXTINCTION MEMORY

The strong correlation between IL activity and recall of extinction suggests a possible causal relationship between the two. However, correlations do not necessarily imply causality. For example, it is possible that IL potentiation has no bearing on behavior, or represents a purely cognitive representation of extinction (Herry & Garcia, 2003). To further test the hypothesis that IL activity is responsible for reduced freezing, we used electrical stimulation of the IL. We reasoned that if IL tone responses are critical for reducing fear the day after extinction, then stimulation mimicking these tone responses should reduce fear in animals that did not receive extinction the previous day. In other words, can IL stimulation simulate extinction memory?

To answer this question, rats were chronically implanted with stimulating electrodes in the IL and given 7 conditioning trials with no extinction (Milad & Quirk, 2002; Milad, Vidal-Gonzalez, & Quirk, 2004). The following day, unstimulated rats showed high freezing to the tone as expected. In contrast, rats that received IL stimulation paired with the tone showed less freezing from the very first tone onward (see Figure 3.5). Stimulation was given only during the first 0.4 s of the 30-s tone, in order to mimic naturally occurring tone responses following extinction. Freezing was reduced in trials paired with stimulation and was also low the following day in the absence of stimulation, suggesting strengthening of extinction memory. These effects were seen at stimulation rates of 100 Hz and also 20 Hz, which closely approximates the firing rates of actual IL neurons. No reduction in freezing was observed if the adjacent PL area was stimulated or if the IL was stimulated during the intertrial interval (Milad & Quirk, 2002). Thus, IL activity is not only correlated with fear reduction, it is also

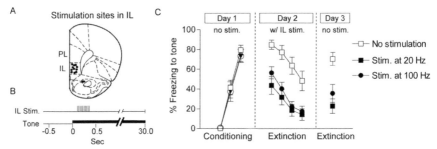

FIGURE 3.5. Infralimbic stimulation reduces conditioned freezing. (A) Location of stimulating electrodes in IL. (B) A single brief train of stimulation was given, 100–400 ms after tone onset, to mimic naturally occurring tone responses of IL neurons. The duration of the tone was 30 s. (C) Groups were matched for freezing levels on Day 1. On Day 2, rats received 8 tones paired with stimulation (at either 20 or 100 Hz). Stimulated rats showed significantly less freezing than unstimulated controls. The following day, freezing remained low in the absence of stimulation, suggesting strengthening of extinction memory. Data shown in blocks of two trials. (Adapted from Milad et al., 2004.)

sufficient for fear reduction. We next focus on the outputs of the IL that could reduce fear.

INFRALIMBIC STIMULATION INHIBITS AMYGDALA OUTPUT NEURONS

The IL projects to various parts of the amygdala, but projections are particularly strong to the intercalated (ITC) cells (Freedman, Insel, & Smith, 2000; McDonald et al., 1996). ITC cells are GABAergic interneurons that inhibit the amygdala central (Ce) nucleus (Royer, Martina, & Pare, 1999). Ce neurons constitute the output of the amygdala and project to the midbrain and hypothalamic sites that generate fear responses. Potentially, this is a circuit by which the IL could inhibit the expression of fear after extinction. To investigate this possibility, we recorded from Ce neurons in anesthetized rats and cats (Quirk, Likhtik, Pelletier, & Pare, 2003). Stimulation of the amygdala basolateral nucleus strongly activated the Ce. However, stimulating the IL shortly prior to the basolateral (BL) nucleus prevented Ce activation (see Figure 3.6A). Increasing the interval between IL and BL stimulation decreased the inhibitory effect. These findings together with others (Rosenkranz, Moore, & Grace, 2003) provide physiological support for the hypothesis that the mPFC inhibits the expression of fear via its projections to the amygdala. If the timing is right, IL activity is able to gate the output of the amygdala via ITC cells (see Figure 3.6B). In addition to inhibiting the expression of fear, the IL may contribute to storage of extinction in the

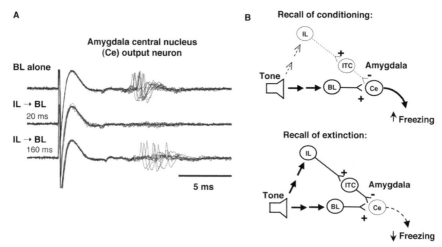

FIGURE 3.6. Infralimbic (IL) stimulation reduces amygdala output. (A) Recordings from an anesthetized cat showing the action potentials of an amygdala central nucleus (Ce) output neuron projecting to the brainstem, in response to stimulation of the basolateral nucleus of the amygdala (BL). Stimulating IL 20 ms prior to BL prevented Ce from being activated. Stimulating IL 160 ms prior to BL had little effect, suggesting that IL can gate the excitability of amygdala output neurons, over a brief time window. (B) Schema of how this circuit might function in conditioning and extinction. When recalling conditioning memory, the tone strongly activates BL and Ce, leading to high freezing levels. When recalling extinction, the tone also activates IL, which in turn activates GABAergic intercalated (ITC) cells in the amygdala. ITC cells inhibit Ce and are able to cancel BL's excitatory effect, resulting in lower freezing. (A is adapted from Quirk et al., 2003. Copyright 2003 by the Society for Neuroscience; B is adapted from Milad et al., 2004.)

amygdala, as suggested by the fact that ITC cells show NMDA-dependent long-term potentiation (Royer & Pare, 2002).

MOLECULAR MECHANISMS OF EXTINCTION CONSOLIDATION

It is well established that long-term memory requires calcium influx through NMDA glutamate receptors, followed by activation of protein kinases, gene expression, and protein synthesis (Kandel, 1997; Silva, Kogan, Frankland, & Kida, 1998). Molecular events underlying acquisition of fear conditioning have been extensively studied (Lamprecht & LeDoux, 2004; Malkani & Rosen, 2000; Ressler, Paschall, Zhou, & Davis, 2002; Shumyatsky et al., 2002), but less is known about extinction. A seminal study by Falls and coworkers (1992) showed that NMDA activation in the amygdala was necessary for extinction of fear-potentiated startle. Rats conditioned to associate a light with a shock were unable to extinguish

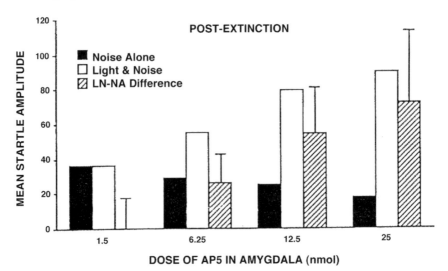

FIGURE 3.7. Blocking NMDA glutamate receptors in the amygdala prevents extinction of fear-potentiated startle. In this study by Falls et al. (1992), rats given light–shock pairings show increased startle responses to a loud noise if delivered in the presence of the light. After multiple days of light-alone trials, this difference extinguishes. Microinfusing the NMDA receptor antagonist AP5 into the basolateral amygdala prevents extinction in a dose-dependent manner. (Adapted from Falls et al., 1992. Copyright 1992 by the Society for Neuroscience.)

this association if extinction trials were given shortly after infusing the NMDA antagonist AP5 into the amygdala (see Figure 3.7). This was the first evidence that extinction uses the same molecular mechanisms as other forms of learning, and strongly supported the "extinction as new learning" hypothesis.

Are NMDA receptors necessary for both short- and long-term phases of extinction learning? We addressed this issue with the systemic NMDA antagonist CPP (Santini, Muller, & Quirk, 2001). Rats injected with CPP learned extinction normally across a 90-min session but were unable to recall extinction the following day (see Figure 3.8A). Thus, NMDA-mediated calcium influx is *not* necessary for acquiring extinction but is necessary for consolidating extinction into a stabile, long-term memory. Therefore, acquisition of extinction may occur via an NMDA-independent mechanism (see Barad & Cain, this volume). What about events downstream of NMDA receptors? Protein kinases have been implicated in extinction of conditioned fear (Lu et al., 2001) as well as extinction of inhibitory avoidance (Cammarota, Bevilaqua, Kerr, Medina, & Izquierdo, 2003). The protein synthesis inhibitor anisomycin prevents extinction of inhibitory avoidance (Vianna, Szapiro, McGaugh, Medina, & Izquierdo, 2001) and conditioned taste aversion (Berman & Dudai, 2001). It is not known,

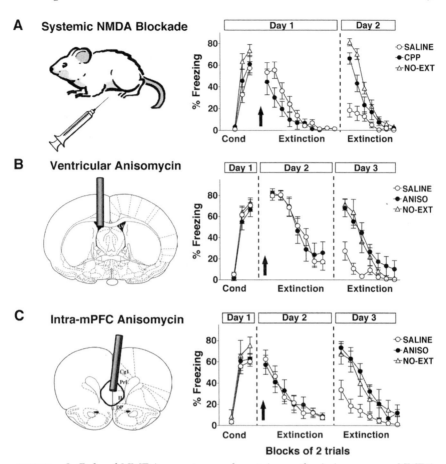

FIGURE 3.8. Role of NMDA receptors and protein synthesis in memory. NMDA receptors and protein synthesis are important for long-term, but not short-term, extinction memory. (A) Rats given the NMDA receptor antagonist CPP systemically can extinguish but cannot recall extinction the following day, indicating that long-term, but not short-term, extinction memory is NMDA-dependent. (Adapted from Santini et al., 2001. Copyright 2001 by the Society for Neuroscience.) (A similar effect is seen when the protein synthesis blocker anisomycin is infused (B) into the lateral ventricle, or (C) directly into the mPFC, suggesting that mPFC is a site of consolidation and storage of extinction. Note that anisomycin-infused rats showed no savings in their rate of relearning of extinction, suggesting amnesia for extinction. Arrows indicate the time of infusion.) (B and C adapted from Santini, Ge, Ren, Peña de Ortiz, & Quirk, 2004. Copyright 2004 by the Society for Neuroscience.)

however, if extinction of cued conditioned fear requires protein synthesis. To address this, we administered anisomycin into the lateral ventricle, which presumably reaches all structures. The effects were similar to mPFC lesions and systemic CPP; namely, rats could learn extinction but could not recall it the next day (see Figure 3.8B). Interestingly, there was no savings in the rate of relearning of extinction, suggesting complete amnesia for extinction learning (Santini et al., 2004). Additional controls showed that this effect was not due to state-dependent learning or toxic side effects. The same results were obtained when anisomycin was infused directly into the mPFC (Figure 3.8C) but not when infused into the insular cortex. Inhibition of mitogen-activated protein kinase (MAPK) in the mPFC also impairs consolidation of extinction (Hugues, Deschaux, & Garcia, 2004). These findings extend the lesion and recording studies by showing that the mPFC is a critical site of storage of fear extinction, rather than simply an expression pathway for extinction stored elsewhere.

SUMMARY AND PREDICTIONS FOR FUTURE EXPERIMENTS

Pavlov predicted the existence of a brain structure that would inhibit the expression of fear after extinction. Converging lines of evidence from rodent studies suggest that this structure is the infralimbic prefrontal cortex: (1) Lesions of the IL interfere with recall of extinction, (2) single units in the IL signal extinction memory, (3) IL stimulation reduces the expression of conditioned fear and strengthens extinction memory, (4) protein synthesis in the IL is necessary for long-term memory of extinction, and (5) IL stimulation inhibits amygdala output neurons. These findings suggest the following model. Extinction is initially learned outside of the mPFC (most likely in the amygdala) via an NMDA-independent process. During consolidation of extinction, auditory inputs to the IL from the amygdala are potentiated via an NMDA- and protein synthesis–dependent process, leading to eventual storage of extinction in the mPFC. A similar relationship between subcortical and cortical structures in memory consolidation has been proposed for inhibitory avoidance (McGaugh, 2000) and spatial learning (Wittenberg & Tsien, 2002). Subsequent exposure to the extinguished stimulus triggers robust IL activity, which would suppress the expression of fear at the level of the amygdala. Note that the fear memory would still be present in the amygdala but would not be able to be expressed due to inhibited output neurons.

Several testable predictions arise from this model: (1) Blocking NMDA receptors in the mPFC during extinction training, or shortly after extinction training, should prevent long-term memory for extinction. (2) Systemic CPP or anisomycin should prevent the development of extinction-induced neuronal plasticity in the IL. (3) Given that expression of extinction is gated by the context (Bouton, 1993; see Bouton & Waddell, this volume), contextual stimuli should be able to gate IL or ITC cell activity, perhaps via hippocampal inputs (Corcoran & Maren, 2001). We are currently exploring these and other possibilities to determine the extent of involvement of the IL in extinction. In addition to projecting to the amygdala, the IL also projects directly to the brainstem and hypothalamic sites that produce fear responses (Floyd, Price, Ferry, Keay, & Bandler, 2000). The IL could therefore suppress fear independently of the amygdala. A prior study of extinction of fear-potentiated startle observed no effect of mPFC lesions (Gewirtz, Falls, & Davis, 1997). Interestingly, the only fear expression center that does not receive direct input from the IL is the pontine area (Hurley et al., 1991; Vertes, 2004), shown to mediate the startle reflex (Lee, Lopez, Meloni, & Davis, 1996). A direct effect of the IL on lower fear centers, then, could potentially explain conflicting observations about the involvement of the mPFC in extinction. Whether the IL exerts its influence via the amygdala or directly on fear centers (or both) remains to be determined.

SIGNIFICANCE FOR PTSD: COMPROMISED EXTINCTION CIRCUITS?

It has been suggested that one of the factors increasing susceptibility to PTSD is deficient extinction of conditioned fear (Charney, 2004; Gorman, Kent, Sullivan, & Coplan, 2000; Vermetten & Bremner, 2002). In fact, PTSD patients appear to be resistant to extinction in experimental fear conditioning (Orr et al., 2000; Peri, Ben-Shakhar, Orr, & Shalev, 2000; Rothbaum, Kozak, Foa, & Whitaker, 2001). The animal models discussed previously predict that PTSD patients would show increased amygdala activity, coupled with decreased mPFC activity, consistent with reduced prefrontal inhibition of the amygdala. Is there any support for such a model from functional brain imaging studies of PTSD patients?

Convergent results from symptom provocation studies indicate that, when exposed to traumatic reminders, PTSD subjects exhibit greater responses within the amygdala (Liberzon et al., 1999; Shin et al., 1997), and smaller responses in medial prefrontal areas (Bremner et al., 1999; Lanius et al., 2003; Shin et al., 1999; Shin et al., 2001), compared to non-PTSD controls (see Bremner, this volume). In fact, a recent study showed an inverse correlation between activity in the ventral mPFC and the amygdala in PTSD (Shin et al., 2004), supporting the hypothesis that PTSD is characterized by a lack of top-down control over the amygdala. Additional support for the involvement of prefrontal areas in PTSD comes from morphometric MRI data (Rauch et al., 2003). PTSD subjects exhibited volumetric decreases within the pregenual (area 32) and subcallosal (area 25) areas, which are homologous to the PL (area 32) and the IL (area 25) in the rat (see Figure 3.9).

The homology between human prefrontal areas compromised in PTSD and rat prefrontal areas involved in extinction suggests that these regions in humans are involved in extinction (Milad, Rauch, Pitman, & Quirk, 2006). Functional imaging studies of extinction in humans are just starting to appear, and the findings bear a striking resemblance to rat models. In normal individuals undergoing fear conditioning and extinction, the

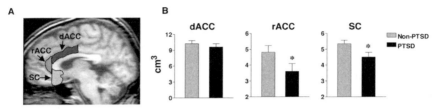

FIGURE 3.9. PTSD subjects show decreased cortical volumes in the rostral anterior cingulate and subcallosal cortex. (A) The parcellation scheme is illustrated on a sample magnetic resonance image. (B) Size of the different subregions of the anterior cingulate cortex in the PTSD subjects and non-PTSD subjects. Only the pericallosal regions (rACC, SC), corresponding to extinction areas in the rat, were significantly smaller in PTSD subjects. ACC: dorsal anterior cingulate; rACC: rostral anterior cingulate; SC: subcallosal cortex. $^*p < 0.05$. (Adapted from Rauch et al., 2003. Copyright 2003 by Lippincott, Williams & Wilkins.)

ability to recall extinction from the previous day was correlated with vmPFC thickness (Milad et al., 2005) and vmPFC activity during extinction training (Phelps, Delgado, Nearing, & LeDoux, 2004), supporting the hypothesis that extinction failure contributes to PTSD.

RELATION TO BROADER THEMES

Understanding the role of the prefrontal cortex in extinction learning connects with other themes discussed in this volume. The work of Meaney and colleagues in rats (see Bagot et al., this volume) shows that subtle differences in early postnatal handling and maternal care affects adult stress responses and inhibitory activity in the mPFC (Caldji, Diorio, & Meaney, 2003; see Bagot et al., this volume). This suggests that the extinction circuits are affected by early life events that may predispose an individual to develop PTSD after trauma. On the positive side, vmPFC thickeness was correlated with extroverted personality traits (Rauch et al., 2005) suggesting that extinction of fear may be important for social interactions. The beneficial effects of cognitive therapy (see Yadin & Foa, this volume) and perhaps religious beliefs (see Boehnlein, this volume) may be mediated via mPFC extinction circuits. In support of this, cognitive appraisal of fearful faces reduces amygdala activation while at the same time increasing prefrontal activation (Hariri, Bookheimer, & Mazziotta, 2000; Hariri, Mattay, Tessitore, Fera, & Weinberger, 2003) consistent with prefrontal inhibition of the amygdala. Prefrontal activation is also correlated with the placebo effect (Wager et al., 2004) and recovery following presentation of negatively valenced emotional stimuli (Jackson et al., 2003). Finally, work on extinction mechanisms could lead to new physiological or pharmacological treatments to augment the effectiveness of exposure-based therapies

(Cain, Blouin, & Barad, 2003; Ressler et al., 2004; see Barad & Cain, this volume). It is likely, therefore, that a fuller understanding of prefrontal–amygdala circuits in extinction will help PTSD sufferers break the cycle of fear.

References

Barrett, D., Shumake, J., Jones, D., & Gonzalez-Lima, F. (2003). Metabolic mapping of mouse brain activity after extinction of a conditioned emotional response. *Journal of Neuroscience, 23*(13), 5740–5749.

Baum, M. (1988). Spontaneous recovery from the effects of flooding (exposure) in animals. *Behaviour Research and Therapy, 26*(2), 185–186.

Berman, D. E., & Dudai, Y. (2001). Memory extinction, learning anew, and learning the new: Dissociations in the molecular machinery of learning in cortex. *Science, 291*(5512), 2417–2419.

Bouton, M. E. (1993). Context, time, and memory retrieval in the interference paradigms of Pavlovian learning. *Psychological Bulletin, 114*(1), 80–99.

Bouton, M. E., & King, D. A. (1983). Contextual control of the extinction of conditioned fear: Tests for the associative value of the context. *Journal of Experimental Psychology: Animal Behavior Processes, 9*(3), 248–265.

Bremner, J. D., Staib, L. H., Kaloupek, D., Southwick, S. M., Soufer, R., & Charney, D. S. (1999). Neural correlates of exposure to traumatic pictures and sound in Vietnam combat veterans with and without posttraumatic stress disorder: A positron emission tomography study. *Biological Psychiatry, 45*(7), 806–816.

Breslau, N., & Kessler, R. C. (2001). The stressor criterion in DSM-IV posttraumatic stress disorder: An empirical investigation. *Biological Psychiatry, 50*(9), 699–704.

Cain, C. K., Blouin, A. M., & Barad, M. (2003). Temporally massed CS presentations generate more fear extinction than spaced presentations. *Journal of Experimental Psychology: Animal Behavior Processes, 29*(4), 323–333.

Caldji, C., Diorio, J., & Meaney, M. J. (2003). Variations in maternal care alter GABA$_A$ receptor subunit expression in brain regions associated with fear. *Neuropsychopharmacology, 28*(11), 1950–1959.

Cammarota, M., Bevilaqua, L. R., Kerr, D., Medina, J. H., & Izquierdo, I. (2003). Inhibition of mRNA and protein synthesis in the CA1 region of the dorsal hippocampus blocks reinstallment of an extinguished conditioned fear response. *Journal of Neuroscience, 23*(3), 737–741.

Charney, D. S. (2004). Psychobiological mechanisms of resilience and vulnerability: Implications for successful adaptation to extreme stress. *American Journal of Psychiatry, 161*(2), 195–216.

Corcoran, K. A., & Maren, S. (2001). Hippocampal inactivation disrupts contextual retrieval of fear memory after extinction. *Journal of Neuroscience, 21*(5), 1720–1726.

Davis, M. (2000). The role of the amygdala in conditioned and unconditioned fear and anxiety. In J. P. Aggleton (Ed.), *The amygdala* (pp. 213–288). Oxford: Oxford University Press.

Delatour, B., & Gisquet-Verrier, P. (2000). Functional role of rat prelimbic-infralimbic cortices in spatial memory: Evidence for their involvement in attention and behavioural flexibility. *Behavioural Brain Research, 109*(1), 113–128.

Falls, W. A., Miserendino, M. J., & Davis, M. (1992). Extinction of fear-potentiated startle: Blockade by infusion of an NMDA antagonist into the amygdala. *Journal of Neuroscience, 12*(3), 854–863.

Floyd, N. S., Price, J. L., Ferry, A. T., Keay, K. A., & Bandler, R. (2000). Orbitomedial prefrontal cortical projections to distinct longitudinal columns of the periaqueductal gray in the rat. *Journal of Comparative Neurology, 422*(4), 556–578.

Foa, E. B. (2000). Psychosocial treatment of posttraumatic stress disorder. *Journal of Clinical Psychiatry, 61*(Suppl 5), 43–48; discussion 49–51.

Freedman, L. J., Insel, T. R., & Smith, Y. (2000). Subcortical projections of area 25 (subgenual cortex) of the macaque monkey. *Journal of Comparative Neurology, 421*(2), 172–188.

Gewirtz, J. C., Falls, W. A., & Davis, M. (1997). Normal conditioned inhibition and extinction of freezing and fear-potentiated startle following electrolytic lesions of medical prefrontal cortex in rats. *Behavioral Neuroscience, 111*(4), 712–726.

Gorman, J. M., Kent, J. M., Sullivan, G. M., & Coplan, J. D. (2000). Neuroanatomical hypothesis of panic disorder, revised. *American Journal of Psychiatry, 157*(4), 493–505.

Hariri, A. R., Bookheimer, S. Y., & Mazziotta, J. C. (2000). Modulating emotional responses: Effects of a neocortical network on the limbic system. *Neuroreport, 11*(1), 43–48.

Hariri, A. R., Mattay, V. S., Tessitore, A., Fera, F., & Weinberger, D. R. (2003). Neocortical modulation of the amygdala response to fearful stimuli. *Biological Psychiatry, 53*(6), 494–501.

Herry, C., & Garcia, R. (2002). Prefrontal cortex long-term potentiation, but not long-term depression, is associated with the maintenance of extinction of learned fear in mice. *Journal of Neuroscience, 22*(2), 577–583.

Herry, C., & Garcia, R. (2003). Behavioral and paired-pulse facilitation analyses of long-lasting depression at excitatory synapses in the medial prefrontal cortex in mice. *Behavioural Brain Research, 146*(1–2), 89–96.

Hugues, S., Deschaux, O., & Garcia, R. (2004). Postextinction infusion of a mitogen-activated protein kinase inhibitor into the medial prefrontal cortex impairs memory of the extinction of conditioned fear. *Learning & Memory, 11*(5), 540–543.

Hurley, K. M., Herbert, H., Moga, M. M., & Saper, C. B. (1991). Efferent projections of the infralimbic cortex of the rat. *Journal of Comparative Neurology, 308*(2), 249–276.

Jackson, D. C., Mueller, C. J., Dolski, I., Dalton, K. M., Nitschke, J. B., Urry, H. L., et al. (2003). Now you feel it, now you don't: Frontal brain electrical asymmetry and individual differences in emotion regulation. *Psychological Science, 14*(6), 612–617.

Kandel, E. R. (1997). Genes, synapses, and long-term memory. *Journal of Cellular Physiology, 173*(2), 124–125.

Konorski, J. (1967). *Integrative activity of the brain.* Chicago: University of Chicago Press.

Lamprecht, R., & LeDoux, J. (2004). Structural plasticity and memory. *Nature Reviews Neuroscience, 5*(1), 45–54.

Lanius, R. A., Williamson, P. C., Hopper, J., Densmore, M., Boksman, K., Gupta, M. A., et al. (2003). Recall of emotional states in posttraumatic stress disorder: An fMRI investigation. *Biological Psychiatry, 53*(3), 204–210.

Lebron, K., Milad, M. R., & Quirk, G. J. (2004). Delayed recall of fear extinction in rats with lesions of ventral medial prefrontal cortex. *Learning & Memory, 11*(5), 544–548.

LeDoux, J. E. (2000). Emotion circuits in the brain. *Annual Review of Neuroscience, 23,* 155–184.

LeDoux, J. E., Xagoraris, A., & Romanski, L. M. (1989). Indelibility of subcortical emotional memories. *Journal of Cognitive Neuroscience, 1,* 238–243.

Lee, Y., Lopez, D. E., Meloni, E. G., & Davis, M. (1996). A primary acoustic startle pathway: Obligatory role of cochlear root neurons and the nucleus reticularis pontis caudalis. *Journal of Neuroscience, 16*(11), 3775–3789.

Liberzon, I., Taylor, S. F., Amdur, R., Jung, T. D., Chamberlain, K. R., Minoshima, S., et al. (1999). Brain activation in PTSD in response to trauma-related stimuli. *Biological Psychiatry, 45*(7), 817–826.

Lin, C. H., Yeh, S. H., Lu, H. Y., & Gean, P. W. (2003). The similarities and diversities of signal pathways leading to consolidation of conditioning and consolidation of extinction of fear memory. *Journal of Neuroscience, 23,* 8310–8317.

Lu, K. T., Walker, D. L., & Davis, M. (2001). Mitogen-activated protein kinase cascade in the basolateral nucleus of amygdala is involved in extinction of fear-potentiated startle. *Journal of Neuroscience, 21*(16), RC162.

Malkani, S., & Rosen, J. B. (2000). Specific induction of early growth response gene 1 in the lateral nucleus of the amygdala following contextual fear conditioning in rats. *Neuroscience, 97*(4), 693–702.

Maren, S. (2001). Neurobiology of Pavlovian fear conditioning. *Annual Review of Neuroscience, 24,* 897–931.

McDonald, A. J., Mascagni, F., & Guo, L. (1996). Projections of the medial and lateral prefrontal cortices to the amygdala: A phaseolus vulgaris leucoagglutinin study in the rat. *Neuroscience, 71*(1), 55–75.

McGaugh, J. L. (2000). Memory – a century of consolidation. *Science, 287*(5451), 248–251.

Milad, M. R., & Quirk, G. J. (2002). Neurons in medial prefrontal cortex signal memory for fear extinction. *Nature, 420*(6911), 70–74.

Milad, M. R., Quinn, B. T., Pitman, R. K., Orr, S. P., Fischl, B., & Rauch, S. L. (2005). Thickness of ventromedial prefrontal cortex in humans is correlated with extinction memory. *Proceedings of the National Academy of Science USA, 102*(30), 10706–10711.

Milad, M. R., Rauch, S. L., Pitman, R. K., & Quirk, G. J. (2006). Fear extinction in rats: Implications for human brain imaging and anxiety disorders. *Biological Psychology, 73*(1), 61–71.

Milad, M. R., Vidal-Gonzalez, I., & Quirk, G. J. (2004). Electrical stimulation of medial prefrontal cortex reduces conditioned fear in a temporally specific manner. *Behavioral Neuroscience, 118*(2), 389–394.

Morgan, M. A., Romanski, L. M., & LeDoux, J. E. (1993). Extinction of emotional learning: Contribution of medial prefrontal cortex. *Neuroscience Letters, 163*(1), 109–113.

Morgan, M. A., Schulkin, J., & LeDoux, J. E. (2003). Ventral medial prefrontal cortex and emotional perseveration: The memory for prior extinction training. *Behavioural Brain Research, 146*(1–2), 121–130.

Myers, K. M., & Davis, M. (2002). Behavioral and neural analysis of extinction. *Neuron, 36*(4), 567–584.

Nair, H. P., Berndt, J. D., Barrett, D., & Gonzalez-Lima, F. (2001). Maturation of extinction behavior in infant rats: Large-scale regional interactions with medial prefrontal cortex, orbitofrontal cortex, and anterior cingulate cortex. *Journal of Neuroscience, 21*(12), 4400–4407.

Orr, S. P., Metzger, L. J., Lasko, N. B., Macklin, M. L., Peri, T., & Pitman, R. K. (2000). De novo conditioning in trauma-exposed individuals with and without posttraumatic stress disorder. *Journal of Abnormal Psychology, 109*(2), 290–298.

Pavlov, I. (1927). *Conditioned reflexes*. London: Oxford University Press.

Paxinos, G., & Watson, C. (1998). *The rat brain in stereotaxic coordinates*. San Diego: Academic Press.

Peri, T., Ben-Shakhar, G., Orr, S. P., & Shalev, A. Y. (2000). Psychophysiologic assessment of aversive conditioning in posttraumatic stress disorder. *Biological Psychiatry, 47*(6), 512–519.

Phelps, E. A., Delgado, M. R., Nearing, K. I., & LeDoux, J. E. (2004). Extinction learning in humans: Role of the amygdala and vmPFC. *Neuron, 43*(6), 897–905.

Quirk, G. J. (2002). Memory for extinction of conditioned fear is long-lasting and persists following spontaneous recovery. *Learning & Memory, 9*(6), 402–407.

Quirk, G. J., Likhtik, E., Pelletier, J. G., & Pare, D. (2003). Stimulation of medial prefrontal cortex decreases the responsiveness of central amygdala output neurons. *Journal of Neuroscience, 23*(25), 8800–8807.

Quirk, G. J., Russo, G. K., Barron, J. L., & Lebron, K. (2000). The role of ventromedial prefrontal cortex in the recovery of extinguished fear. *Journal of Neuroscience, 20*(16), 6225–6231.

Rauch, S. L., Milad, M. R., Orr, S. P., Quinn, B. T., Fischl, B., & Pitman, R. K. (2005). Orbitofrontal thickness, retention of fear extinction, and extraversion. *Neuroreport, 16*(17), 1909–1912.

Rauch, S. L., Shin, L. M., Segal, E., Pitman, R. K., Carson, M. A., McMullin, K., et al. (2003). Selectively reduced regional cortical volumes in post-traumatic stress disorder. *Neuroreport, 14*(7), 913–916.

Rescorla, R. A., & Heth, C. D. (1975). Reinstatement of fear to an extinguished conditioned stimulus. *Journal of Experimental Psychology: Animal Behavior Processes, 1*(1), 88–96.

Ressler, K. J., Paschall, G., Zhou, X. L., & Davis, M. (2002). Regulation of synaptic plasticity genes during consolidation of fear conditioning. *Journal of Neuroscience, 22*(18), 7892–7902.

Ressler, K. J., Rothbaum, B. O., Tannenbaum, L., Anderson, P., Graap, K., & Zimand, E. (2004). Cognitive enhancers as adjuncts to psychotherapy: Use of D-cycloserine in phobic individuals to facilitate extinction of fear. *Archives of General Psychiatry, 61*(11), 1136–1144.

Rosenkranz, J. A., Moore, H., & Grace, A. A. (2003). The prefrontal cortex regulates lateral amygdala neuronal plasticity and responses to previously conditioned stimuli. *Journal of Neuroscience, 23*(35), 11054–11064.

Rothbaum, B. O., Kozak, M. J., Foa, E. B., & Whitaker, D. J. (2001). Posttraumatic stress disorder in rape victims: Autonomic habituation to auditory stimuli. *Journal of Trauma: Injury, Infection and Critical Care, 14*(2), 283–293.

Rothbaum, B. O., & Schwartz, A. C. (2002). Exposure therapy for posttraumatic stress disorder. *American Journal of Psychiatry, 56*(1), 59–75.

Royer, S., Martina, M., & Pare, D. (1999). An inhibitory interface gates impulse traffic between the input and output stations of the amygdala. *Journal of Neuroscience, 19*(23), 10575–10583.

Royer, S., & Pare, D. (2002). Bidirectional synaptic plasticity in intercalated amygdala neurons and the extinction of conditioned fear responses. *Neuroscience, 115*(2), 455–462.

Santini, E., Ge, H., Ren, K., Peña de Ortiz, S., & Quirk, G. J. (2004). Consolidation of fear extinction requires protein synthesis in the medial prefrontal cortex. *Journal of Neuroscience, 24*(25), 5704–5710.

Santini, E., Muller, R. U., & Quirk, G. J. (2001). Consolidation of extinction learning involves transfer from NMDA-independent to NMDA-dependent memory. *Journal of Neuroscience, 21*(22), 9009–9017.

Shin, L. M., McNally, R. J., Kosslyn, S. M., Thompson, W. L., Rauch, S. L., Alpert, N. M., et al. (1997). A positron emission tomographic study of symptom provocation in PTSD. *Annals of the New York Academy of Sciences, 821,* 521–523.

Shin, L. M., McNally, R. J., Kosslyn, S. M., Thompson, W. L., Rauch, S. L., Alpert, N. M., et al. (1999). Regional cerebral blood flow during script-driven imagery in childhood sexual abuse-related PTSD: A PET investigation. *American Journal of Psychiatry, 156*(4), 575–584.

Shin, L. M., Orr, S. P., Carson, M. A., Rauch, S. L., Macklin, M. L., Lasko, N. B., et al. (2004). Regional cerebral blood flow in the amygdala and medial prefrontal cortex during traumatic imagery in male and female Vietnam veterans with PTSD. *Archives of General Psychiatry, 61*(2), 168–176.

Shin, L. M., Whalen, P. J., Pitman, R. K., Bush, G., Macklin, M. L., Lasko, N. B., et al. (2001). An fMRI study of anterior cingulate function in posttraumatic stress disorder. *Biological Psychiatry, 50,* 932–942.

Shumyatsky, G. P., Tsvetkov, E., Malleret, G., Vronskaya, S., Hatton, M., Hampton, L., et al. (2002). Identification of a signaling network in lateral nucleus of amygdala important for inhibiting memory specifically related to learned fear. *Cell, 111*(6), 905–918.

Silva, A. J., Kogan, J. H., Frankland, P. W., & Kida, S. (1998). CREB and memory. *Annual Review of Neuroscience, 21,* 127–148.

Vermetten, E., & Bremner, J. D. (2002). Circuits and systems in stress, I: Preclinical studies. *Depression and Anxiety, 15*(3), 126–147.

Vertes, R. P. (2004). Differential projections of the infralimbic and prelimbic cortex in the rat. *Synapse, 51*(1), 32–58.

Vianna, M. R., Szapiro, G., McGaugh, J. L., Medina, J. H., & Izquierdo, I. (2001). Retrieval of memory for fear-motivated training initiates extinction requiring protein synthesis in the rat hippocampus. *Proceedings of the National Academy of Science USA, 98*(21), 12251–12254.

Wager, T. D., Rilling, J. K., Smith, E. E., Sokolik, A., Casey, K. L., Davidson, R. J., et al. (2004). Placebo-induced changes in fMRI in the anticipation and experience of pain. *Science, 303*(5661), 1162–1167.

Wittenberg, G., & Tsien, J. (2002). An emerging molecular and cellular framework for memory processing by the hipppocampus. *Trends in Neurosciences, 25,* 501.

4

Mechanisms of Fear Extinction: Toward Improved Treatment for Anxiety

Mark Barad and Christopher K. Cain

INTRODUCTION

Extinction is the explicit model for the treatment of human anxiety disorders by behavior and cognitive behavior therapy (Craske, 1999). These therapies depend crucially on deliberate exposure to cues that generate fear or anxiety in patients in order to reduce gradually the amount of distress such cues cause when encountered during the course of the patient's usual activities, and they are extremely effective. They are also based directly on scientific studies of extinction. The first to use such a protocol for a human subject was Mary Cover Jones in 1924. Jones's successful treatment of little Peter, a two-year-old boy with phobias of rabbits, dogs, cats, stuffed animals, and even of shawls, was inspired by Pavlov's extinction of conditioned salivary responses in dogs (Jones, 1924). Later, Joseph Wolpe based his gradual desensitization method of behavior therapy on his own experiments on fear-conditioned cats (Wolpe, 1969). Wolpe's model of behavior therapy remains in active and successful use to this day.

Nevertheless, although behavior therapy is effective, it still suffers from the limitations of all forms of psychotherapy. That is, it is slow, it requires great effort from the patient and therapist, and it does not always work. Even when it does work, patients remain subject to relapses. These drawbacks are only intensified in the context of PTSD, which is notoriously difficult to treat (McFarlane, 1994). Therefore, any scientific advances that facilitate treatment, speed it up, or make it more universally effective or more resistant to relapse will be of significant benefit to the many patients who suffer from PTSD and from a variety of other human anxiety disorders. Fortunately, a renaissance in the study of the mechanisms of extinction in animals, by many scientists including some of the authors of this volume, promises to provide a wide variety of improvements to the practice of behavior therapy. This chapter will summarize some of the important findings from my laboratory, and from several others, and outline how these discoveries are already beginning to alter both our understanding of extinction and the clinical practice of behavior therapy.

A common feature of most anxiety disorders, including PTSD, is that harmless environmental stimuli trigger pathological fear reactions in the patient. To study this phenomenon in the laboratory, scientists typically rely on the conditioned fear paradigm in rodents. Fear conditioning involves the temporal pairing of a harmless cue, such as a light or tone (conditioned stimulus or CS), with an aversive stimulus, usually an electric shock (unconditioned stimulus or US). Following such pairings, rodents exhibit an array of reactions to the CS including increased heart rate, a facilitation of the startle reflex, and behavioral freezing (Davis, 1992). As in the human disorders, these reactions can persist for the lifetime of the rodent without further training (Gale et al., 2004). Extinction training involves repeated presentations of the fear-eliciting CS in the absence of the aversive US. With enough extinction training, fear reactions to the CS can be eliminated entirely. Experimental extinction and human exposure therapy are thought to succeed because nonreinforced cue presentations violate the subject's expectation that the cue predicts danger (Rescorla & Wagner, 1972).

As outlined in Chapter 2, by Bouton and Waddell, extinction is not erasure of the original fearful associations that characterize both conditioned fear in animals and anxiety disorders in humans. While some very recent evidence indicates that extinction training beginning within an hour of acquisition does involve erasure (Myers, Ressler, & Davis, 2006), the statement still holds true for most extinction training. The fundamental argument for this statement is that, even after complete extinction, the original association can return under a variety of circumstances. For example, even completely extinguished fear can return spontaneously after the passage of time (Baum, 1988) or can be "reinstated" by presentations of US alone (Rescorla & Heth, 1975). Furthermore, conditional fear is "renewed" when the CS is presented in a context different from that where extinction took place (Bouton & King, 1983). These phenomena, as well as others, strongly indicate that the original association between cue and US remains intact during extinction and implies that extinction of fear is new learning, learning that something is safe, which inhibits or competes with the expression of an intact fear memory.

In addition to these behavioral findings, a variety of studies indicate that extinction depends largely on a set of molecules common to many other learning protocols. Other results indicate that extinction learning differs in important ways from other forms of learning. Chapter 3, by Quirk, Milad, Santini, and Lebrón, points, for example, to the unusual involvement of the infralimbic prefrontal cortex in controlling extinction learning. Extinction may also differ from other forms of learning on a mechanistic level, both in terms of the training rules that generate the most effective extinction, and, most importantly, in terms of the crucial molecules that contribute to it. This chapter will consider some of this evidence with a special focus on promising new adjuncts to human behavior therapy.

EXTINCTION IS LEARNING: COMMON MOLECULES
WITH OTHER FORMS OF LEARNING

The demonstration that NMDA-type glutamate receptors (NMDAr) in the amygdala were necessary for the extinction of fear-potentiated startle by Mike Davis and his colleagues in 1992 made a crucial molecular contribution to the argument that extinction was a form of learning (Baker & Azorlosa, 1996; Falls, Miserendino, & Davis, 1992). Since the characterization of the contribution of NMDAr to synaptic plasticity in the hippocampus (Collingridge, Kehl, & McLennan, 1983), it has been recognized as a crucial molecule both in changes of synaptic strength and in behavioral learning in animals.

The NMDAr has been of particular interest because it is a molecular coincidence detector (Wigstrom & Gustafsson, 1986). The NMDAr is an ionotropic receptor, a channel that opens to allow the passage of calcium into the postsynaptic cell. The NMDAr acts as a coincidence detector because it requires two simultaneous signals to open and allow calcium into the cell (Brown, Chapman, Kairiss, & Keenan, 1988). Because it is a glutamate receptor, one of those signals is glutamate released into the synapse by the activity of a presynaptic terminal. However, glutamate alone is not enough to open the calcium channel because it is blocked by a magnesium ion at the resting potential. The blockade by magnesium is removed when the postsynaptic cell is depolarized, presumably by nearly simultaneous activity at other synapses of the same cell. In this way, the NMDA receptor acts as a detector for simultaneous presynaptic and postsynaptic activity, and opens only when both signals are present. Such coincidence detection is one of the essential theoretical elements of associative learning (Hebb, 1949), and the discovery of this molecular coincidence detector led to numerous experiments to determine whether it had a role in associative learning, in which an animal learns that two stimuli are linked.

Coincidence detection by the NMDA receptor could clearly mediate associative fear conditioning, and experiments using antagonists of the NMDAr demonstrated that NMDA receptor activity is essential for this learning task (Kim, DeCola, Landeira-Fernandez, & Fanselow, 1991; Miserendino, Sananes, Melia, & Davis, 1990). Experiments like these, and others showing an important role for the NMDAr in spatial learning protocols that require the association of many disparate cues (Morris, Anderson, Lynch, & Baudry, 1986), established the NMDAr as a crucial molecule in many forms of learning. Thus, the finding that the NMDAr also plays a role in extinction supported the conclusion from the psychological evidence that extinction was, in fact, a form of learning.

Extinction has since been shown to share additional molecular mechanisms with other forms of learning. In other systems, NMDA-mediated calcium entry has been shown to activate protein kinases, which phosphorylate substrates important for long-term memory (Nicoll & Malenka, 1999). Some of those kinases have also been implicated in extinction. For example, infusions of MAP kinase inhibitors into the amygdala block both acquisition and extinction of conditional fear (Lu, Walker, & Davis, 2001; Schafe, Nadel, Sullivan, Harris, & LeDoux, 1999). Calcineurin, a phosphatase, has been implicated in both learning and extinction, though with opposing effects. That is, calcineurin appears to act to retard learning because genetic inhibition of this molecule improves hippocampus-dependent learning (Malleret et al., 2001). On the other hand, infusion of calcineurin inhibitors into the amygdala blocks extinction (Lin et al., 2003). Even though the effects of inhibition of calcineurin are opposite in acquisition and extinction learning, it is clear from these experiments that this molecule plays a role in both mechanisms.

It is reasonable to expect that many more molecular parallels will be found between extinction and other forms of learning. As will be clear from the last section of this chapter, such parallels have already begun pointing toward methods that may both accelerate extinction in animals and improve and facilitate treatment for anxiety disorders, including PTSD, in human beings.

EXTINCTION IS LEARNING: MOLECULES SPECIFIC TO EXTINCTION LEARNING

Though there appears to be considerable overlap between the mechanisms of extinction learning and the mechanisms of other forms of learning, differences are beginning to emerge. These mechanistic differences may be particularly important for developing interventions that specifically target extinction without affecting learning in general. A major hint that such differences exist came from a second series of experiments on the role of the NMDAr in extinction of conditioned fear. In the original experiments looking at the role of the NMDAr in extinction, the test for extinction was performed 24 hours after extinction training with NMDAr antagonist infusions into the amygdala (Baker & Azorlosa, 1996; Falls et al., 1992). However, when fear is rated during CS presentations after systemic treatment with NMDAr antagonist CPP, extinction proceeds normally (Santini, Muller, & Quirk, 2001). Lest there be concern that this difference in results is due to differences in the mode of administration (systemic injection versus local injection into the amygdala) or in the drug used (CPP versus APV), these investigators did see a complete block of long-term extinction by CPP

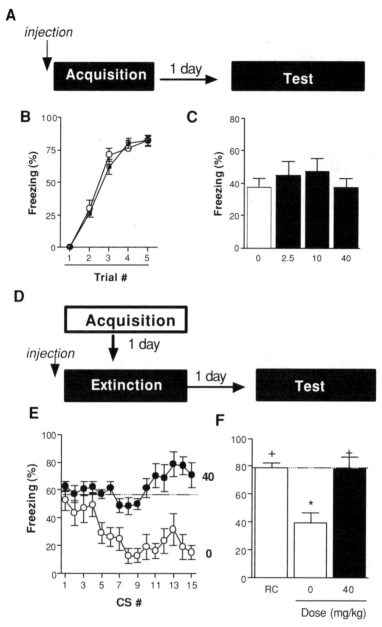

FIGURE 4.1. Nifedipine does not affect cue fear acquisition, but blocks extinction entirely. A, Acquisition: Experimental design. Fifty min after injection of drug or vehicle, mice received five pairings of a 2-min white noise (WN) cue with cotermi-nating 2-s 0.7-mA footshock (2-min intertrial interval, or ITI). B, Freezing during

in a test 24 hours later. These experiments provide strong evidence that, although the NMDAr is crucial for the long-term, 24-hour consolidation of extinction memory, it does not appear to be essential for the initial learning, or induction, of extinction. This is in dramatic contrast to the immediate and essential role that NMDA receptors play in acquisition of fear, spatial/contextual information, and other forms of learning (Campeau, Miserendino, & Davis, 1992; Fanselow & Kim, 1994; Gewirtz & Davis, 1997; Miserendino et al., 1990; Morris et al., 1986; Staubli, Thibault, DiLorenzo, & Lynch, 1989; Tang et al., 1999).

This crucial finding demands that some other molecule be involved in the induction phase of conditioned fear extinction. The most prominent candidates are the L-type voltage-gated calcium channels (LVGCCs). For some time, LVGCCs have been known to make contributions to a variety of forms of synaptic plasticity and long-term potentiation (LTP), though usually in addition to the NMDAr (Christie & Abraham, 1994; Huang & Malenka, 1993; Huber, Mauk, & Kelly, 1995; Johnston, Williams, Jaffe, & Gray, 1992). However, one form of LTP, in the amygdala, has been shown to depend on LVGCCs and not on the NMDAr (Weisskopf, Bauer, & LeDoux, 1999). Because the amygdala plays an important role in fear conditioning and in extinction of fear, these channels have been investigated in both aspects of conditioned fear.

Using blockers of LVGCCs, the evidence for an effect on acquisition of fear has been mixed. With systemic administration there is no block of fear acquisition, either acutely or when measured after 24 hours, over a wide range of doses (see Figures 4.1A through 4.1C; Cain, Blouin, & Barad, 2002). On the other hand, when the LVGCC blocker verapamil was administered by infusion directly into the amygdala, it blocked long-term fear memory but not acute acquisition of fear (Bauer, Schafe, & LeDoux, 2002), whereas NMDA receptor antagonists blocked both acute acquisition of fear and its long-term memory. Thus, although LVGCCs may play a role in the long-term retention of conditioned fear, they do not appear to be

←——————————————————————————————————————

FIGURE 4.1 (*continued*) the five cues that preceded each shock for mice injected with nifedipine (40 mg/kg, *filled squares*) or vehicle (*open circles*). C, Freezing 24 hr later during a 2-min, drug-free cue test in groups treated during training with 0, 2.5, 10, or 40 mg/kg of nifedipine. D, Extinction: Experimental design. One day after training, as in A, mice were injected with drug or vehicle, and, after 50 min, given 60 2-min WN cues (5-s ITI). E, Freezing during the first 15 cues for mice injected with nifedipine (40 mg/kg, *filled squares*) or vehicle (*open circles*). F, Freezing 24 hr later during a 2-min drug-free cue by animals that received no cue presentations on the extinction day (RC), or by animals treated before extinction with 0 or 40 mg/kg of nifedipine. $*p < 0.05$ vs. RC, $^+p < 0.05$ vs. 0 mg/kg of nifedipine. (Adapted from Cain et al., 2002. Copyright 2002 by the Society for Neuroscience.)

necessary for its acquisition, in contrast to NMDAr, which are necessary for both.

On the other hand, LVGCCs appear to be necessary for the induction of extinction learning. When fear-conditioned animals are treated with an LVGCC antagonist during extinction training, they initially show fear equal to controls, but they are unable to extinguish, even after fear in control animals has completely disappeared. Furthermore, no long-term extinction memory appears to have been induced when animals are tested 1 day later either drug free or in the presence of the blocker (see Figures 4.1D through 4.1F; Cain et al., 2002). Thus LVGCCs appear to serve a crucial role in the induction of fear extinction, the first learning protocol so far described to which they are essential.

THE RULES OF EXTINCTION LEARNING

Why should extinction operate via different molecular mechanisms compared to other forms of learning? We may perhaps gain some insight if we look back at the reasons why the NMDA receptor has been so interesting as a candidate in the induction of various forms of associative learning. The NMDAr was thought to be particularly suitable as a switch to generate such learning because it is a molecular coincidence detector, ideally suited to generate associations between two signals, for example, the auditory cue (CS) and the footshock (US) in fear conditioning. However, during extinction, no such association needs to occur because only the CS is presented. Could it be that learning about a CS in isolation does not require a coincidence detector? We have begun to test this hypothesis in our lab using two protocols. In one of these protocols, called *latent inhibition*, animals receive preexposure to the CS for many trials before fear conditioning, and then show less fear than nonpreexposed controls. In another protocol, called *novel object recognition*, animals are familiarized with one of two objects before being asked to choose between the familiar object and a novel object. In both of these protocols, treatment with an LVGCC inhibitor during the preexposure blocks the effect entirely (data not shown; Barad, Blouin, & Cain, 2004). Thus, LVGCCs may be crucial to a whole set of learning processes that depend on learning about a single stimulus or involve inhibitory processes. Regardless of the generality of the role of LVGCCs, they do appear to be specifically involved in the induction of fear extinction learning, but not of fear acquisition. This is powerful evidence that extinction may involve different learning mechanisms than many other forms of learning.

Further evidence of important differences comes from the behavioral level of analysis. One of the most consistent of all learning rules for acquisition learning is that temporally spaced training trials produce more and longer lasting learning than temporally massed trials (Barela, 1999; Carew

& Kandel, 1973; Ebbinghaus, 1885/1913; Fanselow, DeCola, & Young, 1993; Fanselow & Tighe, 1988; Freudenthal et al., 1998; Gibbon, 1977; Humphreys, 1940; Jenkins, Barnes, & Barrera, 1981; Josselyn et al., 2001; Kogan et al., 1997; Scharf et al., 2002; Terrace, Gibbon, Farrell, & Baldock, 1975; Tully, Preat, Boynton, & Del Vecchio, 1994). The spacing of behavioral training has long been taken to be most consistent with the requirement for transcription and translation in long-lasting learning (Bailey, Bartsch, & Kandel, 1996; Goelet, Castellucci, Schacher, & Kandel, 1986). Once short-term processes are saturated by a training session, it seems that further learning depends on the completion of these time-consuming processes.

However, the data for extinction learning has not been so consistent. Although some studies report that spaced training is better in extinction (Baum, Andrus, & Jacobs, 1990; Sheffield, 1949; Westbrook, Smith, & Charnock, 1985), others report that massed training is better (Oler & Baum, 1968; Pavlov, 1927; Reynolds, 1945), and still others that there is no difference (Birch, 1965; Martasian, Smith, Neill, & Rieg, 1992; Schiff, Smith, & Prochaska, 1972; Shipley, 1974; Stanley, 1952).

We recently attempted to resolve this question in our own lab, examining both the acute phase of extinction induction and the long-term memory for extinction 1 or 8 days after fear extinction training in mice. We found that individual CS presentations more efficiently generated extinction induction and retention when they were temporally massed. Interestingly, this appeared to follow, not from a fundamental difference in learning rules, but rather from CS presentations eliciting two opposing mechanisms: one causing extinction, and one that tended to block extinction or even cause increases in fear (see Figure 4.2; Cain, Blouin, & Barad, 2003). This latter process, called *incubation*, can be conceptualized as a rehearsal of the original CS–US association after the presentation of the CS alone, and may strengthen that association (Eysenck, 1968). It seems to be favored by spaced training and acts to retard extinction learning. Massing, on the other hand, favors extinction, which may be thought of as a reevaluation of the likelihood that the CS actually predicts the US occurring. Thus, when we presented blocks of massed CS presentations that were individually sufficient to induce extinction (and thus overcome the incubation brake), we found that extinction was still more effective when such blocks were temporally spaced. Our results suggest that extinction follows a complex relationship regarding the spacing of CS presentations, in which individual presentations are most effective when massed, but that blocks of such massed training are most effective when spaced.

This complex picture presents an interesting challenge to understand the mechanisms underlying it. More importantly, it can begin to provide guidance to improve the pattern of exposure to anxiogenic cues in human patients with anxiety disorders like PTSD. In the future this model may help determine patterns of temporal spacing of such exposures that will most

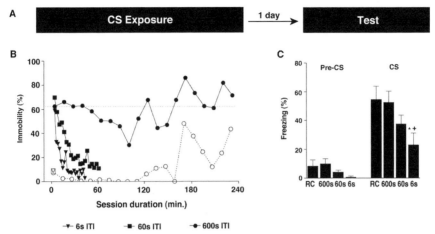

FIGURE 4.2. Temporally massed conditioned stimulus (CS) presentations produce greater cue fear extinction than spaced presentations. A, Experimental design. Animals were trained with two pairings of a 2-min white noise cue (CS) coterminating with a 2-s 0.7-mA footshock. B, Immobility during 2 min prior to the CS (pre-CS) and the 2-min CS presentations 1 day after cue fear acquisition in a different context. All CS presentation groups were presented with 20 CSs; only the ITI varied: 6 s (massed, *filled circles*), 60 s (intermediate, *filled squares*), or 600 s (spaced, *filled triangles*). Open symbols represent immobility during equivalent pre-CS periods. Retention control mice were placed in the chambers for an equivalent period of time but were not presented with any CSs. C, Freezing during a single 2-min CS presentation in the extinction context 1 day after presentations. *$p < .05$ vs. RC; +$p < .05$ vs. spaced.

effectively generate decreases in symptoms in anxiety-disorder patients. For example, it may be most effective to start exposure therapy in the office with long focused exposures to fearful cues, and then to encourage patients to do daily exposure sessions of similar (or even slightly shorter) durations (see Yadin & Foa, this volume).

DESIGNING EFFECTIVE THERAPIES FOR ANXIETY DISORDERS

Generally, all psychiatric treatments in current use are designed to improve symptoms either through drug effects or through psychotherapy. Although the two are frequently combined, there is little theoretical basis and little support in basic or clinical research for the efficacy of the combination. Little work has been done on the biological mechanisms by which psychotherapies work, and less on how the various drugs used for treatment might affect their efficacy. However, as indicated previously, rapid progress is being made in understanding the mechanisms underlying extinction, and extinction is clearly an important mechanism of behavior therapy. Thus, extinction provides a golden opportunity for basic science research on the interactions of medications with a model of therapy to help guide the design of effective combination therapy for anxiety disorders.

One early example of this kind of research was the investigation of the effects of benzodiazepines on extinction of conditioned fear (Bouton, Kenney, & Rosengard, 1990). Benzodiazepines, which include diazepam, chlordiazepoxide, lorazepam, and alprazolam, are the medications most commonly prescribed for anxiety and sleep disorders. However, benzodiazepines given to fearful rats before extinction training produced a dose-dependent blockade of the memory for extinction. Thus, despite their direct anxiolytic effects, benzodiazepines are unlikely to be helpful when combined with behavioral or cognitive behavior therapy. This is quite consistent with the fact that extinction is a form of learning, as benzodiazepines are well known to be amnestic; that is, they interfere with learning (Newman & Reves, 1993). Human studies also generally indicate that benzodiazepine treatment may interfere with the efficacy of cognitive behavior therapy for anxiety (Westra & Stewart, 1998).

On the other hand, at least four pharmacological interventions have been shown to improve extinction learning, and in one case early clinical studies support the efficacy of using this intervention in human anxiety-disorder treatment. Spurred by the important role of noradrenergic transmission in the fight or flight response to frightening situations, our lab has shown that the noradrenergic neurotransmission plays a crucial modulatory role in fear extinction learning (Cain, Blouin, & Barad, 2004). We used systemic injections of either propranolol or yohimbine to probe the role of this neurotransmitter system in the extinction of conditioned fear in mice. Propanolol blocks postsynaptic adrenergic beta receptors, and thus blocks many of the effects of noradrenergic neurotransmission. Yohimbine blocks presynaptic autoinhibitory alpha-2 receptors, and thus potentiates noradrenergic neurotransmission by preventing its autoinhibition. Even though propranolol is commonly used to treat human social phobia (Brantigan, Brantigan, & Joseph, 1982; Hartley, Ungapen, Davie, & Spencer, 1983), we found that propranolol had no effect on extinction generated by temporally massed trials, whereas yohimbine, which tends to be anxiogenic by itself (Bremner, Krystal, Southwick, & Charney, 1996; Tanaka, Yoshida, Emoto, & Ishii, 2000), reduced the number of trials required to generate extinction four-fold (see Figure 4.3). On the other hand, when spaced CS presentations, which normally generate acute incubation and no day-to-day change in fear, were given, propranolol treatment yielded day-to-day *increases* of fear, whereas yohimbine treatment permitted significant extinction to occur (see Figure 4.4). Such results predict that propranolol will be a poor medication to combine with behavior therapy, as suggested by at least one human study (Hafner & Milton, 1977), whereas yohimbine is likely both to accelerate behavior therapy and to help correct for errors in the administration

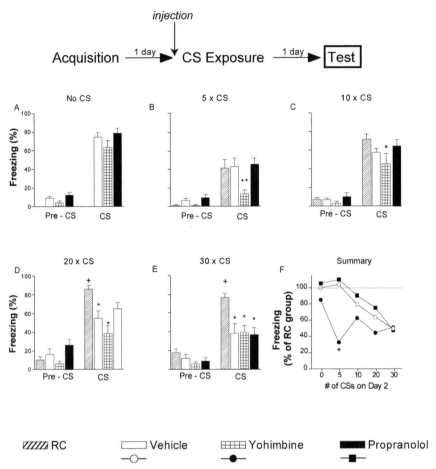

FIGURE 4.3. Yohimbine facilitates long-term cue fear extinction with massed conditioned stimulus (CS) exposures. One day after training with two pairings of a 2-min 80-dB white noise CS coterminating with a 2-s footshock (0.7 mA, 2-min ITI), mice in separate experiments were tested for the effects of vehicle, yohimbine (5 mg/kg, s.c.), and propranolol (10 mg/kg, s.c.) on extinction with 0 (A), 5 (B), 10 (C), 20 (D), or 30 (E) nonreinforced CS presentations (5-s ITI, 7–8 mice/group). Data shown represent freezing during a single 2-min test CS given 1 day after the extinction sessions (drug free). The final summary panel (F) shows the results of the five experiments with fear normalized to freezing in groups of mice that were injected with vehicle and not presented with any extinction CSs on Day 2 (retention control mice, RC). $*p < 0.05$ vs. RC mice; $+p < 0.05$ vs. vehicle-extinction mice. (Reprinted from Cain et al., 2004. Copyright 2004 by Cold Spring Harbor Laboratory Press.)

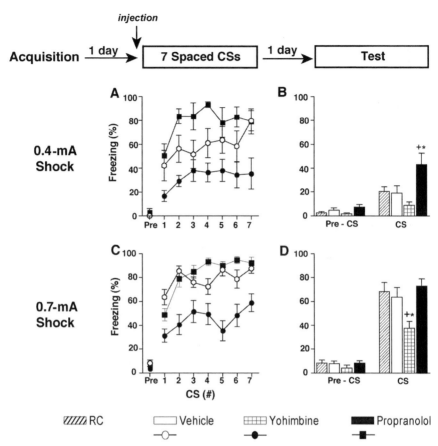

FIGURE 4.4. Effects of yohimbine and propranolol on fear learning. Yohimbine leads to extinction, whereas propranolol leads to incubation, of cue fear when given in conjunction with spaced CS presentations. Separate experiments examined the effect of vehicle, yohimbine (5 mg/kg, s.c.), or propranolol (10 mg/kg, s.c.) on the effect of spaced CS presentations after weak (two pairings of CS coterminating with 0.4-mA footshocks; A and B) or strong (two pairings of CS coterminating with 0.7-mA footshocks; C and D) cue fear conditioning. In each experiment, 1 day after acquisition, mice were injected with vehicle, yohimbine, or propranolol and presented with seven CSs (20-min ITI). A retention control (RC) group received injections of vehicle and spent the same amount of time in the extinction chambers but received no CS presentations. A and C, Freezing during the spaced CS sessions 20 min after injections. B and D, Freezing 1 day later during the final 5-min CS tests (drug free). $*p < 0.05$ vs. RC mice; $+p < 0.05$ vs. vehicle-exposure mice. (Adapted from Cain et al., 2002. Copyright 2002 by the Society for Neuroscience.)

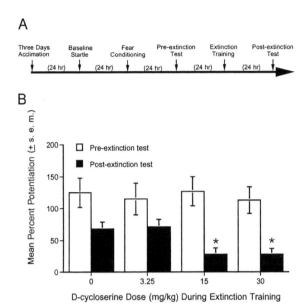

FIGURE 4.5. Dose–response function for the effect of D-cycloserine (DCS) on sub-maximal extinction. A, Timeline of the behavioral procedures for experiment. B, Percentage of fear-potentiated startle measured 24 hr before and 24 hr after a single session of extinction training in rats injected with saline or DCS (3.25, 15, or 30 mg/kg, i.p.) 30 min before nonreinforced cue exposure. DCS dose-dependently facilitated extinction learning. *$p < 0.05$ versus saline after extinction. (Reprinted from Walker, Ressler, Lu, & Davis, 2002. Copyright 2002 by the Society for Neuroscience.)

of behavior therapy (as modeled by temporally spaced CS presentations) that might otherwise interfere with the effectiveness of treatment. We are currently performing human studies based on these experiments in mice.

Another drug that facilitates extinction in animals when injected is sulpiride, an inhibitor of D2-like dopamine receptors (Ponnusamy, Nissim, & Barad, 2005). This is particularly interesting because sulpiride inhibits the excitatory learning that underlies fear conditioning itself, thus differentiating extinction learning from acquisition learning. Like yohimbine, sulpiride also converts an incubation-inducing procedure (spaced CSs) into an effective extinction-inducing procedure.

Still another pharmacological approach that facilitates extinction in rodents is the inhibition of the reuptake or breakdown of endocannabinoids (Chhatwal, Davis, Maguschak, & Ressler, 2005). Endocannabinoids are the natural neurotransmitters that bind to the same receptors that are targeted by the active ingredient in marijuana. These receptors were recently shown to be important for the generation of extinction using "knockout" mice without the cannabinoid CB1 receptors and inhibitors of endocannabinoid neurotransmission (Marsicano et al., 2002). AM404, which extends the action of endocannabinoids at synapses in the brain by preventing their breakdown and reuptake, has now been shown to facilitate extinction when injected into rats before extinction training (Chhatwal et al., 2005).

Studies from Mike Davis and his colleagues have been even more dramatic in demonstrating that effective adjunctive pharmacotherapy can be based on the hypothesis that extinction and behavior therapy are forms of learning. This group used both systemic and intra-amygdala administration of D-cycloserine (DCS). DCS is an agonist at a glycine-binding site on the NMDA receptor and promotes its opening when it binds glutamate (Lehmann, Colpaert, & Canton, 1991). Consistent with the hypothesis that NMDA receptor activity is necessary for long-term extinction learning, a suboptimal number of CS presentations given along with DCS treatment generated significantly more extinction than the CS presentations given along with vehicle, although DCS alone had no effect on fear by itself (see Figure 4.5; Walker et al., 2002). Because DCS has long been used as an antimicrobial treatment, it was possible to test this agent immediately in combination with human anxiety treatment. In a study using just two psychotherapy sessions involving exposure to a virtual-reality glass elevator, DCS treatment generated significantly more subjective and objective improvements in acrophobic subjects than did placebo treatment (Ressler et al., 2004). Thus, the analysis of the mechanisms of extinction learning has already generated a first method for facilitating that learning and increasing the efficacy of human behavioral treatment.

CONCLUSION

The mechanistic analysis of extinction is proceeding rapidly. Consistent with the psychological evidence that extinction is a form of learning and not merely erasure, neurobiological studies have shown that extinction shares several crucial molecular mechanisms with other forms of learning, particularly the NMDA receptor. However, extinction is a special kind of learning. Other evidence indicates that it follows unusual behavioral rules for the optimal temporal patterning of training. Individual CS presentations generate more extinction when massed than when spaced. Induction of extinction also depends on a novel molecular mechanism: Acutely, extinction learning is independent of the NMDA receptor and dependent on LVGCCs. The analysis of the mechanisms of extinction learning is already generating information about what drugs to use, and not to use, to maximize the efficacy of extinction and of anxiety-disorder treatment. Specifically, benzodiazepines probably interfere with extinction (and behavior therapy), just as they do with many other forms of learning. On the other hand, yohimbine, a potentiator of adrenergic transmission; sulpiride, a blocker of D2-like dopamine receptors; AM404, a facilitator of cannabinoid signaling; and DCS, which acts as an agonist at the glycine-binding site of the NMDAr, all facilitate extinction learning. And DCS has already shown promise in improving human anxiety-disorder treatment. More pharmacological adjuncts to behavior therapy will certainly be added to the psychiatric pharmacopoeia soon and will represent not anxiolytic therapies themselves, but rather a new strategy designed to improve therapeutics by facilitating the learning that lies at the heart of anxiety-disorder treatment.

PTSD presents a conundrum for any thoughtful observer. The effects of trauma can be dire, and PTSD is only one such dire consequence. A focus on PTSD, the set of symptoms suffered by some individuals after a trauma, may seem to give insufficient weight to all the societal and political effects of trauma, and to all the ways it disrupts peoples' lives that do not come under the rubric of PTSD. However, like so many psychiatric diagnoses, PTSD identifies a consistent pattern of suffering, and, as will be apparent in the next section of this book, allows scientific clinical trials to find effective treatments for that suffering.

Some of the most effective treatments for PTSD are based on extinction of conditioned fear in animals. Just as the construct of PTSD fails to capture the complexity of human response to trauma, simplified models of conditioned fear and its extinction certainly fail to capture much of the pathology of PTSD, for example, nightmares or emotional numbing. Nevertheless, the study of extinction in animals has already done much to guide psychotherapy for anxiety disorders including PTSD. Some of the clincally relevant findings about the mechanisms of extinction have been reviewed in this chapter. Studies of extinction in animals have led to understanding of the role of context in the response to extinction, and in relapse. They have led to important hypotheses about the optimal patterns and intensities of cue exposure. Most recently, understanding of cellular mechanisms underlying extinction has led to the identification of drugs that can facilitate extinction, and the demonstration that such drugs can facilitate behavioral therapy of human anxiety-disorder patients. Thus, these discoveries made in the animal lab will lead directly to improved treatments to mitigate one of the devastating effects of trauma on human beings.

References

Bailey, C. H., Bartsch, D., & Kandel, E. R. (1996). Toward a molecular definition of long-term memory storage. *Proceedings of the National Academy of Sciences of the United States of America, 93*(24), 13445–13452.

Baker, J. D., & Azorlosa, J. L. (1996). The NMDA antagonist MK-801 blocks the extinction of Pavlovian fear conditioning. *Behavioral Neuroscience, 110*(3), 618–620.

Barad, M., Blouin, A. M., & Cain, C. K. (2004). Like extinction, latent inhibition of conditioned fear in mice is blocked by systemic inhibition of L-type voltage-gated calcium channels. *Learning & Memory, 11*, 536–539.

Barela, P. B. (1999). Theoretical mechanisms underlying the trial-spacing effect in Pavlovian fear conditioning. *Journal of Experimental Psychology: Animal Behavioral Processes, 25*(2), 177–193.

Bauer, E. P., Schafe, G. E., & LeDoux, J. E. (2002). NMDA receptors and L-type voltage-gated calcium channels contribute to long-term potentiation and different components of fear memory formation in the lateral amygdala. *Journal of Neuroscience, 22*(12), 5239–5249.

Baum, M. (1988). Spontaneous recovery from the effects of flooding (exposure) in animals. *Behaviour Research and Therapy, 26*(2), 185–186.

Baum, M., Andrus, T., & Jacobs, W. J. (1990). Extinction of a conditioned emotional response: Massed and distributed exposures. *Behaviour Research and Therapy, 28*(1), 63–68.

Birch, D. (1965). Extended training extinction effect under massed and spaced extinction trials. *Journal of Experimental Psychology, 70*, 315–322.

Bouton, M. E., Kenney, F. A., & Rosengard, C. (1990). State-dependent fear extinction with two benzodiazepine tranquilizers. *Behavioral Neuroscience, 104*(1), 44–55.

Bouton, M. E., & King, D. A. (1983). Contextual control of the extinction of conditioned fear: Tests for the associative value of the context. *Journal of Experimental Psychology: Animal Behavioral Processes, 9*(3), 248–265.

Brantigan, C. O., Brantigan, T. A., & Joseph, N. (1982). Effect of beta blockade and beta stimulation on stage fright. *American Journal of Medicine, 72*(1), 88–94.

Bremner, J. D., Krystal, J. H., Southwick, S. M., & Charney, D. S. (1996). Noradrenergic mechanisms in stress and anxiety, II: Clinical studies. *Synapse, 23*(1), 39–51.

Brown, T. H., Chapman, P. F., Kairiss, E. W., & Keenan, C. L. (1988). Long-term synaptic potentiation. *Science, 242*(4879), 724–728.

Cain, C. K., Blouin, A. M., & Barad, M. (2002). L-type voltage-gated calcium channels are required for extinction, but not for acquisition or expression, of conditioned fear in mice. *Journal of Neuroscience, 22*(20), 9113–9121.

Cain, C. K., Blouin, A. M., & Barad, M. (2003). Temporally massed CS presentations generate more fear extinction than spaced presentations. *Journal of Experimental Psychology: Animal Behavior Processes, 29*(4), 323–333.

Cain, C. K., Blouin, A. M., & Barad, M. (2004). Adrenergic transmission facilitates extinction of conditional fear in mice. *Learning & Memory, 11*(2), 179–187.

Campeau, S., Miserendino, M. J., & Davis, M. (1992). Intra-amygdala infusion of the N-methyl-D-aspartate receptor antagonist AP5 blocks acquisition but not expression of fear-potentiated startle to an auditory conditioned stimulus. *Behavioral Neuroscience, 106*(3), 569–574.

Carew, T. J., & Kandel, E. R. (1973). Acquisition and retention of long-term habituation in Aplysia: Correlation of behavioral and cellular processes. *Science, 182*(117), 1158–1160.

Chhatwal, J. P., Davis, M., Maguschak, K. A., & Ressler, K. J. (2005). Enhancing cannabinoid neurotransmission augments the extinction of conditioned fear. *Neuropsychopharmacology, 30*(3), 516–524.

Christie, B. R., & Abraham, W. C. (1994). L-type voltage-sensitive calcium channel antagonists block heterosynaptic long-term depression in the dentate gyrus of anaesthetized rats. *Neuroscience Letters, 167*(1–2), 41–45.

Collingridge, G. L., Kehl, S. J., & McLennan, H. (1983). Excitatory amino acids in synaptic transmission in the Schaffer collateral-commissural pathway of the rat hippocampus. *Journal of Physiology, 334*, 33–46.

Craske, M. G. (1999). *Anxiety disorders: Psychological approaches to theory and treatment.* Boulder, CO: Westview Press.

Davis, M. (1992). The role of the amygdala in fear and anxiety. *Annual Review of Neuroscience, 15*, 353–375.

Ebbinghaus, H. (1885/1913). *Memory: A contribution to experimental psychology* (H. A. Ruger & C. E. Bussenius, Trans.). New York: Teachers College, Columbia University.

Eysenck, H. J. (1968). A theory of the incubation of anxiety/fear responses. *Behaviour Research and Therapy, 6*(3), 309–321.

Falls, W. A., Miserendino, M. J., & Davis, M. (1992). Extinction of fear-potentiated startle: Blockade by infusion of an NMDA antagonist into the amygdala. *Journal of Neuroscience, 12*(3), 854–863.

Fanselow, M. S., DeCola, J. P., & Young, S. L. (1993). Mechanisms responsible for reduced contextual conditioning with massed unsignaled unconditional stimuli. *Journal of Experimental Psychology: Animal Behavioral Processes, 19*(2), 121–137.

Fanselow, M. S., & Kim, J. J. (1994). Acquisition of contextual Pavlovian fear conditioning is blocked by application of an NMDA receptor antagonist D,L-2-amino-5-phosphonovaleric acid to the basolateral amygdala. *Behavioral Neuroscience, 108*(1), 210–212.

Fanselow, M. S., & Tighe, T. J. (1988). Contextual conditioning with massed versus distributed unconditional stimuli in the absence of explicit conditional stimuli. *Journal of Experimental Psychology: Animal Behavioral Processes, 14*(2), 187–199.

Freudenthal, R., Locatelli, F., Hermitte, G., Maldonado, H., Lafourcade, C., Delorenzi, A., et al. (1998). Kappa-B like DNA-binding activity is enhanced after spaced training that induces long-term memory in the crab *Chasmagnathus*. *Neuroscience Letters, 242*(3), 143–146.

Gale, G., Anagnostaras, S., Godsil, B., Mitchell, S., Nozawa, T., Sage, J., et al. (2004). Role of the basolateral amygdala in the storage of fear memories across the adult lifetime of rats. *Journal of Neuroscience, 24*, 3810–1815.

Gewirtz, J. C., & Davis, M. (1997). Second-order fear conditioning prevented by blocking NMDA receptors in amygdala. *Nature, 388*(6641), 471–474.

Gibbon, J. (1977). Trial and intertrial durations in autoshaping. *Journal of Experimental Psychology: Animal Behavior Processes, 3*(3), 264–284.

Goelet, P., Castellucci, V. F., Schacher, S., & Kandel, E. R. (1986). The long and the short of long-term memory – a molecular framework. *Nature, 322*(6078), 419–422.

Hafner, J., & Milton, F. (1977). The influence of propranolol on the exposure in vivo of agoraphobics. *Psychological Medicine, 7*(3), 419–425.

Hartley, L. R., Ungapen, S., Davie, I., & Spencer, D. J. (1983). The effect of beta adrenergic blocking drugs on speakers' performance and memory. *British Journal Psychiatry, 142*, 512–517.

Hebb, D. O. (1949). *The organization of behavior: A neuropsychological theory*. New York: Wiley.

Huang, Y. Y., & Malenka, R. C. (1993). Examination of TEA-induced synaptic enhancement in area CA1 of the hippocampus: The role of voltage-dependent Ca2+ channels in the induction of LTP. *Journal of Neuroscience, 13*(2), 568–576.

Huber, K. M., Mauk, M. D., & Kelly, P. T. (1995). Distinct LTP induction mechanisms: Contribution of NMDA receptors and voltage-dependent calcium channels. *Journal of Neurophysiology, 73*(1), 270–279.

Humphreys, L. (1940). Distributed practice in the development of the conditioned eyelid reaction. *Journal of General Psychology, 22*, 379–385.

Jenkins, H. M., Barnes, R. A., & Barrera, J. (1981). Why autoshaping depends on trial spacing. In C. Locurto, H. S. Terrace, & J. Gibbon (Eds.), *Autoshaping and conditioning theory*. New York: Academic Press.

Johnston, D., Williams, S., Jaffe, D., & Gray, R. (1992). NMDA-receptor-independent long-term potentiation. *Annual Review of Physiology, 54*, 489–505.

Jones, M. C. (1924). A laboratory study of fear: The case of Peter. *Pedagogical Seminary, 31*, 308–315.

Josselyn, S. A., Shi, C., Carlezon, W. A., Jr., Neve, R. L., Nestler, E. J., & Davis, M. (2001). Long-term memory is facilitated by cAMP response element-binding protein overexpression in the amygdala. *Journal of Neuroscience, 21*(7), 2404–2412.

Kim, J. J., DeCola, J. P., Landeira-Fernandez, J., & Fanselow, M. S. (1991). N-methyl-D-aspartate receptor antagonist APV blocks acquisition but not expression of fear conditioning. *Behavioral Neuroscience, 105*(1), 126–133.

Kogan, J. H., Frankland, P. W., Blendy, J. A., Coblentz, J., Marowitz, Z., Schutz, G., et al. (1997). Spaced training induces normal long-term memory in CREB mutant mice. *Current Biology, 7*(1), 1–11.

Lehmann, J., Colpaert, F., & Canton, H. (1991). Glutamate and glycine co-activate while polyamines merely modulate the NMDA receptor complex. *Progress in Neuro-Psychopharmacology & Biological Psychiatry, 15*(2), 183–190.

Lin, C. H., Yeh, S. H., Leu, T. H., Chang, W. C., Wang, S. T., & Gean, P. W. (2003). Identification of calcineurin as a key signal in the extinction of fear memory. *Journal of Neuroscience, 23*(5), 1574–1579.

Lu, K. T., Walker, D. L., & Davis, M. (2001). Mitogen-activated protein kinase cascade in the basolateral nucleus of amygdala is involved in extinction of fear-potentiated startle. *Journal of Neuroscience, 21*(16), RC162.

Malleret, G., Haditsch, U., Genoux, D., Jones, M. W., Bliss, T. V., Vanhoose, A. M., et al. (2001). Inducible and reversible enhancement of learning, memory, and long-term potentiation by genetic inhibition of calcineurin. *Cell, 104*(5), 675–686.

Marsicano, G., Wotjak, C. T., Azad, S. C., Bisogno, T., Rammes, G., Cascio, M. G., et al. (2002). The endogenous cannabinoid system controls extinction of aversive memories. *Nature, 418*(6897), 530–534.

Martasian, P. J., Smith, N. F., Neill, S. A., & Rieg, T. S. (1992). Retention of massed vs distributed response-prevention treatments in rats and a revised training procedure. *Psychological Reports, 70*(2), 339–355.

McFarlane, A. C. (1994). Individual psychotherapy for post-traumatic stress disorder. *Psychiatric Clinics of North America, 17*(2), 393–408.

Miserendino, M. J., Sananes, C. B., Melia, K. R., & Davis, M. (1990). Blocking of acquisition but not expression of conditioned fear-potentiated startle by NMDA antagonists in the amygdala. *Nature, 345*(6277), 716–718.

Morris, R. G., Anderson, E., Lynch, G. S., & Baudry, M. (1986). Selective impairment of learning and blockade of long-term potentiation by an N-methyl-D-aspartate receptor antagonist, AP5. *Nature, 319*(6056), 774–776.

Myers, K. M., Ressler, K. J., & Davis, M. (2006). Different mechanisms of fear extinction dependent on length of time since fear acquisition. *Learning & Memory, 13*(2), 216–223.

Newman, M., & Reves, J. G. (1993). Pro: Midazolam is the sedative of choice to supplement narcotic anesthesia. *Journal of Cardiothorac and Vascular Anesthesia, 7*(5), 615–619.

Nicoll, R. A., & Malenka, R. C. (1999). Expression mechanisms underlying NMDA receptor-dependent long-term potentiation. *Annals of the New York Academy of Sciences, 868*, 515–525.

Oler, I. D., & Baum, M. (1968). Facilitated extinction of an avoidance response through shortening of the inter-trial interval. *Psychonomic Science, 11*, 323–324.

Pavlov, I. P. (1927). *Conditioned reflexes: An investigation of the physiological activity of the cerebral cortex* (G. V. Anrep, Trans.). New York: Dover.

Ponnusamy, R., Nissim, H. A., & Barad, M. (2005). Systemic blockade of D2-like dopamine receptors facilitates extinction of conditioned fear in mice. *Learning & Memory, 12*(4), 399–406.

Rescorla, R. A., & Heth, C. D. (1975). Reinstatement of fear to an extinguished conditioned stimulus. *Journal of Experimental Psychology: Animal Behavioral Processes, 1*(1), 88–96.

Rescorla, R. A., & Wagner, A. R. (1972). A theory of Pavlovian conditioning: Variations in the effectiveness of reinforcement and nonreinforcement. In A. H. Black & W. F. Prokasy (Eds.), *Classical conditioning II* (pp. 64–99). New York: Appleton-Century-Crofts.

Ressler, K. J., Rothbaum, B. O., Tannenbaum, L., Anderson, P., Graap, K., Zimand, E., et al. (2004). Cognitive enhancers as adjuncts to psychotherapy: Use of D-cycloserine in phobic individuals to facilitate extinction of fear. *Archives of General Psychiatry, 61*(11), 1136–1144.

Reynolds, B. (1945). Extinction of trace conditioned responses as a function of the spacing of trials during the acquisition and extinction series. *Journal of Experimental Psychology, 35*, 81–95.

Santini, E., Muller, R. U., & Quirk, G. J. (2001). Consolidation of extinction learning involves transfer from NMDA-independent to NMDA-dependent memory. *Journal of Neuroscience, 21*(22), 9009–9017.

Schafe, G. E., Nadel, N. V., Sullivan, G. M., Harris, A., & LeDoux, J. E. (1999). Memory consolidation for contextual and auditory fear conditioning is dependent on protein synthesis, PKA, and MAP kinase. *Learning & Memory, 6*(2), 97–110.

Scharf, M. T., Woo, N. H., Lattal, K. M., Young, J. Z., Nguyen, P. V., & Abel, T. (2002). Protein synthesis is required for the enhancement of long-term potentiation and long-term memory by spaced training. *Journal of Neurophysiology, 87*(6), 2770–2777.

Schiff, R., Smith, N., & Prochaska, J. (1972). Extinction of avoidance in rats as a function of duration and number of blocked trials. *Journal of Comparative and Physiological Psychology, 81*, 356–359.

Sheffield, V. F. (1949). Extinction as a function of partial reinforcement and distribution of practice. *Journal of Experimental Psychology, 39*, 511–526.

Shipley, R. H. (1974). Extinction of conditioned fear in rats as a function of several parameters of CS exposure. *Journal of Comparative and Physiological Psychology, 87*(4), 699–707.

Stanley, W. C. (1952). Extinction as a function of the spacing of extinction trials. *Journal of Experimental Psychology, 43*, 249–261.

Staubli, U., Thibault, O., DiLorenzo, M., & Lynch, G. (1989). Antagonism of NMDA receptors impairs acquisition but not retention of olfactory memory. *Behavioral Neuroscience, 103*(1), 54–60.

Tanaka, M., Yoshida, M., Emoto, H., & Ishii, H. (2000). Noradrenaline systems in the hypothalamus, amygdala and locus coeruleus are involved in the provocation of anxiety: Basic studies. *European Journal of Pharmacology, 405*(1–3), 397–406.

Tang, Y. P., Shimizu, E., Dube, G. R., Rampon, C., Kerchner, G. A., Zhuo, M., et al. (1999). Genetic enhancement of learning and memory in mice. *Nature, 401*(6748), 63–69.

Terrace, H. S., Gibbon, J., Farrell, L., & Baldock, M. D. (1975). Temporal factors influencing the acquisition and maintenance of an autoshaped keypeck. *Animal Learning & Behavior, 3*(1), 53–62.

Tully, T., Preat, T., Boynton, S. C., & Del Vecchio, M. (1994). Genetic dissection of consolidated memory in Drosophila. *Cell, 79*(1), 35–47.

Walker, D. L., Ressler, K. J., Lu, K. T., & Davis, M. (2002). Facilitation of conditioned fear extinction by systemic administration or intra-amygdala infusions of D-cycloserine as assessed with fear-potentiated startle in rats. *Journal of Neuroscience, 22*(6), 2343–2351.

Weisskopf, M. G., Bauer, E. P., & LeDoux, J. E. (1999). L-type voltage-gated calcium channels mediate NMDA-independent associative long-term potentiation at thalamic input synapses to the amygdala. *Journal of Neuroscience, 19*(23), 10512–10519.

Westbrook, R. F., Smith, F. J., & Charnock, D. J. (1985). The extinction of an aversion: Role of the interval between non-reinforced presentations of the averted stimulus. *Quarterly Journal of Experimental Psychology: Comparative and Physiological Psychology, 37B*, 255–273.

Westra, H. A., & Stewart, S. H. (1998). Cognitive behavioural therapy and pharmacotherapy: Complementary or contradictory approaches to the treatment of anxiety? *Clinical Psychology Reviews, 18*(3), 307–340.

Wigstrom, H., & Gustafsson, B. (1986). Postsynaptic control of hippocampal long-term potentiation. *Journal of Physiology, 81*(4), 228–236.

Wolpe, J. (1969). *The practice of behavior therapy* (1st ed.). New York: Pergamon Press.

5

Developmental Origins of Neurobiological Vulnerability for PTSD

Rosemary Bagot, Carine Parent, Timothy W. Bredy, Tieyuan Zhang, Alain Gratton, and Michael J. Meaney

The question of vulnerability lies very much at the heart of research on anxiety disorders, such as PTSD (Yehuda, Schmeidler, Wainberg, Binder-Brynes, & Duvdevani, 1998). Surprisingly, only a minority (~25–30%) of humans subjected to even such a profound trauma as rape develop PTSD (Ressnick, Kilpatrick, Dansky, Saunders, & Best, 1993), and early family life serves as a highly significant predictor of vulnerability to PTSD following trauma (Udwin, Boyle, Yule, Bolton, & O'Ryan, 2000). Moreover, many cases of PTSD derive from events that might not be considered as necessarily traumatic by the general population (Breslau et al., 1998), a finding that further underscores the importance of vulnerability. Moreover, there is evidence for the familial transmission of vulnerability to PTSD that is related to alterations in parent–offspring interactions. These findings are not surprising because anxiety reduces parental responsiveness to offspring (e.g., Fleming, 1988, 1999). These findings suggest that early life events might alter the development of neural systems that mediate cognitive and emotional responses to trauma, and thus contribute to individual differences in vulnerability to PTSD.

The question can be rendered more precise in light of the remarkable advances in human clinical studies. First, PTSD research suggests that the probability of chronic PTSD following trauma is related to the magnitude of the initial reaction to the event (Shalev, this volume). Hence, factors that influence the development of individual differences in reactivity are likely of considerable relevance. Second, although it is understandably common for a majority of individuals to show PTSD-like symptomatology in the weeks following trauma, most exhibit a process of recovery over the ensuing months (Shalev, this volume). The processes involved in this recovery appear to map onto those targeted by psychological therapies. Thus, the ability of subjects to "place" the trauma into a specific spatiotemporal context appears to be critical in avoiding chronic PTSD. We suggest that the results of studies with nonhuman, largely rodent models provide evidence that variations in mother–infant interactions over the first week of life stably alter the development of neural systems involved in both cognitive–emotional responses to stress and spatiotemporal information processing. Thus, individual differences in cognitive–emotional systems that process information associated with aversive events may constitute a developmentally determined vulnerability for PTSD.

VARIATIONS IN MOTHER–INFANT INTERACTIONS IN THE RAT

We examine the relation between maternal care and the development of behavioral and endocrine responses to stress using a rather simple model of naturally occurring variations in maternal behavior over the first 6–8 days after birth (Champagne, Francis, Mar, & Meaney, 2003). We characterize individual differences in maternal behavior through direct observation of mother–pup interactions in normally reared animals. These observations reveal considerable variation in two forms of maternal behavior – licking and grooming (LG) of pups and arched-back nursing (ABN) (Stern, 1997). LG includes both body and anogenital licking. ABN, also referred to as "crouching," is characterized by a dam nursing her pups with her back conspicuously arched and legs splayed outward. Although common, it is not the only posture from which dams nurse. A blanket posture represents a more relaxed version of the arched-back position where the mother is almost lying on the suckling pups. This posture provides substantially less opportunity for movement by the pups, such as nipple switching. Dams also nurse from their sides and often will move from one posture to another over the course of a nursing bout.

Interestingly, the frequency of LG and ABN is correlated across animals and thus we are able to define mothers according to both behaviors, as High or Low LG-ABN mothers. For the sake of most of the studies described here, High and Low LG-ABN mothers are females whose scores on both measures were more than 1 standard deviation above (High) or below (Low) the mean for their cohort. Importantly, High and Low LG-ABN mothers do not differ in the amount of contact time with pups; differences in the frequency of LG or ABN do not occur simply as a function of time in contact with pups. High and Low LG-ABN mothers raise a comparable number of pups to weaning and there are no differences in the weaning weights of the pups, suggesting an adequate level of maternal care across the groups. These findings also suggest that we are examining the consequences of variations in maternal care that occur within a normal range. Indeed, the frequency of both pup LG and ABN are normally distributed across large populations of lactating female rats (Champagne et al., 2003).

MATERNAL CARE ALTERS BEHAVIORAL RESPONSES TO STRESS

The critical question concerns the potential consequences of these differences in maternal behavior for the development of behavioral and neuroendocrine responses to stress (Caldji et al., 1998; Liu et al., 1997; Weaver et al., 2004) and to novelty (Caldji et al., 1998; Francis, Diorio, Liu, & Meaney, 1999). As adults, the offspring of the High LG-ABN mothers show decreased startle responses, increased open-field exploration, and shorter latencies to eat food provided in a novel environment. The offspring of Low LG-ABN mothers show greater burying in the defensive-burying paradigm (Menard, Champagne, & Meaney, 2004), which involves an *active* response to a threat. Importantly, these individual differences in behavioral responses to stress are directly related to variations in maternal care (Caldji, Diorio, & Meaney, 2003; Francis et al., 1999). Thus, the behavioral fear responses of the biological offspring of Low LG-ABN mothers cross-fostered within 12 hours of birth to High LG-ABN mothers is indistinguishable from those of the normal adult offspring of High LG-ABN mothers (and vice versa).

MATERNAL CARE ALTERS THE GABA$_A$ RECEPTOR SYSTEM
IN THE AMYGDALA

The maternal effects on behavioral responses to stress and novelty are associated with altered CRF function in the amygdala as well as downstream targets for amygdaloid projections. CRF neurons in the central nucleus of the amygdala project directly to the locus coeruleus and increase the firing rate of locus coeruleus neurons, resulting in increased noradrenaline release in the vast terminal fields of this ascending noradrenergic system. Thus, CRF increases extracellular noradrenaline levels (Valentino, Curtis, Page, Pavcovich, & Florin-Lechner, 1998). The amygdaloid CRF projection to the locus coeruleus is also critical for the expression of behavioral responses to stress (Bakshi, Shelton, & Kalin, 2000; Butler, Weiss, Stout, & Nemeroff, 1990; Davis & Whalen, 2001; Liang et al., 1992; Schulkin, McEwen, & Gold, 1994; Stenzel-Poore, Heinrichs, Rivest, Koob, & Vale, 1994; Swiergiel, Takahashi, & Kalin, 1993). Hence, the CRF neurons in the hypothalamus and the central nucleus of the amygdala serve as important mediators of both behavioral and endocrine responses to stress.

The offspring of the High LG-ABN mothers have decreased CRF receptor levels in the locus coeruleus and increased GABA$_A$/benzodiazepine (BZ) receptor levels in the basolateral and central nucleus of the amygdala, as well as in the locus coeruleus (Caldji et al., 1998, 2003), and decreased CRF mRNA expression in the central nucleus of the amygdala (Francis, Diorio, & Meaney, unpublished data). Predictably, stress-induced increases in levels of noradrenaline in the paraventricular nucleus of the hypothalamus (PVNh) that are normally stimulated by CRF are significantly higher in the offspring of the Low LG-ABN mothers (Caldji, Plotsky, & Meaney, 1999).

Maternal care during the first week of life is associated with stable individual differences in $GABA_A$ receptor subunit expression in brain regions that regulate stress reactivity. The increased $GABA_A$/BZ receptor binding in the basolateral and central nuclei of the amygdala as well as the locus coeruleus of the adult offspring of High LG-ABN mothers provides a mechanism for increased GABAergic inhibition of amygdala–locus coeruleus activity. Fries, Moragues, Caldji, Hellhammer, and Meaney (2004) recently confirmed greater behavioral sensitivity to diazepam (a BZ) in the offspring of High compared with Low LG-ABN mothers. A series of in situ hybridization studies (Caldji et al., 2003) illustrates the molecular mechanism for these differences in receptor binding and suggests that variations in maternal care might actually permanently alter the subunit composition of the $GABA_A$ receptor complex in the offspring. The in situ hybridization technique permits visualization of mRNA levels within anatomically distinct regions of the brain, or even over individual cells.

Because mRNA serves as an intermediate step in protein synthesis from gene transcription, these findings are interpreted as measures of expression (or activity) of a specific gene. The offspring of High LG-ABN mothers show increased levels of the mRNAs for the γ_1 and γ_2 subunits of the $GABA_A$ receptor, which contribute to the formation of a functional BZ binding site. Such differences are not unique to the γ subunits. Levels of mRNA for the α_1 subunit of the $GABA_A$/BZ receptor complex are significantly higher in the amygdala and locus coeruleus of High compared with Low LG-ABN offspring. The α_1 subunit appears to confer higher affinity for GABA, providing the most efficient form of the $GABA_A$ receptor complex. The adult offspring of the Low LG-ABN mothers actually show increased expression of the mRNAs for the α_3 and α_4 subunits in the amygdala and the locus coeruleus. Interestingly, $GABA_A$/BZ receptors composed of the α_3 and α_4 subunits show a reduced affinity for GABA, by comparison to those bearing the α_1 subunit. Moreover, the α_4 subunit does not contribute to the formation of a BZ receptor site. These differences in subunit expression are tissue specific; no such differences are apparent in the hippocampus, hypothalamus, or cortex. Thus, differences in $GABA_A$/BZ receptor binding are not simply due to a deficit in subunit expression in the offspring of the Low LG-ABN mothers, but suggest an apparently "active" attempt to maintain a specific $GABA_A$/BZ receptor profile in selected brain regions.

A critical question concerns the relation between the receptor "profiles" and fear-related behavior. Studies with animals bearing mutations of various $GABA_A$/BZ receptor subunits suggest that mutations of the γ_2 subunit do indeed lead to decreased BZ receptor binding and increased fearfulness. Mice heterozygous for the γ_2 null mutation, $\gamma_2 +/-$ mice, are viable and fertile (the homozygous null mutation is lethal) and display enhanced behavioral inhibition toward aversive stimuli and increased fear conditioning (Crestani et al., 1999; Gunther et al., 1995). However, among the α subunits, it is the α_2 and not the α_1 subunit that has been linked to the anxiolytic effects of BZ treatment; the α_1 subunit is linked to the hypnotic effects (see Rudolph & Mohler, 2004, for a review). Thus, the precise cause–effect relation between the effects of maternal care on $GABA_A/BZ$ receptor subunits and fear remains to be clearly defined. Here, as throughout this area of research, an understanding of the importance of the effects of early environment on gene expression requires a more precise definition at the level of function. However, a recent study (Fries et al., 2004) revealing differences in BZ sensitivity between the adult offspring of High and Low LG-ABN mothers suggests that maternal effects on the expression of $GABA_A/BZ$ receptor subunits is of functional importance. In this study the adult offspring of High LG-ABN mothers showed increased behavioral sensitivity to the anxiolytic effect of acute BZ administration.

Cross-fostering studies (Francis et al., 1999) have revealed evidence for a direct effect of maternal care on individual differences in behavioral fearfulness. Subsequent studies revealed similar findings for both the α_1 and γ_2 $GABA_A$ receptor subunit expression in the amygdala (Caldji et al., 2003). Thus, levels of the mRNA for the α_1 and γ_2 $GABA_A$ receptor subunits in the adult offspring of Low LG-ABN mothers fostered to High LG-ABN mothers shortly after birth are comparable to those of the normal offspring of High LG-ABN mothers. The reciprocal effect is also revealed in cross-fostering studies, and these effects are apparent in the amygdala as well as the locus coeruleus.

Our findings parallel the results of studies on the effects of postnatal handling on the development of fear responses to novelty. Postnatal handling increases BZ receptor binding in the amygdala and locus coeruleus (Caldji, Francis, Sharma, Plotsky, & Meaney, 2000) and decreases noradrenergic responses to stress as well as behavioral fearfulness (Liu, Caldji, Sharma, Plotsky, & Meaney, 2000). Escorihuela (1992) found that acute treatment with the BZ receptor antagonist flumazenil eliminated the effects of postnatal handling on behavioral measures of fear. Interestingly, postnatal handling increases pup LG by rat dams (Lee & Williams, 1975; Liu et al., 1997). Handling infant rat pups is, as it turns out, an intervention that alters the development of individual differences in fearfulness through modifications of parent–offspring interactions. And these effects can be transmitted across generations (Denenberg, 1964; Francis et al., 1999). As adults, female rats handled in infancy are High LG-ABN mothers and the offspring of these females show behavioral responses to novelty that are comparable to those of either postnatally handled animals or the adult offspring of High LG-ABN mothers. These findings suggest that early environmental conditions influence the development of $GABA_A/BZ$ receptor function and might thus contribute to variation in behavioral/emotional responses to stress, providing a neurodevelopmental basis for vulnerability to anxiety disorders.

THE GABA$_A$ RECEPTOR AND VULNERABILITY
TO ANXIETY IN HUMANS

The risk for anxiety disorders is influenced by the quality of early family life. Individuals experiencing parental loss or divorce before the age of 10 are at a seven-times greater risk for anxiety disorders (Tweed, Schoenbach, George, & Blazer, 1989). Likewise, abuse in early life greatly increases the risk of anxiety disorders in adulthood (Brown & Anderson, 1993; Felitti et al., 1998; Stein et al., 1996). In preliminary studies we have found that the maternal care score on the Parental Bonding Index is significantly corre-lated with state anxiety in young adults (Pruessner, Champagne, Meaney, & Dagher, 2004). Evidence from clinical studies is at least consistent with the idea that variation in the GABA$_A$/BZ receptor system in the amygdala might predispose individuals to anxiety disorders.

First, emotionally adverse stimuli activate the human amygdala (Cahill & McGaugh, 1998). Indeed the degree of amygdaloid activation is highly positively correlated ($r = 0.93$) with recall of emotionally disturbing, but not neutral, material. With high temporal resolution fMRI techniques, LaBar, LeDoux, Spencer, and Phelps (1995) found increased amygdala activity during both the acquisition and extinction phases of fear conditioning. Patients with amygdala damage show profound deficits in fear condition-ing (Bechara et al., 1995; LaBar, Gatenby, Gore, LeDoux, & Phelps, 1998). Interestingly, there are considerable individual differences in the degree of amygdaloid activation occurring during fear conditioning, and Fur-mark, Fischer, Wik, Larsson, and Fredrikson (1997) found that the degree of increased blood flow to the amygdala was highly correlated with the strength of a conditioned autonomic fear response.

Studies in humans support the idea that alterations in the GABA$_A$/BZ receptor complex might form the basis of a vulnerability for anxiety dis-orders (Goddard et al., 2004; Gorman, Kent, Sullivan, & Coplan, 2000). Malizia et al. (1998) reported a significant decrease in labelling of the BZ receptor antagonist [^{11}C]flumazenil in the orbitoprefrontal cortex and amygdala/hippocampal region using PET imaging in unmedicated patients with a history of panic disorder. Although preliminary, these findings are certainly consistent with those of pharmacological measures of BZ receptor sensitivity. Glue, Wilson, Coupland, Ball, and Nutt (1995) found that subjects who were high on measures of neuroticism showed reduced sensitivity to the BZ receptor agonist midazolam. Roy-Byrne and colleagues (Roy-Byrne, Cowley, Greenblatt, Shader, & Hommer, 1990; Roy-Byrne, Wingerson, Radant, Greenblatt, & Cowley, 1996) found reduced sensitivity to diazepam in patients with panic disorders and obsessive compulsive disorders and proposed that the reduced BZ receptor sensitivity was related to anxiety. In response to BZ receptor agonists, patients with panic attacks or high levels of general anxiety show decreased BZ-induced amnesia, sedation, and dampening of noradrenergic function than do controls (Melo de Paula, 1984; Oblowitz & Robins, 1983). Goddard et al. (2004) report decreased cortical GABA levels in patients with panic disorders as well as further evidence for decreased cortical BZ sensitivity. The findings are at least consistent with the idea that decreased receptor levels in humans could be related to increased vulnerability to anxiety disorders and that the amygdala is a potentially critical site for BZ action. Clearly we need findings that are more specific for PTSD patients. Taken together with the studies cited previously, these findings suggest that early life events might serve to alter the development of the $GABA_A$ receptor system in brain regions that mediate stress reactivity.

MATERNAL CARE AND COGNITIVE DEVELOPMENT

Tactile stimulation from the mother stimulates the release of growth hormone and inhibits that of adrenal glucocorticoids in the offspring (Levine, 1994; Schanberg, Evoniuk, & Kuhn, 1984). Pups exposed to prolonged periods of maternal separation show increased levels of glucocorticoids and decreased levels of growth hormone. These effects can be reversed by stroking with a brush, a manipulation that mimics the tactile stimulation derived from maternal LG. Maternal deprivation also decreases the expression of brain-derived neurotrophic factor (BDNF) expression in neonates (Roceri, Hendriks, Racagni, Ellenbroek, & Riva, 2002; Zhang, Xing, Levine, Post, & Smith, 1997). The results of these studies suggest that tactile stimulation derived from maternal LG can serve to promote an endocrine or paracrine state that fosters growth and development. cDNA array analyses (Diorio, Weaver, & Meaney, 2000) revealed major classes of maternal effects on hippocampal gene expression in postnatal Day 6 offspring, including (1) genes related to cellular metabolic activity (glucose transporter, cFOS, cytochrome oxydase, LDL receptor, etc.); (2) genes related to glutamate receptor function, including effects on the glycine receptor as well as those mentioned for the NMDA receptor subunits; and (3) genes encoding for growth factors, including BDNF, bFGF, and β-NGF. In each case, expression was more than threefold higher in hippocampal samples from offspring of High compared to Low LG-ABN mothers.

Variations in maternal care are also associated with individual differences in the synaptic development of selected neural systems that mediate cognitive development. As adults, the offspring of High LG-ABN mothers show enhanced spatial learning and memory in the Morris water maze (Liu et al., 2000) as well as in object recognition (Bredy, Humpartzoomian,

Cain, & Meaney, 2003). The performance in both tasks is dependent upon hippocampal function (e.g., Morris, Garrud, Rawlins, & O'Keefe, 1982; Whishaw, 1998), and maternal care has been shown to alter hippocampal synaptogenesis. At both postnatal Day 18 and Day 90, there were significantly increased levels of N-CAM or synaptophysin-like immunoreactivity on Western blots in hippocampal samples from the High LG-ABN offspring, suggesting increased synapse formation or survival. More recent studies reveal significant effects of maternal care on neuronal survival in the hippocampus (Bredy, Zhang, Grant, Diorio, & Meaney, 2004) as well as on hippocampal LTP (Bredy, Humpartzoomian, et al., 2003). Evidence suggests increased long-term survival of neurons generated during the first week of postnatal life in the offspring of High compared with Low LG-ABN mothers.

The influence of the hippocampus in spatial learning is thought to involve, in part at least, cholinergic innervation emerging from the medial septum (e.g., Quirion et al., 1995). In the adult offspring of the High LG-ABN mothers, there is increased hippocampal choline acetyltransferase (ChAT) activity and acetylcholinesterase staining as well as increased hippocampal basal and K^+-stimulated acetylcholine release (Liu et al., 2000). These findings suggest increased cholinergic synaptic number in the hippocampus of the High LG-ABN offspring. Hippocampal BDNF mRNA levels are elevated in the High LG-ABN offspring on Day 8 of life (Liu et al., 2000). BDNF is commonly associated with the survival of cholinergic synapses in the rat forebrain. For example, there is decreased hippocampal ChAT activity in BDNF knockdown mice (Chourbaji et al., 2004).

The expression of BDNF is regulated by NMDA receptor activation, and tactile stimulation increases NMDA receptor expression in the barrel cells of mice (Jablonski, Kossut, & Skangiel-Kramska, 1996). There is increased mRNA expression of both the NR2A and NR2B subunits of the NMDA receptor in the offspring of High compared with Low LG-ABN mothers at postnatal Day 8 (Liu et al., 2000), and these effects on gene expression are associated with increased hippocampal NMDA receptor binding.

Naturally occurring variations in maternal LG and ABN are associated with differences in the development of cholinergic innervation to the hippocampus, as well as differences in the expression of NMDA receptor subunit mRNAs. There is also increased hippocampal NR1 mRNA expression in the adult offspring of High LG-ABN mothers. These findings provide a mechanism for the differences observed in spatial learning and memory in adult animals. In the adult rat, spatial learning and memory is dependent upon hippocampal integrity; lesions of the hippocampus result in profound spatial learning impairments. Moreover, spatial learning is influenced by both cholinergic or NMDA receptor activation or NR1 subunit knockout (McHugh, Blum, Tsien, Tonegawa, & Wilson, 1996; Tang et al., 1999). These findings suggest that maternal care increases hippocampal NMDA receptor levels, resulting in elevated BDNF expression and increased hippocampal synaptogenesis, and thus enhanced spatial learning in adulthood. These results are also consistent with the idea that maternal behavior actively stimulates hippocampal synaptogenesis in the offspring through systems known to mediate experience-dependent neural development (e.g., Schatz, 1990).

Importantly, an NR2B-specific receptor antagonist infused directly into the CA1 region of the hippocampus completely eliminates the group differences in the Morris water maze (Bredy et al., 2004). The NMDA receptor complex, and the NR2B subunit in particular, is interesting because of its importance in synaptic plasticity and hippocampal-dependent learning and memory (Tang et al., 1999). Thus, ifenprodil blocks the effects of postweaning environmental enrichment on spatial learning and memory. Transgenic mice overexpressing the NR2B subunit exhibit enhanced hippocampal LTP and improved learning and memory compared to wild-type controls (Tang et al., 1999). After exposure to environmental enrichment, wild-type mice show an overall improvement in contextual and cued conditioning, fear extinction, and novel object recognition learning, but NR2B transgenic mice show little or no effect of enrichment on performance (Tang, Wang, Feng, Kyin, & Tsien, 2001). One explanation for these findings is that in animals with an overexpression of the NR2B subunit, environmental enrichment provides no further "gain of function." The adult offspring of Low LG-ABN mothers reared under conditions of environmental enrichment show increased hippocampal NR2B expression and synaptic density and performance in the Morris water maze or object-recognition test that is comparable to that of the adult offspring of High LG-ABN mothers. Predictably, the adult offspring of High LG-ABN mothers, which normally exhibit increased NR2B expression, are unaffected by environmental enrichment.

These findings suggest that maternal care in the rat directly influences hippocampal development through effects on the expression of genes involved in both neuron survival and synaptic development. The group differences in performance in the Morris water maze are consistent with a maternal effect on cognitive performance in adulthood. However, the Morris water maze is a model of escape learning that, by definition, involves an aversive component that provides the motivation for escape. The water maze is an interesting task for the current discussion because it provides an opportunity to examine cognitive performance under stressful conditions. In sequence, the animal must contend with (1) removal from the home cage; (2) transport to the testing area; (3) placement into the pool of water, murky at that; and (4) the uncertainty at each stage of testing. Initially, most animals behave in a manner similar to that in an open-field test, circling the perimeter and remaining close to the walls (i.e., thigmotaxis). There is little opportunity for learning so long as the animal refuses to enter the center area of the swim maze where the platform is located. The tendency to remain close to the walls and reluctance to enter the center area is commonly associated with a fear response to the environment. Not surprisingly, thigmotaxis is significantly more prevalent in the offspring of Low compared to High LG-ABN mothers. The difference in thigmotaxis is reversed with postweaning environmental enrichment (Bredy, Humpartzoomian, et al., 2003). Moreover, Smythe and colleagues (Smythe, Bhatnagar, Murphy, Timothy, & Costall, 1998; Smythe, Murphy, & Costall, 1996) showed that blockade of hippocampal cholinergic input results in increased fear behavior under conditions of novelty. The effect is blocked by acute BZ administration. The offspring of Low LG-ABN mothers show decreased hippocampal cholinergic innervation, which might well explain the increased thigmotaxis and thus the impaired performance in the Morris water maze.

Studies with mice bearing a conditional deletion of the trkB gene, which encodes for the trkB receptor, the primary BDNF receptor, restricted to the forebrain are viable and have a normal brain morphology (Minichiello et al., 1999). These so-called trkBCaMKII-CRE mice lack trkB receptors predominantly in the hippocampus and forebrain neocortex. Behavioral analyses of conditional mutant mice revealed a stereotyped hyperlocomotion with an increase of large distance locomotion at the expense of exploratory activity (Zorner et al., 2003). The authors suggest that these peculiar behavioral patterns of trkBCaMKII-CRE mice are caused by impulsivity and stimulus-bound hyperactivity. When exposed to a novel stimulus or environment, activity increases and becomes bound to the most salient stimulus such that in a novel arena the trkBCaMKII-CRE mice run along the wall in a stereotyped manner. Similarly, mice overexpressing the trkB receptor, with the greatest effect in the hippocampus and cortex, show reduced fear behavior and enhanced performance in the Morris water maze.

Indeed, across a wide range of rodent models increased reactivity or emotionality in response to novelty is associated with altered hippocampal plasticity, decreased hippocampal neurogenesis, and impaired performance in the Morris water maze (e.g., Kim and Diamond, 2002; Lemaire, Aurousseau, Le Moal, & Abrous, 1999). Acute increases in levels of adrenal glucocorticoids are commonly associated with decreased hippocampal LTP and impaired performance on hippocampal-dependent cognitive tasks. The hippocampus is also implicated in processing information related to the discrimination between novelty and familiarity (Habib, McIntosh, Wheeler, & Tulving, 2003), and thus the actual nature of the behavioral differences between the offspring of High and Low LG-ABN mothers in settings such as the Morris water maze becomes difficult to disentangle. Rather than becoming lost in the debate over whether such differences emerge due to alterations in emotional *or* cognitive function, which is clearly beyond the scope of resolution at this time, it is probably best to simply restate the findings: The offspring of High and Low LG-ABN mothers differ in hippocampal development and plasticity, behavioral responses to novelty, and performance in tests of hippocampal learning and memory. Although the cause–effect relations embedded within these findings remain to be determined, the important point concerns the pronounced maternal effect on cognitive performance under stressful conditions.

MATERNAL PROGRAMMING OF ATTENTIONAL SYSTEMS

Performance on tests of object recognition or the Morris water maze also depends on the ability of animals to attend to and process relevant stimuli. The medial prefrontal cortex (mPFC) plays a pivotal role in so-called executive functions, where information is processed "on line" through working memory. Neurons within the mPFC are involved in maintaining task-relevant information on line for brief periods (Fuster, 1997) and subserving processes of working memory and sustained attention, both essential components for structuring goal-directed behaviors. Dopamine plays a critical modulatory role, optimizing the activity of mPFC neurons (Murphy, Arnsten, Goldman-Rakic, & Roth, 1996; Williams & Goldman-Rakic, 1995). These functions appear to be modified by postnatal maternal care through effects on genes that influence extracellular dopamine signals in the mPFC.

Prepulse inhibition (PPI) refers to the attenuation of an acoustic startle response (ASR) to a loud noise when it is immediately preceded by a weaker acoustic stimulus (Geyer, Swerdlow, Mansbach, & Braff, 1990). PPI is sensitive to manipulations of mesocorticolimbic dopamine transmission in the nucleus accumbens (Geyer, Krebs-Thomson, Braff, & Swerdlow, 2001; Geyer et al., 1990; Swerdlow, Geyer, & Braff, 2001; Zhang, Forkstam, Engel, & Svensson, 2000) and mPFC (Ellenbroek, Budde, & Cools, 1996). The development of the mesocortical dopamine system and sensory gating, as measured by PPI, is sensitive to postnatal environmental conditions (Brake, Zhang, Diorio, Meaney, & Gratton, 2004; Cilia, Reavill, Hagan, & Jones, 2001; Ellenbroek, van den Kroonenberg, & Cools, 1998; Le Pen & Moreau, 2002; but also see Weiss, Domeney, Moreau, Russig, & Feldon, 2001).

The offspring of Low LG-ABN mothers exhibit decreased PPI and show more pronounced, longer-lasting dopamine stress responses in the left mPFC compared to the offspring of High LG-ABN mothers (Zhang, Chretien, Meaney, & Gratton, 2005). There are no differences in the right mPFC dopamine response to stress. Both the prelimbic and infralimbic areas of the mPFC are involved in the modulation of PPI. Nevertheless, the relationship between frontal dopamine activity and attention is not simple, with evidence that either deficient or excess dopamine produces attentional deficits (Arnsten, 2001). Nevertheless, the stress-induced increase in dopamine in the left mPFC is two or three times higher than that in the offspring of High LG-ABN mothers, which would suggest the possibility of a dopamine-induced disruption of attention and working memory.

Recent findings from the Fleming lab support this idea. Lovic and Fleming (2004) found that, as adults, pups reared artificially in complete absence of maternal care show deficits in reversal learning, forming an attentional set (measured by intradimensional shifts – variation across stimuli within a single category or dimension, e.g., shape, color, etc.), and shifting attention (measured by extradimensional shifts – variation across stimuli and across dimensions), with no deficits in simple and compound stimulus discriminations. In normally reared animals this same pattern of behavior is produced through lesions of either the prefrontal cortex or the hippocampus. The effects of artificial rearing can be at least partially reversed by exposure during the first weeks of life to additional tactile stimulation through stroking pups with an artist's paintbrush, which mimics the tactile stimulation afforded through LG by the rat mother. These findings are consistent with the idea that the tactile stimulation associated with maternal LG alters the mesocortical dopamine system and performance on attentional tests.

The increased dopamine response to stress in the offspring of Low LG-ABN mothers is accompanied by decreased mPFC expression of catechol-*O*-methyl transferase (COMT) by comparison to levels observed in samples from High-LG offspring (Zhang et al., 2005). COMT is a postsynaptic enzyme that methylates dopamine in the mPFC and is the primary mechanism of dopamine clearance in the mPFC (Matsumoto et al., 2003). COMT is highly expressed in the mPFC (Matsumoto et al., 2003), and COMT knockout mice show increases in mPFC dopamine concentrations (Gogos et al., 1998). The increased COMT levels in the mPFC in adult offspring of High compared with Low LG-ABN mothers (Zhang et al., 2005) may contribute to the different cortical dopamine response to stress. However, this effect alone cannot explain the difference in stress-induced mPFC dopamine levels because the alteration in COMT expression, unlike that for the dopamine stress response, is apparent in both hemispheres.

In addition to maternal effects on COMT, there are considerable maternal influences on the development of the mPFC GABAergic system; however, such effects do not involve alterations in GABA$_A$ receptor levels, such as those observed in the amygdala (Caldji, Diorio, Anisman, & Meaney, 2004; Caldji et al., 2003; Caldji et al., 1998). Rather, maternal effects in mPFC GABAergic function involve alterations in glutamic acid decarboxylase (GAD), the rate-limiting synthesizing enzyme for GABA. Throughout the mPFC, levels of the mRNA for both GAD$_{65}$ and GAD$_{67}$ are approximately twofold higher in the offspring of High LG-ABN mothers; differences in protein approximate those of message. Such differences are due to an increased expression within GAD-positive neurons, with no change in the number of GAD-expressing cells. On the basis of differences in subcellular localization and cofactor association (Soghomonian & Martin, 1998), GAD_{67} is thought to be responsible for basal levels of GABA, whereas GAD_{65} is specialized to respond to rapid changes in synaptic demand during intense neuronal activity. Decreased GABAergic regulation could also contribute to the altered mPFC dopamine response to stress in the offspring of Low LG-ABN mothers and attentional deficits.

CONCLUSION

Maternal care alters the expression of genes in brain regions that subserve emotional and cognitive responses to stress. These effects are associated with tissue-specific alterations in gene expression that are sustained into adulthood. Existing evidence suggests a direct effect of maternal care, at least with respect to modifications of the $GAB A_A$ receptor subunit expression. Studies of performance in the Morris water maze suggest a direct link between the changes in gene expression, receptor activity, and brain function.

Taken together, these findings suggest that, in the rat, variations in mother–pup interactions can alter the development of systems that modulate emotional and autonomic responses to stress (through $GABA_A$ receptor systems in the amygdala and locus coeruelus), attentional processing (through dopamine systems in the medial prefrontal cortex), and spatiotemporal information processing (through NMDA receptor systems in the hippocampus). These findings suggest early environmental influences on the development of neural systems that regulate the magnitiude of emotional and autonomic reactions to trauma (for comparable findings with human subjects, see Heim et al., 2000; Pruessner et al., 2004) as well as the ability to process spatial and temporal information effectively under conditions of stress; note, in particular, the impaired performance of the adult offspring of the Low LG-ABN mothers in the Morris water maze (see above). Clearly we are making inferences that cross species boundaries. Nevertheless, these data are consistent with the idea that the quality of early parent–offspring interactions might stably alter neural systems critical for cognitive–emotional function and thus form the basis for vulnerability for chronic PTSD and other anxiety and stress-related disorders.

References

Arnsten, A. F. T. (2001). Stress impairs prefrontal cortical function in rats and monkeys: Role of dopamine D1 and norepinephrine α-1 receptor mechanisms. *Progress in Brain Research, 126,* 183–192.

Bakshi, V. P., Shelton, S. E., & Kalin, N. H. (2000). Neurobiological correlates of defensive behaviors. *Progress in Brain Research, 122,* 105–115.

Bechara, A., Tranel, D., Damasio, H., Adolphs, R., Rockland, C., & Damasio, A. R. (1995). Double dissociation of conditioning and declarative knowledge relative to the amygdala and hippocampus in humans. *Science, 269*(5227), 1115–1118.

Brake, W. G., Zhang, T. Y., Diorio, J., Meaney, M. J., & Gratton, A. (2004). Influence of early postnatal rearing conditions on mesocorticolimbic dopamine and behavioral responses to psychostimulants and stress in adult rats. *European Journal of Neuroscience, 19*, 1863–1874.

Bredy, T. W., Diorio, J., Grant, R., & Meaney, M. J. (2003). Maternal care influences hippocampal neuron survival in the rat. *European Journal of Neuroscience, 18*, 2903–2909.

Bredy, T. W., Humpartzoomian, R. A., Cain, D. P., & Meaney, M. J. (2003). Partial reversal of the effect of maternal care on cognitive function through environmental enrichment. *Neuroscience, 118*, 571–576.

Bredy, T. W., Zhang, T.-Y., Grant, R. J., Diorio, J., & Meaney, M. J. (2004). Peripubertal environmental enrichment reverses the effects of maternal care on hippocampal development and glutamate receptor subunit expression. *European Journal of Neuroscience, 20*, 1355–1362.

Breslau, N., Kessler, R. C., Chilcoat, H. D., Schultz, L. R., Davis, G. C., & Andreski, P. (1998). Trauma and posttraumatic stress disorder in the community: The 1996 Detroit Area Survey of Trauma. *Archives of General Psychiatry, 55*(7), 626–632.

Brown, G. R., & Anderson, B. (1993). Psychiatric morbidity in adult patients with childhood histories of sexual and physical abuse. *American Journal of Psychiatry, 148*, 55–61.

Butler, P. D., Weiss, J. M., Stout, J. C., & Nemeroff, C. B. (1990). Corticotropin-releasing factor produces fear-enhancing and behavioral activating effects following infusion into the locus coeruleus. *Journal of Neuroscience, 10*(1), 176–183.

Cahill, L., & McGaugh, J. L. (1998). Mechanisms of emotional arousal and lasting declarative memory. *Trends in Neurosciences, 21*(7), 294–299.

Caldji, C., Diorio, J., Anisman, H., & Meaney, M. J. (2004). Maternal behavior regulates benzodiazepine/GABA$_A$ receptor subunit expression in brain regions associated with fear in BALB/c and C57BL/6 mice. *Neuropsychopharmacology, 29*(7), 1344–1352.

Caldji, C., Diorio, J., & Meaney, M. J. (2003). Variations in maternal care alter GABA$_A$ receptor subunit expression in brain regions associated with fear. *Neuropsychopharmacology, 28*(11), 1950–1959.

Caldji, C., Francis, D., Sharma, S., Plotsky, P. M., & Meaney, M. J. (2000). The effects of rearing environment on the development of GABA$_A$ and central benzodiazepine receptor levels and novelty-induced fearfulness in the rat. *Neuropsychopharmacology, 22*(3), 219–229.

Caldji, C., Plotsky, P. M., & Meaney, M. J. (1999, October). *Maternal behavior in infancy regulates the in vivo release of noradrenaline in the paraventricular nucleus of the hypothalamus.* Paper presented at Society for Neuroscience Conference, Miami, FL.

Caldji, C., Tannenbaum, B., Sharma, S., Francis, D., Plotsky, P. M., & Meaney, M. J. (1998). Maternal care during infancy regulates the development of neural systems mediating the expression of fearfulness in the rat. *Proceedings of the National Academy of Sciences of the United States of America, 95*(9), 5335–5340.

Champagne, F. A., Francis, D., Mar, A., & Meaney, M. J. (2003). Variations in maternal care in the rat as a mediating influence for the effects of environment on development. *Physiology & Behavior, 79*, 359–371.

Chourbaji, S., Hellweg, R., Brandis, D., Zorner, B., Zacher, C., Lang, U. E., et al. (2004). Mice with reduced brain-derived neurotrophic factor expression show decreased choline acetyltransferase activity, but regular brain monoamine levels and unaltered emotional behavior. *Molecular Brain Research, 121*(1–2), 28–36.

Cilia, J., Reavill, C., Hagan, J. J., & Jones, D. N. (2001). Long-term evaluation of isolation-rearing induced prepulse inhibition deficits in rats. *Psychopharmacology, 156*, 327–337.

Crestani, F., Lorez, M., Baer, K., Essrich, C., Benke, D., Laurent, J., et al. (1999). Decreased GABA$_A$-receptor clustering results in enhanced anxiety and a bias for threat cues. *Nature Neuroscience, 2*(9), 833–839.

Davis, M., & Whalen, P. J. (2001). The amygdala: Vigilance and emotion. *Molecular Psychiatry, 6*(1), 13–34.

Denenberg, V. H. (1964). Critical periods, stimulus input, and emotional reactivity: A theory of infantile stimulation. *Psychological Review, 71*, 335–351.

Diorio, J., Weaver, I. C. G., & Meaney, M. J. (2000). *A DNA array study of hippocampal gene expression regulated by maternal behavior in infancy.* Paper presented at the Society for Neuroscience, New Orleans, LA.

Ellenbroek B. A., Budde, S., & Cools, A. R. (1996). Prepulse inhibition and latent inhibition: The role of dopamine in the medial prefrontal cortex. *Neuroscience, 75*(2), 535–542.

Ellenbroek, B. A., van den Kroonenberg, P. T., & Cools, A. R. (1998). The effects of an early stressful life event on sensorimotor gating in adult rats. *Schizophrenia Research, 30*, 251–260.

Escorihuela, R. M. (1992). Infantile stimulation and the role of benzodiazepine receptor system in adult acquisition of two-way avoidance behavior. *Psychopharmacology, 106*, 282–284.

Felitti, V. J., Anda, R. F., Nordenberg, D., Williamson, D. F., Spitz, A. M., Edwards, V., et al. (1998). Relationship of childhood abuse and household dysfunction to many of the leading causes of death in adults. The Adverse Childhood Experiences (ACE) Study. *American Journal of Preventive Medicine, 14*, 245–258.

Fleming, A. S. (1988). Factors influencing maternal responsiveness in humans: Usefulness of an animal model. *Psychoneuroendocrinology, 13*, 189–212.

Fleming, A. S. (1999). The neurobiology of mother–infant interactions: Experience and central nervous system plasticity across development and generations. *Neuroscience & Biobehavioral Reviews, 23*, 673–685.

Francis, D. D., Diorio, J., Liu, D., & Meaney, M. J. (1999). Nongenomic transmission across generations of maternal behavior and stress responses in the rat. *Science, 286*, 1155–1158.

Francis, D. D., Diorio, J., & Meaney, M. J. (2000). [Corticotrophin-releasing factor expression and function in the amygdala as a function of maternal care]. Unpublished raw data.

Fries, E., Moragues, N., Caldji, C., Hellhammer, D. H., & Meaney, M. J. (2004). Preliminary evidence of altered sensitivity to benzodiazepines as a function of maternal care in the rat. *Annals of the New York Academy of Sciences, 1032*, 320–323.

Furmark, T., Fischer, H., Wik, G., Larsson, M., & Fredrikson, M. (1997). The amygdala and individual differences in human fear conditioning. *Neuroreport, 8*(18), 3957–3960.

Fuster, J. M. (1997). Network memory. *Trends in Neurosciences, 20,* 451–459.

Geyer, M. A., Krebs-Thomson, K., Braff, D. L., & Swerdlow, N. R. (2001). Pharmacological studies of prepulse inhibition models of sensorimotor gating deficits in schizophrenia: A decade in review. *Psychopharmacology, 156,* 117–154.

Geyer, M. A., Swerdlow, N. R., Mansbach, R. S., & Braff, D. L. (1990). Startle response models of sensorimotor gating and habituation deficits in schizophrenia. *Brain Research Bulletin, 25,* 485–498.

Glue, P., Wilson, S., Coupland, N., Ball, D., & Nutt, D. (1995). The relationship between benzodiazepine receptor sensitivity and neuroticism. *Journal of Anxiety Disorders, 9,* 33–45.

Goddard, A. W., Mason, G. F., Appel, M., Rothman, D. L., Gueorguieva, R., & Behar, K. L. (2004). Impaired GABA neuronal response to acute benzodiazepine administration in panic disorder. *American Journal of Psychiatry, 161*(12), 2186–2193.

Gogos, J. A., Morgan, M., Luine, V., Santha, M., Ogawa, S., Pfaff, D., & Karaviorgou, M. (1998). Catechol-O-methyltransferase-deficient mice exhibit sexually dimorphic changes in catecholamine levels and behavior. *Proceedings of the National Academy of Sciences of the United States of America, 95*(17), 9991–9996.

Gorman, J. M., Kent, J. M., Sullivan, G. M., & Coplan, J. D. (2000). Neuroanatomical hypothesis of panic disorder, revised. *American Journal of Psychiatry, 157*(4), 493–505.

Gunther, U., Benson, J., Benke, D., Fritschy, J. M., Reyes, G., Knoflach, F., et al. (1995). Benzodiazepine-insensitive mice generated by targeted disruption of the gamma 2 subunit of gamma-aminobutyric acid type A receptors. *Proceedings of the National Academy of Sciences of the United States of America, 92*(17), 7749–7753.

Habib, R., McIntosh, A. R., Wheeler, M. A., & Tulving, E. (2003). Memory encoding and hippocampally-based novelty/familiarity discrimination networks. *Neuropsychologia, 41,* 271–279.

Heim, C., Newport, D. J., Heit, S., Graham, Y. P., Wilcox, M., Bonsall, R., et al. (2000). Pituitary-adrenal and autonomic responses to stress in women after sexual and physical abuse in childhood. *Journal of the American Medical Association, 284*(5), 592–597.

Jablonski, B., Kossut, M., & Skangiel-Kramska, J. (1996). Transient increase of AMPA and NMDA receptor binding in the barrel cortex of mice after tactile stimulation. *Neurobiology of Learning & Memory, 66,* 36–43.

Kim, J. J., & Diamond, D. M. (2002). The stressed hippocampus, synaptic plasticity and lost memories. *Nature Reviews Neuroscience, 3*(6), 453–462.

LaBar, K. S., Gatenby, J. C., Gore, J. C., LeDoux, J. E., & Phelps, E. A. (1998). Human amygdala activation during conditioned fear acquisition and extinction: A mixed-trial fMRI study. *Neuron, 20*(5), 937–945.

LaBar, K. S., LeDoux, J. E., Spencer, D. D., & Phelps, E. A. (1995). Impaired fear conditioning following unilateral temporal lobectomy in humans. *Journal of Neuroscience, 15*(10), 6846–6855.

Lee, M. H., & Williams, D. I. (1975). Long term changes in nest condition and pup grouping following handling of rat litters. *Developmental Psychobiology, 8*(1), 91–95.

Lemaire, V., Aurousseau, C., Le Moal, M., & Abrous, D. N. (1999). Behavioural trait of reactivity to novelty is related to hippocampal neurogenesis. *European Journal of Neuroscience, 11*, 4006–4014.

Le Pen, G., & Moreau, J. L (2002). Disruption of prepulse inhibition of startle reflex in a neurodevelopmental model of schizophrenia: Reversal by clozapine, olanzapine and risperidone but not by haloperidol. *Neuropsychopharmacology, 27*(1), 1–11.

Levine, S. (1994). The ontogeny of the hypothalamic-pituitary-adrenal axis. The influence of maternal factors. *Annals of the New York Academy of Sciences, 746*, 275–288; discussion 289–293.

Liang, K. C., Melia, K. R., Campeau, S., Falls, W. A., Miserendino, M. J., & Davis, M. (1992). Lesions of the central nucleus of the amygdala but not the paraventricular nucleus of the hypothalamus, block the excitatory effects of corticotrophin-releasing factor on the acoustic startle reflex. *Journal of Neuroscience, 12*(6), 2313–2320.

Liu, D., Caldji, C., Sharma, S., Plotsky, P. M., & Meaney, M. J. (2000). Influence of neonatal rearing conditions on stress-induced adrenocorticotropin responses and norepinephrine release in the hypothalamic paraventricular nucleus. *Journal of Neuroendocrinology, 12*(1), 5–12.

Liu, D., Diorio, J., Tannenbaum, B., Caldji, C., Francis, D., Freedman, A., Sharma, S., Pearson, D., Plotsky, P. M., & Meaney, M. J. (1997). Maternal care, hippocampal glucocorticoid receptors, and hypothalamic-pituitary-adrenal responses to stress. *Science, 277*(5332), 1659–1662.

Lovic, V., & Fleming, A. S. (2004). Artificially-reared female rats show reduced prepulse inhibition and deficits in the attentional set shifting task – Reversal of effects with maternal-like licking stimulation. *Behavioural Brain Research, 148*(1–2), 209–219.

Malizia, A. L., Cunningham, V. J., Bell, C. J., Liddle, P. F., Jones, T., & Nutt, D. J. (1998). Decreased brain $GABA_A$-benzodiazepine receptor binding in panic disorder: Preliminary results from a quantitative PET study. *Archives of General Psychiatry, 55*(8), 715–720.

Matsumoto, M., Weickert, C. S., Akil, M., Lipska, B. K., Hyde, T. M., Herman, M. M., et al. (2003). Catechol *O*-methyltransferase mRNA expression in human and rat brain: Evidence for a role in cortical neuronal function. *Neuroscience, 116*(1), 127–137.

McHugh, T. J., Blum, K. I., Tsien, J. Z., Tonegawa, S., & Wilson, M. A. (1996). Impaired hippocampal representation of space in CA1-specific NMDAR1 knockout mice. *Cell, 87*(7), 1339–1349.

Melo de Paula, A. J. (1984). A comparative study of lormetazepam and flurazepam in the treatment of insomnia. *Clinical Therapeutics, 64*, 500–508.

Menard, J. L., Champagne, D. L., & Meaney, M. J. (2004). Variations of maternal care differentially influence 'fear' reactivity and regional patterns of cFos immunoreactivity in response to the shock-probe burying test. *Neuroscience, 129*(2), 297–308.

Minichiello, L., Korte, M., Wolfer, D., Kuhn, R., Unsicker, K., Cestari, V., Rossi-Arnaud, D., Lipp, H. P., Bonhoeffer, T., & Klein, R. (1999). Essential role for TrkB receptors in hippocampus-mediated learning. *Neuron, 24*(2), 401–414.

Morris, R. G., Garrud, P., Rawlins, J. N., & O'Keefe, J. (1982). Place navigation impaired in rats with hippocampal lesions. *Nature, 297*(5868), 681–683.

Murphy, B. L., Arnsten, A. F., Goldman-Rakic, P. S., & Roth, R. H. (1996). Increased dopamine turnover in the prefrontal cortex impairs spatial working memory performance in rats and monkeys. *Proceedings of the National Academy of Sciences of the United States of America, 93*(3), 1325–1329.

Oblowitz, H., & Robins, A. H. (1983). The effect of clobazam and lorazepam on the psychomotor performance of anxious patients. *British Journal of Clinical Pharmacology, 16*(1), 95–99.

Pruessner, J. C., Champagne, F., Meaney, M. J., & Dagher, A. (2004). Dopamine release in response to a psychological stress in humans and its relationship to early life maternal care: A positron emission tomography study using [11C]raclopride. *Journal of Neuroscience, 24*(11), 2825–2831.

Quirion, R., Wilson, A., Rowe, W., Aubert, I., Richard, J., Doods, H., et al. (1995). Facilitation of acetylcholine release and cognitive performance by an M(2)-muscarinic receptor antagonist in aged memory-impaired. *Journal of Neuroscience, 15*(2), 1455–1462.

Ressnick, H. S., Kilpatrick, D. G., Dansky, B. S., Saunders, B. E., & Best, C. L. (1993). Prevalence of civilian trauma and posttraumatic stress disorder in representative national sample of women. *Journal of Consulting and Clinical Psychology, 61*(6), 984–991.

Roceri, M., Hendriks, W., Racagni, G., Ellenbroek, B. A., & Riva, M. A. (2002). Early maternal deprivation reduces the expression of BDNF and NMDA receptor subunits in the rat hippocampus. *Molecular Psychiatry, 7*(6), 609–616.

Roy-Byrne, P., Wingerson, D. K., Radant, A., Greenblatt, D. J., & Cowley, D. S. (1996). Reduced benzodiazepine sensitivity in patients with panic disorder: Comparison with patients with obsessive-compulsive disorder and normal subjects. *American Journal of Psychiatry, 153*(11), 1444–1449.

Roy-Byrne, P. P., Cowley, D. S., Greenblatt, D. J., Shader, R. I., & Hommer, D. (1990). Reduced benzodiazepine sensitivity in panic disorder. *Archives of General Psychiatry, 47*(6), 534–538.

Rudolph, U., & Mohler, H. (2004). Analysis of GABA$_A$ receptor function and dissection of the pharmacology of benzodiazepines and general anesthetics through mouse genetics. *Annual Review of Pharmacology & Toxicology, 44*, 475–498.

Schanberg, S. M., Evoniuk, G., & Kuhn, C. M. (1984). Tactile and nutritional aspects of maternal care: Specific regulators of neuroendocrine function and cellular development. *Proceedings of the Society for Experimental Biology & Medicine, 175*(2), 135–146.

Schatz, C. J. (1990). Impulse activity and the patterning of connections during CNS development. *Neuron, 5*, 745–756.

Schulkin, J., McEwen, B. S., & Gold, P. W. (1994). Allostasis, amygdala, and anticipatory angst. *Neuroscience & Biobehavioral Reviews, 18*(3), 385–396.

Smythe, J. W., Bhatnagar, S., Murphy, D., Timothy, C., & Costall, B. (1998). The effects of intrahippocampal scopolamine infusions on anxiety in rats as measured by the black–white box test. *Brain Research Bulletin, 45*(1), 89–93.

Smythe, J. W., Murphy, D., & Costall, B. (1996). Benzodiazepine receptor stimulation blocks scopolamine-induced learning impairments in a water maze task. *Brain Research Bulletin, 41*(5), 299–304.

Soghomonian, J. J., & Martin, D. L. (1998). Two isoforms of glutamate decarboxylase: Why? *Trends in Pharmacological Sciences, 19*(12), 500–505.

Stein, M. B., Walker, J. R., Anderson, G., Hazen, A. L., Ross, C. A., Eldridge, G., et al. (1996). Childhood physical and sexual abuse in patients with anxiety disorders and in a community sample. *American Journal of Psychiatry, 153*(2), 275–277.

Stenzel-Poore, M. P., Heinrichs, S. C., Rivest, S., Koob, G. F., & Vale, W. W. (1994). Overproduction of corticotropin-releasing factor in transgenic mice: A genetic model of anxiogenic behavior. *Journal of Neuroscience, 14*(5 Pt 1), 2579–2584.

Stern, J. M. (1997). Offspring-induced nurturance: Animal-human parallels. *Developmental Psychobiology, 31*(1), 19–37.

Swerdlow, N. R., Geyer, M. A., & Braff, D. L. (2001). Neural circuit regulation of prepulse inhibition of startle in the rat: Current knowledge and future challenges. *Psychopharmacology (Berl), 156*(2–3), 194–215.

Swiergiel, A. H., Takahashi, L. K., & Kalin, N. H. (1993). Attenutation of stress-induced behavior by antagonism of corticotropin-releasing factor receptors in the central amygdala in the rat. *Brain Research, 623*(2), 229–234.

Tang, Y. P., Shimizu, E., Dube, G. R., Rampon, C., Kerchner, G. A., Zhuo, M., Liu, G., Tsien, J. Z. (1999). Genetic enhancement of learning and memory in mice. *Nature, 401*(6748), 63–69.

Tang, Y. P., Wang, H., Feng, R., Kyin, M., & Tsien, J. Z. (2001). Differential effects of enrichment on learning and memory function in NR2B transgenic mice. *Neuropharmacology, 41*(6), 779–790.

Tweed, J. L., Schoenbach, V. J., George, L. K., & Blazer, D. G. (1989). The effects of childhood parental death and divorce on six-month history of anxiety disorders. *British Journal of Psychiatry, 154*, 823–828.

Udwin, O., Boyle, S., Yule, W., Bolton, D., & O'Ryan, D. (2000). Risk factors for long-term psychological effects of a disaster experienced in adolescence: Predictors of post traumatic stress disorder. *Journal of Child Psychology and Psychiatry, 41*(8), 969–979.

Valentino, R. J., Curtis, A. L., Page, M. E., Pavcovich, L. A., & Florin-Lechner, S. M. (1998). Activation of the locus ceruleus brain noradrenergic system during stress: Circuitry, consequences, and regulation. *Advances in Pharmacology, 42*, 781–784.

Weaver, I. C., Cervoni, N., Champagne, F. A., D'Alessio, A. C., Sharma, S., Seckl, J. R., et al. (2004). Epigenetic programming by maternal behavior. *Nature Neuroscience, 7*(8), 847–854.

Weiss, I. C., Domeney, A. M., Moreau, J. L., Russig, H., & Feldon, J. (2001). Dissociation between the effects of pre-weaning and/or post-weaning social isolation on prepulse inhibition and latent inhibition in adult Sprague–Dawley rats. *Behavioural Brain Research, 121*(1–2), 207–218.

Whishaw, I. Q. (1998). Place learning in hippocampal rats and the path integration hypothesis. *Neuroscience & Biobehavioral Reviews, 22*(2), 209–220.

Williams, G. V., & Goldman-Rakic, P. S. (1995). Modulation of memory fields by dopamine D1 receptors in prefrontal cortex. *Nature, 376*(6541), 572–575.

Yehuda, R., Schmeidler, J., Wainberg, M., Binder-Brynes, K., & Duvdevani, T. (1998). Vulnerability to posttraumatic stress disorder in adult offspring of Holocaust survivors. *American Journal of Psychiatry, 56*(11), 1838–11839.

Zhang, J., Forkstam, C., Engel, J. A., & Svensson, L. (2000). Role of dopamine in prepulse inhibition of acoustic startle. *Psychopharmacology (Berl), 149*(2), 181–188.

Zhang, L. X., Xing, G. O., Levine, S., Post, R. M., & Smith, M. A. (1997, October). *Maternal deprivation induces neuronal death.* Paper presented at the Society for Neuroscience Conference, New Orleans, LA.

Zhang, T. Y., Chretien, P., Meaney, M. J., & Gratton, A. (2005). Influence of naturally occurring variations in maternal care on prepulse inhibition of acoustic startle and the medial prefrontal cortical dopamine response to stress in adult rats. *Journal of Neuroscience, 25*(6), 1493–1502.

Zorner, B., Wolfer, D. P., Brandis, D., Kretz, O., Zacher, C., Madani, R., et al. (2003). Forebrain-specific trkB-receptor knockout mice: Behaviorally more hyperactive than "depressive." *Biological Psychiatry, 54*(10), 972–982.

6

Does Stress Damage the Brain?

J. Douglas Bremner

INTRODUCTION

In 1980 the American Psychiatric Association (APA) classified posttraumatic stress disorder (PTSD) as a psychiatric disorder for the first time, and listed criteria for inclusion in the *Diagnostic and Statistical Manual III* (Saigh & Bremner, 1999). This is often hailed in the field of psychiatry as a historic time point, when it was first recognized that psychological trauma, that is, things that happen to you when there is no physical injury, can cause changes in your brain and physiological responding. This version of history, enthusiastically passed along as an oral tradition by clinicians and researchers who specialize in PTSD, with no discussion of the history of stress before 1980 or anywhere outside of the United States, is not entirely correct. As discussed elsewhere in this volume, there is a longer history of medical approaches to psychological trauma that stretches back 200 hundred years and includes Europe as well as the United States.

In 1988, the U.S. government allocated funding for research and treatment of PTSD in Vietnam veterans. This was in response to political pressure from Vietnam veterans and led to the establishment of the National Center for PTSD in 1988. The concentration of resources and expertise gave a boost to research in the field of PTSD. At that time, there was no general consensus in American culture that traumatic stress led to real psychiatric disorders. Clinical practices reflected this view. For instance, in a chart review study, we found that prior to 1990 the diagnosis of PTSD was rarely made by psychiatrists, even in VA hospitals where PTSD is now recognized to be the most common psychiatric diagnosis affecting veterans (Bremner, Southwick, Darnell, & Charney, 1996).

RESEARCH ON THE EFFECTS OF STRESS ON THE BRAIN

At the time of the establishment of the National Center for PTSD in 1988, there were only a handful of studies of the biological effects of traumatic stress in humans, despite the thousands of studies in animals showing that stress leads to lasting changes in physiology. At the Clinical Neurosciences Division of the National Center, we were charged with looking at this question.

One brain area sensitive to stress in animals is the hippocampus, which plays a critical role in learning and memory. Studies in animals exposed to stress showed deficits in memory function (Luine, Villages, Martinex, & McEwen, 1994) and damage to the hippocampus (Sapolsky, Uno, Rebert, & Finch, 1990; Uno, Tarara, Else, Suleman, & Sapolsky, 1989). Stress interfered with hippocampal-based mechanisms of memory function, including long-term potentiation (LTP) (Diamond, Fleshner, Ingersoll, & Rose, 1996; Luine et al., 1994). A variety of mechanisms have been proposed for these findings, including elevated levels of glucocorticoids released during stress (Lawrence & Sapolsky, 1994; Sapolsky, 1996), stress-related inhibition of brain-derived neurotrophic factor (BDNF) (Nibuya, Morinobu, & Duman, 1995; Smith, Makino, Kvetnansky, & Post, 1995), or changes in serotonergic function (McEwen et al., 1992), although mechanisms continue to be debated (Leverenz et al., 1999). Since that time studies have shown that stress is associated with an inhibition of neurogenesis (or the growth of new neurons) (Fowler, Liu, Ouimet, & Wang, 2001; Gould, McEwen, Tanapat, Galea, & Fuchs, 1997) in the hippocampus.

Animal studies have demonstrated several agents with potentially beneficial effects on stress-induced hippocampal damage. Antidepressant treatments block the effects of stress and/or promote neurogenesis in the hippocampus (Czeh et al., 2001; Lucassen, Fuchs, & Czeh, 2004; Malberg, Eisch, Nestler, & Duman, 2000; Nibuya et al., 1995; Santarelli et al., 2003). Phenytoin also blocks the effects of stress on the hippocampus, probably through modulation of excitatory amino acid-induced neurotoxicity (Watanabe, Gould, Cameron, Daniels, & McEwen, 1992). Other agents, including tianeptine, dihydroepiandosterone (DHEA), and fluoxetine, have similar effects (Czeh et al., 2001; D'Sa & Duman, 2002; Duman, 2004; Duman, Heninger, & Nestler, 1997; Duman, Malberg, & Nakagawa, 2001; Garcia, 2002; Lucassen et al., 2004; Malberg et al., 2000; McEwen & Chattarji, 2004). These medications may share a common mechanism of action through upregulation of cAMP-response-element–binding protein (CREB), which may lead to regulation of expression of specific target genes involved in structural remodeling of the hippocampus. There is new evidence that neurogenesis is necessary for the behavioral effects of antidepressants (Santarelli et al., 2003; Watanabe, Gould, Daniels, Cameron, & McEwen, 1992), although this continues to be a source of debate (Duman, 2004; Henn & Vollmayr, 2004).

The role of the hippocampus in learning and memory, and the wide range of memory alterations seen in PTSD patients, led to the hypothesis of hippocampal dysfunction in PTSD (Bremner, 2003a; Bremner,

Krystal, Southwick, & Charney, 1995). Initial studies demonstrated deficits in hippocampal-based learning and memory in PTSD (Bremner, Randall, Capelli, et al., 1995; Bremner et al., 1993). Neuroimaging studies subsequently showed alterations in the hippocampus in PTSD. The first neuroimaging study in PTSD was performed using magnetic resonance imaging (MRI) to measure the volume of the hippocampus (Bremner, Randall, Scott, et al., 1995). This study showed an 8% decrease in right hippocampal volume in patients with combat-related PTSD ($N = 26$) in comparison to matched control participants ($N = 22$) ($p < 0.05$). Decreases in right hippocampal volume in the PTSD patients were associated with deficits in short-term memory (Bremner, Randall, Scott, et al., 1995). Findings of smaller hippocampal volume or a reduction in N-acetyl aspartate (NAA) in the hippocampus (a marker of neuronal integrity) in adults with chronic, long-standing PTSD have been replicated several times (Bremner, Randall, Scott, et al., 1995; Bremner, Randall, et al., 1997; Bremner, Vythilingam, Vermetten, Southwick, McGlashan, Nazeer, et al., 2003; Freeman, Cardwell, Karson, & Komoroski, 1998; Gurvits et al., 1996; Schuff et al., 2001; Stein, Koverola, Hanna, Torchia, & McClarty, 1997; Villareale et al., 2002). One study used a specific cognitive task to probe hippocampal function and demonstrated a failure of left hippocampal activation with a memory task in women with abuse-related PTSD. This was significant after controlling for differences in hippocampal volume measured on MRI in the same subjects. Women with PTSD had smaller hippocampal volume than both abused non-PTSD and nonabused non-PTSD women (Bremner, Vythilingam, Vermetten, Southwick, McGlashan, Nazeer, et al., 2003). Studies in children (Carrion et al., 2001; De Bellis, Hall, Boring, Frustaci, & Moritz, 2001; De Bellis et al., 1999) and new-onset PTSD (Bonne et al., 2001; Notestine, Stein, Kennedy, Archibald, & Jernigan, 2002) have not shown smaller hippocampal volume in PTSD, suggesting that chronic PTSD is required for the effect. One study showed a correlation between PTSD symptoms and hippocampal volume in unaffected twin brothers, suggesting a genetic contribution to smaller hippocampal volume (Gilbertson et al., 2002); however, our own study (Bremner, Hoffman, et al., 2003) of twins discordant for PTSD showed smaller hippocampal volume in a pattern consistent with a combined genetic and environmental effect.

There has long been an interest in the relationship between exposure to psychological trauma and deficits in memory function (Buckley, Blanchard, & Neill, 2000; Elzinga & Bremner, 2002). Danish survivors of the WWII concentration camps were noted to have subjective complaints of memory problems in a large number of cases (Thygesen, Hermann, & Willanger, 1970). American POWs from the Korean War had deficits in verbal declarative memory function, with a relative preservation of IQ (Sutker, Winstead, Galina, & Allain, 1991). These studies occurred before the development of the diagnostic category of PTSD, leaving unanswered the question of whether verbal declarative memory deficits are specifically associated with stress-related psychiatric disorders including PTSD.

Subsequent studies have demonstrated verbal declarative memory deficits in PTSD consistent with hippocampal dysfunction (Brewin, 2001; Buckley et al., 2000; Elzinga & Bremner, 2002; Golier & Yehuda, 1998). Several studies, using a variety of measures (including the Wechsler Memory Scale, the visual and verbal components of the Selective Reminding Test, the Auditory Verbal Learning Test, the California Verbal New Learning Test, and the Rivermead Behavioral Memory Test), found specific deficits in verbal declarative memory function, with a relative sparing of visual memory and IQ (Barrett, Green, Morris, Giles, & Croft, 1996; Bremner, Randall, Capelli, et al., 1995; Bremner et al., 1993; Gil, Calev, Greenberg, Kugelmas, & Lerer, 1990; Gilbertson, Gurvits, Lasko, Orr, & Pitman, 2001; Golier et al., 1997; Jenkins, Langlais, Delis, & Cohen, 1998; Moradi, Doost, Taghavi, Yule, & Dalgleish, 1999; Roca & Freeman, 2001; Sachinvala et al., 2000; Uddo, Vasterling, Braily, & Sutker, 1993; Vasterling, Brailey, Constans, & Sutker, 1998; Vasterling et al., 2002; Yehuda et al., 1995). These studies have been conducted in both patients with PTSD related to Vietnam combat (Barrett et al., 1996; Bremner et al., 1993; Gilbertson et al., 2001; Golier et al., 1997; Roca & Freeman, 2001; Sachinvala et al., 2000; Uddo, Vasterling, Braily, & Sutker, 1993; Vasterling, Brailey, Constans, & Sutker, 1998; Vasterling et al., 2002; Yehuda et al., 1995) and to rape (Jenkins et al., 1998), in adults with early childhood abuse (Bremner, Randall, Capelli, et al., 1995), and in traumatized children (Moradi et al., 1999). One study in adult rape survivors showed that verbal declarative memory deficits are specifically associated with PTSD and are not a nonspecific effect of trauma exposure (Jenkins et al., 1998). Another study of women with early childhood sexual abuse in which some, but not all, of the patients had PTSD showed no difference between abused and nonabused women (Stein, Hanna, Vaerum, & Koverola, 1999), while another study was not able to show a difference between Vietnam veterans with and without PTSD (Zalewski, Thompson, & Gottesman, 1994). These studies suggest that traumas such as early abuse with associated PTSD result in deficits in verbal declarative memory. More recently we showed that cognitive deficits in early abuse survivors are specific to PTSD and are not related to the nonspecific effects of abuse (Bremner, Vermetten, Nafzal, & Vythilingam, 2004).

Based on findings related to the effects of antidepressants on neurogenesis, we assessed the effects of the selective serotonin reuptake inhibitor (SSRI) paroxetine on outcomes related to function of the hippocampus. We studied 28 patients with PTSD and treated them for up to a year with variable doses of paroxetine. Twenty-three patients completed the course of treatment, and MRI posttreatment was obtained in 20 patients. Patients who did not complete treatment stopped because of a relapse of substance abuse or were lost to follow-up (possibly because of a treatment

nonresponse). Neuropsychological testing was used to assess hippocampal-based declarative memory function and MRI to assess hippocampal volume before and after treatment. Declarative memory was assessed
with the Wechsler Memory Scale–Revised and Selective Reminding Test.
Patients with PTSD showed a significant improvement in PTSD symptoms with treatment. Treatment resulted in significant improvements in
verbal declarative memory and a 4.6% increase in mean hippocampal volume. These findings suggested that long-term treatment with paroxetine
is associated with improvement of verbal declarative memory deficits and
an increase in hippocampal volume in PTSD (Vermetten, Vythilingam,
Southwick, Charney, & Bremner, 2003).

NEUROHORMONAL RESPONSES TO STRESS

Animal studies show that stress has lasting effects on brain circuits and
systems. A network of brain regions are involved in the stress response,
including the hippocampus, amygdala, cingulate, and prefrontal cortex.
Neurohormonal systems that play roles in stress include the hypothalamic–
pituitary–adrenal (HPA) axis and the noradrenergic system.

The noradrenergic system plays a critical role in stress (Bremner, Krystal,
Southwick, & Charney, 1996a, 1996b). The majority of noradrenergic cell
bodies are located in the locus coeruleus, a nucleus in the dorsal pons region
of the brainstem, with a dense network of axons that extend throughout the cerebral cortex and to multiple cortical and subcortical areas,
including the hippocampus, amygdala, thalamus and hypothalamus, bed
nucleus of stria terminalis, and nucleus accumbens, as well as descending projections that synapse at the level of the thoracic spinal cord (Foote,
Bloom, & Aston-Jones, 1983). Exposure to stressors results in activation of
the locus coeruleus, with release of norepinephrine throughout the brain
(Abercrombie & Jacobs, 1987). Acute stressors such as a cat seeing a dog
or another aggressive cat result in an acute increase in firing of neurons
in the locus coeruleus (E. S. Levine, Litto, & Jacobs, 1990) with increased
release of norepinephrine in the hippocampus and medial prefrontal cortex (Finlay, Zigmond, & Abercrombie, 1995). Chronic stress is associated
with potentiated release of norepinephrine in the hippocampus with exposure to subsequent stressors (Bremner et al., 1996a; Nisenbaum, Zigmond,
Sved, & Abercrombie, 1991).

Norepinephrine sharpens the senses, focuses attention, raises the level
of fear, quickens the heart rate and blood pressure, and in general helps
to prepares us for "fight or flight." The norepinephrine system is like a
fire alarm that alerts all areas of the brain simultaneously. This system
sacrifices the ability to convey specific information to specific parts of the
brain in order to obtain more speed. Norepinephrine focuses the senses
by activating the neuronal systems that process sensory information in

order to assess dangers in the environment rapidly and efficiently. At the same time, norepinephrine causes the heart to beat more rapidly and blood pressure to increase. This allows an "emergency" mobilization of oxygen and nutrients needed for survival to all the cells of the body. The beauty of the system is that the same chemical messenger that "turns on" the brain also stimulates the heart (as well as other bodily organs regulated by the autonomic nervous system) in order to facilitate behavioral responses important for survival in situations of threat or danger. Chronic stress in animals leads to increased levels of norepinephrine (Bremner et al., 1996a).

A variety of studies have found long-term dysregulation of the noradrenergic system in PTSD (Bremner et al., 1996b). Psychophysiology studies have demonstrated an increase in sympathetic responses (heart rate, blood pressure, and galvanic skin response) to traumatic reminders, such as traumatic slides and sounds or traumatic scripts, in PTSD (Pitman, Orr, Forgus, de Jong, & Claiborn, 1987). Studies of norepinephrine in plasma and urine have shown increased levels at baseline, while traumatic reminders result in a potentiated release of norepinephrine in PTSD (McFall, Murburg, Ko, & Veith, 1990). Administration of the α_2 antagonist, yohimbine, which results in an increase of release of norepinephrine in the brain, to PTSD patients resulted in an increase in PTSD-specific symptomatology, as well as greater release of norepinephrine metabolites in plasma (Southwick et al., 1993). Alterations in central metabolic responses to yohimbine were also found in PTSD patients as measured with positron emission tomography (PET) (Bremner, Innis, et al., 1997). Animal studies have shown that increasing norepinephrine release up to a certain level improves cognition and attention, but beyond that point there is a reduction in performance. Using PET, which allows us to measure brain activity while we stimulate norepinephrine release in the brain with medication (yohimbine), we found that lower levels of norepinephrine stimulate brain activity in the prefrontal cortex, but at very high levels (as seen in PTSD) the brain shuts off. The findings are consistent with an inverted U-shaped curve for norepinephrine effects, where lower levels of norepinephrine stimulation increase the efficiency of the brain, whereas very high levels make it more inefficient. Everyone knows that a little bit of stress can be a good thing. For instance, it's always hard to study if you don't have any real reason to learn the material, especially if you don't find it all that interesting. However, we learn better and faster if we have an important exam to study for that we don't want to mess up. But sometimes people get so stressed out that they "choke" and actually do worse. This happens when they release too much norepinephrine in their brains. This concept lies behind the common practice of taking propanolol (which blocks the effects of norepinephrine in the brain) to improve performance during public speaking.

The cortisol system also plays an important role in the stress response. Like norepinephrine, cortisol is released during times of threat and is critical to survival. Cortisol redistributes the energy of our bodies when we are under attack in order to help us survive, suppressing functions that we don't need for immediate survival, including reproduction, the body's immune response, digestion, and the feeling of pain. Cortisol also promotes what we need, increasing heart rate and blood pressure, and shunts energy to the brain and muscles, so we can think fast and make a quick getaway. Although cortisol has actions that are beneficial for short-term survival, it may perform these functions at the expense of long-term viability. For instance, chronically high cortisol levels cause gastric ulcers, thinning of the bones, and possibly even brain damage. Evolution may have preferred the caveman who could survive attacks by wooly mammoths long enough to pass his genes to the next generation, even if it meant that he couldn't remember where he left his favorite spear when he was old. In other words, evolution prefers short-term survival at the expense of long-term function.

Stress is associated with activation of the HPA axis. Corticotropin-releasing factor (CRF) is released from the hypothalamus, with stimulation of adrenocorticotropic hormone (ACTH) release from the pituitary. This results in glucocorticoid (cortisol) release from the adrenal, which in turn has a negative feedback effect on the axis at the level of the pituitary as well as central brain sites including the hypothalamus and hippocampus. In addition to its role in triggering the HPA axis, CRF acts centrally to mediate fear-related behaviors (Arborelius, Owens, Plotsky, & Nemeroff, 1999) (see Bouton and Wadell, this volume) and triggers other neurochemical responses to stress such as the noradrenergic system via the brainstem locus coeruleus (Melia & Duman, 1991).

Exposure to stressful situations is associated with a marked increase in cortisol release from the adrenal gland. Animals with a history of chronic stress, including maternal deprivation, have increased glucocorticoid response to subsequent stressors (see Bagot et al., this volume) (S. Levine, Weiner, & Coe, 1993; Stanton, Gutierrez, & Levine, 1988).

PTSD has been associated with long-term dysregulation of the HPA axis. Baseline levels of urinary cortisol were either decreased or unchanged in chronic PTSD, while decreased levels were found in 24-hour samples of plasma cortisol levels (Bremner, Vermetten, & Kelley, in press; Yehuda, Teicher, Levengood, Trestman, & Siever, 1994). Exposure to a stressor (Bremner, Vythilingam, Vermetten, Adil, et al., 2003) or a traumatic reminder (Elzinga, Schmahl, Vermetten, van Dyck, & Bremner, 2003) was associated with a potentiated release of cortisol, however, in PTSD. Cortisol may also be elevated in the more acute phase of PTSD, although further research is needed in this area. A replicated finding has been a supersuppression of the cortisol response to lower doses of dexamethasone (0.5 mg), a finding which is the opposite of patients with major depression who are nonsuppressers with the standard 1-mg dexamethasone suppression test (DST) (Yehuda et al., 1993). PTSD patients had elevated levels of CRF in the cerebrospinal fluid (Baker et al., 1999; Bremner, Licinio, et al., 1997). One possible explanation of findings to date is that patients with PTSD have an increase in neuronal CRF release, increased central glucocorticoid receptor responsiveness, and resultant low levels of peripheral cortisol due to enhanced negative feedback.

The few studies of the effects of early stress on neurobiology conducted in clinical populations of traumatized children have generally been consistent with findings from animal studies and suggest that early abuse is associated with long-term changes in the HPA axis, although the direction of those changes is not always consistent.

CHANGES IN BRAIN ACTIVITY AFTER STRESS

A network of brain areas, including the amygdala and prefrontal cortex, together with the hippocampus, mediate the stress response. These brain areas are involved with different aspects of memory and visuospatial processing. Dysfunction of this circuit may contribute to symptoms of PTSD (Bremner, 2002, 2003a; Pitman, 2001). The amygdala plays a central role in conditioned fear responses (Davis, 1992; LeDoux, 1993). Stress is associated with increased dendritic arborization in the amygdala (Vyas, Mitra, Shankaranarayana Rao, & Chattarji, 2002; Vyas, Pillai, & Chattarji, 2004). The medial prefrontal cortex consists of several related areas, including the orbitofrontal cortex, anterior cingulate (Area 25 – the subcallosal gyrus – and Area 32), and anterior prefrontal cortex (Area 9) (Devinsky, Morrell, & Vogt, 1995; Vogt, Finch, & Olson, 1992). The medial prefrontal dopaminergic system is one of the most sensitive areas in the brain to even mild stressors (Roth, Tam, Ida, Yang, & Deutch, 1988). Lesions in this area result in a failure to mount the peripheral cortisol and sympathetic response to stress (Devinsky et al., 1995; Vogt et al., 1992). Recently stress has been associated with a reduction in dendritic branching in this area (Radley et al., 2004). This area also has important inhibitory inputs to the amygdala that mediate extinction to fear responding (Morgan & LeDoux, 1995; Quirk, 2002). As discussed earlier in this volume, animals with lesions of the medial prefrontal cortex are unable to extinguish fear responses after trials of fear conditioning (Morgan & LeDoux, 1995; Morgan, Romanski, & LeDoux, 1993). Human subjects with lesions of the prefrontal cortex show dysfunction of normal emotions and an inability to relate in social situations that require correct interpretation of the emotional expressions of others (Damasio, Grabowski, Frank, Galaburda, & Damasio, 1994). These findings suggest that dysfunction of the medial prefrontal cortex may play a role in pathological emotions that sometimes follow exposure to extreme stressors such as childhood sexual abuse.

Functional neuroimaging studies have been performed to map the neural circuitry of PTSD (Bremner, 2003b; Bremner & Vermetten, 2001). These studies are consistent with dysfunction in a network of related brain areas including the amygdala, medial prefrontal cortex, and hippocampus. For example, we measured brain blood flow during exposure to specific reminders of childhood sexual abuse. Twenty-two women with a history of childhood sexual abuse underwent injection of a tracer followed by PET imaging of the brain while listening to neutral and traumatic (personalized childhood sexual abuse events) scripts. Brain blood flow during exposure to traumatic versus neutral scripts was compared between sexually abused women with and without PTSD. Abuse memories were associated with alterations in blood flow in the medial prefrontal cortex, with decreased blood flow in the subcallosal gyrus – Area 25 – and a failure of activation in the anterior cingulate – Area 32. There was also decreased blood flow in the right hippocampus, fusiform/inferior temporal gyrus, supramarginal gyrus, and visual association cortex in PTSD relative to non-PTSD women (Bremner, Narayan, et al., 1999). This study replicated findings of decreased function in the medial prefrontal cortex and increased function in the posterior cingulate in combat-related PTSD during exposure to combat-related slides and sounds (Bremner, Staib, et al., 1999).

In another study, 8 women with childhood sexual abuse and PTSD were compared to 8 women with abuse without PTSD using PET during exposure to script-driven imagery of childhood abuse. The authors found increases in the orbitofrontal cortex and anterior temporal pole in both groups of participants, with greater increases in these areas in the PTSD group. PTSD patients showed a relative failure of anterior cingulate/medial prefrontal cortex activation compared to control participants. The PTSD patients (but not control participants) showed decreased blood flow in anteromedial portions of the prefrontal cortex and left inferior frontal gyrus (L. H. Shin et al., 1999). Several other studies have shown a failure of medial prefrontal cortical activation in PTSD related to other traumas including combat (Bremner, Innis, et al., 1997; Bremner, Vermetten, Vythilingam, et al., 2004; Bremner, Vythilingam, Vermetten, Southwick, McGlashan, Staib, et al., 2003; Lanius et al., 2001; Liberzon et al., 1999; L. H. Shin et al., 1999; L. M. Shin, Orr, et al., 2004; L. M. Shin et al., 2001; Zubieta et al., 1999).

These studies have relied on specific traumatic cues to activate personalized traumatic memories and PTSD symptoms in patients with PTSD. Another method to probe neural circuits in PTSD is to assess neural correlates of retrieval of emotionally valenced declarative memory. In this type of paradigm, instead of using a traditional declarative memory task, such as retrieval of word pairs like "gold–west," which has been the standard of memory research for several decades, words with emotional valence, such as "stench–fear," are utilized (Bremner et al., 2001). If PTSD patients demonstrate a pattern of brain activation during retrieval of emotionally valenced declarative memory that is similar to that seen during exposure to other tasks that stimulate brain networks mediating PTSD symptoms, such as exposure to personalized scripts of childhood trauma or exposure to trauma-related pictures and sounds, then that would provide convergent evidence for dysfunction of a specific neural circuit in the processing of emotional memory in PTSD.

We recently used PET in the examination of neural correlates of retrieval of emotionally valenced declarative memory in 10 women with a history of childhood sexual abuse and the diagnosis of PTSD and 11 women without abuse or PTSD. We hypothesized that retrieval of emotionally valenced words would result in an altered pattern of brain activation in patients with PTSD similar to that seen in prior studies of exposure to cues of personalized traumatic memories. During retrieval of emotionally valenced word pairs, PTSD patients showed greater decreases in blood flow than control participants in an extensive area that included the orbitofrontal cortex, anterior cingulate, and medial prefrontal cortex (Brodmann's Areas 25, 32, and 9), left hippocampus, and fusiform gyrus/inferior temporal gyrus, with increased activation in the posterior cingulate, left inferior parietal cortex, left middle frontal gyrus, and visual association and motor cortex. There were no differences between patients and control participants in patterns of brain activation during retrieval of neutral word pairs. These findings were similar to those of previous imaging studies from our group using trauma-specific stimuli for symptom provocation, adding to the evidence for a dysfunction in PTSD of a network of brain areas involved in memory, including the hippocampus, medial prefrontal cortex, and cingulate (Bremner, Vythilingam, Vermetten, Southwick, McGlashan, Staib, et al., 2003).

Another study examined neural correlates of the Stroop task in sexually abused women with PTSD. The Stroop task involves color naming semantically incongruent words (e.g., name the color of the word "green" printed in the color red). People experience competition or interference between the visual color and the linguistic meaning of the word, which delays their response to this task. The latency to respond gives a measure of the speed of verbal information processing or the degree of interference. The Stroop task has been consistently found to be associated with activation of the anterior cingulate in normal subjects, an effect attributed to the divided attention or inhibition of responses involved in the task. Studies with versions of the Stroop task using emotionally laden words (e.g., name the color of a trauma-specific word like "rape") have found a delay in color naming in patients with PTSD (Foa, Feske, Murdock, Kozak, & McCarthy, 1991). Women with early childhood sexual abuse-related PTSD ($n = 12$) and women with a history of abuse but without PTSD ($n = 9$) underwent PET measurement of cerebral blood flow during exposure to control, color Stroop, and emotional Stroop conditions. Women with abuse with PTSD (but not abused non-PTSD women) had a relative decrease in anterior cingulate blood flow during exposure to the emotional (but not color) classic Stroop task. During the color Stroop there were also relatively greater increases in blood flow in non-PTSD compared with PTSD women in the right visual association cortex, cuneus, and right inferior parietal lobule. These findings were consistent with dysfunction of the anterior cingulate/medial prefrontal cortex in women with early abuse-related PTSD (Bremner, Vermetten, Vythilingam, et al., 2004).

We compared hippocampal function and structure in 33 women with and without early childhood sexual abuse and PTSD. Women with abuse with and without PTSD were studied with PET measurement of brain blood flow while they read and committed to memory a paragraph (verbal memory encoding) compared to a control condition. There were no differences in blood flow during the control task between groups; however, there were significantly greater increases in hippocampal blood flow during verbal memory encoding in abused women without PTSD relative to women with PTSD ($F = 14.93$; df 1,20; $p < 0.001$). Women with PTSD also had smaller left hippocampal volume as measured by MRI compared to abused women without PTSD and nonabused non-PTSD women. Differences in hippocampal activation were statistically significant after controlling for left hippocampal volume, suggesting that the failure of activation was not secondary to smaller hippocampal volume in patients with PTSD. There was a significant relationship between increased dissociative experiences as measured with the Clinician Administered Dissociative States Scale (CADSS) and smaller left hippocampal volume as measured with MRI in abused women as measured with logistic regression (Bremner, Vythilingam, Vermetten, Southwick, McGlashan, Nazeer, et al., 2003). Another study in men and women with Vietnam service and PTSD found a failure of hippocampal activation with a word-stem completion memory task (L. M. Shin, Shin, et al., 2004).

In addition to a failure of hippocampal activation with cognitive tasks, studies found decreased hippocampal activation with symptom provocation in PTSD. Studies have found decreased hippocampal function during traumatic remembrance stimulated with trauma-specific scripts (Bremner, Narayan, et al., 1999), during stimulation of PTSD symptoms with the drug yohimbine (Bremner, Innis, et al., 1997), or during recall of emotionally negative words in PTSD (Bremner, Vythilingam, Vermetten, Southwick, McGlashan, Staib, et al., 2003), although increased function was seen during counting of combat words (L. M. Shin et al., 2001). Increased dissociation and flashbacks during these tasks may lead to (or be caused by) decreased hippocampal function (Brewin, 2001).

Although some studies have demonstrated increased amygdala function in PTSD (Semple et al., 2000), the experience to date suggests that increased amygdala involvement is not necessarily seen in all of the study paradigms applied to PTSD. Although some studies have found amygdala activation with trauma-specific stimuli (Rauch et al., 1996), a larger number have not (Bremner, Innis, et al., 1997; Bremner, Narayan, et al., 1999; Bremner, Staib, et al., 1999; Lanius et al., 2001; Liberzon et al., 1999; L. H. Shin et al., 1999). It is likely that specific tasks are required to show increased amygdala activation in PTSD. For instance, Rauch and colleagues found that exposure to masked fearful faces was associated with greater amygdala activation in PTSD (Rauch et al., 2000). Similarly, we found increased amygdala activation during acquisition of fear in a classical fear conditioning paradigm (Bremner et al., 2005). In summary, increased amygdala function has not been shown to be nonspecifically associated with traumatic remembrance in PTSD; however, there are suggestions that alterations in amygdala activity do play a role in PTSD, probably related to specific mechanisms of the disorder. Further studies are required in this area.

Imaging studies that involve provoking symptoms in adults with PTSD are also consistent with dysfunction in the medial prefrontal cortex/anterior cingulate (Bremner, 2003a). In one study, PTSD symptoms were provoked by activating brain norepinephrine systems with yohimbine (an α_2 noradrenergic receptor antagonist which stimulates norepinephrine release in the brain). Using PET imaging of brain metabolism, PTSD patients showed decreased activity in the orbitofrontal cortex, relative to control participants (Bremner, Innis, et al., 1997). In another study, using an attentional task, decreased baseline blood flow was seen in the medial prefrontal cortex in patients with PTSD and substance abuse (Semple et al., 2000). Other studies have found dysfunction in various subregions of the medial prefrontal cortex/anterior cingulate (Areas 32, 24, and 25), including a failure of activation and decreased function relative to control participants during exposure to traumatic scripts (Bremner, Narayan, et al., 1999; Lanius et al., 2001; Lanius et al., 2003; L. H. Shin et al., 1999; L. M. Shin, Orr, et al., 2004), combat-related slides and/or sounds (Bremner, Staib, et al., 1999; Liberzon et al., 1999), a trauma-specific counting Stroop task (L. M. Shin et al., 2001), and an emotional Stroop task (Bremner, Vermetten, Vythilingam, et al., 2004). For the other parts of the medial prefrontal cortex (orbitofrontal cortex [Area 11], Areas 9 and 10), the findings have been mixed (Zubieta et al., 1999), with about equal numbers of studies showing increases and decreases. At present, it is reasonable to postulate that exposure to standard materials such as traumatic scripts and slides is associated with a relative failure of function in the "extended anterior cingulate" portion of the medial prefrontal cortex (Areas 24, 32, and 25); however, more studies are required to confirm this finding.

Studies have begun to use neuroimaging to examine central receptor function in PTSD. Animal studies showed that chronic stress leads to a decrease in benzodiazepine receptor binding in the frontal cortex. In a recent study, we used single photon emission computed tomography (SPECT) with [^{123}I]Iomazenil (a drug that binds to benzodiazepine receptor sites) to examine the levels of benzodiazepine receptors in patients with combat-related PTSD and healthy control participants. We found a decrease in benzodiazepine receptor binding in the medial prefrontal cortex (Brodmann's Area 9) in 13 patients with combat-related PTSD compared to 13 case-matched healthy control participants (Bremner et al., 2000). These findings are consistent with animal studies of stress showing decreased binding in the frontal lobe.

Functionally, the cingulate cortex has been divided into an anterior portion involved in emotion and selection for action and a posterior portion involved in visuospatial processing (Devinsky et al., 1995). Recent imaging studies in humans, however, have been consistent with a role for the posterior cingulate in processing of emotional and traumatic material in normal individuals (Maddock & Buonocore, 1997). Multiple PET studies found increased posterior cingulate function during stimulation of traumatic memories in PTSD (Bremner, Narayan, et al., 1999; Bremner, Staib, et al., 1999; Lanius et al., 2001; L. M. Shin et al., 1997; L. M. Shin et al., 2001). These findings corroborate the importance of the entire cingulate area in the limbic system response to trauma.

The dorsolateral prefrontal cortex, which includes areas such as the middle and inferior frontal gyri, is involved in cognitive functions, language, and speech (Tulving, Kapur, Craik, Moscovitch, & Houle, 1994). The prefrontal cortex plays an important role in the activation of memory pathways and sustained attention that are elicited during the stress response. This area has functional connections with other regions mediating cognitive and emotional responses to stress, including the motor cortex, parietal cortex, cingulate, hippocampus, and amygdala. Disruption of circuits between the dorsolateral prefrontal cortex and other regions involved in emotion and the stress response (e.g., limbic regions) may lead to disconnection between cognitive and emotional processing and responses to traumatic events.

Several studies have found decreased activity in the dorsolateral prefrontal cortex in PTSD patients when PTSD symptoms are provoked (Bremner, Innis, et al., 1997; Bremner, Narayan, et al., 1999; Rauch et al., 1996; L. H. Shin et al., 1999; L. M. Shin et al., 1997). Decreased activity in this area may be involved in the dysfunctions of memory, speech, and cognition seen in PTSD patients, especially during periods of stress or traumatic reminders. A functional disconnection between "higher" prefrontal cortical areas involved in abstract thought, language, and cognition and "lower" limbic areas that govern primary emotions may underlie unregulated emotions, traumatic dissociative memory recall in PTSD, and difficulties in verbalization of traumatic experiences.

The parietal cortex plays a critical role in the visuospatial processing that is involved in the response to threat (Jonides et al., 1993; Pardo, Fox, &

Raichle, 1991). Several studies have found decreased function in the parietal cortex (Bremner, Innis, et al., 1997; Bremner, Staib, et al., 1999; Rauch et al., 1996; L. H. Shin et al., 1999; L. M. Shin et al., 1997) with a smaller number of studies showing an increase (Bremner, Narayan, et al., 1999; L. M. Shin et al., 2001). These studies are consistent with alterations in parietal and visual association cortical function in PTSD, probably mediating alterations in cognitive functions associated with these areas.

BRAIN IMAGING OF TRAUMA SPECTRUM DISORDERS

I have argued that psychiatric nosology might recognize a spectrum group of trauma-related disorders including PTSD, depression, borderline personality disorder (BPD), and dissociative disorders (Bremner, 2002). This is a departure from the DSM approach of having multiple disorders grouped by symptoms without any theoretical foundation. The DSM view is based on the hope that neurobiology will eventually help us to distinguish different disorders. However, these disorders have high comorbidity and overlapping descriptive language. Neuroimaging has shown common deficits in the anterior cingulate/medial prefrontal cortex and hippocampus in these disorders. For instance, we studied women sexually abused in childhood who had received a primary diagnosis of BPD. About 50% of these women had comorbid PTSD (Schmahl, McGlashan, & Bremner, 2002). Our group (Schmahl, Vermetten, Elzinga, & Bremner, 2003) and others (Driessen et al., 2000) have found smaller hippocampal and amygdala volume in women with histories of abuse and BPD. A consistent finding in these studies is decreased amygdala function.

We have developed a paradigm involving exposure to scripts of an abandonment situation, which is specific to the psychopathology of BPD, and which differentially affects women with BPD compared to PTSD as measured by psychophysiological responding (Schmahl, Elzinga, & Bremner, 2002). We assessed cerebral blood flow with PET in 20 abused women with and without BPD while they listened to scripts describing neutral and personal abandonment events. Memories of abandonment were associated with greater increases in blood flow in the bilateral dorsolateral prefrontal cortex and right cuneus, and greater decreases in the anterior cingulate in women with BPD compared to women without BPD (Schmahl et al., 2003). These findings show some overlap between abused women with BPD and PTSD, specifically in the area of decreased anterior cingulate/medial prefrontal cortical function.

CONCLUSION

The research discussed in this chapter provides evidence for long-term changes in the brain and stress responsive systems in patients with PTSD.

Brain areas affected include the amygdala, hippocampus, and frontal cortex. These changes may lead to both memory problems and maintenance of abnormal fear responses and other symptoms of PTSD.

The studies outlined in this chapter were performed in the medical research model of applying scientific methods to look for the mechanisms underlying the disorder. This method was applied late to PTSD within the field of psychiatry, which in turn was a latecomer to the scientific method within the medical field. The dominance of psychoanalysis led to a delay in research in psychiatry, and popular assumptions that trauma did not lead to real disorders affected the field of psychiatry, in general, and, in particular, PTSD, causing a delay in research in this area compared to disorders such as schizophrenia.

Now that this research enterprise is well under way, current biological studies in PTSD are revealing the impact of trauma on the brain and suggest the usefulness of recognizing a broader category of trauma-related disorders in psychiatric nosology.

References

Abercrombie, E. D., & Jacobs, B. L. (1987). Single-unit response of noradrenergic neurons in the locus coeruleus of freely moving cats, II: Adaptation to chronically presented stressful stimuli. *Journal of Neuroscience, 7*, 2844–2848.

Arborelius, L., Owens, M. J., Plotsky, P. M., & Nemeroff, C. B. (1999). The role of corticotropin-releasing factor in depression and anxiety disorders. *Journal of Endocrinology, 160*, 1–12.

Baker, D. B., West, S. A., Nicholson, W. E., Ekhator, N. N., Kasckow, J. W., Hill, K. K., et al. (1999). Serial CSF corticotropin-releasing hormone levels and adrenocortical activity in combat veterans with posttraumatic stress disorder. *American Journal of Psychiatry, 156*, 585–588.

Barrett, D. H., Green, M. L., Morris, R., Giles, W. H., & Croft, J. B. (1996). Cognitive functioning and posttraumatic stress disorder. *American Journal of Psychiatry, 153*(11), 1492–1494.

Bonne, O., Brandes, D., Gilboa, A., Gomori, J. M., Shenton, M. E., Pitman, R. K., et al. (2001). Longitudinal MRI study of hippocampal volume in trauma survivors with PTSD. *American Journal of Psychiatry, 158*, 1248–1251.

Bremner, J. D. (2002). *Does stress damage the brain? Understanding trauma-related disorders from a mind-body perspective.* New York: W. W. Norton.

Bremner, J. D. (2003a). Functional neuroanatomical correlates of traumatic stress revisited 7 years later, this time with data. *Psychopharmacology Bulletin, 37*(2), 6–25.

Bremner, J. D. (2003b). Long-term effects of childhood abuse on brain and neurobiology. *Child and Adolescent Psychiatric Clinics of North America, 12*(2), 271–292.

Bremner, J. D., Hoffman, M., Vaccarino, V., Afzal, N., Cheema, F. A., Novik, O., et al. (2003, Oct.) *Memory and the hippocampus in Vietnam twins with PTSD.* In E. Vermetten (Chair), *New research from brain imaging studies in PTSD.* Symposium conducted at the Annual Meeting of the International Society for Traumatic Stress Studies, Chicago IL.

Bremner, J. D., Innis, R. B., Ng, C. K., Staib, L., Duncan, J., Bronen, R., et al. (1997). PET measurement of cerebral metabolic correlates of yohimbine administration in posttraumatic stress disorder. *Archives of General Psychiatry, 54,* 246–256.

Bremner, J. D., Innis, R. B., Southwick, S. M., Staib, L. H., Zoghbi, S., & Charney, D. S. (2000). Decreased benzodiazepine receptor binding in frontal cortex in combat-related posttraumatic stress disorder. *American Journal of Psychiatry, 157,* 1120–1126.

Bremner, J. D., Krystal, J. H., Southwick, S. M., & Charney, D. S. (1995). Functional neuroanatomical correlates of the effects of stress on memory. *Journal of Traumatic Stress, 8,* 527–554.

Bremner, J. D., Krystal, J. H., Southwick, S. M., & Charney, D. S. (1996a). Noradrenergic mechanisms in stress and anxiety, I: Preclinical studies. *Synapse, 23,* 28–38.

Bremner, J. D., Krystal, J. H., Southwick, S. M., & Charney, D. S. (1996b). Noradrenergic mechanisms in stress and anxiety, II: Clinical studies. *Synapse, 23,* 39–51.

Bremner, J. D., Licinio, J., Darnell, A., Krystal, J. H., Owens, M., Southwick, S. M., et al. (1997). Elevated CSF corticotropin-releasing factor concentrations in posttraumatic stress disorder. *American Journal of Psychiatry, 154,* 624–629.

Bremner, J. D., Narayan, M., Staib, L. H., Southwick, S. M., McGlashan, T., & Charney, D. S. (1999). Neural correlates of memories of childhood sexual abuse in women with and without posttraumatic stress disorder. *American Journal of Psychiatry, 156,* 1787–1795.

Bremner, J. D., Randall, P. R., Capelli, S., Scott, T. M., McCarthy, G., & Charney, D. S. (1995). Deficits in short-term memory in adult survivors of childhood abuse. *Psychiatry Research, 59,* 97–107.

Bremner, J. D., Randall, P. R., Scott, T. M., Bronen, R. A., Delaney, R. C., Seibyl, J. P., et al. (1995). MRI-based measurement of hippocampal volume in patients with combat-related posttraumatic stress disorder. *American Journal of Psychiatry, 152,* 973–981.

Bremner, J. D., Randall, P. R., Vermetten, E., Staib, L., Bronen, R. A., Mazure, C. M., et al. (1997). MRI-based measurement of hippocampal volume in posttraumatic stress disorder related to childhood physical and sexual abuse: A preliminary report. *Biological Psychiatry, 41,* 23–32.

Bremner, J. D., Scott, T. M., Delaney, R. C., Southwick, S. M., Mason, J. W., Johnson, D. R., et al. (1993). Deficits in short-term memory in post-traumatic stress disorder. *American Journal of Psychiatry, 150,* 1015–1019.

Bremner, J. D., Soufer, R., McCarthy, G., Delaney, R. C., Staib, L. H., Duncan, J. S., et al. (2001). Gender differences in cognitive and neural correlates of remembrance of emotional words. *Psychopharmacology Bulletin, 35,* 55–87.

Bremner, J. D., Southwick, S. M., Darnell, A., & Charney, D. S. (1996). Chronic PTSD in Vietnam combat veterans: Course of illness and substance abuse. *American Journal of Psychiatry, 153,* 369–375.

Bremner, J. D., Staib, L., Kaloupek, D., Southwick, S. M., Soufer, R., & Charney, D. S. (1999). Neural correlates of exposure to traumatic pictures and sound in Vietnam combat veterans with and without posttraumatic stress disorder: A positron emission tomography study. *Biological Psychiatry, 45*, 806–816.

Bremner, J. D., & Vermetten, E. (2001). Stress and development: Behavioral and biological consequences. *Development and Psychopathology, 13*, 473–489.

Bremner, J. D., Vermetten, E., & Kelley, M. E. (in press). Cortisol, dehydroepiandrosterone (DHEA), and estradiol measured over 24 hours in women with childhood sexual abuse–related postraumatic stress disorder. *Journal of Nervous and Mental Disease.*

Bremner, J. D., Vermetten, E., Nafzal, N., & Vythilingam, M. (2004). Deficits in verbal declarative memory function in women with childhood sexual abuse-related posttraumatic stress disorder (PTSD). *Journal of Nervous and Mental Disease, 192*(10), 643–649.

Bremner, J. D., Vermetten, E., Schmahl, C., Vaccarino, V., Vythilingam, M., Afzal, N., et al. (2005). Positron emission tomographic imaging of neural correlates of a fear acquisition and extinction paradigm in women with childhood sexual abuse-related posttraumatic stress disorder. *Psychological Medicine, 35*(6), 791–806.

Bremner, J. D., Vermetten, E., Vythilingam, M., Afzal, N., Schmahl, C., Elzinga, B., & Charney, D. (2004). Neural correlates of the classic color and emotional stroop in women with abuse-related posttraumatic stress disorder. *Biological Psychiatry, 55*(6), 612–620.

Bremner, J. D., Vythilingam, M., Vermetten, E., Adil, J., Khan, S., Nazeer, A., et al. (2003). Cortisol response to a cognitive stress challenge in posttraumatic stress disorder (PTSD) related to childhood abuse. *Psychoneuroendocrinology, 28*, 733–750.

Bremner, J. D., Vythilingam, M., Vermetten, E., Southwick, S. M., McGlashan, T., Nazeer, A., et al. (2003). MRI and PET study of deficits in hippocampal structure and function in women with childhood sexual abuse and posttraumatic stress disorder (PTSD). *American Journal of Psychiatry, 160*, 924–932.

Bremner, J. D., Vythilingam, M., Vermetten, E., Southwick, S. M., McGlashan, T., Staib, L., et al. (2003). Neural correlates of declarative memory for emotionally valenced words in women with posttraumatic stress disorder (PTSD) related to early childhood sexual abuse. *Biological Psychiatry, 53*, 289–299.

Brewin, C. R. (2001). A cognitive neuroscience account of post-traumatic stress disorder and its treatment. *Behaviour Research and Therapy, 39*, 373–393.

Buckley, T. C., Blanchard, E. B., & Neill, W. T. (2000). Information processing and PTSD: A review of the empirical literature. *Clinical Psychology Reviews, 28*(8), 1041–1065.

Carrion, V. G., Weems, C. F., Eliez, S., Patwardhan, A., Brown, W., Ray, R. D., et al. (2001). Attenuation of frontal asymmetry in pediatric posttraumatic stress disorder. *Biological Psychiatry, 50*, 943–951.

Czeh, B., Michaelis, T., Watanabe, T., Frahm, J., de Biurrun, G., van Kampen, M., et al. (2001). Stress-induced changes in cerebral metabolites, hippocampal volume, and cell proliferation are prevented by antidepressant treatment with tianeptine. *Proceedings of the National Academy of Sciences of the United States of America, 98*, 12796–12801.

Damasio, H., Grabowski, T., Frank, R., Galaburda, A. M., & Damasio, A. R. (1994). The return of Phineas Gage: Clues about the brain from the skull of a famous patient. *Science, 264,* 1102–1105.

Davis, M. (1992). The role of the amygdala in fear and anxiety. *Annual Review of Neuroscience, 15,* 353–375.

De Bellis, M. D., Hall, J., Boring, A. M., Frustaci, K., & Moritz, G. (2001). A pilot longitudinal study of hippocampal volumes in pediatric maltreatment-related posttraumatic stress disorder. *Biological Psychiatry, 50,* 305–309.

De Bellis, M. D., Keshavan, M. S., Clark, D. B., Casey, B. J., Giedd, J. N., Boring, A. M., et al. (1999). A. E. Bennett Research Award: Developmental traumatology, part II: Brain development. *Biological Psychiatry, 45,* 1271–1284.

Devinsky, O., Morrell, M. J., & Vogt, B. A. (1995). Contributions of anterior cingulate to behavior. *Brain, 118,* 279–306.

Diamond, D. M., Fleshner, M., Ingersoll, N., & Rose, G. M. (1996). Psychological stress impairs spatial working memory: Relevance to electrophysiological studies of hippocampal function. *Behavioral Neuroscience, 110,* 661–672.

Driessen, M., Herrmann, J., Stahl, K., Zwaan, M., Meier, S., Hill, A., et al. (2000). Magnetic resonance imaging volumes of the hippocampus and the amygdala in women with borderline personality disorder and early traumatization. *Archives of General Psychiatry, 57,* 1115–1122.

D'Sa, C., & Duman, R. S. (2002). Antidepressants and neuroplasticity. *Bipolar Disorders, 4,* 183–194.

Duman, R. S. (2004). Depression: A case of neuronal life and death? *Biological Psychiatry, 56,* 140–145.

Duman, R. S., Heninger, G. R., & Nestler, E. J. (1997). A molecular and cellular theory of depression. *Archives of General Psychiatry, 54,* 597–606.

Duman, R. S., Malberg, J. E., & Nakagawa, S. (2001). Regulation of adult neurogenesis by psychotropic drugs and stress. *Journal of Pharmacology and Experimental Therapeutics, 299,* 401–407.

Elzinga, B. M., & Bremner, J. D. (2002). Are the neural substrates of memory the final common pathway in PTSD? *Journal of Affective Disorders, 70,* 1–17.

Elzinga, B. M., Schmahl, C. S., Vermetten, E., van Dyck, R., & Bremner, J. D. (2003). Higher cortisol levels following exposure to traumatic reminders in abuse-related PTSD. *Neuropsychopharmacology, 28*(9), 1656–1665.

Finlay, J. M., Zigmond, M. J., & Abercrombie, E. D. (1995). Increased dopamine and norepinephrine release in medial prefrontal cortex induced by acute and chronic stress: Effects of diazepam. *Neuroscience, 64,* 619–628.

Foa, E. B., Feske, U., Murdock, T. B., Kozak, M. J., & McCarthy, P. R. (1991). Processing of threat-related information in rape victims. *Journal of Abnormal Psychology, 100,* 156–162.

Foote, S. L., Bloom, F. E., & Aston-Jones, G. (1983). Nucleus locus coeruleus: New evidence of anatomical and physiological specificity. *Physiology & Behavior, 63,* 844–914.

Fowler, C. D., Liu, Y., Ouimet, C., & Wang, Z. (2001). The effects of social environment on adult neurogenesis in the female prairie vole. *Journal of Neurobiology, 51,* 115–128.

Freeman, T. W., Cardwell, D., Karson, C. N., & Komoroski, R. A. (1998). In vivo proton magnetic resonance spectroscopy of the medial temporal lobes of subjects with combat-related posttraumatic stress disorder. *Magnetic Resonance in Medicine, 40,* 66–71.

Garcia, R. (2002). Stress, metaplasticity, and antidepressants. *Current Molecular Medicine, 2,* 629–638.

Gil, T., Calev, A., Greenberg, D., Kugelmas, S., & Lerer, B. (1990). Cognitive functioning in posttraumatic stress disorder. *Journal of Traumatic Stress, 3,* 29–45.

Gilbertson, M. W., Gurvits, T. V., Lasko, N. B., Orr, S. P., & Pitman, R. K. (2001). Multivariate assessment of explicit memory function in combat veterans with posttraumatic stress disorder. *Journal of Traumatic Stress, 14,* 413–420.

Gilbertson, M. W., Shenton, M. E., Ciszewski, A., Kasai, K., Lasko, N. B., Orr, S. P., et al. (2002). Smaller hippocampal volume predicts pathologic vulnerability to psychological trauma. *Nature Neuroscience, 5*(11), 1242–1247.

Golier, J., & Yehuda, R. (1998). Neuroendocrine activity and memory-related impairments in posttraumatic stress disorder. *Development and Psychopathology, 10*(4), 857–869.

Golier, J., Yehuda, R., Cornblatt, B., Harvey, P., Gerber, D., & Levengood, R. (1997). Sustained attention in combat-related posttraumatic stress disorder. *Integrative Physiological & Behavioral Science, 32*(1), 52–61.

Gould, E., McEwen, B. S., Tanapat, P., Galea, L. A. M., & Fuchs, E. (1997). Neurogenesis in the dentate gyrus of the adult tree shrew is regulated by psychosocial stress and NMDA receptor activation. *Journal of Neuroscience, 17,* 2492–2498.

Gurvits, T. G., Shenton, M. R., Hokama, H., Ohta, H., Lasko, N. B., Gilbertson, M. B., et al. (1996). Magnetic resonance imaging study of hippocampal volume in chronic combat-related posttraumatic stress disorder. *Biological Psychiatry, 40,* 192–199.

Henn, F. A., & Vollmayr, B. (2004). Neurogenesis and depression: Etiology or epiphenomenon? *Biological Psychiatry, 56,* 146–150.

Jenkins, M. A., Langlais, P. J., Delis, D., & Cohen, R. (1998). Learning and memory in rape victims with posttraumatic stress disorder. *American Journal of Psychiatry, 155,* 278–279.

Jonides, J., Smith, E. E., Koeppe, R. A., Awh, E., Minoshima, S., & Mintun, M. A. (1993). Spatial working memory in humans as revealed by PET. *Nature, 363,* 623–625.

Lanius, R. A., Williamson, P. C., Boksman, K., Densmore, M., Gupta, M. A., Neufeld, R. W. J., et al. (2002). Brain activation during script-driven imagery induced dissociative responses in PTSD: A functional magnetic resonance imaging investigation. *Biological Psychiatry, 52*(4), 305–311.

Lanius, R. A., Williamson, P. C., Densmore, M., Boksman, K., Gupta, M. A., Neufeld, R. W., et al. (2001). Neural correlates of traumatic memories in posttraumatic stress disorder: A functional MRI investigation. *American Journal of Psychiatry, 158,* 1920–1922.

Lanius, R. A., Williamson, P. C., Hopper, J., Densmore, M., Boksman, K., Gupta, M. A., et al. (2003). Recall of emotional states in posttraumatic stress disorder: An fMRI investigation. *Biological Psychiatry, 53*(3), 204–210.

Lawrence, M. S., & Sapolsky, R. M. (1994). Glucocorticoids accelerate ATP loss following metabolic insults in cultured hippocampal neurons. *Brain Research, 646,* 303–306.

LeDoux, J. L. (1993). In search of systems and synapses. *Annals of the New York Academy of Sciences, 149*–157.

Leverenz, J. B., Wilkinson, C. W., Wamble, M., Corbin, S., Grabber, J. E., Raskind, M. A., et al. (1999). Effect of chronic high-dose exogenous cortisol on hippocampal neuronal number in aged nonhuman primate. *Journal of Neuroscience, 19,* 2356–2361.

Levine, E. S., Litto, W. J., & Jacobs, B. L. (1990). Activity of cat locus coeruleus noradrenergic neurons during the defense reaction. *Brain Research, 531,* 189–195.

Levine, S., Weiner, S. G., & Coe, C. L. (1993). Temporal and social factors influencing behavioral and hormonal responses to separation in mother and infant squirrel monkeys. *Psychoneuroendocrinology, 4,* 297–306.

Liberzon, I., Taylor, S. F., Amdur, R., Jung, T. D., Chamberlain, K. R., Minoshima, S., et al. (1999). Brain activation in PTSD in response to trauma-related stimuli. *Biological Psychiatry, 45,* 817–826.

Lucassen, P. J., Fuchs, E., & Czeh, B. (2004). Antidepressant treatment with tianeptine reduces apoptosis in the hippocampal dentate gyrus and temporal cortex. *European Journal of Neuroscience, 14,* 161–166.

Luine, V., Villages, M., Martinex, C., & McEwen, B. S. (1994). Repeated stress causes reversible impairments of spatial memory performance. *Brain Research, 639,* 167–170.

Maddock, R. J., & Buonocore, M. H. (1997). Activation of left posterior cingulate gyrus by the auditory presentation of threat-related words: An fMRI study. *Psychiatry Research, 75,* 1–14.

Malberg, J. E., Eisch, A. J., Nestler, E. J., & Duman, R. S. (2000). Chronic antidepressant treatment increases neurogenesis in adult rat hippocampus. *Journal of Neuroscience, 20,* 9104–9110.

McEwen, B. S., Angulo, J., Cameron, H., Chao, H. M., Daniels, D., Gannon, M. N., et al. (1992). Paradoxical effects of adrenal steroids on the brain: Protection versus degeneration. *Biological Psychiatry, 31,* 177–199.

McEwen, B. S., & Chattarji, S. (2004). Molecular mechanisms of neuroplasticity and pharmacological implications: The example of tianeptine. *European Neuropsychopharmacology, 14*(Suppl. 5), S497–502.

McFall, M. E., Murburg, M. M., Ko, G. N., & Veith, R. C. (1990). Autonomic responses to stress in Vietnam combat veterans with posttraumatic stress disorder. *Biological Psychiatry, 27,* 1165–1175.

Melia, K. R., & Duman, R. S. (1991). Involvement of corticotropin-releasing factor in chronic stress regulation of the brain noradrenergic system. *Proceedings of the National Academy of Sciences of the United States of America, 88,* 8382–8386.

Moradi, A. R., Doost, H. T., Taghavi, M. R., Yule, W., & Dalgleish, T. (1999). Everyday memory deficits in children and adolescents with PTSD: Performance on the Rivermead Behavioural Memory Test. *Journal of Child Psychology and Psychiatry, 40,* 357–361.

Morgan, C. A., & LeDoux, J. E. (1995). Differential contribution of dorsal and ventral medial prefrontal cortex to the acquisition and extinction of conditioned fear in rats. *Behavioral Neuroscience, 109,* 681–688.

Morgan, C. A., Romanski, L. M., & LeDoux, J. E. (1993). Extinction of emotional learning: Contribution of medial prefrontal cortex. *Neuroscience Letters, 163,* 109–113.

Nibuya, M., Morinobu, S., & Duman, R. S. (1995). Regulation of BDNF and trkB mRNA in rat brain by chronic electroconvulsive seizure and antidepressant drug treatments. *Journal of Neuroscience, 15*, 7539–7547.

Nisenbaum, L. K., Zigmond, M. J., Sved, A. F., & Abercrombie, E. D. (1991). Prior exposure to chronic stress results in enhanced synthesis and release of hippocampal norepinephrine in response to a novel stressor. *Journal of Neuroscience, 11*, 1478–1484.

Notestine, C. F., Stein, M. B., Kennedy, C. M., Archibald, S. L., & Jernigan, T. L. (2002). Brain morphometry in female victims of intimate partner violence with and without posttraumatic stress disorder. *Biological Psychiatry, 51*, 1089–1101.

Pardo, J. V., Fox, P. T., & Raichle, M. E. (1991). Localization of a human system for sustained attention by positron emission tomography. *Nature, 349*, 61–64.

Pitman, R. K. (2001). Investigating the pathogenesis of posttraumatic stress disorder with neuroimaging. *Journal of Clinical Psychiatry, 62*, 47–54.

Pitman, R. K., Orr, S. P., Forgus, D. F., de Jong, J. B., & Claiborn, J. M. (1987). Psychophysiologic assessment of posttraumatic stress disorder imagery in Vietnam combat veterans. *Archives of General Psychiatry, 44*, 970–975.

Quirk, G. J. (2002). Memory for extinction of conditioned fear is long-lasting and persists following spontaneous recovery. *Learning & Memory, 9*, 402–407.

Radley, J. J., Sisti, H. M., Hao, J., Rocher, A. B., McCall, T., Hof, P. R., et al. (2004). Chronic behavioral stress induces apical dendritic reorganization in pyramidal neurons of the medial prefrontal cortex. *Neuroscience, 125*(1), 1–6.

Rauch, S. L., van der Kolk, B. A., Fisler, R. E., Alpert, N. M., Orr, S. P., Savage, C. R., et al. (1996). A symptom provocation study of posttraumatic stress disorder using positron emission tomography and script-driven imagery. *Archives of General Psychiatry, 53*, 380–387.

Rauch, S. L., Whalen, P. J., Shin, L. M., McInerney, S. C., Macklin, M. L., Lasko, N. B., et al. (2000). Exaggerated amygdala response to masked facial stimuli in posttraumatic stress disorder: A functional MRI study. *Biological Psychiatry, 47*(9), 769–776.

Roca, V., & Freeman, T. W. (2001). Complaints of impaired memory in veterans with PTSD. *American Journal of Psychiatry, 158*, 1738.

Roth, R. H., Tam, S. Y., Ida, Y., Yang, J. X., & Deutch, A. Y. (1988). Stress and the mesocorticolimbic dopamine systems. *Annals of the New York Academy of Sciences, 537*, 138–147.

Sachinvala, N., von Scotti, H., McGuire, M., Fairbanks, L., Bakst, K., McGuire, M., et al. (2000). Memory, attention, function, and mood among patients with chronic posttraumatic stress disorder. *Journal of Nervous and Mental Disease, 188*, 818–823.

Saigh, P. A., & Bremner, J. D. (1999). The history of posttraumatic stress disorder. In P. A. Saigh & J. D. Bremner (Eds.), *Posttraumatic stress disorder: A comprehensive text* (pp. 1–17). Needham Heights, MA: Allyn & Bacon.

Santarelli, L., Saxe, M., Gross, C., Surget, A., Battaglia, F., Dulawa, S., et al. (2003). Requirement of hippocampal neurogenesis for the behavioral effects of antidepressants. *Science, 301*(5634), 805–809.

Sapolsky, R. M. (1996). Why stress is bad for your brain. *Science, 273*, 749–750.

Sapolsky, R. M., Uno, H., Rebert, C. S., & Finch, C. E. (1990). Hippocampal damage associated with prolonged glucocorticoid exposure in primates. *Journal of Neuroscience, 10*, 2897–2902.

Schmahl, C. G., Elzinga, B. M., & Bremner, J. D. (2002). Individual differences in psychophysiological reactivity in adults with childhood abuse. *Clinical Psychology and Psychotherapy, 9*, 271–276.

Schmahl, C. G., Elzinga, B. M., Vermetten, E., Sanislow, C., McGlashan, T. H., & Bremner, J. D. (2003). Neural correlates of memories of abandonment in women with and without borderline personality disorder. *Biological Psychiatry, 54*, 42–51.

Schmahl, C. G., McGlashan, T., & Bremner, J. D. (2002). Neurobiological correlates of borderline personality disorder. *Psychopharmacology Bulletin, 36*, 69–87.

Schmahl, C. G., Vermetten, E., Elzinga, B. M., & Bremner, J. D. (2003). Magnetic resonance imaging of hippocampal and amygdala volume in women with childhood abuse and borderline personality disorder. *Psychiatry Research: Neuroimaging, 122*, 193–198.

Schuff, N., Neylan, T. C., Lenoci, M. A., Du, A. T., Weiss, D. S., Marmar, C. R., et al. (2001). Decreased hippocampal N-acetylaspartate in the absence of atrophy in posttraumatic stress disorder. *Biological Psychiatry, 50*, 952–959.

Semple, W. E., Goyer, P., McCormick, R., Donovan, B., Muzic, R. F., Rugle, L., et al. (2000). Higher brain blood flow at amygdala and lower frontal cortex blood flow in PTSD patients with comorbid cocaine and alcohol abuse compared to controls. *Psychiatry, 63*, 65–74.

Shin, L. H., McNally, R. J., Kosslyn, S. M., Thompson, W. L., Rauch, S. L., Alpert, N. M., et al. (1999). Regional cerebral blood flow during script-driven imagery in childhood sexual abuse-related PTSD: A PET investigation. *American Journal of Psychiatry, 156*, 575–584.

Shin, L. M., Kosslyn, S. M., McNally, R. J., Alpert, N. M., Thompson, W. L., Rauch, S. L., et al. (1997). Visual imagery and perception in posttraumatic stress disorder: A positron emission tomographic investigation. *Archives of General Psychiatry, 54*, 233–237.

Shin, L. M., Orr, S. P., Carson, M. A., Rauch, S. L., Macklin, M. L., Lasko, N. B., et al. (2004). Regional cerebral blood flow in the amygdala and medial prefrontal cortex during traumatic imagery in male and female Vietnam veterans with PTSD. *Archives of General Psychiatry, 61*(2), 168–176.

Shin, L. M., Shin, P. S., Heckers, S., Krangel, T. S., Macklin, M. L., Orr, S. P., et al. (2004). Hippocampal function in posttraumatic stress disorder. *Hippocampus, 14*(3), 292–300.

Shin, L. M., Whalen, P. J., Pitman, R. K., Bush, G., Macklin, M. L., Lasko, N. B., et al. (2001). An fMRI study of anterior cingulate function in posttraumatic stress disorder. *Biological Psychiatry, 50*(12), 932–942.

Smith, M. A., Makino, S., Kvetnansky, R., & Post, R. M. (1995). Stress and glucocorticoids affect the expression of brain-derived neurotrophic factor and neurotrophin-3 mRNA in the hippocampus. *Journal of Neuroscience, 15*, 1768–1777.

Southwick, S. M., Krystal, J. H., Morgan, C. A., Johnson, D. R., Nagy, L. M., Nicolaou, A. L., et al. (1993). Abnormal noradrenergic function in posttraumatic stress disorder. *Archives of General Psychiatry, 50*(4), 295–305.

Stanton, M. E., Gutierrez, Y. R., & Levine, S. (1988). Maternal deprivation potentiates pituitary-adrenal stress responses in infant rats. *Behavioral Neuroscience, 102,* 692–700.

Stein, M. B., Hanna, C., Vaerum, V., & Koverola, C. (1999). Memory functioning in adult women traumatized by childhood sexual abuse. *Journal of Traumatic Stress, 12*(3), 527–534.

Stein, M. B., Koverola, C., Hanna, C., Torchia, M. G., & McClarty, B. (1997). Hippocampal volume in women victimized by childhood sexual abuse. *Psychological Medicine, 27,* 951–959.

Sutker, P. B., Winstead, D. K., Galina, Z. H., & Allain, A. N. (1991). Cognitive deficits and psychopathology among former prisoners of war and combat veterans of the Korean conflict. *American Journal of Psychiatry, 148,* 67–72.

Thygesen, P., Hermann, K., & Willanger, R. (1970). Concentration camp survivors in Denmark: Persecution, disease, and compensation. *Danish Medical Bulletin, 17,* 65–108.

Tulving, E., Kapur, S., Craik, F. I. M., Moscovitch, M., & Houle, S. (1994). Hemispheric encoding/retrieval asymmetry in episodic memory: Positron emission tomography findings. *Proceedings of the National Academy of Sciences of the United States of America, 91,* 2016–2020.

Uddo, M., Vasterling, J. J., Braily, K., & Sutker, P. B. (1993). Memory and attention in posttraumatic stress disorder. *Journal of Psychopathology and Behavioral Assessment, 15,* 43–52.

Uno, H., Tarara, R., Else, J. G., Suleman, M. A., & Sapolsky, R. M. (1989). Hippocampal damage associated with prolonged and fatal stress in primates. *Journal of Neuroscience, 9,* 1705–1711.

Vasterling, J. J., Brailey, K., Constans, J. I., & Sutker, P. B. (1998). Attention and memory dysfunction in posttraumatic stress disorder. *Neuropsychology, 12,* 125–133.

Vasterling, J. J., Duke, L. M., Brailey, K., Constans, J. I., Allain, A. N., Jr., & Sutker, P. B. (2002). Attention, learning, and memory performances and intellectual resources in Vietnam veterans: PTSD and no disorder comparisons. *Neuropsychology, 16,* 5–14.

Vermetten, E., Vythilingam, M., Southwick, S. M., Charney, D. S., & Bremner, J. D. (2003). Long-term treatment with paroxetine increases verbal declarative memory and hippocampal volume in posttraumatic stress disorder. *Biological Psychiatry, 54*(7), 693–702.

Villareale, G., Hamilton, D. A., Petropoulos, H., Driscoll, I., Rowland, L. M., Griego, J. A., et al. (2002). Reduced hippocampal volume and total white matter in posttraumatic stress disorder. *Biological Psychiatry, 15,* 119–125.

Vogt, B. A., Finch, D. M., & Olson, C. R. (1992). Functional heterogeneity in cingulate cortex: The anterior executive and posterior evaluative regions. *Cerebral Cortex, 2,* 435–443.

Vyas, A., Mitra, R., Shankaranarayana Rao, B. S., & Chattarji, S. (2002). Chronic stress induces contrasting patterns of dendritic remodeling in hippocampal and amygdaloid neurons. *Journal of Neuroscience, 22*(15), 6810–6818.

Vyas, A., Pillai, A. G., & Chattarji, S. (2004). Recovery after chronic stress fails to reverse amygdaloid neuronal hypertrophy and enhanced anxiety-like behavior. *Neuroscience, 128*(4), 667–673.

Watanabe, Y., Gould, E., Cameron, H. A., Daniels, D. C., & McEwen, B. S. (1992). Phenytoin prevents stress- and corticosterone-induced atrophy of CA3 pyramidal neurons. *Hippocampus, 2,* 431–436.

Watanabe, Y., Gould, E., Daniels, D. C., Cameron, H., & McEwen, B. S. (1992). Tianeptine attenuates stress-induced morphological changes in the hippocampus. *European Journal of Pharmacology, 222,* 157–162.

Yehuda, R., Keefe, R. S., Harvey, P. D., Levengood, R. A., Gerber, D. K., Geni, J., et al. (1995). Learning and memory in combat veterans with posttraumatic stress disorder. *American Journal of Psychiatry, 152,* 137–139.

Yehuda, R., Southwick, S. M., Krystal, J. H., Bremner, J. D., Charney, D. S., & Mason, J. (1993). Enhanced suppression of cortisol with low dose dexamethasone in posttraumatic stress disorder. *American Journal of Psychiatry, 150,* 83–86.

Yehuda, R., Teicher, M. H., Levengood, R. A., Trestman, R. L., & Siever, L. J. (1994). Circadian regulation of basal cortisol levels in posttraumatic stress disorder. *Annals of the New York Academy of Sciences,* 378–380.

Zalewski, C., Thompson, W., & Gottesman, I. (1994). Comparison of neuropsychological test performance in PTSD, generalized anxiety disorder, and control Vietnam veterans. *Assessment, 1,* 133–142.

Zubieta, J.-K., Chinitz, J. A., Lombardi, U., Fig, L. M., Cameron, O. G., & Liberzon, I. (1999). Medial frontal cortex involvement in PTSD symptoms: A SPECT study. *Journal of Psychiatry Research, 33,* 259–264.

7

Somatic Manifestations of Traumatic Stress

Emeran A. Mayer

Traumatic stress can be associated with adverse mental and physical health outcomes (Friedman & Schnurr, 1995; Lamprecht & Sack, 2002). Whereas the impact of traumatic stress on mental health is typically referred to as posttraumatic stress disorder (PTSD), there is a wide range of somatic symptoms and syndromes related to different organ systems that have been reported in association with trauma. These include cardiovascular, gastrointestinal, dermatological, ophthalmological, and gynecological symptoms (Friedman & Schnurr, 1995). Pain problems figure prominently amongst patients' complaints including headaches, musculoskeletal pain, chest pain, abdominal pain, and pelvic pain. Somatic symptoms have been reported after different types of trauma, including sexual abuse, and natural disasters, and have been reported after every military conflict since 1864. This chapter will discuss the relationship of traumatic stress with somatic symptoms focusing on so-called medically unexplained or "functional" syndromes, in particular, irritable bowel syndrome (IBS) and fibromyalgia (FM). Both syndromes are commonly reported by PTSD patients, and affected patients frequently show comorbidity with disorders of mood and affect (Campbell, Clauw, & Keefe, 2003; Mayer, Craske, & Naliboff, 2001; Williams, Brown, Clauw, & Gendreau, 2003).

Somatic responses associated with normal emotions and somatic manifestations of traumatic stress can be conceptualized as normal and pathological outputs of the emotional motor system (EMS; Figure 7.1; Holstege, Bandler, & Saper, 1996). The EMS refers to brain circuits generating parallel outputs to the body and brain that mediate the distinct pattern of the organism's response associated with emotional activation. These outputs include skeleto-motor, autonomic, neuroendocrine, and pain modulatory components. We have proposed a model of altered EMS responsiveness as a crucial pathophysiological mechanism in the development of medically

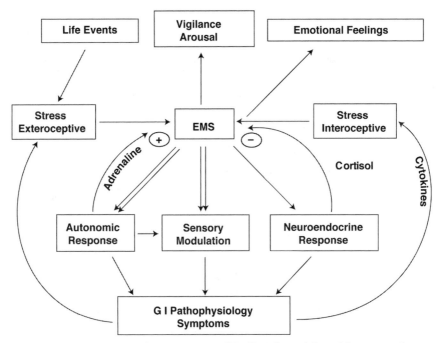

FIGURE 7.1. The emotional motor system (EMS). Adapted from Mayer, 2000b.

unexplained somatic symptoms, PTSD, as well as PTSD with somatic symptoms (Figure 7.2). The trigger for the development of somatic syndromes in vulnerable individuals can be the extreme stress associated with trauma; stressful life events that are sustained but not traumatic; or even the perturbation of physiological homeostasis by infections, injuries, or exposure to harmful substances in susceptible individuals (reviewed in Mayer, Naliboff, Chang, & Coutinho, 2001). According to this model, the development of somatic symptoms is related to the chronic influence of altered outputs of the EMS, in terms of autonomic nervous system (ANS) responses (increased sympathetic nervous system [SNS] drive, decreased cardiovagal tone), altered hypothalamic–pituitary–adrenal (HPA) axis responses (blunted circadian rhythm with increased responses to stress), altered pain modulation (predominance of endogenous pain facilitatory over pain inhibitory modulation), and alterations in monoaminergic arousal systems (hypervigilance, fatigue, sleep alterations).

As with mental health outcomes, the fact that only a minority of individuals exposed to trauma will develop somatic symptoms suggests that vulnerability factors must play a role in the development of these adverse outcomes. Genetic factors as well as aversive early life experiences and possibly severe adult traumatic stress appear to increase the vulnerability

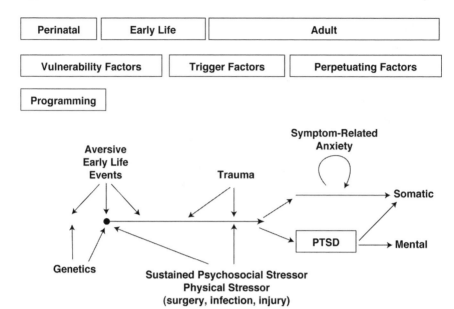

FIGURE 7.2. The effect of genetics and stressors during different life periods on the development of somatic and psychological manifestations of distress.

of developing stress-related somatic manifestations by increasing adult stress responsiveness. Extensive epidemiological as well as animal experimental data support the concept that the quality of the mother–infant interaction plays a prominent role in shaping adult stress responsiveness (see Bagot et al., this volume). Patients with IBS and FM commonly report a history of aversive early life events (Mayer, 2000a), and animal models of compromised mother–infant interactions commonly show evidence for altered stress-induced modulation of visceral and somatic pain (Mayer & Collins, 2002).

In summary, sensitization of central stress circuits through interaction of genetic factors with early life (and possibly prenatal) events may be an important risk factor for the development of somatic symptoms and syndromes following adult traumatic stress. This increased vulnerability may be shared with PTSD and other affective disorders, and may explain both (a) the fact that somatic, as well as mental, manifestations of trauma occur in only a fraction of those exposed to the trauma and (b) the frequent comorbidity of affective and somatic disorders following a traumatic event. Very similar functional somatic symptoms can develop in the general population in the absence of any traumatic experience. In these individuals, other types of psychological (sustained, nontraumatic stress) or physical stressors (infections, injuries) may trigger the development of the somatic symptoms. Individuals who develop these syndromes in the general population may be particularly vulnerable because of genetic and development factors. However, because not all PTSD patients develop somatic symptoms, some predisposition to increased pain perception or somatization may be required, independent of external stressors (Diatchenko et al., 2005).

HISTORICAL PERSPECTIVE

As summarized in a comprehensive review by Lamprecht and Sack (2002), published reports dating back to the late 19th century considered the possible association of traumatic life events with somatic symptoms. For example, in 1866 Erichsen proposed the term "railroad spine syndrome" to refer to a symptom complex (including fatigue, sleep disturbance, dizziness, and pain in the limbs) associated with anxiety, impaired memory, and nightmares following railway accidents, which were common at the time (Erichsen, 1866). Oppenheim (1889), A. B. R. Myers (1870), and da Costa (1871) reported on the frequent symptom reports in trauma survivors related to the heart and coined the term "soldier's heart" or "irritable heart"; the latter term is still being used today to describe a common, stress-sensitive functional syndrome in the general population. Oppenheim described this syndrome as an "abnormal excitability of the cardiac nervous system [which] is an almost constant symptom of traumatic neurosis, only in few instances is there serious cardiac disease" (Oppenheim, 1889). Charcot and Janet emphasized the role of traumatic events in the pathophysiology of hysteria and dissociation (Charcot, 1887; Janet, 1889). Janet hypothesized that emotions that are too powerful for the individual dissociate themselves from conscious experience and voluntary control.

In 1915, during World War I, the term "shell shock syndrome" was introduced to describe combat-related psychiatric, neurological, and somatic symptoms (Myers, 1940). The syndrome, frequently characterized by uncontrollable shaking spells of affected individuals (in German, these unfortunate individuals were referred to as "Schüttler," or "shakers"), was observed both in individuals experiencing direct, combat-related injury as well as in those in whom the extreme stress of combat was sufficient to explain the symptom development. Because no neurological basis for these symptoms could be found in the majority of cases, the military and medical establishment frequently suspected that these individuals complained of symptoms in order to avoid deployment. In 1941, Kardiner proposed the concept of "physioneurosis" for war trauma-related psychiatric and somatic symptoms, emphasizing the integral part of trauma-related somatic symptoms (Kardiner, 1941). Other terms popular in describing these symptoms at the time were "combat fatigue" and "combat exhaustion," emphasizing the prominent role of fatigue in the reported symptom complex. Drawing on Stekel's earlier use of the term "somatization,"

Menninger introduced the concept of "somatization reaction" to describe the great frequency and variety of medically unexplained somatic symptoms among veterans, including the cardiovascular, genitourinary, skin, and gastrointestinal systems (Menninger, 1947). Similar to Janet's concept of somatic expression of uncontrollable emotions, he hypothesized that "the anxiety is relieved in such reactions by channeling the originating impulses through the ANS into visceral organ symptoms and complaints." Following Selye and Fortier's introduction of the "general adaptation syndrome," an increasing number of authors identified alterations in different outputs of the central stress system, for example, in different effector subsystems of the EMS such as the ANS, HPA axis, and ascending arousal systems (reviewed in Lamprecht & Sack, 2002).

In summary, physicians and psychiatrists have recognized the association of various types of traumatic experience with an increased frequency of somatic, medically unexplained symptoms for more than 100 years. Reported symptoms and syndromes suggest involvement of most viscera and organ systems. Even though differences in symptom patterns were described, the cluster of fatigue, musculoskeletal symptoms, and sleep disturbances appears to show significant consistency over time. Theories to explain trauma-related, functional somatic symptoms have gradually evolved from psychoanalytic concepts to models viewing somatic symptoms as persistent bodily consequences of intense emotions, with or without conscious awareness of such emotions.

FUNCTIONAL SYMPTOMS FOLLOWING TRAUMATIC STRESS

Depending on the nature of the trauma (combat, prisoner of war, rape) and the social context in which it occurs, the pattern of trauma- and PTSD-related illness varies. For example, the pattern of symptoms reported by individuals involved in the first Persian Gulf War appears to be different from that of veterans of the Vietnam War and the second Persian Gulf War: While direct trauma-related injury was much more frequent in the latter two conflicts, somatoform symptoms (referred to as Gulf War Related Syndromes) were more common following the first Persian Gulf War, and these symptoms were frequently not associated with a diagnosis of PTSD.

Even though an increased incidence of organic disease following different traumatic events has been reported (reviewed in Friedman & Schnurr, 1995), the relationship of trauma with somatic manifestations has been studied primarily in terms of so-called functional, somatoform, or medically unexplained disorders (e.g., symptoms without a currently identifiable organic cause), including musculoskeletal syndromes (such as FM), fatigue, functional gastrointestinal disorders (such as IBS), gynecological and urological syndromes (such as chronic pelvic pain and interstitial

TABLE 7.1. *Most Frequent Complaints Among the 19,721 Veterans on the Revised Persian Gulf Registry*

Complaints	Frequency	Percentage[a]
Loss of memory and other general symptoms	5,794	29.4
Headache	5,204	26.4
Fatigue	4,639	23.5
Skin rash	4,574	23.2
Muscle/joint pain	4,096	20.8
Sleep disturbances	2,553	12.9
Diarrhea and other GI symptoms	2,352	11.9
Shortness of breath	2,050	10.4
Chest pain	1,041	5.3
Choking sensitivity	939	4.8
Abdominal pain	916	4.6
Other symptoms involving skin and integumentary tissue	692	3.5
Cough	676	3.4
No complaint	1,527	7.7

[a] *Note:* Percentage of 19,721 veterans.

Source: Data as of February 1999, prepared by the VA Environmental Epidemiology Service. Reprinted from VA EES (2002) with permission.

cystitis), and cardiovascular syndromes (such as noncardiac chest pain). This chapter will focus on the functional syndromes commonly associated with PTSD, in particular those characterized by pain and discomfort.

Self-Reported Symptoms

A large literature exists concerning recent war veterans, particularly those returning from Vietnam (reviewed in Friedman & Schnurr, 1995) and the first Gulf War (reviewed in Committee on Identifying Effective Treatments for Gulf War Veterans' Health Problems & Board on Health Promotion and Disease Prevention, 2001; Department of Veterans Affairs Employee Education System [VA EES], 2002; Tables 7.1 and 7.2). In general, the findings support the following concepts:

1. Veterans with a history of war-zone exposure reported poorer health and more health problems relative to control groups (veterans, civilians, twins not exposed to war-zone stress) (Kulka, Fairbank, Jordan, & Weiss, 1990). Reported symptoms include those related to the musculoskeletal, cardiovascular, gastrointestinal, dermatological, and ophthalmological systems.
2. Whenever medical examinations were performed, symptom reporting of various medical problems was rarely associated with

TABLE 7.2. *Distribution of Diagnoses for the 19,721 Veterans on the Revised Persian Gulf Registry*

Diagnosis	Number	Percentage
Musculoskeletal and connective tissue	7,286	36.9
Mental disorders	6,887	34.9
Skin and subcutaneous tissue	3,813	19.3
Respiratory system	3,626	18.4
Digestive system	3,451	17.5
Nervous system	3,441	17.4
Circulatory system	2,083	10.6
Injury and poisoning	2,020	10.2
Infectious diseases	1,785	9.1
Genitourinary system	1,126	5.7
Neoplasm (malignant)	149	0.8
No medical diagnosis	4,664	23.6

Source: Data as of February 1999, prepared by the VA Environmental Epidemiology Service. Reprinted from VA EES (2002) with permission.

detectable organic abnormalities, confirming historical reports of the predominance of medically unexplained symptomatology (Centers for Disease Control [CDC], 1988).

3. The severity of the experienced trauma is typically associated with increased number and severity of medical symptoms.
4. The prevalence of different types of symptoms and comorbidity with PTSD appears to vary with different types of traumatic stress.

In addition to combat-related trauma, a series of reports exist on the role of sexual trauma in the development of somatic symptoms, including gastrointestinal symptoms, chronic abdominal pain, recurrent headaches, and dysuria (Drossman et al., 1990; Felitti, 1991; Kimerling & Calhoun, 1994; Koss, Woodruff, & Koss, 1990; Rapkin, Kames, Darke, Stampler, & Naliboff, 1990; Rimsza, Berg, & Locke, 1988; Schei, 1991; Toomey, Hernandez, Gittelman, & Hulka, 1993; Waigandt, Wallace, Phelps, & Miller, 1990; Walker et al., 1992). These findings can be summarized as follows:

1. Women who have a history of sexual victimization are more likely than control subjects, without such a history, to report multiple somatic symptoms and syndromes and poorer health status.
2. A history of sexual abuse, in particular when experienced during childhood, may be more likely to result in adult chronic pelvic pain symptoms (Drossman et al., 1990; Schei, 1991; Toomey, Hernandez, Gittelman, & Hulka, 1993; Walker et al., 1992) and IBS (Felitti, 1991; Rimsza, Berg & Locke, 1988).

3. Some studies suggest that there is a close relationship between sexual, physical, and verbal abuse (Talley, Boyce, & Jones, 1998) and that it is the context of a "risky family" rather than the specifics of the trauma that is the primary risk factor for adult symptoms (Reppetti, Taylor, & Seeman, 2002).

4. Similar to findings in combat-related somatic syndromes, studies employing comprehensive medical examinations of women who have experienced sexual abuse are usually unable to find physical abnormalities to explain the reported symptoms.

There are also reports suggesting negative health outcomes and exacerbation of previously existing somatic symptoms in individuals having experienced natural disasters, such as earthquakes and hurricanes (Armenian, Melkonian, & Hovanesian, 1998; Kodama et al., 1999; Lutgendorf et al., 1995).

Healthcare Utilization

Published reports about differences in healthcare utilization by individuals exposed to trauma related to prisoner of war status (Beebe, 1975; Page, National Research Council [U.S.], Medical Follow-up Agency, & Institute of Medicine [U.S.], 1992), concentration camp survivors (Eitinger, 1973), sexual abuse (Drossman et al., 1990; Felitti, 1991; Kimerling & Calhoun, 1994; Waigandt et al., 1990), exposure to violent crime (Bergman & Brismar, 1991; Koss et al., 1990; Norris, Kaniasty, & Scheer, 1990), and natural disasters (Abrahams, Price, Whitlock, & Williams, 1976; Adams & Adams, 1984; Bennet, 1970), compared to a control population without exposure, support the following statements:

1. Victims of different types of trauma show increased utilization of the medical, as well as mental, healthcare system.

2. Increased utilization may result in an increased number of outpatient visits, more frequent and longer hospitalization periods, as well as a greater frequency of lifetime surgeries.

3. The severity of the trauma is typically associated with greater utilization rates.

The Relationship of Functional Somatic Syndromes to PTSD

There is a close relationship between combat-related PTSD, poor health outcomes, and somatic symptoms. For example, an increased prevalence of gastrointestinal symptoms in PTSD has been reported in prisoners of war, Vietnam combat veterans (Fass, Kagan, Fullerton, & Mayer, 1995; Irwin et al., 1996), and former hostages (Stam, Akkermans, & Wiegant, 1997). The reported increase in IBS prevalence in women with sexual abuse is highest in those who were raped at gunpoint or perceived a life threat, meeting PTSD criteria (Drossman et al., 1990). This relationship appears to be true for both medically unexplained symptoms as well as for organic morbidity, such as cardiovascular disease, even though the number of publications is more extensive for the latter (Friedman & Schnurr, 1995). Based on their analyses of existing data, the authors suggested that PTSD plays a prominent role in the mediation between trauma exposure and perceived and actual physical health. However, it has to be kept in mind that very similar somatic symptoms are commonly reported by individuals in the general population, as well as by patients in primary care and most medical specialties, for example, in patient populations without a history of trauma or without comorbid PTSD.

Although many individuals exposed to combat or to natural disasters may meet the criteria for PTSD, the great majority of patients developing the same symptoms and syndromes do not have a history of trauma; for example, Gulf War I–related illnesses have been found among those awaiting deployment (VA EES, 2002). Similarly, IBS, FM, headaches, and chronic fatigue syndrome (which are among the syndromes making up the group of Gulf War–related conditions) are some of the most common diagnoses made by primary care physicians and various subspecialties in the general population.

HOW ARE STRESSORS TRANSLATED INTO SOMATIC SYMPTOMS?

The close relationship of emotions and physical responses has been recognized in many healing traditions (Tan, Tillisch, & Mayer, 2004). The role of distinctive bodily responses in the expression of different emotions has been emphasized by LeDoux (1996), whereas Damasio (1994) and Craig (2002) have emphasized the importance of afferent feedback from these bodily responses (e.g., the information about the state of the body) for cognitive and emotional function. Although the traditional concept of stress and trauma has focused on the feelings, thoughts, and memories reported by individuals in association with stressful and traumatic life events, major advances in this area have occurred through examining the biological mechanisms that mediate the detrimental effect of life events on health and on the development of somatic symptoms (McEwen, 1998).

The response to stress is generated by a network of brain structures which include cortical, subcortical, and brainstem components (for review, see Mayer, 2000b). The core of the stress system comprises subregions of the hypothalamus (i.e., the paraventricular nucleus), amygdala, and periaqueductal gray. This basic stress circuit receives input from visceral and somatic afferents and from cortical structures. While afferent input from the periphery informs the brain about a wide range of homeostatic parameters (temperature, blood oxygen levels, pH, food intake), cortical inputs to the central stress system inform the brain about environmental events and threats. In turn, the integrative stress circuit provides outputs to the pituitary and to pontomedullary nuclei, which mediate the neuroendocrine and the autonomic and pain modulatory output to the body, respectively (Bandler, Price, & Keay, 2000; LeDoux, 1996; Sawchenko, Li, & Ericsson, 2000).

An important circuit in the stress response involves reciprocal interactions between corticotropin-releasing factor (CRF) positive neurons of the amygdaloid complex, including the bed nucleus of the stria terminalis, and catecholaminergic neurons of the locus coeruleus complex (Chrousos, 1995; Plotsky, Cunningham, & Widmaier, 1989; Smith et al., 1998; Taché, Martinez, Million, & Rivier, 1999; Taché & Moennikes, 1993; Timpl et al., 1998; Valentino, Miselis, & Pavcovich, 1999). Outputs from the central nucleus of the amygdala, the bed nucleus of the stria terminalis, and the hypothalamus can stimulate noradrenergic outputs from the locus coeruleus to the medial prefrontal cortex, insula, and dorsal anterior cingulate cortex, which in turn project back to the amygdala, forming a feedforward system associated with increased arousal, as well as ANS and HPA axis responses. Circulating glucocorticoids contribute to this feedforward system in the amygdala, but exert inhibitory control via central glucocorticoid receptors located in the hippocampus and in the medial prefrontal cortex (Sternberg, Chrousos, & Gold, 1992). The parallel outputs of this circuit are called the EMS, and its principal pathways are summarized in Figure 7.1 (Mayer, 2000a).

FACTORS INFLUENCING THE RESPONSIVENESS OF THE EMS

As emphasized by McEwen (1998) and LeDoux (1996), the activation of different subcircuits of the EMS in response to real or perceived perturbations of homeostasis serves adaptive functions. Similarly, differences in individual EMS circuits programming the organism to be more vigilant, more aggressive, or more affiliative may be highly adaptive to particular environmental conditions. As suggested by Taylor et al. (2000), the adaptive value of a particular EMS pattern may also be contingent on the sex of the individual. Thus, when challenged with an aggressor, a "fight or flight" response pattern may be most useful for males, whereas a "tend and befriend" pattern may be more adaptive for females, being primarily responsible for the young. The responsiveness and output pattern of the EMS are likely to be under partial genetic control (Eley & Plomin, 1997; Glowa, Sternberg, & Gold, 1992) but show considerable plasticity in response to early life events (Ladd et al., 2000) and to certain types of pathological stress (Flügge, 1996; Fuchs & Fluegge, 1995).

Studies in different patient populations have demonstrated that the quality of the early family environment can serve as a major source of stress vulnerability in later life. Individuals who are the victims of physical, emotional, or sexual abuse are at considerably greater risk for anxiety disorders and depression in later life (Bifulco, Brown, & Adler, 1991; Brown & Anderson, 1993; Hammen, Davila, Brown, Ellicott, & Gitlin, 1992; McCauley et al., 1997; Wissow, 1995). Other less dramatic influences in early life, such as cold and distant parent–child relationships and divorce of the parents or death of the mother before age 10, have also been associated with such enhanced vulnerability later in life (Canetti, Bachar, Galili-Weisstub, De-Nour, & Shalev, 1997; Parker, 1981; Russak & Schwartz, 1997). The enhanced vulnerability is not limited to affective disorders, but extends to a greater risk of chronic illness in general, including a greater risk for development of IBS (Hill & Blendis, 1967; Hislop, 1979; Lowman, Drossman, Cramer, & McKee, 1987). It has been suggested that this influence of early life events is mediated in part by parental influences on the development of neural systems that underlie the expression of behavioral, autonomic, and neuroendocrine responses to stress (Coplan et al., 1996; De Bellis et al., 1994; Francis & Meaney, 1999; Heim, Owens, Plotsky, & Nemeroff, 1997; Meaney et al., 1996; see Bagot et al., this volume).

Studies in animals and men have clearly demonstrated that certain types of pathological stress can alter the responsiveness of feedback systems by downregulation of pre- and/or postsynaptic receptors (adrenergic, serotonergic, and glucocorticoid receptors; Flügge, 1996; Fuchs & Fluegge, 1995) and, in the most severe forms, by structural changes in certain brain regions (Bremner, Licinio, et al., 1997; Fuchs, Uno, & Fluegge, 1995; see Bremner, this volume). Thus, pathological stress can not only activate but also fundamentally change the responsiveness and output of the central stress circuits. These alterations could affect the individual output pathways of the general stress response differentially and in different directions (for example, increase or decrease specific sympathetic outputs, increase or decrease certain vagal outputs, up- or downregulate the HPA axis, and change pain perception). Some of the best characterized alterations in this central adaptation to pathological stress are an increase in CRF synthesis and secretion (Bremner, Licinio, et al., 1997; Imaki, Nahan, Sawchenko, & Vale, 1991; Owens & Nemeroff, 1993), an increase in the activity and sensitivity of central noradrenergic systems (Bremner, Innis, et al., 1997; Curtis, Pavcovich, & Valentino, 1995; Curtis, Pavcovich, & Valentino, 1999; Ladd et al., 2000; Reche & Buffington, 1998), and either a downregulation or a sensitization of glucocorticoid receptors and ACTH release (Yehuda, Giller, Levengood, Southwick, & Siever, 1995). As a consequence of these alterations in the central stress circuitry, secondary changes in receptor systems can occur in spinal (Pertovaara, 1993) or peripheral target cells of the output systems (Yehuda, Boisonaeau, Mason, & Giller, 1993). Thus, in cases of pathological stress resulting in permanent changes in the central stress circuitry, lifelong changes in *peripheral* receptor systems may also be expected. Finally, changes in mood and affect associated with alterations in the stress response have been reported (Gold, Goodwin, & Chrousos, 1988; McEwen, 1998).

Autonomic Nervous System Response

The classical description of the fight or flight response by Cannon (1929) focused on the stereotypic and global activation of the SNS. However, despite the integrated nature of the response to different stressors, there is considerable variability in the specifics of the peripheral output. At the level of the paraventricular nucleus of the hypothalamus, the cells that give rise to major classes of visceromotor projections are separate, suggesting that they are not necessarily called into play in a stereotyped "all or none" manner, but rather that they may be differentially recruited (Swanson & Kuypers, 1980). Evidence supports a functionally distinct branch of the SNS dedicated specifically to immune modulation (Felten, 2000; Jänig & Habler, 2000). Stress-related increases in plasma epinephrine (and glucocorticoids) play an important role in the facilitation of memory in amygdala–hippocampal circuits, including in the development of conditioned fear (Cahill, Prins, Weber, & McGaugh, 1994). Epinephrine-stimulated vagal feedback has also been implicated in the activation of endogenous pain modulation circuits (Fillingim & Maixner, 1995).

In addition to activation of sympathetic pathways, various acute stressors produce a characteristic biphasic pattern of parasympathetic activation, consisting of vagal inhibition and activation of sacral parasympathetic output (Martinez, Rivier, Wang, & Taché, 1997). Similar to the different subclasses of central sympathetic neurons, subpopulations of function- and target-specific vagal motor neurons have been identified. Pathological stress has also been associated with persistent decreases in cardiovagal tone and in cardiovagal responsiveness to stress (Musselman & Nemeroff, 2000; Verrier & Mittleman, 2000).

HPA Axis

The HPA axis is a neuroendocrine response system that is activated by physical and psychological stressors and ultimately results in the release of cortisol (or other glucocorticoids) into the bloodstream. The system was initially understood to increase energy in situations of stress by enhancing the metabolism of protein and fat to increase blood glucose. However, a range of other adaptive effects of increased plasma glucocorticoids has been identified. For example, peripheral glucocorticoids act in parallel with the SNS to suppress the inflammatory response. In addition, stress-induced HPA axis activation is normally regulated by feedback mediated by glucocorticoid receptors in brain regions including the hippocampus and medial prefrontal cortex (McEwen, 1995; Sapolsky, Krey, & McEwen, 1984; see Figure 7.1). This feedback mechanism in response to acute stress can be modified in various chronic disease states. Hyperactivity of the HPA axis manifesting as hypercortisolism, as seen in certain forms of depression, is a classic example of a generalized stress response that has escaped its usual counterregulation (Gold, Goodwin, & Chrousos, 1988). Similar HPA hyperactivity has also been reported in anorexia nervosa (Gold et al., 1986), panic disorder (Gold, Pigot, Kling, Kalogeras, & Chrousos, 1988), and after sexual abuse (De Bellis et al., 1994). A decrease in glucocorticoid receptor expression has been observed in animal models of chronic stress (Jacobson & Sapolsky, 1991) and in adult animals exposed to perinatal stress (Ladd et al., 2000). A decrease in central glucocorticoid receptors may be secondary to a reversible downregulation of the receptor or a permanent destruction of glucocorticoid-containing brain regions (Bremner et al., 1995; Bremner, Licinio, et al., 1997; McEwen, 2000).

A different pattern of stress-induced HPA dysregulation has been described in patients with PTSD (Yehuda et al., 1995), chronic fatigue syndrome (Sternberg, 1993), FM (Crofford et al., 1994), and possibly IBS (Munakata et al., 1998). In some of these populations there is evidence for a highly sensitized HPA axis, characterized by normal or decreased basal cortisol levels and exaggerated HPA axis response to certain stressors. Other findings in these patient populations include an increased number of lymphocyte glucocorticoid receptors, a greater suppression of cortisol to dexamethasone, and a sensitized pituitary gland (Yehuda et al., 1995). Thus, in addition to the classic pattern of increased cortisol levels in response to acute stress, there appears to be a pattern characterized by diminished basal cortisol levels as a result of stronger negative feedback inhibition in certain disorders associated with pathological stress. This diminished cortisol response may be associated with increased central CRF responses to stress (Bremner, Innis, et al., 1997). The different patterns of HPA axis dysregulation may be related to genetic factors and/or develop in response to different patterns of pathological stress (e.g., chronicity, severity).

Modulation of Visceral and Somatic Pain Perception

Although not generally discussed in the context of classic stress responses, modulation of perceptual responses to sensory stimuli originating in the viscera, the musculoskeletal system, or the environment is an integral component of adaptation to stress. In general, the anticipation of potentially harmful stimuli and the related increase in vigilance and attention are associated with an increase of sensitivity in different sensory modalities, including the visual, auditory, and olfactory system. This increase in sensitivity is also observed in the somatosensory system (Porreca, Ossipov, & Gebhart, 2002). On the other hand, the actual experience of noxious stimuli or severe stress is sometimes characterized by a decrease in the sensitivity to environmental stimuli, including a powerful inhibition of pain experience. Both clinical and animal experimental data strongly support the concept of stress- and fear-induced analgesia resulting in decreased somatic pain perception (Basbaum & Fields, 1978; Fanselow, 1986). Stress-induced analgesia is mediated by descending pain inhibitory pathways and, depending on the nature and severity of the stressor, is partially mediated by opioidergic, noradrenergic, glutaminergic, and serotonergic systems (Harris & Feinmann, 1990).

Recent evidence suggests that this stress-induced decrease in somatic pain sensitivity can be accompanied by a stress-induced *increase* in visceral pain sensitivity (Bradesi, Schwetz, McRoberts, Ohning, & Mayer, 2003; Coutinho, Miller, Plotsky, & Mayer, 1999). Certain types of stressor and anxiety states can also be associated with an increase in somatic pain sensitivity (Porreca et al., 2002). For example, Duncan and colleagues have demonstrated that the anticipation of pain in nonhuman primates can activate the same dorsal horn neurons normally activated by actual pain, providing a possible neurobiological basis for the amplification of pain during an anticipated harmful stimulus (Duncan, Bushnell, Bates, & Dubner, 1987). Immediately after injury, pain inhibitory pathways are activated. One way to explain these observations is that both pain facilitatory and inhibitory systems are activated simultaneously in response to stress, the effect at any point in time being determined by the relative contribution of these opposing influences (Porreca et al., 2002; Wei, Dubner, & Ren, 1999). In addition to these phasically responding pain modulation systems, there are tonic pain modulatory influences (including descending serotonergic systems) which bias the system in accordance with the general homeostatic state of the organism (Stables, Kennan, & Gore, 1998).

In addition to the activation of descending systems from the brainstem to the spinal cord, there are ascending systems originating in monoaminergic brainstem nuclei that may contribute to stress-induced modulation of perception of visceral and somatic stimuli. Noradrenergic, serotonergic, and cholinergic neurons that project to cortical (prefrontal cortex) and subcortical regions (including the paraventricular nucleus, amygdala, hippocampus, and nucleus tractus solitarius) play an important role in emotional arousal, attention, and vigilance toward sensory stimuli.

STRESS-RELATED ALTERATIONS OF EMS OUTPUTS IN
THE DEVELOPMENT OF FUNCTIONAL GI SYNDROMES

In this section, I will summarize selected reports of altered autonomic, neuroendocrine, and endogenous sensory modulation in IBS patients, viewing these alterations as changes not in isolation but as alterations in the integrated response to stressors described in Figure 7.2. Analogous alterations, albeit in different patterns, may underlie symptoms in FM and in other less common somatic syndromes.

Changes in ANS Responses

In both healthy humans and animals, stressors have been shown to result in a slowing of gastric emptying (Malagelada, 1991), an increase in distal colonic motility (Welgan, Meshkinpour, & Beeler, 1988; Welgan, Meshkinpour, & Hoehler, 1985), and an acceleration of intestinal transit (Ditto, Miller, & Barr, 1998; Martinez et al., 1997). In the most common functional gastrointestinal disorders, IBS and functional dyspepsia, alterations of autonomic responsiveness are likely to play a role in altered bowel habits and alterations in gastric emptying, respectively. Evidence for such alterations in IBS includes increased responses of distal colonic motility in response to laboratory stress (Welgan et al., 1988) and possibly food intake (Niederau, Faber, & Karaus, 1992), and delayed gastric emptying in a subset of patients (Evans, Bak, Shuter, Hoschl, & Kellow, 1997). A model of IBS, taking into account altered autonomic regulation of gastric and distal colonic function and based on an upregulation of CRF-containing neurons in Barrington's nucleus (part of the locus coeruleus complex), has been proposed by Valentino and coworkers (1999).

There is evidence that decreased cardiovagal tone is present in certain patients with functional dyspepsia (Haug et al., 1994; Hausken et al., 1993) and in subsets of patients with IBS (Hausken et al., 1993; Heitkemper et al., 1998). Recent evidence from patients with functional constipation suggests that despite the heterogeneity of vagal motor neurons, cardiovagal tone, vagal regulation of colonic transit, and vagal regulation of colonic mucosal blood flow may all be reduced in parallel (Emmanuel & Kamm, 1999).

HPA Axis Changes

Alterations in HPA axis function have been demonstrated in diarrhea-predominant IBS patients who showed decreased 24-hr plasma cortisols, blunted cortisol responses, and normal or elevated ACTH responses to noxious rectosigmoid distension (Chang et al., 2005). In contrast, Heitkemper reported that urine cortisol levels obtained immediately after rising were significantly higher in IBS women as compared to control women (Heitkemper et al., 1996). Even though HPA axis responses have not been thoroughly characterized in functional gastrointestinal disorder patients, these preliminary findings suggest the pattern of sensitized glucocorticoid feedback also reported in victims of abuse (Heim et al., 1999), in FM, and in chronic fatigue syndrome (Stratakis & Chrousos, 1995). There is significant overlap in the epidemiology of all these conditions with IBS (Drossman, Creed, & Fava, 1995; Drossman et al., 1990; Moldofsky & Franklin, 1993;

Triadafilopoulos, Simms, & Goldenberg, 1991; Veale, Kavanagh, Fielding, & Fitzgerald, 1991). It remains to be determined whether these HPA axis changes are an epiphenomenon or play a role in symptom generation and pathophysiology of these syndromes.

Changes in Pain Modulation

Suggestive evidence for alterations in stress-induced modulation of viscerosomatic sensitivity comes from human and animal studies. In most published studies IBS patients show cutaneous hypoalgesia (Chang, Mayer, Johnson, FitzGerald, & Naliboff, 2000; Cook, Van Eeden, & Collins, 1987) combined with visceral hypersensitivity (Mayer, Naliboff, & Munakata, 2000), a similar pattern seen in the rat in response to psychological stressors (Coutinho et al., 1999). However, others have reported somatic (lower extremity) thermal hyperalgesia in IBS patients (Verne, Robinson, & Price, 2001), and Giamberardino and colleagues have provided evidence for deep muscular hyperalgesia in IBS patients (Giamberardino, Berkley, Iezzi, de Bigontina, & Vecchiet, 1995). Preliminary results using a psychological laboratory stress in healthy volunteers suggest a stress-induced increase in colonic or rectosigmoid sensitivity to distension (Delvaux, 1999; Dickhaus et al., 2003). Even though all published human studies are open to methodological criticism, they are consistent with reported findings in animals of a differential viscerosomatic pain modulation.

Changes in Brain Activation

Functional brain imaging studies using $H_2{}^{15}O$ positron emission tomography (PET) have shown differences in regional brain activation between IBS patients and healthy control subjects (Naliboff et al., 2000) and between patients with functional (IBS) and inflammatory (mild ulcerative colitis) bowel disease (Chang et al., 2004). In response to aversive visceral stimuli or to anticipation of such stimuli, nonconstipated IBS patients showed greater activation of limbic and paralimbic regions, including the dorsal anterior cingulate cortex and the dorsomedial prefrontal cortex, whereas healthy controls and ulcerative colitis patients showed greater activation of the periaqueductal gray region. Greater activation of the dorsal anterior cingulate cortex has also been reported by others (Mertz et al., 2000). Although these findings need to be confirmed in additional patient samples, they are consistent with the hypothesis that IBS patients activate primarily pain amplification networks, whereas the other two groups, who do not show visceral hypersensitivity, activate brain regions concerned with pain inhibition (periaqueductal gray).

In summary, IBS patients present with a pattern consistent with enhanced stress responsiveness manifested by predicted autonomic and pain modulatory responses and a sensitized glucocorticoid feedback. This response pattern is associated with changes in brain activity in response to the anticipation or experience of aversive visceral stimuli. The blunting of the HPA axis may precede the onset of IBS symptoms and may predispose individuals to develop IBS after an infection. The fact that up to 40% of IBS patients show evidence for increased anxiety (Creed, 1999) suggests a top-down model in which the alterations in the central stress circuits of predisposed individuals are triggered by stressors and play a primary role in pathophysiology.

ANIMAL MODELS OF ENHANCED VULNERABILITY
TO STRESSFUL EVENTS

Considerable progress has been made in the development of different types of animal models of enhanced stress responsiveness (reviewed in Kalin, 1993; Ladd et al., 2000; Mayer & Collins, 2002). In addition to their usefulness for psychiatric research, these models may allow better understanding of the mechanisms underlying some individuals' increased vulnerability to develop somatic symptoms in response to traumatic stress. In addition, they may help in the development of pharmacologic therapies for trauma-related somatic syndromes, such as novel antidepressants and centrally acting drugs (e.g., CRF receptor antagonists).

Interference with the interaction between rat dams and their litter by daily separation of the litter from their dams during postnatal Days 4–18 will result in an alteration of maternal behavior (Ladd et al., 2000). The resulting neonatal stress, in form of compromised mother–infant interaction, results in permanent changes in the central nervous systems of the adult rats, which has been documented at the level of gene expression, neurochemistry, electrophysiology, and morphology (Bakshi & Kalin, 2000; Caldji, Diorio, & Meaney, 2000; Kaufman, Plotsky, Nemeroff, & Charney, 2000; Ladd et al., 2000). A key component of the model is the compromised ability to restrain the synthesis and release of CRF in response to acute psychological stressors (Kaufman, Plotsky, Nemeroff, & Charney, 2000). We have demonstrated that maternally separated rats also show evidence of alterations in stress-induced visceral and somatic pain sensitivity consistent with compromised stress-induced engagement of opioid systems. In addition, colonic motor function in response to stress is enhanced in these animals (Coutinho, Sablad, Miller, et al., 2000; Coutinho et al., 1999; Coutinho, Sablad, Marvizon, et al., 2000; Schwetz et al., 2005). The stress-induced visceral hyperalgesia in adult animals with a history of maternal neonatal separation is abolished by central administration of a CRF_1 receptor antagonist (Million et al., 2006; Schwetz et al., 2005).

The demonstration of enhanced anxiety-like behaviors, hypervigilance, increased vulnerability to anhedonia under stress, alterations in the HPA axis responsiveness, stress-induced visceral hyperalgesia, and enhanced stress-induced colonic motility in adult animals give this model both face and construct validity for enhanced stress responsiveness as a vulnerability factor for IBS as well as for affective disorders, including PTSD. The increased prevalence of functional gastrointestinal symptoms in patients with a history of early adverse life events (Drossman et al., 1990; Drossman, Talley, Leserman, Olden, & Barreiro, 1995; Scarinci, McDonald-Haile, Bradley, & Richter, 1994; Talley, Fett, Zinsmeister, & Melton, 1994; Walker, Katon, Roy-Byrne, Jemelka, & Russo, 1993) further contributes to the similarity of animal model and human condition.

CONCLUSION

The development of somatic symptoms and syndromes following a traumatic experience has been observed for centuries, but a neurobiological understanding of the mechanisms mediating the development of such symptoms has occurred only in the past few decades. The model of a trauma-related alteration in the responsiveness of central stress circuits and the EMS, thereby altering the modulation of various bodily functions and the perception of bodily events, has provided a theoretical framework for better understanding of such common syndromes as FM, IBS, and other chronic pain syndromes. Somatic symptoms with and without associated psychiatric symptoms can be viewed as a maladaptive response of homeostatic afferent systems, related ANS and HPA responses, and the emotional and cognitive responses to such "homeostatic emotions" (Craig, 2003). Such a model has also been useful in the creation of realistic animal models and in the development of both novel biological as well as psychological treatments for these debilitating disorders.

ACKNOWLEDGMENTS

The author would like to thank Teresa Olivas for invaluable editorial services. This work was supported in part by grants from the National Institutes of Health, DK 48351, DK 58173, P50 DK64539, and R24 AT002681.

References

Abrahams, M. J., Price, J., Whitlock, F. A., & Williams, G. (1976). The Brisbane floods, January 1974: Their impact on health. *Medical Journal of Australia, 2*, 936–939.

Adams, P. R., & Adams, G. R. (1984). Mount Saint Helens's ashfall: Evidence for a disaster stress reaction. *American Psychologist, 39*, 252–260.

Armenian, H. K., Melkonian, A. K., & Hovanesian, A. P. (1998). Long term mortality and morbidity related to degree of damage following the 1998 earthquake in Armenia. *American Journal of Epidemiology, 148*, 1077–1084.

Bakshi, V. P., & Kalin, N. H. (2000). Corticotropin-releasing hormone and animal models of anxiety: Gene-environment interactions. *Biological Psychiatry, 48*, 1175–1198.

Bandler, R., Price, J. L., & Keay, K. A. (2000). Brain mediation of active and passive emotional coping. In E. A. Mayer & C. B. Saper (Eds.), *Progress in brain research: Vol. 122. The biological basis for mind body interactions* (pp. 333–349). Amsterdam: Elsevier Science.

Basbaum, A. I., & Fields, H. L. (1978). Endogenous pain control mechanisms: Review and hypothesis. *Annals of Neurology, 4*, 451–462.

Beebe, G. W. (1975). Follow-up studies of World War II and Korean War prisoners, II: Morbidity, disability, and maladjustments. *American Journal of Epidemiology, 101*, 400–422.

Bennet, G. (1970). Bristol floods 1968. Controlled survey of effects on health of local community disaster. *British Medical Journal, 3*, 454–458.

Bergman, B., & Brismar, B. (1991). A 5-year follow-up study of 117 battered women. *American Journal of Public Health, 81*, 1486–1489.

Bifulco, A., Brown, G. W., & Adler, Z. (1991). Early sexual abuse and clinical depression in adult life. *British Journal of Psychiatry, 159*, 115–122.

Bradesi, S., Schwetz, I., McRoberts, J., Ohning, G., & Mayer, E. A. (2003). Chronic water avoidance stress induces visceral hypersensitivity in male Wistar rats. *Gastroenterology, 124*, A671.

Bremner, J. D., Innis, R. B., Ng, C. K., Staib, L. H., Salomon, R. M., Bronen, R. A., et al. (1997). Positron emission tomography measurement of cerebral metabolic correlates of yohimbine administration in combat-related posttraumatic stress disorder. *Archives of General Psychiatry, 54*, 246–254.

Bremner, J. D., Licinio, J., Darnell, A., Krystal, J. H., Owens, M. J., Southwick, S. M., et al. (1997). Elevated CSF corticotropin-releasing factor concentrations in posttraumatic stress disorder. *American Journal of Psychiatry, 154*, 624–629.

Bremner, J. D., Randall, P., Scott, T. M., Bronen, R. A., Scibyl, J. P., Southwick, S. M., et al. (1995). MRI-based measurement of hippocampal volume in patients with combat-related posttraumatic stress disorder. *American Journal of Psychiatry, 152*, 973–981.

Brown, G. R., & Anderson, B. (1993). Psychiatric morbidity in adult inpatients with childhood histories of sexual and physical abuse. *American Journal of Psychiatry, 148*, 55–61.

Cahill, L., Prins, B., Weber, M., & McGaugh, J. L. (1994). β-Adrenergic activation and memory for emotional events. *Nature, 371*, 702–704.

Caldji, C., Diorio, J., & Meaney, M. J. (2000). Variations in maternal care in infancy regulate the development of stress reactivity. *Biological Psychiatry, 48*, 1164–1174.

Campbell, L. C., Clauw, D. J., & Keefe, F. J. (2003). Persistant pain and depression: A biopsychosocial perspective. *Biological Psychiatry, 54*, 399–409.

Canetti, L., Bachar, E., Galili-Weisstub, E., De-Nour, A. K., & Shalev, A. Y. (1997). Parental bonding and mental health in adolescence. *Adolescence, 32*, 381–394.

Cannon, W. B. (1929). Organization for physiological homeostasis. *Physiological Reviews, 9*, 399–431.

Centers for Disease Control. (1988). Health status of Vietnam veterans. III. Reproductive outcomes and child health. The Center for Disease Control Vietnam Experience Study. *Journal of the American Medical Association*, *259*, 2715–2719.

Chang, L., Berman, S. M., Suyenobu, B., Gordon, W. A., Mandelkern, M. A., Naliboff, B. D., et al. (2004). Differences in brain responses to rectal distension between patients with inflammatory and functional GI disorders. *Gastroenterology*, *126*, A106.

Chang, L., Mayer, E. A., Johnson, T., FitzGerald, L., & Naliboff, B. (2000). Differences in somatic perception in female patients with irritable bowel syndrome with and without fibromyalgia. *Pain*, *84*, 297–307.

Chang, L., Sundaresh, S., Baldi, P., Licudine, A., Mayer, M., Vuong, T., et al. (2005). Dysregulation of basal circadian and pulsatile secretion of hypothalamic-pituitary-adrenal (HPA) axis in irritable bowel syndrome and fibromyalgia. *Gastroenterology*, *128*, A620–A621.

Charcot, J. M. (1887). *Leçons sur les maladies du système nerveux, faites à la Salpêtrière*. Paris: Delahaye et Lecrosnier.

Chrousos, G. P. (1995). The hypothalamic–pituitary–adrenal axis and immune-mediated inflammation. *New England Journal of Medicine*, *332*, 1351–1362.

Committee on Identifying Effective Treatments for Gulf War Veterans' Health Problems & Board on Health Promotion and Disease Prevention. (2001). *Gulf War veterans: Treating symptoms and syndromes*. Washington, DC: National Academy Press.

Cook, I. J., Van Eeden, A., & Collins, S. M. (1987). Patients with irritable bowel syndrome have greater pain tolerance than normal subjects. *Gastroenterology*, *93*, 727–733.

Coplan, J. D., Andrews, M. W., Rosenblum, L. A., Owens, M. J., Friedman, S., Gorman, J. M., et al. (1996). Persistent elevations of cerebrospinal fluid concentrations of corticotropin-releasing factor in adult nonhuman primates exposed to early-life stressors: Implications for the pathophysiology of mood and anxiety disorders. *Proceedings of the National Academy of Sciences of the United States of America*, *93*, 1619–1623.

Coutinho, S. V., Miller, J. C., Plotsky, P. M., & Mayer, E. A. (1999). Effect of perinatal stress on responses to colorectal distension in adult rats. *Society for Neuroscience Abstracts*, *25*, 687.

Coutinho, S. V., Sablad, M. R., Marvizon, J. C., Miller, J. C., Zhou, H., Bayati, A. I., et al. (2000). Role of endogenous opioids in stress-induced visceral hyperalgesia in the rat. *Society for Neuroscience Abstracts*, *26*, 2190.

Coutinho, S., Sablad, M., Miller, J., Zhou, H., Lam, A., Bayati, A., et al. (2000). Neonatal maternal separation results in stress-induced visceral hyperalgesia in adult rats: A new model for IBS. *Gastroenterology*, *118*, A637.

Craig, A. D. (2002). How do you feel? Interoception: The sense of the physiological condition of the body. *Nature Reviews Neuroscience*, *3*, 655–666.

Craig, A. D. (2003). A new view of pain as a homeostatic emotion. *Trends in Neurosciences*, *26*, 303–307.

Creed, F. (1999). The relationship between psychosocial parameters and outcome in the irritable bowel syndrome. *American Journal of Medicine*, *107*, 74S–80S.

Crofford, L. J., Pillemer, S. R., Kalogeras, K. T., Cash, J. M., Michelson, D., Kling, M. A., et al. (1994). Hypothalamic-pituitary-adrenal axis perturbations in patients with fibromyalgia. *Arthritis and Rheumatism, 37*, 1583–1592.

Curtis, A. L., Pavcovich, L. A., & Valentino, R. J. (1995). Previous stress alters corticotropin-releasing factor neurotransmission in the locus coeruleus. *Neuroscience, 65*, 541–550.

Curtis, A. L., Pavcovich, L. A., & Valentino, R. J. (1999). Long-term regulation of locus coeruleus sensitivity to corticotropin-releasing factor by swim stress. *Journal of Pharmacology and Experimental Therapeutics, 289*, 1211–1219.

da Costa, J. M. (1871). On irritable heart: A clinical study of a form of functional cardiac disorder and its consequences. *American Journal of Medical Sciences, 61*, 17–52.

Damasio, A. R. (1994). *Descartes' error*. New York: G. P. Putnam's Sons.

De Bellis, M., Chrousos, G. P., Dorn, L. D., Burke, L., Helmers, K., Kling, M. A., et al. (1994). Hypothalamic-pituitary-adrenal axis dysregulation in sexually abused girls. *Journal of Clinical Endocrinology & Metabolism, 78*, 249–255.

Delvaux, M. M. (1999). Stress and visceral perception. *Canadian Journal of Gastroenterology, 13* (Suppl A), 32A–36A.

Department of Veterans Affairs Employee Education System (VA EES). (2002). *A guide to Gulf War veteran's health: Independent study course 1997* (revised June 2001; released March 2002). Washington, DC: Author.

Diatchenko, L., Slade, G. D., Nackley, A. G., Bhalang, K., Sigurdsson, A., Belfer, I., et al. (2005). Genetic basis for individual variations in pain perception and the development of chronic pain condition. *Human Molecular Genetics, 14*, 135–143.

Dickhaus, B., Mayer, E. A., Firooz, N., Stains, J., Conde, F., Olivas, T. I., et al. (2003). Irritable bowel syndrome patients show enhanced modulation of visceral perception by auditory stress. *American Journal of Gastroenterology, 98*, 135–143.

Ditto, B., Miller, S. B., & Barr, R. G. (1998). A one-hour active coping stressor reduces small bowel transit time in healthy young adults. *Psychosomatic Medicine, 60*, 7–10.

Drossman, D. A., Creed, F. H., & Fava, G. A. (1995). Psychosocial aspects of the functional gastrointestinal disorders. *Gastroenterology International, 8*, 47–90.

Drossman, D. A., Leserman, J., Nachman, G., Li, Z. M., Gluck, H., Toomey, T. C., et al. (1990). Sexual and physical abuse in women with functional or organic gastrointestinal disorders. *Annals of Internal Medicine, 113*, 828–833.

Drossman, D. A., Talley, N. J., Leserman, J., Olden, K. W., & Barreiro, M. A. (1995). Sexual and physical abuse and gastrointestinal illness: Review and recommendations. *Annals of Internal Medicine, 123*, 782–794.

Duncan, G. H., Bushnell, M. C., Bates, R., & Dubner, R. (1987). Task-related responses of monkey medullary dorsal horn neurons. *Journal of Neurophysiology, 57*, 289–310.

Eitinger, L. (1973). A follow-up study of the Norwegian concentration camp survivors' mortality and morbidity. *Israel Annals of Psychiatry and Related Disciplines, 11*, 199–209.

Eley, T. C., & Plomin, R. (1997). Genetic analysis of emotionality. *Current Opinion in Neurobiology, 7*, 279–284.

Emmanuel, A. V., & Kamm, M. A. (1999). Laser Doppler measurement of rectal mucosal blood flow. *Gut, 45*, 64–69.

Erichsen, J. E. (1866). *On railway and other injuries of the nervous system*. London: Walton and Maberly.

Evans, P. R., Bak, Y. T., Shuter, B., Hoschl, R., & Kellow, J. E. (1997). Gastroparesis and small bowel dysmotility in irritable bowel syndrome. *Digestive Diseases and Sciences, 42*, 2087–2093.

Fanselow, M. S. (1986). Conditioned fear-induced opiate analgesia: A competing motivational state theory of stress analgesia. *Annals of the New York Academy of Sciences, 467*, 40–54.

Fass, R., Kagan, B., Fullerton, S., & Mayer, E. A. (1995). The prevalence of functional gastrointestinal symptoms in male patients with posttraumatic stress syndrome (PTSD). *Gastroenterology, 108*, A597.

Felitti, V. J. (1991). Long-term medical consequences of incest, rape, and molestation. *Southern Medical Journal, 84*, 328–331.

Felten, D. L. (2000). Neural influence on immune responses: Underlying suppositions and basic principles of neural-immune signaling. In E. A. Mayer & C. B. Saper (Eds.), *Progress in brain research: Vol. 122. The biological basis for mind body interactions* (pp. 381–389). Amsterdam: Elsevier Science.

Fillingim, R. B., & Maixner, W. (1995). Gender differences in the responses to noxious stimuli. *Pain Forum, 4*, 209–221.

Flügge, G. (1996). Alterations in the central nervous α_2-adrenoceptor system under chronic psychosocial stress. *Neuroscience, 75*, 187–196.

Francis, D. D., & Meaney, M. J. (1999). Maternal care and the development of stress responses. *Current Opinion in Neurobiology, 9*, 128–134.

Friedman, M. J., & Schnurr, P. P. (1995). The relationship between trauma, posttraumatic stress disorder, and physical health. In M. J. Friedman, D. S. Charney, & A. Y. Deutch (Eds.), *Neurobiological and clinical consequences of stress from normal adaptation to PTSD* (pp. 507–524). Philadelphia: Lippincott-Raven.

Fuchs, E., & Fluegge, G. (1995). Modulation of binding sites for corticotropin-releasing hormone by chronic psychosocial stress. *Psychoneuroendocrinology, 20*, 33–51.

Fuchs, E., Uno, H., & Fluegge, G. (1995). Chronic psychosocial stress induces morphological alterations in hippocampal pyramidal neurons of the tree shrew. *Brain Research, 673*, 275–282.

Giamberardino, M. A., Berkley, K. J., Iezzi, S., de Bigontina, P., & Vecchiet, L. (1995). Changes in skin and muscle sensitivity in dysmenorrheic vs. normal women as a function of body site and monthly cycle. *Society for Neuroscience Abstracts, 21*, 1638.

Glowa, J. R., Sternberg, E. M., & Gold, P. W. (1992). Differential behavioral response in LEW/N and F344/N rats: Effects of corticotropin releasing hormone. *Progress in Neuro-Psychopharmacology & Biological Psychiatry, 16*, 549–560.

Gold, P. W., Goodwin, F. K., & Chrousos, G. P. (1988). Clinical and biochemical manifestations of depression. Relation to the neurobiology of stress (part 2). *New England Journal of Medicine, 319*, 348–353.

Gold, P. W., Gwirtsman, H., Avgerinos, P., Nieman, L. K., Gallucci, W. T., Kaye, W., et al. (1986). Abnormal hypothalamic-pituitary-adrenal function in anorexia nervosa. Pathophysiological mechanisms in underweight and weight-corrected patients. *New England Journal of Medicine, 314*, 1335–1342.

Gold, P. W., Pigot, T. A., Kling, M. K., Kalogeras, P., & Chrousos, G. P. (1988). Basic and clinical studies with corticotropin releasing hormone: Implications for a possible role in panic disorder. *Psychiatric Clinics of North America, 11*, 327–334.

Hammen, C., Davila, J., Brown, G., Ellicott, A., & Gitlin, M. (1992). Psychiatric history and stress: Predictors of severity of unipolar depression. *Journal of Abnormal Psychology, 101*, 45–52.

Harris, M., & Feinmann, C. (1990). Psychosomatic disorders. In M. K. Mason & J. G. Jones (Eds.), *Oral manifestations of systemic disease*. Philadelphia: W. B. Saunders.

Haug, T. T., Svebak, S., Hausken, T., Wilhelmsen, I., Berstad, A., & Ursin, H. (1994). Low vagal activity as mediating mechanism for the relationship between personality factors and gastric symptoms in functional dyspepsia. *Psychosomatic Medicine, 56*, 181–186.

Hausken, T., Svebak, S., Wilhelmsen, I., Haug, T. T., Olafsen, K., Pettersson, E., et al. (1993). Low vagal tone and antral dysmotility in patients with functional dyspepsia. *Psychosomatic Medicine, 55*, 12–22.

Heim, C., Newport, D. J., Heit, S., Graham, Y. P., Bonsall, R., Miller, A. H., et al. (1999). Pituitary-adrenal responses to CRF stimulation in adult survivors of childhood abuse with and without depression. *Society for Neuroscience Abstracts, 25*, 1454.

Heim, C., Owens, M. J., Plotsky, P. M., & Nemeroff, C. B. (1997). The role of early adverse life events in the etiology of depression and post-traumatic stress disorder. Focus on corticotropin-releasing factor. *Annals of the New York Academy of Sciences, 821*, 194–207.

Heitkemper, M., Burr, R. L., Jarrett, M., Hertig, V., Lustyk, M. K., & Bond, E. F. (1998). Evidence for autonomic nervous system imbalance in women with irritable bowel syndrome. *Digestive Diseases and Sciences, 43*, 2093–2098.

Heitkemper, M., Jarrett, M., Cain, K., Shaver, J., Bond, E., Woods, N. F., et al. (1996). Increased urine catecholamines and cortisol in women with irritable bowel syndrome. *American Journal of Gastroenterology, 91*, 906–913.

Hill, O. W., & Blendis, L. (1967). Physical and psychological evaluation of non-organic abdominal pain. *Gut, 8*, 221–229.

Hislop, I. G. (1979). Childhood deprivation: An antecedent of the irritable bowel syndrome. *Medical Journal of Australia, 1*, 372–374.

Holstege, G., Bandler, R., & Saper, C. B. (1996). *The emotional motor system*. Amsterdam: Elsevier.

Imaki, T., Nahan, J. L., Sawchenko, P. E., & Vale, W. (1991). Differential regulation of corticotropin-releasing factor mRNA in rat brain regions by glucocorticoids and stress. *Journal of Neuroscience, 11*, 585–599.

Irwin, C., Falsetti, S. A., Lydiard, R. B., Ballenger, J. C., Brock, C. D., & Brener, W. (1996). Comorbidity of posttraumatic stress disorder and irritable bowel syndrome. *Journal of Clinical Psychiatry, 57*, 576–578.

Jacobson, L., & Sapolsky, R. (1991). The role of the hippocampus in feedback regulation of the hypothalamic-pituitary-adrenocortical axis. *Endocrine Reviews, 12,* 118–134.

Janet, P. (1889). *L'automatisme psychologique.* Paris: Alcan.

Jänig, W., & Habler, H.-J. (2000). Specificity in the organization of the autonomic nervous system: A basis for precise neural regulation of homeostatic and protective body functions. In E. A. Mayer & C. B. Saper (Eds.), *Progress in brain research: Vol. 122. The biological basis for mind body interactions* (pp. 351–367). Amsterdam: Elsevier Science.

Kalin, N. H. (1993). The neurobiology of fear. *Scientific American, 268,* 94–101.

Kardiner, A. (1941). *The traumatic neuroses of war.* New York: Hoeber.

Kaufman, J., Plotsky, P. M., Nemeroff, C. B., & Charney, D. S. (2000). Effects of early adverse experiences on brain structure and function: Clinical implications. *Biological Psychiatry, 48,* 778–790.

Kimerling, R., & Calhoun, K. S. (1994). Somatic symptoms, social support, and treatment seeking among sexual assault victims. *Journal of Consulting and Clinical Psychology, 62,* 333–340.

Kodama, A., Horikawa, T., Suzuki, T., Ajiki, W., Takashima, T., Harada, S., et al. (1999). Effect of stress on atopic dermatitis: Investigation in patients after the great Hanshin earthquake. *Journal of Allergy and Clinical Immunology, 104,* 173–176.

Koss, M. P., Woodruff, W. J., & Koss, P. G. (1990). Relation of criminal victimization to health perceptions among women medical patients. *Journal of Consulting and Clinical Psychology, 58,* 147–152.

Kulka, R. A., Fairbank, J. A., Jordan, B. K., & Weiss, D. (1990). *Trauma and the Vietnam War generation: Report of findings from the National Vietnam Veterans Readjustment Study.* New York: Brunner/Mazel.

Ladd, C. O., Huot, R. L., Thrivikraman, K. V., Nemeroff, C. B., Meaney, M. J., & Plotsky, P. (2000). Long-term behavioral and neuroendocrine adaptations to adverse early experience. In E. A. Mayer & C. B. Saper (Eds.), *Progress in brain research: Vol. 122. The biological basis for mind body interactions* (pp. 81–103). Amsterdam: Elsevier Science.

Lamprecht, F., & Sack, M. (2002). Posttraumatic stress disorder revisited. *Psychosomatic Medicine, 64,* 222–237.

LeDoux, J. E. (1996). *The emotional brain: The mysterious underpinnings of emotional life.* New York: Simon & Schuster.

Lowman, B. C., Drossman, D. A., Cramer, E. M., & McKee, D. C. (1987). Recollection of childhood events in adults with irritable bowel syndrome. *Journal of Clinical Gastroenterology, 9,* 324–330.

Lutgendorf, S. K., Antoni, M. H., Ironson, G., Fletcher, M. A., Penedo, F., Baum, A., et al. (1995). Physical symptoms of chronic fatigue syndrome are exacerbated by the stress of Hurricane Andrew. *Psychosomatic Medicine, 57,* 310–323.

Malagelada, J.-R. (1991). The gastroduodenal response to stress in man in health and functional dyspepsia. In Y. Taché & D. Wingate (Eds.), *Brain-gut interactions* (pp. 297–305). Boston: CRC Press.

Martinez, V., Rivier, J., Wang, L., & Taché, Y. (1997). Central injection of a new corticotropin-releasing factor (CRF) antagonist, astressin, blocks CRF- and stress-related alterations of gastric and colonic motor function. *Journal of Pharmacology and Experimental Therapeutics, 280,* 754–760.

Mayer, E. A. (2000a). Psychological stress and colitis. *Gut, 46*, 595–596.

Mayer, E. A. (2000b). The neurobiology of stress and gastrointestinal disease. *Gut, 47*, 861–869.

Mayer, E. A., & Collins, S. M. (2002). Evolving pathophysiologic models of functional gastrointestinal disorders. *Gastroenterology, 122*, 2032–2048.

Mayer, E. A., Craske, M. G., & Naliboff, B. D. (2001). Depression, anxiety and the gastrointestinal system. *Journal of Clinical Psychiatry, 62*, 28–36.

Mayer, E. A., Naliboff, B. D., Chang, L., & Coutinho, S. V. (2001). Stress and the gastrointestinal tract, V: Stress and irritable bowel syndrome. *American Journal of Physiology – Gastrointestinal and Liver Physiology, 280*, G519–G524.

Mayer, E. A., Naliboff, B., & Munakata, J. (2000). The evolving neurobiology of gut feelings. In E. A. Mayer & C. B. Saper (Eds.), *Progress in brain research: Vol. 122. The biological basis for mind body interactions* (pp. 195–206). Amsterdam: Elsevier Science.

McCauley, J., Kern, D. E., Kolodner, K., Dill, L., Schroeder, A. F., DeChant, H. K., et al. (1997). Clinical characteristics of women with a history of childhood abuse: Unhealed wounds. *Journal of the American Medical Association, 277*, 1362–1368.

McEwen, B. S. (1995). Adrenal steroid actions on brain. Dissecting the fine line between protection and damage. In J. M. Friedman, D. S. Charney, & A. Y. Deutsch (Eds.), *Neurobiological and clinical consequences of stress: From normal adaptation to PTSD* (pp. 135–150). Philadelphia: Lippincott-Raven.

McEwen, B. S. (1998). Protective and damaging effects of stress mediators. *New England Journal of Medicine, 338*, 171–179.

McEwen, B. S. (2000). Protective and damaging effects of stress mediators: Central role of the brain. In E. A. Mayer & C. B. Saper (Eds.), *Progress in brain research: Vol. 122. The biological basis for mind body interactions* (pp. 25–34). Amsterdam: Elsevier Science.

Meaney, M. J., Diorio, J., Francis, D., Widdowson, J., LaPlante, P., Caldji, C., et al. (1996). Early environmental regulation of forebrain glucocorticoid receptor gene expression: Implications for adrenocortical response to stress. *Developmental Neuroscience, 18*, 49–72.

Menninger, W. C. (1947). Psychosomatic medicine: Somatization reactions. *Psychosomatic Medicine, 9*, 92–97.

Mertz, H., Morgan, V., Tanner, G., Pickens, D., Price, R., Shyr, Y., et al. (2000). Regional cerebral activation in irritable bowel syndrome and control subjects with painful and nonpainful rectal distension. *Gastroenterology, 118*, 842–848.

Million, M., Wang, L., Wang, Y., Adelson, D. W., Yuan, P. Q., Maillot, C., et al. (2006). CRF2 receptor activation prevents colorectal distension induced visceral pain and spinal ERK1/2 phosphorylation in rats. *Gut, 55*, 172–181.

Moldofsky, H., & Franklin, L. A. (1993). Disordered sleep, pain, fatigue, and gastrointestinal symptoms in fibromyalgia, chronic fatigue and irritable bowel syndromes. In E. A. Mayer & H. E. Raybould (Eds.), *Basic and clinical aspects of chronic abdominal pain* (pp. 249–256). New York: Elsevier.

Munakata, J., Mayer, E. A., Chang, L., Schmulson, M., Liu, M., Tougas, G., et al. (1998). Autonomic and neuroendocrine responses to recto-sigmoid stimulation. *Gastroenterology, 114*, 808.

Musselman, D., & Nemeroff, C. B. (2000). Depression really does hurt your heart: Stress, depression, and cardiovascular disease. In E. A. Mayer & C. B. Saper (Eds.), *Progress in brain research: Vol. 122. The biological basis for mind body interactions* (pp. 43–59). Amsterdam: Elsevier Science.

Myers, A. B. R. (1870). *On the etiology and prevalence of diseases of the heart among soldiers.* London: Churchill.

Myers, C. S. (1940). *Shell shock in France, 1914–18.* Cambridge: Cambridge University Press.

Naliboff, B. D., Derbyshire, S. W. G., Munakata, J., Berman, S., Mandelkern, M., Chang, L., et al. (2000). Evidence for decreased activation of central fear circuits by expected aversive visceral stimuli in IBS patients. *Gastroenterology, 118,* A137.

Niederau, C., Faber, S., & Karaus, M. (1992). Cholecystokinin's role in regulation of colonic motility in health and in irritable bowel syndrome. *Gastroenterology, 102,* 1889–1898.

Norris, F. H., Kaniasty, K. Z., & Scheer, D. A. (1990). Use of mental health services among victims of crime: Frequency, correlates, and subsequent recovery. *Journal of Consulting and Clinical Psychology, 58,* 538–547.

Oppenheim, H. (1889). *Die Traumatischen Neurosen, Nach den in der Nervenklinik der Charité in den Letzten 5 Jahren Gesammelten Beobachtungen.* Berlin: Hirschwald.

Owens, M. J., & Nemeroff, C. B. (1993). The role of corticotropin-releasing factor in the pathophysiology of affective and anxiety disorders: Laboratory and clinical studies. *Ciba Foundation Symposium, 172,* 296–316.

Page, W. F., National Research Council (U.S.), Medical Follow-up Agency, & Institute of Medicine (U.S.). (1992). *The health of former prisoners of war: Results from the medical examination survey of former POWs of World War II and the Korean conflict.* Washington, DC: National Academy Press.

Parker, G. (1981). Parental representations of patients with anxiety neurosis. *Acta Psychiatrica Scandinavica, 63,* 33–36.

Pertovaara, A. (1993). Antinociception induced by alpha-2-adrenoceptor agonists, with special emphasis on medetomidine studies. *Progress in Neurobiology, 40,* 691–709.

Plotsky, P. M., Cunningham, E. T., & Widmaier, E. P. (1989). Catecholaminergic modulation of corticotropin-releasing factor and dexamethason secretion. *Endocrine Reviews, 10,* 437–458.

Porreca, F., Ossipov, M. H., & Gebhart, G. F. (2002). Chronic pain and medullary descending facilitation. *Trends in Neurosciences, 25,* 319–325.

Rapkin, A. J., Kames, L. D., Darke, L. L., Stampler, F. M., & Naliboff, B. D. (1990). History of physical and sexual abuse in women with chronic pelvic pain. *Obstetrics and Gynecology, 76,* 92–96.

Reche, A. J., & Buffington, C. A. T. (1998). Increased tyrosine hydroxylase immunoreactivity in the locus coeruleus of cats with interstitial cystitis. *Journal of Urology, 159,* 1045–1048.

Reppetti, R. L., Taylor, S. E., & Seeman, T. E. (2002). Risky families: Family social environments and the mental and physical health of offspring. *Psychological Bulletin, 128,* 330–366.

Rimsza, M. E., Berg, R. A., & Locke, C. (1988). Sexual abuse: Somatic and emotional reactions. *Child Abuse & Neglect, 12,* 201–208.

Russak, L. G., & Schwartz, G. E. (1997). Feelings of parental care predict health status in midlife: A 35-year follow-up of the Harvard Mastery of Stress Study. *Journal of Behavioral Medicine, 20,* 1–11.

Sapolsky, R. M., Krey, L. C., & McEwen, B. S. (1984). Glucocorticoid-sensitive hippocampal neurons are involved in terminating the adrenocortical stress response. *Proceedings of the National Academy of Sciences of the United States of America, 81,* 6174–6177.

Sawchenko, P. E., Li, H.-Y., & Ericsson, A. (2000). Circuits and mechanisms governing hypothalamic responses to stress: A tale of two paradigms. In E. A. Mayer & C. B. Saper (Eds.), *Progress in brain research: Vol. 122. The biological basis for mind body interactions* (pp. 61–78). Amsterdam: Elsevier Science.

Scarinci, I. C., McDonald-Haile, J., Bradley, L. A., & Richter, J. E. (1994). Altered pain perception and psychosocial features among women with gastrointestinal disorders and history of abuse: A preliminary model. *American Journal of Medicine, 97,* 108–118.

Schei, B. (1991). Sexual factors in pelvic pain: A study of women living in physically abusive relationships and of randomly selected controls. *Journal of Psychosomatic Obstetrics and Gynaecology, 12,* 99–108.

Schwetz, I., McRoberts, J. A., Coutinho, S. V., Bradesi, S., Gale, G., Fanselow, M., et al. (2005). Corticotropin releasing factor receptor 1 mediates acute and delayed stress-induced visceral hyperalgesia in maternally separated Long Evans rats. *American Journal of Physiology – Gastrointestinal and Liver Physiology, 289,* G704–712.

Smith, G. W., Aubry, J. M., Dellu, F., Contarino, A., Bilezikjian, L. M., Gold, L. H., Chen, R., Marchuk, Y., Hauser, C., Bentley, C. A., Sawchenko, P. E., Koob, G. F., Vale, W., & Lee, K. F. (1998). Corticotropin releasing factor receptor 1-deficient mice display decreased anxiety, impaired stress response, and aberrant neuroendocrine development. *Neuron, 20,* 1093–1102.

Stables, L. A., Kennan, R. P., & Gore, J. C. (1998). Asymmetric spin-echo imaging of magnetically inhomogeneous systems: Theory, experiment, and numerical studies. *Magnetic Resonance in Medicine, 40,* 432–442.

Stam, R., Akkermans, L. M. A., & Wiegant, V. M. (1997). Trauma and the gut: Interactions between stressful experience and intestinal function. *Gut, 40,* 704–709.

Sternberg, E. M. (1993). Hyperimmune fatigue syndromes: Diseases of the stress response? *Journal of Rheumatology, 20,* 418–421.

Sternberg, E. M., Chrousos, G. P., & Gold, P. W. (1992). The stress response and the regulation of inflammatory disease. *Annals of Internal Medicine, 117,* 854–866.

Stratakis, C. A., & Chrousos, G. P. (1995). Neuroendocrinology and pathophysiology of the stress system. *Annals of the New York Academy of Sciences, 771,* 1–18.

Swanson, L. W., & Kuypers, H. G. J. M. (1980). The paraventricular nucleus of the hypothalamus: Cytoarchitectonic subdivisions and organization of projections to the pituitary, dorsal vagal complex, and spinal cord as demonstrated by retrograde fluorescence double-labeling methods. *Journal of Comparative Neurology, 194,* 555–570.

Taché, Y., Martinez, V., Million, M., & Rivier, J. (1999). Corticotropin-releasing factor and the brain-gut motor response to stress. *Canadian Journal of Gastroenterology, 13*, 18A–25A.

Taché, Y., & Moennikes, H. (1993). CRF in the central nervous system mediates stress-induced stimulation of colonic motor function: Relevance to the patho-physiology of IBS. In E. A. Mayer & H. E. Raybould (Eds.), *Basic and clinical aspects of chronic abdominal pain* (pp. 142–151). Amsterdam: Elsevier.

Talley, N. J., Boyce, P. M., & Jones, M. (1998). Is the association between irritable bowel syndrome and abuse explained by neuroticism? A population based study. *Gut, 42*, 47–53.

Talley, N. J., Fett, S. L., Zinsmeister, A. R., & Melton, L. J., III. (1994). Gastrointestinal tract symptoms and self-reported abuse: A population-based study. *Gastroenterology, 107*, 1040–1049.

Tan, S., Tillisch, K., & Mayer, E. A. (2004). Functional somatic syndromes: Emerging biomedical models and traditional Chinese medicine. *Evidence Based Complementary Alternative Medicine, 1*, 35–40.

Taylor, S. E., Klein, L. C., Lewis, B. P., Gruenewald, T. L., Gurung, R. A. R., & Updegraff, J. A. (2000). Biobehavioral responses to stress in females: Tend-and-befriend, not fight-or-flight. *Psychological Review, 107*, 411–429.

Timpl, P., Spanagel, R., Sillaber, I., Kresse, A., Reul, J. M., Stalla, et al. (1998). Impaired stress response and reduced anxiety in mice lacking a functional corticotropin-releasing hormone receptor. *Nature Genetics, 19*, 162–166.

Toomey, T. C., Hernandez, J. T., Gittelman, D. F., & Hulka, J. F. (1993). Relationship of sexual and physical abuse to pain and psychological assessment variables in chronic pelvic pain patients. *Pain, 53*, 105–109.

Triadafilopoulos, G., Simms, R. W., & Goldenberg, D. L. (1991). Bowel dysfunction in fibromyalgia syndrome. *Digestive Diseases and Sciences, 36*, 59–64.

Valentino, R. J., Miselis, R. R., & Pavcovich, L. A. (1999). Pontine regulation of pelvic viscera: Pharmacological target for pelvic visceral dysfunction. *Trends in Pharmacological Sciences, 20*, 253–260.

Veale, D., Kavanagh, G., Fielding, J. F., & Fitzgerald, O. (1991). Primary fibromyalgia and the irritable bowel syndrome: Different expressions of a common pathogenetic process. *British Journal of Rheumatology, 30*, 220–222.

Verne, G. N., Robinson, M. E., & Price, D. D. (2001). Hypersensitivity to visceral and cutaneous pain in the irritable bowel syndrome. *Pain, 93*, 7–14.

Verrier, R. L., & Mittleman, M. A. (2000). The impact of emotions on the heart. In E. A. Mayer & C. B. Saper (Eds.), *Progress in brain research: Vol. 122. The biological basis for mind body interactions* (pp. 369–380). Amsterdam: Elsevier Science.

Waigandt, A., Wallace, D. L., Phelps, L., & Miller, D. A. (1990). The impact of sexual assault on physical health status. *Journal of Traumatic Stress, 3*, 93–102.

Walker, E. A., Katon, W. J., Hansom, J., Harrop-Griffiths, J., Holm, L., Jones, M. L., et al. (1992). Medical and psychiatric symptoms in women with childhood sexual abuse. *Psychosomatic Medicine, 54*, 658–664.

Walker, E. A., Katon, W. J., Roy-Byrne, P. P., Jemelka, R. P., & Russo, J. (1993). Histories of sexual victimization in patients with irritable bowel syndrome or inflammatory bowel disease. *American Journal of Psychiatry, 150*, 1502–1506.

Wei, F., Dubner, R., & Ren, K. (1999). Nucleus reticularis gigantocellularis and nucleus raphe magnus in the brain stem exert opposite effects on behavioral hyperalgesia and spinal Fos protein expression after peripheral inflammation. *Pain, 80,* 127–141.

Welgan, P., Meshkinpour, H., & Beeler, M. (1988). Effect of anger on colon motor and myoelectric activity in irritable bowel syndrome. *Gastroenterology, 94,* 1150–1156.

Welgan, P., Meshkinpour, H., & Hoehler, F. (1985). The effect of stress on colon motor and electrical activity in irritable bowel syndrome. *Psychosomatic Medicine, 47,* 139–149.

Williams, D. A., Brown, S. C., Clauw, D. J., & Gendreau, R. M. (2003). Self-reported symptoms before and after September 11 in patients with fibromyalgia. *Journal of the American Medical Association, 289,* 1637–1638.

Wissow, L. S. (1995). Child abuse and neglect. *New England Journal of Medicine, 332,* 1425–1431.

Yehuda, R., Boisonaeau, D., Mason, J. W., & Giller, E. L. (1993). Relationship between lymphocyte glucocorticoid receptor number and urinary free cortisol excretion in mood, anxiety, and psychotic disorders. *Biological Psychiatry, 34,* 18–25.

Yehuda, R., Giller, E. L., Jr., Levengood, R. A., Southwick, S. M., & Siever, L. J. (1995). Hypothalamic-pituitary-adrenal functioning in post-traumatic stress disorder: Expanding the concept of the stress response spectrum. In M. J. Friedman, D. S. Charney, & A. Y. Deutch (Eds.), *Neurobiological and clinical consequences of stress: From normal adaptation to post-traumatic stress disorder* (pp. 351–366). Philadelphia: Lippincott-Raven.

CLINICAL PERSPECTIVES ON TRAUMA

C linical issues and concerns about the suffering of individuals are central to the contributions in this section. Clinicians focus on symptoms and signs, which allow them to diagnose specific problems that, in turn, suggest interventions that can alleviate distress. Of course, any diagnosis captures only some elements of an individual's suffering, and clinicians usually work with more encompassing assessments and case formulations that include social or interpersonal problems and predicaments. Clinicians use these formulations to make sense of individuals' suffering and devise problem-solving interventions. Although in the past many clinicians adhered to a particular school of therapy, today a reasoned eclecticism is more common. Effectiveness is the final arbiter of clinical relevance – though judgments of good outcome raise many practical, epistemological, and sociomoral questions (Kirmayer, 2004).

Although much is known about effective interventions for trauma-related disorders, significant controversies and large areas of uncertainty remain (Bisson & Andrew, 2005). Some of the controversies, and much of the uncertainty, reflect the very different sorts of problems and predicaments gathered together under the rubrics of trauma and PTSD. These include disparate responses to events that vary in frequency, severity, and meaning. There are also enormous individual differences in the response to the same violent event, some of which is attributable to constitutional and genetic factors, early child socialization, and the age and developmental stage at which an individual experiences the trauma. Each of the contributions in this section, therefore, must be considered in relation to the types of patients or clinical populations that the authors have in mind.

All of the clinicians contributing to this section were trained in Western settings and most work in developed countries. They write about abused children, survivors of domestic violence, and refugees from war-torn areas. Some have also worked in situations of endemic violence: societies in the midst of war, terrorism, or genocide, or in the day-to-day struggle of refugee camps. However, most clinical work takes place away from the spaces of terror and ongoing violence where many victims of trauma live.

Elna Yadin and Edna Foa review literature on the prevalence, correlates, and underlying cognitive processes implicated in PTSD. They focus largely on individuals who have experienced isolated traumatic events like rape or other forms of assault. They describe some of the "dysfunctional cognitions" found among patients with PTSD, which include a perception of the world as a dangerous place, low self-esteem, and a tendency toward self-blame. They then discuss cognitive behavioral therapy (CBT) approaches to the treatment of PTSD, which include variants of exposure therapy, anxiety management, cognitive therapy, and eye movement desensitization and reprocessing (EMDR). They present the evidence from clinical trials for the superior efficacy of a specific form of CBT using prolonged exposure (with or without the concomitant use of antidepressant medication). This form of CBT uses both audiotaped scripts recounting the specific traumatic experiences of the patient and *in vivo* exposure to reminders of those traumas. This approach has beneficial effects on a range of client outcomes, reducing anxiety, depression, and self-blame, while increasing self-efficacy. This type of treatment does not require highly experienced clinicians; it can be equally successful when administered by community counselors who have received 10 days of training. They conclude with a discussion that aims to dispel some myths concerning the perceived harm to patients of prolonged exposure.

The use of prolonged exposure to reduce or eliminate symptoms of anxiety and PTSD fits with the neurobiological models of extinction presented in Section I. However, the research of Bouton and others also shows that fear can return when the context changes. This accords with the clinical experience of David Kinzie, who discusses the treatment of highly traumatized refugee populations from Somalia, Cambodia, and Guatemala at the Intercultural Psychiatric Program of the Oregon Health and Science University, where patients receive comprehensive care from a team composed of a psychiatrist and a counselor/interpreter who is from the same ethnocultural group. Many of these refugees have experienced massive, multiple, and prolonged exposures to both physical and psychological trauma both in their countries of origin and in refugee camps. As a result, they suffer from a complex mix of problems. In this context, PTSD frequently co-occurs with other psychological and medical disorders and is often a "chronic relapsing disorder." The refugees whom Kinzie treats have suffered multiple losses and typically present with major depression and sometimes with psychotic disorders, as well as PTSD. Their symptoms may be exacerbated by exposure to new stressors (such as the images of the 9/11 attacks), which trigger recall of the original trauma. Kinzie is skeptical about the usefulness of prolonged exposure therapy, which seems naive, unrealistic, and even inhumane for refugees who have suffered multiple severe traumas and losses. He suggests that this model is based on Western cultural assumptions about the value of explicitly talking about distress and directly confronting emotional problems with the expectation that they can be overcome. Instead, Kinzie argues that clinicians must be prepared to provide long-term supportive psychiatric care combined with careful medical assessment and management of physical illnesses like hypertension and diabetes, which appear to be frequent among his PTSD patients.

Based in part on his experience with Israeli soldiers and civilians exposed to war and terrorism, Arieh Shalev argues that experiencing psychologically traumatic events does not fully explain the occurrence of PTSD. Although most people display symptoms of stress after such events, only a minority fail to recover from this initial distress and go on to develop chronic PTSD. Shalev reviews evidence for the relative contribution of triggering and maintaining factors in the development of chronic PTSD. In addition to the importance of fear, he argues that what makes events traumatic is their novelty, incongruity, and associated loss. This approach implies a view of PTSD as a disorder of recovery or restitution, in which the most powerful healing factors involve social solidarity and support.

Bessel van der Kolk addresses the developmental impact of childhood trauma. He argues that the explanatory adequacy of most animal models is constrained by the fact that it is impossible to model some of the uniquely human relational factors that are known to predict the development of PTSD: abandonment, betrayal, helplessness, and submission. He discusses the proposal for a diagnostic construct of "complex PTSD," which aims to capture the varied consequences of exposure in early life to multiple, repeated, and prolonged interpersonal violence (e.g., sexual or physical abuse, war, community violence). Such pervasive developmental insult many result in deformations of personality and profound difficulties in negotiating stable relationships with others over the lifespan.

Derrick Silove gives an account of how he and his network of health care and service providers established urgently needed mental health and other vital services to East Timorese refugees living in Australia and those still living in war-torn East Timor. The chapter focuses on a specific "ecosocial" intervention model, "Adaptation and Development After Persecution and Trauma" (ADAPT), and identifies several cultural challenges and infrastructural problems that they encountered. Silove describes the post-traumatyic stress response as a "normative survival overdrive state (SOS)" that is designed to trigger learned survival reactions in future encounters. He argues that the disorder emerges in the absence of "ecosocial safety signals" and of a newly stabilized context. Silove argues for a broad contextual approach to trauma and mental health problems, allowing for greater community and familial participation in the healing process.

James Boehnlein examines the role of religion and spirituality following trauma. Trauma undermines our sense of the world as just and moral, and challenges religious beliefs and commitments. Most people who have experienced trauma engage in a continuing search for meaning, both to make sense of their past and to come to terms with their altered future. In many cases, meaning is found through religion or spiritual life. Boehnlein finds that psychiatry and religion can either complement each other or conflict in this search for meaning. He emphasizes the importance of recognizing the value of diverse cultural and religious traditions and healing rituals, the necessity of meaning-making and the reestablishment of trust, and the possibility of "spiritual awakening" in the process of recovery.

Cécile Rousseau and Toby Measham, psychiatrists who work with refugee children, adolescents, and their families in clinical and community settings, argue for the necessity of situating their work as clinicians within the larger sociopolitical and cultural context. They critique the application of trauma models in work with refugees, noting the ways in which conventional models bracket off the complex set of emotions of anger, aggression, and moral outrage, which are part of the response to trauma as well as the larger social context of structural violence, which both engenders and obscures the sources of trauma. On the basis of clinical observations, they maintain that trauma can transform a person in positive ways. In their research with children of Cambodian refugees, they found that families that had experienced the greatest trauma were most sure of themselves and proud of their ethnic identity. Khmer-Canadian community members interpreted these results as reflecting the fact that adolescents in families who had experienced such suffering were entrusted with a mission of survival, which gave meaning to the trauma and to their lives. They also point out some of the contradictions implicit in conventional medical and psychiatric practice when faced with the realities of trauma. For example, disclosure, trust, and meaning are highly valued, despite the fact that distrust can be protective "as a survival strategy" and meaninglessness is a primary feature of most profoundly traumatizing events. Indeed, they suggest that therapists' willingness to acknowledge the "absurdity" of violence and suffering may be as important as their ability to coconstruct meaning with their patients. Recognizing the importance of social and cultural context in healing, Rousseau and Measham advocate an approach to therapy that respects the needs of the patient and their entourage by moving back and forth between disclosure and containment of unspeakable suffering.

As can be seen from the range of approaches represented in these chapters, there is significant controversy over what works in therapy. To some extent this reflects differences in patient populations and in how clinicians frame the problems they are addressing. What these clinical methods have in common is various forms of narration, of telling a story to others as a way of making sense of it and of having them bear witness. As James Pennebaker has shown, the process of recounting trauma can itself be healing

(Pennebaker, 1990; Pennebaker, Barger, & Tiebout, 1989; Pennebaker & Beall, 1986). In part, this may be due to a process of self-regulated exposure or extinction, but it seems also to involve a progressive cognitive reorganization and reintegration, which comes about through the process of narration, whether by writing or by talking with someone (Pennebaker & Seagal, 1999; Kloss & Lisman, 2002; Cohn, Mehl, & Pennebaker, 2004). Of course, this retelling is dependent on a safe-enough sociopolitical context in which one can narrate without the fear of further violence or retribution (see the chapters by Dwyer & Santikarma and Lemelson, Kirmayer, & Barad in Section III). We do not know enough about the trade-offs involved in telling one's story or choosing to keep silent in different personal and social contexts. For some individuals, nonverbal modes of expression and articulate forms of silence may be more personally and culturally appropriate and effective strategies for adaptation (Bagilishya, 2000).

In successful psychotherapy, the trauma story that may have remained stuck in an endless loop for years begins to move and transform. As Shalev (this volume) puts it:

In other words, human trauma is essentially embedded in language and in other species-specific complex signaling processes. Emphasizing these top-down brain processes (in which the *meaning* of an event strongly affects the resulting activation of alarm) may hold the key for better understanding resiliency and recovery.

When they earn the trust of their patients and work with them over time, clinicians may be privy to aspects of personal history and experience that are hidden from others. They thus claim a special intimacy with private worlds of suffering. At the same time, clinicians are prone to certain biases based on the limits of what can be known in the clinical setting. The focus in the clinic is on the symptoms and suffering of the individual. Clinicians usually do not see people who are well, and they may have little sense of how their patients are coping in the context of their family, work, or community. Most clinicians trained in individual psychotherapy do not see their patients in ecological context and so must reconstruct their social worlds with information filtered through patients' own perceptions. Hence, clinicians may exaggerate the prevalence of pathology, fail to recognize resilience, and miss the wider social implications of forms of suffering and healing.

Psychiatry and psychology are closely linked to specific cultural concepts of the person, particularly to a form of rugged individualism that emphasizes personal mastery, instrumental control of the environment, competitiveness, and personal achievement.[1] In recent years, this rugged

[1] The classic analysis of American individualism, still relevant today, is de Tocqueville's *Democracy in America* (1835–40/2004). For the links between individualism, psychology, and psychotherapy, see Cushman (1995) and Rose (1996). For cross-cultural comparative perspectives, see Marsella, DeVos, and Hsu (1985) and Marsella and White (1982).

individualism has partially given way to what Robert Bellah (1985) has called "expressive individualism," which puts a premium on open and energetic expression of one's interests, desires, and opinions.[2] In many cultures, however, these individualistic values are not central and emphasis is given instead to the person's duties and responsibilities to family, clan, and community. Expression of strong emotion or distress may be discouraged and suppressed as potentially disruptive to the social order and damaging to both personal and collective well-being (Wellenkamp, 1995; Wikan, 1990). This difference in values and associated differences in the organization of the self may have profound consequences for the design and delivery of culturally appropriate interventions and, indeed, for the place accorded the mental health professions in any given society.

Ways of narrating trauma depend crucially on the social worlds that make available, encourage, or silence particular types of story (Kirmayer, 1996). And this leads us toward the larger issues of the social consequences of remembering and forgetting, the political use of trauma to define collective identity and legitimacy as a wounded and oppressed people, and the links between the explicit forms of trauma we see and the subtler forms of structural violence, which remain hidden or taken for granted, because they are woven into the fabric of everyday life (Farmer, 2004). Although clinical work usually begins with a more local and individual focus, as many of the contributions to this section clearly show, clinicians cannot avoid the social and political contexts and consequences of their work.

References

Bagilishya, D. (2000). Mourning and recovery from trauma: In Rwanda, tears flow within. *Transcultural Psychiatry, 37*(3), 337–354.

Bellah, R. N. (1985). *Habits of the heart: Individualism and commitment in American life.* Berkeley: University of California Press.

Bisson, J., & Andrew, M. (2005). Psychological treatment of post-traumatic stress disorder (PTSD). *Cochrane Database of Systematic Reviews, 2*, CD003388.

Cohn, M. A., Mehl, M. R., & Pennebaker, J. W. (2004). Linguistic markers of psychological change surrounding September 11, 2001. *Psychological Science, 15*(10), 687–693.

Cushman, P. (1995). *Constructing the self, constructing America: A cultural history of psychotherapy.* Boston: Addison-Wesley.

de Toqueville, A. (1835–40/2004). *Democracy in America.* New York: Library of America.

---

[2] For some indication of how these changes in American individualism may have affected attitudes toward traumatic events, see Gladwell (2004). The veteran of World War II was enjoined to "just get over it," whereas current expectations are that traumatic events leave indelible scars. These different models of coping with adversity are part of larger cultural ideologies of the person.

Farmer, P. (2004). An anthropology of structural violence. *Current Anthropology,* 45(3), 304–325.

Gladwell, M. (2004, November 8). Getting over it. *New Yorker,* 75–79.

Kirmayer, L. J. (1996). Landscapes of memory: Trauma, narrative, and dissociation. In P. Antze & M. Lambek (Eds.), *Tense past: Cultural essays in trauma and memory* (pp. 173–198). New York: Routledge.

Kirmayer, L. J. (2004). The cultural diversity of healing: Meaning, metaphor and mechanism. *British Medical Bulletin,* 69(1), 33–48.

Kloss, J. D., & Lisman, S. A. (2002). An exposure-based examination of the effects of written emotional disclosure. *British Journal of Health Psychology,* 7(Pt. 1), 31–46.

Marsella, A., DeVos, G., & Hsu, F. L. K. (Eds.). (1985). *Culture and self: Asian and Western perspectives.* New York: Tavistock.

Marsella, A. J., & White, G. M. (Eds.). (1982). *Cultural conceptions of mental health and therapy.* Dordrecht: D. Reidel.

Pennebaker, J. W. (1990). *Opening up: The healing power of confiding in others.* New York: William Morrow.

Pennebaker, J. W., Barger, S., & Tiebout, J. (1989). Disclosure of traumas and health among Holocaust survivors. *Psychosomatic Medicine,* 51(5), 577–589.

Pennebaker, J. W., & Beall, S. K. (1986). Confronting a traumatic event: Toward understanding of inhibition and disease. *Journal of Abnormal Psychology, 95,* 274–281.

Pennebaker, J. W., & Seagal, J. D. (1999). Forming a story: The health benefits of narrative. *Journal of Clinical Psychology,* 55(10), 1243–1254.

Rose, N. (1996). *Inventing our selves: Psychology, power, and personhood.* Cambridge, U.K.: Cambridge University Press.

Wellenkamp, J. (1995). Cultural similarities and differences regarding emotion disclosure: Some examples from Indonesia and the Pacific. In J. W. Pennebaker (Ed.), *Emotion, disclosure, and health* (pp. 293–309). Washington, DC: American Psychological Association.

Wikan, U. (1990). *Managing turbulent hearts: A Balinese formula for living.* Chicago: University of Chicago Press.

8

Cognitive Behavioral Treatments for Posttraumatic Stress Disorder

Elna Yadin and Edna B. Foa

INTRODUCTION AND DIAGNOSIS OF POSTTRAUMATIC
STRESS DISORDER

The impact of traumatic events and the behavioral sequelae associated with them has been recognized for over 100 years under a variety of different labels, including compensation neurosis, nervous shock, hysteria, and war neurosis. The introduction of posttraumatic stress disorder (PTSD) into the third edition of the *Diagnostic and Statistical Manual of Mental Disorders* (*DSM–III*) in 1980 (APA, 1980) and its placement among the anxiety disorders reflects the perception that anxiety is a core component of an individual's reaction to a traumatic experience. Accordingly, PTSD is an anxiety disorder that develops in some individuals after a traumatic event defined by the *DSM–IV* (APA, 1994) as (1) experiencing, witnessing, or being confronted with an event that involves actual or threatened death or injury, or a threat to their physical integrity or that of others, *and* (2) responding to the event with intense fear, helplessness, or horror.

In addition to experiencing or witnessing a traumatic event, a diagnosis of PTSD requires the individual to meet the following three symptom criteria: (1) At least one reexperiencing symptom, such as distressing recollections of the trauma, distressing dreams of the event, reliving the experience through flashbacks, psychological distress at exposure to internal or external reminders of the event, or physiological reactivity to those trauma reminders. (2) At least three symptoms of persistent avoidance such as making an effort to avoid trauma-related thoughts or feelings, making an effort to avoid trauma-related activities or situations, amnesia for important aspects of the event, diminished interest in activities, detachment from others, restricted range of affect, or a sense of a foreshortened future. (3) At least two symptoms of increased arousal such as sleep disturbances, irritability and outbursts of anger, difficulty concentrating, hypervigilance, or exaggerated startle response. A diagnosis of PTSD requires that the symptoms persist for a minimum of 1 month and the disturbance causes significant distress or impairment in important areas of functioning. When the PTSD symptoms persevere beyond 3 months, PTSD is considered to be chronic. Delayed-onset PTSD is a condition in which the onset of symptoms is at least 6 months after the stressor event.

PREVALENCE OF PTSD

Epidemiological studies indicate that both exposure to traumatic events and the development of PTSD are common. For example, the National Women's Study, a large-scale study of a nationally representative sample of adult women in the United States, found that nearly 70% had experienced one or more traumatic events such as sexual assault, physical assault, homicide of a family member, natural disaster, or serious accident (Resnick, Kilpatrick, Dansky, Saunders, & Best, 1993). Lifetime prevalence of PTSD among women who reported a traumatic event was 17.9%, whereas prevalence of current PTSD was 6.7%. Rates of both lifetime and current PTSD were significantly higher for victims of crime than for victims of noncrime traumatic events. Similarly high rates of exposure to traumatic events and PTSD have been reported in other, more recent epidemiological studies. Thus, for instance, in the U. S. National Comorbidity Survey (Kessler, 2000; Kessler, Sonnega, Bromet, Hughes, & Nelson, 1995), lifetime prevalence of trauma exposure was 60.7% in men and 51.2% in women, and the conditional risk of PTSD was 8.1% in men and 20.4% in women.

The picture emerging from other cultures and countries is similar. For example, the prevalence rate for PTSD among affected individuals randomly selected from two rural communities near the epicenter of a 1999 major earthquake in Taiwan was 10.3% (Lai, Chang, Connor, Lee, & Davidson, 2004). PTSD was associated with high levels of psychosocial impairment and was approximately two times more prevalent in women (18%) than in men (7.7%). Lifetime prevalence rates of exposure to trauma and PTSD in a sample of adults from four cities in Mexico were 76% and 11.2%, respectively. Risk for developing PTSD was shown to be highest in the poorest city, in women (15% vs. 7% in men), and in low socioeconomic status (Norris et al., 2003).

Trauma survivors with a diagnosis of PTSD have been shown to suffer from other psychiatric, marital, occupational, financial, and health problems, all of which take a toll both on their personal quality of life as well as on the public health system. For example, analysis of data from the National Vietnam Veterans Readjustment Study (Zatzick, Marmar, et al., 1997) demonstrated that PTSD in male Vietnam veterans is associated with a broad spectrum of functional impairment that includes diminished well-being, compromised physical health, physical limitations, greater perpetration of violence, and unemployment. Similar functional impairments

were seen in female Vietnam veterans, with the exception of greater perpetration of violence (Zatzick, Weiss, et al., 1997). In a recent study that
examined PTSD and health consequences within the health system of the
Department of Veterans Affairs, a diagnosis of PTSD was associated with a
higher likelihood of circulatory and musculoskeletal disorders, with more
medical conditions, and with poorer health-related quality of life in both
genders (Ouimette et al., 2004). In Chapter 7 of this volume, Emeran Mayer
presents a comprehensive look at the somatic manifestations of traumatic
stress and their devastating health consequences on the sufferers, on their
families, and on society.

Studies examining the impact of PTSD on the utilization of health care
in civilian populations confirm the findings that PTSD in crime victims
is associated with a greater demand for mental health services (Berliner
& New, 1999; Freedy, Resnick, Kilpatrick, Dansky, & Tidwell, 1994). In
a sample of patients presenting at primary care settings, 83% reported at
least one traumatic event in their lifetime, and of the 504 patients evaluated,
185 met diagnostic criteria for PTSD (Bruce et al., 2001). Studies indicated
high rates of comorbidity of psychiatric disorders among individuals with
PTSD, including high rates of alcohol/substance abuse, depression, and
suicide attempts (Kessler, 2000).

Taken together, these results underscore the fact that PTSD is both a
prevalent and debilitating disorder and thus the need to further the understanding of the nature of the disorder for the development and widespread
dissemination of effective treatments.

WHY SOME PEOPLE RECOVER WHILE OTHERS DO NOT: EMOTIONAL PROCESSING THEORY OF CHRONIC PTSD

Emotional processing theory (Foa & Kozak, 1986), originally proposed to
explain the effectiveness of exposure therapy for anxiety disorders in general, has been applied as a useful framework for understanding factors
associated with natural recovery after a trauma, with the failure to recover,
with the development of chronic PTSD, as well as with the mechanisms
underlying treatment for chronic PTSD. A core concept in the theory is
the presence of "fear structures." A fear structure is defined as a cognitive
structure represented in memory as a network of interconnecting elements
that contain information about the feared stimuli; the verbal, physiological, and overt behavioral fear responses; and the meaning of the stimulus
and response elements in the structure. The interconnections among the
various stimulus, response, and meaning elements in the network serve
as a blueprint for escape or avoiding danger. As such, a fear structure
supports adaptive behavior when a person is faced with a realistically
threatening situation. However, a fear structure may become maladaptive when (1) associations among stimulus elements do not accurately

represent the world, (2) physiological and escape/avoidance responses are evoked by harmless stimuli, (3) excessive and easily triggered response elements interfere with other adaptive behavior, and (4) harmless stimulus and response elements are erroneously interpreted as being dangerous. Foa and colleagues (Foa & Riggs, 1993; Foa, Steketee, & Rothbaum, 1989) proposed that the fear structure underlying PTSD is characterized by a particularly large number of harmless stimulus elements that are erroneously associated with the meaning of danger, and by exaggerated responses erroneously interpreted as reflecting self-incompetence.

Foa and Rothbaum (1998) further suggested that factors influencing the development of PTSD in trauma victims can be divided into three clusters: pretrauma factors, factors related to the memory of the traumatic event, and posttrauma factors. Specifically, emotional processing is impeded either when the trauma violates existing knowledge of oneself as extremely competent and of the world as extremely safe or when the trauma primes existing knowledge of oneself as extremely incompetent and of the world as extremely dangerous. With regard to trauma factors, it has been suggested that traumatic memories are fragmented and include representations of intense fear and confusion, of bodily states such as physical pain, of thoughts and ideas that reflect confusion, and of strong images of some of the specific details (Foa & Riggs, 1993). Posttrauma factors that impede recovery are lasting emotional disturbances such as nightmares and sleeplessness, disruption in daily functioning, and reactions and attitudes of others toward the PTSD sufferer's continued symptoms.

The hypothesis that people who fail to recover from PTSD after a trauma exhibit dysfunctional cognitions about themselves and about others was examined by Foa, Ehlers, Clark, Tolin, and Orsillo (1999). In a study with 601 individuals, trauma-related cognitions were compared in individuals who were traumatized and had PTSD, individuals with a history of trauma but without PTSD, and with nontraumatized individuals. Results revealed elevated perceptions of the world as dangerous, low self-worth, and high self-blame in the PTSD group compared to the other two groups. Thus, the erroneous cognitions that underlie PTSD are that the world is extremely dangerous (e.g., people are untrustworthy, no place is safe) and the victim is extremely incompetent (e.g., having PTSD symptoms is a sign of weakness, other people would have prevented the trauma).

COGNITIVE BEHAVIOR THERAPY TREATMENTS FOR PTSD

Several psychological treatments have been developed and evaluated for their efficacy in the treatment of PTSD in the past 15 years. The recognition that the basis of PTSD lies in pathological anxiety and that cognitive behavioral therapy (CBT) is effective for anxiety disorders led to the application of CBT to treating trauma victims with chronic PTSD. Numerous studies have attested to the efficacy of various forms of CBT programs (for recent comprehensive overviews of psychosocial treatments for PTSD, see Foa & Cahill, 2006; Foa, Rothbaum, & Furr, 2003). The cognitive behavioral treatments include variants of exposure therapy, anxiety management, and cognitive therapy. Exposure therapy consists of a set of techniques designed to help patients confront their feared objects, situations, memories, and images. Anxiety management programs typically consist of relaxation training, controlled breathing, positive self-talk and imagery, social skills training, and distraction techniques. Cognitive therapy entails teaching the patient to identify trauma- or symptom-related unhelpful beliefs, to challenge and modify them, and to replace them with alternative, more helpful, and functional beliefs.

Exposure therapy is the most widely studied treatment for PTSD in a variety of trauma victim populations, but anxiety management therapy, cognitive therapy, a combination of these procedures, and, more recently, eye movement desensitization and reprocessing (EMDR) have also been studied (for reviews see Hembree & Foa, 2003; Rothbaum, Meadows, Resick, & Foy, 2000). Briefly, anxiety management therapy focuses on training sufferers to develop coping skills to manage their anxiety, which in turn makes them better able to deal with everyday life situations. Cognitive therapy aims to help PTSD sufferers identify trauma-related irrational and unhelpful beliefs, to challenge them, and to modify or replace them with more rational and helpful ones. In EMDR, patients are asked to generate vivid images, thoughts, feelings, and body sensations associated with the trauma. They are then asked to evaluate the aversive qualities and replace them with alternative cognitions about the trauma and about their own behaviors, all the while tracking a rapidly moving finger or another object which elicits saccadic eye movements.

Prolonged exposure (PE; e.g., Foa & Rothbaum, 1998), one specific exposure therapy protocol, incorporates education about common reactions to trauma, breathing retraining, prolonged and repeated titrated emotionally engaged reliving of the trauma memory, and repeated *in vivo* exposure to trauma-related feared and avoided situations and objects. Foa, Dancu, et al. (1999) conducted a study comparing the outcome of nine sessions of PE delivered over 5 weeks to stress inoculation training (SIT; Meichenbaum, 1974), to the combination of the two (PE+SIT), and to wait-listed controls (WL) in sexually or physically assaulted women with chronic PTSD. They found that all three active treatments reduced severity of PTSD and depression significantly more than the WL comparison group, and these gains were maintained throughout the follow-up period. In the intent-to-treat sample, PE was superior to SIT and PE+SIT on posttreatment anxiety and global social adjustment at follow-up and had larger effect sizes on PTSD severity, depression, and anxiety. The SIT and PE+SIT conditions did not differ significantly from each other on any outcome measure.

Foa and colleagues (Foa et al., 2005) have recently completed a study that compared the outcome of 9 to 12 sessions (extension given to those not showing at least 70% improvement on self-report PTSD severity scale) of PE alone, to PE combined with cognitive restructuring (PE+CR), and to a WL control group in sexually or physically assaulted women with chronic PTSD. CR consisted of challenging and modifying beliefs about the threatening nature of the PTSD symptoms as well as the distorted perception of the world as an entirely dangerous place and the victims as entirely incapable of coping with stress (Foa & Rothbaum, 1998). Contrary to the hypothesis, the findings revealed no added benefit to the combined treatment over PE alone; both conditions produced similarly more benefit on PTSD and depression symptoms compared to the WL control group.

Several recent studies have compared PE with alternative CBT interventions in men and women suffering from PTSD as a result of a variety of traumatic experiences. Paunovic and Ost (2001) evaluated the effects of PE versus PE+CR in a small sample of traumatized refugees with PTSD. They found that both treatments resulted in large improvements on measures of PTSD, anxiety, and depression, which were maintained at follow-up 6 months later.

Resick, Nishith, Weaver, Astin, and Feuer (2002) compared the 9-session PE protocol developed by Foa and colleagues with a 12-session cognitive processing therapy (CPT; Resick & Schnicke, 1992, 1993). CPT was specifically designed to address concerns of rape victims identified by McCann and Pearlman (1990) as well as the symptoms of PTSD. The treatment involved a combination of cognitive restructuring to identify and modify distorted beliefs, focusing on issues of safety, trust, power, esteem, and intimacy, along with an exposure component that consisted of writing a detailed account of the rape and reading it several times during sessions. Both treatments were highly and equally efficacious and superior to a control group receiving minimal attention.

As noted above, Foa and colleagues hypothesized that individuals with chronic PTSD are characterized by the perceptions that the world is entirely dangerous and that they are extremely incompetent. It follows that successful treatment of PTSD would modify these perceptions. In support of this hypothesis, Foa and Rauch (2004) found that PE alone resulted in clinically significant, reliable, and lasting reductions in negative cognitions about self, world, and self-blame. Treatment that combined PE and cognitive restructuring (PE+CR) did not significantly augment these cognitive changes.

Marks, Lovell, Noshirvani, Livanou, and Thrasher (1998) compared 10 sessions of exposure therapy (5 sessions of imaginal exposure followed by 5 sessions of *in vivo* exposure), cognitive restructuring, and their combination with a relaxation control group. The three CBT interventions were found to be equally superior to relaxation in reducing symptom severity, a superiority that was maintained at follow-up assessments. Indeed, at follow-up, the groups that received exposure therapy seemed superior to cognitive restructuring alone. Tarrier et al. (1999) compared 16 one-hour sessions of imaginal prolonged exposure (without *in vivo* exposure) and cognitive therapy. Both groups displayed significant clinical improvement after treatment, with no differences observed between groups. However, the outcome in both groups was inferior to that of other studies in which exposure therapy was used (Devilly & Foa, 2001).

Devilly and Spence (1999) compared a trauma treatment protocol CBT intervention, consisting of imaginal and *in vivo* exposure with SIT, with EMDR (Shapiro, 1995). The components of EMDR were accessing the trauma images and memories, evaluating their aversive qualities, generating alternative cognitive appraisal, focusing on the alternative, and making lateral eye movement while focusing on the response. Both treatments resulted in significant improvement. However, imaginal and *in vivo* exposure with SIT was superior to EMDR both immediately after treatment and at the 3-month follow-up assessment. Indeed, patients in the former treatment maintained their gains at the follow-up whereas those treated with EMDR showed relapse on several measures.

Comparison of the efficacy, speed, and adverse effects of three PTSD treatments (PE, relaxation training, or EMDR) showed that the treatments did not differ in attrition, in the incidence of symptom worsening, or in their effects on numbing and hyperarousal symptoms (Taylor et al., 2003). Compared with EMDR and relaxation training, exposure therapy produced significantly larger reductions in avoidance and reexperiencing symptoms. Relaxation training and EMDR did not differ from one another in speed or efficacy.

A randomized controlled study comparing cognitive behavioral therapy, supportive psychotherapy, or a wait-listed control condition in motor vehicle accident survivors with chronic PTSD showed significantly greater improvement for those in CBT in comparison to the wait list and to the support conditions (Blanchard et al., 2003). The cognitive behavioral therapy consisted of a combination of behavioral and cognitive procedures that included relaxation, exposure (reading the description of the accident out loud and *in vivo* exposures), cognitive therapy (challenging negative self-talk and distorted thinking), behavioral activation, and dealing with anger issues. The CBT condition led to significantly greater reductions in comorbid major depression and generalized anxiety disorder than the other two conditions. These improvements were maintained at 3 months follow-up.

DISSEMINATION OF TREATMENT OF PTSD

Concerns have often been raised that the efficacy of the cognitive behavioral treatments for PTSD reported in the literature is confined to studies conducted in academic research settings with highly selected patient populations. Therefore, another question asked in the above study (Foa et al., 2005) was whether PE and PE+CR could be successfully disseminated to community mental health clinics such as rape counseling centers. The rape counselors from a rape center in Philadelphia (Women Organized Against Rape; WOAR), with Master's degrees in counseling or social work, had not been previously trained in cognitive behavioral therapy and had no prior research skills or experience in delivering manualized treatment protocols. They received 10 days of training, 5 in PE, and 5 in cognitive restructuring, after which they received weekly supervision from cognitive behavior therapy experts in the Center for Treatment and Study of Anxiety (CTSA), who developed the PE. The study was conducted in both clinics, and study participants received treatment at either WOAR or at the CTSA. No differences were found between the two clinics: Treatment administered by the community counselors was as successful as that given by the CBT experts in reducing PTSD symptoms and depression. Moreover, patient factors such as age, race, time since the trauma, and degree of comorbidity and dysfunction did not predict treatment outcome.

A somewhat different dissemination model has been implemented in several PTSD mental health clinics in Israel. In this model, Israeli clinicians with some experience in delivering PE attend a 2- to 4-week course of PE supervisors at the CTSA. Periodically, CTSA experts, with the assistance of the trained supervisors, conducted 5-day PE workshops in Israel modeled on the one conducted for the WOAR counselors. Those who attended the supervisors' course at the CTSA then supervise the newly trained therapists. Preliminary outcome data from a study comparing PE to treatment as usual in an outpatient clinic for veterans with PTSD indicated that combat veterans and terror victims with chronic PTSD ranging from 6 months to 30 years, with or without accompanying physical injury, evidenced a significant decrease in PTSD and depression after treatment with PE delivered by recently trained clinicians (Nacasch et al., 2003). The mean reduction of symptoms was 58%, a reduction that is comparable to that obtained with female victims of sexual and physical abuse in the United States (Foa et al., 2005).

Another study examined the extent to which these positive findings generalize to routine clinical settings with less selected patients and a trauma that affects a whole community (Gillespie, Duffy, Hackmann, & Clarke, 2002). Patients with PTSD resulting from a car bomb, which exploded in the center of Omagh, Northern Ireland, in August 1998, were treated with cognitive therapy, based on Ehlers and Clark (2000). There were no major exclusion criteria, and 53% of the patients had comorbidity with an additional axis I disorder. The therapists were National Health Service staff with heavy caseloads and modest prior training in CBT for PTSD who received a brief training in specialist procedures for PTSD. Significant and substantial improvements in PTSD were observed after an average of eight treatment sessions, with the degree of improvement comparable to that in previously reported research trials. Patients with comorbidities generally required more treatment sessions to achieve similar results, and patients with physical injuries faired worse than patients without physical injuries. Overall, however, the authors concluded that the results indicate that the positive findings obtained in research settings generalize well to a nonselective population treated by community service providers.

COMBINATION OF PROLONGED EXPOSURE AND MEDICATION

Another avenue in the treatment of patients with PTSD has focused on pharmacological intervention, with or without accompanying psychotherapy. The recent emphasis has been on the selective serotonin reuptake inhibitors (SSRIs), which have been the medications for PTSD most extensively studied in double blind, placebo-controlled trials, with the most favorable adverse effect profile (Asnis, Kohn, Henderson, & Brown, 2004). In a recently completed study (Cahill et al., 2004), the effect of sertraline (SRT) on PTSD symptoms was compared to that of sertraline in combination with prolonged exposure (SRT+PE), after an initial 10-week treatment phase with sertraline alone. In a sample of 59 completers, the effect size for both groups was large, but the effect size for the combined group was substantially greater than that for the sertraline-alone group. Furthermore, when the sample of treatment completers was divided into partial and excellent responders according to their degree of response in the sertraline-alone phase, the addition of prolonged exposure significantly improved the outcome of the partial responders whereas continued treatment with sertraline alone in this group did not result in such an improvement.

FURTHER CONSIDERATIONS

Despite the large body of accumulated evidence in support of effective treatments available for the treatment of PTSD, not all sufferers partake in these treatments, and of those who do, not all benefit and some continue to suffer from residual symptoms. Examination of the available literature highlights some contributing factors to treatment failure, such as lack of awareness of the availability of effective treatments, cultural conventions about coping with adversity and seeking help, stigma attached to diagnostic labeling and treatment seeking, limited choices and availability, health care professional attitudes, worries about exacerbation due to the treatment, and palatability of the treatment to the patient.

In a community study conducted at the Duke University Medical Center (Amaya-Jackson et al., 1999), it was found that only 20% of persons with PTSD had seen a mental health professional in the previous

6-month period compared to 71% who had seen a general physician, suggesting the underutilization of mental health resources by PTSD sufferers. The difficulty of seeking treatment, particularly for mental health problems, is even greater in some cultural contexts. For example, surveys after the World Trade Center attacks in 2001 showed that symptoms related to the attacks were found in large numbers of people, and many affected individuals were offered free treatment for their PTSD symptoms (Marshall & Suh, 2003). However, special issues arose such as the influence of culture on the clinical presentation as well as on treatment utilization in this multiethnic community. For example, utilization of mental health services was extremely low in a sample of immigrant Chinese displaced workers, 21% of whom met diagnostic criteria for PTSD (Thiel de Bocanegra & Brickman, 2004). In this survey, the authors reported that the prevalence of PTSD among displaced workers from this ethnic group 8 months after the attack was nearly identical to that found in a community survey of Manhattan residents 2 months after the attack. Only two of the individuals with PTSD, and four others in the sample, had undergone any sort of counseling when the interviews were conducted. In their discussion, the authors highlighted this combination of high symptom levels and low receptiveness to the idea of counseling as an issue requiring creativity in developing strategies to reach those in need of help.

On the other hand, in a review of the literature on mental health in relation to natural disasters such as earthquakes, volcanic eruptions, typhoons, and cyclones throughout Asia (Kokai, Fujii, Shinfuku, & Edwards, 2004), it has been shown that the field of "disaster psychiatry" is beginning to emerge from the stigma attached to mental health. The authors suggest that this change is due in part to the acceptance of the notion of PTSD, which in turn allows greater involvement of mental health professionals, both in providing the needed support and in conducting well-controlled studies.

It is the case that therapists tend not to use evidence-based treatments, including for PTSD. Thus, for instance, a recently conducted survey of psychologists' attitudes toward and utilization of exposure therapy for PTSD (Becker, Zayfert, & Anderson, 2004) revealed that, in spite of the ample research supporting its efficacy, exposure therapy is not completely accepted or widely used. This was true even among psychologists with strong interest and training in behavioral treatments for PTSD. Some of the perceived barriers to implementing this treatment were lack of adequate training and experience in application of exposure therapy, both to PTSD sufferers as well as to individuals with other anxiety disorders. Furthermore, according to the survey, many factors were widely endorsed as contraindications for the use of exposure therapy, indicating a belief that the treatment would lead to an increase in symptoms or to problems in therapy such as worsening in suicidality or substance abuse, and consequently to an increased desire to drop out of treatment. These contraindications included some that are common exclusions from randomized trials (such as psychotic disorders, severe suicidality, homicidality), but also many that have not been demonstrated to be exclusions (such as any dissociative symptoms, or any comorbid disorder). More disturbingly, the results of the survey suggested that clinicians sometimes implement exposure therapy in the presence of real factors that have been indicated as clear exclusion criteria in randomized controlled studies, such as the ongoing presence of the source of the threat and current abuse (Foa, Dancu, et al., 1999; Foa, Rothbaum, Riggs, & Murdock, 1991; Resick et al., 2002). As the authors of the survey suggest, the use of exposure therapy in the presence of empirically supported contraindicated factors may result in poor outcomes and thereby discourage further use.

The discussion about factors limiting the application of evidence-based treatments for PTSD highlights the need for an open dialogue between researchers and clinicians, which would help to dispel some of the myths about the perceived harm to the patient, as well as to create acceptable ways of facilitating the training and use of these efficacious treatments. Several studies examined the following myths (for a review see Cahill & Foa, 2004):

1. PE causes exacerbation of symptoms during treatment and poorer treatment outcome.

    A minority of patients in the recently completed study showed a reliable exacerbation of symptoms during treatment associated with the initiation of imaginal exposure therapy (Foa, Zoellner, Feeny, Hembree, & Alvarez-Conrad, 2002). However, participants who showed symptom worsening early in therapy were no more likely to drop out of treatment than participants who did not experience symptom worsening. Moreover, treatment outcome was not different for participants who showed symptom worsening compared to those who did not (Cahill, Riggs, Rauch, & Foa, 2003).

2. PE increases dropout rates.

    In a paper examining the hypothesis that treatments that include exposure are associated with a higher dropout rate than treatments that do not, a literature search had identified 25 controlled studies of cognitive–behavioral treatment for chronic PTSD that included data on dropouts (Hembree et al., 2003). The results indicated no difference in dropout rates among exposure therapy, cognitive therapy, SIT, and EMDR. These findings are consistent with previous research about the tolerability of exposure therapy.

3. PE is not acceptable to patients.

    A further consideration for the mental health professional, who is faced with a patient with PTSD and who would like to increase the probability of a successful outcome, is to look at patient choice. When treatment options are readily available, the impetus for seeking treatment ultimately lies within the PTSD sufferer, so the factors that influence the decision to seek help are of utmost importance. Zoellner, Feeny, Cochran, and Pruitt (2003) collected data from women with varying degrees of trauma history and subsequent PTSD symptoms, asking about their treatment choice in the event of a hypothetical traumatic scenario. The treatment options were prolonged exposure, sertraline, or no treatment at all. Contrary to the authors' expectations, women were dramatically less likely to consider medication a viable treatment option for chronic PTSD; 6.9% chose sertraline whereas 87.4% chose prolonged exposure.

A better understanding of the factors that play a major role in what treatment options are offered; the relevant individual and cultural aspects that determine a person's treatment choice, compliance, and adherence; as well as the underlying sources of residual symptoms will improve the utilization and outcome of these evidence-based treatments for PTSD. Future research should develop programs that increase the motivation of patients to take advantage of these efficacious treatments and that disseminate treatments to mental health professionals in a way that would help them offer these therapies to their PTSD patients.

ACKNOWLEDGMENT

We would like to thank Shawn Cahill for his generosity in sharing his expertise, as well as for his astute editorial eye.

References

Amaya-Jackson, L., Davidson, J. R., Hughes, D. C., Swartz, M., Reynolds, V., George, L. K., et al. (1999). Functional impairment and utilization of services associated with posttraumatic stress in the community. *Journal of Traumatic Stress, 12*, 709–724.

American Psychiatric Association. (1980). *Diagnostic and statistical manual of mental disorders* (3rd ed.). Washington, DC: Author.

American Psychiatric Association. (1994). *Diagnostic and statistical manual of mental disorders* (4th ed.). Washington, DC: Author.

Asnis, G. M., Kohn, S. R., Henderson, M., & Brown, N. L. (2004). SSRIs versus non-SSRIs in post-traumatic stress disorder: An update with recommendations. *Drugs, 64*, 383–404.

Becker, C. B., Zayfert, C., & Anderson, E. (2004). A survey of psychologists' attitudes towards and utilization of exposure therapy for PTSD. *Behaviour Research and Therapy, 42*, 277–292.

Berliner, L., & New, M. (1999). The impact of health care reform: A survey of victim and offender treatment providers. *Sexual Abuse: Journal of Research and Treatment, 11*, 5–16.

Blanchard, E. B., Hickling, E. J., Devineni, T., Veazey C. H., Galovski, T. E., Mundy, E., et al. (2003). A controlled evaluation of cognitive behavioral therapy for post-traumatic stress in motor vehicle accident survivors. *Behaviour Research and Therapy, 41*, 79–96.

Bruce S. E., Weisberg R. B., Dolan R. T., Machan J. T., Kessler R. C., Manchester G., et al. (2001). Trauma and posttraumatic stress disorder in primary care patients: Primary care companion. *Journal of Clinical Psychiatry, 3*, 211–217.

Cahill, S. P., & Foa, E. B. (2004). A glass half empty or half full? Where we are and directions for future research in the treatment of PTSD. In S. Taylor (Ed.), *Advances in the treatment of posttraumatic stress disorder: Cognitive-behavioral perspectives* (pp. 267–313). New York: Springer.

Cahill, S. P., Foa, E. B., Rothbaum, B. O., Davidson, J. R. T., Connor, K., & Compton, J. (2004). Augmentation of sertraline with cognitive behavior therapy in the treatment of posttraumatic stress disorder: Effects on acute treatment outcome and maintenance of treatment gains. In N. C. Feeny (Chair), *Psychosocial and pharmacological interventions for PTSD: Recent advances.* Symposium conducted at the annual conference of the Anxiety Disorders Association of America, Miami, FL.

Cahill, S. P., Riggs, D. S., Rauch, S. A. M., & Foa, E. B. (2003). *Does prolonged exposure therapy for PTSD make people worse?* Poster session presented at the annual convention of the Anxiety Disorders Association of America, Toronto, Ontario, Canada.

Devilly, G. J., & Foa, E. B. (2001). The investigation of exposure and cognitive therapy: Comment on Tarrier et al. (1999). *Journal of Consulting and Clinical Psychology, 69*, 114–116.

Devilly, G. J., & Spence, S. H. (1999). The relative efficacy and treatment distress of EMDR and a cognitive-behavior trauma treatment protocol in the amelioration of posttraumatic stress disorder. *Journal of Anxiety Disorders, 13*, 131–157.

Ehlers, A., & Clark, D. M. (2000). A cognitive model of posttraumatic stress disorder. *Behaviour Research and Therapy, 38*, 319–345.

Foa, E. B., & Cahill, S. P. (2006). Psychosocial treatments for PTSD: An overview. In Y. Neria, R. Gross, R. Marshall, & E. Susser (Eds.), *9/11: Public health in the wake of terrorist attacks* (pp. 457–474). Cambridge, U.K.: Cambridge University Press.

Foa, E. B., Dancu, C. V., Hembree, E. A., Jaycox, L. H., Meadows, E. A., & Street, G. P. (1999). A comparison of exposure therapy, stress inoculation training, and their combination for reducing posttraumatic stress disorder in female assault victims. *Journal of Consulting and Clinical Psychology, 67*, 194–200.

Foa, E. B., Ehlers, A., Clark, D. M., Tolin, D. F., & Orsillo, S. M. (1999). The Posttraumatic Cognitions Inventory (PTCI): Development and validation. *Psychological Assessment, 11*, 303–314.

Foa, E. B., Hembree, E. A., Cahill, S. P., Rauch, S. A., Riggs, D. S., Feeny, N. C., & Yadin, E. (2005). Randomized trial of prolonged exposure for PTSD with and without cognitive restructuring: Outcome at academic and community clinics. *Journal of Consulting and Clinical Psychology, 73*, 953–964.

Foa, E. B., & Kozak, M. J. (1986). Emotional processing of fear: Exposure to corrective information. *Psychological Bulletin, 99*, 20–35.

Foa, E. B., & Rauch, S. A. M. (2004). Cognitive changes during prolonged exposure versus prolonged exposure and cognitive restructuring in female assault. *Journal of Consulting and Clinical Psychology, 72,* 879–884.

Foa, E. B., & Riggs, D. S. (1993). Post-traumatic stress disorder in rape victims. In J. Oldham, M. B. Riba, & A. Tasman (Eds.), *American Psychiatric Press review of psychiatry* (Vol. 12, pp. 273–303). Washington, DC: American Psychiatric Press.

Foa, E. B., & Rothbaum, B. O. (1998). *Treating the trauma of rape.* New York: Guilford Press.

Foa, E. B., Rothbaum, B. O., & Furr, J. M. (2003). Augmenting exposure therapy with other CBT procedures. *Psychiatric Annals, 33,* 47–53.

Foa, E. B., Rothbaum, B. O., Riggs, D. S., & Murdock, T. B. (1991). Treatment of posttraumatic stress disorder in rape victims: A comparison between cognitive-behavioral procedures and counseling. *Journal of Consulting and Clinical Psychology, 59,* 715–723.

Foa, E. B., Steketee, G., & Rothbaum, B. (1989). Behavioral/cognitive conceptualizations of post-traumatic stress disorder. *Behavior Therapy, 20,* 155–176.

Foa, E. B., Zoellner, L. A., Feeny, N. C., Hembree, E. A., & Alvarez-Conrad, J. (2002). Does imaginal exposure exacerbate PTSD symptoms? *Journal of Consulting and Clinical Psychology, 70,* 1022–1028.

Freedy, J. R., Resnick, H. S., Kilpatrick, D. G., Dansky, B. S., & Tidwell, R. P. (1994). The psychological adjustment of recent crime victims in the criminal justice system. *Journal of Interpersonal Violence, 9,* 450–468.

Gillespie, K., Duffy, M., Hackmann, A., & Clark, D. M. (2002). Community based cognitive therapy in the treatment of posttraumatic stress disorder following the Omagh bomb. *Behaviour Research and Therapy, 40,* 345–357.

Hembree, E. A., & Foa, E. B. (2003). Interventions for trauma-related emotional disturbances in adult victims of crime. *Journal of Traumatic Stress, 16,* 189–201.

Hembree, E. A., Foa, E. B., Dorfan, N. M., Street, G. P., Kowalski, J., & Tu, X. (2003). Do patients drop out prematurely from exposure therapy for PTSD? *Journal of Traumatic Stress, 16,* 555–562.

Kessler, R. C. (2000). Posttraumatic stress disorder: The burden to the individual and to society. *Journal of Clinical Psychiatry, 61*(Suppl. 5), 4–14.

Kessler, R. C., Sonnega, A., Bromet, E., Hughes, M., & Nelson, C. B. (1995). Post-traumatic stress disorder in the National Comorbidity Survey. *Archives of General Psychiatry, 52,* 1048–1060.

Kokai, M., Fujii, S., Shinfuku, N., & Edwards, G. (2004). Natural disaster and mental health in Asia. *Psychiatry and Clinical Neuroscience, 58,* 110–116.

Lai, T. J., Chang C. M., Connor K. M., Lee L. C., & Davidson, J. R. (2004). Full and partial PTSD among earthquake survivors in rural Taiwan. *Journal of Psychiatric Research, 38,* 313–322.

Marks, I., Lovell, K., Noshirvani, H., Livanou, M., & Thrasher, S. (1998). Treatment of posttraumatic stress disorder by exposure and/or cognitive restructuring. *Archives of General Psychiatry, 55,* 317–325.

Marshall, R. D., & Suh, E. J. (2003). Contextualizing trauma: Using evidence-based treatments in a multicultural community after 9/11. *Psychiatry Quarterly, 74,* 401–420.

McCann, I. L., & Pearlman, L. A. (1990). *Psychological trauma and the adult survivor: Theory, therapy, and transformation.* New York: Bruner/Mazel.

Meichenbaum, D. (1974). *Cognitive behavior modification.* Morristown, NJ: General Learning Press.

Nacasch, N., Cohen-Rapperot, G., Polliack, M., Knobler, H. Y., Zohar J., Yadin, E., et al. (2003, April). *Prolonged exposure therapy for PTSD: The dissemination and the preliminary results of the implementation of the treatment protocol in Israel.* Abstract in the Proceedings of the 11th Conference of the Israel Psychiatric Association, Haifa, Israel.

Norris, F. H., Murphy, A. D., Baker, C. K., Perilla, J. L., Rodriguez, F. G., & Rodriguez, J. de J. (2003). Epidemiology of trauma and posttraumatic stress disorder in Mexico. *Journal of Abnormal Psychology, 112,* 646–656.

Ouimette, P., Cronkite, R., Henson, B. R., Prins, A., Gima, K., & Moos, R. H. (2004). Posttraumatic stress disorder and health status among female and male medical patients. *Journal of Traumatic Stress, 17,* 1–9.

Paunovic, N., & Ost, L. G. (2001). Cognitive-behavior therapy vs. exposure therapy in the treatment of PTSD in refugees. *Behaviour Research and Therapy, 39,* 1183–1197.

Resick, P. A., Nishith, P., Weaver, T. L., Astin, M. C., & Feuer, C. A. (2002). A comparison of cognitive-processing therapy with prolonged exposure and a waiting condition for the treatment of chronic posttraumatic stress disorder in female rape victims. *Journal of Consulting and Clinical Psychology, 70,* 867–879.

Resick, P. A., & Schnicke, M. K. (1992). Cognitive processing therapy for sexual assault victims. *Journal of Consulting and Clinical Psychology, 60,* 748–756.

Resick, P. A., & Schnicke, M. K. (1993). *Cognitive processing therapy for rape victims: A treatment manual.* Newbury Park, CA: Sage.

Resnick, H. S., Kilpatrick, D. G., Dansky, B. S., Saunders, B. E., & Best, C. L. (1993). Prevalence of civilian trauma and posttraumatic stress disorder in a representative national sample of women. *Journal of Consulting and Clinical Psychology, 61,* 984–991.

Rothbaum, B. O., Meadows, E. A., Resick, P., & Foy, D. W. (2000). Cognitive-behavioral therapy. In E. B. Foa, T. M. Keane, & M. J. Friedman (Eds.), *Effective treatments for PTSD: Practice guidelines from the International Society for Traumatic Stress* (pp. 320–324). New York: Guilford Press.

Shapiro, F. (1995). *Eye movement desensitization and reprocessing: Basic principles, protocols, and procedures.* New York: Guilford Press.

Tarrier, N., Pilgrim, H., Sommerfield, C., Faragher, B., Reynolds, M., Graham, E., et al. (1999). A randomized trial of cognitive therapy and imaginal exposure in the treatment of chronic posttraumatic stress disorder. *Journal of Consulting and Clinical Psychology, 67,* 13–18.

Thiel de Bocanegra, H., & Brickman, E. (2004). Mental health impact of the World Trade Center attacks on displaced Chinese workers. *Journal of Traumatic Stress, 17,* 55–62.

Taylor, S., Thordarson, D. S., Maxfield, L., Federoff, I. C., Lovell, K., & Ogrodniczuk, J. (2003). Efficacy, speed, and adverse effects of three PTSD treatments: Exposure therapy, relaxation training, and EMDR. *Journal of Consulting and Clinical Psychology, 71,* 330–338.

Zatzick, D. F., Marmar, C. R., Weiss, D. S., Browner, W. S., Metzler, T. J., Golding, J. M., et al. (1997). Posttraumatic stress disorder and functioning and quality of life outcomes in a nationally representative sample of male Vietnam veterans. *American Journal of Psychiatry, 154,* 1690–1695.

Zatzick, D. F., Weiss, D. S., Marmar, C. R., Metzler, T. J., Wells, K., Golding, J. M., et al. (1997). Post-traumatic stress disorder and functioning and quality of life outcomes in female Vietnam veterans. *Military Medicine, 162,* 661–665.

Zoellner, L. A., Feeny, N. C., Cochran B., & Pruitt L. (2003). Treatment choice for PTSD. *Behaviour Research and Therapy, 41,* 879–886.

9

PTSD Among Traumatized Refugees

J. D. Kinzie

Since 1977, the Intercultural Psychiatric Program (formally the Indochinese Psychiatric Program) of the Oregon Health and Science University has been treating refugees from Southeast Asia, that is, Vietnam, Cambodia, and Laos (Kinzie, Tran, Breckenridge, & Bloom, 1980). Over the years, the program has grown to include refugees and immigrants from Russia, Bosnia, Central America, Somalia, Ethiopia, Iran, Afghanistan, and the Kurdish areas of Central Asia. Our clinical method has been consistent over this time. Each patient has one counselor from his or her own ethnic group and one psychiatrist. The counselor acts as an interpreter, case manager, and usually a socialization group leader. The psychiatrist provides the initial evaluation, diagnostic formulation, psychotherapy, and medication management (Kinzie, 1981). Typically, a counselor–psychiatrist team will follow from 50 to 100 patients. As of 2004, the program had 1100 active patients with Vietnamese comprising the largest group. Cambodians, Russians, and Bosnians also were strongly represented. Overall, the program staff have the ability to translate 17 different languages.

Beginning with the Cambodians in 1981 (Kinzie, Fredrickson, Ben, Fleck, & Karls, 1984), we became aware through their psychiatric histories of the massive trauma suffered by these refugees. This prompted us to take more systematic trauma histories from other refugee groups, and we found a high rate in all groups (Kinzie et al., 1990). As civil wars, ethnic cleansing, and tribal violence continued throughout the world, successive waves of refugees coming to the United States became patients in our program. They recounted horrors they had witnessed and endured and their subsequent symptoms. In this chapter, I summarize some of the major findings from 25 years of clinical experience working with traumatized refugees.

THREE CASE VIGNETTES

PTSD among refugees is the story of trauma, usually both psychological and physical, often prolonged and involving extreme cruelty. The stories we hear are of those who have suffered and survived. Below, I present vignettes of three cases from my practice whose stories are representative of the traumas suffered by refugees from their respective countries.

Case 1. Elly

Elly is a Somali woman who is separated from her husband and had been in the United States for about 3 years when she was referred to our clinic with her 16-year-old son, who refused to accompany her. Elly's history revealed a traumatic past and many current symptoms including markedly reduced sleep of about 3 hours per night, frequent startling with recurrent nightmares about past events, and ongoing conflicts with her children. She reports crying much of the time but also feels a deep sadness when she cannot cry. Her thoughts about the past intrude into her consciousness both day and night. She has frequent feelings of anger and irritability and feels that she has very poor memory. She has reduced appetite and is tired much of the time. She relates all of these symptoms to the time when she was stuck in the back with a gun butt during a robbery. She reports times when she hears the voice of someone talking to her, but when she looks around she finds no one is there.

Elly came from a moderately well-off family in Somalia. She married young and reported that her husband treated her well. She had four sons and was pregnant when the war broke out in 1992. First, a gang of thieves broke into her house and stole everything valuable. Later another gang took what remained and forced her family to leave their home. During one of these attacks, her father was tortured, severely mauled, and left to die, but he survived. Sometime during all of this, her mother died "of shock." During the family's flight, a gang accosted them at gunpoint to demand money. They forced Elly into a room to be raped; she received cuts to her arms and was beaten with a gun on her back. When her husband tried to protect her, he was grabbed, taken outside, and shot. Elly rushed outside only to see him die of a massive head wound. From that point on, she remembers very little. Apparently, some neighbors took care of her and the children, and they buried her husband. Later, she married another man who was good to her and took her older son to Kenya. Separated from her second husband, she was able with some financial help to get to the United States with her son and her 10-year-old daughter.

During this difficult clinical interview, Elly's demeanor remained subdued and her speech was slow, hesitant, and so soft that at times it was barely audible. At the end of the history, I said to her that her pain was not due to being hit on her back but was due to a "broken heart" from the death of her husband. Quietly she said "yes" and, for the first time in the interview, cried openly.

Case 2. Yen

When first seen at our clinic, Yen was a 44-year-old separated Cambodian woman with symptoms of disturbed sleep, headaches, and poor concentration. Her psychiatric history was long and complicated, but her symptoms had worsened in the past 6 months. There was a long history of marital conflict. At the time of referral to our clinic, she had separated from her husband and received no support from him. She reported feelings of being overwhelmed, poor appetite, exhaustion, and weakness. She had recurrent nightly dreams of witnessing killings and butchering of people.

Yen was born in a rural area of Cambodia. She describes a happy childhood. She married her current husband at 17 and apparently found out only afterward that he had been married several times before. She suspected him of having multiple affairs throughout their marriage. She contracted pelvic inflammatory disease and had two pregnancies ending in miscarriage. The Pol Pot regime took over Cambodia in 1975 and discovered her father was a schoolteacher, and he was quickly executed. Her mother, a brother and sister, and an uncle and aunt were all killed one evening, apparently in a sadistic way. Yen was tied up several times and threatened with execution but was finally removed to another area where she endured starvation and forced labor. Although she was "like a toothpick" when the Vietnamese invaded, she survived. In her travels to reach the refugee center in Thailand, she endured multiple beatings and robberies. She came to the United States soon after arriving at the refugee camp in Thailand.

Yen told her story in a straightforward, low-key manner but appeared extremely sad, shedding many tears as she described the death of her family. Although she did not spontaneously make the link, when asked, it was clear that she saw her symptoms as caused by the traumatic events in her past.

Case 3. Maria

Maria is a Guatemalan woman in her mid-20s who was referred because of her persistent depression and sense of loss following the death of her mother in Guatemala during the civil war. Apparently, her mother had been a revolutionary figure who may have broadcast some antigovernment information on a clandestine radio station. She eventually was captured and killed. At first, Maria related her symptoms to this event. On further inquiry, however, she described a very chaotic childhood with frequent alcoholic bouts and fighting between her parents. There was also violence directed toward the children. Maria particularly remembers being stripped of her clothes at age 8 and forced to remain outside all night. She hinted that she may have been sexually abused, and later heard (or imagined) her parents talking about offering her as a prostitute. After recounting this history, she acknowledged a great deal of ambivalence toward her mother and admitted feeling some relief when she was killed, which of course was mixed with guilt. Maria fled from the guerrilla activities and eventually found her way to the United States. Now she felt haunted by her mother today, with complex feelings of grief, anger, loss, and love for what she had lost.

THE COMPLEXITY OF TRAUMA EXPOSURE AND RESPONSE

Many refugees have massive, multiple, prolonged, and unpredictable physical and psychological trauma continuing in refugee camps as well as countries of asylum. The implications of these experiences depend on the type and duration of trauma, the patient's personality, coping assets, and culture.

As the case stories presented suggest, exposure to trauma for many refugees is prolonged and complicated. Furthermore, trauma does not end once refugees arrive in host countries (the United States, in our case); they often face economic problems, discrimination, and ongoing violence. Events in the host country can reactivate symptoms.

A Somali woman with multiple symptoms of PTSD and depression was a patient in our clinic. In addition to brutal cruelty during the Somali war in which her husband was killed in front of her, the family was severely threatened and robbed in a refugee camp in Kenya. The family lived in a poor area of our city, and there was a shooting outside her apartment. Her symptoms immediately returned after several months of having been quiescent.

A Guatemalan woman was brought to the clinic several months after the local police had come into her apartment and forcibly removed her sister, who was immediately deported. Her PTSD symptoms had been under some control for the last 15 years. They had started when a student she was hiding from the military was discovered and killed in front of her. Later, her husband was also killed in the ongoing civil war. The patient became a legal resident of the United States but her sister had outstayed her visa. In what was probably a case of mistaken identity, the police had entered her apartment looking for drug dealers. The patient and her teenage children said they could no longer trust anyone here.

It is clear that, for most refugees, there is no single stress or traumatic event, but rather a prolonged series of traumas and losses. Clinically, it is important to do a thorough history of the patient to determine previous stresses and traumas (sometimes occurring early in life, such as child abuse), war related trauma, resettlement trauma, and current trauma.

Often there is no well-defined trauma on which to focus, as most forms of trauma therapy recommend. Many current therapeutic techniques involve some type of reexperiencing or exposure therapy with the goal of slowly decreasing the symptom by desensitization (Kinzie, 2001b; see Yadin & Foa, this volume). The theoretical underpinnings of this form of therapy assume that there has been a failure of extinction of the fear response, which is inappropriate in the current nontraumatic situation. However, this is a naïve and unrealistic assumption for refugees. They have experienced multiple traumas that are thoroughly intertwined, so one cannot pick one and ignore the others. Also the world, for refugees, is often not a safe place – threats and violence continue and the implication that one can "get over" the past seems quite simplistic.

The notion of confronting trauma through exposure reflects a Western concept: We need to face our problems and overcome them. This approach to mastering problems does not make sense for many cultures that emphasize different coping strategies, for example, cultivating the acceptance of one's Karma in Buddhist cultures, or recognizing that one's fate is in Allah's hands in Islamic cultures. The whole concept of openly recounting and confronting trauma may be foreign or even opposed to some core cultural values shared by the patient and his or her family or community.

Finally, some traumas are so existentially profound and disturbing that asking patients to be exposed to reminders of them without exhibiting a response seems cruel and inhumane. Does anyone really think that it is therapeutic to reexperience the murder of your husband in front of you, the burning of a building with your child locked inside, or your mother dying of starvation? Those are always and should be painful memories.

THE CO-OCCURRENCE OF TRAUMA AND LOSS

In addition to trauma, refugees have suffered multiple losses; this leads to the common comorbid diagnosis of depression. Being a refugee almost automatically means multiple losses: the loss of family members through death or separation, but also the loss of the wider social network of extended family or village. The losses continue with migration to a new society because the prescribed and familiar roles of traditional societies as providers, caretakers, and family leaders may be profoundly different or unavailable in an industrial society. This often results in a loss of income and vocation, and many refugees need governmental assistance. This unfamiliar dependence can lead to a loss of self-respect and respect within the community. Finally, the refugee experiences a loss of country, culture, and familiar social institutions. Given these multiple losses, it is not surprising that PTSD is usually associated with depression. In fact, they almost always coexist. The most frequent diagnosis of refugees in our clinic is "PTSD–depression complex."

This has multiple implications for our concepts of refugee trauma. To be relevant to this population, the conceptual model must include both trauma and loss. Animal models based on fear conditioning or human psychological models based only on aversive stimuli experience are incomplete. This also means that the clinical information gathered must include the history of losses as well as symptoms and signs of depression. Treatment clearly must include attention to depression as well as PTSD.

A related issue frequently ignored in PTSD literature is the presence of psychotic symptoms or even frank schizophrenia associated with trauma. Some patients will present with psychotic symptoms congruent with depression, while other psychotic symptoms seem unrelated. At times it is difficult to distinguish between the intrusive thoughts of PTSD and hallucinations or thought insertion. As we have followed patients, many have psychotic symptoms that have responded to antipsychotic medication. A smaller number have schizophrenia with delusions, hallucinations, thought disorder, affective incongruity, and bizarre behavior recognized by the community as mental illness. In the context of trauma and PTSD, these disorders are difficult to treat (Kinzie & Boehnlein, 1989). For example, the fear and hyperarousal of PTSD can exacerbate the psychotic symptoms. On the other hand, we have treated schizophrenia in refugees whose massive PTSD symptoms become apparent only when their psychotic symptoms are controlled.

Table 9.1 shows the high levels of comorbidity among refugees attending our clinic. The majority of patients received a diagnosis of PTSD and depression. PTSD also coexists with psychotic symptoms (requiring antipsychotic medication). Schizophrenia and PSTD, or schizophrenia by itself, has been found in all of the groups we follow. Overall, PTSD is present in conjunction with another diagnosis in 83%, 67%, and 82% of Cambodians, Bosnians, and Somalis, respectively. The reason for the high

TABLE 9.1. *Current Diagnoses Among Cambodian, Bosnian, and Somali Patients Attending the Intercultural Psychiatric Program*

	Cambodian (*n* = 110) %	Bosnian (*n* = 58) %	Somali (*n* = 59) %
PTSD alone	0	0	0
PTSD + depression	79	57	62
PTSD + depression + psychosis	0	5	17
Depression alone	6	19	3
Schizophrenia	7	12	12
Schizophrenia + PTSD	4	5	3
Alcohol dependence	2	0	0
Total with PTSD (including comorbid conditions)	83	67	82

rate of psychosis among the Somalis is unknown. Unlike American veterans with PTSD, alcohol and drug abuse are very uncommon in Buddhist and Muslim patient populations.

CLINICAL COURSE AND TREATMENT RESPONSE

For massively traumatized refugees, the PTSD–depression disorder and the PTSD–psychotic disorders are associated with high levels of impairment and subject to exacerbation under stress. In our first published study of Cambodians who survived the Pol Pot regime, from 1975 to 1979, all 12 had PTSD (Kinzie et al., 1984). After 1 year of treatment, about half had improved and no longer qualified for the diagnosis (Boehnlein, Kinzie, Ben, & Fleck, 1985). It was felt at that time that the disorder was perhaps easier to treat than indicated by the studies of Holocaust survivors. However, subsequently all of these patients had relapses of the full range of symptoms as have the majority of other patients with PTSD. Indeed, the chronicity of the disorder is now recognized to be a primary feature.

In a follow-up study of 23 Cambodian patients treated in our clinic for at least 10–15 years, 11 were asymptomatic, 8 had mild symptoms on the Clinician-Administered PTSD Scale (CAPS = 20–39), 3 had moderate symptoms (CAPS = 50–59), and 1 had severe symptoms (CAPS = 60) (Boehnlein et al., 2004). All continued to receive medication and individual therapy and most also receive a socialization group therapy. PTSD symptoms were still common as were social and vocational impairment (only one was employed). Only four had clinical depression with a score of over 17 on the Hamilton Rating Scale for Depression. On a variety of outcome measures, including symptoms, social improvement, and subjective distress, 10 were judged to have a poor outcome while 13 were relatively improved. All, however, have chosen to remain in treatment, and most have had an exacerbation of symptoms following some stressful life event.

The chronic waxing and waning course of PTSD is clinically impressive, especially compared to the general decline of depressive symptoms in the same patients. This was clearly observed in their response to the media coverage of 9/11, the World Trade Center bombing. The massive TV coverage was closely watched by our patients, who had much anxiety about an event that they barely understood. Many felt Portland itself had been attacked and they would not be safe. Patients described a general increase in their symptoms. We did a study of the clinic population with PTSD using self-report measures of change in symptoms. Patients were asked to rate responses to three questions on a 10-point visual analogue scale from 0 = *none* to 10 = *extremely*: (1) How much did the events affect you? (2) Did you have changes in the frequency or content of your nightmares? (3) Did you have changes in the frequency or content of flashbacks?

TABLE 9.2. *Reactions to 9/11 Events Among Patients with PTSD**

Ethnicity	N	Affect You Mean (SD)	Nightmares Change Mean (SD)	Flashbacks Change Mean (SD)
Vietnamese	42	7.33 (2.34)	6.13 (3.13)	4.65 (3.26)
Cambodians	37	6.65 (3.08)	2.57 (3.18)	5.05 (3.32)
Somalis	17	9.00 (1.27)	6.94 (3.60)	8.00 (3.32)
Laotians	10	7.10 (2.08)	2.40 (2.80)	3.50 (2.32)
Bosnians	18	9.22 (1.31)	4.56 (3.88)	6.50 (3.56)
One-way ANOVA		$F = 5.47$	$F = 9.27$	$F = 4.30$
		$p < .001$	$p < .001$	$p = .003$

* Rated on 10-point visual analogue scale from *none* to *very extreme*

The questions were asked by the attending psychiatrist through the counselor. The answers were the patients' own, either a mark on the scale or a verbal statement of their rating. Although this is a very imprecise rating, it was the only way to access the reactions of a largely illiterate and culturally diverse group rapidly (Kinzie, Boehnlein, Riley, & Sparr, 2002). The mean levels of the reactions of Vietnamese, Cambodian, Somali, Laotian, and Bosnian patients in our clinic to the media coverage of the events of 9/11 are shown in Table 9.2. Clearly, all patients had reactions to watching the events of 9/11, which affected them deeply. Most had an increase in nightmares and flashbacks. The greatest changes were found among the Somalis and Bosnians, probably because of their more recent war trauma but perhaps also because of their Muslim identity. Importantly, the content of the changes in PTSD symptoms of nightmares, flashbacks, and reexperiencing concerned their own war trauma, not the current 9/11 events. This is typical of PTSD, in which new stressors or traumatic events remind patients of their original traumas.

The response to treatment usually follows the phases depicted in Figure 9.1. Depressive symptoms and hyperarousal respond first to treatment, and reexperiencing decreases following treatment with medication such as clonidine (which reduces some of the symptoms related to sympathetic nervous system activation). Avoidance behavior (not wanting to think about the traumatic event and avoiding reminders of it) is difficult to treat and may even be protective in this population. However, under stress or new trauma, as our data on the impact of the events of 9/11 indicate, the full symptoms can return. Over time, each exacerbation is less severe and of shorter duration.

The clinical implication is that treatment needs to be long term (more like the clinical situation for patients with schizophrenia than for those with depression), and recurrences and remissions are to be expected. Short-term

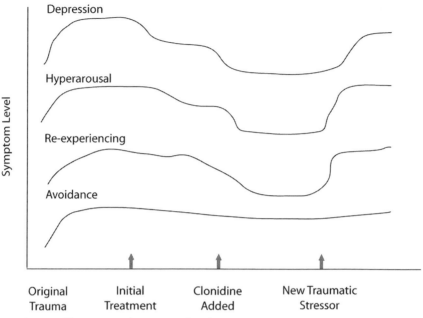

FIGURE 9.1. The course of trauma-related symptoms.

treatment is inappropriate, and a comprehensive clinical approach involving case management and extensive contact is required.

MEDICAL PROBLEMS

Mental health problems are not the only concern in this patient population. Traumatized refugees have a very high prevalence of hypertension and a high prevalence of diabetes. In the course of treating refugees, we became aware of the increasing rate of hypertension among our patients. This was so apparent that for many groups, including Cambodians, Somalis, and Vietnamese, we began to take blood pressures routinely in our clinic. Additionally, we noticed that a relatively large proportion was also being treated for diabetes. This led to an evaluation of hypertension and diabetes within the most traumatized population. We diagnosed hypertension, either by the fact that the patient was treated for hypertension or had a diastolic blood pressure over 140 and/or a systolic over 90. Diabetes was diagnosed if the patient was either being currently treated in the community or had a screening hemoglobin A1c test and a fasting blood sugar of over 120. Our preliminary results indicate that hypertension affects 43% of the patients, all groups being about equally affected. Diabetes affects between 12% to 18% of the refugee patients with the highest percentage found in the Somalis (of whom 48% had hypertension).

The reasons for these findings are unclear. The differences in rates are not related to age, which is comparable across groups. The Vietnamese and Cambodians have resided in the United States about 15 to 20 years longer than the Somalis and may have made changes in their diet or lifestyle, which could explain some of their increased rate of hypertension. Anecdotal information suggests that diabetes is prevalent among Somalis in Africa and of major concern. Of course, another possibility is that those with medical problems went to their primary care physicians and were then selected out for referral to our psychiatric clinic. An important possibility, however, is that chronic PTSD is itself a risk factor for medical problems such as hypertension and diabetes – a finding that has been reported among American veterans (David, Woodward, Esquenazi, & Mellman, 2004).

Whatever the cause of the elevated rates of medical disorders, the clinical implication is quite clear. The separation of mental health from physical health in clinical services may prevent essential diagnosis and treatment. Often primary care physicians cannot make the psychiatric diagnosis, whereas the reverse is true for psychiatrists. Psychiatrists and other mental health practitioners need to be aware of the potential for medical problems and ensure that patients are fully assessed. In our clinic, this has led us to do our own blood pressure and diabetes screening (hemoglobin A1c and fasting blood glucose). Obviously, when medical illness is identified, it is necessary to help patients obtain the proper treatment and ongoing monitoring to ensure compliance.

GUIDELINES FOR TREATMENT

Having detailed some of the issues involved in working with traumatized refugees with PTSD, I will offer some guidelines for treatment. These have been described in detail in other places (Kinzie, 2001a, 2001b) but are summarized here. Treatment planning must take into consideration the clinical setting, staff, and the relationship to the specific refugee communities served.

1. The clinic needs to manage the major psychiatric diagnoses in the refugee population. As we have shown, in addition to PTSD, patients commonly have major depression, psychotic symptoms, and, in some cases, schizophrenia. This requires a comprehensive evaluation and treatment plan that includes medication and case management as well as psychotherapy.

2. The presence of a well-trained, bilingual mental health counselor is required. Interpreters who come and go have little continuity or commitment to the program. Our approach is to train appropriate

people from the patient's own community who become interpreters for the psychiatrist, case managers, and counselors. They provide patients with continuity of care and are the program's representatives to and from the community. Of our current 25 counselors at various levels of training, 24 are from the ethnocultural group they represent and speak the language of that group.

3. Easy access to the clinic is important. For refugees, coming to a clinic may be a very intimidating experience. The clinic must be physically easy to reach, but, more importantly, all of the staff, from the janitor and administrative staff to the director, must like and welcome the refugees. Administrative red tape must be kept to a minimum. Having a critical mass so that refugees do not feel they stand out or are alone is also important. This is sometimes the problem with having refugees attend a general mental health clinic. However, in small refugee communities, attending a psychiatric clinic can result in loss of privacy and potential exposure. As patients improve and function better, they generally are less sensitive about being a "patient." The importance for our counselors of maintaining absolute confidentiality needs to be emphasized because an ill-advised comment in a community setting could damage both patients and the program. Although clearly labeled a "psychiatric program," our clinic is part of a general hospital and therefore does not have the stigma of a freestanding mental health clinic. It is easier to come to the hospital than to a psych clinic.

4. By caring for patients competently, treating them respectfully, and providing relief of their disorders, the clinic can achieve credibility within the community. Indeed, referrals now come from other patients who have appreciated their treatment. Credibility requires that the counselors maintain a professional and confidential approach in their interactions within their own community.

5. Integration of physical and mental health is important. Most refugees do not make the distinction and indeed often present with physical complaints that they link to the traumas they have endured. It is important to take these physical complaints seriously and ensure good access to primary care or family medicine. Because access in the United States is increasingly limited by funding cuts, some of our psychiatrists deal with more straightforward medical issues including obtaining and interpreting routine laboratory tests; assessing blood pressure; and treating arthritis, simple GI complaints, and infections. Clearly, it is important that patients have ready access to integrated care for all their health and social service needs.

6. Psychiatrists with specific competencies are essential to any clinic. The core of a medical program is its physicians. Treating traumatized

refugees is very difficult and requires the most experienced and flexible physicians to do the work. Clinicians need a broad range of skills; dedication to a single form of therapy is inadequate. There is a need for the personal qualities of liking the patient and being able to empathize with the severe difficulties he or she has been through. There is also the need for the basic skills of taking a complete history and formulating the issues (including diagnosis) in a manner that the patient can understand and accept. Treatment in general must include education, support, dynamic interpretation when appropriate, continuity of care, and specific interventions for symptom reduction. Recognizing the long-term relationship and being committed to it is probably the single most significant factor.

7. Reduction of symptoms is an important clinical focus. Patients usually have suffered for a long time and reasonably expect relief of symptoms. Fortunately, this is now possible through our understanding and experience with psychopharmacology. This is a subject unto itself and has been discussed elsewhere (Kinzie & Friedman, 2004).

Despite ethnocultural differences and genetic variations, Western medicine can be very useful across the range of refugee populations. Treatment for depression can proceed with an SSRI antidepressant; if insomnia is a problem, sedative tricyclic antidepressants such as imipramine may be even more useful. Nightmares and symptoms of hyperarousal can be controlled with adrenergic blocking agents such as clonidine or prozasin. Severe agitation and irritability may be reduced by an atypical antipsychotic such as risperidone. It is reasonable to expect to get major symptom relief within a few weeks. Of course, new stressful or traumatic events may bring exacerbations even when patients seem well controlled.

FINAL THOUGHTS

The movement in treatment of PTSD has been increasingly oriented toward specific technical interventions: exposure therapy, cognitive behavior therapy, EMDR, and even specific psychopharmacology. These all involve something being done to or with a patient. This focus on technical interventions seems to leave out the importance of the therapist as a person. For a traumatized refugee whose world has been shattered, and who has been physically and emotionally displaced, the presence of a therapist – who can sit, listen, and empathize with their pain, fear, and loss over time – is the most important treatment ingredient (Kinzie, 2001b). Searching for meaning, sharing experiences, and trusting each other are unique healing experiences and are increasingly rare in medicine as well as in everyday life.

References

Boehnlein, J. K., Kinzie, J. D., Ben, R., & Fleck, J. (1985). One-year follow-up study of posttraumatic stress disorder among survivors of Cambodian concentration camps. *American Journal of Psychiatry, 142*(8), 956–959.

Boehnlein, J. K., Kinzie, J. D., Sekiya, U., Riley, C., Pou, K., & Rosborough, B. (2004). A ten-year treatment outcome study of traumatized Cambodian refugees. *Journal of Nervous and Mental Disease, 192*(10), 658–663.

David, D., Woodward, C., Esquenazi, J., & Mellman, T. A. (2004). Comparison of comorbid physical illnesses among veterans with PTSD and veterans with alcohol dependence. *Psychiatric Services, 55*(1), 82–85.

Kinzie, J. D. (1981). Evaluation and psychotherapy of Indochinese refugee patients. *American Journal of Psychotherapy, 35*(2), 251–261.

Kinzie, J. D. (2001a). Cross-cultural treatment of PTSD. In M. F. Friedman, J. P. Wilson, & J. D. Lindy (Eds.), *Treating psychological trauma and PTSD* (pp. 255–277). New York: Guilford Press.

Kinzie, J. D. (2001b). Psychotherapy for massively traumatized refugees: The therapist variable. *American Journal of Psychotherapy, 55*(4), 475–490.

Kinzie, J. D., & Boehnlein, J. K. (1989). Post-traumatic psychosis among Cambodian refugees. *Journal of Traumatic Stress, 2*(2), 185–198.

Kinzie, J. D., Boehnlein, J. K., Leung, P. K., Moore, L. J., Riley, C., & Smith, D. (1990). The prevalence of posttraumatic stress disorder and its clinical significance among Southeast Asian refugees. *American Journal of Psychiatry, 147*(7), 913–917.

Kinzie, J. D., Boehnlein, J. K., Riley, C., & Sparr, L. (2002). The effects of September 11 on traumatized refugees: Reactivation of posttraumatic stress disorder. *Journal of Nervous and Mental Disease, 190*(7), 437–441.

Kinzie, J. D., Fredrickson, R. H., Ben, R., Fleck, J., & Karls, W. (1984). Posttraumatic stress disorder among survivors of Cambodian concentration camps. *American Journal of Psychiatry, 141*(5), 645–650.

Kinzie, J. D., & Friedman, M. (2004). Psychopharmacology for refugee and asylum-seeker patients. In J. P. Wilson & W. B. Drozdek (Eds.), *Broken spirits: The treatment of traumatized asylum seekers, refugees, war and torture victims* (pp. 579–600). New York: Brunner-Routledge Press.

Kinzie, J. D., Tran, K. A., Breckenridge, A., & Bloom, J. D. (1980). An Indochinese refugee psychiatric clinic: Culturally accepted treatment approaches. *American Journal of Psychiatry, 137*(11), 1429–1432.

10

PTSD: A Disorder of Recovery?

Arieh Y. Shalev

INTRODUCTION: A VIEW OF THE ETIOLOGY OF PTSD

Posttraumatic stress disorder is the better researched consequence of traumatic events. In its current formulation (APA, 1994) the disorder is essentially linked to the triggering event: It cannot be diagnosed in the absence of a traumatic event, and its core symptoms of reexperiencing and avoidance must refer to the traumatic event.

This perspective implies a causal link between the event and subsequent PTSD. Such a link is also intuitively appealing and frequently appears in survivors' narratives. For an external observer as well, the association between a traumatic event and PTSD appears to have some truth to it because many survivors' lives are dramatically changed by an encounter with extreme adversity or evil. Thus, from both the survivor's perspective and that of involved observers, the traumatic event is *the* cause of PTSD.

From a scientific point of view, however, this is only half true because many trauma survivors do not develop PTSD. A traumatic event, accordingly, is a *necessary*, but certainly not a *sufficient* cause of PTSD. If so, then what are the alternatives?

The oldest alternative to simple causation refers to individual differences in vulnerability. Historically, this mainly concerned predisposing factors, an attribution that often carried value judgments. The latter could extend from assuming a personality defect in those who broke down under stress to more understandingly relegating the causality to the wear and tear of the central nervous system by adverse living circumstances (e.g., McEwen, 2000) or birth circumstances (e.g., Meaney et al., 1991; see also Bagot et al., this volume).

More recent formulations suggest that a combination of biological and biographical factors, such as inheritance (e.g., True et al., 1993), child abuse, lower education, lifetime occurrence of mental disorders, and so forth contribute to individual vulnerability (e.g., Brewin, Andrews, & Valentine,

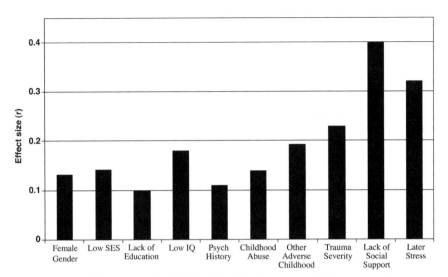

FIGURE 10.1. Risk factors for PTSD. Graphic depiction of Brewin et al. (2000). Adapted with permission from the *Journal of Consulting and Clinical Psychology*. Copyright 2000 by the American Psychological Association.

2000). Accordingly, under traumatic circumstances these potential "cracks" in one's protective shield yield to pressure, and symptoms of neuropsychological illness are expressed as PTSD. PTSD, thereby, epitomizes the way in which the environment can damage a vulnerable psyche (or vulnerable brain). Brewin et al.'s (2000) meta-analysis of risk factors for PTSD optimally expresses this multicausal view (Figure 10.1), giving relative weights to each of many risk factors. Perusal of this figure also shows that factors that follow the traumatic event, such as lack of social support and continuous adversities, increase the likelihood of developing PTSD after exposure.

Computations such as those provided by Brewin et al. (2000) are important in that they quantify the association between putative causal factors and PTSD. However, this type of analysis does not effectively tell us how, where, and when these factors might operate. For example, inherited predisposition can affect the likelihood of being exposed to a traumatic event (Goldberg, True, Eisen, & Henderson, 1990), as well as the intensity of subsequent PTSD symptoms (True et al., 1993). At present, therefore, the translation of risk factor into pathogenic paths is incomplete.

Furthermore, clinicians often encounter risk factors for PTSD in the form of "laundry lists," within which no single factor has enough sensitivity and specificity to predict a case of PTSD concretely from among a cohort of survivors of a traumatic event. It is only when an adult with a history of child abuse has developed PTSD that we can claim to understand and identify the abuse as a plausible contributing factor. This is truly weak support for a causal inference, in that it is based on narrative-driven, post hoc attribution, which can neither be confirmed nor rejected. Not surprisingly, such inferred causality has led to misplaced interventions, focusing on false etiologies (e.g., McNally, 2004). By extension, the entire idea of vulnerability has little practical value as a guideline for eventual prevention of PTSD among survivors, and clinicians usually refer to the severity and the duration of early PTSD symptoms in making clinical decisions.

TRAUMA SEVERITY

The second idea regarding the etiology of PTSD pertains to characteristics of the traumatic event itself, for example, its intensity, duration, and the embedded horror and grotesqueness. As shown in Figure 10.1, most of the literature currently suggests that the traumatic event is but partially responsible for subsequent PTSD (e.g., D. W. King, King, Gudanowski, & Vreven, 1995). Another important distinction concerns the concrete reality of an event, on the one hand, and the *reaction* to the event, on the other hand. The two (i.e., extreme event and intense reaction) are currently embedded in the stressor criterion (criterion A) of the *DSM–IV* definition of PTSD. The *perception* of the event and of subsequent symptoms is also an important component of the current construct of "trauma" (e.g., Ehlers & Steihl, 1995). Shalev, Schreiber, and Galai (1993) have shown a wide array of subjective appraisals of a single terrorist attack, in which a bus was overturned into a steep valley. Surviving passengers who had very similar concrete experiences (i.e., being in the same metal box that rolled over three times, seeing death and destruction) derived extremely different individual meanings, from "having acted extremely well under dire circumstances" to "having failed to prevent the attack."

The fear-conditioning theory of PTSD encompasses both the acute demand and the immediate emotional and bodily responses. This theory postulates that PTSD involves an associative link between an aversive event, an immediate and natural response, and a cue or piece of information that later comes to represent the event. The emphasis here is an immediate imprinting of this link, and its subsequent involuntary activation, in the form of PTSD symptoms (Pitman, Shalev, & Orr, 2000). An initial acquisition of conditioned response is essential for this view of PTSD, although there is also place for subsequent reinforcement via operative conditioning (e.g., successful avoidance). The fear-conditioning model of PTSD, however, does not explain the disorder's repeated intrusive recollections (see also Barad & Cain and Quirk, Milad, Santini, & Lebrón, this volume).

An extension of the previous approach is the cognitive behavioral theory of PTSD, which emphasizes the way in which events are perceived and subsequently construed and mentally elaborated (e.g., Foa, Steketee, & Rothbaum, 1989; Yadin & Foa, this volume). The cognitive behavioral theory effectively combines meaning, emotion, and their subsequent elaboration (or lack thereof). It therefore offers a powerful metaphoric explanation of the way in which the disorder is triggered *and* maintained. The related cognitive behavioral therapy (CBT) successfully couples deconditioning through reexposure and an elaboration of maladaptive meaning propositions. CBT is an effective psychotherapy of both chronic and acute PTSD. An apparent weakness of this theory is that it is still based on assuming fear response. In that sense, the cognitive behavioral theory is an extension of a stress–response model of PTSD.

The most heavily invested biological theory of PTSD pertains to neuroendocrine findings of a hypersensitive HPA axis in chronic PTSD (Yehuda, Giller, Southwick, Lowy, & Mason, 1991; see also Section I of this volume and the chapter by Konner). For the purpose of the argument made in this chapter, this view encompasses vulnerability and an *early response* stance, in that the yet unproven abnormal early response of the HPA axis might reflect prior sensitivities (such as having had prior traumatic experiences; Resnick, Yehuda, Pitman, & Foy, 1995) and peritraumatic occurrence of biological alterations. An apparent weakness of this model is that it builds its case on assuming a dysfunction of a widely distributed neuromodulatory system's functions (the CRF/glucocorticoid and mineralocorticoid array) and draws its evidence from the marginally related peripheral expression of the HPA axis. It nevertheless follows substantial animal literature on the role of the HPA axis in modulating memory imprinting during stress (e.g., Bohus, 1984). As expected from such a distal echo of a widely distributed array of CNS modulators, the relationships are nonspecific; hence, levels of stress hormones cannot diagnose, characterize, or predict PTSD, or otherwise guide clinicians. Importantly, the HPA axis theory of PTSD is also a branch of the more generic stress model of the disorder.

Finally, an elegant psycho-neuroanatomical explanatory model of the development of PTSD (Brewin, Dalgleish, & Joseph, 1996) suggests that traumatic recollections are initially encoded as unelaborated emotional memories and later have to be *transformed* into autobiographical (episodic) memories through reencoding. This transformation involves cross talk between two memory systems, the midbrain "emotional learning" system (focused on the amygdala) and the more widely distributed "episodic memory" storage and retrieval system. As a result of such cross talk, recollections of the traumatic events acquire temporal and spatial tags, and can be voluntarily evoked or abandoned, but do not relentlessly intrude and evoke fear and alarm. This theory is one of the best existing explanations of the repeated and distressful intrusive recollection of traumatic memories in PTSD and of the role of this type of activity in pathogenesis and recovery. Intrusive recollections reflect the above-mentioned amygdala–hippocampus cross talk. Brewin's theory also transcends the stress model of PTSD in that it offers a memory-processing model.

Along the same line, this chapter presents an alternative to the stress theory of PTSD by pointing to the essential etiological roles of novelty, incongruity, and loss. I will argue (a) that the weight of a traumatic event reflects the degree of its grotesqueness and incongruity with previous experiences; (b) that mechanisms related to the processing of such experiences are essentially responsible for the emergence of early PTSD symptoms; and (c) that the persistence of the latter significantly contributes to modifying the central nervous system toward preferentially and indiscriminately misinterpreting inner and external realities as aversive, incongruous, and threatening.

In other words, threat and fear are not enough: PTSD is the result of threatening events that are also horrible and grotesque. "Grotesque" here is to be read as strange, disturbing, or distorted – a type of experience akin to violation of norms for wholeness, bodily integrity, and species-specific survival schemata. Early experiments by Hebb (1946) and later by Humphrey and Keeble (1974) have shown an initial preference to allocate attention to fearsome pictures, prior to learning to avoid them. Along the same line, traumatic recollections might be preferentially attended to during the early aftermath of traumatic events. Such normal initial attention may not properly extinguish in PTSD.

The chapter's underlying thread of evidence comes from the author's longitudinal studies of acute response to traumatic events. The chapter, therefore, summarizes and builds on a series of systematic observations, within which it is framed, and by which it may also be limited. It nonetheless attempts to convey a compelling argument for integrating a specific, representation-driven understanding of the construct of psychological trauma with the current view of traumatic stress.

PTSD DOES NOT DEVELOP WITH TIME

It is now a common knowledge that, in aggregates of survivors, PTSD symptoms are intense and prevalent in the early aftermath of traumatic events, and their frequency and intensity subsequently decline. Data supporting this phenomenon comes from an array of approaches, including epidemiological studies of large cohorts New York residents following the 9/11 attacks (e.g., Galea et al., 2002), retrospective evaluation of a representative sample of the U.S. population (Kessler, Sonnega, Bromet, Hughes, & Nelson, 1995), longitudinal surveys of rape victims (Rothbaum, Foa, Riggs, Murdock, & Walsch, 1992), prospective studies of road traffic accidents (Koren, Arnon, & Klein, 1999), and terror survivors (Shalev & Freedman, 2005).

Figure 10.2 illustrates the progression of PTSD symptoms in survivors of rape and of violent crime accidents (Rothbaum et al., 1992). As can be seen,

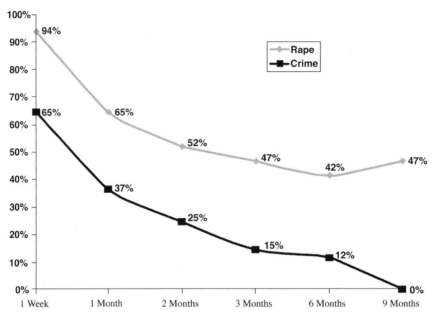

FIGURE 10.2. Proportion of rape survivors and crime victims who express PTSD symptoms at different time intervals after the traumatic event. Based on data from Rothbaum et al. (1992).

even in the absence of residual PTSD, many crime victims expressed the full PTSD syndrome in the period immediately following their traumatic event.

What is less clear is whether the decline in the frequency and the intensity of PTSD symptoms is somehow paralleled by a change in symptom severity among those who develop chronic PTSD. In other words, the question is whether, in the case of chronic PTSD, symptoms change over time or simply remain at the same level. Figure 10.3 illustrates the longitudinal course of PTSD symptoms, depression, and anxiety among injured survivors who did and who did not have PTSD 6 months after the traumatic event (Shalev, Peri, Canetti, & Schreiber, 1996). As can be seen, survivors without PTSD at 6 months had somewhat lower levels of symptoms at 1 week, and their symptoms declined with time. Survivors with PTSD, in contrast, kept expressing the same levels of symptoms across time and symptom domains (i.e., PTSD, depression, and anxiety). In other words, PTSD patients did not develop new symptoms. Rather, they did not lose those that they initially expressed. A similar course of symptoms has been observed in noninjured trauma survivors during a year (Freedman, Brandes, Peri, & Shalev, 1999), in children with PTSD (E. Galili, 2004; personal communication), and in a group of male and female survivors of road traffic accidents (Shalev et al., 1996).

To further illustrate this stable expression of symptoms in individuals who develop PTSD, we analyzed 1 year of longitudinal data in 10 survivors

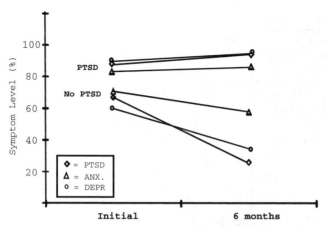

FIGURE 10.3. PTSD anxiety and depression symptoms 1 week and 6 months following a traumatic event in injured survivors with and without PTSD. Based on data from Shalev et al. (1996).

of traumatic events, using individual growth curves (King, King, Salgado, & Shalev, 2003). As can be seen in Figure 10.4 (in which each line represents one individual), symptoms declined among survivors who did not have PTSD at 1 year, but not in those who met diagnostic criteria for PTSD. Expressing similar levels of PTSD symptoms, therefore, is not an artifact

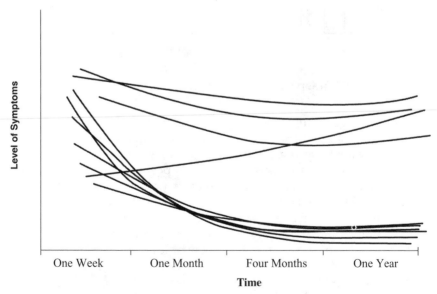

FIGURE 10.4. PTSD symptoms (total impact of events scores) in individual survivors at different time intervals from traumatic events. Reprinted from King et al. (2003) with permission from MBL Communications.

No. cases

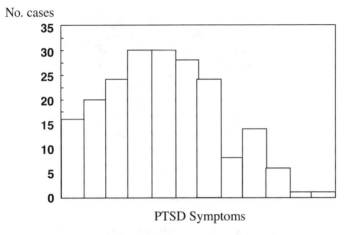

PTSD Symptoms

No. cases

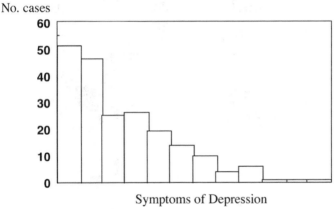

Symptoms of Depression

FIGURE 10.5. PTSD (top) and Beck Depression Inventory (bottom) (Beck, 1988) scores in 239 civilian survivors 1 week following a traumatic event.

of group averages, but rather typical of certain individuals. These observations suggest that PTSD does not "develop," but rather "persists."

An associated question is whether early PTSD symptoms are of "normal" occurrence. Normality is an elusive proposition, but approximations can be drawn from two kinds of data: frequency of a response (within which normal would be what is very frequently expressed) and data on symptom distribution (in which case normality pertains to a pattern of symmetrical distribution around a central trend). Data from studies performed at the early aftermath of the 9/11 attacks show at least one PTSD symptom in about 80% of the U.S. population (Schuster et al., 2001). Data from the above-mentioned Rothbaum et al.'s (1992) study show that PTSD is fully expressed by 94% of rape survivors 1 week after the rape. Figure 10.5 additionally shows a normal distribution of PTSD symptoms, 1 week after a traumatic event, in civilian survivors of traumatic incidents (upper

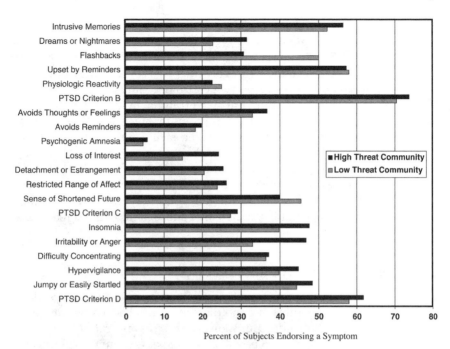

FIGURE 10.6. Frequency of *DSM–IV* PTSD symptoms and symptom criteria in 264 adult residents of two suburbs of Jerusalem during a wave of terror (March 2002). Reprinted from Shalev et al. (2006) with permission from the *American Journal of Psychiatry*, Copyright (2006) American Psychiatric Association.

histogram). Concurrent symptoms of depression (lower histogram) are not normally distributed. Figure 10.6 further illustrates the frequency of PTSD symptoms among 270 Israeli civilians living under continuous threat of terror and shows a frequent endorsement of most PTSD symptoms in the entire sample (Shalev, Tuval-Mashiach, & Hadar, 2004). Because only a subset of this group actually meets PTSD diagnostic criteria, the frequent presence of single PTSD symptoms is part of a normal reaction to adversity.

Thus, on both quantitative accounts, PTSD symptoms are a normal occurrence in the early aftermath of traumatic events or during prolonged exposure to adversities. For readers of earlier literature, this comes as no surprise: In the 1940s Lindemann (1944/1994) described the regular occurrence of a mentally painful condition that included intrusive recollections, emotional numbing, and eventual avoidance at the aftermath of traumatic loss. He furthermore suggested that expressing and communicating these symptoms is a prerequisite for recovery from acute grief, whereas their repression might lead to an "impacted grief" and protracted psychological dysfunction. Lindemann clearly portrayed detachment and what would now be interpreted as episodes of dissociation in which one could hear or otherwise feel or perceive the presence of the deceased with the intensity of a hallucination.

This digression to the literature on grief is not without intent. During the seminal years in which the PTSD construct was conceived, Horowitz's (1976) formulation of "stress response syndrome" similarly equated protracted responses as representing impacted trauma. In fact, what we now call PTSD is essentially composed of symptoms that were first described as acute responses to loss (e.g., intrusive reexperiencing of painful reminders, psychological numbing, attempt to avoid the pain of remembrance). PTSD symptoms of intrusive recall, dissociation, and numbing might, in fact, be a specific response to the incongruous novelty of some aversive events. Detachment, negative affect, and rumination are also typical of depression, and early depression is highly predictive of subsequent PTSD (Freedman et al., 1999; Shalev et al., 1996).

THE NATURE OF INTRUSIVE RECOLLECTIONS

Observations of recent survivors of suicide bombs in Jerusalem (Shalev et al., 2003) suggest that intrusive and distressing recall starts within minutes of a traumatic event, indeed, as soon as survivors are brought to safety. These "flash bulb memories" (Sierra & Berrios, 1999) are anything but verbal and reflective (as would be predicted by the appraisal component of Lazarus and Folkman's (1984) stress, appraisal, and coping model). They are, in fact, uncontrollable, inescapable, intense, and pervasive, often causing feelings more painful than the event itself. The reactions include both alarm and bewilderment. They often concern the most horrendous component of a traumatic experience (e.g., exposure to body parts). They often occur in witnesses (e.g., rescuers, body handlers) who came to the site of adversity only when the threat was over. These early reactions are clearly related to trying to process events that are beyond imagination, overwhelming and grotesque events that could not possibly have occurred. Here again one can see a response to the incongruous novelty of the traumatic event.

But what is the dynamic behind such tormenting and intrusive recall? In an attempt to resolve the paradox of traumatic nightmares, Freud (1920/1957) postulated that traumatic neurosis is a unique exception to the mental apparatus's dynamics of seeking equilibrium (alias "the pleasure principle"). He further suggested that traumatic nightmares are *not* essentially driven by their psychological content, as other dreams, but rather express an automatic "repetition," unrelated to the dynamics of drives, wishes, and their fulfillment. A more recent response (Brewin et al., 1996) suggests that intrusive recollections reflect the converging effect of two systems: the midbrain fear and alarm system and a yet to be described mechanism of solving incongruity and intense novelty (see Barad & Cain, this volume).

BETWEEN FEAR AND HORROR: THE POSTTRAUMATIC TRAP

Together, fear conditioning and posttraumatic rumination constitute a trap, which leaves some survivors in a limbo. The survivors cannot extinguish conditioned fear responses because the latter are rekindled and reinforced by repeated intrusive recall. They are also unable to lead the experience of incongruous novelty to resolution, possibly because of avoidance, associated with the forbidding conditioned response. These two processes, then, become mutually sustaining and perpetuating. With time, they may also lose their original purposefulness and plasticity and become redundant and automatic. The following paragraphs outline the sequence of empirical studies that supports this view.

Strength and Limitation of the Fear-Conditioning Paradigm

- Data from a prospective study of PTSD (Shalev, Sahar, et al., 1998) show that the disorder is preceded by a higher heart rate response to exposure, that is, a higher unconditioned response (UCR) to the traumatic event.
- Replications of these data (e.g., Bryant, Harvey, Guthrie, & Moulds, 2000) further confirm the association between PTSD and strong UCRs.
- Ample data has consistently shown an association between chronic PTSD and elevated physiological responses (heart rate, skin conductance, muscle tension) to traumatic cues (summarized in Orr, Metzger, & Pitman, 2003). This further buttresses the idea that PTSD includes an element of fear conditioned response.
- Data from functional brain imaging studies (reviewed in Liberzon, Britton, & Phan, 2003) consistently shows that the amygdala is centrally involved in mediating the responses to traumatic cues in PTSD. The amygdala is the essential element of the fear-conditioning pathways.
- Data from studies of differential conditioning (e.g., Orr et al., 2000; Peri, Ben-Shakhar, Orr, & Shalev, 2000) shows that PTSD patients may be highly conditionable. Preliminary results additionally show that heightened conditionabilty might precede the traumatic event and predispose expression of PTSD symptoms (Guthrie, 2005).
- A study by Pitman et al. (2002) shows that blocking the biological response that mediates fear conditioning (e.g., reducing the brain's noradrenergic drive by treating survivors with the beta-blocking agent propranolol shortly after a traumatic event) prevents the acquisition of physiological responses to traumatic reminders.
- However, this same study seems to suggest that blocking the acquisition of conditioned fear does not prevent PTSD, but rather specifically reduces the physiological response to reminders.
- These preliminary results illustrate the limits of the fear-conditioning model of PTSD. If PTSD persists despite successful inhibition of conditioned fear responses, then the disorder is not entirely explained by

fear conditioning. Fear conditioning, accordingly, is a necessary – but not sufficient – cause of PTSD.

Progressive "Wear and Tear" of the Response to Strong Auditory Stimuli in PTSD

- Exaggerated startle is one of the *DSM–IV* diagnostic criteria of PTSD. Physiological studies of the startle response in PTSD have yielded conflicting results as to the proper startle reflex (that is, the muscular response to startling stimuli) and more consistent findings of higher and nonhabituating autonomic responses to startling tones (Orr, Lasko, Shalev, & Pitman, 1995; Shalev, Orr, Peri, Schreiber, & Pitman, 1992).
- Shalev, Freedman, et al. (1998) studied the longitudinal course of startle responses and showed that the elevated autonomic responses to startling tones are *not* expressed 1 week following trauma. These responses, however, become clearly expressed 4 months later (Figure 10.7). The responses at 4 months resembled those observed in chronic PTSD.
- Using the same psychophysiological technique in a monozygotic twin study of Vietnam veterans with PTSD, Orr et al. (2003) have further shown that an abnormal autonomic response to startling tones is

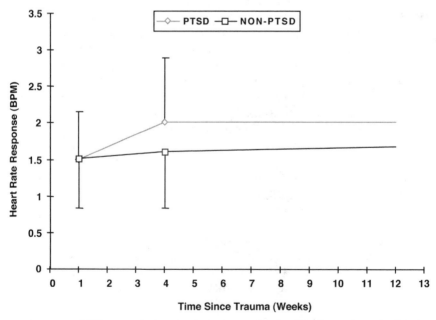

FIGURE 10.7. Differences in heart rate responses to startling tones do not exist at 1 week, but show up 1 month following trauma. Reprinted from Shalev et al. (2000) with permission from the *American Journal of Psychiatry*, Copyright (2000) American Psychiatric Association.

acquired (as opposed to inherited), and that the preconditions for its acquisition are both combat exposure and subsequent PTSD.

These findings first show that the abnormal response to startle is not inherited; otherwise, the two identical twins would have had the same response. It also shows that this response is acquired if both exposure *and* subsequent PTSD occur. In line with the previously described prospective study of startle responses, there is now compelling evidence that an abnormal response to startle is acquired.

The progressive acquisition of abnormal startle responses is important for understanding PTSD. First, these are bodily responses, which cannot be modified by volition and are essentially mediated by subcortical structures of the brain. These are also responses to a neutral stimulus that does not replicate the traumatic event. Therefore, they are not conditioned responses. They tell us, however, that, as PTSD symptoms continue to be expressed, the brain changes the way in which it responds to stimuli in general.

A study of vagal modulation of heart rate responses to neutral stimuli (Sahar, Shalev, & Porges, 2001) similarly suggests that PTSD patients use their alarm system to respond to minor challenges, such as arithmetic computation, which survivors without PTSD address by deactivating the parasympathetic control of the heart rate. What might be happening is that survivors who keep expressing PTSD symptoms progressively learn to preferentially perceive or respond to an array of novel stimuli as if they signaled a threat (e.g., McNally, Kaspi, Riemann, & Zeitlin, 1990).

PUTTING IT ALL TOGETHER

In summary, this chapter proposes that PTSD is a disturbance of recovery from the early and normal response to traumatic events. Underlying this defect of recovery is the mutual activation of two contrasting mechanisms: fear-driven learning and the processing of incongruous novelty. The first has to do with fear, threat, and danger and would lead to avoidance and distancing from the traumatic event and related recollections. The second originates in the need to attend to unthinkable and grotesque experiences initially (Humphrey & Keeble, 1974), presumably through repeated intrusive images. PTSD might be the consequence of unfortunate convergence between the need to remember and the imperative to avoid.

Using an analogy with predigital photography, fear-driven learning reflects a primary imprint of exposure, which the redundant processing of incongruous novelty either fixes or softens and lets fade out. Prior vulnerability confers emulsion sensitivity over which grotesque traumatic experiences may have scorching consequences. Everything is seen and interpreted through the lens of prior experience.

Events become traumatic through both fear *and* horror. This may explain the fact that, in the aftermath of the 9/11 attacks so many civilians who were not under direct threat expressed PTSD symptoms. There has been enough grotesque novelty to defy geographical distances. The 9/11 events also had another hallmark trauma: the total surprise and the sense that "this cannot be truly happening."

Unfortunately "this" happens. Traumatic events can be generally expected even though they remain individually surprising and shocking. "This"will certainly continue to affect numerous new survivors for a lifetime, unless one intervenes in time to prevent the transformation of acute PTSD symptoms into chronic PTSD.

A major context of traumatic events is human interaction and its related discourse. It is within this context that fear responses can either become an illness or subside. To some extent, people are attracted by horror – as reflected by the success of horror movies, or the effective use of the bad and the sensational in marketing and advertisement. In the right context (that is, within good-enough emotional controllability and specific temporal and spatial attribution), people may even learn from allocating attention to terror (i.e., how to protect themselves better, how to localize sources of threat). Primates also initially allocate attention to fearful stimuli, possibly to avoid them better later. The ubiquitous symptoms recorded shortly after 9/11 (Galea et al., 2002), and with them the initial attraction to the repeated TV images of the attacks, might have been such preparatory reactions. Research indicates that one must attend to the subsequent weeks and months.

These ideas imply, for example, that efforts should be made to mitigate the grotesqueness of terrorist attacks, such as by limiting the media's distribution of shocking photos and descriptions. They also imply that the ways in which events are construed, named, or appraised by the public, or by a relevant social group, may have major effects on the way in which they will be processed by individuals, indeed, by the brain where linguistic and semantic cues readily initiate a top-down appraisal of the emotional relevance of an event. In other words, human trauma is essentially embedded in language and in other species-specific complex signaling processes. Emphasizing these top-down brain processes (in which the *meaning* of an event strongly affects the resulting activation of alarm) may hold the key for better understanding resiliency and recovery.

References

American Psychiatric Association. (1994). *Diagnostic and statistical manual of mental disorders* (4th ed.). Washington, DC: Author.

Beck, A. T. (1988). *Beck Depression Inventory*. New York: Psychological Corporation.

Bohus, B. (1984). Humora ...d memory processes: Phys-
iological significance of ...anisms. In J. Delacour (Ed.),
The memory system of the ...roscience (Vol. 4, pp. 337–364).
Singapore: World Scien

Brewin, C. R., Andrews, ... Meta-analysis of risk factors
for posttraumatic stre: ...ed adults. *Journal of Consulting*
and Clinical Psychololo

Brewin, C. R., Dalgleis: ... dual representation theory of
posttraumatic stress ...w, *103*(4), 670–686.

Bryant, R. A., Harvey, ...lds, M. L. (2000). A prospective
study of psychophy ...ess disorder, and posttraumatic
stress disorder. *Jour.* ...09(2), 341–344.

Ehlers, A., & Steihl, R. (1995). Maintena... ...sive memories in posttraumatic
stress disorder: A cognitive approach. *Behavioural and Cognitive Psychotherapy, 23*,
217–249.

Foa, E. B., Steketee, G., & Rothbaum, B. O. (1989). Behavioral/cognitive conceptualization of post-traumatic stress disorder: A cognitive approach. *Behavior Therapy,*
20, 155–176.

Freedman, S. A., Brandes, D., Peri, T., & Shalev, A. (1999). Predictors of chronic
post-traumatic stress disorder. A prospective study. *British Journal of Psychiatry,*
174, 353–359.

Freud, S. (1920/1957). *Beyond the pleasure principle. Standard edition* (Vol. 18). London:
Hogarth Press.

Galea, S., Ahern, J., Resnick, H., Kilpatrick, D., Bucuvalas, M., Gold, J., et al. (2002).
Psychological sequelae of the September 11 terrorist attacks in New York City.
New England Journal of Medicine, 346(13), 982–987.

Goldberg, J., True, W. R., Eisen, S. A., & Henderson, W. G. (1990). A twin study
of the effects of the Vietnam War on posttraumatic stress disorder. *Journal of the*
American Medical Association, 263(9), 1227–1232.

Guthrie, R. M. (2005). *A prospective psychophysiological study of posttraumatic stress*
[dissertation]. Sydney: University of New South Wales.

Hebb, D. O. (1946). On the nature of fear. *Psychological Review, 53*, 259–276.

Horowitz, M. J. (1976). *Stress response syndromes*. New York: Jason Aronson.

Humphrey, N. K., & Keeble, G. R. (1974). The reaction of monkeys to "fearsome"
pictures. *Nature, 251*(5475), 500–502.

Kessler, R. C., Sonnega, A., Bromet, E., Hughes, M., & Nelson, C. B. (1995). Posttraumatic stress disorder in the National Comorbidity Survey. *Archives of General*
Psychiatry, 52(12), 1048–1060.

King, D. W., King, L. A., Gudanowski, D. M., & Vreven, D. L. (1995). Alternative
representations of war zone stressors: Relationships to posttraumatic stress disorder in male and female Vietnam veterans. *Journal of Abnormal Psychology, 104*(1),
184–195.

King, L. A., King, D. W., Salgado, D. M., & Shalev, A. Y. (2003). Contemporary
longitudinal methods for the study of trauma and posttraumatic stress disorder.
CNS Spectrum, 8(9), 686–692.

Koren, D., Arnon, I., & Klein, E. (1999). Acute stress response and posttraumatic
stress disorder in traffic accident victims: A one-year prospective, follow-up
study. *American Journal of Psychiatry, 156*(3), 367–373.

Lazarus, R. S., & Folkman, S. (1984). *Stress, appraisal and coping.* New York: Springer Verlag.

Liberzon, I., Britton, J. C., & Phan, K. L. (2003). Neural correlates of traumatic recall in posttraumatic stress disorder. *Stress, 6*(3), 151–156.

Lindemann, E. (1994). Symptomatology and management of acute grief. *American Journal of Psychiatry, 151*(6 Suppl.), 155–160.

McEwen, B. S. (2000). Allostasis and allostatic load: Implications for neuropsychopharmacology. *Neuropsychopharmacology, 22*(2), 108–124.

McNally, R. J. (2004). Is traumatic amnesia nothing but psychiatric folklore? *Cognitive Behaviour Therapy, 33*(2), 97–101; discussion 102–104, 109–111.

McNally, R. J., Kaspi, S. P., Riemann, B. C., & Zeitlin, S. B. (1990). Selective processing of threat cues in posttraumatic stress disorder. *Journal of Abnormal Psychology, 99*(4), 398–402.

Meaney, M. J., Mitchell, J. B., Aitken, D. H., Bhatnagar, S., Bodnoff, S. R., Iny, L. J., et al. (1991). The effects of neonatal handling on the development of the adrenocortical response to stress: Implications for neuropathology and cognitive deficits in later life. *Psychoneuroendocrinology, 16*(1–3), 85–103.

Orr, S. P., Lasko, N., Shalev, A. Y., & Pitman, R. K. (1995). Physiologic responses to loud tones in Vietnam veterans with PTSD. *Journal of Abnormal Psychology, 104,* 75–82

Orr, S. P., Metzger, L. J., Lasko, N. B., Macklin, M. L., Hu, F. B., Shalev, A. Y., et al. (2003). Physiologic responses to sudden, loud tones in monozygotic twins discordant for combat exposure: Association with posttraumatic stress disorder. *Archives of General Psychiatry, 60*(3), 283–288.

Orr, S. P., Metzger, L. J., Lasko, N. B., Macklin, M. L., Peri, T., & Pitman, R. K. (2000). De novo conditioning in trauma-exposed individuals with and without posttraumatic stress disorder. *Journal of Abnormal Psychology, 109*(2), 290–298.

Orr, S. P., Metzger, L. J., & Pitman, R. K. (2002). Psychophysiology of post-traumatic stress disorder. *Psychiatric Clinics of North America, 25,* 271–293.

Peri, T., Ben-Shakhar, G., Orr, S. P., & Shalev, A. Y. (2000). Psychophysiologic assessment of aversive conditioning in posttraumatic stress disorder. *Biological Psychiatry, 47*(6), 512–519.

Pitman, R. K., Sanders, K. M., Zusman, R. M., Healy, A. R., Cheema, F., Lasko, N. B., et al. (2002). Pilot study of secondary prevention of posttraumatic stress disorder with propranolol. *Biological Psychiatry, 51*(2), 189–192.

Pitman, R. K., Shalev, A. Y., & Orr, S. P. (2000). Post-traumatic stress disorder, emotion, conditioning and memory. In M. S. Gazzaniga (Ed.), *The new cognitive neurosciences* (2nd ed., pp. 1133–1148). Cambridge, MA: MIT Press.

Resnick, H. S., Yehuda, R., Pitman, R. K., & Foy, D. W. (1995). Effect of previous trauma on acute plasma cortisol level following rape. *American Journal of Psychiatry, 152*(11), 1675–1677.

Rothbaum, B. O., Foa, E. B., Riggs, D. S., Murdock, T., & Walsch, W. (1992). A prospective examination of post-traumatic stress disorder in rape victims. *Journal of Traumatic Stress, 5,* 455–475.

Sahar, T., Shalev, A. Y., & Porges, S. W. (2001). Vagal modulation of responses to mental challenge in posttraumatic stress disorder. *Biological Psychiatry, 49*(7), 637–643.

Schuster, M. A., Stein, B. D., Jaycox, L., Collins, R. L., Marshall, G. N., Elliott, M. N., et al. (2001). A national survey of stress reactions after the September 11, 2001, terrorist attacks. *New England Journal of Medicine, 345*(20), 1507–1512.

Shalev, A. Y., Addesky, R., Boker, R., Bargai, N., Cooper, R., Freedman, S., et al. (2003). Clinical intervention for survivors of prolonged adversities. In R. J. Ursano, C. S. Fullerton, & A. E. Norwood (Eds.), *Terrorism and disaster: Individual and community mental health interventions* (pp. 162–186). Cambridge, UK: Cambridge University Press.

Shalev, A. Y., & Freedman, S. (2005). PTSD following terrorist attacks: A prospective evaluation. *American Journal of Psychiatry, 162*(6), 1188–1191.

Shalev, A. Y., Freedman, S., Peri, T., Brandes, D., Sahar, T., Orr, S. P., et al. (1998). Prospective study of posttraumatic stress disorder and depression following trauma. *American Journal of Psychiatry, 155*(5), 630–637.

Shalev, A. Y., Orr, S. P., Peri, T., Schreiber, S., & Pitman, R. K. (1992). Physiologic responses to loud tones in Israeli patients with posttraumatic stress disorder. *Archives of General Psychiatry, 49*(11), 870–875.

Shalev, A. Y., Peri, T., Brandes, D., Freedman, S., Orr, S. P., & Pitman, R. K. (2000). Auditory startle response in trauma survivors with posttraumatic stress disorder: A prospective study. *American Journal of Psychiatry, 157*(2), 255–261.

Shalev, A. Y., Peri, T., Canetti, L., & Schreiber, S. (1996). Predictors of PTSD in injured trauma survivors: A prospective study. *American Journal of Psychiatry, 153*(2), 219–225.

Shalev, A. Y., Sahar, T., Freedman, S., Peri, T., Glick, N., Brandes, D., et al. (1998). A prospective study of heart rate response following trauma and the subsequent development of posttraumatic stress disorder. *Archives of General Psychiatry, 55*(6), 553–559.

Shalev, A. Y., Schreiber, S., & Galai, T. (1993). Early psychiatric responses to traumatic injury. *Journal of Traumatic Stress, 6*, 441–450.

Shalev, A. Y., Tuval, R., Frenkiel-Fishman, S., Hadar, H., & Eth, S. (2006). Psychological responses to continuous terror: A study of two communities in Israel. *American Journal of Psychiatry, 163*, 667–673.

Shalev, A. Y., Tuval-Mashiach, R., & Hadar, H. (2004). Posttraumatic stress disorder as a result of mass trauma. *Journal of Clinical Psychiatry, 65*(Suppl. 1), 4–10.

Sierra, M., & Berrios, G. E. (1999). Flashbulb memories and other repetitive images: A psychiatric perspective. *Comprehensive Psychiatry, 40*, 115–125.

True, W. R., Rice, J., Eisen, S. A., Heath, A. C., Goldberg, J., Lyons, M. J., et al. (1993). A twin study of genetic and environmental contributions to liability for posttraumatic stress symptoms. *Archives of General Psychiatry, 50*(4), 257–264.

Yehuda, R., Giller, E. L., Southwick, S. M., Lowy, M. T., & Mason, J. W. (1991). Hypothalamic-pituitary-adrenal dysfunction in posttraumatic stress disorder. *Biological Psychiatry, 30*(10), 1031–1048.

11

The Developmental Impact of Childhood Trauma

Bessel A. van der Kolk

Childhood trauma, including abuse and neglect, is probably the single most important public health challenge in the United States – a challenge that has the potential to be largely resolved by appropriate prevention and intervention. Each year over 3 million children are reported for abuse and/or neglect in the United States (Wang & Daro, 1997). The effects of abuse and neglect are well documented to persist over time. Although posttraumatic stress disorder (PTSD) has received much attention in the research and clinical literature, it is not the most common psychiatric diagnosis in children with histories of abuse and neglect (Putnam, 2003). Separation anxiety disorder, oppositional defiant disorder, and phobic disorders may all be more frequent diagnoses than PTSD in abused children, and attention-deficit hyperactivity disorder (ADHD) is common as well (Ackerman, Newton, McPherson, Jones, & Dykman, 1998).

Because there is only one trauma-related diagnosis in the fourth edition of the *Diagnostic and Statistical Manual* (*DSM–IV*), the effects of trauma on children are generally described under the rubric of PTSD, with numerous additional comorbid diagnoses to describe the many other psychological and biological functions that are disturbed by life experiences that may overwhelm the coping mechanisms of the growing human organism. When the *DSM–IV* was under development, extensive research was conducted to support the introduction of complex PTSD or disorders of extreme stress not otherwise specified (DESNOS) as an extended diagnosis for children and adults who were victims of prolonged interpersonal abuse (Herman, 1992; van der Kolk, Roth, Pelcovitz, Sunday, & Spinazzola, 2005). Even though the *DSM–IV* PTSD Committee overwhelmingly voted for inclusion of DESNOS as a new diagnosis in the *DSM–IV*, the Steering Committee of the *DSM* decided to list this diagnosis under "Associated Features of PTSD."

The diagnosis of PTSD was created in response to the political demand to capture the serious psychiatric problems suffered by hundreds of thousands of returning Vietnam veterans in the late 1970s. At that time, only a sparse literature on "traumatic neuroses" was available to guide the formulation of diagnostic criteria. Hence, the *DSM* committee had to rely on the clinical descriptions of war neuroses and on a few small studies of predominantly male burn victims (Andreasen & Norris, 1972) and Vietnam veterans (Shatan, Smith, & Haley, 1977) to arrive at meaningful diagnostic criteria. Despite these humble origins, PTSD has been found to be an enormously useful diagnostic construct with wide applicability to different victim populations and with its own unique neurobiology and therapeutics.

Prior to the conceptualization of PTSD, other posttraumatic syndromes were proposed, such as a "rape trauma syndrome" (Burgess & Holstrom, 1974) and a "battered women's syndrome" (Walker, 1984). These high-lighted the effects of assaults on victims' sense of safety, trust, and self-worth; their frequent revictimization; and their loss of a coherent sense of self.

Epidemiological research has shown that whereas men – the initial population studied to establish the diagnostic criteria for PTSD – most frequently are traumatized by accidents, war, assaults, and natural disas-ters, childhood abuse is by far the most frequent cause of traumatization in women (Kessler, Sonnega, Bromet, Hughes, & Nelson, 1995). Between 17% and 33% of women in the general population report histories of sexual and/or physical abuse (Finkelhor, Hotaling, Lewis, & Smith, 1990; Kessler et al., 1995), and in mental health settings, the rates range from 35% to 50% (Cloitre, Cohen, Han, & Edelman, 2001). More than twice as many women report histories of childhood sexual abuse than of (adult) rape, which occurs in approximately 10% of the general population (Breslau, Davis, Andreski, Peterson, & Schultz, 1997; Kessler et al., 1995).

Women are much more likely to be traumatized in the context of inti-mate relationships than men: 63% of the almost 4 million reported assaults on males are by strangers, whereas 62% of the almost 3 million reported attacks on women in the United States are by persons they know (Acierno, Resnick, Kilpatrick, Saunders, & Best, 1999). In the United States, 61% of all rapes occur before victims reach age 18; 29% of forcible rapes occur before the age of 11 (Acierno et al., 1999), usually by family members. Studies of physically and sexually abused children consistently report a range of psy-chological sequelae that are not captured in the PTSD diagnostic criteria. Studies of children also show that the emotion of fear, which has cap-tured the imagination of most neurobiological researchers who use animal models of fear (including those represented in this volume) and taken to represent the essence of trauma, is only one of several emotions reported by childhood trauma victims: Helplessness, depression, shame, grief, and mental collapse are more frequently reported by these trauma victims (van der Kolk et al., 2005).

Relational issues are difficult to address in animal research models of PTSD, with the exception of the fertile studies of rhesus monkeys by Harry Harlow, Steven Suomi, and Gary Kraemer, which have demonstrated the devastating effects of abandonment and maltreatment on the neurobiological development of our primate relatives. Because trauma in the context of intimate relationships is such a cardinal feature in the development of complex psychopathology in children, most animal models of human trauma appear rather naïve in the face of what is known to predict the development of PTSD in human beings: abandonment, betrayal, helplessness, and submission.

DEVELOPMENTAL AND RELATIONAL ISSUES

From its inception it has been clear that PTSD captures only a limited aspect of posttraumatic psychopathology, particularly in children (e.g., Brett, Spitzer, & Williams, 1988; Briere, 1988; Cole & Putnam, 1992; Scheeringa, Zeanah, Drell, & Larrieu, 1995; Scheeringa, Zeanah, Meyers, & Putnam, 2003; Summit, 1983; Terr, 1979). Many studies of traumatized children find problems with unmodulated aggression and impulse control (e.g., Burgess, Hartman, & McCormack, 1987; Cole & Putnam, 1992; Lewis & Shanok, 1981; Steiner, Garcia, & Matthews, 1997), attentional and dissociative problems (e.g., Teicher et al., 2003), and difficulty negotiating relationships with caregivers, peers, and, subsequently, marital partners (e.g., Finkelhor, Hotaling, Lewis, & Smith, 1989; Schneider-Rosen & Cicchetti, 1984).

Histories of childhood physical and sexual assaults also are associated with a host of other psychiatric problems in adolescence and adulthood: substance abuse; borderline and antisocial personality disorders; and eating, dissociative, affective, somatoform, cardiovascular, metabolic, immunological, and sexual disorders (e.g., Breslau et al., 1997; Cloitre, Tardiff, Marzuk, Leon, & Portera, 2001; Dube et al., 2001; Felitti et al., 1998; Finkelhor & Kendall-Tackett, 1997; Herman, Perry, & van der Kolk, 1989; Kilpatrick et al., 2000, 2003; Lyons-Ruth & Jacobovitz, 1999; Margolin & Gordis, 2000; Putnam & Trickett, 1997; van der Kolk, Perry, & Herman, 1991; Wilson, van der Kolk, Burbridge, Fisler, & Kradin, 1999).

Despite the ubiquitous occurrence of numerous posttraumatic problems other than PTSD, the relationship between PTSD and these multiple other symptoms associated with early and/or prolonged trauma has received surprisingly little attention. In the PTSD literature, psychiatric problems that do not fall within the framework of PTSD are generally referred to as "comorbid conditions," as if they occurred independently from the PTSD symptoms. By relegating them to seemingly unrelated comorbid conditions, fundamental trauma-related disturbances may be lost to scientific investigation, and clinicians may run the risk of applying treatment approaches that are not helpful (see Spinazzola et al., 2005).

TRAUMA IN CHILDREN

Most trauma for children begins at home. The vast majority of people (about 80%) responsible for child maltreatment are children's own parents (e.g., Felitti et al., 1998). Inquiry into developmental milestones and family medical history is routine in medical and psychiatric examinations. In contrast, social taboos seem to prevent obtaining information about childhood trauma, abuse, neglect, and other exposures to violence. Traumatic childhood experiences are not only extremely common, but they also have a profound impact on many different areas of functioning. For example, children exposed to alcoholic parents or domestic violence rarely have secure childhoods; their symptomatology tends to be pervasive and multifaceted and is likely to include depression, various medical illnesses, and a variety of impulsive and self-destructive behaviors (Felitti et al., 1998). Approaching each of these problems piecemeal, rather than as expressions of a vast system of internal disorganization, runs the risk of losing sight of the forest in favor of one tree.

The traumatic stress field has adopted the term "complex trauma" to describe the experience of multiple and/or chronic and prolonged, developmentally adverse traumatic events, most often of an interpersonal nature (e.g., sexual or physical abuse, war, community violence) and early-life onset. These exposures often occur within the child's caregiving system and include physical, emotional, and educational neglect and child maltreatment beginning in early childhood.

In the Adverse Childhood Experiences (ACE) study by Kaiser Permanente and the Centers for Disease Control (Felitti et al., 1998), 17,337 adult HMO members responded to a questionnaire about adverse childhood experiences, including childhood abuse, neglect, and family dysfunction. Eleven percent reported having been emotionally abused as a child, 30.1% reported physical abuse, and 19.9% reported sexual abuse; 23.5% reported being exposed to family alcohol abuse and 18.8% to mental illness; 12.5% witnessed their mothers being battered; and 4.9% reported family drug abuse.

The ACE study showed that adverse childhood experiences are vastly more common than previously recognized or acknowledged and that they have a powerful relation to adult health a half-century later. The study unequivocally confirmed earlier investigations that found a highly significant relationship between adverse childhood experiences and depression, suicide attempts, alcoholism, drug abuse, sexual promiscuity, domestic violence, cigarette smoking, obesity, physical inactivity, and sexually transmitted diseases. In addition, the more adverse the childhood experiences were, the more likely a person was to develop heart disease, cancer, stroke, diabetes, skeletal fractures, and liver disease.

Isolated traumatic incidents tend to produce discrete conditioned behavioral and biological responses to reminders of the trauma, such as the PTSD diagnosis seeks to capture (see Section I of this volume). In contrast, chronic maltreatment or inevitable repeated traumatization, such as occurs in children who are exposed to repeated medical or surgical procedures, have pervasive effects on the development of mind and brain. Chronic trauma interferes with neurobiological development and the capacity to integrate sensory, emotional, and cognitive information into a cohesive whole. Developmental trauma sets the stage for unfocused responses to subsequent stress (Cicchetti & Toth, 1995), leading to dramatic increases in the use of medical, correctional, social, and mental health services (Drossman et al., 1990). People with childhood histories of trauma, abuse, and neglect make up almost our entire criminal justice population (Teplin, Abram, McClelland, Dulcan, & Mericle, 2002); physical abuse and neglect are associated with very high rates of arrest for violent offenses. In one prospective study of victims of abuse and neglect, almost half were arrested for nontraffic-related offenses by age 32 (Widom & Maxfield, 1996). Seventy-five percent of perpetrators of child sexual abuse report to have themselves been sexually abused during childhood (Romano & De Luca, 1997). These data suggest that most interpersonal trauma on children is perpetuated by victims who grow up to become perpetrators and/or repeat victims of violence. This tendency to repeat represents an integral aspect of the cycle of violence in our society.

TRAUMA, CAREGIVERS, AND AFFECT TOLERANCE

Children learn to regulate their behavior by anticipating their caregivers' responses to them (Schore, 1994). This interaction allows them to construct what Bowlby called "internal working models" (1980).

A child's internal working models are defined by the internalization of the affective and cognitive characteristics of their primary relationships. Because early experiences occur in the context of a developing brain, neural development and social interaction are inextricably intertwined. As Don Tucker (1992) has said, "For the human brain, the most important information for successful development is conveyed by the social rather than the physical environment. The baby brain must begin participating effectively in the process of social information transmission that offers entry into the culture" (p. 199).

Early patterns of attachment inform the quality of information processing throughout life (Crittenden, 1992). Secure infants learn to trust both what they feel and how they understand the world. This allows them to rely on both their emotions and thoughts to react to any given situation. Their experience of feeling understood provides them with the confidence that they are capable of making good things happen, and that if they do not know how to deal with difficult situations they can find people who can help them figure out a solution. Secure children learn a complex vocabulary to describe their emotions, such as love, hate, plea-sure, disgust, and anger. This allows them to communicate how they feel and to formulate efficient response strategies. Compared to maltreated children, secure children spend more time describing physiological states such as hunger and thirst, as well as emotional states (Cicchetti & White, 1990).

Under most conditions parents are able to help their distressed children restore a sense of safety and control, and the security of the attachment bond mitigates against trauma-induced terror. When trauma occurs in the presence of a supportive, if helpless, caregiver, the child's response is likely to mimic that of the parent – the more disorganized the parent, the more disorganized the child (Browne & Finkelhor, 1986). However, if the dis-tress is overwhelming, or when the caregivers themselves are the source of the distress, children are unable to modulate their arousal. This causes a breakdown in their capacity to process, integrate, and categorize what is happening: At the core of traumatic stress is a breakdown in the capacity to regulate internal states. If the distress does not let up, children dissoci-ate. The relevant sensations, affects, and cognitions cannot be associated; instead, they are dissociated into sensory fragments (van der Kolk & Fisler, 1995) and, as a result, these children cannot comprehend what is happening or devise and execute appropriate plans of action.

When caregivers are emotionally absent, inconsistent, frustrating, vio-lent, intrusive, or neglectful, children are liable to become intolerably dis-tressed and unlikely to develop a sense that the external environment is able to provide relief. Thus, children with insecure attachment patterns have trouble relying on others to help them, while they are unable to regulate their emotional states by themselves. As a result, they experi-ence excessive anxiety, anger, and longings to be taken care of. These feelings may become so extreme as to precipitate dissociative states or self-defeating aggression. Spaced-out and hyperaroused children learn to ignore either what they feel (their emotions) or what they perceive (their cognitions).

When children are unable to achieve a sense of control and stability, they become helpless. If they are unable to grasp what is going on and unable do anything about it to change it, they go immediately from (fearful) stimulus to (fight/flight/freeze) response without being able to learn from the expe-rience. Subsequently, when exposed to reminders of a trauma (sensations, physiological states, images, sounds, situations), they tend to behave as if they were traumatized all over again – as a catastrophe (Streeck-Fischer & van der Kolk, 2000). Many problems of traumatized children can be under-stood as efforts to minimize objective threat and to regulate their emotional distress (Pynoos et al., 1987). Unless caregivers understand the nature of such reenactments, they are liable to label the child as "oppositional," "rebellious," "unmotivated," and "antisocial."

THE DYNAMICS OF CHILDHOOD TRAUMA

Young children, still embedded in the here and now and lacking the capacity to see themselves in the perspective of the larger context, have no choice but to see themselves as the center of the universe: Everything that happens is directly related to their own sensations. Development consists of learning to master and "own" one's experiences and to learn to experience the present as part of one's personal experience over time (Kegan, 1982). Piaget called this "decentration" – moving from being one's reflexes, movements, and sensations to having them.

Predictability and continuity are critical in order to develop a good sense of causality and for learning to categorize experience. Children need to develop categories in order to be able to place any particular experience in a larger context. Only when they can do this will they be able to evaluate what is currently going on and entertain a range of options with which they can affect the outcome of events. Imagining being able to play an active role leads to problem-focused coping (Streeck-Fischer & van der Kolk, 2000).

If children are exposed to unmanageable stress, and if the caregiver does not take over the function of modulating the child's arousal, as occurs when children are exposed to family dysfunction or violence, the child will be unable to organize and categorize its experiences in a coherent fashion. Unlike adults, children do not have the option to report, move away, or otherwise protect themselves – they depend on their caregivers for their very survival. When trauma emanates from within the family, children experience a crisis of loyalty and organize their behavior to survive within their families. Being prevented from articulating what they observe and experience, traumatized children will organize their behavior around keeping the secret, dealing with their helplessness through compliance or defiance, and accommodating in any way they can to entrapment in abusive or neglectful situations (Summit, 1983). When professionals are unaware of children's need to adjust to traumatizing environments and expect that children should behave in accordance with adult standards of self-determination and autonomous, rational choices, these maladaptive behaviors tend to inspire revulsion and rejection. Ignorance of this fact is likely to lead to labeling and stigmatizing children for behaviors that are meant to ensure survival.

Being left to their own devices leaves chronically traumatized children with deficits in emotional self-regulation. This results in problems with self-definition as reflected by (1) a lack of a continuous sense of self; (2) poorly modulated affect and impulse control, including aggression against self and others; and (3) uncertainty about the reliability and predictability of others, which is expressed as distrust, suspiciousness, and problems with intimacy and which results in social isolation (Cole & Putnam, 1992). Chronically traumatized children tend to suffer from distinct alterations in states of consciousness, with amnesia, hypermnesia, dissociation, depersonalization and derealization, flashbacks and nightmares of specific events, school problems, difficulties in attention regulation, and difficulties with orientation in time and space. They also suffer from sensorimotor developmental disorders. They often are literally are "out of touch" with their feelings and often have no language to describe internal states (Cicchetti & White, 1990).

Lacking a sense of predictability interferes with the development of object constancy – a lack of inner representations of their own inner world or their surroundings. As a result, they lack a good sense of cause and effect and of their own contributions to what happens to them. Without internal maps to guide them, they act instead of plan, and show their wishes in their behaviors rather than discussing what they want (Streeck-Fischer & van der Kolk, 2000). Unable to appreciate clearly who they or others are, they have problems enlisting other people as allies on their behalf. Other people are sources of terror or pleasure but rarely fellow human beings with their own sets of needs and desires. They have difficulty appreciating novelty; without a map to compare and contrast, anything new is potentially threatening. What is familiar tends to be experienced as safer, even if it is a predictable source of terror.

These children rarely spontaneously discuss their fears and traumas, and they have little insight into the relationship among what they do, what they feel, and what has happened to them. They tend to communicate the nature of their traumatic past by repeating it in the form of interpersonal enactments, in their play, and in their fantasy lives.

CHILDHOOD TRAUMA AND PSYCHIATRIC ILLNESS

As noted in the introduction to this chapter, PTSD is not the most common psychiatric diagnosis in children with histories of chronic trauma. For example, in one study of 364 abused children (Ackerman et al., 1998), the most common diagnoses in order of frequency were separation anxiety disorder, oppositional defiant disorder, phobic disorders, PTSD, and ADHD. These diagnoses reflect the fact that studies of traumatized children find they tend to have problems with aggression and impulse control (Lewis & Shanok, 1981; Steiner et al., 1997), attentional problems and dissociative symptoms (Teicher et al., 2003), and relationship difficulties with family, peers, and, eventually, intimate partners (Schneider-Rosen & Cicchetti, 1984).

Histories of childhood physical and sexual assaults are associated with a host of other psychiatric diagnoses in adolescence and adulthood: substance abuse; borderline and antisocial personality disorders; and eating, dissociative, affective, somatoform, cardiovascular, metabolic, immunological, and sexual disorders (van der Kolk, 2003).

The results of the *DSM–IV* field trial suggested that trauma has its most pervasive impact during the first decade of life and becomes more circumscribed, that is, more like "pure" PTSD, with age (van der Kolk et al., 2005). The diagnosis of PTSD is not developmentally sensitive and does not adequately describe the impact of exposure to childhood trauma on the developing child. Because multiple abused infants and children often experience developmental delays across a broad spectrum, including cognitive, language, motor, and socialization skills (Culp, Heide, & Richardson, 1987), they tend to display very complex disturbances with a variety of different, often fluctuating, presentations.

However, because there currently is no other diagnostic entity that describes the pervasive impact of trauma on child development, these children are given a range of comorbid diagnoses as if they occurred independently from the PTSD symptoms, none of which do justice to the spectrum of problems of traumatized children, and none of which provide guidelines on what is needed for effective prevention and intervention. By relegating the full spectrum of trauma-related problems to seemingly unrelated comorbid conditions, fundamental trauma-related disturbances may be lost to scientific investigation, and clinicians may run the risk of applying treatment approaches that are not helpful.

TOWARD A DIAGNOSIS OF DEVELOPMENTAL TRAUMA DISORDER

The question of how best to organize the very complex emotional, behavioral, and neurobiological sequelae of childhood trauma has vexed clinicians for several decades. Because the *DSM–IV* has a diagnosis for adult-onset trauma, PTSD, this label often is applied to traumatized children as well. However, the majority of traumatized children do not meet diagnostic criteria for PTSD (Kiser, Heston, Millsap, & Pruitt, 1991), and PTSD cannot capture the multiplicity of exposures over critical developmental periods. Moreover, the PTSD diagnosis does not capture the developmental impact of childhood trauma: the complex disruptions of affect regulation; the disturbed attachment patterns; the rapid behavioral regressions and shifts in emotional states; the loss of autonomous strivings; the aggressive behavior against self and others; the failure to achieve developmental competencies; the loss of bodily regulation in the areas of sleep, food, and self-care; the altered schemas of the world; the anticipatory behavior and traumatic expectations; the multiple somatic problems, from gastrointestinal distress to headaches; the apparent lack of awareness of danger and resulting self-endangering behaviors; the self-hatred and self-blame; and the chronic feelings of ineffectiveness.

Interestingly, many forms of interpersonal trauma, in particular psychological maltreatment, neglect, separation from caregivers, traumatic loss, and inappropriate sexual behavior, do not necessarily meet the *DSM–IV*

"Criterion A" definition for a traumatic event, which requires, in part, an experience involving "actual or threatened death or serious injury, or a threat to the physical integrity of self or others" (APA, 1994, p. 427). Children exposed to these common types of interpersonal adversity thus typically would not qualify for a PTSD diagnosis unless they also were exposed to experiences or events that qualify as traumatic, even if they have symptoms that would otherwise warrant a PTSD diagnosis. This finding has several implications for the diagnosis and treatment of traumatized children and adolescents. Non–Criterion A forms of childhood trauma exposure – such as psychological/emotional abuse and traumatic loss – have been demonstrated to be associated with PTSD symptoms and self-regulatory impairments in children (Basile, Arias, Desai, & Thompson, 2004) and into adulthood (Higgins & McCabe, 2003; Zlotknick et al., 1996). Thus, classification of traumatic events may need to be defined more broadly, and treatment may need to address directly the sequelae of these interpersonal adversities, given their prevalence and potentially severe negative effects on children's development and emotional health.

The Complex Trauma Task Force of the National Child Traumatic Stress Network has been concerned about the need for a more precise diagnosis for children with complex histories. In an attempt to delineate more clearly what these children suffer from and to serve as a guide for rational therapeutics, this task force has started to conceptualize a new diagnosis provisionally called "developmental trauma disorder."[1] This proposed diagnosis is organized around the issue of triggered dysregulation in response to traumatic reminders, stimulus generalization, and the anticipatory organization of behavior to prevent the recurrence of the trauma impact (see Table 11.1).

This provisional developmental trauma disorder is predicated on the notion that multiple exposures to interpersonal trauma, such as abandonment, betrayal, physical or sexual assaults, or witnessing domestic violence, have consistent and predictable consequences that affect many areas of functioning. These experiences engender (1) intense affects such as rage, betrayal, fear, resignation, defeat, and shame and (2) efforts to ward off the recurrence of those emotions, including the avoidance of experiences that precipitate them or engaging in behaviors that convey a subjective sense of control in the face of potential threats. (3) These children tend to behaviorally reenact their traumas either as perpetrators, in aggressive or sexual acting out against other children, or in frozen avoidance reactions. (4) Their physiological dysregulation may lead to multiple somatic

---

[1] The members of the NCTSD Developmental Trauma Disorders Task Force are Marylene Cloitre, Julian Ford, Alicia Lieberman, Frank Putnam, Robert Pynoos, Glenn Saxe, Michael Scheeringa, Joseph Spinazzola, and Bessel van der Kolk, with input from Michael DeBellis, Allan Steinberg, and Martin Teicher.

TABLE 11.1. *Diagnostic Criteria for Developmental Trauma Disorder (Proposed by the National Child Traumatic Stress Network Task Force on DSM–V)*

A. Exposure
   - Multiple or chronic exposure to one or more forms of developmentally adverse interpersonal trauma (abandonment, betrayal, physical assaults, sexual assaults, threats to bodily integrity, coercive practices, emotional abuse, witnessing violence and death)
   - Subjective experience (rage, betrayal, fear, resignation, defeat, shame)

B. Triggered pattern of repeated dysregulation in response to trauma cues. Dysregulation (high or low) in presence of cues. Changes persist and do not return to baseline; not reduced in intensity by conscious awareness.
   - Affective
   - Somatic (physiological, motoric, medical)
   - Behavioral (e.g., reenactment, cutting)
   - Cognitive (thinking that it is happening again, confusion, dissociation, depersonalization)
   - Relational (clinging, oppositional, distrustful, compliant)
   - Self-attribution (self-hate and blame)

C. Persistently altered attributions and expectancies
   - Negative self-attribution
   - Distrust protective caretaker
   - Loss of expectancy of protection by others
   - Loss of trust in social agencies to protect
   - Lack of recourse to social justice/retribution
   - Inevitability of future victimization

D. Functional impairment
   - Educational
   - Familial
   - Peer
   - Legal
   - Vocational

problems, such as headaches and stomachaches, in response to fearful and helpless emotions.

Persistent sensitivity to reminders interferes with the development of emotion regulation and causes long-term emotional dysregulation and precipitous behavior changes. Their over- and underreactivity is manifested on multiple levels: emotional, physical, behavioral, cognitive, and relational. They have fearful, enraged, or avoidant emotional reactions to minor stimuli that would have no significant impact on secure children. After having become aroused, these children have a great deal of difficulty restoring homeostasis and returning to baseline. Insight and understanding about the origins of their reactions seems to have little effect.

In addition to the conditioned physiological and emotional responses to reminders characteristic of PTSD, complexly traumatized children develop a view of the world that incorporates their betrayal and hurt. They anticipate and expect the trauma to recur and respond with hyperactivity, aggression, defeat, or freeze responses to minor stresses.

Their cognition is affected by reminders, so they tend to become confused, dissociated, and disoriented when faced with stressful stimuli. They easily misinterpret events in the direction of a return of trauma and helplessness, which causes them to be constantly on guard, frightened, and overreactive. Finally, expectations of a return of the trauma permeate their relationships. This is expressed as negative self-attributions, loss of trust in caretakers, and loss of the belief that some somebody will look after them and make feel safe. They tend to lose the expectation that they will be protected and act accordingly. As a result, they organize their relationships around the expectation or prevention of abandonment or victimization. This is expressed as excessive clinging, compliance, oppositional defiance, and distrustful behavior, and they may be preoccupied with retribution and revenge.

All of these problems are expressed in dysfunction in multiple areas of functioning: education, family, peer relationships, problems with the legal system, and problems in maintaining jobs.

TREATMENT IMPLICATIONS

In the treatment of traumatized children and adolescents, there often is a painful dilemma of whether to keep them in the care of people or institutions who are sources of hurt and threat, or whether to play into abandonment and separation distress by taking the child away from familiar environments and people to whom they are intensely attached but who are likely to cause further substantial damage (Streeck-Fischer & van der Kolk, 2000).

Exposure Treatment

In recent years there has been an advocacy of "exposure treatment" as the treatment of choice for PTSD. This advocacy is based on the notions that during traumatic experiences people fail to integrate their traumatic memories (van der Kolk & Fisler, 1995) and that they need to be desensitized from their traumatic fears by confronting them. Although this notion is basically valid, it ignores the core issue that people need to be in a state of relative physiological homeostasis to be able to integrate their dissociated traumatic memories. Once people feel physically safe (as measured by self-reports and such variables as sympathetic nervous system activation and heart rate variability), they seem to regain the courage to be able to face the unacceptable and terrifying experiences of their past. Research has shown that such somatically based therapies as EMDR (Sack, Hopper, & Lamprecht, 2004) and yoga (van der Kolk et al., 2005) create a state of decreased autonomic arousal that facilitates the processing of traumatic memories and help them change from fragmented sensory imprints into personal narratives without physiological arousal after exposure (van der Kolk et al., in press).

We recently reviewed the treatment outcome literature of PTSD and found that (1) very few studies reported on the fate of the dropouts and those with negative treatment outcome and that (2) the selection criteria for current PTSD treatment studies by and large exclude typical treatment-seeking clinical populations.

Establishing Safety and Competence

Complexly traumatized children need to be helped to engage their attention in pursuits that (1) do not remind them of trauma-related triggers and that (2) give them a sense of pleasure and mastery. Safety, predictability, and fun are essential for the establishment of the capacity to observe what is going on, put it into a larger context, and initiate physiological and motoric self-regulation. Before addressing anything else these children need to be helped with how to react differently from their habitual fight/flight/freeze reactions (Streek-Fischer & van der Kolk, 2000). Only after children develop the capacity to focus on pleasurable activities without becoming disorganized do they have a chance to develop the capacity to play with other children, engage in simple group activities, and deal with more complex issues.

Dealing with Traumatic Reenactments

After having been multiply traumatized, the imprint of the trauma becomes lodged in many aspects of the child's make-up. This is manifested in multiple ways: for example, as fearful reactions, aggressive and sexual acting out, avoidance, and uncontrolled emotional reactions. Unless this tendency to repeat the trauma is recognized, the response of the environment is likely to be a replay of the original traumatizing, abusive, but familiar relationships. Because these children are prone to experience anything novel, including rules and other protective interventions, as punishments, they tend to regard their teachers and therapists who try to establish safety as perpetrators (Streek-Fischer & van der Kolk, 2000).

Attention to the Body: Integration and Mastery

Mastery is most of all a physical experience – the feeling of being in charge, calm, and able to engage in focused efforts to accomplished the goals one sets for oneself. These children experience the trauma-related hyperarousal and numbing on a deeply somatic level. Their hyperarousal is immediately apparent in their inability to relax and by their high degree of irritability. Children with "frozen" reactions need to be helped to reawaken their curiosity and to explore their surroundings. They avoid engagement in activities because any task may unexpectedly turn into a traumatic trigger. Neutral, fun tasks and physical games can provide them with knowledge of what it feels like to be relaxed and to feel a sense of physical mastery.

At the center of the therapeutic work with terrified children is helping them realize that they are repeating their early experiences and helping them find new ways of coping by developing new connections among their experiences, emotions, and physical reactions. Unfortunately, all too often, medications take the place of helping children acquire the skills necessary to deal with and master their uncomfortable physical sensations. In clinical settings it still is common to establish a sense of mastery and capacity to regulate the child's physiological arousal by fostering play, engaging in soothing physical activities, and participating in physical activities such as "improv exercises" and sensory integration techniques (Macy et al., 2004; Spinazzola et al., 2005). In order to process their traumatic experiences, traumatized children first need to develop a safe space where they can look at their traumas without repeating them and making them real once again (Streeck-Fischer & van der Kolk, 2000).

References

Acierno, R., Resnick, H. S., Kilpatrick, D. G., Saunders, B. E., & Best, C. L. (1999). Risk factors for rape, physical assault, and posttraumatic stress disorder in women: Examination of differential multivariate relationships. *Journal of Anxiety Disorders, 13*(6), 541–563.

Ackerman, P. T., Newton, J. E. O., McPherson, W. B., Jones, J. G., & Dykman, R. A. (1998). Prevalence of posttraumatic stress disorder and other psychiatric diagnoses in three groups of abused children (sexual, physical, and both). *Child Abuse & Neglect, 22*(8), 759–774.

American Psychiatric Association. (1994). *Diagnostic and statistical manual of mental disorders* (4th ed.). Washington, DC: Author.

Andreasen, N. J. C., & Norris, A. S. (1972). Long-term adjustment and adaptation mechanisms in severely burned adults. *Journal of Nervous and Mental Disease, 154,* 352–362.

Basile, K. C., Arias, I., Desai, S., & Thompson, M. P. (2004). The differential association of intimate partner physical, sexual, psychological, and stalking violence and posttraumatic stress symptoms in a nationally representative sample of women. *Journal of Traumatic Stress, 17*(5), 413–421.

Bowlby, J. (1980). *Attachment and loss* (Vol. 3). New York: Basic Books.

Breslau, N., Davis, G. C., Andreski, P., Peterson, E. L., & Schultz, L. R. (1997). Sex differences in posttraumatic stress disorder. *Archives of General Psychiatry, 54*(11), 1044–1048.

Brett, E., Spitzer, R., & Williams, J. (1988). DSM III-R criteria for posttraumatic stress disorder. *American Journal of Psychiatry, 145*, 1232–1236.

Briere, J. (1988). The long-term clinical correlates of childhood sexual victimization. *Annals of the New York Academy of Sciences, 528*, 327–334.

Browne, A., & Finkelhor, D. (1986). Impact of child abuse: A review of the research. *Psychological Bulletin, 99*, 66–77.

Burgess, A. W., Hartman, C. R., & McCormack, A. (1987). Abused to abuser: Antecedents of socially deviant behavior. *American Journal of Psychiatry, 144*, 1431–1436.

Burgess, A. W., & Holmstrom, L. L. (1974). Rape trauma syndrome. *American Journal of Psychiatry, 131*, 981–986.

Cicchetti, D., & Toth, S. D. (1995). Developmental psychopathology and disorders of affect. In D. Cicchetti & D. Cohen (Eds.), *Developmental psychopathology, Vol. 2: Risk, disorder, and adaptation. Wiley series on personality processes* (pp. 369–420). New York: Wiley.

Cicchetti, D., & White, J. (1990). Emotion and developmental psychopathology. In N. Stein, B. Leventhal, & T. Trebasso (Eds.), *Psychological and biological approaches to emotion* (pp. 359–382). Hillsdale, NJ: Erlbaum.

Cloitre, M., Cohen, L., Han, H., & Edelman, R. (2001). Posttraumatic stress disorder and extent of trauma exposure as correlates of medical problems and perceived health among women with childhood abuse. *Women and Health, 34*, 1–17.

Cloitre, M., Tardiff, K., Marzuk, P. M., Leon, A. C., & Portera, L. (2001). Consequences of childhood abuse among male psychiatric inpatients: Dual roles as victims and perpetrators. *Journal of Traumatic Stress, 14*(1), 47–61.

Cole, P., & Putnam, F. W. (1992). Effect of incest on self and social functioning: A developmental psychopathology perspective. *Journal of Consulting and Clinical Psychology, 60*, 174–184.

Crittenden, P. M. (1992). Treatment of anxious attachment in infancy and early childhood. *Development and Psychopathology, 4*, 575–602.

Culp, R. E., Heide, J., & Richardson, M. T. (1987). Maltreated children's developmental scores: Treatment versus nontreatment. *Child Abuse & Neglect, 11*(1), 29–34.

Drossman, D. A., Leserman, J., Nachman, G., Li, Z. M., Gluck, H., Toomey, T. C., et al. (1990). Sexual and physical abuse in women with functional or organic gastrointestinal disorders. *Annals of Internal Medicine, 113*(11), 828–833.

Dube, S. R., Anda, R. F., Felitti, V. J., Chapman, D. P., Williamson, D. F., & Giles, W. H. (2001). Childhood abuse, household dysfunction, and the risk of attempted suicide throughout the life span: Findings from the Adverse Childhood Experiences Study. *Journal of the American Medical Association, 286*(24), 3089–3096.

Felitti, V. J., Anda, R. F., Nordenberg, D., Williamson, D. F., Spitz, A. M., Edwards, V., et al. (1998). Relationship of childhood abuse and household dysfunction to many of the leading causes of death in adults: The Adverse Childhood Experiences (ACE) study. *American Journal of Preventive Medicine, 14*, 245–258.

Finkelhor, D., Hotaling, G., Lewis, I. A., & Smith, C. (1989). Sexual abuse and its relationship to later sexual satisfaction, marital status, religion, and attitudes. *Journal of Interpersonal Violence, 4*, 279–399.

Finkelhor, D., Hotaling, G., Lewis, I. A., & Smith, C. (1990). Sexual abuse in a national survey of adult men and women: Prevalence, characteristics, and risk factors. *Child Abuse & Neglect, 14*(1), 19–28.

Finkelhor, D., & Kendall-Tackett, K. (1997). A developmental perspective on the childhood impact of crime, abuse and violent victimization. In D. Cicchetti & S. Toth (Eds.), *Rochester symposium on developmental psychopathology and developmental perspectives on trauma* (pp. 1–32). Rochester, NY: University of Rochester Press.

Herman, J. L. (1992). *Trauma and recovery*. New York: Basic Books.

Herman, J. L., Perry, J. C., & van der Kolk, B. A. (1989). Childhood trauma in borderline personality disorder. *American Journal of Psychiatry, 22,* 231–237.

Higgins, D. J., & McCabe, M. P. (2003). Maltreatment and family dysfunction in childhood and the subsequent adjustment of children and adults. *Journal of Family Violence, 18*(2), 107–120.

Kegan, R. (1982). *The evolving self*. Cambridge, MA: Harvard University Press.

Kessler, R. C., Sonnega, A., Bromet, E., Hughes, M., & Nelson, C. B. (1995). Posttraumatic stress disorder in the national comorbidity survey. *Archives of General Psychiatry, 52,* 1048–1060.

Kilpatrick, D. G., Acierno, R., Saunders, B. E., Resnick, H. S., Best, C. L., & Schnurr, P. P. (2000). Risk factors for adolescent substance abuse and dependence: Data from a national sample. *Journal of Consulting and Clinical Psychology, 68*(1), 19–30.

Kilpatrick, D. G., Ruggeiro, K. J., Acierno, R., Saunders, B. E., Resnick, H. S., & Best, C. L. (2003). Violence and risk of PTSD, major depression, substance abuse/dependence and comorbidity: Results from the National Survey of Adolescents. *Journal of Consulting and Clinical Psychology, 71,* 692–700.

Kiser, L. J., Heston, J., Millsap, P. A., & Pruitt, D. C. (1991). Physical and sexual abuse in childhood: Relationship with posttraumatic stress disorder. *Journal of the American Academy of Child & Adolescent Psychiatry, 30,* 776–783.

Lewis, D. O., & Shanok, S. S. (1981). Perinatal difficulties, head and face trauma, and child abuse in the medical histories of seriously delinquent children. *American Journal of Psychiatry, 136*(4A), 419–423.

Lyons-Ruth, K., & Jacobovitz, D. (1999). Attachment disorganization: Unresolved loss, relational violence and lapses in behavioral and attentional strategies. In J. Cassidy & P. Shaver (Eds.), *Handbook of attachment theory and research* (pp. 520–554). New York: Guilford Press.

Macy, R. D., Behar, L., Paulson, R., Delman, J., Schmid, L., & Smith, S. F. (2004). Community-based, acute posttraumatic stress management: A description and evaluation of a psychosocial-intervention continuum. *Harvard Review of Psychiatry, 12*(4), 217–228.

Margolin, G., & Gordis, E. B. (2000). The effects of family and community violence on children. *Annual Review of Psychology, 51,* 445–479.

Putnam, F. (2003). Ten-year research update review: Child sexual abuse. *Journal of the American Academy of Child & Adolescent Psychiatry, 43,* 269–278.

Putnam, F., & Trickett, P. K. (1997). The psychobiological effects of sexual abuse, a longitudinal study. *Annals of the New York Academy of Sciences, 821,* 150–159.

Pynoos, R. S., Frederick, C. J., Nader, K., Arroyo, W., Steinberg, A., Eth, S., et al. (1987). Life threat and posttraumatic stress in school age children. *Archives of General Psychiatry, 44,* 1057–1063.

Romano, E., & De Luca, R. V. (1997). Exploring the relationship between childhood sexual abuse and adult sexual perpetration. *Journal of Family Violence, 12*(1), 85–99.

Sack, M., Hopper, J. W., & Lamprecht, F. (2004). Low respiratory sinus arrhythmia and prolonged psychophysiological arousal in posttraumatic stress disorder: Heart rate dynamics and individual differences in arousal regulation. *Biological Psychiatry, 55*(3), 284–290.

Scheeringa, M. S., Zeanah, C. H., Drell, M. J., & Larrieu, J. (1995). Two approaches to the diagnosis of posttraumatic stress disorder in infancy and early childhood. *Journal of the American Academy of Child & Adolescent Psychiatry, 34*(2), 191–200.

Scheeringa, M. S., Zeanah, C. H., Meyers, L., & Putnam, F. W. (2003). New findings on alternative criteria for PTSD in preschool children. *Journal of the American Academy of Child & Adolescent Psychiatry, 42*(5), 561–570.

Schneider-Rosen, K., & Cicchetti, D. (1984). The relationship between affect and cognition in maltreated infants: Quality of attachment and the development of visual self-recognition. *Child Development, 55*, 648–658.

Schore, A. (1994). *Affect regulation and the origin of the self: The neurobiology of emotional development.* Hillsdale, NJ: Erlbaum.

Shatan, C. F., Smith, J., & Haley, S. (1977, October). *Johnny comes marching home: DSM III and combat stress.* Paper presented at the 130th Annual Meeting of the American Psychiatric Association, Toronto, Ontario, Canada.

Spinazzola, J., Ford, J. D., Zucker, M., van der Kolk, B. A., Silva, S., Smith, S. F., et al. (2005). Survey evaluates complex trauma exposure, outcome and intervention among children and adolescents. *Psychiatric Annals, 35*(5), 433–442.

Steiner, H., Garcia, I. G., & Matthews, Z. (1997). Posttraumatic stress disorder in incarcerated juvenile delinquents. *Journal of the American Academy of Child & Adolescent Psychiatry, 36*(3), 357–365.

Streeck-Fischer, A., & van der Kolk, B. A. (2000). Down will come baby, cradle and all: Diagnostic and therapeutic implications of chronic trauma on child development. *Australian and New Zealand Journal of Psychiatry, 34*(6), 903–918.

Summit, R. C. (1983). The child sexual abuse accommodation syndrome. *Child Abuse & Neglect, 7*(2), 177–193.

Teicher, M. H., Andersen, S. L., Polcari, A., Anderson, C. M., Navalta, C. P., & Kim, D. M. (2003). The neurobiological consequences of early stress and childhood maltreatment. *Neuroscience & Biobehavioral Reviews, 27*(1–2), 33–44.

Teplin, L. A., Abram, K. M., McClelland, G. M., Dulcan, M. K., & Mericle, A. A. (2002). Psychiatric disorders in youth in juvenile detention. *Archives of General Psychiatry, 59*(12), 1133–1143.

Terr, L. C. (1979). Children of Chowchilla: A study of psychic trauma. *Psychoanalytic Study of the Child, 34*, 552–623.

Tucker, D. M. (1992). Developing emotions and cortical networks. In M. R. Gunnar & C. A. Nelson (Eds.), *Minnesota symposium on child psychology* (Vol. 24, pp. 75–128). Hillsdale, NJ: Erlbaum.

van der Kolk, B. A. (2003). The neurobiology of childhood trauma and abuse. *Child and Adolescent Psychiatric Clinics of North America, 12*, 293–317.

van der Kolk, B. A., & Fisler, R. (1995). Dissociation and the fragmentary nature of traumatic memories: Overview and exploratory study. *Journal of Traumatic Stress, 9*, 505–525.

van der Kolk, B. A., Perry, J. C., & Herman, J. L. (1991). Childhood origins of self-destructive behavior. *American Journal of Psychiatry, 148*, 1665–1671.

van der Kolk, B. A., Roth, S., Pelcovitz, D., Sunday, S., & Spinazzola, J. (2005). Disorders of extreme stress: The empirical foundation of a complex adaptation to trauma. *Journal of Traumatic Stress, 18*(5), 389–401.

van der Kolk, B. A., Spinazzola, J., Hopper, J., Blaustein, M., Korn, D., Hopper, E., et al. (in press). A double blind controlled study of EMDR, fluoxetine and pill placebo in the treatment of PTSD. *Journal of Clinical Psychiatry.*

Walker, L. E. (1984). *The battered woman syndrome.* New York: Springer.

Wang, C. T., & Daro, D. (1997). *Current trends in child abuse reporting and fatalities: The results of the 1997 annual fifty state survey.* Chicago: Prevent Child Abuse America.

Widom, C. S., & Maxfield, M. G. (1996). A prospective examination of risk for violence among abused and neglected children. *Annals of the New York Academy of Sciences, 794*, 224–237.

Wilson, S. N., van der Kolk, B. A., Burbridge, J., Fisler, R., & Kradin, R. (1999). Phenotype of blood lymphocytes in PTSD suggests chronic immune activation. *Psychosomatics, 40*, 222–225.

Zlotnick, C., Zakriski, A. L., Shea, M. T., Costello, E., Begin, A., Pearlstein, T., et al. (1996). The long-term sequelae of sexual abuse: Support for a complex posttraumatic stress disorder. *Journal of Traumatic Stress, 9*(2), 195–205.

12

Adaptation, Ecosocial Safety Signals, and the Trajectory of PTSD

Derrick Silove

INTERNATIONAL CONCERNS ABOUT PTSD

In recent years, Western concepts of psychological trauma have come under increasing challenge, particularly from a transcultural perspective (see Silove, 1999a). The evolving critique is based on several loosely interrelated assertions (Summerfield, 1999): that the psychiatric category posttraumatic stress disorder (PTSD) has its roots in the historical and social imperatives of the 1970s when there was a need to vindicate and advocate for Vietnam combat veterans returning to a hostile public reception in the USA; that, in turn, the medicalization of PTSD spawned a self-sustaining and self-serving trauma counseling industry; and that the consequences, intentional or otherwise, have been to encourage a culture of victimization, compensation seeking, and unrealistic expectations. Concerns have been raised, in particular, about the proliferation of psychological debriefing after disasters, in spite of mounting evidence that indiscriminate interventions of that type may be ineffective, and in some cases injurious, to natural recovery (Raphael & Wilson, 2000). The added concern is that the professional appropriation of psychological trauma may undermine communal support mechanisms that traditionally provided comfort to survivors.

Such concerns are particularly relevant to conflict-affected countries that lack the resources and skills to apply best practice treatments for PTSD. Issues of feasibility and affordability make it impossible to offer best practice interventions (whether pharmacological or cognitive behavioral) on a mass scale to the large portion of trauma-affected populations meeting criteria for PTSD soon after major humanitarian disasters. The ongoing controversy over PTSD and its relevance to postconflict countries may confuse donors, planners, and emerging service developers, damaging the case for promoting mental health services in general (Silove, Ekblad, & Mollica, 2000). Excessive dissent in the field reinforces the stereotype that mental health professionals are factionalized and driven by sectarian

ideologies, the potential consequence being that the whole area of mental health, already prone to stigmatization, may be neglected (Silove, Ekblad, et al. 2000).

By focusing on the distinction between normative and pathological responses to the stresses of war and conflict, it may be possible to refine thinking about the resources that need to be committed to dedicated clinical programs in settings of humanitarian crisis. The present chapter focuses on this issue, exploring general principles underlying communal adaptation after mass conflict (Silove, 1999a; Silove, 2004) and using that framework to offer an evolutionary-learning theory of PTSD (Silove, 1998) based on the notion of survival learning.

DRAWING INFERENCES FROM CONTEMPORARY RESEARCH

The scientific literature focusing on refugees and postconflict populations in the developing world tends to paint a picture of traumatic stress, generally represented by diagnoses of PTSD and major depression, as being at epidemic levels in these settings (K. de Jong, Mulhern, Ford, van der Kam, & Kleber, 2000; Modvig et al., 2000). Epidemiologic studies undertaken across diverse cultures and sites, such as in refugee camps, in countries during or soon after armed conflict, and among recently repatriated or resettled populations (Mollica et al., 1993; Mollica et al., 1999; Turner, Bowie, Dunn, Shapo, & Yule, 2003), have tended to yield rates of PTSD that are many times higher than in countries not affected by mass upheaval. PTSD across these diverse postconflict populations commonly reaches prevalence figures of 20–35%, and sometimes as high as 99% (K. de Jong et al., 2000). In addition, a robust dose–effect relationship has emerged, with greater exposure to trauma being associated with higher levels of PTSD symptoms (Mollica et al., 1998; Silove, Sinnerbrink, Field, Manicavasagar, & Steel, 1997). These findings may be interpreted as suggesting a linear causal model of PTSD; that is, antecedent exposure to trauma leads predictably to PTSD, and the greater the exposure (or the more grotesque and novel the stimulus; see Shalev, this volume), the more probable it is that persons will suffer severe symptoms.

CAUTION IN INTERPRETING RESEARCH FINDINGS

Nevertheless, findings from epidemiologic studies undertaken across contexts need to be tempered by several considerations. First, PTSD symptoms are ubiquitous after mass exposure to trauma (Yehuda, 2002), suggesting that their presence in the immediate aftermath of these events may represent a normative reaction to life threat. Second, in spite of such early symptoms, most persons exposed to trauma of any type do not develop disabling, chronic PTSD, suggesting that there may be powerful cultural, social, and individual psychobiological mechanisms that protect the majority of exposed persons from that morbid outcome. Third, rates of PTSD vary substantially across contexts (J. de Jong et al., 2001), raising questions of whether broad cultural and ecosocial factors may influence morbid outcomes. Fourth, disability associated with PTSD is variable, with some studies showing remarkably low levels of dysfunction where PTSD is the only disorder (Mollica et al., 1999; Momartin, Silove, Manicavasagar, & Steel, 2003, 2004). That observation suggests that in some cultural and social contexts, PTSD may impact less on the functional capacity of affected persons. Fifth, and related to the foregoing, it is noteworthy across several contexts that even when treatment services are available, only a minority of persons with PTSD seeks professional assistance (J. de Jong & Komproe, 2002). Sixth, even when morbid psychological reactions occur, their type, severity, and social consequences are diverse, extending beyond PTSD to depression, anxiety, grief, anger, somatoform complaints, and other maladaptive behavioural responses (Silove, 1999a).

I will draw on these considerations in the sections that follow in order to outline a general ecosocial framework for understanding trauma in the context of mass violence and persecution and, second, within that conceptual structure, to posit a heuristic evolutionarily based model of PTSD as a *survival overdrive state* (SOS).

A GENERAL MODEL OF ADAPTATION AND DEVELOPMENT AFTER PERSECUTION AND TRAUMA (THE ADAPT MODEL)

Previously, I have outlined an ecosocial model of trauma (Ekblad & Jaransen, 2004; Silove, 1999a; Silove, 2004) that extends beyond (but incorporates) concepts relevant to PTSD (see Table 12.1). In countries beset by systemic violence, persecution, and gross human rights violations, trauma is pervasive – over a billion persons in the contemporary world have been exposed to such experiences. Social, cultural, historical, and political influences undoubtedly shape individual psychological interpretations of these complex events. For example, adherence to religion and dedication to a political cause each may moderate the impact of torture and other traumas in generating risk to PTSD (Basoglu, Jaranson, Mollica, & Kastrup, 2001). At the same time, although the contextual particularities of each instance of mass violence are of paramount importance, there may be some core universal adaptive responses that can be discerned across settings. I have suggested (Silove, 1999a) that in stable societies, five broad psychosocial pillars support a platform of social equilibrium and that these systems have mirror-image representations in the intrapsychic domain and in the wider social milieu. In stable and harmonious societies, individual and social systems are broadly in synchrony and are mutually supportive, but that nexus breaks down when whole populations are threatened by mass violence and persecution.

TABLE 12.1. *The ADAPT Model: Five Proposed Adaptive Systems and the Threats that Undermine Them*

System	Threat: Past, Present, and Future	Normative Psychological Responses	Normative Adaptive Responses	Multilevel Forms of Assistance	Negative Outcomes if Adaptive Responses Fail
Security	Ongoing violence and threats, forced repatriation, poverty, lack of food, absence of medical care, uncontrolled behaviour of mentally ill	Fear, anxiety, hypervigilance, insecurity	Security seeking, protectiveness, vigilance	Conditions that promote personal and social security	Anxiety, posttraumatic stress disorder
Bonds, family, networks	Forced separation, losses, disappearances	Grief, separation anxiety	Parental protectiveness, attention to restoring families and networks	Tracing and reuniting families, promoting mourning and remembrance	Complicated grief, pathological separation anxiety, depression
Justice and HR	Discrimination, racism, humiliation, degradation, rejection, incarceration, dehumanization	Suspicion, lack of trust in authorities, anger	Sensitisation to justice, universalism, human rights, promoting and demanding	Applying social justice principles across all interventions	Pathological anger, loss of trust, paranoia
Roles and identity	Dispossession and deprivation, genocide, ethnic cleansing, denial of rights to work, residency, and self-support	Aimlessness, liminality, loss of sense of belonging and efficacy	Role confusion, recreation of new or hybrid roles and identities	Creation of foundations for empowerment: work, study, social, and political organization, cultural revival	Loss of direction, giving up, persisting aimlessness or inactivity
Meaning	Destruction of places of worship and shrines, banning of religious practices, suppression of spiritual, political, and cultural aspirations and practices	Loss of coherence, anomie, cultural disintegration	Rediscovery or regeneration of culture and religion, pursuit of social and political causes	Promotion of respect and institutions for religious, political, cultural, and other practices, recording history	Isolation, discontinuity, fragmentation, loss of coherence

The five psychosocial domains disrupted by such ecosocial threats subserve functions of (1) safety and security; (2) interpersonal and communal bonding; (3) justice; (4) maintenance of roles and identities; and (5) preservation of social coherence and existential meaning in the political, religious, spiritual, and cultural realms.

At the collective level, societies attempt to defend the institutions subserving these functions when they are threatened and they strive to recreate them when they are destroyed, with each society actively mobilizing material resources and culture-specific knowledge and skills in the process of repair. At the individual level, threats to these domains may trigger specific neural networks that promote survival and adaptive responses, with the strongest evidence relating to the first two identified domains (life threat and interpersonal bonds). Life threat triggers limbic, autonomic, and cortical mechanisms that initiate flight and fight responses. Traumatic loss, in turn, provokes separation anxiety, intense searching, or grieving, reactions that are likely to derive from specific neural substrates although the expression of these responses is strongly influenced by culture. Further investigation is warranted to define possible psychophysiologic responses when the other three domains are threatened, for example, the underlying mechanisms that provoke anger when communities are exposed to gross injustices (Silove, 1999a).

Humanitarian responses to situations of mass conflict generally aim to restore the key components identified by the ADAPT model (Table 12.1) by establishing conditions of safety, security, and predictability; by initiating processes to trace and reunite families and kinship groups; by creating effective systems of justice; by constructing social and economic platforms that promote productive roles, which, in turn, allow the reestablishment of identities; and by assisting in the regeneration of institutions (religious, political, social, cultural) that restore a sense of meaning and coherence.

DIVERSE MEANINGS, DIVERSE OUTCOMES

Consistent with the ADAPT model is the notion that complex humanitarian disasters are accompanied by traumas with multiple meanings and diverse impacts (Silove, 1999a). A young adult son who is rendered helpless while watching his father being tortured, humiliated, and finally killed in front of the whole family is confronted by threats relating to all the five domains identified by the ADAPT model: threats to his own life; traumatic loss of his father; an acute sense of injustice; an abrupt role change in which he may have to assume leadership of the family; and existential challenges to meaning systems that previously provided a coherent sense of self, society, and life.

Studies of patterns of trauma-related psychiatric morbidity have tended to focus largely on the first two domains of the ADAPT model. PTSD appears to be a relatively specific response to life threat, whereas traumatic loss in some survivors leads to complicated grief reactions, with the two morbid outcomes being distinct (Momartin et al., 2003, 2004). Depression appears to be an intermediate and possibly secondary reaction, associated with the persistence of both patterns as well as ongoing stresses in the posttraumatic environment (Momartin et al., 2004).

THE NEXUS BETWEEN LIFE THREAT AND PTSD

Life Threat

A key question, and the one to which I will devote the remainder of this chapter, is the link between life threat and PTSD. The distinction between life-threatening reactions and other anxiety-provoking stimuli may be important in delineating continuities and discontinuities between PTSD and other anxiety disorders. Such distinctions may be difficult to make when studying laboratory animals.

Intrusions and Memory

The unique feature of PTSD, and one not accounted for by classical conditioning (Silove, 1998; see Shalev, this volume), is the reexperiencing of trauma memories encompassed by criterion B of *DSM–IV*. The unbidden and emotionally disturbing recovery of intense trauma memories, a feature often considered pathognomonic of PTSD, has spawned extensive research into the neuropsychology of working memory (Galletly, Clark, McFarlane, & Weber, 2001). The key hypothesis is that PTSD may represent a pathological block to normal memory consolidation, resulting in trauma memories being retained in short-term storage, thereby allowing rapid and inappropriate triggering of recall by an ever-increasing range of conditioned environmental cues. Various limbic brain centers or circuits have been incriminated, including the hippocampus and the amygdala.

A dynamic neurophysiologic model presented in this volume (see Bouton & Waddell) suggests that there is a dysregulation in the balance between orbitofrontal cortical inhibitory and limbic excitatory pathways responsible for learned fear responses. Representing a critical step forward, research has matched neurophysiologic and behavioral data to show that conditioned fear responses are never extinguished, and that active cortical learning via separate but parallel pathways is critical to the successful inhibition of such fear responses. Such findings may be of immense importance to understanding possible mechanisms underlying PTSD and its trajectory over time.

Survival Learning

It does not make evolutionary sense for survival learning to be extinguishable by simple conditioning. Hence, in theory, survival responses should differ from other fears such as phobias that represent an aberrant response to environmental stimuli that are not inherently threatening. (Admittedly, this distinction may not be absolute because some phobia-inducing stimuli such as heights and confined spaces may have been life threatening in earlier historical contexts.) The gap in classical conditioning theory in explaining memory intrusions may provide the necessary clue to an expanded formulation in which posttraumatic stress (PTS), rather than being a pathological reaction *ab initio*, may represent a normative evolutionarily primitive response to life threat (Silove, 1998).

From an evolutionary perspective, survival learning provoked by immediate mortal threat would constitute the most important mechanism protecting a species from extinction, so the efficiency and refinement of that system would assume high "design" priority at an early stage of speciation. It would make sense if in early hominids, durable single-event learning, particularly in relation to novel mortal threats, was well established to ensure that survivors of the first encounter with that source of danger would establish instantaneous and reflexive defensive reactions if they encounter cues signalling salient threat, without the need for future direct exposure to the actual source of the threat. Failure to learn after the first encounter would risk death the second time around. Speculatively, such learning mechanisms were established at a time in evolution when the human cortex (and associated capacities to evaluate, communicate, and plan) was relatively poorly developed. Within that context, the flashbacks of PTSD might be understood as a highly efficient single-event survival-learning mechanism. Maintaining strong representations of the trauma event in multiple sensory modalities within working memory, at least for a short period after the aftermath of trauma exposure, would promote associative learning, linking salient environmental cues to the risk of return of the threat, thereby generating a highly tuned and rapidly responsive survival response repertoire to that threat in the future. Linking memory retrieval to psychophysiologic and emotional fear responses, and in turn to instantaneous behavioral defensive reactions, would increase the chances of survival. In that respect, the two symptom domains of PTSD (avoidance and arousal) that follow intrusions might be seen as potentially adaptive, coinciding with primitive defensive reactions of flight and readiness for fight, respectively.

In summary, the early features of what has become known as PTSD in fact may be better regarded as a normative survival overdrive state (SOS), a mechanism that putatively has its roots in evolutionarily archaic psychobiological survival mechanisms. In that respect, the reaction is *future* rather than *past* directed in that it is designed to trigger learned survival reactions when the organism is next confronted with the salient danger or environmental cues signaling the return of the threat. The subjective experience may be unpleasant, but the forces of evolution are directed principally toward survival rather than to ensuring the subjective comfort of the individual.

Persistence and Disability

The SOS response, once activated, is highly dynamic with excitatory and inhibitory brain mechanisms modulating its expression. This balance is necessary to ensure that, over time, the system can be reset serially according to changing contexts so that survivors do not overreact to irrelevant cues, thereby developing rigid responses that reduce their capacity for everyday functioning and for future adaptations when confronted with other threats.

Indeed, it is precisely this rigidity and inflexibility of the response that may transform into clinically relevant PTSD and its associated disabilities. The key question, therefore, as indicated by Shalev in this volume, is why the ubiquitous early PTS reaction becomes chronic and self-sustaining. Clearly, several interrelated factors including genetic, developmental, cognitive, and environmental influences determine the course and outcome of PTS, but here I will give emphasis to the relevance of ecosocial safety signals and the stabilizing impact of context as determining factors at a population-wide level. The challenge in so doing is to link population-wide studies across a diversity of cultures to advances made in laboratory experimentation reported in this volume. Preliminary data (Bouton & Waddell, this volume) identifying possible discrete brain centers that differentiate between immediate startle responses (the amygdala) and longer term anxiety that is future directed (subserved, it appears, by the bed nucleus of the stria terminalis) may advance understanding about how the experience of past trauma becomes linked to a heightened preparedness to deal with future danger. Importantly, time elapsed since the trauma and ongoing contextual signals appear to be critical to the trajectory of learned fear responses.

Humans cannot be subjected to the highly controlled experimental conditions of the animal laboratory, so we need to turn to observations derived from quasi-experimental social conditions that may throw light on why PTS persists under certain conditions. Geopolitical shifts in refugee policies (Silove, Steel, et al., 2000) represent just such a social experiment that has drastically changed the nature of posttraumatic environments for displaced persons previously exposed to trauma. As such, I will draw contrasts between research undertaken by our group on the mental health of Vietnamese refugees in Sydney and on more recently arrived asylum seekers living in the same city. I also will make reference to preliminary data from East Timor, findings that raise important questions about the influence of recovery environments on the outcome of PTS symptoms.

Asylum Seekers in Australia

For several years, our research group in Sydney has focused on the mental health and psychological well-being of asylum seekers entering Australia. In the past decade, successive Australian governments have implemented stringent policies of deterrence aimed at discouraging asylum seekers from entering the country (Silove, 2002; Silove, Steel, et al., 2000). Historically, Australia's approach to this issue can be divided into two distinct if overlapping epochs. Prior to the early 1990s, refugees (most of whom were screened and accepted overseas) were offered permanent residency; access to a wide array of resettlement, health, employment, and educational services; and unrestricted opportunities to participate in the host society. During the 1990s, with the increasing influx of asylum seekers (persons applying for refugee status after arrival in Australia), a series of restrictive measures were introduced including mandatory, indefinite detention of the minority arriving without any entry papers; and restrictions in government financial support and access to health care, education, and work for those allowed to live in the community (Silove, 2002; Silove, Steel, et al., 2000); and, more recently, the issuing of temporary visas with the expectation that refugees will be repatriated once permits lapse. These communities therefore face the ever-present risk of forced repatriation to conditions of insecurity and possible future persecution. Concurrently, Australia has continued to accept refugees for permanent resettlement as long as they are selected and screened in other countries, thereby creating a two-tier system with members of the same ethnic community arbitrarily being granted either permanent or temporary asylum.

Clinical impressions have suggested that previously trauma-affected asylum seekers with insecure residency continue to experience prolonged and often deteriorating PTSD reactions, unlike their permanently resettled refugee counterparts. Studies examining the impact of postmigration stresses on PTSD symptoms have tended to support these clinical observations, suggesting that a combination of factors including social, cultural, and economic deprivations; enforced and prolonged separation from families; and the ever-present fear of repatriation, all encourage the persistence of PTSD and related symptoms of depression (see Silove, 2002). Time and context add to risk, with the longer the period persons live in states of insecurity or threat, particularly detention, the more likely they are to experience worsening of traumatic stress symptoms (Steel et al., 2004).

In an unfortunate way, this social experiment has created specific conditions that provide an in vivo test of the impact of ongoing ecosocial insecurity in maintaining the SOS response. Asylum seekers are reminded repeatedly both of the past traumas they have suffered and the threat of future persecution should they be repatriated. In that regard, compared to the officials who assess their refugee claims (see Kirmayer, this volume), their capacity to imagine and rehearse potentially threatening events in the future is based on concrete past life experiences.

The Vietnamese Refugees

Policies applied to the 100,000 Vietnamese refugees arriving in Australia from the late 1970s through to the early 1990s contrast starkly with those pursued for more recently arrived asylum seekers. In spite of early public concerns about the arrival of the Vietnamese boat people, government policy at the time focused on rapid resettlement of these refugees with arrivals being offered permanent residency and unrestricted access to services, education, and work opportunities.

In the late 1990s, we undertook a study of a random population sample of 1100 Vietnamese adults living in Sydney (Steel, Silove, Phan, & Bauman, 2002), comparing the data with a large Australia-wide population study that used identical case-finding methods. Both populations had a 12-month prevalence for PTSD of 3.5%. A retrospective analysis allowed us to examine the relevance of two key variables, time since trauma and quantum of trauma (less or more than three traumatic events) as predictors of the trajectory of PTSD, anxiety, and depression in the Vietnamese. Trauma quantum was a strong predictor of risk of psychiatric morbidity, in keeping with the dose–response relationship now established in both the refugee and general trauma literature. Importantly, however, time was a powerful moderator, with increasing time since trauma being associated with a stepwise improvement in morbidity across those with moderate and severe trauma exposure. After 10 years, those with moderate trauma exposure reverted to levels of morbidity amongst their non-trauma-affected compatriots. Time also greatly reduced the risk of morbidity in those with severe levels of trauma, but a small subgroup remained ill even after 10 years. In summary, time had a healing effect on traumatic stress in permanently settled Vietnamese but had the opposite effect on asylum seekers living under persistent states of insecurity.

East Timorese

Studies and general observations derived from working with the East Timorese population further illustrate the impact of context and time on the unfolding of PTSD symptoms.

Background

East Timor is a half-island territory with a population of 1 million persons located north of Australia and to the east of the main Indonesian archipelago. The territory was a Portuguese colony for 400 years. The Japanese invaded the territory during World War II, and the subsequent jungle war was accompanied by mass human rights violations perpetrated against the indigenous community because of its support for the retreating allied forces (Silove, 1999b). Portugal restored its sovereignty after the war, but an independence movement gained ground, leading to a short civil war in 1974–5, an upheaval that created the pretext for the invasion by Indonesia. Twenty-four years of low-intensity civil conflict ensued with the indigenous resistance movement waging a guerrilla war against the occupying Indonesian military. During that period, 200,000 East Timorese died as a consequence of forced displacements, bombing of villages, famine, and consequent epidemics of communicable diseases. Widespread human rights violations occurred including arbitrary detentions and killings, rape, torture, and exile of political leaders (Silove, 1999b). In 1999, a referendum was held, the outcome being overwhelming public support for independence. Leading up to the referendum and in the immediate aftermath, Indonesian-supported militia systematically destroyed 70% of the built infrastructure of the territory and forcibly displaced 80% of the population. The Australian army followed by a United Nations force gradually restored order, and in 2002, East Timor (Timor Leste) became an independent country.

Until renewed violence broke out in 2006, a notable feature of the post-1999 period was the level of stability established in the country, setting it apart from other contemporary postconflict nations (for example, Iraq, Afghanistan, Sri Lanka), where, as a rule, acute episodes of major hostilities have been interspersed with long periods of instability and low-grade conflict.

Mental Health Interventions

After the 1975 invasion of East Timor, several thousand refugees fled the territory, many to Australia. These early arrivals were given permanent residency. The Australian government changed its policy in the 1990s, however, rejecting the right of recently arrived East Timorese to seek asylum in that country. The result was a prolonged and complex legal battle in which East Timorese asylum seekers challenged the host government's rejection of their right to seek refuge (Silove et al., 2002).

The Service for the Treatment and Rehabilitation of Torture and Trauma Survivors (STARTTS) in the state of New South Wales, in conjunction with the Psychiatry Research and Teaching Unit, University of New South Wales, initiated a researcher-advocacy program with the aim of assisting East Timorese asylum seekers by documenting their plight and providing immediate support and referral for members facing psychosocial and health-related difficulties (Silove et al., 2002). Asylum seekers presenting for assistance reported extensive exposure to human rights violations, and over 50% met criteria for PTSD and depression. As among other asylum groups, postmigration stresses were prominent, particularly fears of forced repatriation and anxieties about immediate survival (Silove et al., 2002).

Following the humanitarian crisis of 1999, our group initiated the Psychosocial Recovery and Development in East Timor (PRADET) program supported by AusAID, the Australian federal government overseas development agency (Zwi & Silove, 2002). In 2000, another international group published data from an epidemiologic study undertaken within months of the major conflagration in East Timor toward the end of 1999 (Modvig et al., 2000). They used the Harvard Trauma Questionnaire, the same measure that our group had employed with asylum seekers in Sydney. The epidemiologic study undertaken in the immediate aftermath of widespread violence and persecution revealed high levels of PTSD (34%) across the territory.

Nevertheless, in establishing a community-based crisis mental health service, we predicted that those seeking urgent care would present with a diversity of problems, not only PTSD (Silove et al., 2004). In other postconflict settings, it has become evident that persons with severe mental and neuropsychiatric illnesses such as psychosis, severe depression, and epilepsy often are the first patients to present for treatment (Silove, Ekblad, et al., 2000). Persons with untreated psychosis and severe mood disorders such as manic depression are likely to be severely disabled, and some are disruptive, violent, suicidal, or at risk of abuse and neglect, particularly in the chaotic setting of conflict-affected environments (Silove, Ekblad, et al., 2000). In contrast, even though PTSD reactions are common, many persons are able to continue functioning in spite of symptoms. A retrospective analysis of the case profile of early presentations to the PRADET service (Silove et al., 2004) confirmed our expectations, with the majority of persons having diagnoses of psychosis and only a minority manifesting symptoms of PTSD.

Preliminary data from an ongoing epidemiologic survey undertaking in East Timor in 2004, during a period of prolonged peace prior to the upheaval of 2006, suggest that the community prevalence of PTSD may be many times lower than the 34% recorded in 2000. Although that observation needs to be confirmed, if true, it suggests that the East Timorese community has experienced a remarkable recovery from early traumatic stress symptoms even though very few have received counseling or other interventions aimed specifically at treating PTSD. At the same time, as amongst resettled Vietnamese refugees, there is a sizeable minority of East Timorese who continue to suffer severe and disabling symptoms, and they deserve active intervention.

DISCUSSION: IMPLICATIONS FOR UNDERSTANDING TRAUMATIC STRESS REACTIONS

Sampling and other methodological differences caution against too close a comparison across the studies described. Nevertheless, some tentative inferences may be drawn about the relevance of context and time in relation to the persistence and/or recovery of PTSD symptoms. All samples described had suffered major trauma and, consistent with the large body of literature in the field, there was a reliable relationship between trauma exposure and risk of PTSD. At the same time, the ecosocial conditions in which survivors found themselves in the posttraumatic phase appeared to be important in determining the trajectory of symptoms. Survivor groups faced with ongoing insecurities and future threat, such as the asylum seekers in Australia, tended to experience persisting PTS symptoms that were complicated by depression and general psychosocial disabilities. Those living in secure and predictable environments, such as the Vietnamese in Australia and the East Timorese studied 4.5 years after armed conflict in their home country, appeared to manifest low (but not negligible) levels of PTSD symptoms.

Several tentative parallels thus can be drawn between the laboratory experiments reported in this volume and the context-related level of symptoms among the Vietnamese and asylum seeker groups, respectively. There is a growing consensus from laboratory experiments that learned fear responses are never fully extinguished but can be held in check by inhibitory cortical mechanisms, a process based on active learning (Bouton & Waddell, this volume). Context and time appear to be critical to the balance of inhibitory and excitatory processes. These findings support the possibility that ecosocial safety or threat signals can exert a powerful influence in determining the balance between excitatory and inhibitory circuits governing ongoing fear responses. For the Vietnamese and the East Timorese studied in their home country in 2004, political and social signals all converged to signify long-term safety and stability, whereas precisely the converse message continues to be sent to asylum seekers, that is, one of immediate threat to survival and longer term risk of repatriation to situations of danger. In that respect, distinctions between shorter and longer term aversive stimuli and their impact on discrete brain pathways are particularly illuminating in relation to the persistence of traumatic stress reactions in refugees. Bouton and Waddell (this volume) report interesting if preliminary data suggesting that distinct networks may underlie learned fear and anticipatory fear responses and that these networks are linked. The impact of changing environmental conditions on the interaction between these brain centers may throw important light on why the acute traumatic stress reaction becomes chronic and disabling in some survivors.

Humans are imbued with imagination, an asset suppressed by the rigid legalistic protocols imposed on the refugee determination process applied to asylum seekers (Kirmayer, this volume). Paradoxically, imagination also works to the detriment of asylum seekers insofar as their vivid experiences of past trauma and the images they generate provide fertile ground for anxieties about the future, fears that are constantly provoked by the real risk of ultimate repatriation to places of danger. In that sense, past, present, and future converge to generate a life of endless terror. Under these conditions, it is not surprising that ecosocial threats play a central role in the failure to recover from initial PTS reactions (see Shalev, this volume).

IMPLICATIONS FOR INTERVENTIONS

Several implications for intervention emanate from both the ADAPT and SOS theories of mass trauma. Attention to repair of the ecosocial system is overwhelmingly salient both in conflict-affected countries and in all other settings where traumatized populations reside. It may well be that deficiencies in peace-keeping operations and in the protection regimes offered to refugees and asylum seekers (Kirmayer, this volume) account much more for the persistence of PTSD in affected populations than has been previously assumed. In essence, there is much to be said for the argument that peace and security provide the best immediate therapy for the majority of populations exposed to mass violence and displacement.

Clearly, a complex matrix of social and cultural influences may enhance the sense of security offered by conditions of physical safety. For both the East Timorese in the home country and the Vietnamese in Australia, important recovery factors were at play, including the freedom to pursue religious and cultural practices. During our studies, it has been clear that the Vietnamese feel fortunate in being given the opportunity to settle and prosper in Australia. In East Timor, there is a strong sense that past sufferings have been vindicated by the achievement of national independence. At the same time, other factors, such as frustrations about the failure to prosecute perpetrators of past human rights violations and slow progress in economic development may be at the heart of recent uprisings in that country. These social signifiers of success and vindication contrast with those confronting many other trauma-affected populations such as asylum seekers and possibly even Vietnam combat veterans where the sense of failure, defeat, and alienation may create enduring vulnerability. The impact of these broader issues relating to justice, identity, and existential meaning on the SOS response require further definition and research.

In practical terms, a multilevel response to traumatic stress according to the ADAPT model is warranted for populations exposed to mass violence. Most persons can be expected to recover spontaneously if the social and cultural environment is supportive. Given constraints in cost, logistics, and skills, it is not feasible to provide extensive individual interventions for traumatic stress in low-income countries exposed to mass violence. The evidence referred to herein suggests that such mass interventions may not be necessary. Hence, the dictum "not too early, not too late" may be germane in relation to PTS reactions. On the one hand, indiscriminate interventions in the early phase are not warranted, especially in settings of ongoing threat and danger (see Yadin & Foa, this volume). At the same time, there is a minority of persons who continue to suffer PTSD in the longer term in spite of the stabilization of the social environment, and these persons often are hidden from view. Further research is needed to uncover the precise interaction of risk factors that determine these morbid outcomes in the minority (see Shalev, this volume). Persons with severe and unremitting PTSD living in postconflict countries certainly warrant attention, and further work is needed to establish how best practice treatments can be adapted to non-Western cultural contexts in order to ensure their acceptability and effectiveness.

References

Basoglu, M., Jaranson, J., Mollica, R., & Kastrup, M. (2001). Torture and mental health: A researcher overview. In E. Gerrity, T. Keane, & F. Tuma (Eds.), *The mental health consequences of torture* (pp. 35–65). New York: Plenum.

de Jong, J. T., & Komproe, I. H. (2002). Closing the gap between psychiatric epidemiology and mental health in post-conflict situations. *Lancet, 359*(9320), 1793–1794.

de Jong, J. T., Komproe, I. H., Van Ommeren, M., El Masri, M., Araya, M., Khaled, N., et al. (2001). Lifetime events and posttraumatic stress disorder in 4 postconflict settings. *Journal of the American Medical Association, 286*(5), 555–562.

de Jong, K., Mulhern, M., Ford, N., van der Kam, S., & Kleber, R. (2000). The trauma of war in Sierra Leone. *Lancet, 355*(9220), 2067–2068.

Ekblad, S., & Jaranson, J. (2004). Psychosocial rehabilitation. In J. Wilson & B. Drozdek (Eds.), *Broken spirits* (pp. 609–636). New York: Brunner/Routledge.

Galletly, C., Clark, C. R., McFarlane, A. C., & Weber, D. L. (2001). Working memory in posttraumatic stress disorder – an event-related potential study. *Journal of Traumatic Stress, 14*(2), 295–309.

Modvig, J., Pagaduan-Lopez, J., Rodenburg, J., Salud, C. M., Cabigon, R. V., & Panelo, C. I. (2000). Torture and trauma in post-conflict East Timor. *Lancet, 356*(9243), 1763.

Mollica, R. F., Donelan, K., Tor, S., Lavelle, J., Elias, C., Frankel, M., et al. (1993). The effect of trauma and confinement on functional health and mental health status of Cambodians living in Thailand-Cambodia border camps. *Journal of the American Medical Association, 270*(5), 581–586.

Mollica, R. F., McInnes, K., Pham, T., Smith Fawzi, M. C., Murphy, E., & Lin, L. (1998). The dose-effect relationships between torture and psychiatric symptoms in Vietnamese ex-political detainees and a comparison group. *Journal of Nervous and Mental Disease, 186*(9), 543–553.

Mollica, R. F., McInnes, K., Sarajlic, N., Lavelle, J., Sarajlic, I., & Massagli, M. P. (1999). Disability associated with psychiatric comorbidity and health status in Bosnian refugees living in Croatia. *Journal of the American Medical Association, 282*(5), 433–439.

Momartin, S., Silove, D., Manicavasagar, V., & Steel, Z. (2003). Dimensions of trauma associated with posttraumatic stress disorder (PTSD) caseness, severity and functional impairment: A study of Bosnian refugees resettled in Australia. *Social Science & Medicine, 57*(5), 775–781.

Momartin, S., Silove, D., Manicavasagar, V., & Steel, Z. (2004). Comorbidity of PTSD and depression: Associations with trauma exposure, symptom severity and functional impairment in Bosnian refugees resettled in Australia. *Journal of Affective Disorders, 80*(2–3), 231–238.

Raphael, B., & Wilson, J. (2000). Introduction and overview: Key issues in the conceptualization of debriefing. In B. Raphael & J. Wilson (Eds.), *Psychological debriefing theory, practice and evidence* (pp. 1–17). Cambridge, UK: Cambridge University Press.

Silove, D. (1998). Is posttraumatic stress disorder an overlearned survival response? An evolutionary-learning hypothesis. *Psychiatry, 61*(2), 181–190.

Silove, D. (1999a). The psychosocial effects of torture, mass human rights violations, and refugee trauma: Toward an integrated conceptual framework. *Journal of Nervous and Mental Disease, 187*(4), 200–207.

Silove, D. (1999b). Health and human rights of the East Timorese. *Lancet, 353*(9169), 2067.

Silove, D. (2002). The asylum debacle in Australia: A challenge for psychiatry. *Australian and New Zealand Journal of Psychiatry, 36*(3), 290–296.

Silove, D. (2004). The global challenge of asylum. In J. P. Wilson & B. Drozdek (Eds.), *Broken spirits* (pp. 13–32). New York: Brunner-Routledge.

Silove, D., Coello, M., Tang, K., Aroche, J., Soares, M., Lingam, R., et al. (2002). Towards a researcher-advocacy model for asylum seekers: A pilot study amongst East Timorese living in Australia. *Transcultural Psychiatry, 39*(4), 452–468.

Silove, D., Ekblad, S., & Mollica, R. (2000). The rights of the severely mentally ill in post-conflict societies. *Lancet, 355*(9214), 1548–1549.

Silove, D., Manicavasagar, V., Baker, K., Mausiri, M., Soares, M., de Carvalho, F., et al. (2004). Indices of social risk among first attenders of an emergency mental health service in post-conflict East Timor: An exploratory investigation. *Australian and New Zealand Journal of Psychiatry, 38*(11–12), 929–932.

Silove, D., Sinnerbrink, I., Field, A., Manicavasagar, V., & Steel, Z. (1997). Anxiety, depression and PTSD in asylum-seekers: Associations with pre-migration trauma and post-migration stressors. *British Journal of Psychiatry, 170*, 351–357.

Silove, D., Steel, Z., & Watters, C. (2000). Policies of deterrence and the mental health of asylum seekers. *Journal of the American Medical Association, 284*(5), 604–611.

Steel, Z., Momartin, S., Bateman, C., Hafshejani, A., Silove, D. M., Everson, N., et al. (2004). Psychiatric status of asylum seeker families held for a protracted period in a remote detention centre in Australia. *Australian and New Zealand Journal of Public Health, 28*(6), 527–536.

Steel, Z., Silove, D., Phan, T., & Bauman, A. (2002). Long-term effect of psychological trauma on the mental health of Vietnamese refugees resettled in Australia: A population-based study. *Lancet, 360*(9339), 1056–1062.

Summerfield, D. (1999). A critique of seven assumptions behind psychological trauma programmes in war-affected areas. *Social Science & Medicine, 48*(10), 1449–1462.

Turner, S. W., Bowie, C., Dunn, G., Shapo, L., & Yule, W. (2003). Mental health of Kosovan Albanian refugees in the UK. *British Journal of Psychiatry, 182,* 444–448.

Yehuda, R. (2002). Post-traumatic stress disorder. *New England Journal of Medicine, 346*(2), 108–114.

Zwi, A. B., & Silove, D. (2002). Hearing the voices: Mental health services in East Timor. *Lancet, 360*(Suppl.), s45–46.

13

Religion and Spirituality After Trauma

James K. Boehnlein

Traumatic events often leave survivors with a number of perplexing and unanswered questions. These questions frequently are not recognized by the survivor in the immediate period after the acute trauma, but their ultimate resolution often determines the degree of optimum posttraumatic adjustment, both intrapersonal and interpersonal. These questions frequently involve an encounter with the ultimate questions of human existence, such as the capriciousness of life and death, the meaning of loss, and the moral complexities of good and evil. Frequent examples include: Why did this occur? I am a good person and have led a good life. Why did this happen to me? Did I do something to cause this to happen? Why did God allow this to happen? Will the perpetrators of evil be punished? I have lost so much; is life worth living anymore? What do I have to live for? My life is so painful now and has no purpose – will it be better in the next life?

Many of these questions that survivors and clinicians grapple with in long-term recovery involve complex religious and spiritual questions and have no easy answers. They are often painful and challenge a person's core belief systems (personal, secular, and religious). The process of confronting these questions and attempting resolution frequently involves an examination of previously stable cultural and religious assumptions that were the foundations of a person's life: I am safe; God is watching over me and my family; good will prevail over evil and a good life will be rewarded; I am a good person and would never wish evil on others for any reason; this life is hard, but after death I will be reunited with my loved ones and be happy.

This chapter will explore the roots and the process of resolution of these religious and spiritual issues following trauma. After an introductory section that will define and highlight essential religious and spiritual themes relevant to this topic, various posttraumatic psychological issues related to religion and spirituality will be considered. This will be followed by a discussion of clinical issues, including healing in the context of religion and spiritual belief systems, psychotherapy, and interpersonal and social reintegration, along with specific case examples.

My perspectives are grounded in two decades of clinical work with refugees from Southeast Asia and Central America who have experienced war trauma, American veterans and prisoners of war from World War II and Vietnam, and civilian trauma survivors. Regardless of cultural, ethnic, or religious background, a common characteristic that I have noted in working with these very diverse populations is that most individuals are continually searching for meaning both for their traumatic experiences and for their future. This is often mediated through a religious or spiritual belief system. Those in the mental health professions in a wide range of clinical settings often will encounter this exploration for meaning in their work with traumatized patients because the search for meaning occurs frequently in psychotherapy, in addition to a person's solitary personal search or with the counsel of clergy. I will primarily focus on the specific challenges that the clinician likely will confront with the trauma survivor during the course of treatment, with a specific focus on psychotherapy that considers the individual as an integral part of a social and cultural fabric. As Rousseau and Measham note in this volume, traumatic suffering has both positive and negative effects, continues to change over time, is profoundly influenced by context, and can be a source of transformation for the survivor.

RELIGION AND SPIRITUALITY

Religion and spirituality are important and, until recently, neglected topics in psychology and psychiatry, particularly in the treatment of trauma survivors. In the contemporary era, the biological and social sciences and the humanities are frequently in conflict in their attempts to describe the natural world and human behavior. However, there is also a great deal of convergence among their concepts and constructs that is often obscured. Psychiatry and religion both draw on rich traditions of human thought and practice, and psychiatry is the branch of medicine that most prominently incorporates the humanities and social sciences in its scientific base and in its treatment of illness; moreover, psychiatry has often needed to go beyond the world of natural science into the realm of philosophy in its attempts to explain the full range of human behavior, particularly behavior following intense trauma and violence (Boehnlein, 2000). Psychiatry and religion actually can offer parallel and complementary frames of reference for understanding and describing the human experience, along with illuminating how identity is defined and how it is affected by interpersonal and social processes. Yet, at the same time, psychiatry and religion can be in conflict, particularly in the realm of faith. Psychiatry is a scientific discipline that demands proof of assertions or beliefs about how the mind works and about human behavior. However, religious beliefs are often based on revelation or faith and ultimately cannot be proven in the scientific sense. Therefore, there can be conflict between science and religion, particularly if adherents in either realm demand that beliefs, assertions, or values be judged using perspectives not accepted by the other. When culture is added to the mix, there can be even more tension among belief systems.

All religions in every culture offer some type of explanation of how the universe was created, how life is maintained, and what happens when life ceases to exist (Boehnlein, 2000). And all religions attempt to give their followers explanations for life's meaning, including rationales for the reality of human suffering, within a context of cultural symbols, beliefs, and practices. As the anthropologist Clifford Geertz (1973) has noted, from the perspective of the individual as part of a social unit, religion serves as a source of conceptions of the world, the self, and the relations between them. Spirituality is often more difficult to define because it is less codified within a specific tradition and frequently is more elusive psychologically and emotionally. But, it also incorporates ultimate values and meanings that inform life, and often spirituality bridges the domains of religion and science. Seaward (1991) has described the human spirit as an integration of three facets: an insightful relationship with oneself and others, a strong personal value system, and a meaningful purpose to one's life. It also involves an awareness of the degree of connectedness between oneself and the natural and supernatural environment. Spirituality refers to personal concerns with the transcendent – with something sacred and ultimate – and may or may not be embedded in a formal, established religious tradition (Plante & Sherman, 2001). Spirituality can be explored and experienced from both intellectual and emotional perspectives, and both on an individual level or within the interpersonal and social context of a religious community. So spirituality is not necessarily dependent on a specific historical or dogmatic tradition, and each person may develop and evolve an individual tradition in experiencing the transcendent. Spiritual experiences can be, and often are, intensely emotional and life-changing for some individuals.

Even within various organized religious traditions there are myriad accepted ways of exploring spiritual concerns, and there are often similarities in how subgroups within various religious traditions explore spirituality. Examples of subgroups that are found in the major religions of the world include contemplatives, mystics, and fundamentalists. Even though beliefs and traditions may vary greatly across the groups, the processes through which adherents in the same subgroups deal with spiritual concerns are often very similar. An implicit struggle between secular and religious perspectives has taken place in the understanding of spirituality over the past century; a secular perspective is manifest in an emphasis on the place of

values within a spiritual orientation rather than theistic or formally religious beliefs (Favazza, 2004; Galanter, Larson, & Rubenstone, 1991).

PSYCHOLOGICAL CHALLENGES AFTER TRAUMA RELATED
TO RELIGION AND SPIRITUALITY

People who experience intense trauma often undergo a deep moral crisis
(Marin, 1981), and it may take years, or even a lifetime, to reconstitute a
solid foundation of values and beliefs. The traumatic experience may also
be the individual's first encounter with evil (Sparr & Fergueson, 2000). Evil
is absolute wrongdoing that leaves no room for account or expiation; evil
is not merely the opposite of good but inimical to it, and true evil aims at
destroying moral distinctions themselves (Neiman, 2002).

Janoff-Bulman (1985) has stated that three basic assumptions held by the
survivor may be destroyed by the trauma: (1) the belief in one's personal
invulnerability; (2) the perception of the world as understandable; and
(3) the view of oneself in a positive light. The basic trust in oneself and
others can be permanently affected.

The cultural traditions of the survivor may strongly influence the degree
of control that he or she feels in the future, or even whether or not a sense
of control or the ability to proactively control events is considered possible or valuable. For example, in many Eastern traditions, meditation offers
a means of transcending the illusions of everyday life, achieving a state
of nonjudgmental detachment, or passively observing one's own mind
(Tan & Dong, 2001). Therefore, in Eastern traditions it may be considered
more acceptable, or even desirable, after trauma to adopt or maintain a
more detached or nonjudgmental view of traumatic events. However, a
survivor who had been raised in a Western culture that maintains the value
of proactive control in influencing life events may become demoralized if,
for the first time, the ability to influence events seems to be totally out of
one's control. Yet, regardless of whether the survivor has been raised in
Eastern or Western traditions, he or she may still struggle with the challenge of an altered meaning or purpose in life. In the West, a new meaning
may be more strongly defined in more personal terms, such as individual
achievement or generativity, whereas in the East a meaningful life after
trauma may be constructed around the value of one's social roles in the
family and community and the success of effectively fulfilling those roles.
The construction of meaning is a long process that involves many different elements – personal, familial, sociopolitical, cultural, and religious
(Rousseau & Measham, this volume).

In order to come to terms with the meaning of the event, the survivor
must first mourn the losses that occurred during the trauma, be they material, human, or symbolic. Because one of the central roles of religion is to
place loss in a context of meaning and purpose, mourning can be facilitated

by religious belief and ritual. The bereaved person does not have to be religious in a formal sense; however, how the person was socialized to reconcile the pain of loss is important (Eisenbruch, 1984). The use of ritual can reinforce central cultural beliefs that reestablish the concept that there is some order in the universe (Levi-Strauss, 1979). In cultures that highly value social connectedness and intricately connect identity with social role and affiliation, grief and the pain of loss are more likely to be worked through in a social context and with collective ritual. This may allow those who are mourning to have greater access to a wider variety of effective options for dealing with emotional pain. As described elsewhere in this volume by BenEzer, the ritual re-telling by Ethiopian Jews of their traumatic migration story from Ethiopia to Israel serves to reaffirm identity, mourn past losses, and enhance integration into Israeli society.

Collective ritual may be exclusively secular or religious, but in cultures in which there has been an intermixing of religious traditions with secular ritual over many centuries, there may be numerous rituals that represent a hybridization of the two. Even in cultures that more highly value individual autonomy and action, along with internalization of feeling and expression, group ritual at times of great loss and mourning can offer a collective efficacy that goes beyond each individual.

Rituals that enable individuals and groups to deal with loss and death frequently include elements of majority and folk religions in various combinations, secular culture, and personal beliefs and values. In cultures throughout the world, death is universally followed by some sort of passage ceremony, both for the deceased who are removed to the symbolic world of the dead and for the immediate survivors who are removed from their status and roles lost when the death occurred (Rosenblatt, Walsh, & Jackson, 1976). The process of grief and mourning is facilitated by the continuity of meaning that is developed over generations in the rituals of any given culture. Prayer in Buddhism, Islam, Christianity, and Judaism, frequently facilitated by an acknowledged leader or member of the clergy, is utilized individually and collectively to help the survivor to separate emotionally from the deceased, connect with others in the present, and focus on the future.

There also can be profound changes in the survivor's sense of identity after trauma. This can be the case particularly with a person who has taken pride in an ability to be proactive and to control life events. The trauma may seriously alter this sense of the self and impact future decision making. Yet, individuals whose posttraumatic cognitive processing includes significant thinking about the event and its potential meaning and significance are more likely to report experiencing posttraumatic growth (Calhoun, Cann, Tedeschi, & McMillan, 2000). However, if the traumatic experience required the person to make split-second life or death decisions that impacted the survival of others, the outcome may negatively and profoundly impact

one's sense of self as a good and moral person. The nature of the relationship between religious faith and negative life events can be complex:
For some individuals, religious faith may enhance the ability to cope with
negative life events; whereas for others, negative life events may result in
greater religious faith (Connor, Davidson, & Lee, 2003).

Yet, experiencing massive trauma can also result in a collapse of faith.
The human experience of useless cruelty, such as in the Holocaust, where
the goal of the perpetrators is the suffering of others solely for the sake
of suffering rather than for a military or political aim (Langer, 1998), is
an apt example. It illustrates well the problem of theodicy, the difficulty
of defending divine justice in the face of great evil and suffering; if God
is all-loving he would not be able to tolerate the appalling suffering that
is evident in the created order and, if he is almighty, he would be able
to do something about it (Bowker, 1970). So, the problem of evil can be
expressed in theological or secular terms, but it is fundamentally a problem
about the intelligibility of the world as a whole; the problem of evil belongs
essentially neither to ethics nor to metaphyisics, but forms a link between
the two (Neiman, 2002).

The following case (Boehnlein, 1987, p. 768) illustrates the clinical significance of the confluence of religious belief, ritual, and perceived self-image
in the process of mourning after trauma. It also illustrates how illness is
shaped by cultural factors governing the perception and understanding of
personal experience (Kleinman, Eisenberg, & Good, 1978).

A 45-year-old widow was referred for psychiatric evaluation because of anorexia
and slow, yet steady, weight loss. She had numerous symptoms of major depression, but also admitted to a number of subjectively disturbing symptoms of posttraumatic stress disorder such as nightmares and intrusive thoughts of her war
experiences, numbing of emotional feeling for loved ones, and startle reactions
accompanying loud noises or knocks at the door.

With antidepressant medication, there was substantial improvement in her
nightmares and startle reactions, yet she remained chronically depressed, with
a pervasive feeling of helplessness and hopelessness.

Three months after the start of treatment, she had an exacerbation of symptoms
(particularly nightmares) associated with family financial problems and also associated with receipt of a letter from a younger sister who had recently become seriously ill in a Thai refugee camp. Nightmare themes, as before, centered around the
violent deaths of many family members who had perished during the Pol Pot years.

During that session she spontaneously related an excruciating tale of an experience during the Pol Pot era which had haunted her for many years in her nightmares and daily thoughts. In her presence, her father had committed suicide with
an overdose of medication because of his fear of the impending discovery, by Khmer
Rouge forces, of his former position as a military officer in the Lon Nol government
(the regime overthrown by the Khmer Rouge); this discovery would have meant
certain death. The patient engaged in a physical struggle with her father in an
attempt to extract the medication from him, but was too weak to do so because of

prolonged starvation and malnutrition. She described her failure and helplessness at not being able to prevent his suicide. She felt like crying constantly after his death, but refrained, as any sign of tears would have been a sign of weakness to Pol Pot forces and subsequently would have led to her own execution. She went on the describe her great concern that her father's body had not been cremated, but instead had been buried at a mass grave; there was a brief covert family ceremony marking his death. In attempting to come to terms with her father's death, she remained concerned that the manner of his death (suicide) and the lack of cremation may have eternally affected his reincarnation.

This woman's religious beliefs had a significant influence upon her views of her father's fate after death, along with her feelings of personal responsibility in not being able to prevent his suicide. As the eldest child she had felt responsible for ensuring that Buddhist burial ceremonies for her deceased father were adhered to closely. Although that had been impossible during the Khmer Rouge era, this perceived lack of responsibility continued to haunt her.

The search for meaning often leads to an encounter with religious beliefs and spiritual practices that, as Sparr and Fergueson (2000) describe, provide an explanatory framework of symbols and concepts within a behavioral context of ritual and social interaction. They note that Judaism holds open the possibility of being restored to a right relationship with God through atonement; Christianity teaches that repentance for sin, accompanied by turning to God and asking to be united with Christ's sacrifice, brings forgiveness and the gift of a new life (Christian trauma survivors often mention the loss of God as one of their greatest losses); Buddhism incorporates the acceptance of life as it comes, including traumatic events (reincarnation is a major tenet of Buddhism, along with Karma, the belief that a person's actions in this life will affect one's existence in the next). In Islam, given that death to an individual is divinely ordained, the survivor need not bear the guilt of a loss (Elbedour, Baker, Shalhoub-Kevorkian, Irwin, & Belmaker, 1999). In most of the religions of the world, pain, suffering, atonement, and forgiveness are interrelated in theology and in everyday life. The relative importance of each, and their interaction, may vary among the major religions, but they are central issues that affect recovery from great trauma and loss. The following are examples from specific religious traditions (Bowker, 1970; Schimmel, 2002):

1. What a religious tradition has to say about suffering often reveals what it believes about the nature and purpose of existence. Suffering as purposeful, or considered as a way of atonement, has allowed Jewish communities to survive intense and relentless persecution. In Judaic tradition, the existence of suffering and death is located in the choices of man. In Islam God's, not man's, power and control is paramount, and suffering must be a part of the purposes of God. It is seen as a punishment for sin or as a test, but it also builds character and reveals a man's true nature. In the Quran endurance and

acceptance are considered worthwhile because of greater rewards to come, and suffering can be used as an instrument to resist evil. In Hinduism, suffering is seen as the essence of the universe, a result of conflict and tension, but it is only a problem as long as it appears to be an inescapable truth. For Buddhists, suffering is inescapable in the current life, and should be accepted, but can be relieved by reincarnation in the next life. Overall, it is striking to note that all major religious traditions start with the facts of suffering as they are, not with suffering as a theoretical problem.

2. The concept of forgiveness is intricately connected with the practical problems of pain, suffering, and trauma in the religions of the world. In Christian and Judaic understandings of forgiveness, reconciliation is an ultimate goal of forgiveness, even though reconciliation does not necessarily imply or depend on forgiveness. In Buddhist teaching, whatever one does in this life one gets back in return. If actions are tainted with evil and have not been atoned for, evil is returned in the next life.

Religious traditions in the West generally include a more active approach to suffering and trauma, whereas Eastern traditions prescribe a somewhat more reflective position. Both of these traditions can be seen in psychotherapeutic approaches to trauma recovery. In PTSD recovery, spiritual awakening can play a role in relieving survivor guilt (Khouzam & Kissmeyer, 1997). And there are a number of similarities between the spiritual process of repentance and the process of psychotherapy as, in both processes, the individual undertakes a journey of transformation that includes painful introspection; the working through of rage, guilt, or shame related to the experience of evil optimally involves seeking a proper balance of justice, repentance, and forgiveness (Schimmel, 2002). This is not an easy task, however, for the survivor. Normal and expected human interactions such as anger, hate, and the urge for revenge can be overwhelming, thus preventing resolution of the intense mix of emotions that occur after trauma.

It is conceivable that many of the posttraumatic symptoms that are described in a variety of different ethnic groups represent a universal human response to the cognitive disruption of a sense of order and meaning, which comes from a stable system of culturally specific beliefs and values. It is even possible to understand some of the symptoms of PTSD as a search for meaning; for example, revisiting or even obsessing about the trauma may be a part of a normal urge to integrate and understand a dreadful experience (Konner, this volume). Individuals experience great cognitive dissonance between what they observe and experience in reality and what they previously believed were stable, secure, and predictable relationships, not only with other individuals, but also with the metaphysical or spiritual. A desire to be spiritual leads people to form an identification with mythic systems, which are composed of three elements (Sparr & Fergueson, 2000, pp. 115–116): (1) a symbolic narrative that portrays the relationship between the individual and ultimate eternal transcendent reality (e.g., the Gospels, Vision Quest stories), (2) a system of rituals used to unite the individual with the ultimate eternal transcendent reality, and (3) interpretive concepts (theology) that define and explain the spiritual. These concepts are used to interpret human experience in the context of the symbolic narrative (i.e., they give meaning to life experience). Mythic systems often become formalized and institutionalized into religions.

Because of early identification, a mythic system may be a person's only available source for interpreting life experience. When traumatic stress elicits profound spiritual questions about good, evil, right, wrong, and the meaning of human existence, people naturally turn to their identified mythic system to find answers. With some investigative encouragement, people with PTSD may describe mythic interpretations of their traumatic experience.

As BenEzer has noted elsewhere in this volume in his description of the journey of Ethiopian Jews, myth is a story that can make sense of untidy and traumatic memory and a system of communication that can enhance the evolution of individual and collective identity.

THE ROLE OF THE HEALING PROCESS IN RESTRUCTURING VALUES AND MEANING AFTER TRAUMA

The complex existential and spiritual issues associated with trauma and loss are central to both religious faith and the process of posttraumatic recovery. Shils (1975) has noted that when empirically observable events contradict the rules of life that designate the individual's and the society's appropriate relationship with core values, there is a need to reaffirm and reinterpret that relationship.

That reinterpretation may involve a restructuring of one's relationship with not only cognitive structures of meaning and order in the universe, but also one's relationship with the society at large. This task involves the ability not only to mourn the losses of the past (personal, material, and symbolic), but also to trust again those who might provide some sense of security and hope for the present and future (healers, such as clergy and health professionals, family, and friends). For immigrants and refugees who have experienced much trauma, this task also exists concurrently with the stresses of migration and subsequent acculturation that are, in themselves, immensely challenging. These stresses also exist alongside changes in religious beliefs and practice that occur during acculturation. Immigrants and refugees, through community integration, marriage, or other factors, adopt other forms of religious practice that often complement their traditional practice that had evolved through generations.

For example, Southeast Asian refugees of different cultural backgrounds, who had developed religious traditions over centuries that fused beliefs and practices of animism and Buddhism, have adopted various Christian practices after immigration that center around important life transitions such as birth, marriage, and death.

The cognitive reinterpretation of one's central values and relationship with the environment following trauma may be similar cross-culturally, but the specific practical form that this process takes is related to culturally specific healing forms, including symbolic systems and ritual performance. The ability of healers to help people within their own cultural system depends on individual and group perception of healers as effective; worthy of respect; and able to provide a safe, secure, and predictable environment for the healing process (Boehnlein, 1987). For healers, whether traditional or Western, working with an ethnic group that is both acculturating and collectively recovering from trauma, success also depends on bridging the symbolic systems of ritual and myth that exist both in the acculturating group and the majority society. For example, the Western health professional needs to know how to present possibly effective treatments (such as medication or certain verbal interpretations) to individuals from another ethnic group in a culturally appropriate manner, and he/she must also attempt to understand how patients interpret the trauma within their own secular and religious systems. Modes of treatment involving a hybridization of myths and symbols may evolve over time through a process similar to the process that healing systems undergo during normal acculturation.

The evolution of new healing forms that span different cultural systems of thought and action may theoretically parallel similar processes that Wallace (1966, 1970) has described in the development of revitalization movements in religion and other social systems. According to Wallace, revitalization movements reduce the level of stress prevalent in systems of dogma, myth, and ritual by reestablishing some sense of internal organization and consistency. Cultural elements that had previously appeared to be contradictory are restructured in a meaningful form by creative individuals with some societal-sanctioned authority; this also serves as a process of cultural innovation and renewal. This process can lead to an ultimate strengthening of both individual qualities and social bonds necessary for posttraumatic recovery. Yet this process also may fail if the immigrant community after resettlement is disrupted by continuous stress from crime, poverty, or internal migration that prevents long-term stability.

THE THERAPEUTIC RELATIONSHIP

The healing relationship with a health care provider, psychotherapist, member of the clergy, or other socially sanctioned healer can serve as an initial catalyst for the survivor's attempt to build a renewed sense of trust and meaning in life. This security and acceptance can provide what Bowlby (1973) has called a "secure base" that allows the survivor to begin to explore a new world and interact with others once again. In the realm of society and culture, the healer can assist the survivor in slowly rebuilding his or her connections to the altered cultural foundations in life that contribute to self-identity and meaning and to recover some degree of control over his or her environment (Boehnlein, 1987). Religious beliefs, institutions, and rituals can help to build that secure base by giving some individuals a known and predictable foundation from which to face an unpredictable future. Religious belief systems throughout the world provide followers with constructs for dealing with loss, death, and the unpredictability of the future after loss or trauma. Additionally, the social structure and function of religious rituals allow trauma survivors to receive support from other people and to build and strengthen social bonds that can help them to survive future challenges or traumas.

The appropriate mix of emphasis in therapy on the individual or social/interpersonal aspects of recovery will depend on the overall values of the specific ethnic group or culture. For example, does the culture more highly value individualism, proactiveness, and control over one's environment, or does the culture more strongly value a high degree of social affiliation and a clearly defined social role as core elements of identity and self-worth? Of course, it is also vitally important in treatment to consider individual demographic factors (age, education, degree of identification with one's culture) and not make blanket assumptions because a person is part of a specific ethnic or cultural group.

The therapist frequently encounters great challenges in deciding to what degree he or she can assist the recovery of the trauma survivor by either supporting or challenging traditional religious or spiritual belief systems. This decision is influenced by the therapist's clinical judgment about the degree of moral pain experienced by the survivor, by the degree of understanding of the foundations of meaning in the survivor's religious and cultural background, and by countertransference feelings related to personal and cross-cultural experiences. Moral pain is the emotional discomfort that a survivor feels that results from the dissonance between what is witnessed or experienced in the traumatic event and what was previously experienced or expected in life. Expectations may have been based on moral or religious precepts that were learned or practiced throughout life, and the foundations of these expectations may have been shaken by the traumatic experience, including emergent decisions made by the survivor during the trauma. Classic examples include moral decisions faced by combatants during war that are far removed from what had been previously confronted prior to combat, such as irreconcilable life and death choices that involve split-second decisions to kill or be killed. A specific example would be a young soldier in the stress of combat having to decide whether a child approaching his combat unit carrying a bag is presenting a gift or an explosive device.

In these cases it is important for the therapist to listen carefully to the survivor over time to determine what constitutes his/her foundation of morality and meaning. The foundation may consist of fixed and unwavering ideals and precepts based in a specific religious tradition. In any given individual, this may either provide a solid foundation from which the survivor can experience solace, understanding, and forgiveness, or it can contribute to irreconcilable guilt and endless searching for an elusive forgiveness. Moreover, the underpinnings of this foundation may be undergoing evolution and change as the survivor searches for comprehensible explanations for ambivalent feelings, complicated moral questions, or behavior during the trauma that the survivor now regrets.

In these therapeutic situations, the therapist can slowly guide the survivor along a path of reconciliation, recognizing and supporting the survivor's strengths, while at the same time encouraging the survivor to utilize other available social, family, or religious supports. This journey may take many years as the survivor negotiates life transitions in education, work, and social relationships that, in turn, influence impressions of self, others, religion/spirituality, and one's place in the world. It is important to recognize that suffering – experiencing, enduring, and transcending pain and tribulation – is a social, intersubjective process (Kleinman, 1999).

Because of the absolute split between good and evil in many mythic systems, Sparr and Fergueson (2000, p. 117) note that some survivors believe that their encounter with evil during the traumatic experience has permanently defiled them:

One veteran told his therapist that he was "Satan's child" because of his war experiences. The therapist explained to the veteran that this was an irrational and superstitious idea that was being used to avoid responsibility. Although the therapist's explanation may have had intellectual merit, it overlooked the personal impact of the man's encounter with evil and his mythic identification. Calling himself "Satan's child" was, in part, a way of understanding and giving meaning to his experience. The veteran abandoned therapy because he felt the therapist had discounted his ideas.

Challenging the survivor's system of meaning that may be adversely affecting the ability to recover from trauma is a delicate and sometimes unpredictable process in treatment.

A young Buddhist woman was assaulted as a teenager on several occasions by security forces in an Asian country after being jailed during a peaceful protest advocating for greater civil rights for her minority group. The assault was extremely traumatic for her and she suffered from numerous PTSD symptoms for more than a decade afterwards. These symptoms included insomnia, nightmares, startle reactions, intrusive thoughts, flashbacks, and emotional withdrawal, and they significantly affected her interpersonal relationships and overall social functioning.

Initially, antidepressant treatment allowed for some blunting of the most intense PTSD symptoms, but it took some time to gain trust in the psychotherapeutic process. The therapist created an accepting, safe, and non-confrontative environment in sessions that occurred only every 3–4 weeks, at the patient's request; she stated that more frequent sessions would be too intense for her psychologically.

While describing why it was so difficult for her to discuss her traumatic experiences, and why she had not done so previously before starting therapy, she stated that no matter how much she had tried to struggle with a solution over the years, she felt emotionally paralyzed by trying to resolve who was responsible for her trauma – the security forces who had abused her or she herself. Because of her Buddhist beliefs, she believed that her Karma was responsible for her being singled out for the assault, and she believed she could do nothing about it. However, if she blamed the perpetrators, she would become extremely angry and upset, thus perpetuating an endless cycle of intrusive thoughts, ruminations, anxiety, and hyperarousal. And there was ultimately no way to confront those who had assaulted her.

Over a long period of time, therapy focused on what appeared on the surface to be an unreconcilable ambivalence between blaming herself and blaming others. The therapeutic process did not focus on challenging her religious belief systems that were very fixed, but instead focused on other aspects of Buddhism that would better ameliorate the intense ambivalence. Specifically, within the context of her Buddhist beliefs, acceptance of what had happened was suggested, along with concurrent acknowledgment of the strong character traits that not only had allowed her to survive the assaults, but also had allowed her to go on with her life and graduate from college, despite little social support. An independent spirit was fostered and encouraged, while at the same time a secure base was provided in therapy (Bowlby, 1973) to allow for the development of both greater self-confidence and greater ease in interpersonal relationships.

Greater levels of personal resilience have been associated with more favorable outcomes in PTSD (Connor et al., 2003). Religion and spirituality may contribute to this resilience by providing guidance for the survivor on complicated moral questions, along with a social network of individuals with shared values and beliefs who can provide support and guidance. Also, success in psychotherapy in the treatment of PTSD requires overt questioning, on the part of the patient and the clinician, of the congruence of their respective models of illness causation and ideas for treatment. It also allows for discussion that focuses on beliefs and values, which are central concerns for trauma survivors. It is essential for the clinician to be aware of the importance of fostering an environment of safety, security, and trust. It is also important to be aware of subtle signs of internal distress that are communicated by patients, either through affect or behavior.

From the clinician's perspective, dealing with one's own emotional responses can be very challenging. When working with trauma survivors, the therapist will be confronted with a broad and intense range of personal emotions and may go back and forth between the extremes of insensitivity and overidentification as a way of dealing with his or her own emotional reactions to horrific stories (Kinzie & Boehnlein, 1993). The therapeutic process will require the therapist to think about and confront moral issues in treatment and to consider the complexity and often overwhelming nature of good and evil in the world. As treatment proceeds, patients can be encouraged to explore alternative paths to health, to obtain broad-based information, to discuss their thoughts and feelings with others and the therapist, and to reestablish religious or cultural ties that had been destroyed by the trauma and its aftermath.

This mutual therapeutic encounter with complex moral questions concerning good and evil can also present immense emotional challenges for the therapist. The therapist inevitably must confront personal feelings about life and death, the fragility of existence, and the problem of evil. Moreover, the therapist also has the challenge of creating meaning for one's professional work with survivors who have confronted evil and are struggling to find coherent answers to often unanswerable questions. To abandon the attempt to comprehend evil is to abandon every basis for confronting it, in thought as in practice (Neiman, 2002). This inevitably requires the therapist to examine his or her own attitudes toward religion and spirituality, and it requires a journey from the therapist along a road that has constant detours, twists, and turns. This journey requires steady questioning, observation, reflection, and dedication as a healer.

The long-term course of treatment in PTSD, particularly related to the component of religion and spirituality, is truly a process of struggle and growth for clinician and patient. The most complex and private issues of life are confronted in a collaborative process that continually changes both therapist and patient. The struggle for meaning, purpose, identity, and relationships with others is indeed an ongoing existential engagement with the spiritual dimension of life.

References

Boehnlein, J. K. (1987). Clinical relevance of grief and mourning among Cambodian refugees. *Social Science & Medicine, 25*(7), 765–772.

Boehnlein, J. K. (2000). Introduction. In J. K. Boehnlein (Ed.), *Psychiatry and religion: The convergence of mind and spirit* (pp. xv–xx). Washington, DC: American Psychiatric Press.

Bowker, J. (1970). *Problems of suffering in religions of the world.* New York: Cambridge University Press.

Bowlby, J. (1973). *Attachment and loss: Separation* (Vol. 2). New York: Basic Books.

Calhoun, L. G., Cann, A., Tedeschi, R. G., & McMillan, J. (2000). A correlational test of the relationship between posttraumatic growth, religion, and cognitive processing. *Journal of Traumatic Stress, 13*(3), 521–527.

Connor, K. M., Davidson, J. R., & Lee, L. C. (2003). Spirituality, resilience, and anger in survivors of violent trauma: A community survey. *Journal of Traumatic Stress, 16*(5), 487–494.

Eisenbruch, M. (1984). Cross-cultural aspects of bereavement. II: Ethnic and cultural variations in the development of bereavement practices. *Culture Medicine and Psychiatry, 8*(4), 315–347.

Elbedour, S., Baker, A., Shalhoub-Kevorkian, N., Irwin, M., & Belmaker, R. H. (1999). Psychological responses in family members after the Hebron massacre. *Depression and Anxiety, 9*(1), 27–31.

Favazza, A. (2004). *PsychoBible: Behavior, religion and the Holy Book.* Charlottesville, VA: Pitchstone Publishing.

Galanter, M., Larson, D., & Rubenstone, E. (1991). Christian psychiatry: The impact of evangelical belief on clinical practice. *American Journal of Psychiatry, 148*(1), 90–95.

Geertz, C. (1973). *The interpretation of cultures.* New York: Basic Books.

Janoff-Bulman, R. (1985). The aftermath of victimization: Rebuilding shattered assumptions. In C. R. Figley (Ed.), *Trauma and its wake* (Vol. 1, pp. 15–33). New York: Brunner/Mazel.

Khouzam, H. R., & Kissmeyer, P. (1997). Antidepressant treatment, posttraumatic stress disorder, survivor guilt, and spiritual awakening. *Journal of Traumatic Stress, 10*(4), 691–696.

Kinzie, J. D., & Boehnlein, J. K. (1993). Psychotherapy of the victims of massive violence: Countertransference and ethical issues. *American Journal of Psychotherapy, 47*(1), 90–102.

Kleinman, A. (1999). Experience and its moral modes: Culture, human conditions and disorder. In G. B. Petersen (Ed.), *The Tanner Lectures on human values* (Vol. 20, pp. 357–420). Salt Lake City: University of Utah Press.

Kleinman, A., Eisenberg, L., & Good, B. (1978). Culture, illness, and care: Clinical lessons from anthropologic and cross-cultural research. *Annals of Internal Medicine, 88*(2), 251–258.

Langer, L. L. (1998). *Preempting the Holocaust.* New Haven, CT: Yale University Press.

Levi-Strauss, C. (1979). *Myth and meaning.* New York: Schocken Books.

Marin, P. (1981). Living in moral pain. *Psychology Today, 6,* 68–74.

Neiman, S. (2002). *Evil in modern thought: An alternative history of philosophy.* Princeton, NJ: Princeton University Press.

Plante, T. G., & Sherman, A. C. (2001). Research on faith and health. In T. G. Plante & A. C. Sherman (Eds.), *Faith and health: Psychological perspectives* (pp. 1–12). New York: Guilford Press.

Rosenblatt, P. C., Walsh, R. P., & Jackson, D. A. (1976). *Grief and mourning in cross-cultural perspective.* New Haven, CT: HRAF Press.

Schimmel, S. (2002). *Wounds not healed by time: The power of repentance and forgiveness.* Oxford, UK: Oxford University Press.

Seaward, B. L. (1991). Spiritual wellbeing: A health education model. *Journal of Health Education, 22,* 166–169.

Shils, E. (1975). *Center and periphery: Essays in macrosociology.* Chicago: University of Chicago Press.

Sparr, L. F., & Fergueson, J. F. (2000). Moral and spiritual issues following traumatization. In J. K. Boehnlein (Ed.), *Psychiatry and religion: The convergence of mind and spirit* (pp. 109–123). Washington, DC: American Psychiatric Press.

Tan, S. Y., & Dong, N. J. (2001). Spiritual interventions in healing and wholeness. In T. G. Plante & A. C. Sherman (Eds.), *Faith and health: Psychological perspectives* (pp. 291–310). New York: Guilford Press.

Wallace, A. (1966). *Religion: An anthropological view.* New York: Random House.

Wallace, A. (1970). *Culture and personality.* New York: Random House.

14

Posttraumatic Suffering as a Source of Transformation: A Clinical Perspective

Cécile Rousseau and Toby Measham

When confronted with catastrophic trauma, our immediate response as clinicians is to focus on efforts to ensure survival. Organized violence, such as warfare, provokes a wide range of responses, including the urgent, moral need to condemn such crimes against humanity. The emergency pushes us to rely on our previously acquired knowledge and know-how. Once the initial crisis has faded, however, we tend to neglect the equally important task of creating spaces in which to rethink and adapt our interventions.

In order to work effectively in the field of trauma, we need to locate and identify our roles as clinicians and as members of institutions in a particular sociopolitical, historical, and cultural discourse on trauma. Contextualization is a necessary prerequisite to effective clinical work in trauma therapy. An important part of our work involves a continual questioning and examination of the complexity of social violence, including our own implicit role in the process, in order to avoid unwitting participation in the very forms of social violence we seek to address (Kleinman & Kleinman, 1997a). We also recognize that we need to strike a delicate balance between questioning the dominant models and supporting them. When models are too severely questioned and when the necessarily aggressive aspects of all types of treatment are too harshly critiqued, there is a real risk that the criticism will provoke a state of paralysis and a withdrawal of efforts to address the origins and consequences of organized violence. We believe that trying to change a system from within is better than doing nothing to help people. Clinicians need to question, understand, contain, and even help transform the effects of organized violence by recognizing them and by assuming a share of the collective political responsibility for their occurrence (Ricoeur, 2000a).

Our desire as clinicians to heal people suffering from the consequences of war is tied to our fluctuating awareness of local, national, and political responsibilities. These responsibilities are being transformed by globalization, as an emerging global worldview is calling into question traditional notions of proximity and distance. At the same time, healing interventions remain embedded in a discourse of political correctness. This discourse, by its very nature, denies our own relationship with organized violence. As a result, humanitarian and clinical programs set up to address the consequences of war are guided primarily by theories of victimology and the posttraumatic model. It is therefore critical to identify and examine the larger context in which this clinical work is situated, including the intimate connections between clinicians, institutions, and the social construction of violence.

This paper expresses the thinking of the Transcultural Child Psychiatry Team of McGill University, a clinical, research, and teaching group that works with refugee families in Montreal, Canada. Our work partially reflects a North American worldview, but it is also influenced by European perceptions, given Montreal's unique position in Canada. In addition, our collaboration with practitioners and leading experts from non-Euro-American traditions, both within Canada and internationally, has both enriched our thinking and called into question the dominant Euro-American model for the psychological treatment of trauma. We are also influenced by the dual institutional bases of McGill University's Division of Social and Transcultural Psychiatry, first set up as a joint venture between the Departments of Psychiatry and Anthropology at McGill in 1955, and the Montreal Children's Hospital, which has a long tradition of serving Montreal's diverse community and has offered an innovative multiculturalism program addressing issues of culture in service delivery since 1986. Finally, the Transcultural Child Psychiatry Team is part of a greater Montreal network of individuals and groups who are interested in expanding current models of mental health to incorporate community approaches. Our work thus moves beyond the defined boundaries of medicine and academia to collaborate with community groups and international institutions addressing and questioning mental health problems from diverse perspectives. Although this paper reflects the current viewpoint of our clinical team, we consider it a work in progress.

This chapter will outline our perceptions of the limitations of current dominant theoretical models addressing the understanding and treatment of the consequences of war. Our objective is to illustrate how we have tried to rethink our clinical work in the light of these limitations. We will provide examples from both our hospital-based and community-based work to illustrate how we have tried to address the complexities of individual and collective experiences of organized violence.

THE VICTIM–AGGRESSOR DICHOTOMY: A DENIAL OF SHARED HUMANITY AND OF OUR OWN AGGRESSION

Violence in "peaceful" Euro-American societies is essentially constructed as something perpetrated and experienced by individuals. From this individualistic perspective, there are two types of participants: aggressors, who need to be identified, controlled, punished, and reformed or healed; and victims, who are accorded distinct rights, as long as they can prove that they have been wronged. In this context, power is seen as a force that is exercised to uphold the good and promote life and that has no potential to be abused. All occurrences of violence are represented as psychopathological and a scandal (Marange, 2001).

According to Marange, the idealism of peaceful societies makes us experience violence as something other than ourselves, both locally and globally. Communal and state-sponsored violence is represented as something totally foreign to "peaceful" societies, occurring somewhere "out there" and belonging mainly to a non-Western world characterized by barbarism, radicalism, and dictatorial régimes. Our need to create spaces where violent interactions can be played out, always at a distance from ourselves, can be viewed as a result of the denial of this and other forms of "clean" violence that characterize our societies (De Certeau, 1987). These virtual spaces present images of the other as either a barbaric and uncivilized aggressor or as a defenseless victim totally dependent on our aid (Kleinman & Kleinman, 1997b).

The common notion linking violence uniquely to one party shapes our worldview and our view of history. It is grounded in a self-preservation mechanism that serves to obscure the ordinary brutality caused by the inequalities inherent in all of our societies. It limits our capacity to confront the complexities of conflict and legitimizes a crusade against violence both at home and "out there." This mechanism reinforces socially constructed categories of exclusion and inequality. As clinicians, we participate in this mechanism, whether actively, unconsciously, or reluctantly.

The ascendancy of victimology and criminology as disciplinary fields is a by-product of this dichotomy between victims and aggressors. Victims, at least in North America, are perceived as essentially weak, powerless, and nonaggressive. The social construction of victimhood is reflected in psychiatric nosology. In the *DSM–IV* construct of PTSD, anger is recognized only as an essentially physiological epiphenomenon of autonomic nervous dysfunction, where it is characterized by irritability (APA, 1994). The psychological experience of aggression, including the expression of anger in reaction to profound betrayal by one's fellow humans as well as the expression of anger as a desire for revenge, is not covered by this posttraumatic model.

The dichotomy between victim and aggressor also limits the ways in which we understand the reactions of clinicians who work with traumatized persons. For example, "vicarious traumatization" is now widely recognized as a secondary disorder in which the patient's posttraumatic symptoms are transmitted to the therapist (Peltzer, 1996). However, there is an institutional and social denial of therapists' anger toward their patients for exposing them to this violence. Both patient and therapist are perceived as victims and, by definition, lack any aggressiveness.

THE NOTION OF TRAUMA AS SOLELY PATHOLOGICAL

The categorically constructed understanding of trauma as pathological dominates North American clinical models and underlies the *DSM–IV* diagnostic classification of posttraumatic stress disorder (PTSD). This fails to acknowledge that traumatic suffering has both positive and negative effects, is subject to change over time, and is profoundly influenced by social context.

Meta-analyses of epidemiological studies have demonstrated that, on average, only 20% of those who experience traumatic events develop post-traumatic stress syndrome (Yehuda & McFarlane, 1995). Two possibilities have been suggested to account for this low incidence: Either people who have experienced trauma may develop other kinds of problems, or they may be resilient and overcome the effects of trauma. Despite this evidence indicating that most people do not respond to trauma exposure with specific psychopathology, trauma is increasingly referred to as an experience that almost universally results in emotional and sometimes even cognitive disabilities.

As a result of this model the debilitating effects of trauma are emphasized, but little attention is paid to the individual and collective strengths that can come out of terrible experiences (Sigal, 1998). When strengths are identified, these are usually treated as anecdotal observations, as if they were individual exceptions to the rule. This conceptualization of the effects of traumatic experiences as necessarily pathological exists within the clinical framework, despite the fact that the majority of clinicians whose work deals with the effects of war and organized violence have witnessed the emergence of a sense of solidarity and even feelings of tenderness from horror. Although there is ample documentation of these observations, there has been little systematic investigation of the positive effects of trauma – as if there were perhaps something indecent in pursuing this line of inquiry (Sigal, 1995).

Nonetheless, a small number of quantitative studies of resiliency have shown these positive effects. For instance, a longitudinal study examining the emotional and behavioral well-being of Cambodian adolescents in Montreal whose families had come to Canada as refugees found that children whose families had experienced trauma before their birth had fewer externalizing symptoms (Rousseau, Drapeau, & Platt, 2000; Rousseau, Drapeau, & Rahimi, 2003). They also exhibited fewer risk behaviors, such as drug use, than their Quebec-born peers. The families' experiences of trauma during the Pol Pot régime also influenced the youngsters' self-perception and group identity. Children whose families had experienced the greatest trauma were most sure of themselves and most proud of their ethnic identity. Thus, intergenerational transmission of trauma had a positive effect on these adolescents (Rousseau et al., 2000; Rousseau, Drapeau, & Rahimi, 2003). Khmer community members interpreted these results as reflecting an implicit mission entrusted to adolescents in families who had experienced suffering, whereby the meaning of the trauma had a protective influence on the course of their future lives.

Other quantitative research has attempted to identify how people are strengthened by trauma. Studies have shown an increase in altruistic behavior following traumatic experiences, as well as an increase in planning behavior and a more positive perception of one's capacities (Dalianis-Karambatzakis, 1994; Ferren, 1999; Lyons, 1991; Macksoud & Aber, 1996; Sigal, 1998). However, these studies have had little effect on counteracting the near-universal belief that the effects of trauma on individuals and groups are always pathological. This points to the need to question the social utility of maintaining the dominant models of victimology and the medicalization of suffering. Models that pathologize trauma account for only one facet of the complex experience.

THE LIMITED KNOWLEDGE BASE OF CURRENT MODELS OF TRAUMA

The most serious problem with current models of trauma is that they are reified as representing a universal reality, rather than being recognized as concepts derived from a knowledge base that remains impoverished by its inability to incorporate nonmedical and non-Western sources of knowledge. The primacy of Western scientific, and particularly biomedical, knowledge remains unquestioned in these models, and they are promoted within our own societies and exported globally without any acknowledgment of their limits or deficits. One unfortunate result of this process is that conventional models of trauma serve to maintain the social order by perpetuating unequal power relations and particular representations of the other. Clinical models that aim to address the effects of trauma by drawing only from this biomedical knowledge base may harm as well as help, as they paradoxically may serve to maintain social inequalities and structural violence.

THE DICHOTOMY BETWEEN HEALTH AND DISABILITY

A diagnosis of PTSD requires three groups of symptoms – reliving the traumatic event, avoidance of trauma-related stimuli and numbing of general responsiveness, and hyperarousal – with the disturbance causing clinically significant distress or impairment in social, occupational, or other important areas of functioning. Although the classification requires that the disordered individual simultaneously relive trauma and avoid related stimuli, it does not describe how these types of symptoms might coexist. Which symptoms predominate? How does the transition from one group of symptoms to the other affect clinical status?

Research has shown that people who undergo trauma may continue to be able to function despite experiencing symptoms that wax and wane over a long period, depending on internal and external environmental factors (Kinzie, this volume; see also Kinzie, Sack, Angell, Clarke, & Rath, 1989; Mollica, 2001; Tousignant, 1997). During this time, the traumatic experience continues to transform the individual. It is clinically naïve to expect that, following catastrophic trauma, health will be manifested either by an enduring absence of symptoms or by a return to a previous state. Instead, the effect of psychic trauma may be to transform the person, who is also continuing on a developmental trajectory. The manifestation of symptoms is one aspect of the metamorphosis to a new state of equilibrium.

A side effect of this dichotomy between health and disability is the equally polarized view of the adaptive strategies available to people who have experienced trauma. Strategies are objectified and usually assigned a positive or negative valence. Thus, for example, disclosure is regarded as a helpful way to address the effects of trauma. The positive effects of disclosure are upheld by "expert consensus" in the clinical recommendations for the treatment of PTSD in children by the American Academy of Child and Adolescent Psychiatry (AACAP, 1997) despite the absence of research to support this claim. Clinicians who respect the wishes of their young patients not to address painful aspects of their past are viewed with suspicion, as if they may be colluding with their patients' defenses, which are deemed to be inappropriate denial and avoidance. Similarly, trust is valued, whereas distrust is seen essentially as a symptom, thus robbing it of its central protective role as a survival strategy both in time of war and during the process of adaptation in the host country. Meaning is valued and absurdity ignored. Thus, there has been a good deal of clinical work recognizing the importance of making sense of one's traumatic experiences, either by embracing the past or by exploring a number of different pathways. The devastating effects of the absurdity of many traumatic events have also been addressed (M. Viñar & Viñar, 1989). Yet, there is tendency to deny that meaninglessness is an integral part of the experience of trauma for many people. Premature attempts by clinicians to make sense of seemingly absurd events or failure to acknowledge feelings of absurdity can increase patients' sense of isolation. For this reason, acknowledging the absurdity of catastrophic experiences may be as important for the therapeutic process as finding meaning. Other dichotomies that have frequently been assigned positive and negative valences are isolation as opposed to reestablishment of social ties and dissociation as opposed to good contact with reality.

INTRODUCING MOVEMENT IN THE RECONSTRUCTION PROCESS

Clinicians who work with traumatized individuals are familiar with the oscillation between these poles, both within the therapeutic context and in the patient's external world. These oscillations can be seen as approaching and distancing maneuvers that serve to regulate the patients' affective experience and social positioning. Our own clinical experience, as well as research data, suggests that adopting either one of these strategies is not in and of itself psychopathological; instead, we have found that sticking exclusively to one of the strategies may indicate trouble. In other words, presenting as always disclosing, trustful, seeking meaning, reestablishing social bonds, and being in touch with reality may be just as pathological as saying nothing, being distrustful, being unable to find any meaning in one's experiences, isolating oneself, and dissociating. In our clinical practice, gaining even the slightest ability to move back and forth between two opposing strategies is seen as a key moment in which an individual or group begins to emerge from a predominantly inward-looking state of stupor and disconnection or begins to contain a process previously characterized by being overwhelmed by uncontainable traumatic experiences that were being constantly transmitted to others for containment.

This back-and-forth movement must always be linked to context. The ability to oscillate between two opposing strategies or poles of experience is considered to be adaptive if it is consistent with the reality of internal and external safety. This is of particular relevance to clinicians working with people who have experienced organized violence. A clinician may mistakenly diagnose PTSD at the onset of therapy when a patient presents during the asylum-seeking process. However, this highly fraught situation, like the experience of war, is in fact an ongoing state of peril. There is a very real possibility that the patient's claim for asylum may be rejected. Clinicians need to acknowledge to themselves and their patients that they cannot guarantee this basic aspect of security and that they themselves are part of an imperfect society. Otherwise, patients may feel doubly betrayed when they share their suffering in a therapeutic context that falsely promises hope or a cure. A patient's distancing efforts need to be equally respected in this context, and the adaptive function of taking those first hesitant steps toward another needs to be recognized, as the patient is preparing to deal with the possibility that newly established social ties with the host country may be broken.

DISCLOSURE AND SILENCE

Many clinicians believe that there is a relationship between a person's disclosure of traumatic events and psychological adaptation to trauma. Important in this paradigm are both the collective and individual values associated with disclosure as a reparative mechanism to address trauma. For example, bearing witness is a valued means by which Holocaust survivors can address their traumatic experiences both individually and collectively, in which a goal of "never again" is attached to the significance of these disclosures (Kirmayer, 1996). Current models of trauma treatment also value the role of telling, with such interventions as "debriefing" after traumatic events, as well as cognitive behavior therapy models predicated on exposure and response prevention mechanisms (see Yadin & Foa, this volume). Similarly, workshops and groups that encourage people to relate their traumatic experiences verbally or symbolically (through art or play, for example) are considered to have positive therapeutic value. Non-Western traditions, however, may value avoidance of any discussion of traumatic events just as highly and consider other mechanisms, such as a return to tradition, to be a means of repairing trauma (Dwyer & Santikarma, this volume; Rousseau, Morales, & Foxen, 2001). Ricoeur's (1976) work on the generation of meaning from past experiences, which introduces the concept of a dialectic between approaching the past and moving away from it, is relevant here. Avoidance and disclosure may represent different moments in the ongoing process of collective response to massive trauma.

Movements toward and away from expressing traumatic experience can similarly be seen on an individual level in the reparative process. Pennebaker (1985) has identified a group of Holocaust survivors that he describes as "super-repressors," because they did very well despite maintaining complete silence about their concentration camp experiences.

An investigation of the role of disclosure in children's adaptation following trauma has led to the concept of modulated disclosure (Measham, 2002). In the case of a family's experience of traumatic events, healthy adaptation for the developing child is hypothesized to be supported by a modulated disclosure of traumatic events by parents to children. What is important for children who have experienced war trauma may not be so much what their parents tell them about their experiences but, rather, what particular aspects should be disclosed and when disclosure occurs, according to the child's developmental needs. The goal is for parents to assume the role of gatekeepers of the past for the sake of their children's well-being. Children are given enough knowledge and guidance in order to make sense of their experiences while not being overwhelmed by disclosures that they are psychologically unable to handle.

DISTRUST AND TRUST

In a study of the refugee status determination process, we interviewed former members of the Canadian Immigration and Refugee Board (Rousseau & Foxen, 2005). One of them told us, "The idea of setting up a relationship of trust is a bit nonsensical.... Why should they trust us?...There is no reason to trust." This person was talking about not just the fundamental mistrust of institutions common in those who have lived under a totalitarian régime or the shattering of basic trust that results from trauma, but also the uneven power relationship that characterizes the refugee in the immigration system and in the host country as a whole. The situation of clinicians is not radically different, given our position in a society that considers refugees to be potential liars and views them with suspicion (see Kirmayer, this volume). Host country citizens are often ambivalent about asylum seekers. A wary approach to interpersonal relationships can be protective during the adaptation process, as newcomers try to avoid further disappointment by the inevitable limitations of humanity, as well as the more specific disappointments associated with our multicultural societies, in which minorities continue to experience intolerance and exclusion.

Establishment or reestablishment of trust may not begin in the clinical setting, but clinicians' capacity to maintain a bond in spite of distrust may shift the patient's attention toward the possibility of renewed trust, though at first it may be limited to internalized representations of loved ones or to an intimate relationship with spiritual or religious figures. It is tempting for the patient to see the therapist and the host society as radically distinct from the terror-provoking context of their trauma, but the massive investment and the inevitable disillusion that follows this idealized perspective can often be as problematic as deep distrust itself (Peltzer, 1996).

In North America, the current concerns with national security parallel the idea of trust in the therapeutic relationship. Establishing security by any means with the intention of creating a perimeter to exclude the unidentified "enemy" fuels distrust and fear, as any sign of otherness becomes suspicious. In the therapeutic setting, we prefer to work with the notion of *relative safety*. Safety depends on anchors and holding but may involve a protected space – partly internal, partly external – in an uncertain world where violence and aggression can occur.

MEMORY AND FORGETFULNESS

De Certeau (1987) argues that forgetfulness is as much an active process as remembering. In the continual remodeling of personal and collective histories, forgetfulness plays the role of erasing or dimming the intensity of unbearable or confusing aspects of the experience. Forgetfulness is often a key element in achieving coherence, which is always partial, stripped of its complexity. In recent work with communities in the highlands of Peru that have been devastated by the war between the army and the *Sendero Luminoso* ("Shining Path"), we were struck by the contrast between the memory work being done by the truth commission and nongovernmental organizations and the simultaneous desire to forget strongly expressed by the Quechua villagers. Memories of the recent past were not safe because the aggressors were either still around (in the case of the army) or making a comeback, in the case of the Shining Path. Furthermore, the villagers could not mourn the loss of the dreams and hopes for social change they had had at the beginning of the war because of the association with the subsequent horror. They could not recognize themselves in the skewed image of the past, in which they were portrayed as passive victims, and they felt that this view would not serve to reestablish justice.

When, what, and how much a person or a group needs to remember and to forget are complex questions. History must be written and transmitted to future generations, but the costs associated with a simplistic account of the collective experience should also be considered. In treatment programs and clinical processes, how can memory support the construction of meaning without either imposing a single voice or becoming overwhelmed by complexity and thus provoking chaos?

MEANING AND ABSURDITY

Fighting against absurdity is a central task both for the therapist and patient in trauma work. The construction of meaning is a long process that involves many different signifiers – sociopolitical, religious, cultural, familial, and personal (Bracken, 2002). Multiplicity of meaning sometimes facilitates the expression of different dimensions of the experience that are neither globally understandable nor transmissible. In a study of Rwandan adolescents who survived the 1994 massacres, Ehrensaft (2002) describes a pattern in which multiple meanings gravitate around a core meaning or around two opposite meanings. She shows how multiple meanings can reflect a flexible relationship to the past and are usually associated with resilience. For other adolescents, however, multiplicity reflects confusion and may represent either avoidance of an unacceptable meaning (for example, family responsibility for horrific events) or an attempt to overcome the sense of absurdity (Ehrensaft, 2002). It is important to recognize that in most cases of severe trauma, the pervasive feeling of absurdity remains and is transmitted to the therapist. Being able to understand this feeling as an essential part of human experience may at times be just as important as reframing the perception and using one's own sense of purpose to restore a meaningful universe. This sense of absurdity can extend to a disruption in our relationship with a religious and spiritual universe. Among the most serious symptoms in severely traumatized persons is the loss of faith. Its clinical accompaniment is captured by a turning to suicide as a solution. In these situations, reestablishing fragments of meaning must be anchored to a recognition of the radical doubt that these people have experienced when faced with a universe without any purpose. The clinician's contact with his or her own existential doubt and his or her own brief experiences of feelings of absurdity stemming from confrontations with horror, violence, and suffering may begin to bridge the gap with the patient. In this precarious proximity, a respectful search for shared meanings may be more acceptable than an imposition of a coherent narrative, because the latter will likely trigger anger and be experienced as a push toward certainties that the patient has rejected.

INTERVENTION AND PREVENTION

The clinic can play an important role as one of the powerful voices that speaks of trauma, but it is at the same time inherently limited, given that it can never address more than a small part of the effects of trauma and rarely has an impact on society at large. The clinical encounter can, however, open up unique spaces that enable and even encourage patients to put some distance between themselves and the group with which they identify, introducing a kind of movement that the group's collective reconstruction does not facilitate. This distinct space of expression may be especially useful when the collective reconstruction of meaning sacrifices the well-being of certain individuals for the sake of group harmony, as occurs in some cases of political rape (Atlani & Rousseau, 2000). The clinic, with its many tools, may also relieve suffering, offer consolation, and become a visible sign of solidarity.

The opening of avenues for expression suggests other areas of intervention that could be further developed, focusing on community programs that can serve as transitional spaces. When invested with clinical sensitivity, such community programs can help patients reestablish social ties and rebuild a meaningful world. There are many community or institutional projects that could play this role (Tolfree, 1996), but they have not often been assessed and their role in the reconstruction process remains largely unknown. To articulate this clinical sensitivity we now turn to a discussion of some of the key concepts behind the development of our clinical practice and prevention programs.

WORKING "ON" OR "AROUND" TRAUMA

Case Vignette: Lullabies

James is a 13-year-old from West Africa. This quiet, obedient boy was referred to the Transcultural Child Psychiatry Team by his school because he sometimes had strange outbursts of anger which terrified his teacher. The initial interview revealed that the outbursts were within the standard range of oppositional behavior and that what might be more terrifying to the school staff was James's story.

James had arrived in Canada 6 months before the interview. He had lived for more than 3 years in an orphanage in his homeland after having been saved from war in circumstances that remain unclear. From the bits and pieces that are known, it seems that he was the youngest child in a large family and that all the other members were killed with machetes, probably in front of him. His hands were cut off, and his forearms were burned with gasoline.

James never talked about any of that. He also refused to speak his mother tongue with the African psychologist on the team. He came to see the psychologist regularly and always began the sessions with the same ritual. He would ask permission to call his school and announce to the person who answered the phone, "Hello, I am James X"– emphasizing his new name – then add "I am calling to inform you that I am at the hospital." He did this in spite of the fact that the school knew he had a weekly appointment. He then went on to talk about his life in Canada, played, and even helped his therapist, doing precise artwork with his two forearms. After a few months, he received confirmation that he was accepted as a refugee. A couple of weeks later he stopped calling the school and asked his therapist to bring in some African music, lullabies that he hummed softly. Little by little he reclaimed his mother tongue and disclosed fragments of his history, the other story, structured around traditional proverbs, daily gestures, and familiar smells. He still got angry from time to time, but the school staff were no longer afraid of him.

Most posttraumatic therapeutic approaches focus on the traumatic event and associated memories. The therapeutic aim of direct exposure, which involves either desensitization, flooding or implosive therapy, and other variants of *in vivo* or imaginary exposure (including EMDR), is to modify behavioral and physiological responses to the traumatic memory. Cognitive approaches emphasize patterns of perception and interpretation, attentional processes, and memory integration with the aim of reframing perception and reassigning meaning to alter the associated psychological condition. For communities, truth commissions and bearing witness provide other reparative strategies centered on the sharing of traumatic memories (Foxen, 2002). In all these approaches, meaning is constructed *from* trauma; webs of relationships between life before and after are spun outward from this core. The traumatic experience is seen as a major source of disruption, which thus also becomes central to the reestablishment of continuity.

Documentation of reconstruction in community and clinical processes suggests that continuity also can be woven *around* trauma, when the emphasis shifts toward elements of the past (traditional, religious, familial, or personal) that structure the person's present and that therefore indirectly represent the possibility of surviving the traumatic experience. This indirect approach to trauma may confer a particular intensity to daily life or to rituals that represent personal and historical continuity and can sometimes be at least as important in the therapeutic encounter as a direct focus on trauma (Rousseau et al., 2001).

In James's story, two moments related to this process can be distinguished. First, in the precarity of the asylum application, he needed to establish a maximum distance from the past, to the point of rejecting, or denying, his own identity: He clung to his Canadian name and called the school to reassure himself by reaffirming that he was now in Canada, as a different person, and that everybody (the therapist and the school) acknowledged and agreed with this version of the story. The acceptance of his refugee claim opened the door to reestablishing some links with the past, first in the form of nonspecific attachment memories (lullabies), which structured a link between past attachment figures and the therapist. He then moved toward a more direct exploration of the past: wanting to understand how he had survived and what were the roots of his present strength. In his case, continuity was established *around* trauma, in widening circles, that contained and connected an increasing range of his life experiences.

REPRESENTING AMBIVALENCE AS A NECESSITY

Clinicians who adopt a strong position of advocacy for vulnerable groups like refugees may be tempted to disassociate themselves from mainstream society and its institutions, which are often rightly portrayed as unhelpful and discriminatory, if not openly hostile (Suárez-Orozco, 2000). In his distinction among criminal, moral, and political responsibility, Ricoeur (2000b) underscores the subject's duty to assume, at least partially, responsibility for society's neglect or abuse of marginal or minority groups. From this point of view, clinicians, even when they belong to a minority, simultaneously represent both mainstream society with its multiple sources of frustration and a critique of this society, and they can thus embody the patient's ambivalence toward the new milieu. Representing ambivalence in this way may enable the patient to mourn the loss of expectations about the host society, while establishing links with "good enough" aspects of this society. At a personal level, this process parallels the patient's discovery of the therapist's dangerous side. Recognizing the aggressor in the therapist and in oneself is one of the most terrifying consequences of trauma. If patients can cope with the fact that the clinician is similar in some aspects to the aggressor – and if the therapist can survive being viewed this way, while at the same time being experienced as radically different – then patients may come to grips with their ambivalence about themselves and others and reconcile in some small way with human nature.

Although professional associations working with children advocate for moral clarity to give meaning to organized violence (AACAP, 1997), the role of ambivalence in the partial resolution of intercommunity tensions in multiethnic neighborhoods should also be considered (Apfel & Simon, 2000). For example, we recently conducted an elementary school–based pilot project for recent immigrant children that was designed to decrease anxiety, reduce intergroup tensions associated with the Iraq war, and address the common gap between the ways that traumatic events covered by the media are understood at home and at school (Rousseau & Machouf,

2005). Once a week, the children brought in a newspaper story or other media information that they wanted to discuss. They could propose written media in any language, and the material they shared represented the diversity of viewpoints and experiences in the face of this international situation. They were deeply disturbed by the events, and they expressed empathy for all the parties involved: the American families of the 9/11 drama, the Iraqi families suffering from the war, the prisoners of war, and so on. They decided to write a joint letter to Saddam Hussein and George Bush, which they published in their school newspaper. They were proud of their efforts, and although they recognized their relative impotence they expressed the wish for other public spaces where they could have a voice. During the project, the children demonstrated that they could handle ambivalent feelings that allowed them not to betray their families and communities, while enabling them to understand some aspects of host society positions. The project helped them to create group solidarity and work together to gain a sense of control. The results underscored the fact that the multiplicity of meanings associated with international events should be addressed when planning a prevention program in multiethnic schools.

ARTICULATING THE THERAPEUTIC AND POLITICAL SPACE

The medicalization of sociopolitical issues and of the resultant social suffering has been discussed by social scientists (Kleinman, 1997a), but the problematic effects of this institutional and clinical tendency to shift social dysfunction to individuals are still not well documented. Most studies tend to overlook the systemic variables that could describe the consequences of medicalization or else consider them as "noise," rather than giving them the attention they deserve. At the clinical level, this situation represents a dilemma, as clinicians may unwillingly participate in and thus reinforce a process that they might otherwise critique.

This may lead clinicians either to pursue clinical action without taking into account the wider political context or to withdraw from clinical practice, retreating into critical research, which requires less compromise than the clinical world. Another possibility would be to introduce an acknowledged political dimension into clinical practice. This would take place first at the symbolic level. According to M. U. Viñar (1993), the efficacy of the therapeutic framework is based on the capacity to recreate a space that represents social, legal, and political dimensions and that can bridge the gap between personal experience and history and collective memory. This bridging can also take place directly in the legal or political arena through advocacy work. Being involved in immigration procedures is neither easy nor rewarding for clinicians. The status of expert on a pedestal implies a capacity to determine certainties and demonstrate the truth. Using the power associated with professional expertise can be particularly difficult for clinicians struggling to make sense of their patients' uncertainties and multiple, sometimes contradictory, stories – even when they are convinced that patients' experiences are authentic.

Case Vignette: Jacob's Injury

Rebecca is a young Nigerian woman, referred to the Transcultural Child Psychiatry Team by her social worker, who was worried about her attachment to her 18-month-old baby. Rebecca had arrived in Canada 20 months before the consultation and had obtained refugee status. In Nigeria, Rebecca had been arrested and jailed because of her family's political activities. She was repeatedly tortured and gang-raped but finally escaped thanks to the compassion of one of her guards, who was also one of her assailants. She later realized that she had become pregnant from these multiple aggressions and, by the time she got to Canada, it was too late to consider an abortion. During the interview, she told her story in a monotone with an expressionless face.

At the start of the interview, her toddler had immediately run toward the clinician and climbed onto her lap, clearly ignoring his mother. When the clinician asked her about the little boy's name, Rebecca suddenly came back to life and appeared very upset. "It was terrible," she said. When she gave birth at the hospital, they forced her to give the baby her own family name, her father's name – which identified her child as a child of rape. "These children [named after their maternal grandfather] kill their parents," she said. She then explained that this was very shameful and that she could not hear her son's name without thinking about this shame. She needed to hide it from the community. When the clinician asked her about the name she would like to give the child, she lit up. She wanted to call him Jacob. She began telling her version of the Bible story: the ladder to Heaven, the struggle between Jacob and the angel, Jacob's injury. The clinician pointed out how her son was like Jacob, both injured and exceptional. Rebecca then asked, "Help me to change his name."

Requests for help in resolving everyday problems are not trivial in the therapeutic process. The negotiation of the challenges of resettlement and the trials of daily life raise sociopolitical and emotional dimensions of the relationship with the host country and, by extension, with the therapist. Supporting patients and helping them to have a voice in institutional settings, as illustrated by Rebecca's story, allows the clinician to embody compassion through solidarity and, at times, advocacy.

AGENCY, CREATIVITY, AND TRANSFORMATION

Individuals and communities are not passively transformed by a traumatic experience. To varying degrees, they actively engage and take part in their own transformation. In the process of adjusting internal reality to external reality, transitional spaces are key. Through creative expression, they provide a transformative power that can channel overwhelming emotions;

facilitate the interplay of multiple, contradictory meanings; and, through the transmission of fragments of the experience, reforge social bonds.

Community meeting places like schools or community groups may be ideal settings for creative expression programs. Contrary to clinical settings they are nonstigmatizing and are closely linked to everyday life. In the past decade, we have developed several creative expression workshops for newly arrived immigrant and refugee youths in Montreal's multiethnic schools. Workshops for preschoolers are organized around sand play. Drawing and storytelling are the central components of the program for elementary schoolchildren (Rousseau, 1999; Rousseau, Lacroix, Bagilishya, & Heusch, 2003; Rousseau, Singh, Lacroix, Bagilishya, & Measham, 2004), whereas theatre is the chosen mode of expression for adolescents (Rousseau, de la Aldea, Viger Rojas, & Foxen, 2005). The theater program is based on Augusto Boal's "Forum theatre" (1995, 1979/2000) and Jonathan Fox's "playback theater" (Fox, 1981, 1994; Fox & Dauber, 1999). Playback theater is a type of improvisational theater that aims to achieve personal and social transformation through sharing a theater experience within a ritual space (Fox, 1981). It places the marginalized and excluded in the position of subject, which can empower them to change themselves and their environment (Boal, 1979/2000).

Within a safe and respectful atmosphere, a play director coordinates and contains the story told by an adolescent as it unfolds, while actors and musicians gather the information in order to play the story back to the teller and the group. The stories told can be transformed and replayed through alternative scenarios developed by the group of adolescents. The idea is to alter the situation to empower the storyteller and the others, either by changing the meaning, building a relationship, or creating an opening or dialogue with others that was missing from the original story. This part of the workshop becomes a collective effort, focusing on cocreating a story or situation where the adolescents look for alternatives to their first reactions and strategies.

The goal of the workshops is to provide a safe environment for expression while not forcing it, allowing the children to relate their experiences indirectly through the use of metaphor. Although the stories told or made up by the children often allude to terrible trauma, they can also be read as a discovery of personal and collective strengths. The recognition that learning and growth can come from enduring suffering, witnessing the suffering of others, and experiencing solidarity offers a glimpse of hope and empowerment.

CONCLUSION

In this chapter, we have argued that, rather than understanding trauma as solely producing psychopathology, it is more helpful in clinical practice to conceptualize the traumatic experience as a process that triggers a transformation or metamorphosis that evokes both strengths and vul-nerabilities. In contexts where therapy shares common ground with the social violence it is intended to relieve, clinicians need to focus on relative safety by reestablishing movement between opposing strategies of dis-closure and containment. Clinical work needs to include a sociopolitical dimension, where spaces for the multiplicity of meanings and voices can be negotiated. The two goals of treatment can thus be conceptualized as simultaneously supporting individual healing and contributing to efforts to build a world that promotes the respectful coexistence of interdependent societies.

Clinicians involved in the reconstruction process must accept the ten-sion between acquiring knowledge to better understand and help indi-viduals and communities who have suffered trauma and coping with the uncertainty that stems from our limited capacity to grasp the complexity associated with these experiences and their multifaceted consequences. Accepting our ignorance is a key step in recognizing the potential for per-sonal metamorphosis through trauma.

References

AACAP Official Action. (1997). Practice parameters for the assessment and treat-ment of children and adolescents with schizophrenia. *Journal of the American Academy of Child & Adolescent Psychiatry, 36*(10), 177S–192S.

American Psychiatric Association. (1994). *Diagnostic and statistical manual of mental disorders* (4th ed.). Washington, DC: Author.

Apfel, R. J., & Simon, B. (2000). Mitigating discontents with children in war: An ongoing psychoanalytic inquiry. In A. C. G. M. Robben & M. M. Suárez-Orozco (Eds.), *Cultures under siege: Collective violence and trauma* (pp. 102–130). Cam-bridge, UK: Cambridge University Press.

Atlani, L., & Rousseau, C. (2000). The politics of culture in humanitarian aid to women refugees who have experienced sexual violence. *Transcultural Psychiatric Review, 37*(3), 435–449.

Boal, A. (1995). *The rainbow of desire: The Boal method of theatre and therapy*. London: Routledge.

Boal, A. (2000). *Theatre of the oppressed*. London: Pluto Press. (Original work pub-lished 1979)

Bracken, P. J. (2002). *Trauma: Culture, meaning and philosophy*. London: Whurr.

Dalianis-Karambatzakis, A. M. (1994). *Children in turmoil during the Greek Civil War 1946–49: Today's adults. A longitudinal study on children confined with their mothers in prison*. Stockholm: Karolinska Institutet, Department of Woman and Child Health, Child and Adolescent Psychiatry Unit.

De Certeau, M. (1987). Corps torturés, paroles capturées. In L. Giard (Ed.), *Cahiers pour un temps* (pp. 61–70). Paris: Centre Georges Pompidou.

Ehrensaft, E. (2002). *The relationship between resilience, adversity and meaning con-struction among Rwandan refugee adolescents exposed to armed conflict*. Unpublished doctoral dissertation, Université du Québec à Montréal, Montréal.

Ferren, P. M. (1999). Comparing perceived self-efficacy among adolescent Bosnian and Croatian refugees with and without posttraumatic stress disorder. *Journal of Traumatic Stress, 12*(3), 405–420.

Fox, J. (1981). Playback theater: The community sees itself. In G. Schattner & R. Courney (Eds.), *Drawing and therapy* (Vol. 2 [Adults], pp. 295–306). New York: Drama Book Specialists.

Fox, J. (1994). *Acts of service: Spontaneity, commitment, tradition in the nonscripted theatre.* New Paltz, NY: Tusitala.

Fox, J., & Dauber, H. (Eds.). (1999). *Gathering voices: Essays on playback theatre.* New Paltz, NY: Tusitala.

Foxen, P. (2002). *K'iche' Maya in a re-imagined world: Transnational perspectives on identity.* Unpublished doctoral dissertation, McGill University, Montréal, Québec.

Kinzie, J. D., Sack, W. H., Angell, R. H., Clarke, G., & Rath, B. (1989). A three-year follow-up of Cambodian young people traumatized as children. *Journal of the American Academy of Child & Adolescent Psychiatry, 28*, 501–504.

Kirmayer, L. J. (1996). Landscapes of memory: Trauma, narrative, and dissociation. In P. A. M. Lambek (Ed.), *Tense past: Cultural essays in trauma and memory* (pp. 173–198). New York: Routledge.

Kleinman, A., & Kleinman, J. (1997a). Introduction. In A. Kleinman, V. Das, & A. M. Lock (Eds.), *Social suffering.* Berkeley: University of California Press.

Kleinman, A., & Kleinman, J. (1997b). The appeal of experience, the dismay of images: Cultural appropriations of suffering in our times. In A. Kleinman, V. Das, & M. Lock (Eds.), *Social suffering* (pp. 1–24). Berkeley: University of California Press.

Lyons, J. A. (1991). Strategies for assessing the potential for positive adjustment following trauma. *Journal of Traumatic Stress, 4*(1), 93–111.

Macksoud, M. S., & Aber, J. L. (1996). The war experiences and psychosocial development of children in Lebanon. *Child Development, 67*, 70–88.

Marange, V. (2001). *Éthique et violence: Critique de la vie pacifiée.* France: L'Harmattan.

Measham, T. (2002). *Children's representations of war trauma and family separation in play.* Unpublished master's thesis, McGill University, Montréal, Québec.

Mollica, R. (2001). The trauma story: A phenomenological approach to the traumatic life experiences of refugee survivors. *Psychiatry, 64*(1), 60–63.

Peltzer, K. (1996). Counselling and psychotherapy of victims of organised violence in sociocultural context. Frankfurt: IKO – Verlag für Interkulturelle Kommunkation.

Pennebaker, J. W. (1985). Traumatic experience and psychosomatic disease: Exploring the roles of behavioural inhibition, obsession, and confiding. *Canadian Psychology, 26*(2), 82–95.

Ricoeur, P. (1976). Speaking and writing. In P. Ricoeur (Ed.), *Interpretation theory: Discourse and the surplus of meaning* (pp. 25–95). Fort Worth, TX: Texas Christian University Press.

Ricoeur, P. (2000a). Devant l'inacceptable: Le juge, l'historien, l'écrivain. In R. Rohrlich (Ed.), *Philosophie – La philosophie devant la Shoah* (Vol. 67, pp. 3–18). Paris: In Les Éditions de Minuit.

Ricoeur, P. (2000b). *La mémoire, l'histoire, l'oubli.* Paris: Éditions du Seuil.

Rousseau, C. (1999). Playing around with a story. *Transcultural Psychiatry, 36*(4), 447–450.

Rousseau, C., de la Aldea, E., Viger Rojas, M., & Foxen, P. (2005). After the NGO's departure: Changing memory strategies of young Mayan refugees who returned to Guatemala as a community. *Anthropology & Medicine, 12*(1), 3–21.

Rousseau, C., Drapeau, A., & Platt, R. (2000). Living conditions and emotional profiles of young Cambodians, Central Americans and Québécois youth. *Canadian Journal of Psychiatry, 45*(10), 905–911.

Rousseau, C., Drapeau, A., & Rahimi, S. (2003). The complexity of trauma response: A four-year follow-up of adolescent Cambodian refugees. *Child Abuse & Neglect, 27*, 1277–1290.

Rousseau, C., & Foxen, P. (2005). Constructing and deconstructing the myth of the lying refugee: Paradoxes of power and justice in an administrative immigration tribunal. In E. van Dongen (Ed.), *Lying and illness: Power and performance* (pp. 56–91). Amsterdam: Het Spinhuis Publishers.

Rousseau, C., Lacroix, L., Bagilishya, D., & Heusch, N. (2003). Working with myths: Creative expression workshops for immigrant and refugee children in a school setting. *Journal of the American Art Therapy Association, 20*(1), 3–10.

Rousseau, C., & Machouf, A. (2005). *Moral clarity or ambivalence? Preventive pilot project to attenuate the impact of war in Iraq in Canadian multiethnic schools.* Manuscript submitted for publication.

Rousseau, C., Morales, M., & Foxen, P. (2001). Going home: Giving voice to memory strategies of young Mayan refugees who returned to Guatemala as a community. *Culture, Medicine and Psychiatry, 25*(2), 135–168.

Rousseau, C., Singh, A., Lacroix, L., Bagilishya, D., & Measham, T. (2004). Creative expression workshops for immigrant and refugee – Clinical perspective. *Journal of the American Academy of Child & Adolescent Psychiatry, 43*(2), 235–238.

Sigal, J. J. (1995). Resilience in survivors, their children and their grandchildren. *Echoes of the Holocaust: Bulletin of the Jerusalem Center for Research into the Late Effects of the Holocaust (Talbieh Mental Health Center, Jerusalem, Israel), 4*, 9–14.

Sigal, J. J. (1998). Long-term effects of the holocaust: Empirical evidence for resilience in the first, second, and third generation. *Psychoanalytic Review, 85*(4), 579–585.

Suárez-Orozco, C. (2000). Identities under siege: Immigration stress and social mirroring among the children of immigrants. In A. C. G. M. Robben & M. M. Suárez-Orozco (Eds.), *Cultures under siege: Collective violence and trauma* (pp. 194–226). Cambridge, UK: Cambridge University Press.

Tolfree, D. (1996). *Restoring playfulness: Different approaches to assisting children who are psychologically affected by war or displacement.* Stockholm: Rädda Barnen – Swedish Save the Children.

Tousignant, M. (1997). Refugees and immigrants in Quebec. In I. Al-Issa & M. Tousignant (Eds.), *Ethnicity, immigration, and psychopathology* (pp. 57–70). New York: Plenum Press.

Viñar, M., & Viñar, M. (1989). *Exil et torture.* Paris: Éditions Denoël.

Viñar, M. U. (1993). *Children affected by organized violence in South America.* Paper presented at the Children: War and Persecution conference, Hamburg, Germany.

Yehuda, R., & McFarlane, A. C. (1995). Conflict between current knowledge about post-traumatic stress disorder and its original conceptual basis. *American Journal of Psychiatry, 152*(12), 1705–1713.

CULTURAL PERSPECTIVES ON TRAUMA

The preceding sections have made the case that there are universal aspects of the biological and psychological response to trauma. A comprehensive understanding of trauma, however, must explore how collective cultural meanings articulate with the individual psychological and biological responses identified through neuroscience and clinical research. This is true for individual idiosyncratic experiences no less than the large-scale social catastrophes of genocide and war that are the concern of the many of the chapters in this section.

This section presents reflections on the meanings of trauma from anthropological perspectives. The contributors represent the subfields of physical, psychological, and cultural anthropology. They examine the social construction of our concepts of trauma, its political and rhetorical uses, and the role of social and cultural knowledge and practice in both individual and collective responses to violence.

Physical anthropology is concerned with integrating an evolutionary understanding of biology with an appreciation of humans as fundamentally cultural beings. The task of the psychological anthropologist is to understand the influence of culture on the dynamics of individual experience (and the emergence of cultural phenomena through the interaction of individuals). A central tenet of psychological anthropology holds that individual meaning has a collective dimension that resides in shared knowledge, institutions, and practices. Hence, individual experience cannot be reduced to individual cognition or psychodynamics, but requires close attention to the cultural and historical contexts of experience. This is equally true of trauma and its aftermath. Many traumatic events arise from complex social situations, and all acquire tangled social, cultural, and political meanings over time. The ways that individuals make sense of their suffering are embedded in and interact with these larger social meanings. These different levels of meaning need not be consonant or in harmony. The collective remembering or forgetting of trauma can serve powerful political interests that work against the possibility of individual or communal healing. Individual acts of remembering or commemoration may serve state or community purposes or constitute acts of resistance.

Anthropologist and physician Melvin Konner provides an evolutionary and cross-cultural perspective on trauma. He supports his evolutionary claims by fieldwork among the !Kung San hunter-gatherers of Botswana, whose way of life may be similar in some respects to the circumstances during which many human characteristics evolved. Everyday life for the !Kung was punctuated by what many would perceive to be trauma, primarily in the form of physical danger, uncertainty associated with subsistence on hunting or gathering food, and loss (50% of children died before the age of 15, primarily by infectious diseases, accidents, or violent injury). Nonetheless, the level of social support within a relatively small group of people was high.

Konner describes the positive attributes of the "fight or flight" system, as well as the stress system hormone cortisol. He argues that successful coping with life's (inevitable) stress is evolutionarily adaptive and can even be "rewarding and sometimes exhilarating." He stresses that humans are resilient creatures, primarily because of the availability of social support and the possibilities of adaptability, self-reliance, and reinforcement via the cognitive perception of stress or trauma as a surmountable challenge. Konner does not question the reality of PTSD as a disabling condition, but raises thoughtful questions concerning its etiology, diagnostic criteria, and treatment, as well as its representation in the mass media. Finally, he cautions against an unreflective acceptance of the posttraumatic model as a biological certainty when "the typical response to time-constrained trauma is recovery over time."

The following chapters explore key issues pertaining to traumatic memory in its personal and collective forms. Several of the chapters examine the social context and reconstruction of memory and the diverse models of expression or suppression of memory and emotion in relation to notions of psychological health and well-being. These chapters make it clear that political, social, and cultural implications of disclosing or repressing traumatic memories and experiences must be more fully addressed by clinicians as well as researchers.

Allan Young, a medical anthropologist who has long studied the social construction and politics of PTSD within U.S. psychiatry, begins by raising the basic problem of mimesis. Mimesis is a general term for the processes by which we construct representations that mimic or stand in for reality. Mimesis is clearly evident in the many processes that underlie memory. Recollection is not simply veridical recall but a process of reconstructing and reorganizing experiences according to cultural models or templates. Cultural knowledge provides models that individuals use to make sense of and narrate their own experiences, and these cultural constructions become the reality we inhabit. As a result, it is often difficult to tell when a person is describing what they have actually experienced in the past or rather what they have come to understand after the fact by reformulating their memory and experience in accord with cultural models. Although both mimetic and nonmimetic processes play a role in shaping the expression of trauma, there is a persistent confusion between reasons and causes throughout the research, including both clinical and cultural studies literature on trauma and PTSD (Young, 1995).

This leads Young to challenge some of the assumptions of trauma theorists who claim that the memory of a traumatic event is either repressed or "unrepresentable" until its meaning is discovered belatedly or "recovered." The theory that every traumatic memory inevitably goes through a period of latency before it is recognized and experienced (so that every traumatic memory is, in a sense, "recovered") derives from Freud's final monograph, *Moses and Monotheism*, on the cross-generational transmission of collective memory (Freud, 1939/1959; see also Young, 1992). However, Young cites the careful review of trauma and memory by Richard McNally to support his claim that declarative memory is continuous in most cases of PTSD (McNally, 2003). He argues here and elsewhere that the clinical and cultural phenomena that are being explained by trauma theorists reflect a circular process in which prevalent cultural models link psychiatric symptoms to a past event in narratives that therefore cannot be used as evidence of a preexisting causal connection.

The next chapter, by cultural psychiatrist Laurence J. Kirmayer, addresses the breakdown of mimesis when "performances" of trauma narratives are subject to frank disbelief. Kirmayer focuses on the need for asylum seekers to present a consistent story about their previous lives in order to gain refugee status in Canada. Refugees must tell their personal stories in very specific narrative formats, which are subject to intense scrutiny and scepticism by the psychiatric and legal systems. The failure of the clinical imagination to bridge the disparate worlds that refugees experience reflects both the foreign and uncanny quality of patients' experiences as well as cultural differences in self-presentation, self-understanding, memory, and identity. Two different versions of the truth often coexist and may conflict. On the one hand, psychiatrists understand patients' stories as efforts to make sense of and adapt to terrible trials. On the other hand, the Immigration and Refugee Board (IRB) assesses the refugee's narrative in terms of whether it is "true" vis-à-vis some set of historically likely events. A narrative account that correlates with the posttraumatic stress model is double edged – it may legitimate the individual's suffering and provide sufficient cause for asylum, but it may also erode credibility by suggesting a "stock story provided by psychiatry" if the IRB does not perceive the refugee's narrative as being sufficiently, and uniquely, "truthful." Kirmayer illustrates the different functions of social imagination in the construction, interpretation, and assessment of the truth value of narratives of identity and affliction.

Continuing this exploration of the narrative shaping of traumatic experience, Gadi BenEzer discusses the Ethiopian Jewish exodus from North Africa to Israel during the period 1977–85. He argues for the importance of the journey narrative as a way to understand collective trauma and suffering. The collective narrative the Ethiopian Jews forged of their harrowing journey – which had powerful precedent in Biblical texts and prophecy – has failed to gain wide acceptance in Israel. The narratives of exodus emphasized three themes that gave coherence and meaning to the stories: Jewish identity, the role of suffering, and the value of heroism and inner strength. According to BenEzer, these three themes reflect the Ethiopian Jews' cultural identification with the Biblical exodus out of Egypt and anticipate their identification with and integration into Israeli society, which is guided by a similar collective ethos, including a shared belief in Jewish identity. The Ethiopian Jews felt that as a group they would be strongly identified with and valorized once they settled in Israel. Instead, they experienced a continual struggle to be accepted as Jews and to overcome a perception as being helpless and highly dependent on their host society, instead of exceedingly "brave and resourceful." Israel's reception of the Ethiopian Jews challenged the cultural meaning of their journey and their collective identity. The threat to meaning making influenced the transformation of a factual journey into a more formalized, self-sustaining myth, which BenEzer suggests could serve the Ethiopian Jewish community as a crucial means for opening up a political and social space in the Israeli consciousness.

Anthropologists Leslie Dwyer and Degung Santikarma discuss how the effects of trauma are embedded in the fabric of Indonesian political, social, and cultural life. They describe how trauma and PTSD became salient psychological concepts in Indonesia after the Balinese nightclub bombings in 2002. These same concepts, however, were not extended to acknowledge the suffering caused by the state-sanctioned mass murder of over one million people in Indonesia during the anticommunist sweep of 1965–66. Public memory was suppressed under Soeharto's New Order regime (1965–98). Yet Dwyer and Santikarma argue that the implicit references to 1965–66 have pervaded language, society, culture, and politics such that the violence "continues to reverberate through social networks, marking everyday life and molding imaginations of the future." The recent nightclub bombings triggered traumatic responses for many Balinese survivors of the 1965–66 massacre (see Kinzie, this volume). Post-Soeharto efforts to confront the atrocities directly by creating a National Truth and Reconciliation Commission have "stalled" because of the lack of trust in the current political climate.

Anthropologist Alex Hinton's fieldwork in Cambodia provides the basis for an exploration of how specific aspects of narrative – metaphors and other local idioms of distress – mediate an individual's experiences and responses to trauma. Hinton characterizes the state of being under extreme terror as one of "fear, withdrawal, isolation, and silence." Hinton points out that maintaining equilibrium, or the "middle path" in Buddhism, is crucial to social and physical well-being, which are highly interrelated, whereas "talking through" the experiences may unleash toxic forces. Hinton argues that it is essential to take into account both cultural idioms of distress and cultural approaches to healing in the treatment of PTSD. He relativizes our own "folk understanding" of PTSD as a medical disorder and suggests that this conceptualization diverts our gaze from the ways in which suffering is mediated by political, social, moral, and historical circumstances.

In a concluding chapter, Robert Lemelson and the coeditors consider how the different levels of explanation developed by the contributors to this book can be brought together to understand traumatic experience in context. The chapter is anchored with three case vignettes of Indonesians who have endured individual and collective trauma but whose life trajectories and responses are markedly different. Although all three have symptoms that fit the model of PTSD, other personal, social, and cultural issues supervene to give meaning to their suffering. Understanding trauma requires that we consider the interaction of processes at multiple levels over time. The complexity of this interaction – and the ongoing efforts of individuals to position themselves in ways that are socially valued and adaptive – results in many competing narratives. The decision to privilege one story reflects explanatory interests and values. An overarching or grand narrative that integrates biological and clinical perspectives on trauma must consider the social, cultural, and political significance of these alternative accounts of human suffering.

References

Freud, S. (1959). Moses and monotheism. In J. Strachey (Ed. and Trans.), *The standard edition of the complete psychological works of Sigmund Freud (Vol. 23)*. London: Hogarth Press. (Original work published 1939)

McNally, R. J. (2003). *Remembering trauma*. Cambridge, MA: Harvard University Press, Belknap Press.

Young, A. (1992). The return of "the return of the repressed." *Transcultural Psychiatric Research Review, 28*, 235–243.

Young, A. (1995). Reasons and causes for post-traumatic stress disorder. *Transcultural Psychiatric Research Review, 32*(3), 287–298.

15

Trauma, Adaptation, and Resilience: A Cross-Cultural and Evolutionary Perspective

Melvin Konner

Trauma and its consequences are a focus of intense interest. Posttraumatic stress disorder (PTSD), although not a new diagnosis – "war psychosis" and "shell shock" were long recognized – has recently been applied to a very wide range of negative experiences (Jones et al., 2003; Jones & Wessely, 2004; McHugh, 1999; A. Young, 1995). The definition has broadened beyond extremely severe and abnormal circumstances, such as war, rape, or devastating natural disasters, to encompass stresses in normal life – ongoing aspects of work and relationships and childhood emotional stress in the range that might once have been considered normal. Although physical, sexual, and severe emotional abuse – not to mention torture and concentration-camp experiences – surely deserve this label, the word *trauma* is no longer restricted to such extremes.

In the popular imagination and for some mental health professionals, it means far more – including residence in the city where a terrorist attack has occurred or viewing traumas on the television news – and we often hear recommendations for immediate psychological intervention. In fact, extensive evidence shows that resilience and/or independent recovery are by far the most common responses to potentially traumatic experiences (PTEs) in both adults (Bonanno, 2004, 2005) and children (Masten, 2001). Furthermore, research and clinical experience question the value of and point to the possible harm due to widely urged mental health interventions following PTEs (Rose, Bisson, Churchill, & Wessely, 2002; Rose, Bisson, & Wessely, 2003; Wessely, 2005; Wessely & Deahl, 2003). Although psychiatry has tried to restrict PTSD to established criteria (American Psychiatric Association [APA], 1994), some mental health professionals and many media pundits have abused the label, with potentially negative consequences for public mental health.

This chapter sets psychological trauma in the broad context of human evolution and culture. First, I consider stress in the original human environment, that of hunting and gathering, with an emphasis on the !Kung San or Bushmen of Botswana, who are in some ways representative. Second, I review basic stress physiology and consider the distinction (originally made by Hans Selye) between *dis*tress and *eu*stress, and how the distinction aids our understanding of resilience. Third, I raise some questions about the concepts of psychological trauma and PTSD, about inappropriate uses of these concepts, and about interventions often urged or performed after PTEs. I conclude with some inferences about the role of stress in human experience.

HUNTER-GATHERER ADAPTATIONS

In the mid-twentieth century anthropologists became interested in studying living hunter-gatherers to model the circumstances in which our species evolved (Lee & DeVore, 1968a) and attempted to document their subsistence ecology and social organization. Classical studies had included those of Australian aborigines, Eskimo, Amazonian hunter-gatherers (HGs), and many others throughout the world (Lee & DeVore, 1968b). More systematic, multidisciplinary, quantitative studies were subsequently done on the Hadza of Tanzania (Hawkes, O'Connell, & Jones, 1991; Hurtado, Hawkes, Hill, & Kaplan, 1985), the Ache of Paraguay (Hill & Hurtado, 1999), the Agta of the Philippines (Griffin & Estioko-Griffin, 1985), the Efe Pygmies of Zaire (Bailey, 1991; Peacock, 1991), and the Bushmen of Southern Africa (Lee, 1979a; Silberbauer, 1981), among others (Lee & Daly, 1999).

These groups represent some aspects of our environment of evolutionary adaptedness (EEA), although given the variation among them and among past populations, the phrase should be pluralized to EEAs. These are, or were, the contexts for which natural selection prepared us, and from which we have departed only in the past 10,000 years, a short time in evolutionary terms. No one claims that the whole range of EEAs is observable among recent HGs, who have occupied only some of the wide range of ecological situations available to our ancestors. However, we also have extensive archeological, paleodemographic, and paleopathological evidence (Keenleyside, 1998; Reinhard, Fink, & Skiles, 2003; Tague, 1994) that – with the studies of recent HGs – leads to reasonable models of life during human evolution (Hewlett, 1991; Kelly, 1995; Winterhalder & Smith, 1981).

Certain generalizations are possible: (1) Groups were usually small, ranging in size from 15 to 40 people related through blood or marriage, but could be larger in ecologically rich settings; (2) they were usually nomadic, moving with changing subsistence opportunities, and flexible in composition, size, and adaptive strategies, although they could be sedentary in richer settings; (3) daily life involved physical challenge, vigorous exercise, and occasional hunger; (4) disease, mainly infectious rather than chronic, produced high rates of mortality especially in infancy and early childhood, with consequent frequent experience of loss; (5) virtually all activities were done in a highly social context with people one knew well; (6) privacy was limited, but creative expression in the arts was possible; and (7) conflicts and problems were dealt with through extensive group discussions, but could result in separation or violence.

This applies to most of human history, so it is often said that we are HGs in business suits and skyscrapers. The industrial revolution, in evolutionary perspective, happened only a moment ago, and several of these generalizations – notably for our purposes the physical challenges of life, the role of hunger and infectious disease, and the high infant and child mortality – apply to all premodern societies. Direct fossil and archeological evidence demonstrates rates of injury consistent with substantial violence and/or accidental trauma (Keeley, 1996; LeBlanc & Register, 2003), periodic food shortages (Gaulin & Konner, 1977; Whiting, 1958), and high levels of premature mortality in premodern populations generally (Hammel & Howell, 1987). Nutritional stress and infectious disease may have increased after the transition to agriculture (Armelagos, Goodman, & Jacobs, 1991; Cohen & Armelagos, 1984), but HG life was physically and psychologically stressful. As for nonhuman animals, and by inference the prehuman phases of our evolution, premature mortality and the stresses implied by it were if anything greater than in any human populations (P. H. Harvey, 1990; Hill et al., 2001).

Baby and child care were also distinctive in HG societies (Konner, 2005), despite variations, including (1) frequent breast feeding (up to four times per hour); (2) late weaning (at least 2 and up to 4 years); (3) close mother–infant contact, including skin-to-skin carrying and adjacent sleeping until weaning; (4) prompt response to infant crying and indulgent response to other infant and child demands; (5) maternal primacy in attachment; (6) more father involvement than in most societies; (7) a gradual transition to a multi-aged play group of mixed sex; (8) usually less assignment of responsibility in the sense of chores or schooling in middle childhood, with learning through observation and play; (9) liberal premarital sexual mores with sex play in middle childhood and adolescent sexuality; and (10) late menarche, limiting childbearing until the late teens or later. These generalizations have withstood the test of sophisticated new research in at least five HG societies (Konner, 2005). Because early experience plays a role in resilience, this pattern may buffer people against lifelong stress.

However, the great majority of HG children experienced loss and grief through the death of siblings, parents, or others, as well as their own life-threatening illnesses. Thus HG childhood was far from idyllic, but most frustration and loss did not come from parentally imposed stresses. Still, physical punishment and ridicule were used by parents among the !Kung (Shostak, 1981), children were required to forage for themselves among the Hadza (Blurton Jones, 1993), and the experience of loss was virtually universal.

The !Kung San (Bushmen) of Botswana, among whom I did field research for two years, are typical in many ways. Physiologically and psychologically they resemble human beings anywhere, but in subsistence ecology they – along with other HG groups – represent that of our ancestors (Lee, 1979a; Lee & DeVore, 1976; Marshall, 1976a). The environment is semiarid, and the soil is sandy with relatively sparse vegetation, but it provides ample plant food for people's needs. Like most HGs, their population density averaged less than one person per square mile, but was concentrated in villages with high social contact.

Women gathered plants, providing 70% of the diet by weight, retrieved water; collected firewood; and did 90% of the infant and child care. Nevertheless, they enjoyed largely equal relationships with men, had strong female friendships, and sometimes took lovers (Shostak, 1981, 2000). They gathered two to three days per week in highly social small groups. The staff of life was the fruit and nut of the mongongo tree, and women walked an average of 6 miles each way to the groves, carrying one or two infants or small children both ways plus 30 pounds of nuts on the way back. Men hunted at about the same frequency, alone or in groups, but hunts were necessarily quiet. Eland, oryx, kudu, wildebeest, duiker, steenbok, and giraffe were among their prey. Game such as oryx and warthog, which stand and resist, were hunted with dogs and spears by small groups of men, the other animals by one or two men with deadly poisoned arrows. Some carried scars of hand combat with leopards; others were killed by lions or hyenas.

Women had if anything a greater ordeal of physical courage: At least in the higher parities, childbirth was ideally supposed to be managed by the parturient woman alone (Konner & Shostak, 1987). The loss of at least one child, usually in infancy and early childhood, was common. Because of intensive breast feeding, average birth spacing was 4 years. Infants were in skin-to-skin contact with someone at least 90% of waking hours in the first months, declining to 25% at 18 months. Mother and infant slept on the same skin mat. Toddlers made a gradual transition to a multi-aged, mixed-sex play group. Children had little responsibility but tended to forage for themselves casually, and younger children were often cared for by older ones, especially girls. Information and skills passed mainly from older to younger children, not mainly from adults to children.

Play groups were frequently out of sight of adults, and sexual curiosity took its course. Adults did not approve of sexual play but made little effort to discourage it, viewing it as inevitable and even healthy. Most children also could observe sexual intercourse at some time during childhood. Overall, the effect seems to be that sex is less taboo, less frightening, and less unknown. However, the transition from the playful sex of childhood to the real sex of adulthood could be difficult, especially for girls, half of whom were married before their first menstruation (about age 16.5), typically to men about 10 years older. Although in principle the husband's advances would be delayed until menarche, the transition was stressful for many (Konner & Shostak, 1986; Shostak, 1981).

Overall patterns of fertility and mortality are well established (Howell, 1979). Prospective study of the age at menarche (marked by a dramatic ritual) gives a mean of 16.6 years, with the majority passing this milestone between 16 and 18 (Howell, 1979, p. 178). The average age at first birth was 19 years, almost all between 17 and 22 (p. 128). Completed fertility was 4.7 live births per woman, with the last birth in the mid-30s. Mortality patterns were typical of most human populations before the nineteenth century. Half of all children died before age 15, 20% in the first year. Life expectancy at birth was 32 years, at age 15, 55 (40 more years). Only 20% of neonates reached age 60, but some lived well into their 80s. Most deaths were due to infectious diseases such as gastrointestinal infection, pneumonia, tuberculosis, malaria, and wound infections, but some were due to accidental or violent injury, and the parasite burden was high. The central ritual was a healing dance in which trained men danced until in a trance state and attempted to heal through laying on of hands with a specific form of trembling and shrieking, a formidable display of individual and communal support (Lee, 1982; Marshall, 1981).

A village camp was a small circle of huts, each holding a family in a hemisphere of grass just large enough to lie down in. The camp included perhaps 30 people, but group structure was flexible, varying between 10 and 40, and moved with seasonal vagaries of food and water availability. People changed groups at times; conflicts were often resolved by group fission. The fragments might coalesce again months later or form the nuclei of new bands (Lee, 1979; Marshall, 1976b).

War was unknown in recent generations, although ambushes and deadly intervillage raids occurred in the past (Wilhelm, 1953). Conflicts were often resolved by the sharing of food and other goods and by talking, sometimes half or all the night, sometimes for weeks on end. Few social or economic distinctions could be maintained; the ethic of sharing strongly pressured a person to part with any visible wealth (Wiessner, 1982, 1996). Stinginess led to social ostracism, intolerable where survival requires mutual aid.

Mental illnesses both major and minor occurred. Homicide exceeded levels in American cities (Lee, 1979), despite the application of the phrase "the harmless people" to this group. Other undesirable behaviors, such as selfishness, deceit, adolescent rebellion, adultery, desertion, and child abuse also occurred, but for methodological reasons it is impossible to compare their rates to those in industrial societies. The lack of privacy provides stresses just as crowding and high levels of contact with strangers may be stressful for us. Morbidity, mortality, and the uncertainties of the daily food quest took their psychological toll.

In summary, during the 98% of human history that took place in our environments of evolutionary adaptedness – the environments in and for which our genomes evolved – we survived periodic hunger; extreme physical exertion; natural disasters such as storms, fire, earthquakes, tidal waves, and volcanic eruptions; attacks by lions, leopards, hyenas, wolves, wild dogs, and many other predators; defensive attacks by large prey we were hunting; attacks by other humans; a heavy burden of infectious and parasitic illness; and frequent loss of loved ones. Many of these stresses persisted through almost the whole of the 10 millennia since the invention of agriculture. It is possible that our common generalized anxiety disorders (GAD) are the evolutionary legacy of a world in which mild recurring fear was adaptive (Nesse & Lloyd, 1992). Yet we not only survived; in some respects we thrived.

STRESS PHYSIOLOGY: *DIS*TRESS, *EU*STRESS, AND RESILIENCE

Because our genomes were formed in those conditions, we must be programmed to adapt to stress. Indeed, for hundreds of millions of years, stress was ubiquitous for all species ancestral to us; stress is of the essence of evolution by natural selection and close to the essence of life itself (Sapolsky, Romero, & Munck, 2000). It has been said of stress responses that "[t]hese changes are normally adaptive and improve the chances of the individual for survival," and that the behavioral component of the response includes many positive as well as negative features, such as "increased arousal, alertness, and vigilance, improved cognition, and focused attention, as well as euphoria or dysphoria" (Chrousos, 1998, p. 312). Some men speak of their combat experiences in strangely positive terms, as the time in their past when they felt most alive, or even as the best time (Terkel, 1984). Adventurous people say similar things about experiences that cause fear and stress in themselves and others, and seek such experiences (McCormick, 2001). Any model of stress effects must take into account such positive consequences, as well as the ubiquity of stress.

In mammals, a wide variety of stresses both physical and psychological results in a predictable suite of responses (Figure 15.1), sometimes called the general adaptation syndrome (GAS) (Sapolsky, 1992a; Selye, 1936, 1976, 1936/1998). Part of this syndrome is sympathetic nervous system (SNS) activation, also known as the "fight or flight" response. Essential aspects of this part of the response were established by the 1920s (Cannon, 1915/1963, 1927). The SNS initiates increases in cardiac and respiratory rates; mobilization of blood glucose; arterial dilation in heart, lung, and voluntary muscle; sweating; pupillary dilation; bladder emptying; and sensory heightening and draws blood flow and energy away from digestion

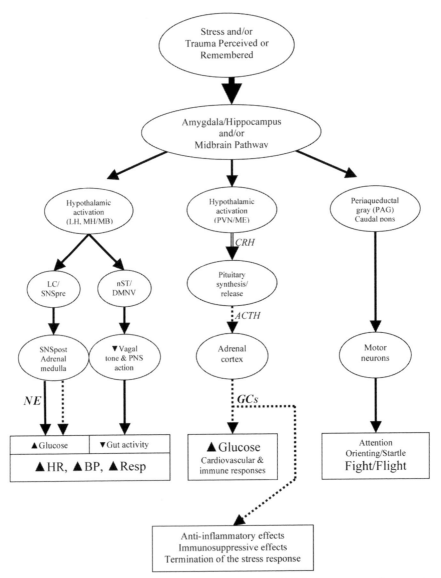

FIGURE 15.1. Simplified model of the stress response. Solid arrows, neural connections; dotted arrows, hormones in general circulation; double arrow, pituitary portal vessels; LH, lateral hypothalamus; MH, medial hypothalamus; MB, mammilary bodies; PVN, periventricular nucleus; ME, median eminence; PAG, periaqueductal gray; LC, locus ceruleus; SNSpre, preganglionic sympathetic nervous system; SNSpost, postganglionic SNS; nST, nucleus of the solitary tract; DMNV, dorsal motor nucleus of the vagus; PNS, parasympathetic nervous system; HR, heart rate; BP, blood pressure; Resp, respiration; CRH, corticotrophin-releasing hormone; ACTH, adrenocorticotropic hormone; GCs, glucocorticoids; NE, norepinephrine; Epi, epinephrine (adrenaline).

and reproduction. Its activation is twofold: faster, mediated by noradrenergic (norepinephrine-secreting, NE) neurons, and slower, mediated by secretion of adrenaline (epinephrine, E) by the adrenal medulla, or core of the adrenal gland. Although E acts as a hormone, this is phylogenetically and embryologically neural tissue similar to NE neurons, but E, which the adrenal medulla releases into the bloodstream, is a modified form of NE that is hundreds of times more potent. NE neurons within the brain are also activated.

Another component of the stress response, added to Cannon's model by Hans Selye (Selye, 1936), is activation of the hypothalamic–pituitary–adrenal (HPA) axis. Perception of stress by the limbic system, especially the amygdala and hippocampus, activates hypothalamic neurons that secrete corticotropin-releasing factor or hormone (CRF/CRH) into the anterior pituitary, where it stimulates the synthesis and secretion of corticotropin (adrenocorticotropic hormone, ACTH). At the adrenal cortex (the outer adrenal gland), ACTH stimulates the synthesis and release of cortisol, a glucocorticoid (GC) and principal stress hormone. Like E, GCs mobilize blood glucose for fight, flight, or other responses to stress and have both positive and negative effects on cognitive function (K. Erickson, Drevets, & Schulkin, 2003). GCs, over time, also can damage hippocampal and other neurons (Sapolsky, 1992b). But the discovery in the late 1940s that GCs have healing properties changed views about the GAS, suggesting the HPA axis has a role not just in mobilizing the organism in acute stress, but also in modulating and terminating that response.

The two components of the stress response are synergistic. During vertebrate evolution the adrenal medulla and adrenal cortex tissues changed their anatomical positions (Norris, 1997). In lower vertebrates they are adjacent, but mammalian evolution brought them into increasing juxtaposition until the medulla was surrounded by the cortex (hence, their names). The functional explanation is that the cortex supplies GCs to the medulla, where they are cofactors for the enzyme (phenylethanolamine *N*-methyl transferase) that converts NE to the far more potent E, greatly increasing the efficiency of the stress response. Brain NE neurons are also probably involved in directing the hypothalamus to release CRF.

We can now understand what is obvious to all who study natural history or evolution: Life itself is stress and coping, and because of the competition entailed in natural (including sexual) selection, individuals are continually providing stresses for each other even beyond other environmental stresses (Konner, 2002; Sapolsky, 2001; Sapolsky et al., 2000). Success in evolution requires superior coping with stress. In an important sense, every change in the stimulus envelope is a kind of stress, or at least a challenge, to which the organism must respond both physiologically and psychologically according to genetic programs modulated by individual experience.

Attention is the minimal change needed for an organism to respond to changing stimuli; the next step is arousal, then frustration, fear, or pain, depending on the nature and strength of the stimulus (Davis & Whalen, 2001; Ursin & Kadda, 1960; Zald, 2003), a process that is largely subcortical (Liddell et al., 2005; Ohman, 2005). This continuum of arousal and stress demands a corresponding continuum of response and action – adaptation or coping. Because of the internal discomfort, however mild, caused by many stimulus changes, successful coping is rewarding and sometimes exhilarating. Human infants as young as 3 or 4 months of age show wary attention to a moderately unfamiliar stimulus and smile when they have recognized or assimilated it (Super, Kagan, Morrison, Haith, & Weiffenbach, 1972; Zelazo & Komer, 1971). This is how we learn, grow psychologically, and liberate ourselves a little from the grip of the genes. It is also how evolution liberated higher organisms from the simple, mechanical, genetically dominated behavior of lower ones. Some helping professionals seem to think that the ideal condition for an organism is the absence of stress. This notion runs counter to all we know about life under natural conditions and violates the logic of our own subjective experience.

This is why Selye named the stress response the *general adaptation syndrome*: It is at the heart of adaptation itself. He also made a vital, often overlooked distinction: Some stress is negative and can impair future function, whereas other stress is positive, producing effective coping and enhancing the organism's long-term function. He called these *"di*stress" and *"eu*stress," respectively (Selye, 1975). Unfortunately for simplicity, this is not a categorical distinction, and it is not always clear where to draw the line.

What *is* clear is that humans, to one degree or another, are resilient, even in the face of severe stresses. We have already considered the environments of human evolutionary adaptedness, where both eustress and distress are ubiquitous; so is resilience. Some people seek severe stresses, as in extreme sports and dangerous occupations (Haynes, Miles, & Clements, 2000), and people can be arrayed on a continuum of sensation seeking that has cross-cultural validity (Neria, Solomon, Ginzburg, & Dekel, 2000; Wang et al., 2000). Sensation seekers differ physiologically from others (Zuckerman, 1984, 1990; Zuckerman, Buchsbaum, & Murphy, 1980); they are not immune to trauma, but they are courageous and resilient. Several studies show that the most resilient athletes are also the best (Holt & Dunn, 2004; Martin-Krumm, Sarrazin, Peterson, & Famose, 2003; Mummery, Schofield, & Perry, 2004; Schinke & Jerome, 2002). Decorated Israeli war veterans score higher than other war veterans on sensation seeking and have low levels of PTSD symptomatology (Neria et al., 2000).

More relevant to the average person are life history studies of ordinary individuals. A longitudinal, prospective study of 94 men who were in college in the early 1940s followed the subjects for half a century. After 35 years of follow-up (Vaillant, 1977), many of the men were happy and successful by self-report as well as external criteria, whereas others were unhappy or failures. Extensive data from the men's childhoods, with follow-up from college up to advanced age, supported several conclusions.

First, a stable, loving early family life appears to confer advantage; men with bleak childhoods tended to remain unhappy despite externally defined success. Some seemed well adapted but could not form intimate relationships; one, aware of his impairment, stated that he could do nothing about it. This observation is consistent with other longitudinal studies, with growing clinical evidence (Heim, Plotsky, & Nemeroff, 2004), and with voluminous experimental data from animal models showing that early positive nurturance enhances lifelong resilience both psychologically and physiologically (Bennett et al., 2002; Champagne, Francis, Mar, & Meaney, 2003; Francis, Szegda, Campbell, Martin, & Insel, 2003; Sanchez, Ladd, & Plotsky, 2001; Sanchez et al., 2005; Suomi, 2002).

A second conclusion was that stress is not necessarily unhealthy or bad. One third of the men in this study spent at least 10 days in continuous combat in World War II. All 94 subjects suffered major personal grief, setbacks, disappointments, and losses during adulthood. None of these life events, per se, predicted poor adjustment. About a famous man not in the study but whom he interviewed, Vaillant asked, "How can I give a logical explanation for the growth of Roy Campanella, a great Brooklyn catcher who at thirty-six broke his neck, was paralyzed in all four limbs; yet at fifty the crippled Campanella seemed a greater man . . . than Campanella the baseball star had seemed at thirty" (Vaillant, 1977, p. 239). Similar things have been said about Christopher Reeve, the actor who became quadriplegic after a fall from horseback and who went on to greater performances and a forceful leadership role in the cause of the disabled. Vaillant echoed Selye: "It is not stress that kills us. It is effective adaptation to stress that permits us to live" (Vaillant, 1977, p. 374).

In the 1990s, the follow-up was extended another 15 years and compared with longitudinal studies of two other samples: 40 women who, as children in the 1920s, had been intellectually gifted, and about 300 men from poor families in Boston, followed from junior high school into their 70s. All three groups displayed considerable variation, but many subjects had transcended adversity, suggesting that human mental life has a self-healing bias. Eleven men, chosen from the poor sample because of extremely bad childhoods, had seemed at age 25 to be psychologically damaged beyond repair; 50 years later 8 of the 11 were doing well. "Man is born broken," Vaillant concluded, but "he lives by mending" (Vaillant, 1993, p. 287).

Summarizing another longitudinal study of adult Americans, Jean Mac-Farlane wrote, "Many of the most outstanding mature adults in our entire group, many who are well integrated, highly competent and/or creative . . . are recruited from those who were confronted with very difficult

situations and whose characteristic responses during childhood and adolescence seemed to us to compound their problems" (Vaillant, 1977, p. 299).
In still another prospective longitudinal study, 698 infants born in Kauai,
Hawaii, in 1955 were followed for over 40 years (Werner, 1989, 1997; Werner
& Smith, 2001). About one third of them had severe deprivations and losses
in early childhood, yet in their 30s and 40s one third of those – about one
ninth of the total sample – developed into "competent, confident, and caring adults" (Werner, 1997, p. 103). In retrospective interviews the participants most frequently cited two protective factors: a significant supportive
person outside their dysfunctional immediate families and a strong individual tendency to make the best of life.

POSTTRAUMATIC STRESS DISORDER: SOME QUESTIONS

PTSD is unusual among psychiatric diagnoses (Breslau, Chase, & Anthony,
2002). First, it is one of few diagnoses in the *Diagnostic and Statistical
Manual of Mental Disorders*, fourth edition (*DSM–IV*; APA, 1994), dependent on etiology, which has otherwise largely been eliminated from *DSM*
because of uncertain causality. Although considering etiology is the rule
in the rest of medical diagnosis (as insisted on by Rudolf Virchow, Robert
Koch, and other founders of modern medicine), in most physical illnesses
the anatomical, physiological, and/or metabolic pathways of the disease
process are largely known. With the exception of those caused by chemical agents, no psychiatric diagnosis, certainly not PTSD, has met these
criteria.

Second, PTSD is unusual in that the criteria prominently include the
characteristics of an *external* event (Eagle, 2002); for most *DSM* diagnoses,
criteria are mainly symptoms, signs, course of illness, and other characteristics of the patient. On such criteria PTSD overlaps extensively with other
diagnoses, hence the need for reference to external events. Again, in the
rest of medicine, external factors – infectious agents, toxins, trauma – are
often cited in diagnostic criteria. However, the pathways in the body from
external agent to physical or metabolic breakdown are largely known and
thoroughly justify the diagnostic consideration of the agent.

Third, most patients resist being labeled with psychiatric diagnoses, and
PTSD may result in such resistance for some patients, but other patients
want and seek the PTSD label. Psychiatric symptoms may be less stigmatizing if caused by a traumatic experience, especially if others were
responsible. Legal issues of compensation enter into some patients' efforts
to receive the diagnosis just as they do with back pain, whiplash, and other
potentially trauma-induced physical ailments. Up to 94% of individuals
receiving the PTSD diagnosis within the Veterans Administration system
apply for compensation benefits, and high levels of disability can result
in payments of $2,000 per month or more. Factitious PTSD in this context

has been repeatedly described, and some veterans carrying or seeking the PTSD diagnosis have been shown to have had no combat exposure, despite their claims to the contrary (Lynn & Belza, 1984; Sparr & Pankratz, 1983). Exaggerated or imagined episodes of combat stress may be deliberate or unintentional in different cases.

Among veterans who are inpatients being treated for PTSD, compensation appears to worsen symptom description (Fontana & Rosenheck, 1998), although this effect may not apply to outpatients. A number of studies have shown that memories of combat become worse over time and that the severity of the remembered combat exposure is correlated with the severity of current PTSD and other symptoms (Southwick, Morgan, Nicolaou, & Charney, 1997; Wessely et al., 2003). In a study of 460 U.S. soldiers who had served in Somalia, subjects remembered more combat exposure as time passed, and "severity of posttraumatic symptomatology was uniquely associated with this change, indicating a possible systematic bias in which severity of symptoms leads to increased reports of stressor frequency" (Roemer, Litz, Orsillo, Ehlich, & Friedman, 1998, p. 597).

In the civilian context, worker's compensation may serve as an incentive, as does some litigation. Authorities on psychiatry and law state that PTSD forms an important new kind of tort, increasingly figuring in civil cases (Lindahl, 2004; Pitman & Sparr, 1998; Sparr & Pitman, 1999), and that the diagnosis in these settings is subject to trivialization and abuse both within (Grisso & Vincent, 2005; Rosen, 1996) and outside the United States (Eagle, 2002; Fabra, 2002, 2003; Tennant, 2004). Efforts to develop tests that discriminate between PTSD sufferers and people trying to simulate the symptom pattern factitiously have not been successful (Hickling, Blanchard, Mundy, & Galovski, 2002), and experiments show that coaching simulators of PTSD enhances their ability to evade detection (Bury & Bagby, 2002).

In addition, PTSD is among the psychiatric diagnoses that have been in flux for many years (McHugh, 1999). During World War I "shell shock" was defined but was thought to be more physical than psychological, due literally to the shock wave of the explosion (A. Young, 1995). However, it was recognized that some men came back with specifically psychological damage, and such diagnoses as hysteria and neurasthenia were applied. By World War II, a book titled *Traumatic Neuroses of War* defined emotional disorders resulting from the psychological stress of combat (Kardiner, 1941).

The recognition of a disorder called "Vietnam War: Post-Vietnam Syndrome" markedly raised awareness of combat-related psychological damage (Davis, 1992). Veterans returning from this particular war may have been especially vulnerable due to hostility at home and a general sense of failure as the war ended unfavorably for the United States. This is consistent with research on the importance of cognitive framing of trauma to the likelihood of later symptoms. However, the essence of the etiology for many men was combat itself. It is also clear that similar symptoms can arise in the wake of many other kinds of trauma (Schnurr, Friedman, & Bernardy, 2002; Yehuda, 2002b).

PTSD entered the *DSM* in 1980 (*DSM–III*) and expanded greatly thereafter (A. Young, 1995, 2000). There is no doubt that this is partly due to the recognition of an important and previously under-recognized disorder. However, it is well established that culture influences *DSM* diagnoses (Konner, 1995; Nuckolls, 1992; Summerfield, 2002). For example, in the early *DSM*s there was an illness called "homosexuality." This was transformed over the decades until the sole reference to sexual orientation became a subset of Sexual Disorder Not Otherwise Specified: "persistent and marked distress about sexual orientation" (APA, 1994, p. 538), which also occured in heterosexuals. Premenstrual syndrome (PMS) evolved into a diagnostic category for research purposes only: premenstrual dysphoric disorder, a subset of Depressive Disorder Not Otherwise Specified (pp. 715–18).

In addition to changes in diagnostic categories in response to cultural influence, application of the labels may depend on cultural differences. For example, through the 1970s diagnoses in the schizophrenia spectrum were applied far more frequently in the United States than in the United Kingdom, which diagnosed bipolar disorder and other mood disorder spectrum labels to the same patients (Pope & Lipinski, 1978), with important implications for treatment. In the past decade there has been a very large expansion in the diagnosis attention-deficit/hyperactivity disorder, including a widening application to adults (Kanapaux, 2002; Rutter, 1998). Bulimia is a relatively new diagnostic category clearly influenced by culture; binging and purging was a culturally accepted practice among well-to-do ancient Romans. This does not condone the practice nor deny its different meaning in a culture that disapproves it; here, bulimia is a disorder. But it does show the power of culture over behaviors we consider symptoms. Probably a culture of exaggerated concern about body image and a subculture of extreme dieting and even binging and purging have increased bulimia's frequency. Finally, there are marked sex differences in the application of diagnoses on *DSM* Axis II, personality disorders that tend to be stable. Antisocial personality disorder is far more often applied to males than females, for example, whereas histrionic personality disorder is far more often applied to females (Nuckolls, 1992). This could be because of a legitimate sex difference in the underlying processes, but it could also be influenced by gender stereotypes.

Regardless of the specific application of the labels, psychiatric diagnosis has important weaknesses as well as negative consequences (McHugh, 1999). It was shown decades ago that it is relatively easy to feign psychosis well enough to be given a diagnosis of major mental illness. Eight different individuals, all free of noteworthy mental illness, were admitted to

12 different psychiatric hospitals and held several weeks until discharge (Rosenhan, 1973). Even when appropriately applied, psychiatric labels carry a significant social stigma with economic consequences and sometimes tend to shift the locus of control from the individual to the health care system, potentially weakening self-reliance and self-healing. They can result from or encourage malingering, and some patients succumb to the temptations of the secondary gains of illness, which can also slow recovery (Franklin, Repasky, Thompson, Shelton, & Uddo, 2002). With the exception of substance abuse disorders, some organic syndromes, and possibly PTSD, no diagnosis in *DSM–IV* has a known etiology, and none has a medical test that qualifies for routine use. Given that psychiatric treatment, whether pharmacological or psychological, is not without risk, these general questions about diagnosis should give us pause.

As for PTSD itself, the diagnosis has come into very widespread use on the basis of research that does not always meet the highest scientific standards (McHugh, 1999). In some settings political and moral judgments play important roles (Eagle, 2002). Media sources have repeatedly invoked the label inappropriately after PTEs in the news, but mental health professionals have often cooperated in the abuse of this and related diagnoses – as after September 11, 2001.

For example, Richard Mollica, MD, director of the Harvard Program in Refugee Trauma, was quoted in the October 17, 2001, issue of the *Journal of the American Medical Association* as saying, "starting around the Thanksgiving holiday and through the New Year, a major mental health crisis will emerge in the city and surrounding area" (Stephenson, 2001, p. 1824). Allen Keller, MD, director of the Bellevue/NYU Program for Survivors of Torture, was quoted as saying,

Arguably, the entire city has been exposed to horrible trauma, and primary care physicians... need to touch base with all of their patients and be very conscious that when individuals present with somatic complaints – stomachaches, headaches, what have you – those problems may be manifestations of stress reactions from these recent horrible events. (p. 1824)

Spencer Eth, MD, medical director of Behavioral Health Services at Saint Vincent Catholic Medical Centers in New York, was quoted in September 2001 on the mental health website HealthRising.com as expecting "huge increases in the prevalence of traumatic grief, depression, posttraumatic stress disorder and substance abuse in the New York City metropolitan area at the least. This is an unprecedented disaster, and its psychiatric toll will be enormous" (Kaplan, 2001). James Nininger, MD, then president of the New York State Psychiatric Association, wrote in a letter in the *New York Times* of September 30, 2001, that the psychiatric problems caused by the attacks would continue to emerge for years, not just in people directly affected, or even just in New Yorkers, but "also among those who viewed the horrific scenes on TV." In other words, billions of people throughout the world.

The projected avalanche of trauma-related mental illness never materialized. A random-digit-dialed telephone survey of adult Manhattanites 6 months after 9/11 showed a prevalence of probable PTSD of 0.6% (Galea et al., 2003). Total utilization of mental health services in Manhattan went from 16.9% in the 30 days before that date to 19.4% in the 30 days following it (Boscarino, Galea, Ahern, Resnick, & Vlahov, 2002). A study comparing the 22-week period following 9/11 with the same period in the 2 previous years surveyed Washington, D.C.–area residents for mental health clinic utilization (Hoge, Pavlin, & Milliken, 2002); there was no overall increase, although there were significant increases in utilization by children with anxiety and stress reactions, as well as an increase in adult adjustment reactions, which are not mental disorders. A Centers for Disease Control random-digit-dialed telephone survey of residents of Connecticut, New Jersey, and New York between October 11 and December 31, 2001, was published in their respected *Morbidity and Mortality Weekly Report* (Centers for Disease Control, 2002). They found that 50% of people participated in a memorial service; 75% had "problems attributed to the attacks," of whom 12% reported "getting help," mostly from family, friends, and neighbors; 48% experienced anger; 3% of alcohol drinkers said they drank more; and 21% of smokers said they smoked more. One percent of nonsmokers said they had started to smoke. (Percentages of those who decreased or ceased usage were not reported.) Twenty-seven percent reported that they missed work, most because of evacuation or transportation problems. Eighty percent said they watched more media coverage than usual. Nothing mentioned in this document falls into the category of morbidity, much less mortality; nowhere does it suggest that all these responses are adaptations, most of them healthy ones. In fact, one study that considered the possibility of positive psychological effects of the September 11 tragedy found them. A self-report on-line questionnaire based on the Values in Action Classification of Strengths was completed by 4,817 Americans in the two months following that date, and showed increases in gratitude, hope, kindness, leadership, love, spirituality, and teamwork; ten months after September 11, the effect was attenuated but still present (Peterson & Seligman, 2003).

Who gets PTSD after a PTE, and why? This holds great practical and theoretical interest. Most prospective studies begin just after the trauma, which limits our knowledge of what symptoms may have preceded it. Pre-trauma neuroticism strongly predicted PTSD among women who suffered a pregnancy loss (Engelhard, van den Hout, & Kindt, 2003). However, in a prospective study of World War II combat exposure, psychological vulnerability before combat exposure predicted later non-specific psychiatric symptoms but not PTSD, while combat exposure itself predicted PTSD symptoms but not other kinds of psychopathology (K. A. Lee, et al., 1995). A meta-analysis of 68 studies showed that seven variables predicted PTSD: prior trauma, prior psychological adjustment, family history of psychopathology, perceived life threat during the trauma, posttrauma social support, peritraumatic emotional responses, and peritraumatic dissociation, with the last factor having the strongest association (Ozer, Best, Lipsey, & Weiss, 2003).

Some studies of identical twins discordant for combat exposure support the role of combat in symptoms of PTSD (Roy-Byrne et al., 2004) and in one of its physiological markers, increased heart-rate response to a sudden loud noise (Orr et al., 2003). In another genetically controlled study, however, 222 monozygotic and 184 dizygotic twin pairs were compared on exposure to trauma and PTSD symptoms; concordance was higher in the monozygotic twin pairs for both risk of exposure to trauma and (given a trauma) the likelihood that PTSD would develop (Stein, Jang, Taylor, Vernon, & Livesley, 2002), suggesting a genetic continuum of vulnerability. Lower intelligence and negative personality traits are pretrauma behavioral predictors (McNally, 2003a). Smaller hippocampal volume has been found in several studies of PTSD victims (Hull, 2002; Lindauer et al., 2004; Villarreal et al., 2002). However, a study of twins discordant for combat exposure showed that the non-combat-exposed twin had reduced hippocampal volume comparable to that of the exposed twin, and that PTSD symptom severity in the combat-exposed twin could be predicted from the hippocampal volume of his non-combat-exposed brother as well as from his own (Gilbertson et al., 2002; Sapolsky, 2002).

A related problem is comorbidity, which complicates the diagnosis and raises questions about pretrauma symptoms and vulnerability. A variety of psychiatric disorders, prominently including substance abuse disorders, appear comorbidly with PTSD and often have symptoms that overlap with those of PTSD. In the National Comorbidity Survey (NCS) of almost 6,000 subjects, pretrauma history of affective disorder predicted PTSD in women and both a history of anxiety disorder and parental mental illness predicted it in men (Bromet, Sonnega, & Kessler, 1998). Other studies have found a variety of comorbid psychiatric disorders. In one typical study over 40% of subjects with PTSD also met criteria for major depression, although these were considered separate and distinguishable, especially by peritraumatic anxiety and dissociation (Shalev et al., 1998). A sample of Gulf War veterans were prospectively studied in a cross-lagged model that showed that PTSD and major depression interacted reciprocally over time to worsen each other's symptoms, except that one PTSD symptom, hyperarousability, appeared to precede but not follow major depression (D. J. Erickson, Wolfe, King, King, & Sharkansky, 2001).

Another approach to the comorbidity question is factor analysis of psychiatric disorders in large community samples such as the NCS (Krueger,

1999), which yielded three dimensions: an anxiety–misery factor (representing mainly mood disorders), a fear factor (phobias and panic), and an externalizing disorders factor (antisocial personality and substance abuse). A subsequent study using a separate subsample of the NCS yielded the same three factors using a different factor-analytic method (Cox, Clara, & Enns, 2002). This second study considered PTSD in relation to the factors and showed that PTSD loads moderately (.39), with mood disorders and generalized anxiety, on the anxiety–misery factor but weakly on the externalizing (.14) and fear (.10) dimensions.

DSM–IV Axis II disorders, especially borderline, obsessive-compulsive, avoidant, and paranoid but also schizotypal and self-defeating personality disorders, have also been shown to be very common among PTSD patients (Southwick, Yehuda, & Giller, 1993). Axis II disorders are by definition not the result of substances, injury, or particular stresses, so they must precede the trauma in many PTSD patients with Axis II diagnoses and could increase vulnerability.

Twin studies are particularly useful. A study of comorbidity in combat-discordant Vietnam-era twins showed that identical twins among men with PTSD had significantly more mood disorder symptoms than identical twins among non-PTSD combat controls or dizygotic twins among those with PTSD; this and other findings in the study suggested that major depression, GAD, and panic disorder are part of a postcombat syndrome and that a shared genetic vulnerability contributes to the association between PTSD and major depression, and between PTSD and dysthymia (Koenen et al., 2003). A similar study showed that part of the vulnerability for PTSD comes from preexisting childhood conduct disorder or adult antisocial personality disorder (Koenen, 1999). Clearly some comorbid psychiatric disorders precede the trauma and may be markers of preexisting vulnerability. Is the PTSD label becoming a substitute for such diagnoses as depression, anxiety, and panic disorder, among many others – not to mention normal emotions such as grief, fear, and rage? We simply do not at present have research that answers this question.

Consider the analogy of certain disorders associated with pregnancy and delivery. Gestational diabetes mellitus Type 2 (GDM) and preeclampsia (hypertension of pregnancy with proteinuria) are by definition pregnancy-induced diseases. However, even if these conditions are not apparent before pregnancy, they often persist long after it and may become chronic or chronically recurring. The incidence of chronic noninsulin-dependent diabetes mellitus (NIDDM) may be as high as 50% of women who previously received the diagnosis of GDM (O'Sullivan, 1991; Tan, Tan, Lim, Tan, & Lim, 2002) without prior evidence of diabetes. In one study, about a fourth of women with GDM had NIDDM 1 year postpartum and another 15% had impaired glucose tolerance (Metzger et al., 1985). Some of these women probably had undetected pregestational impairment of glucose tolerance unmasked by pregnancy whereas in others the chronic problem was induced by pregnancy. Another prospective study showed that 14.8% of women with severe preeclampsia or eclampsia (diagnoses given only in pregnancy) went on to develop chronic hypertension, as opposed to 5.6% of a control group (Sibai, el-Nazer, & Gonzalez-Ruiz, 1986). Patients may be euglycemic or normotensive, respectively, for months to years, before late-onset NIDDM or chronic hypertension develop.

Physicians are interested in the patient's history and want to know, for example, that a 35-year-old woman with NIDDM developed glucose intolerance or hypertension for the first time during a pregnancy at age 28. But they do not use the terms "gestational diabetes" or "pregnancy-induced hypertension" to refer to such a patient. PTSD patients, however, are referred to by this label regardless of how long it has been since the trauma or whether there are comorbid disorders (depression, anxiety-spectrum disorders, OCD, substance abuse) that overlap in symptom picture with PTSD. Standard psychiatric references state that the differential diagnosis of PTSD and these disorders (Davidson, 1995) is difficult and that the most important clues are the first onset after occurrence of a trauma and the presence of trauma-specific intrusive memories and dreams. Neither of these differentiating criteria, considered critical, would clearly distinguish an underlying disorder unmasked by trauma from a disorder caused by trauma.

Depression and the anxiety disorders are now known to be genetically linked (Kendler, Neale, Kessler, Heath, & Eaves, 1992), and some anxiety-spectrum disorders respond well to the same neurotransmitter reuptake inhibitors effective in depression, even when highly serotonin selective; the same medications are also effective in OCD, although often at higher doses (Boerner & Moller, 1999; Kilts, 2003; Vaswani, Linda, & Ramesh, 2003). Even the HPA-axis abnormalities considered distinctive of PTSD are found in some studies to occur in depression and other disorders and to be tied more to depression than to trauma history (Newport, Heim, Bonsall, Miller, & Nemeroff, 2004; Smith et al., 1989). These findings suggest the possibility of a biological continuum with PTSD of some important psychiatric disorders that can be difficult to distinguish from PTSD. Furthermore, stressful life events in the recent past have always been taken into account in the *DSM* diagnosis of mood disorders. The term "diathesis" was used by older physicians to mean "a constitution or condition of the body which makes the tissues react in special ways to certain extrinsic stimuli and thus tends to make the person more than usually susceptible to certain diseases" (Dorland, 1965). It is likely that a constitutional predisposition to mood and/or anxiety disorders (and perhaps dissociative disorders) is a diathesis for psychiatric trauma, which can unmask these disorders or the underlying tendency toward them. This concept has received little attention in the PTSD research literature and in the clinical pragmatics of differential diagnosis.

Many studies have begun with subjects with psychiatric symptoms and probed strongly for a variety of past experiences presumed to have been traumatic, including events and processes common in family life. We know that this approach often distorts memory and that overly eager mental health workers, police officers, and other authority figures can create "memories" of things that did not happen (Loftus, 2000, 2003). This alone should encourage caution in our efforts to elicit memories of trauma retrospectively, sometimes many years after the fact. That the diagnostic criteria for PTSD include "inability to recall an important aspect of the trauma" (APA, p. 428) increases the risk of memory distortion by authority figures during interviews. Repressed memories exist (Loftus, 1993), but the process of eliciting or reconstructing them is fraught with problems.

During the 1980s some clinicians began expanding the diagnosis of multiple personality disorder (MPD), itself presumed to be linked to PTSD, from a rare disorder to a very common one and then to a rare one again (McHugh, 1995; McHugh, Lief, Freyd, & Fetkewicz, 2004; McHugh & Putnam, 1995). During the heyday of the diagnosis, popular clinical manuals advised clinicians to reinterpret a remarkable range of symptoms as evidence of MPD and other dissociative disorders and to presume the existence of past trauma that, it was believed, would explain the "MPD" (McNally, 2003b). Many patients spontaneously or under strong "therapeutic" encouragement remembered things that could not have occurred – abduction by space aliens and baby-sacrificing rituals – and were clearly products of dissociation, suggestion, or both. This wave of clinical enthusiasm had the unfortunate affect of raising doubts about the suffering of real PTSD patients (Ofshe & Waters, 1994; Wright, 1994).

Is there a risk of repeating this mistake today? Some studies enroll subjects with continuing stresses – advanced cancer, for example – confounding PTSD with ongoing stress itself (Jacobsen et al., 2002). Some purport to investigate the PTSD resulting from head trauma, completely confounding the psychological sequelae of the trauma with physical brain damage (Mollica, Henderson, & Tor, 2002; Williams, Evans, Wilson, & Needham, 2002). Some mental health professionals claim to be able, through retrospective interviews, to find trauma in the past of a large proportion of depressed patients; given the broad definition of trauma and the fact that we have all had unpleasant experiences, this is a questionable research strategy. Furthermore, given the weight of evidence supporting genetic influences on depression, we may be in danger of using the trauma concept to turn a trigger of illness into a presumed cause.

As with false memories of childhood abuse, preconceived notions about PTSD treatment have sometimes led to interventions that were neither welcome nor helpful (McHugh, 1999). It is fortunate that two widely accepted treatments for PTSD, psychotherapy (Bradley, Greene, Russ, Dutra, & Westen, 2005) and both selective serotonin and serotonin/NE reuptake inhibitors (SSRIs and SNRIs; Gorman & Kent, 1999; Schoenfeld, Marmar, & Neylan, 2004), are also effective in depression, GAD, and OCD, reducing the risk that misdiagnosis and/or comorbidity will result in inappropriate treatment. Exposure therapy is effective in PTSD (Rothbaum & Schwartz, 2002) but may be inappropriate in comorbid or misdiagnosed depression or OCD. Other approaches to PTSD may be ineffective or harmful. A 20-year retrospective on inpatient treatment found its results to be disappointing by objective and subjective measures (Rosenheck, Fontana, & Errera, 1997). Debriefing has been repeatedly shown in meta-analyses to be ineffective in preventing PTSD (Rose et al., 2002; Wessely & Deahl, 2003), and some studies, including two randomized controlled trials, have suggested that debriefing and similar immediate posttrauma counseling may increase the risk (Bisson, Jenkins, Alexander, & Bannister, 1997; Mayou, Ehlers, & Bryant, 2002). Because it is well established that cognitive framing of trauma affects the likelihood of PTSD (Ali, Dunmore, Clark, & Ehlers, 2002; Dunmore, Clark, & Ehlers, 2001; Ehlers & Clark, 2000), such effects may be the result of negative cognitive framing in some debriefing procedures.

PTSD is real (Schnurr et al., 2002; Yehuda, 2002b). People who have been through concentration camps, combat, natural disasters, serious auto accidents, and rape (among other stresses outside of normal life) are vulnerable to it and deserve help. Its physiology may be distinct from that of ongoing stress – depressed instead of elevated cortisol (Yehuda, 2002a) – although this remains controversial (Newport et al., 2004; E. A. Young & Breslau, 2004). It is disabling to many, with symptoms such as vigilance, fear, anger, light and easily disturbed sleep, revisiting and rehearsing the trauma, avoiding people and places associated with the trauma, withdrawing generally, and maintaining a muted level of affect. All these disturbing symptoms can become chronic and impairing and deserve to be clinically addressed.

Nevertheless, the typical response to acute psychological trauma is recovery over time. Symptoms in the immediate aftermath of the trauma, now known in *DSM–IV* as acute stress disorder (A. G. Harvey & Bryant, 2002), decline with time in most and resolve in many. For example, 52 men who experienced a severe avalanche showed a decrease in stress reactions from 3 weeks to 4 months and a persistent reduction at 12 months, whereas only subjects who experienced repeated stress exposure over the 12 months had increased symptoms (Johnsen, Eid, Laberg, & Thayer, 2002). Of 84 primary care patients who met the criteria for PTSD on presentation, 2 years later 69% no longer met the full criteria and 18% had a full recovery, with comorbid disorders predicting worse outcomes (Zlotnick et al., 2004). In

106 consecutive patients admitted to a trauma unit with severe accidental injuries, 5 met full and 22 met some criteria for PTSD 2 weeks after the trauma; at 12-month follow-up, the numbers had declined to 2 and 13, respectively (Schnyder, Moergeli, Klaghofer, & Buddeberg, 2001).

Of course, not everyone exposed to even severe stressors develops PTSD (Yehuda, 2002b). A review of PTSD following terrorist attacks worldwide showed an incidence of 28% in those closely affected (Gidron, 2002). The *lifetime* prevalence of PTSD in 140 war journalists, who often experience multiple and ongoing stressors, was 28.6% (Feinstein, Owen, & Blair, 2002). Of 77 individuals exposed to a mass shooting spree at a courthouse, 5% developed PTSD (Johnson, North, & Smith, 2002). A 3-year follow-up of victims of serious automobile accidents showed an 11% incidence of PTSD, predicted by persistent health and financial problems, litigation, and several peritraumatic variables (Mayou et al., 2002). Studies of resilience are far less common than studies of PTSD itself, yet these may hold the clues to primary and secondary prevention.

For certain victims of trauma the pre- or posttraumatic cognitive framing of the experience may be critical (Ehlers & Clark, 2000). PTSD after combat is strongly associated with low motivation to serve in the military (Z. Kaplan et al., 2002). Ordinary citizens are much more likely than members of security forces to suffer PTSD after terrorist attacks (Gidron, 2002); the latter's objective experience is the same or worse, but the cognitive preparation and framing are very different. In 181 male firefighters who worked as rescue workers in the Oklahoma City bombing of 1995, 13% had PTSD, compared with 23% of male primary victims (North et al., 2002). Vietnam veterans who suffer from PTSD show improvement if they care for their grandchildren (Hierholzer, 2004); might similar positive, active experiences help other trauma victims cope, even though these activities take place outside the mental health system? Many ongoing investigations are considering the value of intervention by mental health professionals after acute stress, but we should not ignore the healing resources of family and community.

CONCLUSION: STRESS, RESILIENCE, AND ADAPTATION

This chapter began with a description of life in our environments of evolutionary adaptedness, finding it to be stressful and subject to frequent trauma, yet indicative of the great human capacity for resilience. It went on to consider the physiological bases of normal and abnormal responses to stress and, to the extent we understand it, resilience. Finally, it raised some questions about the diagnosis and treatment of PTSD as currently construed in the mental health professions and the media.

A greatly simplified and speculative model of three possible responses to acute stress is shown in Figure 15.2. It proposes a possible continuum of stress responsiveness, construed to include three broad types of

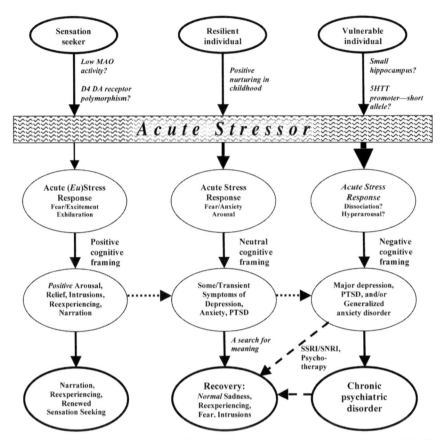

FIGURE 15.2. A speculative model of three responses to acute stress. MAO, monoamine oxidase; DA, dopamine; 5HTT, serotonin transporter; SSRI/SNRI, serotonin selective/serotonin-norepinephrine reuptake inhibitors; dotted arrows, unlikely but possible transformations; dashed arrows, response to treatment.

people. The first, sensation seekers, are the small proportion who desire and seek out experiences that would be stressful to most people. Studies suggest that they may share biological markers including low activity of the enzyme monoamine oxidase (MAO) and a particular polymorphism of the D4 dopamine receptor (Zuckerman & Kuhlman, 2000). These people find novel, stressful, and dangerous experiences desirable and exhilarating, especially if positively framed and sought. The second and largest group is fairly resilient in the face of serious stress but develops acute stress responses which, if they persisted, might qualify as psychiatric disorders. However, few do persist. The third category consists of the minority who are vulnerable to the development of psychiatric illness during and after acute stress. This group may develop PTSD, depressive disorders, and/or GAD in the wake of the stress, and symptoms may persist for years. Small hippocampal volume may be a marker of vulnerability. Carriers and/or homozygotes for an allele for the shorter of two promoters of the serotonin transporter gene are vulnerable to depression and some other psychiatric problems following serious psychological stress (Caspi et al., 2003; Grabe et al., 2005; Kendler, Kuhn, Vittum, Prescott, & Riley, 2005).

This is a speculative model advanced for heuristic purposes, and it has many possible flaws. For example, the first and third categories may not be independent or mutually exclusive and therefore may not be actual ends of the proposed continuum. However, because it is clear that some people are exceptionally resilient in the face of severe stress, the continuum is probably real.

I did not and do not challenge the existence of PTSD nor the all-too-real suffering of those who have it. I have simply reviewed studies and trends that suggest that PTSD is a problematic diagnosis, that it has been overapplied, that it is sometimes exaggerated or factitious, that there are incentives for such distortions, that culture and media influence it and other psychiatric diagnoses, that a great majority of PTSD sufferers also have other psychiatric diagnoses whose symptoms often overlap with those of PTSD, and that little is known about the antecedents of PTSD that make some individuals more vulnerable than others. Most important, I have tried to emphasize that most of us, like our evolutionary and historical predecessors, are resilient.

Where does this resilience come from? I would point to three possible sources. First, social and family supports in ancestral settings were extremely strong, even more so during childhood, and these bonds of aid and empathy are protective. Second, people are far more resilient than some mental health professionals would have us believe, and the experience of self-reliance and survival in these challenging environments must have strengthened resilience. Third, cognitive framing of stress and responses to stress in these cultures emphasized strength, resilience, and the necessity to survive to meet other stresses and to protect dependents.

Because these were the conditions under which we evolved, it is not surprising that we have a GAS consisting of predictable and often appropriate, although sometimes excessive, physiological responses encoded in the genes. Following Selye, we distinguished between *dis*tress and *eu*stress and emphasized that eustress – normal stress – is the essence of life itself. *Dis*tress is also central to life, and the responses organisms make to it determine whether they survive and reproduce. Thus, coping with distress has determined the course of our evolution, and consequently we are relatively good at it. What about the exceptional distress represented by trauma? This too was common in evolution, and the adaptive response produced by thousands of generations of selection was "Let's get on with life."

Still, many must have failed. It does no good to say they were selected against, because in our modern culture we properly insist on buffering those who are less resilient against some severe stresses that others weather more easily. We do not say, with natural selection, "The devil take the hindmost." We intervene. This is fine, provided the intervention does more good than harm.

HGs had levels of mortality from infectious disease that we would not countenance for a moment. The fact that deadly microbes were ubiquitous and natural carries little weight, and that is as it should be. However, we have often prescribed antibiotics unnecessarily, producing adverse instead of salutary effects for many individuals (for example, by killing good bacteria) and damaging the public health by selecting for and breeding antibiotic-resistant organisms. Furthermore, we overestimate the importance of antibiotics in bringing about the great decline in mortality in modern times; in reality, such variables as nutrition, plumbing, pest control, and other community-level factors accounted for almost all of it (McKeown, 1995). We also underestimated the ability of patients to fight infectious diseases with the adaptations provided by a highly evolved immune system. Analogies are limited, but it is possible that our scientific and medical arrogance could once again lead us to overtreat and overintervene, this time in the psychological realm.

Consider the symptoms of PTSD itself in the light of our evolutionary history. In the human EEAs, an adaptive response to stress might include a needed vigilance (with lighter sleep), appropriate fear and/or anger, revisiting and rehearsing the trauma to consolidate its lessons, and avoiding or withdrawing from sources of danger. In some situations even a general withdrawal and a pattern of muted affect – for example, if bravado or anger had helped to cause the trauma – might be adaptive. These symptoms may be less adaptive in a culture like ours, and in any case they would not be adaptive if they become chronic. But the question is not whether PTSD can be debilitating; rather, it is where we draw the line between resilience and vulnerability and whether our interventions sometimes do more harm than good.

Would the Vietnam veterans, with the same combat experience, have been as vulnerable to PTSD if they had been welcomed home as heroes? Would the people of London suffering the blitz have been better off if Churchill, instead of saying, "Death and sorrow will be companions of our journey; hardship our garment; constancy and valor our only shield. We must be united, we must be undaunted. We must be inflexible" (Churchill, 2003), had said, "We'd better send in thousands of trauma counselors"? The stiff upper lip is a famous British cultural adaptation; Churchill believed in it, and he addressed his beleaguered nation in words that helped to make it real. Many people rise to stresses when they are encouraged to believe that they can and that much depends on them, and succumb when they are told that they cannot. After September 11, some mental health authorities predicted a nationwide epidemic of PTSD. Similar predictions were made in the media immediately following the July 7, 2005, terrorist bombings in London, and the counterproductive potential for such predictions raised legitimate concern (Wessely, 2005). This is the kind of thing that prevents people, legislators included, from taking the mental health professions seriously. It also diminishes the suffering of those at or near (in distance or relationship) ground zero.

What actually happened after September 11, of course, was that the American people entered into a new era of vigilance, revisiting and rehearsing the event, learning from it as much as possible, and, yes, getting very angry at the perpetrators and all who gave them comfort. This was a healthy and adaptive response to the trauma and has allowed almost all Americans to adjust without clinical intervention. No doubt many of those who experienced the event at or near ground zero or who lost loved ones in it required and will continue to require help. But many others, even among those close to the event, channeled their grief into adaptive paths, such as agitating for and getting an independent commission to revisit and rehearse the event with them at a national level, going to fight against Al Qaeda in Afghanistan, or learning more about Islamic culture and Islamist terrorism. It is intriguing that in some studies the intrusive memories in PTSD patients are of the warning signs of the forthcoming trauma, rather than or in addition to the trauma itself (Ehlers et al., 2002); this strongly suggests an adaptive mechanism for avoidance learning.

Finally, it is possible to construe some of the symptoms of PTSD as a search for meaning. Revisiting and even to some extent obsessing about the trauma is in part a normal urge to integrate and understand a dreadful experience. Thinking about it and incorporating it into one's own life story is in part a product of the human drive toward narrative, and talking about it can reflect a normal need for a listening ear. Memory – remembrance – has value in itself; it is a part of our selves even when it is bad.

Consider the stories of two combat veterans. One, a Vietnam veteran speaking many years after the war, said,

I can't get the memories out of my mind! The images come flooding back in vivid detail, triggered by the most inconsequential things, like a door slamming or the smell of stir-fried pork. Last night, I went to bed, was having a good sleep for a change. Then in the early morning a storm-front passed through and there was a bolt of crackling thunder. I awoke instantly, frozen in fear. I am right back in Viet Nam, in the middle of the monsoon season at my guard post. I am sure I'll get hit in the next volley and convinced I will die. My hands are freezing, yet sweat pours from my entire body. I feel each hair on the back of my neck standing on end. I can't catch my breath and my heart is pounding. I smell a damp sulfur smell. Suddenly I see what's left of my buddy Troy, his head on a bamboo platter, sent back to our camp by the Viet Cong. Propaganda messages are stuffed between his clenched teeth. The next bolt of lightning and clap of thunder makes me jump so much that I fall to the floor. (Davis, 1992, p. 470)

The second, a World War II veteran, spoke more than 60 years after his event:

I was hid behind a big tree that was knocked down or fallen. And I could see these Germans in the woods across this big field. And I saw this young kid crawling up a ditch straight towards my tree. So I let him crawl, I didn't fire at him, but when he got up, within three or four foot of me, I screamed at him to surrender, and instead of surrendering, he started to pull his gun towards me, which was instant death for him. But this young man, he was a blond, blue-eyed, fair-skinned, so handsome, he was like a little angel, but I still had to shoot him, and it didn't bother me the first night, because I went to sleep, I was so tired, but . . . the second night, I woke up crying [voice breaks] because that kid was there [voice breaks]. And to this day I wake up many nights crying . . . over this kid. I still see him in my dreams. And I don't know how to get him off my mind. (Robertson, 2005)

At first glance the two statements seem similar. The first contains evidence of symptoms meeting most of the *DSM–IV* criteria for PTSD, and the speaker's pain and need for help are palpable, even many years after his horrific experience. The second, especially when heard in spoken form, feels very different. It is a poignant reminiscence of a tragic event in which a soldier had no choice but to kill a beautiful young man much like himself. Yes – 6 decades later – his sleep is disturbed, his thoughts are intrusive, he sometimes wakes up crying, he does not quite know how to get the boy he killed completely off his mind. If he should ask for help, of course he should get it, but he does not appear to view his condition as psychopathology. This, I would argue, is not PTSD. It seems, rather, a fairly normal reexperiencing of a life-changing event, a tragic moment in which he was forced to kill another human being. Why should such an event not be remembered, intrusively or otherwise? Why should it not cause sadness? These memories are part of the meaning of this man's life, of a conscience troubled permanently by a uniquely powerful act, of an identity forged in part by that act and that experience. They show, to himself and others, how very much he cares about human life, and they help to keep the memory of that angelic-looking German boy alive.

Viktor Frankl, a psychiatrist who spent 3 years as a prisoner in Auschwitz, emerged with the belief that suffering must be dealt with through a search for meaning, and he developed a method of psychotherapy based on that belief (Frankl, 1984). Finding meaning in suffering and in life is, he believed, the best and perhaps the only way for a human being to adapt. He recounted the story, first set down by a German bishop, of a Jewish woman who a few years after World War II wore a bracelet with baby teeth set in gold. Questioned by a doctor, she explained, "This tooth here belonged to Esther, this one to Miriam," and so on. These teeth had been saved, one from each of her nine children, all of whom were murdered in Auschwitz. "How can you live with such a bracelet?" the doctor asked.

"I am now," she answered quietly, "in charge of an orphanage in Israel" (Frankl, 2000, p. 142).

Not everyone who experiences severe trauma – even violent rape, even Auschwitz – develops PTSD. It is essential for us to understand who does and who does not, and what the psychological markers are, not just of vulnerability but also of resilience. Unless research is designed with this question in mind, PTSD runs not just the risk of becoming a passing fad, like the MPD of a decade ago, leaving truly needy people in its wake, but a self-fulfilling prophecy in which some people become psychologically debilitated because they are told that they will. Most people should be told that they are resilient, not just because it is a healthy message, but because it is the legacy of our biological evolution and is usually true. Then, and only then, can we identify the minority among us that is not so resilient and direct the scarce resources of clinical intervention where they are needed and where they belong.

ACKNOWLEDGMENTS

I thank Mark Barad for criticisms of an early draft that resulted in major changes and improvements in this chapter and Brandon Kohrt for suggesting an important addition.

References

Ali, T., Dunmore, E., Clark, D., & Ehlers, A. (2002). The role of negative beliefs in posttraumatic stress disorder: A comparison of assault victims and non victims. *Behavioural and Cognitive Psychotherapy, 30*(3), 249–257.

American Psychiatric Association (APA). (1994). *Diagnostic and statistical manual of mental disorders* (4th ed.). Washington, DC: Author.

Armelagos, G., Goodman, A., & Jacobs, K. (1991). The origins of agriculture: Population growth during a period of declining health. *Population and Environment, 13*, 9–22.

Bailey, R. C. (1991). *The behavioral ecology of Efe Pygmy men in the Ituri forest, Zaire* (Paper No. 86). Ann Arbor: Museum of Anthropology, University of Michigan.

Bennett, A. J., Lesch, K. P., Heils, A., Long, J. C., Lorenz, J. G., Shoaf, S. E., et al. (2002). Early experience and serotonin transporter gene variation interact to influence primate CNS function. *Molecular Psychiatry, 7*(1), 118–122.

Bisson, J. I., Jenkins, P. L., Alexander, J., & Bannister, C. (1997). Randomised controlled trial of psychological debriefing for victims of acute burn trauma. *British Journal of Psychiatry, 171*, 78–81.

Blurton Jones, N. (1993). The lives of hunter-gatherer children: Effects of parental behavior and parental reproductive strategy. In M. E. Pereira & L. A. Fairbanks (Eds.), *Juvenile primates: Life history, development, and behavior* (pp. 309–326). New York: Oxford.

Boerner, R. J., & Moller, H. J. (1999). The importance of new antidepressants in the treatment of anxiety/depressive disorders. *Pharmacopsychiatry, 32*(4), 119–126.

Bonanno, G. A. (2004). Loss, trauma, and human resilience: Have we underestimated the human capacity to thrive after extremely aversive events? *American Psychologist, 59*(1), 20–28.

Bonanno, G. A. (2005). Clarifying and extending the construct of adult resilience. *American Psychologist, 60*(3), 265–267.

Boscarino, J. A., Galea, S., Ahern, J., Resnick, H., & Vlahov, D. (2002). Utilization of mental health services following the September 11th terrorist attacks in Manhattan, New York City. *International Journal of Emergency Mental Health, 4*(3), 143–156.

Bradley, R., Greene, J., Russ, E., Dutra, L., & Westen, D. (2005). A multidimensional meta-analysis of psychotherapy for PTSD [erratum appears in *American Journal of Psychiatry, 162*(4), 832]. *American Journal of Psychiatry, 162*(2), 214–227.

Breslau, N., Chase, G. A., & Anthony, J. C. (2002). The uniqueness of the DSM definition of post-traumatic stress disorder: Implications for research. *Psychological Medicine, 32*(4), 573–576.

Bromet, E., Sonnega, A., & Kessler, R. C. (1998). Risk factors for DSM-III-R posttraumatic stress disorder: Findings from the National Comorbidity Survey. *American Journal of Epidemiology, 147*(4), 353–361.

Bury, A. S., & Bagby, R. M. (2002). The detection of feigned uncoached and coached posttraumatic stress disorder with the MMPI-2 in a sample of workplace accident victims. *Psychological Assessment, 14*(4), 472–484.

Cannon, W. B. (1927). The James-Lange theory of emotions: A critical examination and an alternative theory. *American Journal of Psychology, 39*, 106–124.

Cannon, W. B. (1963). *Bodily changes in pain, hunger, fear, and rage.* New York: Harper & Row. (Original work published 1915)

Caspi, A., Sugden, K., Moffitt, T. E., Taylor, A., Craig, I. W., Harrington, H., et al. (2003). Influence of life stress on depression: Moderation by a polymorphism in the 5-HTT gene. *Science, 301*(5631), 386–389.

Centers for Disease Control. (2002). Psychological and emotional effects of the September 11 attacks on the World Trade Center – Connecticut, New Jersey, and New York, 2001. *Morbidity & Mortality Weekly Report, 51*(35), 784–786.

Champagne, F. A., Francis, D. D., Mar, A., & Meaney, M. J. (2003). Variations in maternal care in the rat as a mediating influence for the effects of environment on development. *Physiology & Behavior, 79*(3), 359–371.

Chrousos, G. P. (1998). Stressors, stress, and neuroendocrine integration of the adaptive response. The 1997 Hans Selye Memorial Lecture. *Annals of the New York Academy of Sciences, 851*, 311–335.

Churchill, W. (2003). Speech to the House of Commons, October 8, 1940. *Finest Hour: Journal of the Churchill Centre, 120*, 6.

Cohen, M. N., & Armelagos, G. J. (Eds.). (1984). *Paleopathology at the origins of agriculture.* New York: Academic Press.

Cox, B. J., Clara, I. P., & Enns, M. W. (2002). Posttraumatic stress disorder and the structure of common mental disorders. *Depression and Anxiety, 15*(4), 168–171.

Davidson, J. R. T. (1995). Posttraumatic stress disorder and acute stress disorder. In H. I. Kaplan & B. J. Sadock (Eds.), *Comprehensive textbook of psychiatry/VI* (6th ed., Vol. 1, pp. 1227–1236). Baltimore, MD: Williams & Wilkins.

Davis, M. (1992). Analysis of aversive memories using the fear-potentiated startle paradigm. In L. R. Squire & N. Butters (Eds.), *Neuropsychology of memory* (2nd ed., pp. 470–484). New York: Guilford Press.

Davis, M., & Whalen, P. J. (2001). The amygdala: Vigilance and emotion. *Molecular Psychiatry, 6*(1), 13–34.

Dorland, W. A. N. (Ed.). (1965). *Dorland's illustrated medical dictionary* (24th ed.). Philadelphia: W. B. Saunders.

Dunmore, E., Clark, D. M., & Ehlers, A. (2001). A prospective investigation of the role of cognitive factors in persistent posttraumatic stress disorder (PTSD) after physical or sexual assault. *Behaviour Research and Therapy, 39*(9), 1063–1084.

Eagle, G. T. (2002). Posttraumatic stress disorder (PTSD): The malleable diagnosis? *South African Journal of Psychology, 32*(2), 37–42.

Ehlers, A., & Clark, D. M. (2000). A cognitive model of posttraumatic stress disorder. *Behaviour Research and Therapy, 38*(4), 319–345.

Ehlers, A., Hackmann, A., Steil, R., Clohessy, S., Wenninger, K., & Winter, H. (2002). The nature of intrusive memories after trauma: The warning signal hypothesis. *Behaviour Research and Therapy, 40*(9), 995–1002.

Engelhard, I. M., van den Hout, M. A., & Kindt, M. (2003). The relationship between neuroticism, pre-traumatic stress, and post-traumatic stress: A prospective study. *Personality & Individual Differences, 35*(2), 381–388.

Erickson, D. J., Wolfe, J., King, D. W., King, L. A., & Sharkansky, E. J. (2001). Posttraumatic stress disorder and depression symptomatology in a sample of Gulf War veterans: A prospective analysis. *Journal of Consulting and Clinical Psychology, 69*(1), 41–49.

Erickson, K., Drevets, W., & Schulkin, J. (2003). Glucocorticoid regulation of diverse cognitive functions in normal and pathological emotional states. *Neuroscience & Biobehavioral Reviews, 27*(3), 233–246.

Fabra, M. (2002). Das sogenannte Traumakriterium (A-Kriterium des DSM-IV) der Posttraumatischen Belastungsstorung und seine Bedeutung fur die Sozial- und Sachversicherung (I). [The so-called trauma criterium (A – Criterium of DSM-IV) in posttraumatic stress disorder and its significance for social and legal insurance (I)]. *Versicherungsmedizin, 54*(4), 179–181.

Fabra, M. (2003). Das sogenannte Traumakriterium (A-Kriterium des DSM-IV) der Posttraumatischen Belastungsstorung und seine Bedeutung fur die Sozial- und Sachversicherung (II). [The so-called trauma criterium (A – Criterium in DSM-IV) of post-traumatic stress disorder and its significance for social and legal insurance (II)]. *Versicherungsmedizin, 55*(1), 19–26.

Feinstein, A., Owen, J., & Blair, N. (2002). A hazardous profession: War, journalists, and psychopathology. *American Journal of Psychiatry, 159*(9), 1570–1575.

Fontana, A., & Rosenheck, R. (1998). Effects of compensation-seeking on treatment outcomes among veterans with posttraumatic stress disorder. *Journal of Nervous and Mental Disease, 186*(4), 223–230.

Francis, D. D., Szegda, K., Campbell, G., Martin, W. D., & Insel, T. R. (2003). Epigenetic sources of behavioral differences in mice. *Nature Neuroscience, 6*(5), 445–446.

Frankl, V. E. (1984). *Man's search for meaning: An introduction to logotherapy* (3rd ed.). New York: Simon & Schuster.

Frankl, V. E. (2000). *Man's search for ultimate meaning: A psychological exploration of the religious quest.* New York: Perseus.

Franklin, C. L., Repasky, S. A., Thompson, K. E., Shelton, S. A., & Uddo, M. (2002). Differentiating overreporting and extreme distress: MMPI-2 use with compensation-seeking veterans with PTSD. *Journal of Personality Assessment, 79*(2), 274–285.

Galea, S., Vlahov, D., Resnick, H., Ahern, J., Susser, E., Gold, J., et al. (2003). Trends of probable post-traumatic stress disorder in New York City after the September 11 terrorist attacks. *American Journal of Epidemiology, 158*(6), 514–524.

Gaulin, S., & Konner, M. J. (1977). On the natural diet of primates, including humans. In R. J. Wurtman & J. J. Wurtman (Eds.), *Nutrition and the brain.* New York: Raven Press.

Gidron, Y. (2002). Posttraumatic stress disorder after terrorist attacks: A review. *Journal of Nervous and Mental Disease, 190*(2), 118–121.

Gilbertson, M. W., Shenton, M. E., Ciszewski, A., Kasai, K., Lasko, N. B., Orr, S. P., et al. (2002). Smaller hippocampal volume predicts pathologic vulnerability to psychological trauma. *Nature Neuroscience, 5*(11), 1242–1247.

Gorman, J. M., & Kent, J. M. (1999). SSRIs and SNRIs: Broad spectrum of efficacy beyond major depression. *Journal of Clinical Psychiatry, 60*(Suppl. 4), 33–39.

Grabe, H. J., Lange, M., Wolff, B., Volzke, H., Lucht, M., Freyberger, H. J., et al. (2005). Mental and physical distress is modulated by a polymorphism in the 5-HT transporter gene interacting with social stressors and chronic disease burden. *Molecular Psychiatry, 10*(2), 220–224.

Griffin, P. B., & Estioko-Griffin, A. (Eds.). (1985). *The Agta of Northeastern Luzon: Recent studies.* Cebu City, Philippines: San Carlos Publications.

Grisso, T., & Vincent, G. M. (2005). The empirical limits of forensic mental health assessment. *Law & Human Behavior, 29*(1), 1–5.

Hammel, E. A., & Howell, N. (1987). Research in population and culture: An evolutionary framework. *Current Anthropology, 28*(2), 141–160.

Harvey, A. G., & Bryant, R. A. (2002). Acute stress disorder: A synthesis and critique. *Psychological Bulletin, 128*(6), 886–902.

Harvey, P. H. (1990). Life-history variation: Size and mortality patterns. In C. J. DeRousseau (Ed.), *Primate life history and evolution* (pp. 81–88). New York: Wiley-Liss.

Hawkes, K., O'Connell, J. F., & Jones, N. G. (1991). Hunting income patterns among the Hadza: Big game, common goods, foraging goals, and the evolution of the human diet. *Philosophical Transactions of the Royal Society of London. Series B, Biological Sciences, 334*, 243–250.

Haynes, C. A., Miles, J. N. V., & Clements, K. (2000). A confirmatory factor analysis of two models of sensation seeking. *Personality & Individual Differences, 29*(5), 823–839.

Heim, C., Plotsky, P., & Nemeroff, C. (2004). Importance of studying the contributions of early adverse experience to neurobiological findings in depression. *Neuropsychopharmacology 4*, 641–648.

Hewlett, B. S. (1991). Demography and childcare in preindustrial societies. *Journal of Anthropological Research, 47*(1), 1–37.

Hickling, E. J., Blanchard, E. B., Mundy, E., & Galovski, T. E. (2002). Detection of malingered MVA related posttraumatic stress disorder: An investigation of the ability to detect professional actors by experienced clinicians, psychological tests and psychophysiological assessment. *Journal of Forensic Psychology Practice, 2*(1), 33–54.

Hierholzer, R. (2004). Improvement in PTSD patients who care for their grandchildren. *American Journal of Psychiatry, 161*(1), 176–177.

Hill, K., Boesch, C., Goodall, J., Pusey, A., Williams, J., & Wrangham, R. (2001). Mortality rates among wild chimpanzees. *Journal of Human Evolution, 40*(5), 437–450.

Hill, K., & Hurtado, M. (1999). The Aché of Paraguay. In R. B. Lee & R. Daly (Eds.), *The Cambridge encyclopedia of hunters and gatherers* (p. 92). Cambridge, England: Cambridge University Press.

Hoge, C. W., Pavlin, J. A., & Milliken, C. S. (2002). Psychological sequelae of September 11. Comment with author's reply. *New England Journal of Medicine, 347*(6), 443–445.

Holt, N. L., & Dunn, J. G. H. (2004). Toward a grounded theory of the psychosocial competencies and environmental conditions associated with soccer success. *Journal of Applied Sport Psychology, 16*(3), 199–219.

Howell, N. (1979). *Demography of the Dobe !Kung.* New York: Academic Press, 1979.

Hull, A. M. (2002). Neuroimaging findings in post-traumatic stress. *British Journal of Psychiatry, 181*(2), 102–110.

Hurtado, A. M., Hawkes, K., Hill, K., & Kaplan, H. (1985). Female subsistence strategies among Ache hunter-gatherers of Eastern Paraguay. *Human Ecology, 13*, 1–27.

Jacobsen, P. B., Sadler, I. J., Booth-Jones, M., Soety, E., Weitzner, M. A., & Fields, K. K. (2002). Predictors of posttraumatic stress disorder symptomatology following bone marrow transplantation for cancer. *Journal of Consulting and Clinical Psychology, 70*(1), 235–240.

Johnsen, B. H., Eid, J., Laberg, J. C., & Thayer, J. F. (2002). The effect of sensitization and coping style on post-traumatic stress symptoms and quality of life: Two longitudinal studies. *Scandinavian Journal of Psychology, 43*(2), 181–188.

Johnson, S. D., North, C. S., & Smith, E. M. (2002). Psychiatric disorders among victims of a courthouse shooting spree: A three-year follow-up study. *Community Mental Health Journal, 38*(3), 181–194.

Jones, E., Vermaas, R. H., McCartney, H., Beech, C., Palmer, I., Hyams, K., et al. (2003). Flashbacks and post-traumatic stress disorder: The genesis of a 20th-century diagnosis. *British Journal of Psychiatry, 182*, 158–163.

Jones, E., & Wessely, S. (2004). Hearts, guts and minds: Somatisation in the military from 1900. *Journal of Psychosomatic Research, 56*(4), 425–429.

Kanapaux, W. (2002). ADHD – Overcoming the specter of overdiagnosis. *Psychiatric Times, XIX*(8), http://www.psychiatrictimes.com/showArticle.jhtml?articleID=175802195.

Kaplan, A. (2001). Sept. 11 – Anticipated mental health consequences and what we can do now. http://www.healthrising.com/stories/sept11.html.

Kaplan, Z., Weiser, M., Reichenberg, A., Rabinowitz, J., Caspi, A., Bodner, E., et al. (2002). Motivation to serve in the military influences vulnerability to future posttraumatic stress disorder. *Psychiatry Research, 109*(1), 45–49.

Kardiner, A. (1941). *The traumatic neuroses of war*. Washington, DC: National research council, Committee on problems of neurotic behavior [Menasha, Wis.: George Banta publishing company].

Keeley, L. H. (1996). *War before civilization: The myth of the peaceful savage*. New York: Oxford University Press.

Keenleyside, A. (1998). Skeletal evidence of health and disease in pre-contact Alaskan Eskimos and Aleuts. *American Journal of Physical Anthropology, 107*(1), 51–70.

Kelly, R. L. (1995). *The foraging spectrum: Diversity in hunter-gatherer lifeways*. Washington, DC: Smithsonian Institution Press.

Kendler, K. S., Kuhn, J. W., Vittum, J., Prescott, C. A., & Riley, B. (2005). The interaction of stressful life events and a serotonin transporter polymorphism in the prediction of episodes of major depression: A replication. *Archives of General Psychiatry, 62*(5), 529–535.

Kendler, K. S., Neale, M. C., Kessler, R. C., Heath, A. C., & Eaves, L. J. (1992). Major depression and generalized anxiety disorder: Same genes, (partly) different environments. *Archives of General Psychiatry, 49*, 716–722.

Kilts, C. (2003). In vivo neuroimaging correlates of the efficacy of paroxetine in the treatment of mood and anxiety disorders. *Psychopharmacology Bulletin, 37*(Suppl. 1), 19–28.

Koenen, K. C. (1999). *The comorbidity of post-traumatic stress disorder and antisocial personality disorder: An epidemiological and genetic study (men, twins)*. Unpublished manuscript, Boston University, Boston, MA.

Koenen, K. C., Lyons, M. J., Goldberg, J., Simpson, J., Williams, W. M., Toomey, R., et al. (2003). A high risk twin study of combat-related PTSD comorbidity. *Twin Research, 6*(3), 218–226.

Konner, M. (1995). Anthropology and psychiatry. In H. Kaplan & B. Sadock (Eds.), *Comprehensive textbook of psychiatry* (6th ed., pp. 283–299). Baltimore: Williams and Wilkins.

Konner, M. (2005). Hunter-gatherer infancy and childhood: The !Kung and others. In B. S. Hewlett & M. E. Lamb (Eds.), *Hunter-gatherer childhoods: Evolutionary, developmental & cultural perspectives*. New Brunswick, NJ: AldineTransaction Publishers.

Konner, M. J. (2002). *The tangled wing: Biological constraints on the human spirit* (2nd ed.). New York: Holt/Times Books.

Konner, M. J., & Shostak, M. J. (1986). Adolescent pregnancy and childbearing: An anthropological perspective. In J. B. Lancaster & B. A. Hamburg (Eds.), *School-age pregnancy and childbearing: Biosocial dimensions*. New York: Aldine.

Konner, M. J., & Shostak, M. J. (1987). Timing and management of birth among the !Kung: Biocultural interaction in reproductive adaptation. *Cultural Anthropology, 2*, 11–28.

Krueger, R. F. (1999). The structure of common mental disorders. *Archives of General Psychiatry, 56*(10), 921–926.

LeBlanc, S., & Register, K. E. (2003). *Constant battles: The myth of the peaceful, noble savage*. New York: St. Martin's Press.

Lee, K. A., Vaillant, G. E., Torrey, W. C., & Elder, G. H. (1995). A 50-year prospective study of the psychological sequelae of World War II combat. *American Journal of Psychiatry, 152*(4), 516–522.

Lee, R. B. (1979). *The !Kung San. Men, women and work in a foraging society.* Cambridge, England: Cambridge University Press.

Lee, R. B. (1982). The sociology of !Kung bushman trance performances. In R. Prince (Ed.), *Trance and possession states.* Montreal: R. M. Bucke Memorial Society.

Lee, R. B., & Daly, R. (Eds.). (1999). *The Cambridge encyclopedia of hunters and gatherers.* Cambridge, England: Cambridge University Press.

Lee, R. B., & DeVore, I. (1968a). *Man the hunter.* Chicago: Aldine.

Lee, R. B., & DeVore, I. (1968b). Problems in the study of hunters and gatherers. In R. B. Lee & I. DeVore (Eds.), *Man the hunter* (pp. 3–12). Chicago: Aldine.

Lee, R. B., & DeVore, I. (Eds.). (1976). *Kalahari hunter-gatherers: Studies of the !Kung San and their neighbors.* Cambridge, MA: Harvard University Press.

Liddell, B. J., Brown, K. J., Kemp, A. H., Barton, M. J., Das, P., Peduto, A., et al. (2005). A direct brainstem-amygdala-cortical "alarm" system for subliminal signals of fear. *Neuroimage, 24*(1), 235–243.

Lindahl, M. W. (2004). A new development in PTSD and the law: The case of Fairfax County v. Mottram. *Journal of Traumatic Stress, 17*(6), 543–546.

Lindauer, R. J. L., Vlieger, E.-J., Jalink, M., Olff, M., Carlier, I. V. E., Majoie, C. B. L. M., et al. (2004). Smaller hippocampal volume in Dutch police officers with posttraumatic stress disorder. *Biological Psychiatry, 56*(5), 356–363.

Loftus, E. F. (1993). The reality of repressed memories. *American Psychologist, 48*(5), 518–537.

Loftus, E. F. (2000). Remembering what never happened. In E. Tulving (Ed.), *Memory, consciousness, and the brain: The Tallinn Conference* (pp. 106–118). Philadelphia: Psychology Press.

Loftus, E. F. (2003). Make-believe memories. *American Psychologist, 58*(11), 867–873.

Lynn, E. J., & Belza, M. (1984). Factitious posttraumatic stress disorder: The veteran who never got to Vietnam. *Hospital & Community Psychiatry, 35*(7), 697–701.

Marshall, L. (1976a). *The !Kung of Nyae Nyae.* Cambridge, MA: Harvard University Press.

Marshall, L. (1976b). Sharing, talking, and giving: Relief of social tensions among the !Kung. In R. B. Lee & I. DeVore (Eds.), *Kalahari hunter-gatherers: Studies of the !Kung San and their neighbors* (pp. 349–371). Cambridge, MA: Harvard University Press.

Marshall, L. (1981). The medicine dance of the !Kung bushmen. *Africa, 39*, 347–381.

Martin-Krumm, C. P., Sarrazin, P. G., Peterson, C., & Famose, J.-P. (2003). Explanatory style and resilience after sports failure. *Personality & Individual Differences, 35*(7), 1685–1695.

Masten, A. S. (2001). Ordinary magic. Resilience processes in development. *American Psychologist, 56*(3), 227–238.

Mayou, R. A., Ehlers, A., & Bryant, B. (2002). Posttraumatic stress disorder after motor vehicle accidents: 3-year follow-up of a prospective longitudinal study. *Behaviour Research and Therapy, 40*(6), 665–675.

McCormick, H. (2001, January 7). The boating report: Britain follows the exploits of a folk hero. *New York Times,* final edition, sec. 8, p. 7.

McHugh, P. R. (1995). Witches, multiple personalities, and other psychiatric artifacts. *Nature Medicine, 1*(2), 110–114.

McHugh, P. R. (1999). How psychiatry lost its way. *Commentary, 108*, 32–38.

McHugh, P. R., Lief, H. I., Freyd, P. P., & Fetkewicz, J. M. (2004). From refusal to reconciliation: Family relationships after an accusation based on recovered memories. *Journal of Nervous and Mental Disease, 192*(8), 525–531.

McHugh, P. R., & Putnam, F. W. (1995). Resolved: Multiple personality disorder is an individually and socially created artifact. *Journal of the American Academy of Child & Adolescent Psychiatry, 34*(7), 957–962; discussion 962–953.

McKeown, T. (1995). *The origins of human disease.* Oxford, England: Blackwell.

McNally, R. J. (2003a). Psychological mechanisms in acute response to trauma. *Biological Psychiatry, 53*(9), 779–786.

McNally, R. J. (2003b). *Remembering trauma.* Cambridge, MA: Harvard University Press.

Metzger, B. E., Bybee, D. E., Freinkel, N., Phelps, R. L., Radvany, R. M., & Vaisrub, N. (1985). Gestational diabetes mellitus. Correlations between the phenotypic and genotypic characteristics of the mother and abnormal glucose tolerance during the first year postpartum. *Diabetes, 34*(Suppl. 2), 111–115.

Mollica, R. F., Henderson, D. C., & Tor, S. (2002). Psychiatric effects of traumatic brain injury events in Cambodian survivors of mass violence. *British Journal of Psychiatry, 181*(4), 339–347.

Mummery, W., Schofield, G., & Perry, C. (2004). Bouncing back: The role of coping style, social support and self-concept in resilience of sport performance. *Athletic Insight: Online Journal of Sport Psychology, 6*(3), http://www.athleticinsight.com/Vol6Iss3/BouncingBack.htm.

Neria, Y., Solomon, Z., Ginzburg, K., & Dekel, R. (2000). Sensation seeking, wartime performance, and long-term adjustment among Israeli war veterans. *Personality & Individual Differences, 29*(5), 921–932.

Nesse, R. M., & Lloyd, A. T. (1992). The evolution of psychodynamic mechanisms. In J. H. Barkow, L. Cosmides, & J. Tooby (Eds.), *The adapted mind: Evolutionary psychology and the generation of culture* (pp. 601–624). New York: Oxford University Press.

Newport, D. J., Heim, C., Bonsall, R., Miller, A. H., & Nemeroff, C. B. (2004). Pituitary-adrenal responses to standard and low-dose dexamethasone suppression tests in adult survivors of child abuse. *Biological Psychiatry, 55*(1), 10–20.

Norris, D. O. (1997). *Vertebrate endocrinology* (3rd ed.). San Diego: Academic Press.

North, C. S., Tivis, L., McMillen, J. C., Pfefferbaum, B., Spitznagel, E. L., Cox, J., et al. (2002). Psychiatric disorders in rescue workers after the Oklahoma City bombing. *American Journal of Psychiatry, 159*(5), 857–859.

Nuckolls, C. W. (Ed.). (1992). The cultural construction of diagnostic categories: The case of American psychiatry [Special issue]. *Social Science and Medicine, 35*(1).

Ofshe, R., & Waters, E. (1994). *Making monsters: False memories, psychotherapy, and sexual hysteria.* New York: Charles Scribner's Sons.

Ohman, A. (2005). The role of the amygdala in human fear: Automatic detection of threat. *Psychoneuroendocrinology, 30*(10), 953–958.

Orr, S. P., Metzger, L. J., Lasko, N. B., Macklin, M. L., Hu, F. B., Shalev, A. Y., et al. (2003). Physiologic responses to sudden, loud tones in monozygotic twins discordant for combat exposure: Association with posttraumatic stress disorder. *Archives of General Psychiatry, 60*(3), 283–288.

O'Sullivan, J. B. (1991). Diabetes mellitus after GDM. *Diabetes, 40*(Suppl. 2), 131–135.

Ozer, E. J., Best, S. R., Lipsey, T. L., & Weiss, D. S. (2003). Predictors of posttraumatic stress disorder and symptoms in adults: A meta-analysis. *Psychological Bulletin, 129*(1), 52–73.

Peacock, N. R. (1991). Rethinking the sexual division of labor: Reproduction and women's work among the Efe. In M. di Leonardo (Ed.), *Gender at the crossroads of knowledge: Feminist anthropology in the postmodern era* (pp. 339–360). Berkeley: University of California Press.

Peterson, C., & Seligman, M. E. P. (2003). Character strengths before and after September 11. *Psychological Science, 14*(4), 381–384.

Pitman, R. K., & Sparr, L. F. (1998). PTSD and the law. *PTSD Research Quarterly, 9*(2), 1–8.

Pope, H., & Lipinski, J. (1978). Diagnosis in schizophrenia and manic-depressive illness. *Archives of General Psychiatry, 35,* 811.

Reinhard, K., Fink, T. M., & Skiles, J. (2003). A case of megacolon in Rio Grande valley as a possible case of Chagas disease. *Memorias do Instituto Oswaldo Cruz, 98*(Suppl. 1), 165–172.

Robertson, J. (2005). Joseph Robertson, age 86, talks to his son-in-law about a World War II experience [Radio broadcast; Webcast at http://www.npr.org/templates/story/story.php?storyId=5008155], *NPR StoryCorps Oral History Project.* USA: National Public Radio.

Roemer, L., Litz, B. T., Orsillo, S. M., Ehlich, P. J., & Friedman, M. J. (1998). Increases in retrospective accounts of war-zone exposure over time: The role of PTSD symptom severity. *Journal of Traumatic Stress, 11*(3), 597–605.

Rose, S., Bisson, J., Churchill, R., & Wessely, S. (2002). Psychological debriefing for preventing post traumatic stress disorder (PTSD) [update of *Cochrane Database Systemic Reviews, 3,* CD000560; PMID: 11686967]. *Cochrane Database of Systematic Reviews, 2,* CD000560.

Rose, S., Bisson, J., & Wessely, S. (2003). A systematic review of single-session psychological interventions ('debriefing') following trauma. *Psychotherapy & Psychosomatics, 72*(4), 176–184.

Rosen, G. M. (1996). Posttraumatic stress disorder, pulp fiction, and the press. *Bulletin of the American Academy of Psychiatry & the Law, 24*(2), 267–269.

Rosenhan, D. L. (1973). On being sane in insane places. *Science, 179,* 250–258.

Rosenheck, R., Fontana, A., & Errera, P. (1997). Inpatient treatment of war-related posttraumatic stress disorder: A 20-year perspective. *Journal of Traumatic Stress, 10*(3), 407–413.

Rothbaum, B. O., & Schwartz, A. C. (2002). Exposure therapy for posttraumatic stress disorder. *American Journal of Psychotherapy, 56*(1), 59–75.

Roy-Byrne, P., Arguelles, L., Vitek, M. E., Goldberg, J., Keane, T. M., True, W. R., et al. (2004). Persistence and change of PTSD symptomatology: A longitudinal co-twin control analysis of the Vietnam Era Twin Registry. *Social Psychiatry and Psychiatric Epidemiology, 39*(9), 681–685.

Rutter, M. (1998). Routes from research to clinical practice in child psychiatry: Retrospect and prospect. *Journal of Child Psychology and Psychiatry, 39*(6), 805–816.

Sanchez, M. M., Ladd, C. O., & Plotsky, P. M. (2001). Early adverse experience as a developmental risk factor for later psychopathology: Evidence from rodent and primate models. *Development and Psychopathology, 13*(3), 419–449.

Sanchez, M. M., Noble, P. M., Lyon, C. K., Plotsky, P. M., Davis, M., Nemeroff, C. B., et al. (2005). Alterations in diurnal cortisol rhythm and acoustic startle response in nonhuman primates with adverse rearing. *Biological Psychiatry, 57*(4), 373–381.

Sapolsky, R. M. (1992a). Neuroendocrinology of the stress-response. In J. B. Becker, S. M. Breedlove, & D. Crews (Eds.), *Behavioral endocrinology* (pp. 287–324). Cambridge, MA: MIT Press.

Sapolsky, R. M. (1992b). *Stress, the aging brain, and the mechanisms of neuron death.* Cambridge, MA: MIT Press.

Sapolsky, R. M. (2001). *A primate's memoir: A neuroscientist's unconventional life among the baboons.* New York: Scribner.

Sapolsky, R. M. (2002). Chicken, eggs and hippocampal atrophy. *Nature Neuroscience, 5*(11), 1111–1113.

Sapolsky, R. M., Romero, L. M., & Munck, A. U. (2000). How do glucocorticoids influence stress responses? Integrating permissive, suppressive, stimulatory, and preparative actions. *Endocrine Reviews, 21*(1), 55–89.

Schinke, R. J., & Jerome, W. C. (2002). Understanding and refining the resilience of elite athletes: An intervention strategy. *Athletic Insight: Online Journal of Sport Psychology, 4*(3), http://www.athleticinsight.com/Vol4Iss3/ResilienceIntervention.htm.

Schnurr, P. P., Friedman, M. J., & Bernardy, N. C. (2002). Research on posttraumatic stress disorder: Epidemiology, pathophysiology, and assessment. *Journal of Clinical Psychology, 58*(8), 877–889.

Schnyder, U., Moergeli, H., Klaghofer, R., & Buddeberg, C. (2001). Incidence and prediction of posttraumatic stress disorder symptoms in severely injured accident victims. *American Journal of Psychiatry, 158*(4), 594–599.

Schoenfeld, F. B., Marmar, C. R., & Neylan, T. C. (2004). Current concepts in pharmacotherapy for posttraumatic stress disorder. *Psychiatric Services, 55*(5), 519–531.

Selye, H. (1936). A syndrome produced by diverse nocuous agents. *Nature, 138*, 32.

Selye, H. (1975). Stress and distress. *Comprehensive Therapy, 1*(8), 9–13.

Selye, H. (1976). Forty years of stress research: Principal remaining problems and misconceptions. *Canadian Medical Association Journal, 115*(1), 53–56.

Selye, H. (1998). A syndrome produced by diverse nocuous agents. *Journal of Neuropsychiatry & Clinical Neurosciences, 10*(2), 230–231. (Original work published 1936)

Shalev, A. Y., Freedman, S., Peri, T., Brandes, D., Sahar, T., Orr, S. P., et al. (1998). Prospective study of posttraumatic stress disorder and depression following trauma. *American Journal of Psychiatry, 155*(5), 630–637.

Shostak, M. (1981). *Nisa: The life and words of a !Kung woman.* Cambridge, MA: Harvard University Press.

Shostak, M. (2000). *Return to Nisa.* Cambridge, MA: Harvard University Press.

Sibai, B. M., el-Nazer, A., & Gonzalez-Ruiz, A. (1986). Severe preeclampsia-eclampsia in young primigravid women: Subsequent pregnancy outcome and remote prognosis. *American Journal of Obstetrics & Gynecology, 155*(5), 1011–1016.

Silberbauer, G. B. (1981). *Hunter and habitat in the central Kalahari desert.* Cambridge, England: Cambridge University Press.

Smith, M. A., Davidson, J., Ritchie, J. C., Kudler, H., Lipper, S., Chappell, P., et al. (1989). The corticotropin-releasing hormone test in patients with posttraumatic stress disorder. *Biological Psychiatry, 26*(4), 349–355.

Southwick, S. M., Morgan, C., Nicolaou, A. L., & Charney, D. S. (1997). Consistency of memory for combat-related traumatic events in veterans of Operation Desert Storm. *American Journal of Psychiatry, 154*(2), 173–177.

Southwick, S. M., Yehuda, R., & Giller, E. L. (1993). Personality disorders in treatment-seeking combat veterans with posttraumatic stress disorder. *American Journal of Psychiatry, 150*(7), 1020–1023.

Sparr, L., & Pankratz, L. D. (1983). Factitious posttraumatic stress disorder. *American Journal of Psychiatry, 140*(8), 1016–1019.

Sparr, L. F., & Pitman, R. K. (Eds.). (1999). *Forensic assessment of traumatized adults.* In P. A. Saigh & J. D. Bremner (Eds.), *Posttraumatic stress disorder: A comprehensive text* (pp. 284–308). Boston: Allyn and Bacon.

Stein, M. B., Jang, K. L., Taylor, S., Vernon, P. A., & Livesley, W. J. (2002). Genetic and environmental influences on trauma exposure and posttraumatic stress disorder symptoms: A twin study. *American Journal of Psychiatry, 159*(10), 1675–1681.

Stephenson, J. (2001). Medical, mental health communities mobilize to cope with terror's psychological aftermath. *Journal of the American Medical Association, 286*(15), 1823–1825.

Summerfield, D. (2002). ICD and DSM are contemporary cultural documents. *British Medical Journal, 324*(7342), 914.

Suomi, S. J. (2002). Parents, peers, and the process of socialization in primates. In J. G. Borkowski, S. L. Ramey, & M. Bristol-Power (Eds.), *Parenting and the child's world: Influences on academic, intellectual, and social-emotional development* (pp. 265–279). Mahwah, NJ: Lawrence Erlbaum.

Super, C., Kagan, J., Morrison, F., Haith, M., & Weiffenbach, J. (1972). Discrepancy and attention in the five-month infant. *Genetic Psychology Monographs, 85,* 305–331.

Tague, R. G. (1994). Maternal mortality or prolonged growth: Age at death and pelvic size in three prehistoric Amerindian populations. *American Journal of Physical Anthropology, 95*(1), 27–40.

Tan, H. H., Tan, H. K., Lim, H. S., Tan, A. S. A., & Lim, S. C. (2002). Gestational diabetes mellitus: A call for systematic tracing. *Annals of the Academy of Medicine, Singapore, 31*(3), 281–284.

Tennant, C. (2004). Psychological trauma: Psychiatry and the law in conflict. *Australian and New Zealand Journal of Psychiatry, 38*(5), 344–347.

Terkel, S. (1984). *"The good war": An oral history of World War Two.* New York: Pantheon Books.

Ursin, H., & Kaada, B. R. (1960). Functional localization with the amygdaloid complex in the cat. *Electroencephalography and Clinical Neurology, 12,* 1–20.

Vaillant, G. (1977). *Adaptation to life.* Boston: Little, Brown.

Vaillant, G. E. (1993). *The wisdom of the ego.* Cambridge, MA: Harvard University Press.

Vaswani, M., Linda, F. K., & Ramesh, S. (2003). Role of selective serotonin reuptake inhibitors in psychiatric disorders: A comprehensive review. *Progress in Neuro-Psychopharmacology & Biological Psychiatry, 27*(1), 85–102.

Villarreal, G., Hamilton, D. A., Petropoulos, H., Driscoll, I., Rowland, L. M., Griego, J. A., et al. (2002). Reduced hippocampal volume and total white matter volume in posttraumatic stress disorder. *Biological Psychiatry, 52*(2), 119–125.

Wang, W., Wu, Y.-X., Peng, Z.-G., Lu, S.-W., Yu, L., Wang, G.-P., et al. (2000). Test of sensation seeking in a Chinese sample. *Personality & Individual Differences, 28*(1), 169–179.

Werner, E. E. (1989). High-risk children in young adulthood: A longitudinal study from birth to 32 years. *American Journal of Orthopsychiatry, 59*(1), 72–81.

Werner, E. E. (1997). Vulnerable but invincible: High-risk children from birth to adulthood. *Acta Paediatrica Supplement, 422*, 103–105.

Werner, E. E., & Smith, R. S. (2001). *Journeys from childhood to midlife: Risk, resilience, and recovery.* Ithaca, NY: Cornell University Press.

Wessely, S. (2005). Victimhood and resilience. *New England Journal of Medicine, 353*(6), 548–550.

Wessely, S., & Deahl, M. (2003). Psychological debriefing is a waste of time. *British Journal of Psychiatry, 183*, 12–14.

Wessely, S., Unwin, C., Hotopf, M., Hull, L., Ismail, K., Nicolaou, V., et al. (2003). Stability of recall of military hazards over time. Evidence from the Persian Gulf War of 1991. *British Journal of Psychiatry, 183*, 314–322.

Whiting, M. (1958). *A cross-cultural nutrition survey.* Unpublished doctoral dissertation, Harvard School of Public Health, Cambridge, MA.

Wiessner, P. (1982). Risk, reciprocity and social influences on !Kung San economics. In E. Leacock & R. B. Lee (Eds.), *Politics and history in band societies.* Cambridge, England: Cambridge University Press.

Wiessner, P. (1996). Leveling the hunter: Constraints on the status quest in foraging societies. In P. Wiessner & W. Schiefenhövel (Eds.), *Food and the status quest: An interdisciplinary perspective* (pp. 171–191). Providence: Berghahn Books.

Wilhelm, J. H. (1953). Die !Kung-Buschleute. *Jahrbuch des Museums für Völkerkunde Leipzig, 12*, 91–189.

Williams, W. H., Evans, J. J., Wilson, B. A., & Needham, P. (2002). Prevalence of post-traumatic stress disorder symptoms after severe traumatic brain injury in a representative community sample. *Brain Injury, 16*(8), 673–679.

Winterhalder, B., & Smith, E. A. (Eds.). (1981). *Hunter-gatherer foraging strategies: Ethnographic and archeological analyses.* Chicago: University of Chicago Press.

Wright, L. (1994). *Remembering Satan.* New York: Alfred A. Knopf.

Yehuda, R. (2002a). Current status of cortisol findings in post-traumatic stress disorder. *Psychiatric Clinics of North America, 25*(2), 341–368, vii.

Yehuda, R. (2002b). Post-traumatic stress disorder. *New England Journal of Medicine, 346*(2), 108–114.

Young, A. (1995). *The harmony of illusions: Inventing post-traumatic stress disorder.* Princeton, NJ: Princeton University Press.

Young, A. (2000). An alternative history of traumatic stress. In D. Meichenbaum (Series Ed.) & A. Y. Shalev, R. Yehuda, & A. C. McFarlane (Vol. Eds.), *The Plenum series on stress and coping: International handbook of human response to trauma* (pp. 51–66). New York: Kluwer/Plenum.

Young, E. A., & Breslau, N. (2004). Cortisol and catecholamines in posttraumatic stress disorder: An epidemiologic community study. *Archives of General Psychiatry, 61*(4), 394–401.

Zald, D. H. (2003). The human amygdala and the emotional evaluation of sensory stimuli. *Brain Research Reviews, 41*(1), 88–123.

Zelazo, P. R., & Komer, M. J. (1971). Infant smiling to nonsocial stimuli and the recognition hypothesis. *Child Development, 42,* 1327–1339.

Zlotnick, C., Rodriguez, B. F., Weisberg, R. B., Bruce, S. E., Spencer, M. A., Culpepper, L., et al. (2004). Chronicity in posttraumatic stress disorder and predictors of the course of posttraumatic stress disorder among primary care patients. *Journal of Nervous and Mental Disease, 192*(2), 153–159.

Zuckerman, M. (1984). Sensation seeking: A comparative approach to a human trait. *Behavioral and Brain Sciences, 7,* 413–471.

Zuckerman, M. (1990). The psychophysiology of sensation seeking. *Journal of Personality, 58,* 313–345.

Zuckerman, M., Buchsbaum, M. S., & Murphy, D. L. (1980). Sensation seeking and its biological correlates. *Psychological Bulletin, 88,* 187–214.

Zuckerman, M., & Kuhlman, D. M. (2000). Personality and risk-taking: Common biosocial factors. *Journal of Personality, 68*(6), 999–1029.

16

Bruno and the Holy Fool: Myth, Mimesis, and the Transmission of Traumatic Memories

Allan Young

One of the ways in which people make collective sense of the world is by connecting the present time to past time through participation in myth and ritual. In some rituals, people make the connection through conventional symbols and perfunctory displays of emotion. The annual Remembrance Day ceremony in Britain and Canada, commemorating the war dead, is an example. In another class of rituals, people engage the past through myth and mimesis. By *myth* I mean a narrative that is historically problematic and is shared by a group of people who believe that it is credible, explains their collective identity, and illuminates their present condition. The "truth" of these narratives and collective memories resides less in their "factuality" than their "actuality" (Assmann, 1997, p. 9). *Mimesis* refers to efforts, often in the context of ritual, aimed at imitating or identifying with people and tropes (figurative descriptions of people) from the past.

This chapter explores how myth and mimesis are linked to trauma and its signature condition, posttraumatic stress disorder (PTSD). For reasons that will become obvious, I begin with an old ritual, the Passover *seder*, and an even older myth, the Exodus narrative. The seder comprises a ritual meal and a collection of recitations, prayers, and songs, set down in a text called a *haggadah*. In the course of the seder, participants are admonished to identify themselves with their ancestors' experiences during their bondage in Egypt and the journey through the Sinai. The elements of the ritual meal – unleavened bread, bitter herbs, salt water, and so forth – are symbolic of the harshness of life in bondage and the desert. The earliest haggadahs date to the tenth century. Thousands of versions have circulated since then: traditional Ashkenazi versions and Sephardi versions, as well as recent versions tailored to the sensibilities of vegetarians, socialists, secular humanists, Jews for Jesus, and others.

We might include Sigmund Freud's final monograph, *Moses and Monotheism* (1939/1959), among these texts. In Freud's Exodus narrative, there were two Moses. The first Moses was an Egyptian prince who led the Hebrew slaves out of Egypt and imposed an exacting form of ethical monotheism that Freud traced to the Pharaoh Akhenaten. After a while, the Hebrews grew weary of this austere code, and they murdered Moses. Their memory of the murder and Mosaic monotheism were then forgotten (repressed). A century later, their descendants united with a tribe of monotheistic Semites, the Midianites, whose leader was also called Moses. The repressed memories were now recalled: Freud called this "the return of the repressed." As time passed, the population conflated the two monotheistic deities: the abstract, ethical god of the Egyptian Moses and the vengeful volcano god of the Midianites. Once more, the murder and the Mosaic religion were forgotten. Centuries later, the principles of ethical monotheism returned to group consciousness, but memory of the murder remained repressed and a source of unconscious collective guilt. This situation continues in our own time.[1]

Freud had two goals in writing *Moses and Monotheism*. First, he "wanted to explain the origin of the special character of the Jewish people, a character which is probably what has made their survival to the present day possible." And he concluded that "the man Moses impressed this character on them by giving them a religion which increased their self-esteem so much that they thought themselves superior to all other peoples." The Mosaic religion had also "forced upon the people an advance in intellectuality which, important enough in itself, opened the way, in addition, to the appreciation of intellectual work and to further renunciations of instinct" (Freud 1939/1959, p. 123). Freud's second goal was to find the source of the virulent strain of anti-Semitism that continued to afflict the Jews. Christianity had departed from Judaism by rejecting Jewish exceptionalism ("the chosen people") and by memorializing the murder of the Egyptian Moses through the crucifixion story. And these facts explain Christianity's traditional reproach to the Jews: "They will not accept it as true that they murdered God, whereas we admit it and have been cleansed of that guilt." The Jews, for their part, have found it impossible to admit that they did indeed murder God (Moses). "In a certain sense they have in that way taken a tragic load of guilt on themselves; they have been made to pay a heavy penance for it" (Freud, 1939/1959, p. 136; cf. Lacoue-Labarthe & Nancy, 1989).

---

[1] Freud cites Ernst Sellin's *Mose und seine Bedeutung für die israelistisch-jüdische Religionsgeschichte* (Sellin, 1922) in support of his historical reconstruction. "Indeed, the correlations to *Moses and Monotheism* are so striking that we must wonder if Sellin's work merely confirmed Freud's prior intuition or whether it was the reading of the book that triggered his own thinking" (Yerushalmi, 1991, p. 25). At the time of publication, Sellin's account was regarded by historians of ancient Egypt as mere speculation, and it is remembered today only because of its connection to Freud. See Assmann (1997, chap. 5) for an expert's assessment.

MYTH, RITUAL, AND THEORY

Myth

Freud's myth explains three origins: Jewish collective identity, Christianity, and anti-Semitism. It is organized around the following claims. The Jews are a historical product, created by a man (the Egyptian Moses). The originary event (the return of the repressed) was the perpetrators' posttraumatic reaction to their crime (the memory of the murder, rather than the murder). Everything that happens later in the myth is secondary to this event. Like the Passover seder, *Moses and Monotheism* discloses a past that is not dead because it is not even past. The seder's theme is that Jews in the diaspora follow a path of the Hebrews crossing the Sinai, toward a redemptive arrival in the land of Israel. Freud's theme is that the situation of Jews in anti-Semitic Europe (c. 1939) was predetermined by their collective past and their repressed memory of the murder of Moses.

Ritual

The seder's ritual meal restricts participatory access to the past (the Exodus) to Jews. These participants are enjoined to experience the narrated events of the Exodus as though it is it happening to you now. *Moses and Monotheism* provides another possibility, engagement through an unrestricted medium – via the transmission of traumatic memory (the "return of the repressed"). In Freud's account, transmission is a transgenerational phenomenon incorporating a lapse:

A traumatized generation → *B* amnesic generations → *C* return of the repressed

Theory

Freud died soon after finishing *Moses and Monotheism*, having written nothing more about the mythic potential of traumatic memory. Interest in the subject reemerged during the 1990s, in a discourse now called *trauma theory*. The theory reflects the continuing interest in Freud and psychoanalytic ideas in North American and Western European universities and developments dating to the 1970s: the successful struggle to make traumatic memory part of post-*DSM–III* American psychiatry, and the growing popularity of memory-based (postmodern) theories of knowledge in the humanities and social sciences. Trauma theory picks up where Freud left off – the genealogy is explicit – and makes the transgenerational phenomenon described in *Moses and Monotheism* our template – that is to say, the means with which we might collectively engage our own collective traumatic past in order to fully grasp our unique historical condition. Our collective trauma is the Holocaust.

At first glance there seems to be a disconnection between what happened in *Moses and Monotheism* and the Holocaust, undermining the psychological appropriateness of the template. Generation A is composed of perpetrators, whereas the Holocaust Jews are victims. But trauma theory asks us to understand that the two groups are equal in the crucial sense: They are equally traumatized, even if the slayers of Moses are self-traumatized perpetrators. What is the transmission mechanism of trauma across generations? How might memory survive the utter forgetfulness of the B generations? We must be able to answer this question if we are to justify and understand our own traumatic connection to the Holocaust.

SOLUTION 1: LATENCY

This solution is based on the idea that individual trauma (PTSD) and collective trauma (the murder of the Egyptian Moses) are intrinsically similar. According to the theory, "latency" or "belatedness" is an inevitable feature of individual trauma. In *Moses and Monotheism*, it is revealed in the amnesia of the B generations. To understand what Freud is describing here, the theory says, one must first understand the meaning of latency in clinical cases of PTSD. So the following progression of templates is proposed:

PSTD → collective memory in generation *C* → collective memory today
latency X   *latency Y*   *latency Z*

This theory claims that "the theory of individual trauma contains within it the core of the trauma of a larger history." The relation between individual and collective is intrinsic, not analogic: "historical or generational trauma is in some sense presupposed in the theory of individual trauma, which is what I believe is implicit in Freud's texts" (Caruth, 1992, pp. 71 and 136; see also pp. 6, 7, 17, 23, 62, 101).

Latency is inevitable because trauma is initially incomprehensible; it "takes place too soon, too suddenly, too unexpectedly, to be fully grasped by consciousness" (Caruth, 1996, p. 4). Trauma's meaning is completely understood only retrospectively – a condition that Freud called *Nachträglichkeit*, or afterwardness. Collective memory of the Holocaust follows the pattern exactly. The return of the repressed occurs in the early 1960s, with the Eichmann trial in Jerusalem. Previous to the trial, the "Holocaust" did not exist. That is to say, although evidence of the existence of the death camps had circulated since 1942, the Holocaust did not exist as a discrete, knowable trauma for another two decades. Although Israel received 300,000 survivors, there were few efforts to commemorate the Holocaust before 1960. Contemporary literature, historiography, school texts, and official events targeted resistors – ghetto fighters and partisans – rather than victims (Zertal, 2000, p. 101).[2] The historical basis for this claim, that latency is inevitable, spans the entire period of medical interest in posttraumatic syndromes, from "railway spine," to which Freud calls attention in *Moses and Monotheism*, to current work on PTSD (for a historical perspective, see Leys, 2000; Micale & Lerner, 2001; Young, 1995).

Trauma theory presumes that latency is a single thing during this period, and this justifies believing that latencies *X*, *Y*, and *Z* are intrinsically similar. But the presumption is incorrect: The phenomena that the theory describes as latency are not one thing but rather four kinds:

1. *Posttraumatic amnesia*. The victim cannot retrieve his traumatic memory unassisted. This is trauma theory's paradigmatic case.
2. *Delayed-onset PTSD*. The posttraumatic syndrome is preceded by an asymptomatic period, during which declarative memory of the traumatic event is continuous. Trauma theory presumes that, during the asymptomatic period, traumatic memory remains dormant like the disorder's other features or, alternatively, the event is remembered but its meaning and significance are inaccessible.
3. *Traumatic memory fails to consolidate*. This condition is associated with severe *shock* (surprise plus sensory overload) or neurological immaturity (trauma experienced by very young children). The consensus in neuropsychiatry is that no episodic memory is formed in these circumstances. Trauma theory claims otherwise: There is a memory; it cannot be represented (narrated) but is acted out, typically as a "body memory."
4. *Displacement*. This condition was often observed by army doctors during World War I and is the basis for Freud's comments on traumatic neurosis in *Beyond the Pleasure Principle* (Freud 1920/1950). In these cases, the posttraumatic syndrome is created through a sequence of etiological events. An initial shock (typically a concussive explosion) is followed by a period of unconsciousness, followed by a frightening second event (e.g., the victim awakes and discovers that he is buried alive). There is no episodic memory of the shock, but the individual's memory of the second event is continuous. Trauma theory conflates the events, reducing type 4 to type 3 (no declarative memory).

In other words, trauma theory compresses four kinds of latency into two kinds. In the first kind, memory is inaccessible because it is *repressed*.

---

[2] See Novick (1999, chaps. 6 & 7), for a detailed historical account of the "Holocaust" in the United States in the years leading up to the Eichmann trial; see also Mintz (2001).

In the other kind, access is impossible because the memory is *unrepresentable*. Remembering occurs through *Nachträglichkeit*, in which an active memory's meaning is discovered belatedly (e.g., the Holocaust) or, alternatively, by bringing repressed memories into consciousness, as in recovered memory therapy. In trauma theory, both kinds of forgetting and remembering are bracketed under the concept of the return of the repressed.

Trauma theory claims that that latency is inevitable; memories are initially either repressed or unrepresentable. But this is empirically incorrect: Declarative memory is continuous in most cases of PTSD, even if patients are sometimes initially unwilling or unable to communicate their experiences. Now look at the minority of instances that might be characterized by latency. Richard McNally's recent book, *Remembering Trauma* (2003), includes a rigorous and comprehensive review of clinical and experimental evidence relating to repressed memory and its most important clinical manifestation, the recovered memory phenomenon. He argues persuasively that nearly all reports of posttraumatic amnesia occurring in the absence of neurological injury are problematic, although one should not assume that it never occurs. If McNally is correct, this reduces the relevant cases of PTSD to instances where latency has been detected via *Nachträglichkeit*. But even these remaining cases cannot be presumed to provide evidence for the delayed recollection and impact of trauma. I will return to this point in a moment, when I consider the subject of mimesis.

Our original question asked, How is traumatic memory transmitted within populations? The first solution is based on the idea that individual trauma (PTSD) and collective trauma (reactions to the murder of the Egyptian Moses and the Holocaust) follow intrinsically similar pathways (event → latency → memory). Advocates of trauma theory want to believe that latency is inevitable, but this is untrue. Only a minority of individual cases conceivably fit the profile.

SOLUTION 2: A POST-LAMARCKIAN FREUD

Another possibility is *Lamarckian memory*, the transmission of collective knowledge through genetic inheritance. This was Freud's solution in *Moses and Monotheism* and also in *Totem and Taboo* (1913/1958), in which he describes the patricide in the time of the primal horde that is a prologue to the murder of Moses. However, Freud's confidence in Lamarckian memory was an embarrassment to his supporters even in 1939.

Richard J. Bernstein (1998) argues that, although Freud refers to Lamarckian inheritance, he really had something different in mind:

Latency simultaneously involves *both* forgetting and (unconscious) remembering. This is what happens in the genesis of an individual traumatic neurosis, and, according to Freud, it is what happened in the course of Jewish history. Without the appeal to this psychoanalytic understanding of latency [and the dynamic unconscious], it would not be possible to explain the "remarkable fact" of the gap. (pp. 42–43)

If I understand Bernstein's position correctly, he is saying that the return of the repressed is doubly determined, a consequence of recovered memory together with *Nachträglichkeit*. Unconscious remembering in generation B becomes conscious in generation C, but its full meaning is grasped retrospectively. His solution works if one accepts the authority of the psychoanalytic understanding of latency. But what is this understanding? Bernstein writes that the "temporality of latency and trauma is extremely complex" (p. 42). Is he referring to something different from the four kinds of latency described in the preceding section? We are left in the dark.

SOLUTION 3: CONTAGION

The idea behind *contagion* is that traumatic memories can be passed from one person to another in such a way that the transmitted memories find a place in the recipient's mind or consciousness, where they produce an effect that resembles the donor's experience, including depression, anxiety, dysfunctional patterns of behavior, and vulnerability to pathology following exposure to trauma-level stressors (Yehuda, Schmiedler, Giller, Siever, & Binder-Brynes, 1998; Yehuda, Schmiedler, Wainberg, Binder-Brynes, & Duvdevani, 1998). The forms of contagion most often reported in the traumatic stress literature are "vicarious PTSD" (affecting psychotherapists) and "intergenerational PTSD" (studied mainly in the offspring of Holocaust survivors). To diagnose contagion, one must discover similar content (intrusive images, dreams, thoughts) in the minds of the donor and recipient (see "Item c" and "Item e" of the Compassion Fatigue Scale in Boscarino, Figley, & Adams, 2004). For example,

The affront to the sense of self . . . can be so overwhelming that . . . [therapists] exhibit the same characteristics as their patients . . . [and] experience a change in their interactions with the world, themselves and their families. They may begin to have intrusive thoughts, nightmares, and generalized anxiety. At this point, therapists themselves clearly need supervision and assistance in coping with their traumas. (Cerney 1995, p. 137; see also Catherall, 1995; Figley, 1995; Munroe et al., 1995; Valent, 1995)

[I] have a problem with buying my children clothes with vertical stripes. Silly? Perhaps. But in my parent's photo album is a picture of my father in his concentration camp garb. I carry that photo in my mental album, too. (Kurtz, 1995, p. 45, cited in Kellermann, 2001, p. 259)

What is "contagion"? It is presumed to be a distinctive mechanism for transmitting and incorporating the traumatic past. In practice, it is a cultural metaphor borrowed from medicine and attached to bits of distressful knowledge that recipients have generally obtained from a firsthand source and are unable to assimilate or accommodate. If there is something distinctive about this operation, it is in the way in which the distress (in contrast to the knowledge) is explained and communicated. This solution, in common with the preceding ones, is best described as mimesis.

MIMESIS

Mimesis is an individual or collective effort aimed at imitating or mirroring some source – another person, trope, myth, template, or an imagined reality. Mimesis can take the form of a self-conscious and voluntary performance, during which the performer observes himself as an object. These performances can be consciously or unconsciously strategic, aimed at enhancing the performer's self-identity or influencing his audience. The opposite is also possible, and there are instances of mimesis – clinical suggestion, hypnosis, and possession, for instance – in which a performer abandons his autonomy and submits himself to someone else's design. The phenomenon of clinical transference, as it is described by psychoanalysts, is likewise a mimetic performance, in which the client acts out a past event or relationship. The task of the analyst is to transform the clinical encounter into a *transference neurosis*, in which the client becomes conscious of his (her) mimesis, becomes an object of self-observation, and understands the past in a new way.

Two kinds of traumatic mimesis are recognized in contemporary psychiatry: fictitious PTSD (also called "malingering") and factitious PTSD. In the fictitious case, the individual self-consciously tells a lie about his past in order to assume an altered and advantageous identity. The performance can be superficial (simply telling lies) or an attempt to live the lies, in order to be more convincing. In the factitious case, a person appropriates autobiographical memory and altered identity from someone, real or fictional, and pushes the origins of the memory out of awareness, even to the point of forgetting (cryptomnesia). Sometimes fictitious and factitious PTSD are parts of a single process, in which a mimesis transmutes itself from a self-conscious and self-observed condition into a transformed consciousness and inner identity: a change from mimetic representation ("specular self-distantiation") to mimetic presentation ("nonspecular absorption in a traumatic scenario") (Leys 2000, p. 275; see also Benjamin, 1933/1999; Borch-Jacobsen, 1992, p. 39; Taussig, 1993). Binjamin Wilkomirski will provide an example of this process later in the chapter.

The psychiatric literature on fictitious and factitious PTSD is focused on cases involving forensic issues, notably Vietnam War veterans and putative victims of childhood sexual abuse. There is a third variety of traumatic mimesis, less frequently mentioned but more pervasive. It is the mirror image of the disorder described in the *DSMs*, where PTSD is organized into a familiar sequence of causes and effects. A disturbing event installs a memory that is indelible and distressful and that drives PTSD's characteristic syndrome (avoidance, numbing, autonomic arousal, etc.). The mimetic condition reverses the sequence of events:

Iconic form: event → memory → syndrome

Mimetic form: symptoms → memory

In the mimetic case, the sequence begins with a bona fide psychiatric condition, typically depression and anxiety. The patient, who is often guided by a therapist, chooses a real autobiographical memory that qualifies, post hoc, as the origin of the same condition. The patient now infuses the recalled memory with an intense emotion that it did not originally possess. The reclaimed memory is meaningful in a new way. It is distressful and can be a source of additional symptoms, including intrusive thoughts and phobic behavior. In other words, the belated traumatic memory is an example of guided or induced *Nachträglichkeit*.

INTERIM SUMMARY

In other words, there is no plausible way to explain the transmission of collective memory as it is described in *Moses and Monotheism*.[3] A variety of explanations have been proposed: Lamarckian inheritance, unconscious memory, parallels between individual and collective trauma, and contagion. Each fails, and one must conclude that "the return of the repressed," a notion essential to trauma theory, is mythic in the same way that the Biblical account of Exodus is mythic. The corresponding ritual attitude is mimesis: a collective effort to enact the myth, about which I will have more to say in a moment. Like all myths, the return of the repressed has to be understood in its historical context. But what is the context? One response is to situate Freud's book and theory in the political conditions of the 1930s – the triumph of National Socialism, the *Anschluss* with Austria, Freud's forced exile to England. I have a different context in mind, namely, developments in psychiatry and intellectual discourse that come to fruition decades after Freud's death and that profoundly alter attitudes to memory.

WHY MEMORY? THE PERSPECTIVE OF PSYCHIATRY

PTSD is based on memory. Memory is the mechanism that connects the disorder's precipitating event (traumatic stressor) to its characteristic syndrome. Without a presumptive memory, the syndrome loses its nosological identity. When clinical and literary mimesis imitates PTSD and its ancestral

---

[3] See Kansteiner (2002) for a systematic review of collective memory studies.

conditions, the performances are likewise based on traumatic memory – fictitious, factitious, retrospective, mythic. The connection between memory and the posttraumatic syndrome is now generally taken for granted. This is relatively recent development. Researchers at the Institute of Psychiatry in London have examined the pension files of nearly 2,000 British war veterans, from the Boer War to the 1991 Persian Gulf War, diagnosed with postcombat syndromes (Jones, Hodgins-Vermaas, et al., 2002; Jones, Palmer, & Wessely, 2002; Jones, Vermass, Beech, et al., 2003; Jones, Vermass, McCartney, et al., 2003; Jones & Wessely, 2001). Organic disorders and psychoses were excluded. Medical assessment procedures remained fairly constant throughout this period; examiners made detailed clinical notes and recorded the servicemen's explanations for their symptoms. The researchers' statistical analysis identifies three overlapping clusters of symptoms: a somatic weakness cluster, a cardiac cluster, and a neuropsychiatric cluster. The prevalence of clusters changed over time: The somatic weakness cluster predominates during the early period, whereas the neuropsychiatric cluster predominates from World War II onward.

Improvements in diagnosis explain part of the variation over time. But changes in medical culture – how patients and claimants chose to report their symptoms and how doctors interpreted the symptoms – seem to have been more important. Syndromes are shaped by clinical practices, technologies, metrics, expectations, and explanatory models that will determine the rules of inclusion and exclusion: whether a given experience, attribution, or self-report will count as relevant (e.g., as a real symptom or precipitant) or incidental. Likewise, clinical presentations and self-assessments are shaped by claimants' knowledge of current medical models and diagnostic classifications; their knowledge of clinicians' expectations; and their understanding of the cultural, economic, and institutional significance attributed to particular symptoms. The philosopher of science Ian Hacking (1995) refers to this intrinsically mimetic process as "looping."[4]

Where does the PTSD syndrome fit into this historical picture? The disorder's manifest symptoms (everything minus *DSM* criterion A) are dispersed over all three clusters, from the Boer War onward. When a traumatic stressor (criterion A) is added to our definition, the syndrome becomes specific to the neuropsychiatric cluster and coincides, more or less, with World War I diagnoses like shell shock and traumatic neurasthenia. One must wait until PTSD's memory mechanism is added to the definition in *DSM–III* (APA, 1980) before we arrive at the disorder with which we are now familiar. Prior to this point, the association between traumatic

---

[4] See also Shorter (1992, pp. 1–2, pp. 307–314) on "symptom pool" and "disease template"; for additional historical evidence, see Hyams, Wignall, and Roswell (1996, p. 402); Cox (2001); Crouthamel (2002); Eghigian (2001); Kaufmann (1999); Killen (2003); and Shephard (2000).

memory and the posttraumatic syndrome was not taken for granted nor was it yet part of the looping process described by Hacking. In other words, the association is a product of history and not a fact of nature. This is *not* the same thing as saying that the posttraumatic syndrome is, in every case, a product of the looping process. Rather, clinicians and researchers are often unable to differentiate between the two kinds of cases and, consequently, we do not know the percentage of diagnosed cases that are products of looping.

WHY MEMORY? THE PERSPECTIVE OF TRAUMA THEORY

Trauma theory's subject is collective memory: why particular events are singled out for remembering, how memories are transmitted. The fascination with memory is a result of (1) developments within psychiatry, making PTSD and traumatic memory part of the official nosology; (2) a shift affecting influential writers in a variety of academic disciplines, from traditional forms of historiography to a postmodern, memory-based approach (Eval, 2004); and (3) emergent notions of autobiographical personhood and techniques for narrating the self, in the culture at large (Bruner, 1990, 2003; for an opposing position see Strawson, 2004).

In 1976 a book called *Keywords: A Vocabulary of Culture and Society* was published. Its author was Raymond Williams, a widely read literary scholar and commentator on things cultural. Williams's choice of keywords gives a snapshot of the intellectual horizons and rhetoric of the times, and it reserved no space for "memory" or "trauma." Today these words are an indispensable part of the rhetorical tool kit of scholars in the humanities and social sciences. This addition, prioritizing personal experience, was accompanied by important disappearances: the rapid decline of so-called grand theories or master narratives (structuralism, Marxism, modernization theory, and so on) and the rejection of methodologies, narrative structures, standards of evidence, and epistemologies tainted by an extended list of "isms," including empiricism and scientism, but not Freudianism.

History based on documentary evidence would be replaced by counterhistory based on memory – not memory in the conventional sense, but essentially a new social epistemology that would be attentive to the dissenting and resisting voices that had been previously ignored, and to the various forms of nonverbal remembering inscribed on people's bodies and encoded in rituals, sanctified geographies, and artifacts. The features of memory that professional historians had instinctively distrusted as obstacles to objectivity and truth – namely, memory's fragmentary, allusive, and transient nature – were transformed into memory's distinctive virtues. Memory unprocessed, unappropriated, and unnarrated by experts, memory "naked and immediate, saturated with eventfulness," would give us unique access to our collective, chaotic past and our confusing present time (Roth & Salas, 2001, pp. 1–3). One can see the obvious importance of trauma and traumatic memory: "For . . . scholars interested in memory as a metahistorical category, 'trauma' is the key to [the most] authentic forms of memory, and memories shaped by trauma are the most likely to subvert totalizing varieties of historicism" (Klein, 2000, p. 138). We live in a post-traumatic age. From World War I onward, humankind has experienced an unending series of collective traumas, incomprehensible events that defy representation.[5]

Our history is Hegel's "vast slaughter bench" without Hegel's dialectical spirit and promised apotheosis of reason. And in our posttraumatic age, it is said, the Holocaust is the "limit event," the royal road to understanding our historical condition. "During the 1990s, deconstruction and its derivative forms were repeatedly charged with nihilism and political impotence"; the postmodern response was to deflect these criticisms by shifting to "an engagement with the real" via the medium of traumatic memory (Roth & Salas, 2001, p. 2). Trauma is reality at ground zero. Language is unable to fully contain or convey this reality. It is because trauma is irreducible to any system of signifiers that it cannot be confined to psychiatry. Psychiatry can help us to understand the clinical aspects of trauma, but psychiatry cannot be the ultimate authority or frame of meaning.

When we confront traumatic memory, our obligation is to listen and bear witness to the survivors' suffering and testimony. This is the "ethical response to the fragility of representation and the woundedness of consciousness" (Roth & Salas, 2001, p. 2). This kind of "listening" includes reading: "Each text would be, in effect, a site of trauma with which the reader would have to engage" (Berger, 1997, p. 576; see also Leys, 2000, p. 284). However,

How does one listen to what is impossible? . . . [It] may no longer be simply a choice: to be able to listen to the impossible, that is, is also *to have been chosen by it, before the possibility of mastering it with knowledge*. This is its danger – the danger, as some have put it, of the trauma's "contagion," of *the traumatization of the ones who listen*. . . . But it is also its only possibility for transmission. (Caruth, 1996, p. 10, my emphasis)

Bearing witness is painful, especially with Holocaust memory, because it challenges our beliefs about the meaningfulness of history and the limits to human suffering. This is the critical moment, when one must choose between trauma theory and traditional historical narrative:

Narrative fetishism . . . is the way an inability or refusal to mourn emplots traumatic events. . . . [It] releases one from the burden of having to reconstitute one's self-identity under 'posttraumatic' conditions; in narrative fetishism, the 'post' is indefinitely postponed. (Santner, 1992, p. 144; compare this with LaCapra, 1994, p. 193)

---

[5] See Bellamy (1997) for a superb review and comprehensive analysis.

History (it is said) replaces the victims' voice with document-fed narratives aimed at making a true chaos artificially meaningful. The standards of historiography – objectivity, empiricism – thus constitute a technology of avoidance and an obstacle to mimetic worldly knowledge.[6]

THE ORIGINS OF THE HOLOCAUST

Trauma theory understands that Freud's Exodus narrative is a myth. (Freud himself said it could be considered a work of fiction.) But the myth encapsulates a truth, the return of the repressed. The post-Holocaust reception of the Holocaust exemplifies this truth. The Nazi state capitulated in May 1945. Photographs, films, radio, and print journalism broadcast images and accounts describing the death camps. Testimony and documentation presented at the Nuremburg Trials produced additional information. The images of the death camps were traumatic; audiences were unable to connect what they saw into something meaningful. The collective memories of the Holocaust incubated for 15 years, until the Eichmann trial, after which it gradually became possible to recognize "the Holocaust" as a discrete constellation of events (e.g., Felman, 2002, chap. 3).

This chronology is essentially correct. The term *Holocaust* dates to the Eichmann trial; the death camps did not receive the attention that one might reasonably expect. But "latency" had nothing do with these developments. The course of events was determined by politics and culture rather than trauma psychology. The lack of attention given to Holocaust suffering in American news papers and magazines in the 1945–1960 period can be explained mainly in terms of latent anti-Semitism and the fear of anti-Semitism (Novick, 1999). Holocaust memories were not given prominence in Israeli public life during this period, but this was the result of political decisions by David Ben-Gurion and not posttraumatic forgetting. The Hebrew word *Shoah* was used during World War II to identify the persecution and destruction of European Jews by Nazis and other fascists as an event different from the pogroms and massacres of the past. During the Eichmann trial, the term was translated and transferred into English reportage as "Holocaust." The term signified neither a discovery nor a revelation. Its distinctiveness was in emphasizing the Jewishness of Nazi murderers.

---

[6] For an incisive critique, see Klein (2000): "*trauma, mourning, sublime, apocalypse, fragment, identity, redemption, healing, catharsis, cure, witnessing, testimony, ritual, piety, soul.* This is not the vocabulary of a secular, critical practice. That such a vocabulary should emerge from the most theoretically engaged texts, and that it should advertise itself as a critique of metaphysics, is all the more remarkable" (p. 45). Klein's targets include Caruth (1995, 1996); LaCapara (1994, 1998); and Roth (1995).

The most interesting Holocaust development has been its sacralization, the construction of collective mimetic rituals and sacred sites. There is "the March of the Living," an annual concentration camp odyssey organized for Jewish high school students. For gentiles as well, there is the Washington Holocaust Museum, where visitors receive "identity cards" pairing them to Holocaust victims and survivors. The visitor's journey through the museum leads mimetically to the twin's fate:

[W]e might imagine the museum as . . . a *transferential space*. [W]hat occurs in these public spaces . . . might be exactly the inverse of the psychoanalytic process. That is, these spaces instill in us "symptoms" or "prosthetic memories" through which we . . . have an experiential relationship.

There is a simultaneous negotiation with the object [an exhibit of victims' shoes] and with a person's own archive of experiences. At the same moment that we experience the shoes as *their* shoes – which could very well be *our* shoes – we feel our own shoes on our feet. (Landsberg, 2004, p. 135)

Holocaust awareness and Holocaust uniqueness are important issues for many American Jews. The Holocaust has become a source of cultural identity, a supplement, and for some people a replacement for traditional sources of group cohesion, namely, religious practices and institutions on the one hand and ambient anti-Semitism on the other.

Where does this history of the Holocaust lead us? According to trauma theory, Freud's Exodus narrative is a myth that embeds a truth that is illustrated by the discovery of the Holocaust. But the pattern does not match the history of the Holocaust. This history, as documented by Peter Novick (1999) and Idith Zertal (2000), has no pattern. It is product of contingency – driven by collective anxieties concerning ethnic cohesion and continuity, and rooted in variety of extrinsic and unlikely influences, including declining synagogue attendance and trends in intermarriage between Jews and gentiles.

These themes – Holocaust self-identity, the mimetic transmission of traumatic memory, historical contingency – are illustrated in the following sections, devoted to the life, works, and public reception of Binjamin Wilkomirski.

BINJAMIN WILKOMIRSKI

Binjamin Wilkomirski's memoir, *Fragments: Memoirs of a Childhood, 1939–1948*, was published in German in 1995; the following year it was published in English (Wilkomirski, 1996) and subsequently in French, Hebrew, Italian, Dutch, and other languages. The book describes Wilkomirski's early childhood, a journey that took him from Riga (Latvia) to Poland, where he lived from age 3 to 6, first in Majdanek concentration camp and then Auschwitz-Birkenau. At the end of the war, he was sent to a Jewish orphanage in Krakow; at age 7, he was sent to Switzerland, where he was given the name Bruno Dössekker. According to Wilkomirski, the book's title, *Fragments*, describes his memories: "a rubble field of isolated images and events. Shards of memory with hard knife-sharp edges, which still cut flesh if touched today." The memoir was praised by most reviewers and won several distinctions, including the National Jewish Book Award and an award from the American Orthopsychiatric Association.

In 1998, an Israeli-born Swiss citizen named Daniel Ganzfried raised doubts concerning the authenticity of Wilkomirski's account. Bruno's birth certificate and school records indicate that he was born in Switzerland in 1941 and spent his entire childhood there. Before receiving the name Dössekker, his family name had been Grosjean. Ganzfried claimed that Bruno's knowledge of Nazi extermination camps had been obtained secondhand, from reading books and touring the camps and their museums. Bruno denounced Ganzfried's findings and proposed an alternative explanation. The bureaucrat responsible for the refugee paperwork had confused Bruno with a Swiss orphan named Grosjean.

The literary agency responsible for Wilkomirski's book hired Swiss historian Stefan Mächler to investigate Bruno's past and prepare a report, which was published in 2000 (Mächler, 2001a, 2001b). Independent investigations, conducted by Elena Lappin and Philip Gourevitch, were published in 1999. The investigators interviewed Wilkomirski, people who knew Bruno before he was Wilkomirski, people mentioned in *Fragments*, and Holocaust survivors. Mächler also examined official records relating to Bruno's birth and childhood.

Mächler reports that Bruno's mother was an unmarried Swiss woman, a Protestant, from whom he was taken at age two. The next two years were spent in foster homes, where he was the ward of a physically abusive woman with severe mental illness. Bruno was next domiciled in a Swiss children's home for nine months, together with Jewish refugee children. At age four, he was adopted by a middle-aged childless couple, named Dössekker, and his wife. Dr. Dössekker wanted his adopted son to follow him into medicine, but Bruno became an instrument maker and clarinetist instead. From adolescence onward, Bruno collected histories of the Holocaust and the autobiographies of survivors. In the 1970s, he began to visit concentration camps' sites and museums.

A CHRONOLOGY OF WILKOMIRSKI'S HOLOCAUST MEMORIES

Late 1940s: According to Wilkomirski, the Dössekkers instruct the adopted child to forget everything about his life before joining them, just "as one forgets a bad dream."

Late 1950s: Bruno tells classmates that he came to Switzerland from one of the Baltic states. He has a reputation for lying about himself, but when confronted he would immediately confess, "that was just a moment that came over me" (Gourevitch, 1999, p. 57).

1960s and 1970s: Close friends from Zurich recall frequent conversations, in which "he told us that he been in the Warsaw Ghetto, and was saved from the Holocaust by a Swiss nanny, who brought him here" (Lappin, 1999, p. 59).

1979 to 1982: He meets Elitsur Bernstein, an Israeli psychologist living in Switzerland. Bernstein has come to Bruno for music lessons, and they become close friends. Bernstein describes their friendship as "the story of how, through a lengthy collaborative process of trial and error, he helped Bruno Dössekker become Binjamin Wilkomirski." Bernstein returns to Israel but remains in contact with Wilkomirski. "Wilkomirski" emerges but its origin is uncertain. Bernstein tells this story: He came to Bruno's apartment one day and noticed a picture of a rabbi on the wall. He told Bruno that this is the last rabbi of Wilkomir (Poland). Bruno "turned pale" and informed Bernstein "that his last name might not be Dössekker but Wilkomirski." On the other hand, a former friend traced "Wilkomirski" to a concert, featuring the Polish violinist Wanda Wilkomirska. During the performance, Bruno's companion comments on a physical resemblance between Bruno and Wanda (Gourevitch, 1999, p. 58–59).

Summer 1991: Bernstein returns to Zurich for a visit. Wilkomirski tells him about recurring dreams and nightmares with concentration camp motifs. Bernstein tells him to find a therapist and "get his dreams and nightmares out of his system." Wilkomirski's partner, Verena Piller, agrees. Wilkomirski undergoes psychotherapy. Later, he tells Bernstein that therapy allowed him "'to find words' for the memories that terrified him, and to sort out the jumble of 'pre-verbal' images in his mind" (Gourevitch, 1999, p. 59).

September 1991 to 1992: Wilkomirski faxes the first chapters of *Fragments* to Bernstein. Bernstein asks him, "Are you sure that these are your memories?" Wilkomirski tells him that his memories were never forgotten and therapy had simply permitted him to give words to what had been inchoate. Bernstein says that the recollections had been stored in the form of "body memories" (Gourevitch, 1999, p. 60).

1995: Wilkomirski is invited by the University of Ostrava (Czechoslovakia) to give a lecture, titled "Childhood memory as a historical source ... with examples of child survivors of the Shoah (Holocaust)." Wilkomirski describes a therapy that he has devised with Bernstein and employed "as an experiment on himself." He tells his audience that survivors possess inaccessible but "photographically exact images in memory." His therapy overcomes these psychological barriers: repression, denial, fragmentation, screen memories. Wilkomirski is proof of its efficacy (Mächler 2001a, pp. 247–251, 358).

In the same year, *Fragments* is published. Wilkomirski goes on a European tour – a series of recitals, really. On a typical occasion, he appears on stage, wearing a scarf resembling the shawl (*tallit*) that Jewish men wear during prayer. He performs on his clarinet Max Bruch's version of *Kol Nidre*, a most sacred Jewish liturgical chant. A professional actor reads selected passages from *Fragments*. Wilkomirski sobs on stage (Mächler, 2001a, p. 116). Wilkomirski travels to the United States where he is interviewed, accepts awards, and is the honored guest of the Holocaust Museum. "'He cried everywhere we brought him,' said Wilkomirski's American publisher.... 'I told him that if he didn't stop crying, I'd send him home.... I've published Primo Levi, Elie Wiesel, Aharon Appelfeld – I know a lot of survivors – and one thing they have in common is that they don't cry. This guy couldn't stop'" (Gourevitch, 1999, p. 51).

1999/2000: Wilkomirski "vehemently denies...that the book is to be understood as recovered memory. 'Never in my life have I forgotten what I wrote in my book....I had NOTHING TO RE-DISCOVER AGAIN!'" (Mächler, 2001a, p. 251). "When I was a youngster...I spent hours...at a secret place in our garden, loudly speaking and repeating all I could remember....I felt extremely unhappy. I wanted to go back to Poland, to cross Poland, to go home into the birchwoods of the Baltics!" (Lappin, 1999, p. 54).

AUDIENCES

Let us turn from Bruno to the people who read his book and described their impressions. We can speak of three audiences. The first is composed of people who read *Fragments* before Wilkomirski was exposed, when it was reasonable to believe that the man and his memories were authentic. Even then, there were people who smelled something fishy. Yet there were also knowledgeable people, including Elie Wiesel and other Holocaust survivors, who praised the book for its veracity and success in capturing the consciousness of a small child in this extreme situation. Audiences 2 and 3 are people who read or re-read Bruno's book after he was exposed. Audience 2 is composed of people who believe that Wilkomirski is a literary fraud and a charlatan; audience 3 believes that Bruno is a kind of Holy Fool.

Robert Alter, a professor at Berkeley, is part of audience 2. He attributes Wilkomirski's initial success to a "winning combination of concentration camp testimony and histrionic Yiddishkeit [that] succeeded in bringing...droves of admiring souls, some innocently fooled, some charlatans themselves" (p. 37). The charlatans included Laura Gabrowski, a woman who described herself as Wilkomirski's "childhood friend" in the concentration camps and the Krakow orphanage. Bruno claimed to recognize Laura after a hiatus of 40 years. On this occasion, they broke down and wept in the presence of photo journalists. Laura wasn't Gabrowski any more than Bruno was Wilkomirski. She was subsequently revealed to be a native-born American named Laurel Willson, the author of a bogus autobiography chronicling her experiences with recovered memory, multiple personality, violent sexual trauma, and satanic cults.

Literary hoaxes of the Wilkomirski type are a well-established phenomenon. In 1704, George Psalmanazar, a Frenchman by birth and breeding, published a book titled *An Historical and Geographical Description of Formosa*, in which he claimed to be the first and only native of Formosa to reach Europe. Like Bruno, he made many public appearances, at which he described his fictive homeland. His book gripped readers with eye witness descriptions of the pleasures of polygamy and the horrors of human sacrifice, cannibalism, and infanticide. It was just what the public wanted. When his cover was blown, Psalmanazar faded into obscurity. Wilkomirski, on the other hand, did not fade away. How do we explain the continuing sympathy for Bruno (audience 3), and the impression that he is more than a fake, even if he is something less than an eyewitness? This is Alter's (2001) answer:

At least two prevalent pathologies of everyday contemporary life are manifested in the Wilkomirski affair.... There is the notion, which one can trace back to the founding texts of literary modernism, ... that authenticity can be realized only in the inferno of extreme crisis.... And there is also the contemporary disposition ... to conceive of the Jews not as real people living in history and with their own internal divisions, manifest imperfections, and concrete political aspirations, but rather as emblematic figures in an allegorical masque of timeless human suffering ... in which they themselves have become deeply complicit. (pp. 37–38)

How should we describe Bruno's traumatic mimesis? Did it start as self-conscious playacting and gradually evolve into a truly factitious phenomenon, perhaps in the period between his European tour and his welcome in Washington as the honored guest of the American Holocaust Museum? What is clear is that his Jewish identity gradually changed after Mächler's exposé and when, in 2002, DNA testing established a match between Bruno and the Swiss national who had been his mother's paramour before Bruno's birth. In a recent interview, Bruno has described Jews in very negative terms, as being ultra nationalistic, arrogant with Gentiles, and phonies who exploit a traditional victim role in order to deflect criticism and extort indemnification. The Jews murdered in the Holocaust were real victims, he told the interviewer, but the living Jews are predators living off the Holocaust industry. How should we interpret his change of attitude? Is anti-Semitism to be Bruno's way out of factitious PTSD?

THE HOLY FOOL

The people in Bruno's third audience see things differently. Stephan Feuchtwang, a social anthropologist and expert on religion, understands that Bruno's autobiographical details – born in Riga in 1939, transported to an extermination camp in 1941, and so forth – do not meet the standard of "empirical verifiability." In this respect, they are similar to the problematic "times and locations" underpinned by "religious faith and theological truth." Like the Biblical Exodus, "[t]he Holocaust is a sacred truth . . . both for [Wilkomirski] and his detractors." Through its connection with this sacred truth, *Fragments* can "stand as a work of reminder, like a modern myth – itself an icon by which others can share a horror and a loss, beyond the circumstantial detail" (Feuchtwang, 2003, pp. 81–84). Thus, these mimetic engagements with the past – Bruno's role-playing, the reader's act of bearing witness – acquire the authority and potency of myth and ritual.

Compare Feuchtwang's anthropology of the sacred with Norman Finkelstein's account. Finkelstein is the author of a disputatious book titled *The Holocaust Industry*. He is a dedicated anti-Zionist, and his heart's desire is to see the State of Israel replaced by a Palestinian state. He believes that the sacredness and Jewishness of the Holocaust were manufactured by Zionists to guarantee political support from the United States, justify war crimes against Palestinians, and extort funds from Germany and Switzerland. Like Feuchtwang, Finkelstein describes the Wilkomirski affair as "iconic," only this time it is an icon of deception and greed (Finkelstein, 2000). There is neither sacred truth nor mimesis in this account. Thus, Finkelstein and the posttraumatic Bruno arrive at the same place.

Feuchtwang believes that Bruno made the Holocaust into "an icon of his unremembered childhood" (p. 82). He is not alone in this opinion. Betty Jean Lifton, who is herself an adopted person, a clinical psychologist, and the author of three books on the psychology of adopted children, takes Bruno's unremembered childhood a step further. In an article on the Wilkomirski affair, she writes that many adopted children feel like "survivors" but with a significant difference: they cannot know what they have survived. Of course, the trauma of adoption is not equal to the cumulative trauma of child survivors of the Holocaust, but "to a young child the pain and deprivation may feel similar . . . a feeling of being abandoned, alone, and powerless." The adopted child is the recipient of an identity, a "role" that is given to him or her by the adopted parents. "Like many adoptees, Bruno would speak of himself as being a 'good actor,' 'playing the rules of the game' . . . , and would have difficulty shaking off his 'imposter self'" (Lifton, 2002, pp. 1–2; see also Ford, King, & Hollander, 1988, and Pfefferbaum, Allen, Lindsey, & Whittlesey, 1999). The metamorphosis of

Bruno into Binjamin was the next step: The imposter self is reborn in mythic time, before he was Grosjean.

CONCLUSION

Claude Levi-Strauss wrote that myths are "good for thinking with": useful devices for making sense of experience. Levi-Strauss was thinking about life in tribal and traditional societies, but we too have useful myths. Freud's *Moses and Monotheism* and its account of the return of the repressed are good for thinking with, but not, as intended, for understanding the human mind, the intellectual trajectory of the Jews, or the origins of Christian anti-Semitism. Freud's *Moses and Monotheism* is good for thinking about psychiatry.

Freud's book is about collective memory and how it can be transmitted between generations. Today we are inclined to think of "collective memory" as something similar to "oral history" – simply a collection of beliefs, opinions, and impressions shared by some group about some period in the past. But Freud's myth leads us, inadvertently, in a different direction. It is useful exactly where he gets things wrong, namely, Freud's solution to the puzzle he created: How is memory transmitted over or through amnesic generations? It is a silly question only if you think that myths are silly. (Trauma theory veers in the opposite direction. It wants its myths to be true and not merely useful.) Freud's solution is implausible. However, there is no problem in finding a satisfactory answer, with the help of anthropology, history, philosophy, and evolutionary biology. And the answer is mimesis.

Earlier generations of trauma doctors also knew this solution and wrote about it in terms of autosuggestion, heterosuggestion, and hysteria. This was the period when psychiatric engagement with traumatic memory was clouded by the "culture of suspicion" (1880s to the 1920s). PTSD was intended, by its framers, to terminate the culture of suspicion and its characteristic abuse, blaming the victim for his own affliction. Simultaneously they purged psychiatry of any clinical interest in mimesis. From 1980 forward, it was sufficient to understand only iconic memory. Factitious memory would never again be more than a side issue.

Yet there are occasional reminders of the time when traumatic memory was an object of intellectual curiosity and healthy skepticism. The Bruno/Binjamin affair is one of these reminders.

References

Alter, R. (2001, 30 April). Arbeit macht fraud. *New Republic*, 35–38.
Assmann, J. (1997). *Moses the Egyptian: The memory of Egypt in western monotheism.* Cambridge, MA: Harvard University Press.

Bellamy, E. J. (1997). *Affective genealogies: Psychoanalysis, postmodernism, and the "Jewish Question" after Auschwitz*. London, NE: University of Nebraska Press.

Benjamin, W. (1999). On the mimetic faculty. In *Walter Benjamin: Selected writings, volume 2, 1927–1934* (pp. 720–722). Cambridge, MA: Harvard University Press. (Original work published 1933)

Berger, J. (1997). Trauma and literary theory. *Contemporary Literature, 38*, 569–582.

Bernstein, R. J. (1998). *Freud and the legacy of Moses*. Cambridge, UK: Cambridge University Press.

Borch-Jacobsen, M. (1992). *The emotional tie: Psychoanalysis, mimesis, and affect*. Stanford, CA: Stanford University Press.

Boscarino, J. A., Figley, C. R., & Adams, R. E. (2004). Compassion fatigue following the September 11 terrorist attacks: A study of secondary trauma among New York City social workers. *International Journal of Emergency Mental Health, 6*(2), 57–66.

Bruner, J. (1990). *Acts of meaning*. Cambridge, MA: Harvard University Press.

Bruner, J. (2003). *Making stories: Law, literature, life*. Cambridge, MA: Harvard University Press.

Caruth, C. (Ed.). (1995). *Trauma: Explorations in memory*. Baltimore: Johns Hopkins University Press.

Caruth, C. (1996). *Unclaimed experience: Trauma, narrative, and history*. Baltimore: Johns Hopkins University Press.

Catherall, D. (1995). Preventing institutional secondary traumatic stress disorder. In C. R. Figley (Ed.), *Compassion fatigue: Coping with secondary traumatic stress in those who treat the traumatized* (pp. 232–248). London: Brunner/Mazel.

Cerney, M. S. (1995). Treating the "heroic treaters." In C. R. Figley (Ed.), *Compassion fatigue: Coping with secondary traumatic stress in those who treat the traumatized* (pp. 131–149). London: Brunner/Mazel.

Cox, C. (2001). Invisible wounds: The American Legion, shell-shocked veterans, and American society, 1919–1924. In P. Lerner and M. Micale (Eds), *Traumatic pasts: History, psychiatry and trauma in the modern age, 1860–1930* (pp. 280–305). Cambridge, UK: Cambridge University Press.

Crouthamel, J. (2002). War neurosis versus savings psychosis: Working-class politics and psychological trauma in Weimar Germany. *Journal of Contemporary History, 37*, 163–182.

Eghigian, G. (2001). The German welfare state as a discourse of trauma. In P. Lerner & M. Micale (Eds.), *Traumatic pasts: History, psychiatry and trauma in the modern age, 1860–1930* (pp. 92–112). Cambridge, UK: Cambridge University Press.

Eval, G. (2004). Identity and trauma: Two forms of will to memory. *History and Memory, 16*, 5–36.

Feldman, S. (2002). *The juridical unconscious: Trials and traumas in the twentieth century*. Cambridge, MA: Harvard University Press.

Feuchtwang, S. (2003). Loss: Transmissions, recognitions, authorisations. In S. Radstone & K. Hodgkin (Eds.), *Regimes of memory* (pp. 76–89). London: Routledge.

Figley, C. R. (1995). Compassion fatigue as secondary traumatic stress disorder: An overview. In C. R. Figley (Ed.), *Compassion fatigue: Coping with secondary traumatic stress disorders in those who treat the traumatized* (pp. 1–20). London: Brunner/Mazel.

Finkelstein, M. (2000). *The Holocaust industry: Reflections on the exploitation of Jewish suffering*. London: Verso.

Ford, C. V., King, B. H., & Hollander, M. H. (1988). Lies and liars: Psychiatric aspects of prevarication. *American Journal of Psychiatry, 145*, 554–562.

Freud, S. (1950). Beyond the pleasure principle. In J. Strachey (Ed. and Trans.), *The standard edition of the complete psychological works of Sigmund Freud* (Vol. 18). London: Hogarth Press. (Original work published 1920)

Freud, S. (1958). Totem and taboo. In J. Strachey (Ed. and Trans.), *The standard edition of the complete psychological works of Sigmund Freud* (Vol. 13). London: Hogarth Press. (Original work published 1912–1913)

Freud, S. (1959). Moses and monotheism. In J. Strachey (Ed. and Trans.), *The standard edition of the complete psychological works of Sigmund Freud* (Vol. 23). London: Hogarth Press. (Original work published 1939)

Gourevitch, P. (1999, 14 June). The memory thief. *The New Yorker*, 48–68.

Hacking, I. (1995). The looping effect of human kinds. In D. Sperber, D. Premack, & A. J. Premack (Eds.), *Causal cognition: A multidisciplinary debate* (pp. 351–383). Oxford: Oxford University Press.

Hyams, K. C., Wignall, F. S., & Roswell, R. (1996). War syndromes and their evaluation: From the U.S. Civil War to the Persian Gulf War. *Annals of Internal Medicine, 125*(5), 398–405.

Jones, E., Hodgins-Vermaas, R., McCartney, H., Everitt, B., Beech, C., Poynter, D., et al. (2002). Post-combat syndromes from the Boer War to the Gulf War: A cluster analysis of their nature and attribution. *British Medical Journal, 324*(7333), 321–324.

Jones, E., Palmer, I., & Wessely, S. (2002). War pensions (1900–1945): Changing models of psychological understanding. *British Journal of Psychiatry, 180*, 374–379.

Jones, E., Vermaas, R. H., Beech, C., Palmer, I., Hyams, K., & Wessely, S. (2003). Mortality and postcombat disorders: U.K. veterans of the Boer War and World War I. *Military Medicine, 168*(5), 414–418.

Jones, E., Vermaas, R. H., McCartney, H., Beech, C., Palmer, I., Hyams, K., et al. (2003). Flashbacks and post-traumatic stress disorder: The genesis of a 20th-century diagnosis. *British Journal of Psychiatry, 182*, 158–163.

Jones, E., & Wessely, S. (2001). Psychiatric battle casualties: An intra- and interwar comparison. *British Journal of Psychiatry, 178*, 242–247.

Kansteiner, W. (2002). Finding meaning in memory: A methodological critique of collective memory studies. *History and Theory, 41*, 179–197.

Kaufmann, D. (1999). Science as cultural practice: Psychiatry in the First World War and Weimar Germany. *Journal of Contemporary History, 34*, 125–144.

Kellermann, N. P. E. (2001). Transmission of Holocaust trauma: An integrative view. *Psychiatry: Interpersonal and Biological Processes, 64*, 256–267.

Killen, A. (2003). From shock to *schreck*: Psychiatrists, telephone operators and traumatic neurosis in Germany, 1900–26. *Journal of Contemporary History, 38*, 201–220.

Klein, K. E. (2000). On the emergence of memory in historical discourse. *Representations, 69*, 127–150.

Kurtz, C. (1995). *Jewish Action Magazine*. New York: Orthodox Union of America.

LaCapra, D. (1994). *Representing the Holocaust: History, theory, trauma*. Ithaca, NY: Cornell University Press.

LaCapra, D. (1998). *History and memory after Auschwitz*. Ithaca, NY: Cornell University Press.

Lacoue-Labarthe, P., & Nancy, J.-L. (1989). "From where is psychoanalysis possible?" (Part II of "The Jewish people do not dream"). *Stanford Literature Review, 8*, 39–55.

Landsberg, A. (2004). *Prosthetic memory: The transformation of American remembrance in the age of mass culture*. New York: Columbia University Press.

Lappin, E. (1999). The man with two heads. *Granta, 66*, 7–65.

Leys, R. (2000). *Trauma: A genealogy*. Chicago: University of Chicago Press.

Lifton, B. J. (2002, September/October). Wilkomirski the adoptee. *Tikkun, 17*.

Mächler, S. (2001a). *The Wilkomirski affair: A study in biographical truth* (J. E. Woods, Trans.). New York: Schocken Books.

Mächler, S. (2001b). Wilkomirski the victim: Individual remembering as social interaction and public event. *History and Memory, 13*, 59–95.

McNally, R. J. (2003). *Remembering trauma*. Cambridge, MA: Harvard University Press, Belknap Press.

Micale, M. S., & Lerner, P. F. (Eds.). (2001). *Traumatic pasts: History, psychiatry, and trauma in the modern age, 1870–1930*. New York: Cambridge University Press.

Mintz, A. L. (2001). *Popular culture and the shaping of Holocaust memory in America*. Seattle: University of Washington Press.

Munroe, J. F., Shay, J., Fisher, L., Makary, C., Rapperport, K., & Zimering, R. (1995). Preventing compassion fatigue: A treatment team model. In C. R. Figley (Ed.), *Compassion fatigue: Coping with secondary traumatic stress disorder in those who treat the traumatized* (pp. 209–231). New York: Brunner/Mazel.

Novick, P. (1999). *The Holocaust in American life*. Boston: Houghton Mifflin.

Pfefferbaum, B., Allen, J. R., Lindsey, E. D., & Whittlesey, S. W. (1999). Fabricated trauma exposure: An analysis of cognitive, behavioral, and emotional factors. *Psychiatry, 62*(4), 293–302.

Roth, M. S. (1995). *The ironist's cage: Memory, trauma and the construction of history*. New York: Columbia University Press.

Roth, M. S., & Salas, C. G. (2001). Introduction. In M. S. Roth & C. G. Salas (Eds.), *Disturbing remains: Memory, history and crises in the twentieth century* (pp. 1–13). Los Angeles: Getty Research Institute.

Santner, E. L. (1992). History beyond the pleasure principle: Some thoughts on the representation of trauma. In S. Friedlander (Ed.), *Probing the limits of representation: Nazism and the "Final Solution"* (pp. 143–154). Cambridge, MA: Harvard University Press.

Sellin, E. (1922). *Mose und seine Bedeutung für die israelitisch-jüdische Religionsgeschichte* [microform]. Leipzig: A. Deichert.

Shephard, B. (2000). *A war of nerves: Soldiers and psychiatrists, 1914–1994*. London: Jonathan Cape. (Published in the U.S. as *A war of nerves: Soldiers and psychiatrists in the twentieth century*, 2001, Cambridge, MA: Harvard University Press)

Shorter, E. (1992). *From paralysis to fatigue: A history of psychosomatic illness in the modern era*. New York: Free Press.

Strawson, G. (2004, 15 October). A fallacy of our age. *Times Literary Supplement*, 17–18.

Taussig, M. (1993). *Mimesis and alterity*. New York: Routledge.

Valent, P. (1995). Survival strategies: A framework for understanding secondary traumatic stress and coping in helpers. In C. R. Figley (Ed.), *Compassion fatigue: Coping with secondary traumatic stress disorder in helpers*. New York: Brunner/Mazel.

Wilkomirski, B. (1996). *Fragments: Memoirs of a wartime childhood*. New York: Schocken Books.

Yehuda, R., Schmeidler, J., Giller, E. L., Jr., Siever, L. J., & Binder-Brynes, K. (1998). Relationship between posttraumatic stress disorder characteristics of Holocaust survivors and their adult offspring. *American Journal of Psychiatry, 155*(6), 841–843.

Yehuda, R., Schmeidler, J., Wainberg, M., Binder-Brynes, K., & Duvdevani, T. (1998). Vulnerability to posttraumatic stress disorder in adult offspring of Holocaust survivors. *American Journal of Psychiatry, 155*(9), 1163–1171.

Yerushalmi, Y. H. (1991). *Freud's Moses: Judaism terminable and interminable*. New Haven: Yale University Press.

Young, A. (1995). *The harmony of illusions: Inventing posttraumatic stress disorder*. Princeton, NJ: Princeton University Press.

Zertal, I. (2000). From the people's hall to the Wailing Wall: A study in memory, fear, and war. *Representations, 69*, 96–126.

17

Failures of Imagination: The Refugee's Predicament

Laurence J. Kirmayer

> There is such a thing as absolute power over narrative. Those who secure this privilege for themselves can arrange stories about others pretty much where, and as, they like. Just as in corrupt, totalitarian regimes, those who exercise power over others can do anything.
>
> (Achebe, 2000)

INTRODUCTION

Understanding stories of suffering and healing depends on a shared world of assumptions, ideas, values, and motivations. When stories deviate from our expectations for plausibility, intelligibility, order, and coherence, we have several options: We can expand our vision of the possible; we can interpret the narratives as defective, indicating cognitive dysfunction or some other form of psychopathology; or we can question the motives and credibility of the narrator.

The clinical encounter is a microcosm of the larger social world, and the interpretation of stories told in the clinical setting depends crucially on knowledge of that wider social sphere. When the social worlds of patient and clinician are substantially different or unshared, the stories they tell each other may be mutually unintelligible. In this chapter, I examine this problem of the intelligibility and credibility of clinical narratives in a special setting: the psychiatric assessment of asylum seekers in the context of a cultural consultation service (Kirmayer, Groleau, Guzder, Blake, & Jarvis, 2003). This example throws into relief some basic questions about the grounding of clinical narratives and the social consequences of "clinical epistemology."

TRUTH AND FICTION IN NARRATIVES OF THE SELF

The world we live in is constructed not only of brute facts, but equally of imagination. In consequence, our responses to trauma, loss, and dislocation are profoundly influenced by what and how we imagine the world to be. My focus here is on the role of imagination in the narratives of psychiatry, particularly in the setting of the care of persons seeking refuge (refugee claimants or asylum seekers). I want to consider several different sorts of failures of imagination that illustrate the tacit dimensions of narration in psychiatry.

The role of imagination is apparent in psychiatric settings when patients try to convey unusual experiences to others. The exceptional form and content of some narratives may be interpreted in terms of psychopathology (as in psychotic disorders). During training, psychiatrists come to understand the strange narratives of psychosis using a model of the nature of psychotic pathology to slot various experiences into categories as symptoms (delusions, ideas of reference, hallucinations, paranoid ideation). This reduces the meaning of the patient's story to a series of signs or indices of illness and may foreclose the search for any larger narrative coherence (Kirmayer, Corin, & Jarvis, 2004).

A second challenge to the clinician's imagination comes from patient narratives that involve life circumstances that are outside the bounds of the clinician's experience. This is sometimes the case with people who describe terrible brutality in their families; such accounts violate our notions of the family and of a just world and are, in some ways, difficult to imagine (Kirmayer, 1996). Generally, we do not want to acknowledge the violence of everyday life – except, perhaps, when it is framed as entertainment, where the very unreality of the setting neutralizes its threat. Refugees seen in psychiatric settings may face a more profound version of this failure of imagination (Kirmayer, 2002).

Refugee claimants may be referred for psychiatric consultation because of the distress they suffer from the sequelae of torture, loss of family and home, and profound uncertainty about their futures due to the prolonged waiting period for determination of the validity of their claim for official refugee status. In the course of psychiatric evaluation, clinician and patient co-construct narratives that surround, contain, and situate symptoms and suffering in ways that give them multiple levels of meaning. For the clinician, one layer of meaning concerns symptoms as indices of a specific diagnostic entity or disorder. Thus, the refugee's account of anxiety, depression, recurrent nightmares, easy startling, and intrusive thoughts may be interpreted as symptoms of a recognizable syndrome: posttraumatic stress disorder (PTSD) (Silove, 1999). This gives a causal account of persistent symptoms, linking them to terrible events in the past and offering the reassurance that the symptoms are expectable and not evidence of some special pathology or moral weakness. At the same time, the meaning of the violence the person has suffered may be explored in terms of social and political conflicts beyond his or her control.

The stories that are told in clinical settings to make sense of and master symptoms and suffering exist against a backdrop of equally important stories that warrant the refugee's decision to flee and his claim for asylum. These stories need not fit together in perfect register; indeed, they may conflict. And there is a third set of stories refugees must construct, having to do with the sort of future they imagine, where safety and a new life can be found. The creation and harmonization of these narratives demands imagination. By acknowledging the complexity of these epistemic processes, we can begin to understand the dilemmas that refugees face in terms of failures of imagination in several distinct domains.

First, there is the failure of the refugee's own imagination, faced with the need to bridge one world and the next. These disparate worlds, cleaved apart by the violence of oppression, torture, and forced migration, represent the world of everyday routine, community order, and family roots in their countries of origin; the supervening worlds of violence, disorder, and flight created by war and political upheaval; and the new order of the quotidian represented by the place where they seek asylum. Many refugees are able to bridge these worlds or live with their radical disjuncture, but others suffer from this cleavage (Beiser, 1999). Their suffering is rooted in reality, but it can also be understood as a failure of imagination to bridge disparate worlds – a failure that has both personal and social consequences across generations (Rousseau & Drapeau, 2001).

For the individual, imagination serves the functions of establishing continuity, creating a space where the worlds of the past, present, and future can be connected and dwelt within. Socially, the refugee's own imagination is needed to convey his or her predicament to others who lack the same firsthand experience of catastrophe and who may have many psychological and political reasons to resist understanding the dimensions of that experience. The psychological reasons for resistance or denial have to do with the ways we defend ourselves from vicarious pain by turning away from others. The political reasons are equally familiar, reflecting the ways we create geographical and ethnic boundaries to justify and protect our power and privilege.

A second locus of concern is the failure of the clinical imagination to conceive and understand the refugee's predicament. In clinical settings, the onus for communicating the refugee's predicament is not simply on the refugee but also on his or her clinical interlocutors. The clinical imagination can be conceived of in at least two fundamentally different ways: the limited imagination of preformed categories delivered by psychiatric nosology or theories of psychopathology, and a more open-ended *imagining with the other* that occurs in close listening, witnessing, and some forms of psychotherapy. The privileged position of the clinician allows us to hear stories to which we would not otherwise be privy and to create a protected space where imaginative constructions can unfold.

The clinical imagination is rooted not only in the compendia of diseases in textbooks and the concentration of illness in hospitals, but also in the everyday experience of clinicians as citizens who read newspapers, absorb mass media representations of the world, and live under circumstances profoundly different than those from which the refugee is escaping. The ability to imaginatively reconstruct this world depends on having the right mental furniture or building blocks – which many clinicians may lack because they have not had relevant experiences – but it also requires a willingness to enter into (imaginative) spaces of terror.

Clinicians' difficulties in receiving and understanding the refugee's story are redoubled in the juridical context of the Immigration and Refugee Board (IRB) hearing. Here refugee claimants must defend their versions of events against adversaries who, because they understand their job as first and foremost to identify fakes, may challenge the refugee's story based on inconsistencies and imprecision. In some cases, the questions and deliberation of IRB members reveal a view of narration, and an underlying epistemology, that fails to account for the pervasive effects of trauma in memory, recollection, and reconstruction.

Immigration and Citizenship Canada has produced a report detailing some of the issues involved in assessing the credibility of claims for refugee status and the testimony given in IRB hearings (IRB Legal Services, 1998). Section 2.6.2 of this document identifies specific circumstances of the claimant which may affect the assessment of credibility including "nervousness caused by testifying before a tribunal, the trauma associated with testifying about a trying event such as an arrest or torture, and cultural differences such as the claimant's experiences with officials in the home country or the claimant's cultural and educational background." However, evidence from clinical consultations and the systematic review of cases undertaken by Rousseau and colleagues indicates that in many instances IRB members approach refugee claimants' testimony with little consideration of these complexities (Rousseau, Crépeau, Foxen, & Houle, 2002). The members of the IRB treat the claimant's narrative as a rhetorical act of positioning designed to claim specific social status. They hold an implicit epistemology in which a credible and truthful account is isomorphic with a single sequence of events. A truthful story is a fixed, reliable, and reproducible account of historically verifiable events. Because the precise sequence and details of events prior to migration usually are unverifiable outside the refugee's narrative, the IRB must rely on research dossiers that provide the background for generic accounts and their experience with previous claimants. As such, the claimant's account is suspect even before it is uttered.

THE WORK OF NARRATIVE

Imagination is basic to the understanding of any story. Through imagination we construct images. Narrative provides the temporal structure that binds these images to a plot. Narration is the construction of a sequence, scene, and scenario that invokes or implies a whole world as its larger context (Turner, 1996). Recent work in cognitive science shows how the semantic structure of narratives is based on the construction of representational spaces (Fauconnier, 1997). Most narratives involve multiple spaces, which are blended to allow reasoning with representations rooted in multiple structures. This capacity to blend disparate representational spaces forms the basis of metaphorical and analogical thinking (Fauconnier & Turner, 2002). However, to follow another person's account, we need to make certain that the worlds and their furnishings invoked by the speaker contain sufficient elements familiar to the listener. Most communication is not the transmission of packets of completely new information, but the evocation of the already known to build new configurations. Both the form and context of narratives influence this process of evocation, which is regulated not only by the semantic fields activated by familiar words and phrases, but also by the social context of speech and the affectively charged and socially scripted relationship between speaker and listener as conversational partners (Kirmayer, 2000). In what follows, I explore the co-construction of narratives of self and other in the clinical and juridical encounter with refugees.

EPISTEMOLOGY OF THE PERSONAL INFORMATION FORM

A person is a refugee under the 1951 UN Convention on the basis of the fact that he has a "well-founded fear of being persecuted for reasons of race, religion, nationality, membership of a particular social group, or political opinion" and is outside the country of his nationality and unable or unwilling to return for reasons of safety (United Nations High Commissioner for Refugees [UNHCR], 1997). To gain official status as a refugee, one must have a personal story that fits with some larger account of what is happening to people of a certain background from a certain part of the world. The fit of an individual's narrative with a master narrative is therefore crucial. This master narrative is only partially fixed by international convention. Like any story, it has local versions that are interpreted through a set of social practices in specific settings. In Canada, these interpretive practices centre on the institution of the IRB.

After arriving in Canada, the first formal step in the adjudication of refugee status is the completion of a Personal Information Form or PIF (IRB, 2001c). This form is provided within 10 days of arrival and must be returned within 28 days of receipt. The PIF is a narrative account of the identity, background, and biography of the claimant, including traumas and threats the individual has faced that justify the claim for refugee status. The form for the PIF asks for details of the claimant's language, nationality, ethnic groups, religion, education, military service, work history, travel, prior claims for refugee status, and any crimes or offences. Item 37 asks for the "reasons why the claimant is making a claim for refugee protection and the facts that support the claim." The PIF includes a signed declaration that the information given by the claimant is "complete, true and correct" and that "the claimant knows that the declaration is of the same force and effect as if made under oath."[1] If completed without an interpreter, then claimants must sign a further declaration that they can read the language of the form and that they understand what information is required. If the form is completed with the help of an interpreter, the interpreter must sign a declaration that he or she is proficient in the languages understood by the client, that they were able to communicate fully, that all forms were interpreted to the claimant, and that the claimant understood what was interpreted.

Although the information in the PIF is provided to the IRB to adjudicate the case of the claimant, if deemed relevant, a claimant's PIF may be used to evaluate the claims of other individuals, with some limited protection for the privacy of the claimant (the IRB must make "reasonable efforts" to notify the claimant in writing that his or her testimony will be used in another case). However, "the Division must not disclose personal or other information if there is a serious possibility that it will endanger the life, liberty or security of any person or is likely to cause an injustice" (IRB, 2001b). The narratives of the PIF thus occupy a special social space or liminal zone at the margins of Canadian society, where these narrators have very limited control over the political use of their stories.[2]

Refugees may tell stories of their migration in other settings, to family and friends, employers, clinicians, and other helpers (in social services, etc.), but the PIF is an official account that provides the raw data for the IRB determination of eligibility under the statutes. The clinical narratives provided by refugees have aspects or elements that are both "spontaneous" and elicited. Disagreements among narrators and inconsistencies between consecutive retellings are inevitable under such circumstances for a wide range of reasons: The events recounted may have been a long time ago; they are complex and the speaker has only partial knowledge; they were highly charged or traumatic; the speaker, to survive psychologically, may have tried to forget; the speaker, to survive socially, may have been prohibited from speaking (and hence recollecting) certain details or events; or the speaker may have tried to develop and present (and, ultimately, believe in) alternative stories and, perhaps, to develop one version that will maximize his or her chances of acceptance into a safe haven. As a result of all of these

---

[1] This and all subsequent IRB-related quotations come from the official Web site, www.cisr.gc.ca, accessed February 10, 2003.

[2] A colleague who came to Canada as a refugee recalls receiving the transcript of his IRB hearing in the mail for verification. He found it distinctly unnerving to have these stories, which would be extremely dangerous for him in his country of origin, pass through the public mail and sit, unprotected, in his mailbox.

factors, the stories available to the speaker may be fragmentary, multiple, contradictory, and, insofar as they are consistent, may be formulaic – presenting a fixed narrative that fits a template rather than a living narrative that renegotiates the meaning of events.

The PIF is written shortly after arrival during a time of anxiety and radical uncertainty, when the asylum seeker lacks a definite social status and familiar context with which to anchor and stabilize his self-understanding. The PIF narrative must be composed in English or French, with limited linguistic ability, or, if written in another language, translated (introducing all of the difficulties of accurate translation). Generally, it is composed with limited understanding of the purpose and interpretive frame through which it will be read. If the PIF writer tries to anticipate the biases of the IRB reader, he must recognise that any trace of this effort will cast doubt on his account. Hence, he is caught in an infinite regress, seeking a story that will be credible in its balance of the expected events and idiosyncratic detail.

Of course, the refugee's story is not only his own but also necessarily invokes the voices of others. After Bakhtin we recognize that all narratives are heteroglossic or intertextual – composed of quotations, explicit references, and allusions to other voices – and that these other voices can give authority, depth, and texture to an individual's story. The refugee's narrative poses a particular dilemma in this regard, for the voices it invokes are mostly absent and, even when they can be conjured, they are liable to speak a foreign idiom, unfamiliar to the audience in a new land (DeSantis, 2001). The antiphony that would intensify the emotional import of the refugee's story of suffering may be so faint as to be inaudible and, without this call and response, the refugee's story may seem flat or perforated.

Once committed to paper and filed, the story in the PIF becomes an official version of events – a yardstick against which subsequent versions will be measured for their veridicality and completeness. The addition of information may be possible with proper efforts (revised pages of the form must be submitted in triplicate with any changes to the original document underlined), but subtraction or contradiction of information in the PIF is likely to be met with great suspicion.

THE ARENA OF DOUBT

The IRB is the official institution charged with adjudicating claims for refugee status. It is Canada's largest independent administrative tribunal, part of the state apparatus designed to fulfill Canada's obligations as set out in the international conventions on refugees and human rights "by processing the refugee protection claims that come before it" (IRB, 2001a). Part of the procedure of the IRB is a formal hearing in which the refugee claimant can answer questions related to his or her case. The PIF is reviewed at the

IRB hearing, and the refugee is cross-examined. Although the situation of the IRB tribunal is not supposed to be adversarial, in fact, the members of the IRB sometimes adopt a sceptical stance.[3] The cross-examiner looks for inconsistencies, contradictions, and elements of the story that are hard to understand or credit.

The refugee claimant is questioned on unclear or contradictory details to obtain a satisfactory answer (one that will resolve the interlocutors' doubt), but the goal is often to catch the refugee claimant in a more obvious inconsistency or contradiction. Any incongruity is then pounced on as evidence of his untruthfulness and self-serving lies, which have a ready-made explanation in the presumed motivation to get into Canada illegally to enjoy the benefits of a wealthy society.

The context of recollection and examination is profoundly challenging and stressful for obvious reasons. The Refugee Division is not bound by any legal or technical rules of evidence. Although it is not supposed to be adversarial, the hearing is founded on doubt of the credibility of the refugee claimant and aimed not toward welcoming those deserving of safe haven but identifying those who illicitly seek to take advantage of Canadians. The adjudication of refugee status occurs before a tribunal in a formal setting; it occurs outside other social spaces and with an almost complete absence of other recourse or resources; it occurs in a second or third language for the speaker, who may have an interpreter also operating in a second or third language, and both of whom may be unable to follow the nuances of questions, attitudes, or expectations or be able to convey their own specific meanings.

This context of examination raises critical issues for several reasons: (1) it violates the sort of cognitive generosity necessary to make conversations go smoothly (these include the standard Gricean maxims as well as other ways we fill in the gaps in fragmentary or inconsistent accounts by assuming the relevance of the details a narrator provides (Sperber & Wilson, 1986); (2) it undermines the trust necessary to feel relaxed in an exchange and therefore makes regulation of affect and search of memory more difficult; (3) it may evoke elements of situations of hostile interrogation and undermining of the self that occurred in the refugee's past experience with officials; and (4) the power over the refugee claimant's fate that is wielded by the IRB may give moments of confrontation or dispute some of the quality of total negation or annihilation of the self experienced in torture.

More broadly, the examination and interpretation of the refugee's claims often occurs in the absence of shared cultural background knowledge that would render stories intelligible and motivations credible. Thus, Daniel

---

[3] The process of the IRB is captured in *Asylum* (National Film Board of Canada, Montreal, 1998), a remarkable documentary film by Gary Beitel that follows the experiences of three refugee claimants and takes the viewer behind the closed doors of the tribunal hearing.

points out that many refugees from South Asia share a notion of personhood that is not centred on the individual but on extended networks (Daniel, 2002), and this makes determinations of how directly they have been and are threatened, how personal and individual their own vulnerability, difficult to determine from a frame that privileges the isolable individual of Western psychology.

The members of the IRB are political appointees with limited background and training in refugee-related issues and none at all in mental health. They face a difficult task and their decisions are sometimes contentious. Rousseau and colleagues (2002) examined a series of cases where there were disagreements between the IRB determination and the assessment of clinicians familiar with the person seeking asylum. A systematic review revealed major errors in legal procedure, psychological conflicts, and cultural misunderstandings (Rousseau et al., 2002).

In Rousseau's study, legal procedural errors were identified in almost 90% of the cases reviewed, mainly incorrect handling of evidence, lack of knowledge of political conditions in the claimant's country of origin, and problems interpreting administrative and international law. Rules of conduct and politeness were breached in 28% of cases.

In one case, the Chair declared from the outset that she did not want to hear the claimant's story as she suspected that he would tell the same story she had already read in the PIF. She rejected the counsel's request that he be allowed to ask clarifying questions of the claimant, and asked the Refugee Claim Officer to proceed with her questions. (Rousseau et al., 2002)

Psychological issues were evident in the review of problematic cases due to the difficulty of dealing with refugee's stories, which are laden with horrific events. The review of transcripts of the hearings revealed evidence of massive avoidance of the traumatic content of these narratives in 75% of cases. Lack of empathy, overt expressions of prejudice, and cynical or sarcastic responses were present in 50 to 75% of cases. In one third of cases, there were clear signs of emotional distress in the IRB members.

In one of the cases, an expert psychological report was given, detailing the post-traumatic stress syndrome suffered by the claimant after he was tortured; pictures taken immediately after his arrival in Canada were provided showing his body covered with cigarette burns. The health professional had conducted six consecutive interviews of the claimant, making a thorough assessment of his condition and relating it to the details of his story. The claim was rejected. During the hearing, one of the Board members said that he always took expert psychological reports "with a grain of salt." Later in the hearing it was discovered that he had not even read the report and the Chair had to interrupt the proceedings to allow the Board member to read it. The Chair herself commented on the fact that she herself was a smoker, implying that she did not give much weight to the cigarette burn marks or the expert opinion that these were sequelae of torture. (Rousseau et al., 2002)

Cultural issues included lack of understanding of the social and political context in the refugee's country of origin, difficulties assessing the family and social relationships of the claimant, frank prejudice and stereotyping, and difficulty communicating.

In several cases, the Board Members' concept of family life in a country at war, in low-intensity conflict, or in situations of persecution was simplistic or false. They seemed unable to envisage situations where localized violence reigns as conflicting groups struggle for power, or where the military or police are involved in corruption, intimidation and abuse of power.... Board Members also often seem incredulous at the arbitrary behaviour of the authorities (police, army, government) as recounted by claimants. The notion that terror and persecution are implemented precisely through arbitrariness, chaos and impunity seems difficult for them to grasp, and the inability of claimants to provide a rational reason for such abusive behaviour leads them to further doubt their story. (Rousseau et al., 2002)

The disturbing breaches of etiquette, procedure, understanding, and even compassion cannot be attributed simply to ignorance or ill will on the part of the IRB members. Instead, they reflect an unexamined conflict of cultural and conceptual frames. As Rousseau and colleagues argue,

[T]he primary function of the Board members is to evaluate the credibility of witnesses. In the manner of a jury, the members make decisions based on common sense in order to draw conclusions as to the credibility of the refugee claimant. However, it is the assumption of the existence of a "common sense", especially in matters concerning the determination of refugee status, that we find problematic.... From a cultural perspective, it is erroneous to assume that the reference point for this "common sense" is to be found in Canadian cultural norms and representations. The testimonies and events presented by refugee claimants generally have little or nothing in common with the daily life of the decision-makers. (Rousseau et al., 2002)

The dilemma is that the assumptions of "common sense" and everyday life break down in the encounter with the refugee's experience. To some extent, this can be understood as following from the limited cultural, geographical, and historical knowledge of the IRB members. This could be remedied by providing more detailed background. But there are reasons for the failure of understanding that go beyond mere lack of information and have to do with the ways in which the listeners conceive of stories and their potential truths.

THE RATIONALITY OF IMAGINATION

The doubt and disdain that sometimes mark the IRB tribunal hearing are very different from the sympathetic listening and effort to co-construct a story that characterize the typical clinical encounter. The mental health practitioner, particularly the psychotherapist, aims to create a seamless narrative that is functional for the patient – a story to live by. Even under these circumstances there are often breakdowns in the collaborative effort because of differences in models and metaphors (Kirmayer, 2000). Of course, there are other clinical settings with different epistemologies and different uses for stories: for example, the forensic evaluation where client motivations are suspect (people have every reason to lie, if they can do it effectively), the case manager trying to administer limited social resources by assessing "legitimate" need, or the clinician doing disability assessments for an insurance company. These situations may be more analogous to that of the gatekeepers of the IRB.[4]

In diagnostic assessments, clinicians are interested in the inconsistencies or contradictions in a patient's story, but for the purposes of identifying specific psychological dynamics or neurological dysfunctions (Kirmayer, 1994). To maintain rapport and provide support, they may limit their level of confrontation of gaps or inconsistencies in the patient's story. The psychotherapeutic situation generally offers much greater cognitive and emotional generosity, which fills in the gaps in patients' stories to titrate their anxiety, help them find coherence and build trust. This narrative smoothing works against discovering inconsistency and contradiction – or, at least, narrows the story down to specific areas of therapeutic interest (as in cognitive therapy or psychoanalysis).

The clinical concern is not with challenging the patients' accounts but discovering what will promote and sustain therapeutic imagination – understood as the capacity to reconfigure one's self-narrative in order to live a personally and socially valued life. The result is a narrative that may be frail in the forensic context but that derives its rhetorical force and conviction from the adoption of a specific psychological model of the self and its development. Although this narrative is reflected in popular notions of self and personhood, for the individual in psychotherapy it functions as an unofficial narrative that the patient carries like a keepsake – a private version of the self, a snapshot of an intimate personal history, to be carried close to the heart and consulted when one needs a moment of affirmation of the enduring presence of the past or of one's heroic survival.

There is another narrative that is recorded in disjointed form by the psychiatrist in case notes, diagnostic formulations, and letters of consultation. This official psychiatric narrative is deposited in hospital or clinic records, as well as in letters written to lawyers, courts, bureaucrats, and other health professionals. However, the official narrative also is a trace of more evanescent narratives: the ones told as part of clinical conversations (which may be appropriated and told by patients in other settings, as when

---

4 Some forms of psychotherapy may also employ a hermeneutics of suspicion, in which the clinician is analogous to a detective. Freud wrote many of his case histories in this style although most contemporary clinicians would find this stance countertherapeutic.

patients make use of a diagnostic label or clinical understanding); those told in case conferences or informal colloquy with colleagues (which may be looser, even scatological, and serve the function of regulating painful emotions arising from the challenges of clinical work); and those that occur in the inner monologue of the clinician trying to make sense of puzzling experiences (such transient narratives in therapists' inner theatre of the mind) are the very stuff of clinical reasoning.

Although the narratives of clinical autobiography and psychodynamic formulation may fit specific causal models, their underlying logic is not closely aligned with scientific reasoning or rationality. Clinical reasoning by patient and clinician is not monological but driven by multiple images and prototypes. Hence, metaphoric language dominates the imagination, and strong images demand priority of place in the reconstruction of events. The resultant accounts tend to be polyvocal and contradictory. They are held together not by logical consistency but by the way they cohabit one body and biography and the ways they actively engage each other in conflict or argument that need not be resolved.

The narrating self imagined in the clinical context is a *relational self*, created by a personal history of relationships and constantly engaged in renegotiating its identity through dialogue with significant others. In contrast, the members of IRB imagine an *adamantine self* – obdurate and unchanging – that fits the assumptions they make about the nature of narrative truth (Kirmayer, 2002). Indeed, the adamantine self is a necessary fiction for the juridical process of the tribunal. A univocal, rational self can give an unambiguous account of events and an honest reading of its own motivations, which can then be used to decide the refugee status of the person. The irony is that this fictive entity is invoked in circumstances that effectively conspire against its appearance.

IMAGINING AN ETHICAL RESPONSE

In focusing on the difficulties that refugees face telling and having others credit their stories, it is important to emphasize that their reception in Canada in recent years has been among the best in the world. As a country of immigrants, Canada's response to refugees reflects not just humanitarian commitments but its self-definition as a multicultural society (Ignatieff, 2000; Kymlicka, 1995). Officially, "the IRB contributes to shaping Canada's social fabric by playing a part in achieving the objectives of the Government to make Canada a strong society open to diversity and innovation in which people can live in security" (IRB, 2001a). Hence, the problems we identify in the Canadian context are likely to be greatly exacerbated under regimes with less tolerance for or interest in the plight of refugees.

Since the 1951 Geneva Convention, many states have become less committed to protecting refugees (Wilde, 2001). The use of detention for asylum seekers has increased (Silove, Steel, & Watters, 2000). The concerns about security provoked by the terrorist attack of September 11 have been used to justify more restrictive policies and practices. For example, the United States–Canada "Safe Third Country Agreement," which requires that asylum seekers claim protection in the first safe country they arrive in, means that asylum seekers who land first in the United States can no longer make their way to Canada. Other barriers have multiplied rapidly in the wake of the terror of 9/11 and the predicament of refugees has been both politicized and criminalized (Malik & Mulay, 2002).

[M]ainstream policy in some countries categorizes the causes of migration in a binary fashion, either as 'political' – in which case the immigrants are 'legal' and 'refugees' – or 'economic' – in which case immigrants are, in refugee terms, 'illegal'. Under such a binary system, allowing for overlap between the two categories can lead to an elision of both. (Wilde, 2001)

The anxieties provoked by terrorist attacks and their subsequent political manipulation to encourage a preoccupation with national ("homeland") security make it harder to remember that the very existence of stateless persons is a call to a moral order higher than nationalism or self-interested protectionism (Ignatieff, 2000). Article 14 of the Universal Declaration of Human Rights states that "everyone has the right to seek and enjoy in other countries asylum from persecution" (UNHCR, 1997). Refugees live in a state of displacement and exile, occupying a non-place outside the usual protections of state and community (Bauman, 2002). This predicament is what makes the extension of basic human rights to refugees so morally and politically essential (Dummett, 2001).

Policies of deterrence against refugees and the pervasive suspicion that distorts their reception have been justified on the assumption that many people in impoverished regions of the world want to move to the wealthy urban centers of the West. This assumption, however, is not warranted. The UNHCR *Handbook on Procedures and Criteria for Determining Refugee Status* reminds the reader that "it may be assumed that, unless he seeks adventure or just wishes to see the world, a person would not normally abandon his home and country without some compelling reason" (UNHCR, 1992, chap. 1, article 39). Given freedom of movement, some people would seek economic opportunities elsewhere but most would strive to remain connected to their places of origin.

The natural desire to return to one's home has new modes of expression in the age of electronic networking and telecommunications. People who choose to migrate now can easily maintain ties with their places of origin and, if they return, can also maintain new links with the country of migration; hence, "transnationality" has become a common mode of configuring identity (Appadurai, 1996; Glick-Schiller & Fouron, 1990; Portes, 1999). This transnationality takes two main forms: portable and confluent identities, in which people's sense of national identity moves with them across borders to colonize and change the texture of local worlds even as their own identity takes up elements of the new context; and *extraterritoriality*, in which the individual becomes free-floating, occupying spaces of indeterminacy with ambiguous governance and allegiances.

Extraterritoriality may be freely chosen by some individuals seeking a cosmopolitan identity but it is forced on refugees in flight and may persist long after resettlement due to enduring uncertainties of citizenship status, persistent fears about the plight of loved ones left behind, and the ambivalence of exile. Whether experienced as exile or asylum, however, the credibility and coherence of refugees' narratives of identity depends on the social imagination, and the limited exchange of images and information makes it easy to discredit the radical otherness of the refugee's experience, to assimilate it to familiar forms, to judge his or her story against conventional local norms, and, hence, to view him or her as deviant or defective (Pickering, 2001).

Disbelief when faced with the refugee's story serves defensive or protective functions. It keeps individuals from encountering a destabilizing otherness that would call their assumptive world into question. More importantly, it keeps the privileged from having to recognize the legitimacy (and urgency) of the moral claims of large numbers of less advantaged people, not only for our compassion or concern but also for a share of our resources, time, and space.

These issues are general features of the contemporary scene in which psychiatry is only a bit player. Psychiatry has its own technical procedures and clinical epistemology, but clinicians are deeply embedded in a political and economic system that sustains them. The psychiatrist performing an evaluation that may be used in a refugee hearing may find tensions between a clinical orientation and interpretation and the judicial consequences of assessment and labelling. The resolution of these tensions involves taking a professional stance with political implications. The claim that psychiatry is a technical enterprise may be advanced to deny this political dimension, but once clinicians are asked to take part in the larger system of refugee determination, there is no neutrality: Even the refusal to give an opinion conveys a distinct message with political import. Of course, the psychiatrist is also a citizen and may be just as reluctant to accept newcomers whom he believes threaten his power and privilege as the conservative politician, newspaper columnist, or IRB member.

Psychiatrists are called on to warrant the reality of refugee stories by establishing the mental capacity and general credibility of patients (who may be disqualified by being labelled as antisocial, malingering, or otherwise manipulative, often with the broad label of personality disorder). They may also be asked to assess the likelihood that individuals' fears are well founded and that they have the psychological sequelae of severe trauma. The diagnosis of PTSD has functioned this way – as a discrete diagnostic entity that warrants the history of past torture or other form of assault. Unfortunately, PTSD has no sharp boundaries as a diagnostic entity (Young, 1995) and cannot function with the same degree of certainty with which a bone X-ray showing a specific type of healed fracture might confirm a history of a specific type of torture. Nevertheless, the label of PTSD provides the nidus for a narrative; it serves as a core truth, fact, or datum that influences the interpretation of longer, more idiosyncratic biographical narratives. It may come as a novel account to the survivor of torture and offer some relief by explaining persistent symptoms and hence making them less threatening. For the IRB, the narrative of PTSD has quickly become a stock story provided by psychiatry – one they expect to hear and that in itself carries little new information. By telling the same story again and again, psychiatrists erode the credibility of their consultations and ultimately nullify their impact.

Of course, there is a much larger story to be told. Elided by the PTSD story are the more profound and pervasive effects of massive human rights violations that are central to the refugee's predicament (Silove, 1999). Nor does the violence endured by the refugees end with migration; it is embedded in the structures of most receiving societies (Silove, Steel, & Watters, 2000). Indeed, the mental health outcomes of migration depend on the quality of reception by the host society, including opportunities to find a firm footing through work and social status and to build a new life for one's family and children (Beiser, 1999). This larger story is not subtended by PTSD, but it is not one that the IRB wants to hear, even if its own deliberations are best understood as a chapter in this ongoing saga.

CONCLUSION

The tendency to reduce symptoms to signs in contemporary psychiatric practice works to elide the patient's story and undermine experiential truth. Deploying a hermeneutics of suspicion, psychoanalytic theory and therapy have tended to treat symptoms and stories as screens for other deeper stories that are harder to tell. With perseverance, patients may be brought to recollect and reveal this deeper truth. It is arguable whether this is the excavation of an existing but suppressed experiential truth or really a process of mimesis – the creation of a new account of the self, consistent with the ideology of psychoanalytic theory (Gellner, 1985).

Nevertheless, models of psychopathology may help us to empathize with those whose minds do not work like our own and even lead people to feel that they better understand their own inconsistent selves. Similarly, models of the social world may help us to empathize with those whose life histories and experiences do not accord with our own. Over time, psychiatrists' patients do manage to teach their doctors something about varied social worlds, just as the members of the IRB can become more worldly and aware of the divides of culture and context. But for others who come from afar, differences in language, background knowledge, and rhetorical style make their experiences difficult to convey. Of course, refugees find others reluctant to listen to the horrors they have endured. Those who have escaped extremes of chaos and violence threaten us with the rupture of our ordinary worlds, presenting us with elements of the random, arbitrary, and uncanny that defy the possibility of any conventional explanation or account and challenge our need for order and coherence:

Unlike men and women who have never known exile, whose biography is shaped by and large by social class and environment, to be a refugee is to have sheer chance govern one's fate, which in the end guarantees a life so absurd in most cases that it defeats anyone's powers of comprehension. (Simic, 2003)

We might expect that clinicians accustomed to confronting the absurdities of madness would have an easier time than most imagining their patients' real-world predicaments. However, psychiatrists receive their information about diverse social and cultural worlds from the same sources that saturate the airwaves. Most of our knowledge of the world comes to us filtered through mass media that impose their own distorting perspectives, exoticizing the other, ignoring the mundane, and hence failing to convey the texture of everyday life in a way that would provide the mental furnishings we need to create a conceptual model that captures the other's world of experience.

Perversely, the media do manage to fill our heads with ideas about the other, but the stereotypes we absorb are more likely to be obstacles than bridges to entering other worlds. It is not that it is difficult for us to take up a new idea when it fits with our prejudices. On the obverse of disbelief is the vast territory of credulity. Umberto Eco writes of the persistence of the fable of the *Protocols of the Elders of Zion* in anti-Semitic discourse (Eco, 1994). This never-ending story moved from the realm of fantasy to political reality with its origins as a malicious fabrication conveniently forgotten or ignored (Bronner, 2000). The lesson is clear. We must struggle to create a social space in which imagination is given free reign but that is well stocked with accurate stories about the world that protect it from the extremes of credulity and disbelief.

The stories we find credible depend on a backdrop of narratives in constant circulation controlled by interests that are not neutral and would have us imagine our world in a certain way. This is not the best of all possible worlds. And imagination is the only faculty we have that lets us see beyond the horizon of convention.

ACKNOWLEDGMENT

This chapter is adapted from Kirmayer (2003) with permission from *Anthropology & Medicine*, http://www.tandf.co.uk. Earlier versions were presented at the "Culture and Medical/Psychiatric Narratives Conference" of the Medical Anthropology Group of the Royal Anthropological Institute, University of Bristol, U.K., September 21, 2002, and the Foundation for Psychocultural Research–UCLA conference "Posttraumatic Stress Disorder: Biological, Clinical, and Cultural Approaches to Trauma's Effects," Los Angeles, December 13, 2002.

References

Achebe, C. (2000). *Home and exile*. Oxford, UK: Oxford University Press.

Appadurai, A. (1996). *Modernity at large: Cultural dimensions of globalization*. Minneapolis: University of Minnesota Press.

Bauman, Z. (2002). *Society under siege*. Cambridge, UK: Blackwell.

Beiser, M. (1999). *Strangers at the gate: The 'boat people's' first ten years in Canada*. Toronto: University of Toronto Press.

Bronner, S. E. (2000). *A rumor about the Jews: Reflections on antisemitism and the protocols of the learned elders of Zion*. New York: St. Martin's Press.

Daniel, E. V. (2002). The refugee: A discourse on displacement. In J. MacClancy (Ed.), *Exotic no more: Anthropology on the front lines* (pp. 270–286). Chicago: University of Chicago Press.

DeSantis, A. D. (2001). Caught between two worlds: Bakhtin's dialogism in the exile experience. *Journal of Refugee Studies, 14*(1), 1–19.

Dummett, M. A. E. (2001). *On immigration and refugees*. New York: Routledge.

Eco, U. (1994). *Six walks in the fictional woods*. Cambridge, MA: Harvard University Press.

Fauconnier, G. (1997). *Mappings in thought and language*. Cambridge, UK: Cambridge University Press.

Fauconnier, G., & Turner, M. (2002). *The way we think: Conceptual blending and the mind's hidden complexities*. New York: Basic Books.

Gellner, E. (1985). *The psychoanalytic movement*. London: Paladin Books.

Glick-Schiller, N., & Fouron, G. (1990). "Everywhere we go, we are in danger": Ti Manno and the emergence of a Haitian transnational identity. *American Ethnologist, 17*(2), 329–347.

Ignatieff, M. (2000). *The rights revolution*. Vancouver: House of Anansi Press.

Immigration and Refugee Board. (2001a, rev. February 13, 2003). *About the IRB*. Retrieved February 16, 2003, from http://www.irb.gc.ca/en/about/index_e.htm.

Immigration and Refugee Board. (2001b, rev. June 14, 2002). *Current legislation*. Retrieved February 15, 2003, from www.irb.gc.ca/en/about/rules/index_e.htm.

Immigration and Refugee Board. (2001c, rev. June 14, 2002). *Personal information form*. Retrieved February 15, 2003, from http://www.irb.gc.ca/en/forms/PIForm_e.htm.

Immigration and Refugee Board Legal Services. (1998, rev. June 14, 2002). *Assessment of credibility in the context of CRDD hearings.* Retrieved February 15, 2003, from www.irb.gc.ca/en/about/rules/index_e.htm.

Kirmayer, L. J. (1994). Improvisation and authority in illness meaning. *Culture, Medicine and Psychiatry, 18*(2), 183–214.

Kirmayer, L. J. (1996). Landscapes of memory: Trauma, narrative and dissociation. In P. Antze & M. Lambek (Eds.), *Tense past: Cultural essays on memory and trauma* (pp. 173–198). London: Routledge.

Kirmayer, L. J. (2000). Broken narratives: Clinical encounters and the poetics of illness experience. In C. Mattingly & L. Garro (Eds.), *Narrative and the cultural construction of illness and healing* (pp. 153–180). Berkeley: University of California Press.

Kirmayer, L. J. (2002). The refugee's predicament. *L'Évolution Psychiatrique, 67,* 724–742.

Kirmayer, L. J. (2003). Failures of imagination: The refugee's narrative in psychiatry. *Anthropology & Medicine, 10*(2), 167–185.

Kirmayer, L. J., Corin, E., & Jarvis, G. E. (2004). Inside knowledge: Cultural constructions of insight in psychosis. In X. F. Amador & A. S. David (Eds.), *Insight in psychosis* (2nd ed., pp. 197–229). New York: Oxford University Press.

Kirmayer, L. J., Groleau, D., Guzder, J., Blake, C., & Jarvis, E. (2003). Cultural consultation: A model of mental health service for multicultural societies. *Canadian Journal of Psychiatry, 48*(2), 145–153.

Kymlicka, W. (1995). *Multicultural citizenship.* Oxford: Oxford University Press.

Malik, L., & Mulay, S. (2002, December 24). No room at the inn. *Globe and Mail,* 17.

Pickering, S. (2001). Common sense and original deviancy: News discourses and asylum seekers in Australia. *Journal of Refugee Studies, 14*(2), 169–186.

Portes, A. (1999). Conclusion: Towards a new world – The origins and effects of transnational activities. *Ethnic and Racial Studies, 22*(2), 463–477.

Rousseau, C., Crépeau, F., Foxen, P., & Houle, F. (2002). The complexity of determining refugeehood: A multidisciplinary analysis of the decision-making process of the Canadian Immigration and Refugee Board. *Journal of Refugee Studies, 15*(1), 43–70.

Rousseau, C., & Drapeau, A. (2001). Stories of refugees embodied in their children's lives: Transmission through words and silence in different cultures. In Y. Danielli (Ed.), *International handbook of multigenerational legacies of trauma.* New York: Plenum Press.

Silove, D. (1999). The psychosocial effects of torture, mass human rights violations, and refugee trauma. *Journal of Nervous and Mental Disease, 187*(4), 200–207.

Silove, D., Steel, Z., & Watters, C. (2000). Policies of deterrence and the mental health of asylum seekers. *Journal of the American Medical Association, 284*(5), 604–611.

Simic, C. (2003). Conspiracy of silence. *New York Review of Books, 50*(3), 8–10.

Sperber, D., & Wilson, D. (1986). *Relevance: Communication and cognition.* Cambridge, MA: Harvard University Press.

Turner, M. (1996). *The literary mind.* New York: Oxford University Press.

United Nations High Commissioner for Refugees (UNHCR). (1992). *Handbook on procedures and criteria for determining refugee status under the 1951 convention and the 1967 protocol relating to the status of refugees.* Geneva: United Nations High Commission on Refugees.

United Nations High Commissioner for Refugees (UNHCR). (1997). *The state of the world's refugees, 1997–98: A humanitarian agenda.* New York: Oxford University Press.

Wilde, R. (2001). The refugee convention at 50: Forced migration policy at the turn of the century. *Journal of Refugee Studies, 14*(2), 135–150.

Young, A. (1995). *The harmony of illusions: Inventing posttraumatic stress disorder.* Princeton, NJ: Princeton University Press.

18

Trauma, Culture, and Myth: Narratives of the Ethiopian Jewish Exodus

Gadi BenEzer

This chapter focuses on the way traumatic experience during a group's return from exile can turn into a social myth and on the role played by aspects within the group's culture in this mythologizing process. More specifically, the chapter deals with the journey of the Ethiopian Jews via Sudan to Israel during the 1980s and the meaning it acquired for the people who underwent this journey. I argue, on the basis of my clinical and ethnographic research (BenEzer, 2002), that migration journeys are unjustifiably ignored in migration and refugee studies, as well as in traumatology. Powerful processes occur on such journeys that affect the individual and community in life-changing ways and shape their initial encounter with, and adaptation to, their new society. In what follows, I shall discuss the transformation of the individual stories of the journey of Ethiopian Jews into a collective myth in Israel.

THE JOURNEY: FACTS AND MEANING

The exodus to Israel was motivated by an ancient, recurring dream of the Ethiopian Jewish community that "the time will arrive" in which they will return to their homeland, the land of their ancestors (BenEzer, 2002). In 1862, a respected elder of the community named Abba Mahari announced that "the time has arrived," and thousands of members of the community started to walk with him from the Gondar area, near Lake Tana, toward Israel. When they arrived at the Red Sea, or the Takaze river in Tigray province, according to another traditional account, Abba Mahari pointed his stick toward the sea, like Moses, his forefather 3100 years earlier, and waited for the waters to part and let them pass. When this did not happen, they waited for some days and then decided that "the time has not yet arrived" and that Abba Mahari had experienced only a prophetic dream. Those who remained after this difficult journey returned to their villages and continued to wait for the "ripening of time" (Ben-Dor, 1987).

In 1977, members of the community again perceived that "the time has arrived" and reembarked on the journey to Israel. Over the next few years, 20,000 people, a significant portion of the entire Ethiopian Jewish community, started to walk toward Israel, though, in fact, they were travelling in the opposite direction, toward the Ethiopian–Sudanese border, believing that when they reached the Sudanese border, they would somehow immediately be conveyed to Israel. Their journey was illegal and highly traumatic. Ethiopia at that time was under the control of a Communist–Marxist regime (the Dergue) and even a desire to leave the country, let alone actually trying to escape, was considered a reactionary ideological statement and a serious crime that could lead to a death sentence. Even the move from one district to another required permission by the government.

A veil of secrecy, therefore, shrouded the departure on the journey. The migrants[1] did whatever they could to hide their plans and, many times, left in great haste. In addition to the clandestine nature of their journey, it had an extremely traumatic quality. This occurred in part because of the harsh conditions on the trek. Walking toward the Sudanese border took an average of 3–5 weeks. For many, however, it took much longer due to various obstacles and misfortunes on the way. They suffered from lack of water, food, sleep, and other basic human needs while walking at night along difficult mountain trails. They experienced bandit attacks, government incarcerations, torture, kidnapping, rape, diseases, and death. Arriving in Sudan, they endured an average of 1–2 years in refugee conditions, which included exposure to many of the same obstacles and forms of violence. Some of the problems they faced along that journey and in Sudan were directly related to their Jewish identity and their wish to arrive in Israel. Of the 20,0000 who set out on the trek between 1977 and 1985, about 1 in 5 (4,000 people) did not survive the journey.

In my research project (BenEzer, 2002), I conducted narrative interviews with 45 young people and analyzed their personal stories. Three central themes were found to be the major dimensions of meaning through which Ethiopian Jews constructed their journey experience: the centrality of

---

[1] While the Ethiopian Jews started their migration process as ideological migrants, many of those left behind were then pushed out of their homes by their Christian or Muslim neighbours, thus turning them into refugees. In any event, all of them went through a refugee state in Sudan. Nevertheless, all continued to view themselves along the whole journey as ideological migrants or exiles, returning to their historical homeland. For the choice of the more inclusive term "migrants" in this context, and its use in preference to "immigrants" or "emigrants," see BenEzer (2002, p. 206, n2).

Jewish identity, the significance of suffering, and the importance of bravery and inner strength.

Jewish Identity

The narratives of the Ethiopian Jews showed that Jewish identity was one of the central themes of the journey (BenEzer, 2002, chap. 4). It was expressed by the individuals in relation to themselves and their group, as well as in relation to non-Jews. First, Jewish identity played a crucial role in the decision to migrate. This decision was described as the fulfillment of the ancient dream of the exiled to return to "Yerussalem." This dream was handed down from one generation to the next and completely integrated into family and community life. For example, Shmuel, one of my interviewees, told me how his father used to talk with him about Yerussalem when they were ploughing the field together. His father would say, "You know my son, the land that we are plowing is not our land. Our land is far away, in Yerussalem" (BenEzer, 2002, p. 61).[2] Others related how when a parent or an elderly person wanted to praise a child and bless them they would say, "May you reach your homeland" or "May you arrive in Zion." Children's dreams were often interpreted as foretelling a future when they would reach Israel and "you shall never have to leave again." Thus, the migration dream was kept very much alive throughout the years, so much so that it served as a blueprint for action. Ethiopian Jews believed that when the time arrived they would go back to their homeland. They perceived the return to Israel as a rectification of the situation of exile. They saw themselves as a part returning to the whole, a drop, a stream, or a river that would rejoin the sea so that one could no longer distinguish between river and sea. They believed that, once in Israel, among their brethren, they would feel more complete (BenEzer, 2002, p. 60).

It is important to note how in all phases of this journey, from the preparations, through the Ethiopian trek, and during the long stay in Sudan, the Jewish identity of these wayfarers was strengthened and consolidated. In their eyes, the journey was led by God. The message to set out was given by Him; as Elazar, one of my interviewees, explained, "We did not start this whole thing [the migration]; rather, our time has arrived. . . . No one told us other than the blessed God. A feeling seized us that called to us: 'Go! Go!' These are God's words." God also guided them on the strenuous walk. He gave them the strength to go on walking with no rest, saved them from dangers, assisted them when they were suddenly attacked by enemies, and miraculously put ideas into their minds about how to save themselves or their loved ones.

---

[2] All quotations from narratives in this chapter are taken from the larger study of the migration journey of Ethiopian Jews (BenEzer, 2002).

In addition to their belief in God, Jewish identity was expressed along the journey in their efforts to keep the Jewish religious laws and customs – observing the Sabbath, Passover, food restrictions (*kashrut*), and purity/impurity of women and men, among others. There are many stories of groups that were chased by robbers (*shifta*) or by army patrols, and though they were close to the Sudanese border and could cross it and thus get rid of those chasing them, they stopped running because the Sabbath had arrived. As a result of that they were captured, sometimes tortured, and many times brought back to their villages hundreds of miles distant. An 11-year-old girl spoke of how, in Sudan, the adults hid the children when food was brought to them so that the children would not be tempted to eat nonkosher food.

Burial was also problematic, particularly in Sudan. Many buried their relatives at night and kept their mouths tightly closed by biting on their clothing so that no one would hear their crying and wailing. A 10-year-old girl described how she had to hold her dead baby sister in her arms for 4 days in the Sudanese refugee camp because she did not know where to bury her and she was the only one left of all her relatives.

Jewish identity was also strengthened by the community's sense of isolation on the walking journey and in Sudan. They were constantly threatened by Christian and Muslim villagers, as well as soldiers and other government officials, who tried to expose their identity and destination. Thus, the wayfarers felt they were Jews crossing a hostile sea of Gentiles (non-Jews), while hiding their community's secret of the migration to Israel.

Suffering

The second theme through which the Ethiopian immigrants understand their journey concerns physical as well as emotional suffering. In the physical sense, their suffering relates to the objective difficulties and obstacles of the journey as well as to the problems caused by other people. They had to cross high mountain passes and deep gorges, strong waters and desert areas. They had to move quickly and without stopping, often walking at night, navigating narrow mountainous trails, sometimes without sleep, knowing that if they did not go fast enough they might lose contact with the other wayfarers and get lost on their way. Many fell, were injured, and were then forced to stay behind and wait for relatives to carry them back to their village where they could recuperate and start out on the trail again. The wayfarers went through periods of severe deprivation of food or water and suffered from various diseases, some typical of lowlands, such as malaria, others caused by river parasites. They had to hide from wild animals and from human predators – soldiers or thieves, who controlled the trails during the long civil war in Ethiopia. Many were incarcerated on their way, interrogated, tortured, and brought back to their villages time and again. Others were robbed of their money, clothes, malaria pills, as well as the food and water they carried. Adolescent girls and young women were raped or kidnapped, and to this day, some remain captive in Sudan or Saudi Arabia. In Sudan, many became sick, and the death toll rose dramatically. At one point, in the Um Rakuba camp in Sudan, 15 Jewish Ethiopians were dying each day.

In addition to the physical suffering there was also mental pain. The migrants suffered as a result of separation from members of their family. This pain was accentuated because, according to Ethiopian culture, a person separated from his or her family is considered incomplete (BenEzer, 1990). The disintegration of the families was caused, first, by the need to leave their villages secretly and thus not in large groups. Both extended and nuclear families had to split up for the journey. Second, according to Ethiopian cultural code, a person's obligation toward his or her parents is stronger (hierarchically more important) than the obligation to his or her children. This contributed to the splitting apart of nuclear families because a husband or wife sometimes stayed behind until his or her own parents were able to move, while sending their partner off with some of the children. Third, families broke apart due to the hurdles and difficulties of the walking journey and its misfortunes, as well as the high toll of death in Sudan. Many still feel the typical survivor guilt because they were able to stay alive while their relatives died. Moreover, they often felt guilty because they had to bury their dead in an undignified way that did not give their loved ones the respect they deserved. This might be conceived of as a sort of "cultural survivor guilt."

Another aspect of the mental suffering is related to the traumatic experiences of humiliation and contempt they underwent as individuals or as a group of Jews, from Sudanese police and army forces. Daniel, for example, experienced a trauma related to humiliation. During his stay in Sudan, he tried to escape with a group of friends from the refugee camp, Um Rakuba, to the town of Gedaref. Unfortunately, they were captured by the Sudanese and imprisoned. Daniel was shouted at, beaten, and accused of being head of a *shifta* (outlaws) gang. He continues his account of the event:

Then, on the second day there, the prison commander came, called me, and when I approached him, he took out a pair of big scissors and told his people to shave my hair. I was frightened but even more I was *angry*. Because ... the commander said all kinds of things to me [insults related to his Jewishness]. And so they started, two of his men, one started here [points to one side of his head] and the other ... [silence] they took off all my hair! On that day I was ... on that day ... [finds it difficult to go on] I went inside myself [quiet]. [I realised that] if I said anything, if I let out one word, then they could do as they wished. So eh – I shut down my mind. They cursed me with all kinds of curses [talks very quietly] and so on – and later [long pause], the sun was, what shall I tell you, the sun was *strong* and I was thinking of the sun, [being] without hair [whispers]...I shall never forget that day [keeps quiet for some time]. This is the worst – I suffered worst, I suffered very much. They made me bald, they did – [unclear]. So I became enraged. On that day I thought of my parents. Why had I come? How had I come to be separated from them? What did I have in Sudan? and so on. I had a day... [which was] very sad [very long silence]...they were laughing at me while they were cutting my hair, they were making fun of my hair.

It seems to me that the shaving of his hair was a severe narcissistic blow (Sandler, 1960; Sandler, Dreher, & Drews, 1991) for Daniel, affecting his self-image, and therefore was experienced as traumatic.[3]

In addition to such humiliations, many went through experiences of helplessness and mental torture. Girls, for example, suffered severe emotional pain when they were forced to watch their brothers or friends being tortured, being forced to stand in the burning sun for 3 or 4 days, or hanging upside down for long periods of time. Others were raped and some lost interest in living. Boys and men sometimes experienced intense helplessness at not being able to protect their sisters or other female relatives or school friends, for whom they felt responsible.

Bravery and Inner Strength

The third theme that constituted the meaning of the journey was that of bravery and inner strength. This theme brought together those aspects of the narratives in which the interviewees expressed a feeling of great achievement and those moments or actions in which their powers and potentials were brought to a maximum or stretched even beyond that. This theme seems closely related to the concept of *gobez* (also *govez*) within Ethiopian culture (BenEzer, 2002, p. 120). The central meaning of *gobez* is a person who is brave. *Gobez* is the great Amhara virtue that traditionally embodies fierceness, hardiness, and general male competence (Rosen 1987, p. 58). Its core image is of a person who could cope with a long walking

---

[3] In my view, the subject of humiliation as a distinct source of trauma is insufficiently dealt with in the literature on children in war, refugees, and migrants in their transition process. In my study, it was a common source of trauma. It seems that the experience of being intentionally humiliated by another human being constitutes for many individuals a narcissistic injury of an immense magnitude, which effectively traumatizes them. Their self-image and self-esteem are affected, and the person finds this blow difficult to absorb and recover from. As an Ethiopian proverb claims in relation to verbal abuse, "Curses [insults] are of such a nature that, once uttered, they keep being [hurtfully] spoken in your mind." Of course, it is not curses alone that we are concerned with here, but also with other humiliating measures. When verbal abuse includes insults to one's ethnic group, it adds another dimension of suffering and traumatization (see BenEzer, 2002, for a possible explanation of this and the general subject of traumatic humiliation).

journey in the mountainous trails while subsisting on a handful of dried chickpeas, standing up to the powers of nature and to hostile people. It is particularly relevant for adolescent males and young persons and also extends to female competence.

The image of the *gobez* seemed to play a role in the experience of young people on the journey. Their narratives told of how they strived to actualize this virtue. This became clear, first of all, in their stories of endurance and determination on the journey. Many of them related how even the decision to set out on the journey – in spite of the government warnings and the known dangers of the trail – had been an act of determination. To that one might add the ability to walk without stopping while enduring the lack of food, water, and sleep. In addition, their inner strength was expressed in acts of courage and heroism, such as standing up to government officials or robbers on the trek and saving the lives of relatives or other people.

Amos, for example, saved his brother from drowning in the rushing water of the river that flows between Ethiopia and Sudan, and ran away from the soldiers of the border patrol who were trying to catch them. He narrates,

The soldiers lit the Bauza, "What's that? What's that" Do you know how we ran? What a run for both of us! I gave my brother one shoe. His shoes were gone in the river. Each of us, then, had one shoe. And there were thorns there. These thorns got into our legs. We ran, ran and ran. Without any idea where the place was [the right direction]. We didn't know.... If we headed towards the Sudanese border-guards we would be killed. So we were escaping. And the darkness of the night was absolute. And, do you know, it was hills. Hills. But all of it is full of thorn bushes. So all our body was [covered with our] blood. You know, all was blood! If the thorn caught us we pulled it out by force, and half of it was left in our legs or part of our flesh was left there on the tree [bush]. And we – what a run! Do you know what a run!

And then, there are those who are called Lehawi. The Lehawi – they kill people. If they find people, they have a knife, what shall I tell you, it can be one meter long. So if they find you, that's what they do to you [shows me a throat cutting gesture]. It's your end. You are turned into pieces. And we got there. All that running – yet at the end we arrived where the Lehawi were. Then I heard: "Oh-Oh!" So I said to my brother: "What's that?" Now, he fell down at the area where the Lehawi were. And I couldn't hear him because of his throat, we didn't have water so his throat got hoarse.... I told him: "I am o.k., I am fine. I shall seize you by your hand and run. I shall pull you. I shall run forward." And I grabbed his hand and – what a run! You know, I made him fall as I dragged him. We were running and running. We wanted to move from where we were, to get away from there. Nothing else mattered. Then he said to me: "Our cousin, they probably killed him. We shall die here too. Why do you think that we shall get out of here alive?" And I said: "We shall live! With God's help we shall live! I shall just grab you and run." ... Where we shall arrive – I didn't know. I just continued running. What a run it was!

Amos ran the whole night, dragging his brother. Finally, when the sun came out they saw a person walking along the same path. They approached him and asked for directions to a small border town toward which they had thought they were running. He told them that they were already past it and were actually quite near to Gedaref. They were amazed. "Is that so? Is it really so?"

The theme of bravery and inner strength was expressed also in acts of resourcefulness on the various phases of the journey. For example, by hiding one's money inside one's walking stick before setting out on the journey, or by the decision of women and adolescent girls to wear their most worn-out and filthy clothes for the journey in order to avoid possible rape. Some invented sophisticated cover stories to tell the officials or others who might catch them on their first day of escape, for example, that they were going to a wedding in a distant village. Leadership among adolescents was also felt as an expression of inner strength, even bravery. According to Ethiopian cultural code, adolescents are supposed to obey adults and elders of the community and not take the lead. During the journey, however, roles were sometimes reversed. Some youngsters took upon themselves the responsibility of leading others, mainly the adults and elderly, on the walking journey or found ways to get their families out of the refugee camps to better places. Others participated in the network of organizations that helped get people out of Sudan or distributed the small sums of money available for survival in the camps. Some came in contact with members of the Israeli intelligence service, the Mossad, and became temporary agents of this service. Sometimes they were caught and tortured but did not reveal its secrets. This contributed to their positive self-image, as well as to the way others viewed them – as people possessing tremendous strength, even as heroes.

The Development of a Central Image of the Journey

These three themes through which the Ethiopian Jews view their journey – the commitment to Jewish identity, the endurance of suffering, and the bravery and inner strength they displayed – are crystallized and consolidated within one central image of the journey stemming from their cultural heritage: the Biblical exodus out of Egypt. That is, Ethiopian Jews saw themselves as reliving and reexperiencing the journey of their forefathers, the Israelites, who set out of bondage and embarked on a difficult and lengthy journey to the land of Israel. Like the early Israelites, they were also guided by God to God's country; they were nourished by His help and by His ability to care for them. The Ethiopian Jews, like the Israelites, had to struggle against various physical difficulties, face enemies on their way, and endure tremendous suffering. And they, too, often committed acts of courage and heroism.

My interviewees associated various experiences on their journey with those of the Israelites in the desert. Brehanu recalled,

When we went out of Ethiopia, the haste in which the food was prepared reminded me of my father's stories of how the Israelites prepared their *matzot* (unleavened bread). I said to my father: "This is like the Exodus out of Egypt." He replied: "This is true, and it is good that you recalled it. It is exactly the same."

Marito, a 9-year-old girl, recounts how they had been safe on their way because the clouds covered them. This resonates with the story of how safety was ensured by means of clouds in the original story of the Israelites' exodus out of Egypt:

It was summer then, a very intense summer, yet all the time that we walked, whenever we were out of the bush, we were covered by clouds so that the sun never touched us. We said: "God is making this happen."

Shaul describes a particularly moving experience when he had already been some years in Israel and was invited – though he was still very young – to lead the Passover ceremony for fellow Ethiopian Jews who had just arrived. A major aspect of this ceremony is the reading of the *Haggadah*, the mythical story of the exodus of the Israelites. At a certain point, every person present is asked to feel as if he or she were the one going out of Egypt. When Shaul reached that passage he said to them, "I don't have to explain *to you* what it means to go out of Egypt." He then recounted, "In their faces I saw full agreement to that sentence, they had really felt the Exodus out of Egypt. There was a lot of excitement and emotion on their faces."

ETHIOPIAN JEWS ENCOUNTER ISRAEL

Following their journey, the Ethiopian Jews arrived in Israel with a heightened sense of Jewish identity and an already emerging Israeli identity (BenEzer, 2002, pp. 86, 180). They felt that as individuals and as a community they had been tested, selected, and purified[4] through their suffering and had therefore earned their "right" to enter Israel, God's land, and to participate fully in Israeli society. They had developed and consolidated a self-image as a brave and resourceful people who had successfully stood up to the many challenges of the journey. The three dimensions of their self-perception following the journey – namely, the ethos of Jewishness (or Jewish identity), of suffering, and of bravery and heroism – corresponded to themes of identity or cultural ethos that already played a major role in Israeli society.[5]

---

[4] On the cultural origin of this purification process within Ethiopian Jewish culture, see BenEzer (2002).

[5] For more on the ethos of Israeli society, see BenEzer (2002, chap. 8).

The ethos of Jewishness relates to the fact that although more than 80% of Jews living in Israel are secular, the ethnic identity of Jewish Israelis is still strongly connected to their Jewish origins, even if it is as a cultural heritage rather than a religious practice. This Jewish identity is present in everyday life through various aspects such as the calendar, official holidays and working days, obligatory subjects within the state educational system, the foundations of the legal system and the law, the institutions of marriage and divorce, restrictions on selling certain food in supermarkets and stores, and so forth. In short, although Israel is not only a country for Jews, it is also still, to a large extent, a Jewish country and there is an important "ethnoreligious" dimension related to Judaism in the identity of most Israeli Jews.

Suffering is another ethos in Israeli society. It is connected, in part, to the legacy of the Holocaust, which has become the heritage not only of the survivors but of all Israelis (Segev, 1992, p. 475). The Holocaust serves as the ultimate image of horror for Israelis and is connected, in their minds, to thousands of years of suffering during exile – from the exilic period of Biblical times; through the sufferings of Hamman, Petlura, and the pogroms of Chmielnicki;[6] to the present. Although Israelis did not want to see themselves as the continuation of the people of the Exile, they certainly took upon themselves, especially from the time of Eichmann's trial in the 1960s onward, the heritage of suffering of the Jewish people.

The ethos of bravery in Israelis society was created, at least in its main part, around a few symbolic images. These were the *halutz* (pioneer), the *tzabar* (native-born Israeli), and *the new Hebrew*, which was actually the basis of the first two terms. The Zionist ideologists who were involved in the building of the new Israel resisted the image of the Jews of the Diaspora, who were portrayed as submissive and accommodating, compromising themselves and their self-respect. This derogatory description was contrasted with the new person, the Israeli *halutz* and his or her offspring the *tzabar*. The ethos of bravery was further expressed in aspects connected more directly to acts of heroism within the army, or of "defenders of the land." This can be observed in the concept of "battle heritage" (Almog, 1993, 1997) and in the inscriptions on memorials and tombstones in Israel (Almog, 1991). The latter is related, according to Almog's semiological analysis, to the development of a "civil religion" (Bellah, 1964; Don-Yehiya & Leibman, 1983)[7] in Israel in which the myth of bravery plays an important role.

---

[6] These are the names of the leaders of some of the social disasters inflicted upon Jews at various historical times.

[7] The concept was first used by Jean-Jacques Rousseau in his book *The Social Contract* (Almog, 1991). Robert Bellah later developed this concept into a sociological theory of the development of nationalistic rituals (Bellah, 1964). The sociologists Don-Yehiya and Liebman (1983) have applied this theory to Israeli nationalism.

In view of the correspondence between the ethos of Israeli society and the self-concept that Ethiopian Jews consolidated during their journey, it was reasonable to assume that the Israeli society would see the Ethiopian Jews as having strong resemblance to itself, at least in relation to these all-important dimensions of identity, and would thus embrace them whole-heartedly and accept them as their brethren. The reality of the encounter of Ethiopian Jews with Israeli society, however, was not as expected. From the point of view of the Ethiopian Jews, it might be summed up as a failure to feel the sense of completeness and belonging they had expected and, instead, to experience a continuing struggle to realize their self-concept and identity.

Solomon, one of my interviewees, expressed vividly the frustration and disappointment at the rough reception he received at his journey's end:

When the airplane landed in Israel, the joy of it was beyond description. Suddenly you forgot all the hardships you suffered, for a moment you put it aside, and . . . [I felt] as if I was floating in the air out of happiness. Then they took us into the night. It was raining, we saw the orange groves on our way, and we said to each other: "Look. Here it is! The oranges. As we were told, the land of milk and honey! We are seeing it. It actually starts." Then we arrived at the absorption center, and relatives started visiting us, and we were so tired, and they brought us the fruits of the country, and the joy was incredible. . . . And then, slowly, you start observing something strange . . . as if you were once in a place, [where] you had a certain dream, and now you encounter something . . . for a moment it is hard to accept it. Because . . . your expectations were different, your dreams were different, and then, all the hardships you went through in order to realize it, and for a moment, when you see that things are different from what you expected, you begin to be disappointed. Asking yourself, "Where have I actually arrived?" Because it is not the place. . . . There were in fact people who asked if they had reached the right place . . . and "Is it the place I dreamt of all my life?" Suddenly Shabbat arrived, and there were cars driving on a Shabbat. . . . And the bureaucracy . . . and when they used the word *cushi* [black] . . . this was such an insult . . . and when people used it in a certain tone it would infuriate me. Not only me but many of us felt: "Did we come for *this*? Is this the reception we deserve? What we went through, what we suffered, no one asks us, how many family members we have lost, no one asks us, but instead, they say this word!" . . . And the problem with the [Chief] Rabbinate! . . . And people think that we had come because of hunger. This enrages me! It makes my blood boil! After everything we have suffered on the journey because of our Jewishness!

This passage reflects the major problems within the encounter with Israeli society. First, it conveys the Ethiopian Jews' feeling that the heritage of their journey was neither confirmed nor acknowledged. The authenticity of their own Jewish identity had been put into question; their suffering and trauma was not recognized and appreciated; and, instead of acquiring an image of being brave and resourceful people, they were (and still are) viewed by Israelis as a helpless, dependent, resourceless people who were saved from starvation by the Israelis. Second, Solomon's words point to some major social problems encountered by Ethiopian immigrant Jews in Israel, including the problem of skin color.

Arriving in Israel, the question of the authenticity of Ethiopian Jewish identity resurfaced. In 1973 Ethiopian Jews were recognized officially as Jews, following previous rulings of religious (*Halachic*) authorities in the 16th century and many other rabbis along the following centuries. The renewed rabbinical statement was crucial for the decision to bring the Ethiopian Jews to Israel under the "Law of Return" (1975). Nevertheless, on their arrival, the Israeli Chief Rabbinate demanded a process of symbolic conversion to Judaism, whereby the Ethiopian Jews were asked to undergo a ceremony of immersion in water (*mikveh*) and blessing for women, and, for the men, retrieving a drop of blood from their penises as a symbol of renewed circumcision. This decision was as unintelligible to the Ethiopian Jews as it was for many veteran Israelis. It rekindled the whole issue of who is a Jew that is linked to the dormant issue of the relationship between state and religion in Israel. Many of the Ethiopian community felt humiliated and rejected by Israeli establishment and refused to undergo this ceremony. They perceived that although they had endured a long arduous journey hoping to feel more complete among their brethren, their fellow Jews did not accept them.

In addition, many people in Israel did not recognize the extreme suffering they had undergone, thus denying them the moral entrance ticket (or social visa) to Israeli society, which they felt they had rightly earned by suffering on the journey.[8]

The image of the community as brave and resourceful people also did not find any resonance within Israeli society. This occurred, at least in part, because of the need of Israeli society to maintain its self-image as the brave rescuers of troubled Jews around the world (Troen & Pinkus, 1992). This made it difficult to relate to Ethiopian Jews as heroes. Contributing to that lack of resonance was the wide media coverage of the famine in Ethiopia and Sudan that coincided with the news of "Operation Moses" in January 1985.[9] That media coverage inscribed a message of hungry, needy Ethiopians in the minds of many Israelis that was in sharp contrast to Ethiopian Jews' self-perception.

---

[8] A sense of unacknowledged suffering is not uncommon among survivors of traumatic experiences; they often feel extremely isolated because no other person can really understand what they have gone through (Agger, 1994; Herman, 1992). In the case of the Ethiopian Jews, however, this feeling of isolation stems more directly from their feeling that Israeli society has failed to recognize the real reason for their suffering.

[9] Bob Geldof's "concert for the poor," with the participation of scores of celebrated artists, took place in Britain at that time, with hundreds of thousands contributing to "the hungry people of Ethiopia" (Oxford, 1994; Pankhurst, 1992; Smith, 1994).

Stereotypes related to the Ethiopian Jews' black skin color and to their African origin also contributed to the development of pejorative images such as "primitive," "helpless," and "ignorant" in the eyes of Israelis. Being "black" in Israel aroused prejudices and various stereotypes as well as primitive fears of the strange and alien. As one of my interviewees said, "And this word *cushi* [meaning black in Hebrew but also a slave] when I first heard it I did not understand; and when I realized what it means, I couldn't believe it. Am I someone's slave? I was hurt." This racist stereotype was reinforced by a history of agricultural and industrial support given by the Israeli government to Ethiopia during the 1960s and 1970s. Many Israelis held an image of Ethiopians as people who "need to be taught everything" and that Israeli society had a duty to "raise them up." This, once more, was in absolute contrast with the Ethiopian Jews' self-image as resourceful people who had creatively and courageously coped with the difficult journey.

Moreover, Israel is a highly security-conscious society where people believe in the importance of identifying and categorizing people on the street in order to distinguish between "Us" and "Them" (with "Them" being Arabs who could turn out to be potential terrorists). In this social context, Ethiopian Jews posed, at the time they arrived in Israel in the 1980s, a threat for Israelis because they did not fit easily into any of the existing categories. They challenged the stereotypes based on easily recognized visual characeristics that assisted in identifying people in Israeli public places. This aroused fears among Israelis, which resulted in specific reactions of various kinds (BenEzer, 1992). There were many instances in which Ethiopian Jewish youngsters, even soldiers on leave, were stopped by police patrols, checked for identity cards, and sometimes beaten for pretending to be Jews. It took nearly 10 years for Israelis to develop a clear social category of "Ethiopian-black-Jewish-immigrant," thereby diminishing this suspicion and fear.[10]

A different cultural code also set Ethiopian Jews apart from many others in Israeli society. In particular, their code of communication, especially the ways of expressing respect toward authority figures, was a source of many cross-cultural misunderstandings (BenEzer, 1987). This code includes specific body language, such as ways of shaking hands, avoiding eye contact, and audibly inhaling air as an expression of listening attentively. It also includes the effort to refrain from refusing authority figures, and never saying "no." This led to situations in which the immigrants made

---

[10] The arrival of the "foreign workers" in Israel, mainly in the mid-1990s, many of whom were illegal migrants and among whom are many black people, has complicated the situation yet again. With rising unemployment, immigration laws were tightened and immigration police would sometimes make mistakes of identity and harass Ethiopian Jews, checking their homes as if they were illegal foreign workers to be deported.

appointments that were not kept or said "yes" when they did not really mean it. Unfortunately, the cultural styles of communication were misread by other Israelis, who were thus deterred from approaching or maintaining contact with Ethiopian immigrants.

The Ethiopian Jewish immigrants have suffered from a persistent condition of liminality in their identity and belonging within Israeli society. Their self-concept as brave Jewish people, who suffered tremendously in order to reach Israel, has not been confirmed and acknowledged; and their skin color and different cultural codes set them apart from mainstream Israeli society. They also lack the previous strength of their own community and extended family, which were weakened or broken by the demands of their journey as well as by Israeli policies of resettlement.

Jewish identity and the image of the exodus served as an ideology for Ethiopian Jews. This ideology helped them make sense of their hardships and cope with their harrowing experiences. The symbol of the Israelite exodus, which wove together the themes of the journey, also served to connect them to their origins during a time of great change, when they stepped outside of the known structure of their former cultural world (Turner, 1967, 1974). This experience of liminality (Turner, 1969; van Gennep, 1909) reconfirmed what was most important to them and the reason for their migration, that is, their Jewish identity.

Thus, the meaning of the journey served as an ideological protective layer during their traumatic passage. A sense of belonging and a Jewish identity shared with other Israelis could have served the same way during the difficult process of adaptation to Israel. However, the dilemmas of belonging and identity within Israeli society deprived them of what was most important during their time of transition and undermined their understanding of the trauma of the journey.

The questioning of their self-perception following the journey, in particular the doubt cast upon their Jewish identity, has had (and continues to exert) a tremendous psychological effect on the Ethiopian Jews in Israel. It threatened to strip the meaning from their exodus and especially from the traumatic events they endured. Even deaths could suddenly seem meaningless. The death of a parent or a child is fraught with emotion; stripping it of its previous meaning as part of a purification process led by God could be psychologically harmful. Cultural ideologies and collective myths provide a protective and supportive way to frame experiences, which may help individuals cope with traumatic events.[11] In recent years, a variety of studies have found that adolescents cope better with refugee camp situations when they have a reason for survival or some ideology to

---

[11] This has been shown by theorists and practitioners such as Victor Frankl in his book about the Nazi concentration camps, *Man's Search for Meaning* (1970); by Jerome Frank in *Persuasion and Healing* (1961); and by Bruno Bettelheim in *The Informed Heart* (1970).

fight for (M. Dynes, personal communication, 1991; Punamaki-Gitai, 1992; Reynell, 1989). Destabilizing the Ethiopian Jews' identity and their own understanding of the journey has deprived them of a crucial integrative narrative during the stressful time of resettlement.

TRAUMA, CULTURE, AND MYTH

In the face of their reception by Israeli society, many Ethiopian Jews have felt that, in a sense, the journey to Israel has not yet ended. In their words, "we arrived – yet we did not arrive"; that is to say, we have reached the land of Israel but have not yet reached Israeli society. Their symbolic journey must continue until the wider society recognizes and affirms their self-image. Throughout their ongoing struggle and efforts to integrate into Israeli society – which has involved strikes and engaging the prime minister and the Israeli supreme court[12] – the journey, or rather the story of the journey, has occupied a central place and is acquiring the characteristics of a collective myth.

I am using the concept of myth following Raphael Samuel and Paul Thompson (1990), who do not view it as a "mere archaic relic but a potent force in everyday life, part of our collective unconscious" (p. 20). Furthermore, these authors claim that "old myths are constantly reworked and new myths continually created as people make sense of untidy and traumatic memories and give meaning to their lives" (p. 20). The psychologist Rollo May (1991) writes in his study of myths in the United States, "The myth is a drama which begins as a historical event and takes on its special character as a way of orienting people to reality. The myth, or story, carries

---

[12] There was a prolonged sit-down strike of community leaders and many others in front of the Israeli Chief Rabbinate's building in Jerusalem. This took place during 1985 and is considered by many to be the first watershed in the Ethiopian Jews' sense of belonging in Israel (BenEzer, 2005). Various religious and secular groups, in Israel and among Jews around the world, got involved in this struggle. Of course, some of these groups, such as Reform Jews in the United States and Israel, had their own interests in this struggle. For example, the potential recognition of the legitimacy their own (non-Orthodox) marriage ceremonies might become possible if Ethiopian rabbis (*Kessoch*) were recognized as legitimate officiates at such marriages. Prime Minister Peres was involved in trying to mediate in this conflict. Appealing to the Supreme Court of Israel, the Ethiopian Jews won some recognition for part of their demands. The second watershed was "the spilling of the blood scandal" in 1996 (BenEzer, 2005), in which the blood of soldiers of Ethiopian origin, who had donated blood like other soldiers, was secretly thrown away without informing them, for fear that it might be contaminated by the HIV virus. The uproar, when this was revealed by an Israeli journalist, was unprecedented. Up to this point, leaders of the community had prided themselves in their lectures to other Israelis on the fact that "our skin might be different, but our blood is the same. . . . And since we contributed blood while in the army, it is already flowing in the veins of other Israelis." When it was revealed that their blood was actually thrown away, they were deeply hurt and insulted.

the values of the society: through the myth the individual finds his sense of identity" (p. 26). Myths are especially potent when a collective identity is at risk. In his study of a small commune outside Marseilles, Lucien Aschieri has shown how "for a threatened community, memory must above all serve to emphasize a sense of common identity" (Thompson, 1988, p. 145). Myths can also serve, according to Roland Barthes (1957), as a "system of communication." Rossanna Basso, for example, pointed out in her study of a children's strike that events or actions could be the subject of myth "if there is a collective action that puts them at the center of a system of communication" (1990, p. 68). Following these and other scholars, I think of myth not as an untrue story but as a living memory, either of recent or long-past events, which continues to play a role in peoples' lives and is a living force in the present.

The story of the journey of the Ethiopian Jews seems to have acquired these characteristics of a myth: It is a story that makes sense of untidy and traumatic memories; it is a means of finding and keeping one's identity; and it has become a system of communication, a vehicle for conveying desired messages within the Ethiopian immigrant community as well as to Israeli society.

My ethnographic research indicates that the Ethiopian immigrants recount the journey on various occasions. Obviously, it is retold on memorial days for their loved ones who did not survive the journey. This is true regarding both private ceremonies as well as those that are held by the whole community. A forest of remembrance has been created at Ramat Rachel, near Jerusalem, where relatives have planted a tree for each of those who perished on the journey. A memorial ceremony is held in this forest every year, during which the events of the journey are recounted. The story of the journey is told, however, not only on holy days and formal occasions. It is also narrated among friends and relatives, between generations and within the same age group. The elderly often recall and share their journey experiences when they sit together during the *buna* ritual, the traditional Ethiopian ceremony of coffee drinking. Youngsters often recall the journey when they meet at home on school vacations, returning from their boarding schools.

Retelling the story of the journey among themselves serves several functions (BenEzer, 2002). The first function is reaffirmation of collective identity. Through the story important elements within Ethiopian Jews' identity are restated. The story incorporates the history of the community: the traditions concerning the ways in which they originally arrived in Ethiopia, the state of exile, their existence as an ethnoreligious minority, their sense of not belonging, and the prophecies of return. It thus connects their recent past (the journey) to their more distant (Ethiopian) and mythical (Hebrew) past. The story of the journey restates their Jewish identity as well as rehearses cultural codes and rituals. This reaffirmation of their identity is extremely important for them as a minority in a process of integration into a new society, especially because major elements of their identity and self-concept have been put under question within Israeli society.

The second function of the telling of the story among themselves is group cohesion. The story reminds the members of the community of their mutual fate, their sharing of adversity, and their success in overcoming challenges. It thus connects them to each other and strengthens their sense of togetherness, of being one entity. Sharing a common past also brings a sense of direction to the present and realigns them for their journey into the future.

Recounting the journey serves a third function – tapping into a source of strength. Remembering their forefathers' struggle to maintain their distinct community in spite of hardships gives them the strength to deal with the unexpected hardships of their resettlement. It thus serves as a spring from which they draw the energy needed for their coping.

The story of the journey also plays a central role in the dialogue that has evolved between Ethiopian Jews and Israeli society. The story serves as a means through which Ethiopian Jews promote their view of themselves. This is manifested, for example, in interviews with members of the Ethiopian community in the media in which the interviewees, though asked about other subjects, seize every opportunity to relate their story to the Israeli public. Part of my research followed a group of 29 distinguished members of the Ethiopian Jewish community who were invited to talk about their community to classes of Israeli students or to practitioners and other agencies' workers. Fully 95% of the speakers devoted at least a third of their presentation to the journey, and 80% opened their speech with this subject (BenEzer, 2002).

The journey is central to how Ethiopian Jews view their experiences in Israel: It serves as spectacles through which they see their integration into Israeli society. Through the journey story, they try to convey to Israeli society those aspects of their identity that are most important to them. Their Jewish identity is conveyed through explaining the reason for their journey, a return home, and through stories of Jewish martyrdom – kidush hashem – that are included in the narratives of the journey. By narrating their stories they also relate their suffering on the journey and their bravery and heroism, which contradict Israeli perceptions of them as a helpless and powerless people. Last, transmitting their view of the journey as reexperiencing the Exodus of the Israelites out of Egypt is a powerful way to convey the idea that they share the same ancestors with present-day Israelis.

The story of the journey is a myth in the making. First- and secondhand memory transmitted within and outside the group is being condensed and reworked into a collective story with essential meanings for the community.

The study of the different processes of transmission of memory has been carried furthest among the anthropologists and historians of Africa, due to their special dependence on oral sources (Thompson, 1988, p. 143). Some Africanists have tried to disentangle the process by which immediate memory is transformed into formal tradition. This can sometimes be quite rapid: The lives of African prophets, for example, can be transformed into myths within a space of 2 or 3 years (BenEzer, 2002). Africanist Joseph Miller studied the transmission of memory of the Angolan war of 1861. He has shown that when memory passes beyond personal oral histories, which are eyewitness accounts, and beyond informal memory, which includes secondhand accounts, the story changes. The societies he studied synthesized the memory into "a simplified, stylized account which concentrates on the meaning of the story" (Miller, 1977, cited in Thompson, 2000, p. 167).

For the Ethiopian community in Israel, people who directly experienced the journey are still the majority of those telling the story today. Nevertheless, it seems to be in the midst of a change from a personal story into a collective memory, "a simplified, stylized account which concentrates on [its dimensions of] meaning." For example, one of my interviewees, Tamar, said at the beginning of her account that she "has nothing to tell about" because "I did not suffer as much as most of the others in the community did. . . . My journey was not as difficult as it had been for others." Thus, while willing to relate her own story, she complemented it by filling in the aspect of suffering that she perceived as an important feature of the communal experience of the journey. Tamar, therefore, like some other narrators of the journey stories in my research, is already orienting herself according to collective aspects of the story as if these were coordinates to which her personal account should refer.

Moreover, the story is being told and is owned by people who have not gone through the journey – people who reached Israel in different ways or youngsters who were born in Israel. Such was the case of a young woman in a recent workshop that I conducted who chose the journey as her personal subject for presentation. Although she herself did not go through the journey, she related to it explicitly as *her* story. She belonged to this story and it belonged to her.

Israel is a country of immigrants. It is interesting to note that various groups of immigrants (*aliyot*) have created different myths around their immigration process. These myths relate to their past identities, the ways they were received in Israel, the hardships they went through, or their contributions to their new society (BenEzer, 2002). Often, these myths serve as a means to legitimate claims for certain political or social rights. For example, the myth of the *halutz* – the pioneering Israeli – or the *tzabar*, the born Israeli, created by Ashkenazi Jews (mainly of European origin), was maintained in order to preserve the power of the social elite and as a means to motivate others toward a certain model of conduct. The myth of the disadvantaged (or discriminated) North African group also served as a way of penetrating into the political arena and of promoting a social recognition.

Almog (1993) writes about the "Zionist myth of the 1948 generation," and other scholars, such as Yablonka (1998) and Segev (1992), relate various myths that play a role within Israeli society in their discussion of the ways Holocaust survivors were received in Israel.

Thus, the first settlers, who came mainly from eastern and central Europe in the past century and built the first little villages and towns, presented society at large with the myth of "the drying of the swamps"; the second and third immigration waves (aliya), coming in the 1920s and later mainly from Russia, the Ukraine, and the Baltic republics, created the "New Person" and the "religion of (manual) work." The North African Jews in particular created the myth of discrimination, which includes an idealized picture of their previous existence in Morocco. On the other hand, those who do not have a myth surrounding their immigration wave seem to be missing as a distinct group in Israeli consciousness, like, for example, the Egyptian Jews in Israel.

The story of the traumatic journey of the Ethiopian Jews coming back from exile, which is turning into a myth, is thus extremely important because it serves as a means of opening up a space for the group in the Israeli consciousness. In this way, traumatic experience acquires a social meaning that, on the one hand, helps in coping with the previous trauma while, on the other hand, it serves as a sustainable, protective device against further traumatization during the integration process. In 2005, after some 20 years of struggle, there are some signs that the Ethiopian myth is successfully recognized by Israeli society. A formal national Israeli ceremony for those who died in Sudan was declared by the government, and a national memorial is to be built on Mount Hertzl, where all sacred national events are celebrated. At the same time there continue to be many incidents that subvert the meaning of the journey. We still do not know how this process will continue to unfold and whether the story of the journey will finally be part of the Israeli tapestry of social myths or a footnote on the way to social marginality and communal rage. We do know, however, that in this process trauma, culture, and myth are increasingly intertwined.

References

Agger, I. (1994). *The blue room: Trauma and testimony among refugee women: A psychosocial exploration*. London: Zed Books.

Almog, O. (1991). War memorials in Israel: A semiological analysis. *Megamot, 34*(2), 179–210.

Almog, O. (1993). The Zionist myths of the fighting *Tsabar* of the 1948 generation. *Maarachot, 333*, 40–48.

Almog, O. (1997). *The Tsabar: A people*. Tel-Aviv: Am Oved Publishers.

Barthes, R. (1957). *Mythologies*. Paris: Editions du Seuil.

Basso, R. (1990). Myths in contemporary oral transmission: A children's strike. In R. Samuel & P. Thompson (Eds.), *The myths we live by*. London and New York: Routledge.

Bellah, R. (1964). Religion evolution. *American Sociological Review, 29*, 358–374.

Ben-Dor, S. (1987). The journey towards Eretz Israel: The story of Abba Mahari. *Pe'amim, 33*, 5–32.

BenEzer, G. (1987). Cross-cultural misunderstandings: The case of Ethiopian immigrant Jews in Israeli society. In M. Ashkenazi & A. Weingrod (Eds.), *Ethiopian Jews and Israel*. New Brunswick, UK: Transaction Books.

BenEzer, G. (1990). Anorexia nervosa or an Ethiopian coping style? *Mind and Human Interaction, 2*(2), 36–39.

BenEzer, G. (1992). *As light within a clay pot: Immigration and absorption of Ethiopian Jews*. Jerusalem: Rubin Mass.

BenEzer, G. (2002). *The Ethiopian Jewish exodus: Narratives of the migration journey to Israel 1977–1985*. New York: Routledge.

BenEzer, G. (2005). A test of honor for Israeli society: Reflections following 27 years of integration of Ethiopian Jewish immigrants in Israel. In R. Rosenthal (Ed.), *The heart of the matter: Israeli agenda for social change and different politics (in honor of Yair Tzaban)*. Tel Aviv: Am Oved.

Bettelheim, B. (1970). *The informed heart: Autonomy in a mass age*. London: Paladin.

Don-Yehiya, E., & Liebman, C. S. (1983). *Civil religion in Israel: Traditional Judaism and political culture in the Jewish state*. Berkeley: University of California Press.

Frank, J. D. (1961). *Persuasion and healing: A comparative study of psychotherapy*. Baltimore: Johns Hopkins Press.

Frankl, V. (1970). *Man's search for meaning*. Tel Aviv: Am Oved.

Herman, J. L. (1992). *Trauma and recovery*. New York: Basic Books.

May, R. (1991). *The cry for myth*. New York: Norton.

Oxford, E. (1994, December 23). Well, did they feed the world? *Independent*, p. 1.

Pankhurst, A. (1992). *Resettlement and famine in Ethiopia: The villagers' experience*. Manchester, UK: Manchester University Press.

Punamaki-Gitai, R. L. (1992). "Natural healing processes" and experiences of political violence. Paper presented at the Third Annual Meeting of the International Research and Advisory Panel on Refugees and Other Displaced Persons (IRAP), Refugees Studies Programme, University of Oxford, Oxford, UK.

Reynell, J. (1989). *Political pawns: Refugees on the Thai Kampuchean border*. Oxford: Refugee Studies Programme, University of Oxford.

Rosen, C. (1987). Core symbols of Ethiopian identity and their role in understanding the Beta Israel today. In M. Ashkenazi & A. Weingrod (Eds.), *Ethiopian Jews in Israel*. New Brunswick, UK: Transaction Books.

Samuel, R., & Thompson, P. R. (1990). *The myths we live by*. London: Routledge.

Sandler, J. (1960). The background of safety. *International Journal of Psycho-Analysis, 41*, 352–356.

Sandler, J., Dreher, A. U., & Drews, S. (1991). An approach to conceptual research in psychoanalysis illustrated by a consideration of psychic trauma. *International Journal of Psycho-Analysis, 18*, 113–141.

Segev, T. (1992). *The seventh million: The Israelis and the Holocaust*. Jerusalem: Keter and Domino Press.

Smith, G. (1994, December 12). And there's still no snow in Africa. *Independent*, p. 3.

Thompson, P. R. (1988). *The voice of the past: Oral history* (2nd ed.). Oxford, UK: Oxford University Press.

Thompson, P. R. (2000). *The voice of the past: Oral history* (3rd ed.). Oxford, UK: Oxford University Press.

Troen, S. I., & Pinkus, B. (Eds.). (1992). *Organising rescue: Jewish national solidarity in the modern period*. London: Frank Cass.

Turner, V. W. (1967). Betwixt and between: The liminal period in rites de passage. In V. W. Turner (Ed.), *The forest of symbols: Aspects of Ndembu ritual*. Ithaca, NY: Cornell University Press.

Turner, V. W. (1969). *The ritual process*. London: Routledge and Kegan Paul.

Turner, V. W. (1974). Pilgrimages as social processes. In V. W. Turner (Ed.), *Dramas, fields and metaphors: Symbolic action in human society*. Ithaca, NY: Cornell University Press.

van Gennep, A. (1909). *The rites of passage*. London: Routledge and Kegan Paul.

Yablonka, H. T. (1998). *Survivors of the Holocaust: Israel after the war*. New York: MacMillan and New York University Press.

19

Posttraumatic Politics: Violence, Memory, and Biomedical Discourse in Bali

Leslie Dwyer and Degung Santikarma

In June 2004, as we were preparing this chapter[1] on the emergence of discourses of trauma in Indonesia, two incidents occurred. The first was a conversation between Santikarma and Bre Redana, an editor at *Kompas*, an Indonesian newspaper. After hearing that we were writing about trauma, Redana asked Santikarma to explain something. Why were a number of social welfare organizations in Jakarta changing the names of their programs from "crisis centers" (*krisis center*) to "trauma clinics" (*klinik trauma*)? Both *krisis* and *trauma* – the words borrowed directly from English – were, they agreed, far from neutral terms. "Crisis" had entered widespread usage in Indonesia in 1998, when the "Asian economic crisis," along with a "crisis of legitimacy" of former President Soeharto's government, were claimed by scholars and journalists to have ushered in the end of 32 years of dictatorship and the new era of political possibility known as *reformasi*. So popular had the word "crisis" grown that for many Indonesians it came to signal a generic lack: *krisis moneter* or "monetary crisis" (usually abbreviated as *krismon*) meant that people no longer had money; *krisis kepemimpinan* or "leadership crisis" meant that no one had belief in those in power; and *"saya lagi krisis"* or "I'm in a crisis," with one's empty hands extended, meant that one had nothing to spare. But what, they

[1] Sections of this essay are taken from a paper prepared for the Foundation for Psychocultural Research Fourth Annual Workshop on Integrating Biological, Clinical, and Sociocultural Approaches to Trauma's Effects, Yogyakarta, Indonesia, July 28–31, 2004. It is based on ongoing collaborative field research in Bali, begun in 1998, on the cultural, political, and emotional aftermath of the violence of 1965–66. This research has been funded by a MacArthur Foundation research and writing grant, an H. F. Guggenheim Foundation research grant, and a grant from the Haverford College Faculty Research Fund. For discussions of many of the ideas we present here, we thank Byron Good, Mary-Jo DelVecchio-Good, Hildred Geertz, Gung Ayu Ratih, and John Roosa. Special thanks are due to Robert Lemelson, whose support of critical thought about trauma and of recognizing injustice in Indonesia has been inspirational to our project.

wondered, did it mean for a rhetoric of "crisis" to be replaced by a language of "trauma"?

An easy explanation for the shift would be to view it as a mirror of changing international funding priorities, in turn reflecting a post–September 11 interest in psychosocial repair in the wake of terrorism. But did this move also reference something more broad and complex about how Indonesians were imagining themselves as subjects of history? If *krisis* had come to signal a temporary jarring condition of absence in which society as a whole suffered, what did it mean to speak now of *trauma*, with its implications of personal victimization, of the deep-rooted presence of pain? And why did it seem necessary for a "center," with its connotations of community, to become a *klinik*, a space where individual pathology could be addressed by experts? They arrived at no answers, only a strong sense that these were important questions to consider.

The second incident was a performance art project organized by a collective of young Balinese artists calling themselves Klinik Seni Taxu ("Taxu Art Clinic"). This performance, which opened at the Cemeti Art House gallery in Yogyakarta, Java, on June 9, 2004, was entitled "Memasak Sejarah" ("Cooking History"). On the opening night, the artists, dressed in traditional Balinese ritual attire, washed and chopped and cooked sweet potatoes – a food associated with Indonesia's poor – for their audience, who were then invited to share the meal. Only after the meal was finished did the artists inform the audience that they had grown the sweet potatoes on a field in west Bali that covered a hidden mass grave from 1965, the year when state-sponsored terror began its sweep across Indonesia, leaving some 1 million alleged communists dead and Soeharto's New Order regime ascending to power.[2]

One of the young artists, Ngurah Suryawan, explained that the aim of the performance – which culminated in a number of audience members vomiting in disgust – was to move away from the "exoticization of violence" he claimed characterized media coverage of the conflicts that had emerged after Soeharto's resignation, in which violence was reduced to the reemergence of "primordial sentiments" in the absence of state control. He argued that by evoking the history of 1965, which had long been suppressed under the New Order, the links among violence, entrenched political repression, and injustice could be exposed. What the artists had

---

[2] For more on the events of September 30, 1965, and their political ramifications, see Anderson, McVey, and Bunnell (1971), Cribb (1990), and Crouch (1978). For an overview of the events in Bali, see Robinson (1995). For an examination of the cultural and political repercussions of the violence in Bali, see Dwyer (2004) and Dwyer and Santikarma (2003). For discussions of the important place that "1965" as history, imaginary, and threat has held in state discourse and public culture, see Anderson (1994), Pemberton (1994), Shiraishi (1997), Siegel (1998a), and Steedly (1993).

intended, Suryawan said, was to "traumatize" the audience into an embodied relationship with history that could substitute social memory of atrocity for a willful forgetting (N. Suryawan, personal communication, June 13, 2004).[3]

In this chapter, we take these two incidents and some of the questions they raise as entryways into an exploration of the social and political life of discourses of trauma in Indonesia. Such a starting point, we realize, might seem oddly anecdotal or irrelevant to those used to thinking about trauma in clinical or laboratory contexts. Recognizing that these incidents might seem to point away from the biological and experiential reality of trauma toward its naïve popularization or political/artistic manipulation, we wish to make our theoretical orientation clear from the outset. We begin from the premise that trauma is most productively understood not as a universal human response to certain inherently traumatizing events unassimilable by the human psyche, but rather as a socially positioned process. Trauma, in this view, includes, first, identifying what constitutes experience that cannot or should not be integrated into everyday life; second, engaging in culturally mediated responses that may range from withdrawal to resistance, from alienation to solidarity, and from disruption to the creation of new forms of emotion and interaction; and third – depending on the cultures of treatment present in a given setting – formulating means of attempting to alleviate distress.

To emphasize the embeddedness of trauma in social, cultural, and political relations is not to ignore the importance of scientific research on the biology of fear, arousal, pain, or memory (see Section I of this volume). It is, however, to stress that trauma is always more than a biological state.[4] Like any experience of embodied suffering, it emerges and takes on force and meaning in dialogue with a host of cultural, ethical, and political discourses that address what it means to suffer and what – and whose – pain should be ameliorated (see Biehl, 2005; DelVecchio-Good, Brodwin, Good, & Kleinman, 1994; French, 2004; James, 2004; Kleinman & Desjarlais, 1995). Just as "crisis" – and its counterpoint, "stability" – can be understood not as empirical givens but as culturally and politically produced attributions of particular historical conditions (see Aretxaga, 2003; Greenhouse, 2002; Spyer, 2003), so designations of and attempts to respond to trauma can be seen as drawing on and producing political subjectivities that delineate what constitutes the normal, the disordered, and the utterly unthinkable. Especially when events viewed as traumatizing are caused

---

[3] For more information on the exhibition, see the Web site of the Cemeti Art House (www.cemetiarthouse.com).

[4] Biehl (2005) frames a similar point as follows: "This is not to say that mental disorders are basically a matter of social construction, but rather that such disorders do take form at the most personal juncture between the subject, his or her biology, and the intersubjective and technical recoding of 'normal' ways of being in local worlds" (p. 316).

by human agency, as in the case of terrorism or political violence in Indonesia, we suggest that limiting our understandings of trauma to a naturalistic model of generic physiological response and universally applicable treatment neglects to account for the varied contexts through which experience is rendered traumatic and emotion and social engagements are targeted for attempts at transformation or cure. To separate attempts to produce trauma from its phenomenology, its identification, and its treatment is to ignore the social networks that both give rise to suffering and potentially make healing from it possible.

Likewise, we argue that the diagnosis and treatment of PTSD, often viewed by natural scientists and clinicians in terms of individuals' pathological responses to acute stressor(s), must be placed within frameworks that transcend the boundaries of the clinic to account for the lived experience of both patients and those survivors of violence who reject or do not qualify for such categorization. Clinical settings are specific social, cultural, political, and economic domains that can and should be studied for the particular practices and conceptual frameworks that arise within them; however, what takes place within their walls both draws on and shapes more general understandings. Similarly, the biomedical discourses that set limits and create possibilities for engaging embodied phenomena impact not only clinicians and patients but also broader cultural and political fields as they are spread through social interaction, popular media, and the narratives created to justify and promote practices of diagnosis and treatment. And perhaps most importantly, a focus on the social and political life of discourses of trauma allows us to grasp the processes by which the aftermath of certain kinds of events – and not others – are marked by the emergence of clinical spaces.

Grounding our theoretical concerns ethnographically, we begin by tracing the emergence of "trauma" in Indonesian psychiatry, public culture, and the language of humanitarian aid organizations at work in the archipelago. We argue that the use of the Indonesianized word *trauma* and the diagnostic category PTSD emerged not out of a unidirectional export trajectory in which Western knowledge of human biology and behavior is disseminated to a scientifically underdeveloped world, but out of the social and political relations that coalesced at a particular juncture in Indonesian history. The fall of Soeharto's dictatorship in 1998 made it possible for many Indonesians to speak publicly – often for the first time – about certain kinds of violence and the terrible psychic damage it has caused. It has also enabled international and national actors to engage more directly in projects seeking to transform Indonesian society and subjectivity in the name of development, democratization, transitional justice, or the protection of various strategic interests.[5]

---

[5] See Dwyer and Santikarma (2004) for a discussion of how projects to promote "reconciliation" in the post-Soeharto era have delineated certain politically appropriate forms of

We caution, however, that the introduction of concepts of trauma in Indonesia has not been without its ambivalences and complexities. If for many Indonesian clinicians and patients *trauma* references the lingering effects of a long history of repressive rule and the violence that marked it, for the international aid organizations supporting programs of postconflict social repair, trauma has been tightly tied to a contemporary politics in which terrorism is of primary concern. Focusing on the case of Bali, where an outpouring of international aid in the aftermath of the October 2002 terrorist bombings led to the creation of highly publicized programs for the treatment of PTSD, we show how discourses of trauma have not only influenced clinical practice but also produced social and political contest. Attention to the psychological sequelae of violence has had the effect – welcomed by many Balinese – of opening social spaces closed by the Soeharto regime where acknowledgement of the emotional implications of political terror could take place. However, by framing the terrorist bombings as an event of extraordinary, unprecedented horror – as an exemplary site of trauma – PTSD programs have not only tended to negate the experiences of tens of thousands of Balinese survivors of one of the worst mass crimes of the 20th century, the state-sanctioned anticommunist violence of 1965–66, but also have risked ignoring the continuing suffering of Balinese living with structures of social and economic inequality that became even more pronounced after the bombings. In their broader discursive effects, PTSD programs have also served to bolster relations of power by demarcating forms of subjectivity considered appropriate to citizenship, ethnic identity, and capitalism in the form of cultural tourism.

We conclude by suggesting that such issues raise concerns about the social life of trauma and the treatment of suffering that extend beyond the borders of Bali. As Breslau (2004) has noted, programs to identify and assist those said to be experiencing PTSD in the wake of political violence, natural disasters, terrorism, and forced migration have expanded rapidly over the past decade, to the point that they have become packaged as a standard component of humanitarian relief efforts and postconflict aid programs. As trauma increasingly serves as a lens through which to frame and address varied forms of suffering across the globe, attention to how it engages with particular social, cultural, and political contexts becomes increasingly important. In our insistence on the social location of trauma, our analysis joins an emergent anthropological literature exploring how violence and other presumed triggers of trauma may be experienced through cultural frameworks quite different from those described in the Western clinical literature (e.g., Goldstein, 2003; O'Nell, 2000; Scheper-Hughes, 1992) and

subjectivity for Indonesian victims of violence, in the name of postconflict peacemaking and nation building. Discourses of "trauma," we suggest, have been linked in Indonesia (and elsewhere) to those of "reconciliation" in their framing of psychological and moral orientations as key concerns of the state and the international development apparatus.

how, as French says, "culture has been created around PTSD" (2004, p. 211) as the diagnostic category and attendant modes of evaluating and intervening in the psychological spread across the globe (see Gross, 2004; Han, 2004; James, 2004; Zarowsky, 2004).

Yet our hope is that such work is taken not merely to represent local interpretations of or reactions to PTSD, or to the kinds of events said to spark it – for example, to present simply a "Balinese response" to terrorism or a "Balinese critique" of biomedical models of mental health. Such analyses risk relegating culture to the fixed context in which global forms of experience and knowledge are read, interpreted, and possibly resisted, rather than being constitutive of claims to universality and the production of their allure and authority. Rather, we hope to show that what is often thought to be unproblematically universal – including ways of embodying, evaluating, and addressing psychological distress – are, as Tsing (2005) reminds us, "charged and enacted in the sticky materiality of practical encounters" (p. 1) at the same time that their global assumptions and pretensions create new relations of both power and collaboration. In short, we consider Balinese experiences to offer not just a case study in trauma, but also a call to reconsider the ethics, politics, and cultural assumptions of the concept itself.

THE EMERGENCE OF "TRAUMA" IN INDONESIA

During the era of Soeharto's New Order regime (1966–98), the word "trauma" was rarely heard in Indonesia. Although other terms borrowed from an English-language psychological vocabulary, including *depresi* and *stres*, were spread by the mass media through a host of advice and lifestyle programs and publications, trauma was generally restricted to the esoteric realm of imported scientific literature. Trauma first entered limited popular circulation in media accounts of the violence that preceded Soeharto's fall from power, especially in discussions of the May 1998 riots and the thousands of ethnic Chinese women who were terrorized or raped by gangs said to have been backed by the military.[6] Yet even as *trauma* began to signal the effects of a striking moment of general social upheaval, it also served to reinscribe the marginality of those – ethnic Chinese, women, the urban masses – who had long been imagined to inhabit the edges of Indonesian society and to prescribe a "cure" based on compliance with state authority. If Indonesia as a whole was in *krisis*, those said to be suffering from

---

[6] Siegel (1998b) interprets this new discourse of trauma as engaging with older Indonesian discourses of the supernatural, in which history emerges to haunt the present. His analysis does not, however, trace the routes by which notions of trauma emerged in Indonesia, thus missing the opportunity to explore the broader power relations in which they are embedded.

trauma were the nation's disempowered, whose affliction was viewed as yet another sign of their inability to be integrated into full national belonging. Combined with widespread stigma attached to psychiatric or psychological treatment for mental health, such discourses ensured that, even where such care was available, few Indonesians were willing to seek treatment for trauma-related problems.[7]

In the clinical realm,[8] the use of PTSD as a diagnostic category was likewise rare in New Order Indonesia, where biomedically trained mental health practitioners overwhelmingly tended to focus on disorders considered to arise from purely organic rather than social causes, such as schizophrenia or psychosis. Lemelson (2003) has suggested that clinicians in Bali have also tended not to diagnose other mental illnesses, such as bipolar disorders or obsessive–compulsive disorder, because the scientific knowledge or medications needed to identify and treat such problems have been unavailable or prohibitively expensive. However, in the case of PTSD – a disorder whose identification is premised on the destructive presence not only of individual psychopathology but also on a traumatizing event precipitating it – the barriers to its entrance into the clinical lexicon have been much more deeply entrenched, reflecting Indonesian psychiatry's embeddedness in broader currents of power. During 32 years of a military-backed dictatorship, the state security apparatus was responsible for carrying out many of the acts of violence, terror, and dislocation perpetrated against Indonesians. Corruption in the police force and judicial system and censorship of the media similarly ensured that domestic and community violence often went unaddressed publicly.

Especially in Bali, where approximately 80% of the population directly or indirectly depends on tourism for their economic survival, there have been strong incentives for perpetrators and victims of violence alike to censor the recounting of memories of conflict or public discussions of its

---

[7] That the first Indonesians said to be suffering from trauma were ethnic Chinese women (see Siegel 1998b) delineated, we would suggest, a particularly marginal subject position for those experiencing psychological distress in the aftermath of violence. This stood in contrast to the ways the designation of traumatic victimhood has often been commodified, with victims jockeying for recognition and access to resources, as described by James (2004) in her discussion of the "trauma portfolios" of Haitians.

[8] This realm, it should be noted, is indeed a small one. Estimates for the number of psychiatrists practicing in Indonesia range from 400 to 600 for a population of approximately 220 million. Estimates for the number of practicing psychologists range from 2,000 to 10,000, although most of these are said to be working for private industry as human resource consultants. Mental health treatment for victims of violence, where it has been available, has been frequently provided by nonspecialist physicians or healthcare workers or, more commonly, by community activists working for social welfare organizations. Biomedical discourses of mental health and illness have thus been spread to Indonesia's population less through personal interactions with clinicians than through engagement with public culture.

continuing occurrence in order to maintain touristic images of a peaceful, premodern Bali immune from the stresses of the contemporary world.[9] Given such a background, it is perhaps unsurprising that Balinese psychiatrists have been unlikely to diagnose a disorder often connected to political or domestic violence, or long-term structural inequalities and state repression, aspects of Balinese life and history whose acknowledgment was suppressed by the New Order state and the tourism industry (Santikarma, 2003b). In such a context, the psychiatric diagnosis of PTSD could be viewed less as a neutral scientific endeavor or as an advance in biomedical knowledge and practice than as a political act, which by acknowledging the presence of traumatic events in Indonesia intervenes not only in the possibilities for understanding individual suffering but also for imagining society, the inequalities that mark it, and one's room for agency within it.

This social and political milieu underwent a radical shift, however, on October 12, 2002. That evening, bombs exploded in two crowded nightclubs in the Kuta Beach tourist district of Bali, leading to 202 deaths and over 300 injuries. Because the majority of the victims were Western tourists, the international media focused considerable attention on the events, with the press in Australia, where Bali has long been a popular holiday destination, going so far as to dub the bombings "Australia's 9/11." In the aftermath of the Kuta blasts, hundreds of journalists, police, and forensic investigators descended on Bali from across the world, subjecting what, with the echoes of September 11th strong in the air, was now called "Ground Zero" to intense scrutiny. Teams of Western forensic scientists combed through the rubble of the blasts, identifying bodies and unearthing the clues that eventually led to the arrests and convictions of the Indonesian Islamists involved in the planning and execution of the attacks. At the same time, scores of foreign medical personnel and humanitarian aid workers arrived to treat the wounded and to address the social damage caused by the bombings.

Although a number of countries, including Australia, Japan, and members of the European Union, offered assistance to Bali in the aftermath of the bombings, the United States Agency for International Development (USAID) was among the largest donors, committing over US$5 million to projects to address the impacts of the bombings. Much of this assistance was channeled through USAID Indonesia's Office for Conflict Prevention and Response (OCPR), which in the year prior to the bombings had not considered Bali to be problematic enough to place on its funding agenda,

---

[9] On the production of romantic images of Bali, see Boon (1977) and Vickers (1989). On the erasure of violence in Balinese touristic discourses, see Dwyer (in press), Santikarma (2001, 2003a), and Zurbuchen and Santikarma (2004).

viewing the island, long described in tourist literature as an oasis of social harmony, as having little need for peace building. But if the OCPR's entry into Bali signaled a radical shift in the way the island was now viewed by the development industry – from a relaxing weekend retreat for the Jakarta-based consultant to a site of transnational terror requiring substantial international aid – many of their programs reiterated long-standing assumptions about Balinese history, culture, and emotion. The supposed inherently peaceful nature of Balinese society and of the Balinese themselves was not questioned; rather, interventions were framed by the slogan "Bali Recovery," implying that the challenge now facing the island was how to return it to what it had been prior to the bombings. In turn, the bombings themselves were portrayed through a lens, fixed into focus by coverage of the incidents of 9/11, that viewed terror as fundamentally disconnected from the workings of the society under attack, as a historical aberration with little relation to Bali itself.

This mass-mediated attention to the bombing and its effects was not, however, trained evenly across the cultural and political landscape. While the dead were being identified and social distress diagnosed, sites of potential political disorder were also being mapped. Surveillance, by both the state and local village militias known as *pecalang*, was turned on Bali's gateways, with all who would enter Bali asked to show their national identity cards. Acting on authorization from the provincial government, *pecalang* in ethnically mixed areas of the island carried out what were called "sweeping" raids, checking the identity cards of non-Balinese residents and exacting payment from Indonesian immigrants who wished to remain on the island.[10] Yet even as Bali's landscape was being surveyed for potential dangers, investing ethnic and religious difference with sinister new meaning, these sweepings were rarely mentioned in the local press or acknowledged by Balinese cultural observers in their conversations with Western journalists. The lines of demarcation erected around Bali after the bombing had taken the form not only of security officers manning entry ports, but also of a symbolic boundary that isolated Bali as free from the effects of encounter with historical complexity or conflict. Bali could be victimized by violence, but its essence remained stable and, above all, safe. Bali had become a terrorist target, but terror itself was alien to Balinese.

In a November 2002 fact sheet on the impact of the bombings in Bali, the OCPR's subcontracting agency acknowledged a potential for conflict to arise in the wake of the bombings. The document's greatest emphasis, however, was not on addressing the historical or political context for possible social tensions but on "image rehabilitation" – both for potential

---

[10] See International Crisis Group (2003) and Santikarma (2003a).

tourists and for the Balinese themselves – as the key to Bali's recovery, stating,

> Bali's image and self-image has [sic] been fundamentally damaged. Many in Bali have spent the past few weeks introspecting to determine whether there was something in themselves that caused this tragedy to be thrust upon the island. . . . USAID will seek to support those groups who will work to rehabilitate Bali's self-image and who will carry out activities that promote harmonious relations throughout Bali's diverse society. . . . In addition to activities aimed at preserving Bali's multi-ethnic harmony, USAID is supporting activities that repair and strengthen Bali's image of itself. USAID is funding a number of local organizations to carry out an integrated cleanup and rehabilitation of Bali's physical environment. . . . In addition, USAID is supporting organizations that address Bali's psycho-social needs in the aftermath of the bombing. These activities include clinical and cultural approaches to counseling and a media outreach to affected populations. (Development Alternatives, Inc., 2002)

On one level, this document's message seems quite simple: If the key to Bali's development is tourism, an industry that produces and distributes alluring representations to attract visitors, it would be appropriate to aid Balinese in polishing their now-tarnished image to stimulate development. Although Bali's physical environment was not damaged by the blasts (with the exception of a several-hundred-square-meter area around the actual bomb site), funding efforts to "clean up" Bali would make sense as a way to render the island more attractive in tourists' eyes. Likewise, with violence proven to be one of the most potent disincentives to tourism, supporting programs to promote interethnic harmony promised benefits that exceeded the humanitarian dictum that peace is a good in and of itself.

But what of Bali's "self-image?" Why was it so important not only for Bali to "look good" but also for the Balinese to "feel better?" In the weeks after the bombings, a small number of Balinese intellectuals, most of whom were proponents of cultural conservatism in the face of rampant tourism development, suggested that the bombing of the nightclub, with its "whites only" policy, its reputation for a hedonism notable even for Kuta, and its location in the most overdeveloped area of Bali, exposed a dark side of tourism that demanded attention. Such statements, stripped of much of their critical import and posed against the large-scale state-sponsored post-bomb Hindu-Balinese rituals – rituals that were described in the Western media, in crude translation, as "re-balancing the cosmos" or "placating the angry gods" who had allowed the bombings to occur[11] – were taken as evidence that Balinese, rather than responding to terrorism with anger

---

[11] For a critique of understandings of Balinese ritual that claim "balance" to be their organizing principle, see Geertz (1994, 2004). Geertz suggests that such notions are recent imports to Bali, derived from modernist Hindu teachings in India and influenced by (mis)interpretations of Western scholars.

or vengeance, blamed themselves for the bombings. In stark contrast to post-9/11 New York, where any suggestion that the terrorist attacks might signal something problematic about the United States' actions in the world was met with heated outcry, Balinese were painted as naïvely failing to see the broader politics at work outside their insular island.

One of the goals of post-bomb programming was therefore to effect a delicate balance in Balinese subjectivity: to restore the "self-image" of Balinese who felt themselves at fault, thus enabling them to be healthy participants in the project of repairing their island's image, while at the same time discouraging any anger toward ethnic others, which might explode into a new bar to tourism. In the months after the bombings, we talked to hundreds of Balinese and found none who expressed the opinion that they had been to blame for the bombings, and many who were indeed angry, not only that the bombings had occurred but also at the resurgent Islam they blamed for the attacks. Yet the spectre of a damaged self-image continued to haunt international media accounts, functioning to construct parallels between Western and Balinese victims of transnational terror networks while at the same time maintaining Bali's exotic and attractive difference.

It was in such a discursive context that programs to identify and treat Balinese suffering from PTSD and to raise awareness of the disorder were inaugurated. The organization most involved in trauma work, a U.S.-based nonprofit organization, provided clinical treatment to approximately 200 Indonesians whom they identified as suffering from post-bomb PTSD. The scope of influence of these programs, however, extended much further than these numbers suggest. A large-scale campaign, financed by a roster of international organizations, worked to spread community knowledge of PTSD and its symptoms and encourage Balinese to seek treatment. Programs included placing large advertisements in Bali's major newspaper, holding radio call-in shows, buying television airtime to host a weekly talk show devoted to PTSD, and sponsoring a *wayang trauma* – a shadow puppet play in which the characters display posttraumatic symptoms, including nightmares, flashbacks, and exaggerated startle responses, and receive advice on how to treat them, which was performed in schools and villages across the island and screened on television, reaching an audience estimated at over 50,000.

Many Balinese we spoke with were ambivalent about these initiatives, given that clinical treatment was, during the first stages of the program, offered only to those small numbers of "direct victims" who had incurred PTSD through proximity to the blast, not to the large numbers of those experiencing depression, anxiety, or despair from the severe economic fallout caused by the drop in tourism or the mandatory financial contributions required for the state-sponsored post-bomb rituals. Especially for those whose lives had little to do with the tourist center of Kuta, the focus of these extensive media outreach programs on individuals' symptoms of

PTSD seemed to have little relevance to their struggles to hold families and communities together in the face of a sudden economic downturn whose ramifications extended out across the island. But even for those who had been nowhere near the blast nor sought out PTSD treatment, these programs succeeded in introducing *trauma* into a common Balinese lexicon. A year after the blasts, there were few Balinese we met who were unfamiliar with the word "trauma" applied not only to individual suffering but also to Balinese as an imagined cultural whole, victimized and in desperate need of a recovery grounded not in critical social and historical analysis but in bolstering a cultural self-confidence and idealized notions of citizenship suitable for promotion by a revitalized tourism industry.

MEMORY, TRAUMA, AND TREACHEROUS SPEECH

At first glance, the landscape surrounding Pak Nyoman appears abandoned and traceless, marked only by small hillocks and a carpet of wild grass.... For Pak Nyoman, however, this place is instead a field of terror, saturated with memory. It stands as silent witness to a night in 1965 when Balinese were hauled one by one off of trucks and made to stand on its ground. After fleeing in fear, Pak Nyoman heard shots exploding and watched as a squad of Balinese paramilitaries herded their victims, thumbs tied behind their backs, to line up before four wide holes that men of the village had been forced to prepare. By Pak Nyoman's count, around 220 people met their end on this field, under the deadly command of rifle-wielding soldiers.

Near another beach, around 20 kilometers to the south, dozens of foreign tourists stand transfixed, their heads bowed in sadness before a small shrine crafted from young bamboo stalks sprouting their first leaves.... "Ground Zero" has become an arena opening onto memory: memories of the 202 people who were buried in the ruins, burnt by the horrific explosions.... And it is not only the victims' families who are bound by the collective memory that has emerged from the rubble of the Sari Club. The traffic that passes along the main road bordering the ruins moves slowly. Drivers pause to take a brief look, and bus passengers jostle to hang their heads from the windows, eager to become momentary witnesses to human brutality.

Two fields of terror, each of which claimed more than 200 human lives. One has become a center of public attention, with debates raging over how best to commemorate it with a monument. The other lies hidden, with neither gravestone nor ceremony to mark it. One has produced witnesses who pile into the courtroom to make public their memories. The other has witnesses who are silenced, and perpetrators who are not only free but have been called heroes. One has become a site of pilgrimage, a mandatory stop on the Bali tourist itinerary. The other has been erased from the historical map, visited only by one man who still remains beholden to memory.[12]

Attempts to address the effects of violence in Bali did not, however, enter a vacant social and political field. Despite the international media's shock

---

[12] Translated excerpt from Santikarma (2003c). For an English-language version of this essay, see Santikarma (2004).

and horror at the Bali bombings and the governor of Bali's statement in December 2002 that the blasts were "the worst tragedy the island has experienced" (Beratha, 2002), this was far from the first time mass violence had taken place in Bali. From December 1965 to March 1966, some 80,000–100,000 Balinese (approximately 5–8% of the island's population) were killed as alleged communists,[13] and tens of thousands of others sexually assaulted, imprisoned without trial, widowed, orphaned, or left to survive as they could within severely fragmented communities. For over three decades after the violence, survivors continued to suffer political repression from the "clean environment" (*bersih lingkungan*) policy of the New Order government, which claimed that spouses, parents, siblings, children, and even grandchildren of those marked as communists were "infected" by political uncleanliness and thus were to be subject to strict government surveillance and barred from full social participation.

This history, despite its scale, brutality, and continuing relevance, was not addressed by PTSD programs in Bali, nor were survivors of 1965–66 offered participation in clinical treatment. There are a number of possible explanations for this omission, including a widespread sense on the part of observers of Indonesia that the events of 1965–66 belong firmly in the distant past and a hesitance to draw parallels between the state-sponsored massacre of alleged communists and contemporary antistate terrorism. There has also, historically, been a reluctance on the part of U.S., U.K., and Australian donor agencies to involve themselves in addressing 1965–66, given their governments' prior support for the Indonesian military's goal of destroying the Indonesian Communist Party (PKI) (see Robinson, 1995). And there is, of course, the fact that funds raised specifically for victims of particular disasters are not in practice easily transferable to those seen as suffering from other causes.

But although aid organizations may draw boundaries around particular events or populations, it is far more difficult for Balinese to sustain such categorizations in their everyday lives. Many survivors of 1965–66 described their feelings of terror, panic, or despair being reactivated after witnessing graphic television footage of the bombings. Other Balinese viewed the

---

[13] The exact number of Indonesians killed is unknown and will likely remain so, despite recent efforts at fact-finding by victims' advocacy groups such as the Yayasan Penelitian Korban Pembantaian (Foundation for Research on the Victims of Massacre). Estimates for the number killed across Indonesia have ranged from around 300,000 deaths to as many as 3 million, with a figure of 1 million frequently cited in academic and journalistic accounts of the violence. Robinson (1995) cites 80,000 for Bali, while local activists engaged in fact-finding projects often cite a figure of 100,000. The politics of numbering the dead is, of course, far from straightforward, speaking both to the state's desire to block access to nonofficial historical research and to activists' desires to ground calls for attention to the violence in statistical claims of its significance.

bombings through a political lens that has long posed 1965 as an icon of disorder and threat, worrying that any criticism of government policy to address terrorism could be read as a sign of subversion. Yet this ongoing presence of the past makes it crucial, we argue, to bring an awareness of 1965–66 and its continuing effects to bear on discussions of trauma in Bali. The powerful hold that the history of 1965–66 has had on both the national political imagination and local social relations comprises a fundamental aspect of the ways Balinese now understand violence and imagine the limits and possibilities of recovery from it.

Engaging with the history of 1965–66 not only illuminates the context in which trauma discourse is embedded in Bali, but it also leads us directly toward one of the most crucial aspects of trauma: the place of memory in the phenomenology and treatment of posttraumatic experience. Studies of trauma and PTSD are above all studies of memory and its effects – of the terrible impact on individuals and families of violence and terror, of efforts to forget and the intrusion of painful memories, of the consequences of such memories for individual psychological development and functioning, and of their sequelae in everyday social lives. Such studies often focus rather narrowly on individuals and individual psychology. However, in recent years, scholars from diverse disciplines have begun to look closely at forgetting, repressing, remembering, or reworking memories as social processes. They have discussed "how societies remember" (Connerton, 1989) or how they refuse to recall, and have investigated specific social mechanisms – from ritual to myth to informal narrative to formal truth and reconciliation commissions – established to reconsider history and to engage traumatic memory communally.

In Bali, post-bomb PTSD programs directly addressed the issue of traumatic memory in their outreach materials, framing it as a challenge to social functioning. For example, one organization sponsored the placement of large public service advertisements in Bali's major newspapers with the headline *"Ingin Melupakan?"* or "Do You Want to Forget?" The trauma shadow play echoed the notion that memory was a problematic bar to recovery, describing a key theme of the performance as how "taking what is negative and putting a mask over it can transform it into a positive energy to harness your emotions, your anger, and your sorrow" (Yayasan Kemanusiaan Ibu Pertiwi, 2002). Through such narratives, trauma programs spread assumptions about the intrusion of history into the mind as a troubling symptom and the importance of gaining control over the past in order to move beyond it.

A focus on 1965–66 makes it clear, however, that for many survivors of violence, forgetting or remembering are far more complex matters than empowering sufferers to gain conscious mastery over history. Memory is not simply a matter of individual agency, but rather is embedded in past and present social and political relations. For most Balinese, the violence of 1965–66 is not an event definitively past against which one can take a distanced stance. It is not something that one intentionally chooses to either "remember" by way of, say, a Truth Commission or an updated national curriculum, or to "forget" by way of erasure from the mass media or official histories or through more personal attempts to deny or disregard. It is not, as some Western psychological models might encourage us to think, an experience located safely in individual or social history, recovery from which involves a "working through" or "letting go" of a destructive past, or the arrival at "closure" through an imposition of meaningful narrative on the chaos of pathologically insistent and fragmentary memory. Rather, the events of 1965–66 have channeled and dammed possibilities for speech, social action, and religious and cultural meaning.

In part, this endurance of the events of 1965–66 has been an effect of the New Order state's persistent attempts to promote its version of history to authorize ongoing political oppression. The state's strategies for discursive management included not only the repressive imposition of silence upon survivors, but also an enthusiastic program of commemoration and symbolic control of history. Under Soeharto, public debate of the events of 1965–66 was banned. For a new generation of Indonesians, the halting tales their parents might have told of their experiences – or the deep silences they may have effected to preserve their safety – were drowned out by the insistent rhetoric of the New Order, which staged regular "remembrances" of the state's victory over communism and which spread images of communist evil and bloodthirstiness through the school curriculum, public monuments, and propaganda pieces. Up until Soeharto's fall – and even after – state officials animated the specter of communism, dismissing almost any sort of social or political protest as the work of "formless organizations" of communist sympathizers or as the result of provocation by "remnants" of the PKI. Warnings to remain on guard against communism were typically expressed in the command *awas bahaya laten PKI/komunisme* – "beware of the latent danger of the PKI/communism" – rendering communism less a matter of party affiliation or intellectual position than an invisible but inevitable aspect of any virtually any challenge to Soeharto or his military regime.[14]

The continuing power of 1965–66 to shape Balinese social life and subjectivity has also been an artifact of the context in which the killings and their aftermath were embedded in Bali. Violence became entangled in local communities and kin groups, as neighbors killed neighbors and relatives killed relatives, and the very assumptions and expectations brought to bear on

[14] Honna (2001) details how Indonesian military ideology framed and reframed the notion of "communism" from 1966 to 1998 to address changing threats to its power, ranging from pro-democracy activism to globalization. Heryanto (1999) discusses the deployment of and resistances to the term "communist" under the New Order.

social life shifted.[15] Given such a context, moving past or working through memory is a highly complex cultural and political negotiation, rather than a self-evident goal of treatment. As one Balinese man, who lost his brother to the violence and was himself imprisoned for three years for membership in a leftist high school organization, told us after we apologized for asking him questions that we thought might have brought traumatic memories to the surface, "It's not you who has made me remember. I will have these memories until I also am dead. It is these memories that make me know I'm still alive."

Just as memory, in this case, can be understood to entail a deeply ethical position essential to the construction of selfhood, it must also be seen as something that takes place not in clinical isolation but in engagement with one's everyday social world and those who inhabit it. For most Balinese with whom we discussed memories of 1965–66, attending not only to what people remember but also to how and where and with whom, memory emerges in relation to a social landscape, as victims of violence encounter those they believe responsible for their suffering in regular community interaction. The maintenance of memories of 1965–66 is often seen as essential for navigating a social terrain made treacherous by the open possibility of violence, at the same time as memory and the emotions it entails are often socially managed through strategies of temporary concealment that rarely reach a state of "closure."

A focus on 1965–66 and its aftermath also leads us to consider the discursive landscapes that emerge from violence. Both traumatic memory and treatment to address posttraumatic suffering, although not limited to the linguistic, are nevertheless deeply implicated in it. Memory often emerges into consciousness in dialogue with imagined interlocutors – or potential informers – whereas clinical spaces rely on spoken narratives for diagnosis and monitoring, if not therapy. Yet speaking memories of violence is not always a straightforward process. Indeed, the intensity and openness of public discussion of the Bali bombings, and the attention paid by international organizations to its traumatic effects, pose a stark contrast to the public silence that has prevailed around 1965–66.

For decades, those who lived through the terror have feared that any challenges to official state history could unleash new state violence and suppression of human rights. Even with Soeharto's exit from the presidency in 1998, the historical narratives that were used by his regime to create a kind of mythic charter for its existence, justifying its absolute rule as a benevolent protection against communism, seemed to have been invested with lingering powers. Three decades of warnings by the state to be on guard against an ever-present threat of communism – a threat left

---

[15] For fuller discussion of the intimate dimensions of the violence in Bali, see Dwyer (2004) and Dwyer and Santikarma (2003, in press).

sinisterly vague – endowed speech about 1965–66 with an almost uncanny ability to evoke fears of violent retribution. With the 1966 law banning both the PKI and what the Indonesian state called "Marxist–Leninist ideology" still intact, many survivors remain uncertain as to the very legality of speaking about their experiences. Even after the fall of Soeharto, national history textbooks still retain the New Order's version of the events, making no mention whatsoever of the vast numbers of those slaughtered in the violence.[16]

Although the dismantling of the New Order has undoubtedly loosened restrictions on the press and on freedoms of speech and assembly, this new openness has reflected unevenly in the lives of those affected by the violence. The ambivalence many survivors feel about articulating memory indexes not only their fears of state repression, but also the forms violence took as it became embedded in their communities, which were exhorted by the state to participate in annihilating communism "down to its roots" (*sampai ke akar-akarnya*) by uncovering and destroying the intimate "enemy under the blanket" (*musuh dalam selimut*), be they neighbor, spouse, sibling, or friend. There has often been a reluctance to make public what Veena Das (2000) has called "poisonous knowledge," the implicit understanding that violence does not necessarily create solidarity among victims but rather exposes normally hidden possibilities of betrayals, reprisals, and social tensions within families and communities. In Bali, unlike many other places in Indonesia, most of those who lived through the violence have remained in the same communities, tied by customary law (*adat*) and ritual practice to their villages and temples of origin. Those who carried out violence regularly come face to face with those they terrorized on the streets, in the markets, and at communal ceremonies. Speaking about 1965–66 does not, in such contexts, place a narrator in relation only to the state and its dark history – or only to a clinician, sympathetic or otherwise – but channels memory through the complex local politics of the present in which speech may become a treacherous instrument of harm.

In Bali, the violence has also entered into an economy of memory, in which particular versions of the past become narratively packaged and standardized as tourism commodities, whereas other histories are viewed as lacking in value or even undermining the smooth functioning of this market. With so many Balinese dependent on tourism for their livelihoods, it has been, survivors say, often painfully hard to voice publicly memories that threaten to destabilize the linkage stressed by government officials

---

[16] The national high school and junior high school textbooks were revised in 1999 to include a brief statement that the history of 1965 is debated by historians. The high school textbooks also include a new section presenting differing theories about the alleged coup and whether it really was carried out by the PKI. These books still do not make mention of the violence against alleged communists.

and the tourism industry between foreign arrivals and the production of images of peace.

This is not to imply, however, that the state was successful at completely repressing or silencing memory or precluding processes of remembering and signifying suffering. In Bali, memory may take non-narrative forms familiar to Western clinicians, including recurring nightmares, suicidal impulses, domestic violence, and depression. But Balinese also speak about memory as being located not only in individual or collective recollection but also in the material world as traces of the past (*laad*) that shape how social space is used and interpreted. Memories too painful or politically dangerous to be uttered may also take forms that avoid spoken language altogether, or may shift into indirect registers, most commonly as debates over ritual practice, especially those centered around death and the rebirth of souls. Some of the family members of those killed in 1965–66 maintain more direct contact with their lost relatives, communicating through spirit mediums (*balian peluasan*), hearing their whispers (*pawisik*) in dreams, or speaking with the voices of those dead considered to have become deified ancestors in trance (*kerauhan*), reasserting the social influence of the dead denied by the state. Another means by which memory has often been articulated is in the form of circulating stories concerned with karmic retribution, including stories of killers who died young, fell ill, or suffered various misfortunes of supernatural origin. Such local histories, spread through community networks by rumor and gossip, exist in stark counterpoint to official government narratives, reaching as they do for a realm of justice and historical diagnosis outside the control of the state apparatus. Yet they share the same premise: The violent past is very much a present matter, the articulation of which is fraught with tension and ambivalence.

POSTTRAUMATIC POLITICS

Another crucial concern that a focus on the violence of 1965–66 brings to our understanding of trauma and PTSD is the political context and implications of psychiatric discourses and treatment programs, and how the subjectivities they delineate in defining pathology participate in relations of power. The importance of this issue was made clear to us one afternoon, 10 months after the Bali bombings, when we were visited in Bali by a dozen university students and human rights activists. These young people had read a newspaper article in which Santikarma had discussed the politics of remembering violence in Indonesia, arguing that the experiences of those hundreds of thousands of Indonesians who still lived with deeply painful memories of 1965–66 were not being acknowledged by the new post-bomb surge of interest in the individual effects of terror (Santikarma, 2003b). They had come, they said, to talk about a concern of many of those involved in human rights activism in Bali.

Small grassroots non-governmental organizations (NGOs) that had for years struggled to find material and political support for their work protecting indigenous or women's rights, advocating for democratization or new labor regulations, documenting state and military human rights abuses and corruption, or providing legal aid to the politically and economically disenfranchised were now being solicited by international aid organizations to integrate post-bombing PTSD awareness activities into their programming. This opportunity had left many activists deeply ambivalent. On the one hand, they said, they sympathized with those killed or traumatized by the bombings and their families. Many of the activists were also eager to gain a measure of financial stability and international or national recognition for their organizations, which they hoped to capitalize on to fund future projects. But others were concerned that the wave of new interest in PTSD as a matter of individual suffering threatened to drown out the voices of those working against more dangerous long-term structures of violence and inequality. The divide on this issue had grown so wide, they claimed, that it threatened to split at least one respected human rights NGO into opposing "pro-PTSD" and "anti-PTSD" factions. What they needed to understand, they told us, was whether participation in PTSD programs was compatible with their commitment to social justice. "What we need to know to make our decision," one young man explained, "is what's political about PTSD?"

Most theorizing about PTSD has not engaged such questions. Many individual mental health practitioners have certainly recognized through their day-to-day contacts with victims of violence that the work in which they are engaged has a political background and political implications. Indeed, Breslau (2004) notes that among many of those engaged in international mental health work there has emerged what he calls a culture of "PTSD activism," in which diagnosis of the disorder among particular populations is seen as a crucial step in calling for international attention to certain conflicts or disasters. A small but influential number of these clinicians have sought to reframe traditional assumptions about the neutrality of the therapist's role and the private nature of the clinical encounter to position themselves as "partisan witnesses" (see Sanford, 2003), taking professional responsibility for supporting human rights and making space in treatment for "therapeutic testimony" with explicitly political aims (e.g., McGorry, 1995; Weine & Laub, 1995).

However, the majority of the literature on PTSD has not engaged such themes, but has focused instead on the disorder's relevance as an analytic or treatment model implemented within psychiatric institutions or on debates among mental health professionals about its etiology, symptomatology, or treatment. Likewise, the bulk of trauma research has chosen the laboratory, the clinic, or a group of persons said to be suffering from PTSD as the site of research. A growing body of critical literature has explored the PTSD model's genesis within a particular historical and political context

(Young, 1995), its continued embeddedness within Western notions of self and body as analytically separable from broader social fields (Alexander, Eyerman, Giesen, Smelser, & Sztompka, 2004), and the ramifications of what Kleinman (1995) has called "the medicalization of violence," in which the wide-ranging cultural, social, and political effects of violence tend to be reduced to individual pathology deemed to require the specific intervention of medical experts (Ong, 1995; Summerfield, 1999). Yet to date, comparatively little scholarship has examined how PTSD, as both a biomedical category and a discourse that channels particular theories of memory, emotion, subjectivity, history, and society, as well as funds for research, treatment, and humanitarian intervention, has been interpreted, appropriated, or critiqued by the communities it is being used to identify and treat.

Such a focus is crucial, however, to a better understanding of trauma, its effects, and its amelioration. Ethnographic attention to the social and political life of PTSD as it is spread across the globe by biomedical literature, clinicians, and humanitarian agencies offers the opportunity to examine how survivors of violence live not only with the embodied aftereffects of terror but also with the framings that are offered to interpret such experiences. It allows us to understand how people may resist incorporation into discursive regimes that recast their experiences as illness and, conversely, how PTSD programs may be selective in their identification of populations to target for attention based on assumptions as to what constitutes sufficient psychic pain and which events are extraordinary enough to warrant the implementation of treatment programs. Grounding theories of PTSD in subjects' experience of suffering not only provides a means of giving voice to those whose struggles take place outside the scope of the clinic, but also holds the potential to assist in the creation of more appropriate and effective means of alleviating individual and social distress.

Most of the lay Balinese responses to the model of PTSD put forth in the months following the Bali bombings took as their starting point the premise that categories of suffering are inherently cultural and political discourses that must be evaluated within local frameworks. For example, Balinese we spoke with tended to describe their emotional distress in the aftermath of the attacks not as individual pathology but as shared confusion (*bingung*), shock (*mekesyab*), or panic (*genting*). Although some Balinese used the newly introduced term *trauma* – usually in the plural ("*kita kena trauma*") – others used local terms such as *ngeb*, a form of withdrawal from ordinary social interaction that may be collective, which is generally not thought of as an illness (*penyakit*) and often has political connotations as a form of resistance against unjust authority.[17] These narratives were in

---

[17] This notion of withdrawal as an assertive expression of conflict or resistance is also found in the Balinese practice of *puik*, when two or more individuals enact silence and social

keeping with traditional Balinese taxonomies of mental illness that locate emotional disorder in disturbed relationships with both the visible (*sekala*) and invisible (*niskala*) realms of life, including interactions with family, neighbors, ancestors, gods, spirits, and demons (see Connor 1990, 1995; Jennaway, 2002; Lemelson, 2003; Wikan, 1990).

They fit poorly, however, with PTSD treatment models that saw the encounter between clinician and patient, rather than social and spiritual relations, as the appropriate site of addressing emotional distress. They also, in the case of *ngeb*, contradicted psychiatric diagnostic tools that view "avoidance" as a pathological symptom of illness indicating a retreat from social reality, rather than an assertive act of social commentary.[18] Yet despite these obvious cultural contrasts, Balinese critiques of the PTSD model have not, for the most part, been culturalist critiques that seek to explain illness and its treatment through reference to fixed, shared patterns of belief and behavior. After the bombings, local biomedically trained psychiatrists and psychologists did, in ways quite resonant with Western discourses of cultural competence or cultural sensitivity, tend to caution against the blunt application of PTSD models in Bali because of differences between Western and Balinese culture. They noted that Balinese place great emphasis on spiritual and ritual approaches to healing and spoke of the need to recognize such orientations in PTSD treatment programs in order to make them appropriate for their patients.

Yet critiques by Balinese nonclinicians tended not to follow such lines. Rather than constructing a dichotomy between an essential, homogenous Balinese culture and (an equally homogenous) Western medicine and asserting wariness of the latter, those Balinese we spoke with in the months after the bombing claimed that they had no hesitancy about the Western origins or secular orientations of PTSD treatment programs in Bali, having had long experience of relying on both local healers and biomedically focused clinicians to address their various health concerns. What was at stake for them was not "culture" as an abstract field of norms, but the divides of history, power, and social position that became more painfully visible after the bombings, showing up any notion of unitary "Balineseness" as a tenuous construction.

In the aftermath of the bombings, the majority of those Balinese with whom we spoke identified the traumatic event that had caused them the

avoidance against each other, or in practices of failing to *ngayah*, offer labor for the rituals or other events held by those claiming higher status than oneself. It also references the popular Balinese expression *koh ngomong*, roughly translatable as "fed up with speaking," in which silence becomes a pointed commentary on an excess of "empty" speech.

[18] According to the *DSM–IV–TR*, "persistent avoidance of stimuli associated with the trauma, and numbering of general responsiveness" is one of the six definitive diagnostic criteria of PTSD (APA, 2000). We would argue that what constitutes avoidance, much less responsiveness, is highly locally variable.

most suffering not as the deaths of 202 people in the explosions, but as the economic and political aftershock of terrorism. For example, Pak Ketut, a tour guide who dropped a group of British vacationers at the Sari Club hours before it was engulfed by explosions, described to us his restlessness, inability to concentrate, tendency to startle, and repetitive dreams of the faces of the tourists he had left at the site of their deaths. Yet after hearing that free care was available for Balinese suffering from bomb-related PTSD, he insisted that he was in no way a candidate for psychiatric treatment. He responded that, for Balinese, "death is something usual, something we know how to deal with," referencing the highly elaborated set of traditional Balinese rituals that work to ensure the spiritual well-being of the deceased and their families and to protect the living from the spiritual pollution (*sebel*) of contact with the dead.[19] His statements also evoked the fact that death is far from unusual on an island whose maternal and child mortality rates far exceed those of the industrialized West, where life expectancy averages only in the mid-60s, and where medical treatment for serious illnesses is outside the financial wherewithal of most people.

What Pak Ketut claimed to be most concerned with, and what he attributed his symptoms to, was the fact that within a month of the bombings he had been summarily laid off from his position at a hotel – part of a well-known international chain – where he had worked for the past 15 years. Pak Ketut – like many other Balinese – pointed to the exploitative labor relations that often occur in the Balinese tourism industry, allowing local workers – unlike their Western counterparts who may be employed by the same multinational corporations – little recourse to unemployment or severance compensation. He also noted the pressure exerted by the Indonesian police and military against the few organized attempts to protest unfair labor policies after the bombings, and the claim by government officials that any visible manifestation of dissent was a "social ill" (*penyakit sosial*) that was counterproductive to the quest to restore touristic images of Bali,[20] a claim that resonated neatly with previous state attempts to deny

[19] By referencing traditional Balinese ritual, we do not mean to imply that death ritual has been immune from historical change or contemporary contest. Indeed, the rituals held after the Kuta bombings produced a high degree of debate, with various factions within the Parisadha Hindu Dharma Indonesia, the national state-sponsored Hindu governing organization, fiercely debating whether the rituals that were to be held should be those for victims of natural disaster – a position that would have erased any notion of agency in the commission of terror – or for victims of war – a position that would have cast Muslims as the enemy. Lay Balinese likewise debated whether it was appropriate for them to be asked to hold (and pay for) separate rituals in each household and village temple to address the spiritual pollution of the bombings.

[20] See Good and DelVecchio-Good (2001) on the New Order regime's tendency to pathologize social protest using colonially influenced notions of *amuk*.

the suffering of victims of 1965–66 in the name of social and economic development.

Pak Ketut's emphasis on the social and political context of trauma has, we suggest, implications not only for the work of social scientists but also clinicians. Indeed, it is in such contexts that symptoms are read as either reasonable or pathological responses to political conditions. For example, "avoidance of stimuli associated with the trauma" is cited in the *DSM–IV–TR* as one of the primary criteria for diagnosing PTSD (American Psychiatric Association [APA], 2000). Thus, a New Yorker who persistently avoids lower Manhattan in the wake of the World Trade Center attacks and a Balinese who, claiming to be experiencing *ngeb*, avoids returning to the Kuta Beach tourist district where the bombings occurred might, on a PTSD diagnostic instrument, show certain similarities. They would, however, be responding to very different political situations. In the New Yorker's case, it might be possible to identify a certain measure of emotional and behavioral inconsistency with the reality of a potential threat. In the Balinese case, however, where the Indonesian government has not responded to terrorism with the dramatic security measures implemented in the United States and where political tensions rooted in extreme economic inequalities, a long history of state repression, the post-Soeharto rise of local militias, and newly hardened ethnic and religious divisions appear to be growing, the fear that traumatic events may repeat themselves is grounded in a very different contemporary reality, one saturated with previous experiences of political violence and the lessons learned from it about how to protect oneself and loved ones. For Balinese, it would be irrational to imagine that terror had retreated safely into the past, leaving only the task of coming to terms with a horror now historical. At the very least, there is something ironic about using USAID funds to treat Balinese for symptoms of avoidance, at the same time as the U.S. State Department has issued a blanket warning for Americans against all nonessential travel to Indonesia, singling out Kuta and other places where tourists are known to gather for special mention.

Balinese responses to post-bomb PTSD programs point not only to how individuals' experiences and embodied expressions of trauma unfold within cultural and political contexts, but also to the fact that the boundaries separating the clinic from the broader social arena are, to a large extent, fluid and porous. PTSD treatment programs, even when they are framed as purely biomedical interventions, are far from immune from complicity in politics. In the Bali case, where neither survivors of episodes of violence other than the October 2002 bombings nor those who experienced emotional suffering due to very real readings of the foreshortened possibilities for employment, education, or future economic success were offered participation in the highly publicized PTSD programs, those who felt that their pain was being ignored or downplayed often expressed resentment.

Pak Wayan Santa, one of the leaders of the of the Bali chapter of the Yayasan Pelelitian Korban Pembunuhan (YPKP, the Foundation for Research into Victims of Massacre), an Indonesian organization involved in fact-finding and victims' advocacy related to 1965–66, was one of those dubious of the exclusive attention trained on the victims of the bombings by humanitarian agencies. Pak Santa framed his critique by first describing his memories of 1965, when he was a high school student active in a leftist youth group. After escaping from a group of machete-wielding paramilitaries, he was arrested and detained without trial for several years under conditions of extreme brutality. He faced social, political, and economic discrimination after his release, losing the job he had managed to find in a hotel after his employer performed a background check and discovered he was a former political prisoner. Pak Santa then recounted his continuing nightmares, depression, and pervasive fear, claiming that a fair number of the 1965–66 survivors he knew suffered similar emotional difficulties.

He told a story of how, in 2000, he had tried to organize group therapy sessions for other members of the YPKP, but he could not find a local clinician willing to work with victims of 1965–66, who are frequently still stigmatized either as "communists" whose punishment was just or as politically infectious people with whom public contact could lead to one's own ostracism. "All we could find was a 'trainer' from the John Robert Powers School of Personality Development," Pak Santa recounted, referring to a U.S.-based for-profit franchise offering courses in "self-management," "image projection," and "social graces" popular among Balinese tourism industry personnel who wish to improve their professional persona. As Pak Santa related,

He came and met with us and told us to think positive thoughts and not be trapped in the past, and that if we were feeling tense to imagine ourselves sitting on a beautiful white sand beach. Most of us were confused, and some of us were angry, too, hearing him talk as if we were the ones who had the problem, as opposed to the state having made problems for us. Finally one older man, a poor man, stood up and said, "Why should I think about a beach? I'm a fisherman – I see the beach every day and all it makes me think about is hard work! You sound like a tour guide, not a doctor!"

This exchange, amusing as it might be, does hide some bitter realities. Treatment for those in distress depends on the presence of a social and political space in which their experience can be recognized as painful and problematic, rather than as mundane, malingering, or deserved (James, 2004). Indeed, as Breslau (2004) notes, the discourse of trauma "deals fundamentally with the legitimacy of suffering" (p. 15). It is also linked to social and political processes through which certain kinds of events are identified as harboring the risk of producing large numbers of cases of mental illness. For international organizations without a wide pool of local expertise to draw on and which are themselves beholden to government or private donor interests, this generally involves drawing comparisons with what is known of the psychological effects of other events seen as similar, as well as considering how trauma treatment might provide broader economic and political benefits. Local clinicians or activists seeking to access funding for their efforts often must reproduce such framings, constructing their descriptions of local conditions in terms that resonate with international categories and priorities (Breslau, 2004; Watters, 2001). Likewise, those seeking medical treatment or social resources must often represent themselves as one-dimensional patients suffering psychopathology rather than as complex political actors (Gross, 2004; Zarowsky, 2004). As Ong has described in the case of aid programs for Cambodian refugees in the United States, "Getting the money is tied to the official designation of Cambodians as a 'depressed' minority" (Ong, 1995, p. 1247).

In Bali, support for the treatment of trauma has likewise been contingent on the construction of particular internationally resonant narratives, including that of similarity between the Kuta bombings and the terrorist attacks of 9/11, and of the bombings as an extraordinary violent event unprecedented in Balinese history, enacted upon victims untainted by blame. The experiences of survivors of 1965–66, which fit poorly with such models, have remained unaddressed, leaving them in a discursive "zone of social abandonment" (Biehl, 2005) in which access to care depends on denial of their experience – on a fisherman imagining his reality from the perspective of a tourist. Not only do such models fail to recognize certain forms of suffering, but also by refusing to analyze the political conditions of their production they can engage only with presumed individual pathology, rather than the broader "pathologies of power" (Farmer, 2003) in which distress is embedded. Instead of seeking to dismantle the binds – at once material and discursive – restricting victims of violence, it becomes the victims' own responsibility not to be "trapped in the past."

The Balinese case also demonstrates how PTSD programs, especially when they include educational or public awareness components designed to encourage potential clients to seek treatment, may also have important political effects as they enter broader discursive fields. In the post-9/11 United States, PTSD models were used to treat those who had been in the vicinity of the World Trade Center. Yet PTSD discourse, which was spread past the walls of the laboratory and clinic through the media and public health apparatus, had a social and political impact extending far out from Ground Zero. Discussions of the high rates of PTSD said to be experienced by Americans after September 11 engaged with a public culture that equated the experience of trauma with victimization and with conservative nationalist rhetoric about an America under attack, strengthening battle lines between good and innocent victims and evil perpetrators of senseless acts of aggression. Likewise in Bali, descriptions of the bombings

as "shattering" Balinese life or "destroying" Bali's tourism-driven image
as a peaceful island paradise presumed a stable pre-bomb Bali, erasing
the experiences of contest, conflict, and past violence. By characterizing
PTSD in their educational materials as "a normal response to extraordinary events," the program coordinators no doubt wished to lessen the
strong social stigma attached to psychiatric treatment in Bali. But they also
helped to spread a sense that Bali was indeed experiencing remarkable
violence, that the causes of this were located elsewhere, that through its
relations with Western experts and techniques Bali could recover, and that
the aim of treatment was to put the past behind, rather than to question
power relations in the present in which suffering might be implicated.
Albeit for the most part unwittingly, focus by medical and aid industry
"experts" on the trauma of the bombings as a singularly horrific event
authorized inattention to the presence of long-term structures of violence
and inequality that have caused arguably far more psychic damage to
Balinese.

It is important as well to recognize that discourses of psychic and social
healing from violence are not solely the province of biomedicine. Rather,
they engage with a broader political context and are often used by social
actors seeking to shift or maintain relations of power. PTSD, with its aura of
scientific fact, can become an especially powerful rhetorical tool. This point
has been made for the case of South Africa, where "trauma" became a new
key word authorizing the dismantling of many of the social and political
structures of apartheid, the granting of monetary reparations to victims,
and the dissemination, through the Truth and Reconciliation Commission
(TRC), of personal narratives of structural and political violence. Trauma
can be seen here as a tool of liberation, yet Lund argues that the discourse
of healing that emerged out of the South African TRC also worked to "cast
apartheid as an illness turning South Africans into victims requiring the
ministrations of a new nationalism" (2003, p. 89). In Bali, where the term
"trauma" escaped its origins in clinical discourse to stand for the experiences of an entire ethnic group, PTSD programs likewise became not
simply clinical endeavors but a rationale for reconstructing Balinese society in ways that privileged tourism capital and government authority and
silenced local dissent.

To take such critiques seriously is not, of course, to deny the intense
suffering that those who have lived through violence and terror have
experienced, nor the relief that individuals may obtain through psychiatric
treatment – indeed, a knowledgeable and sensitive clinician was precisely
what Pak Santa and his friends were seeking. Nor is it to cast aside what
is known from clinical and basic science research about the psychological
effects of trauma on individuals, how traumatic memories are stored and
processed in human brains, or how they shape psychological and emotional functioning. And it is certainly not to deny the commitment of those

who seek, through clinical or humanitarian programs, to acknowledge and ameliorate the suffering of victims of violence, whose pain is so often denied by perpetrators, states, and societies.

It is, however, to shift focus to the social, political, and economic discourses that render trauma visible or that, through their inattention, authorize the continuing destructive presence of other forms of violence. It is to question what relations of power and meaning make a "clinic" seem more sensible than a "center," and how the authority of experts is created and contested in such spaces. It is to recognize that clinical interventions may have unintended – even perverse – effects as they intervene in landscapes of postconflict memory that are fundamentally social and political. It is to push past simplistic models of "cultural competence" in designing local programs to address suffering, recognizing that contests over who gets to define "culture" may be deeply implicated in the conflicts that provoke trauma. And it is, ultimately, to open to discussion the crucial question of how clinicians can be incorporated into broader struggles to create more inclusive responses to suffering and to prevent the perpetuation of various forms of violence, from the blunt trauma of terrorism and mass murder to the insidious trauma of ongoing repression, silence, and disregard.

References

Alexander, J. C., Eyerman, R., Giesen, B., Smelser, N. J., & Sztompka, P. (2004). *Cultural trauma and collective identity.* Berkeley: University of California Press.

American Psychiatric Association. (2000). *Diagnostic and statistical manual of mental disorders* (4th ed., text rev.). Washington, DC: Author.

Anderson, B. (1994). *Language and power: Exploring political cultures in Indonesia.* Ithaca, NY: Cornell University Press.

Anderson, B. R. O. G., McVey, R. T., & Bunnell, F. P. (1971). *A preliminary analysis of the October 1, 1965, coup in Indonesia.* Ithaca, NY: Modern Indonesia Project, Cornell University.

Aretxaga, B. (2003). Maddening states. *Annual Review of Anthropology, 32,* 393–410.

Beratha, Dewa Made. (2002, December 11–12). The Kuta tragedy and the present-day Bali (A report by the Governor of Bali). Paper presented at a meeting of the Association of Southeast Asian Nations (ASEAN) National Tourism Organizations (NTO), Denpasar, Bali, Indonesia.

Biehl, J. (2005). *Vita: Life in a zone of social abandonment.* Berkeley: University of California Press.

Boon, J. (1977). *The anthropological romance of Bali 1597–1972: Dynamic perspectives in marriage and caste, politics and religion.* New York: Cambridge University Press.

Breslau, J. (2004). Cultures of trauma: Anthropological views of posttraumatic stress disorder in international health. *Culture, Medicine and Psychiatry, 28,* 113–126.

Connerton, P. (1989). *How societies remember.* New York: Cambridge University Press.

Connor, L. (1990). Séances and spirits of the dead: Context and idiom in symbolic healing. *Oceania, 60,* 345–359.

Connor, L. (1995). Acquiring invisible strength: A Balinese discourse on health and well-being. *Indonesia Circle, 66*, 124–153.

Cribb, R. (Ed.). (1990). *The Indonesian killings of 1965–1966: Studies from Java and Bali* (Papers on Southeast Asia, Vol. 21). Clayton, Victoria, Australia: Centre of Southeast Asian Studies, Monash University.

Crouch, H. A. (1978). *The army and politics in Indonesia*. Ithaca, NY: Cornell University Press.

Das, V. (2000). The act of witnessing: Violence, poisonous knowledge and subjectivity. In V. Das, A. Kleinman, M. Pamphele, & P. Reynolds (Eds.), *Violence and subjectivity* (pp. 205–225). Berkeley: University of California Press.

DelVecchio-Good, M.-J., Brodwin, P. E., Good, B. J., & Kleinman, A. (1994). *Pain as human experience: An anthropological perspective*. Berkeley: University of California Press.

Development Alternatives, Inc. (2002). *Program support initiative (PSI) semi-annual performance report, June 1–November 30, 2002*. Bethesda, MD: Author.

Dwyer, L. (2004, August). The intimacy of terror: Gender and the violence of 1965–66 in Bali, Indonesia. *Intersections: Gender, history and culture in the Asian context, 10*. Retrieved 18 June 2006 from http://wwwsshe.murdoch.edu.au/intersections/issue10/dwyer.html.

Dwyer, L. (in press). A politics of silence: Violence, memory and treacherous speech in post-1965 Bali. In A. Hinton & K. O'Neill (Eds.), *Genocide, truth, memory and representations*. Durham, NC: Duke University Press.

Dwyer, L., & Santikarma, D. (2003). When the world turned to chaos: The violence of 1965–66 in Bali, Indonesia. In B. Kiernan & R. Gellately (Eds.), *The spectre of genocide: Mass murder in historical perspective*. New York: Cambridge University Press.

Dwyer, L., & Santikarma, D. (2004, April). *Democratic subjects and civil selves: Reading "reconciliation" in Indonesia*. Paper presented at the H. F. Guggenheim Foundation conference on "Exporting Democracy," Ascona, Switzerland.

Dwyer, L., & Santikarma, D. (in press). Speaking from the shadows: Memories of massacre in Bali. In B. Pouligny, S. Chesterman, & A. Schnabel (Eds.), *Mass crime and post-conflict peace building*. Tokyo: United Nations University Press.

Farmer, P. (2003). *Pathologies of power: Health, human rights, and the new war on the poor*. Berkeley: University of California Press.

French, L. (2004). Commentary. *Culture, Medicine and Psychiatry, 28*, 211–220.

Geertz, H. (1994). *Images of power: Balinese paintings made for Gregory Bateson and Margaret Mead*. Honolulu: University of Hawaii Press.

Geertz, H. (2004). *The life of a Balinese temple: Artistry, imagination, and history in a peasant village*. Honolulu: University of Hawaii Press.

Goldstein, D. M. (2003). *Laughter out of place: Race, class, violence, and sexuality in a Rio shantytown*. Berkeley: University of California Press.

Good, B. J., & DelVecchio-Good, M.-J. (2001, June). "Why do the masses so easily run amuk?" Madness and violence in Indonesian politics. *Latitudes 5*, 10–19.

Greenhouse, C. J. (2002). Introduction: Altered state, altered lives. In C. J. Greenhouse, E. Mertz, & K. B. Warren (Eds.), *Ethnography in unstable places: Everyday lives in contexts of dramatic political change*. Durham, NC: Duke University Press.

Gross, C. S. (2004). Struggling with imaginaries of trauma and trust: The refugee experience in Switzerland. *Culture, Medicine and Psychiatry, 28*, 151–167.

International Crisis Group. (2003, November 7). *The perils of private security in Indonesia: Guards and militias on Bali and Lombok* (Asia Report No. 67). Jakarta/Brussels: Author.

Han, C. (2004). The work of indebtedness: The traumatic present of late capitalist Chile. *Culture, Medicine and Psychiatry, 28*(2), 169–187.

Heryanto, A. (1999). Where communism never dies: Violence, trauma and narration in the last Cold War capitalist authoritarian state. *International Journal of Cultural Studies, 2*(2), 147–177.

Honna, J. (2001). Military ideology in response to democratic pressures during the late Soeharto era: Political and institutional contexts. In B. Anderson (Ed.), *Violence and the state in Suharto's Indonesia*. Ithaca, NY: Cornell Southeast Asia Program Publications.

James, E. C. (2004). The political economy of "trauma" in Haiti in the democratic era of insecurity. *Culture, Medicine and Psychiatry, 28*, 127–149.

Jennaway, M. (2002). *Sisters and lovers: Women and desire in Bali*. Lanham, MD: Rowman & Littlefield.

Kleinman, A., & Desjarlais, R. (1995). Violence, culture, and the politics of trauma. In Kleinman, A., *Writing at the margin: Discourse between anthropology and medicine* (pp. 173–192). Berkeley: University of California Press.

Lemelson, R. (2003). Obsessive-compulsive disorder in Bali: The cultural shaping of a neuropsychiatric diagnosis. *Transcultural Psychiatry, 40*(3), 377–408.

Lund, G. (2003). "Healing the nation": Medicolonial discourse and the state of emergency from apartheid to truth and reconciliation. *Cultural Critique, 54*, 88–119.

McGorry, P. (1995). Working with survivors of torture and trauma: The Victorian Foundation for Survivors perspective. *Australian and New Zealand Journal of Psychiatry 19*(3), 463–472.

O'Nell, T. D. (2000). "Coming home" among Northern Plains Vietnam veterans: Psychological transformations in pragmatic perspective. *Ethos, 27*(4), 441–465.

Ong, A. (1995). Making the biopolitical subject: Cambodian immigrants, refugee medicine and cultural citizenship in California. *Social Science & Medicine, 40*(9), 1243–1257.

Pemberton, J. (1994). *On the subject of "Java."* Ithaca, NY: Cornell University Press.

Robinson, G. (1995). *The dark side of paradise: Political violence in Bali*. Ithaca, NY: Cornell University Press.

Sanford, V. (2003). *Buried secrets: Truth and human rights in Guatemala*. New York: Palgrave MacMillan.

Santikarma, D. (2001). The power of "Balinese culture." In U. Ramsayer (Ed.), *Bali: Living in two worlds*. Basel: Museum der Kulture and Verlag Schwabe & Co.

Santikarma, D. (2003a, January/March). The model militia: A new security force in Bali is cloaked in tradition. *Inside Indonesia*. Retrieved 18 June 2006 from http://www.insideindonesia.org/edit73/Degung%20pecalangan.htm.

Santikarma, D. (2003b, May 18). Dari stres ke trauma: Politik ingatan dan kekerasan di Bali [From stress to trauma: The politics of memory and violence in Bali]. *Kompas*. Retrieved 18 June 2006 from http://www.kompas.com/kompas-cetak/0305/18/seni/314556.htm.

Santikarma, D. (2003c, August 18). Monumen, dokumen dan kekerasan massal: Politik representasi kekerassan di Bali. [Monument, document and mass violence: Politics of representing violence in Bali]. *Kompas*. Retrieved 18 June 2006 from http://www.kompas.com/kompas-cetak/0308/01/opini/466246.htm.

Santikarma, D. (2004). Monument, document and mass grave. In M. Zurbuchen (Ed.), *Beginning to remember: The past in the Indonesian present*. Seattle: University of Washington Press.

Scheper-Hughes, N. (1992). *Death without weeping: The violence of everyday life in Brazil*. Berkeley: University of California Press.

Shiraishi, S. (1997). *Young heroes: The Indonesian family in politics*. Ithaca, NY: Cornell University, Southeast Asia Program Publications.

Siegel, J. T. (1998a). *A new criminal type in Jakarta: Counter-revolution today*. Durham, NC: Duke University Press.

Siegel, J. T. (1998b). Early thoughts on the violence of May 13 and 14 in Jakarta. *Indonesia, 66*, 75–108.

Spyer, P. (2003). One slip of the pen: Some notes on writing violence in Maluku. In G. Anan & H. Schulte-Nordholt (Eds.), *Indonesia in transition: Work in progress*. Yogyakarta: Pustaka Pelajar.

Steedly, M. M. (1993). *Hanging without a rope: Narrative experience in Colonial and postcolonial Karoland*. Princeton, NJ: Princeton University Press.

Summerfield, D. (1999). A critique of seven assumptions behind psychological trauma programmes in war-affected areas. *Social Science & Medicine, 48*, 1449–1462.

Tsing, A. L. (2005). *Friction: An ethnography of global connection*. Princeton, NJ: Princeton University Press.

Vickers, A. (1989). *Bali: A paradise created*. Ringwood: Penguin Books Australia.

Watters, C. (2001). Emerging paradigms in the mental health care of refugees. *Social Science & Medicine, 52*, 1709–1718.

Weine, S., & Laub, D. (1995). Narrative constructions of historical realities in testimony with Bosnian survivors of "ethnic cleansing." *Psychiatry, 58*(3), 246–260.

Wikan, U. (1990). *Managing turbulent hearts: A Balinese formula for living*. Chicago: University of Chicago Press.

Yayasan Kemanusiaan Ibu Pertiwi. (2002, December 15). *Newsletter 1*(2). Retrieved 18 June 2006 from http://www.ykip.org/news_newsltr_121502.asp.

Young, A. (1995). *The harmony of illusions: Inventing posttraumatic stress disorder*. Princeton, NJ: Princeton University Press.

Zarowsky, C. (2004). Writing trauma: Emotion, ethnography, and the politics of suffering among Somali returnees in Ethiopia. *Culture, Medicine and Psychiatry, 28*, 189–209.

Zurbuchen, M., & Santikarma, D. (2004, February). *Bali after the bombing: Land, livelihoods, and legacies of violence*. Paper presented at the Yale University Agrarian Studies Colloquium Series, New Haven, CT.

20

Terror and Trauma in the Cambodian Genocide

Alexander Hinton

> I continue to think of revenge. But this thought of revenge, it doesn't know how to stop. And we should not have this thought or the matter will grow and keep going on and on for a long time. We should be a person who thinks and acts in accordance with *dhamma*. [A person who seeks revenge] only creates misery for our society. It is a germ in society. But I continue to think of revenge.... The people who killed my brother, who put down his name to get into the truck, are all alive, living in my village. To this day, I still really want revenge. I keep observing them. But, I don't know what to do.... The government forbids it.
>
> – Chlat, whose brother's family was executed by Khmer Rouge

There were many ways to die during Democratic Kampuchea (DK), the genocidal period of Khmer Rouge rule in Cambodia (1975–1979). Some starved to death. Others died from malnutrition and illness. Many more were executed, often *en masse*, in a genocide that took the lives of more than 1.7 of Cambodia's 8 million inhabitants (Kiernan, 1996) – almost a quarter of the population. Such numbers are almost incomprehensible, yet they fail to take account of the toll such death and destruction took on the survivors, who suffered the loss of friends and loved ones; struggled on in a world of privation and relentless work; tried to survive for another day in a time in which fear, terror, and trauma were omnipresent; and, after DK, attempted to piece together their fractured lives in a society that had been turned upside down.

Their success in doing so is remarkable, though signs of lingering trauma emerge at times. Drawing on an interview I had with Yum, a Cambodian woman who lost her husband and several family members during DK, this chapter argues that the way in which Cambodians like Yum experience, respond to, and view trauma can be grasped only through an understanding of ontologically resonant local knowledge in Cambodia. In other words, a reading of trauma in terms of a straightforward Western biomedical model of trauma or posttraumatic stress disorder misses crucial aspects of the Cambodian experience.

YUM'S STORY

Yum, a widow in her mid-50s, provides an illustration of this point. Although widows often bear stigma in Cambodia, Yum stood out in "Banyan," a village where I conducted ethnographic research, for her intelligence, charisma, wealth, and the respect she received from others. During the People's Republic of Kampuchea, run by a socialist government that had been placed in power after Vietnamese troops routed the Khmer Rouge in January 1979, Yum had been selected to be the head of the local Women's Association. Her duties included helping orphans, widows, and the families of absent soldiers; she also acted as a sort of mediator/counselor for families that were having marital problems, including cases of domestic abuse. One of the legacies of civil war and violence in Cambodia is the large number of female-headed households and a skewed female–male ratio (though these numbers have started to even out in recent years) due to higher male mortality rates (Boua, 1982; Ebihara & Ledgerwood, 2002).

Yum's high stature in the community was reflected by the fact that, despite their mother being a widow, her daughters had married well and her son was learning to be a jeweler. She also had the distinction of having a traditional Khmer house raised on piles that was unique in the village for being enclosed at the bottom by cement, making a sort of garage. Although this extravagance was likely facilitated by the wealth of one of her son-in-laws, Yum was also somewhat of an entrepreneur, having her son-in-laws farm her land with the occasional help of hired laborers while she earned money by doing things like preparing lunch each day for a group of doctors at a local hospital. A motivating force in the village and a respected elder, Yum became an elderly "nun" (*yeay chi*) soon after her last daughter had married and now spends much of her time at the large monastic compound near Banyan.

When I first met Yum, I was immediately impressed by her intelligence and grace. She spoke with a broad smile that would collapse when she began speaking about the Khmer Rouge period, often repeating herself as she told me how much she hated the Khmer Rouge and how difficult life had been at that time: "There was such incredible suffering, Leak! Oh, so much misery." Much of Yum's anger centered around the killing of her husband, Saruon, who had been an officer in the Lon Nol army, the Khmer Rouge's hated enemy during the five-year civil war that preceded DK. The first time she told me about her husband's death Yum's voice cracked a bit and she shed a few tears, but she quickly regained her composure and continued talking. Yum seemed like an ideal informant, and I asked her if she would do some in-depth interviews about her life, one of which would focus on DK. She readily agreed.

Yum grew up in Battambang, often called the "rice bowl" of Cambodia because of the region's bountiful harvests. Two events from her childhood stick out in Yum's mind: the death of her father, to whom she was very close, when she was just twelve; and, around the same time, the year-long illness of her sister following childbirth. As a result of these two events, Yum had to drop out of school to help support her family. In 1961, when she was 20, Yum married Saruon and moved to Phnom Penh, where she frequently became sick (*chheu*). She lived there as the U.S. war in Vietnam intensified in the 1960s, slowly bleeding into Cambodian soil as the country's ruler, King Sihanouk, desperately tried to maintain neutrality in a conflict that demanded people take sides (see Becker, 1998; Chandler, 1991; Kiernan, 1985; Short, 2005). Sihanouk was deposed by his pro-U.S. general, Lon Nol, in 1970, an event that sparked violent protests and led tens of thousands of Cambodians to follow their beloved King in joining the Khmer Rouge. For the next 5 years, as the Khmer Rouge slowly surrounded Phnom Penh and the other urban centers controlled by Lon Nol, Yum watched the capital fill with refugees, many of whom lived in extreme poverty. Yum was more fortunate. Although she and Saruon were forced to move closer to the heart of Phnom Penh to avoid enemy ordnance, Yum's business acumen enabled the family to live fairly comfortably.

When the Khmer Rouge, a Maoist-inspired group of rebels led by the charismatic Pol Pot, victoriously entered Phnom Penh on April 17, 1975, everything changed. They immediately set out to transform Cambodian society radically, beginning with the rustication of the entire urban population (Becker, 1998; Chandler, 1999; Kiernan, 1996; Short, 2005). Everyone in Phnom Penh was told to evacuate. Yum recalled that when the Khmer Rouge entered Phnom Penh, Saruon was on patrol and wearing his uniform. Some Khmer Rouge cadre "ordered him to take it off. At first he didn't agree, so they fired a shot right between his feet and then shot up his motorcycle, the one he rode every day. So he took off his uniform and left, returning to his elder sibling's house [where we were staying]." Later that day, the Khmer Rouge ordered everyone to leave the city, threatening to execute anyone who remained.

Yum's extended family joined hundreds of thousands of other people from Phnom Penh in making the slow journey out of the capital in sweltering heat. She continued, "We quickly prepared our things and loaded them in my husband's older brother's car before departing. It took us a really long time to leave Phnom Penh. Each day we were only able to travel a short distance." Along the way, the evacuees witnessed a collage of images: tens of thousands of people inching their way along the packed roads, hospital patients being pushed along in wheel chairs and hospital beds, bloated corpses of the war dead, women giving birth on the side of the road, and executions.

After 10 days, Yum's group arrived, hungry and exhausted, at Chraoy Ambel, where they "weren't given rice or anything else there – we were supposed to solve any problems ourselves." Yum's family quickly learned about the world of deception, double-speak, terror, and violence in which Cambodians would live for more than three and a half more years.

After we arrived at Chraoy Ambel, the Khmer Rouge announced, "Anyone who was an officer before can have the same rank [in the new regime] and return to your former place of work." When we had arrived at Chraoy Ambel, they had sent me to sleep in the large home of an old grandmother. This woman didn't have a sarong, so she asked me for one and I gave it to her. Afterwards, she whispered to me, "Even if you had rank before, don't tell them. Whenever someone tells them this, they are taken away and executed." So I didn't let my husband tell [the Khmer Rouge]. But when I told my elder brother-in-law this – he had been a colonel – he didn't believe me. He said, "There is no way in the world that they will kill people." He told them the truth in the morning. That evening they arrested him and sent him to "go study." He was executed at once.

Hinton: How did you feel?

I was terrified, but I didn't dare cry. Even if you were terrified, you couldn't do this. Whatever you might suffer (*dukkha*), you didn't dare say anything. My brother-in-law's wife cried when they took her husband away. She kept going to ask about him, so they took the entire family away and killed them, too.... It's like a saying [the Khmer Rouge] said, "To dig up the grass, one must dig up the roots." This meant that they wanted to kill an entire family line, so that not even a single person survived.

Following this devastating experience, Yum's family was sent to another village, Praek Pothi. Here, yet again, local officials conducted research on people's backgrounds and announced that former soldiers would be given the same rank in the new regime. Some elderly villagers warned Yum to lie and tell the Khmer Rouge that her husband had been a pedicab driver. They did this, but the local officials "didn't believe it.... They were ready to take my husband to the district office when some of the village elders intervened and said that we were telling the truth about his work – that he had driven a pedicab and guarded the house of a rich person. So he was released."

Yum soon discovered what his fate might have been. While taking a shortcut through the jungle, she suddenly came across a camp where former Lon Nol soldiers were being held before execution. "They were so thin," Yum told me, "And, they didn't have any food. There were so many of them, maybe 300 soldiers sitting there.... Oh, Leak [my Khmer name],

I was so terrified that my knees became weak. . . . I was terrified that the guards would see me and kill me. So I ran." However, a guard saw her and began to question her. "'Where are you going?' he asked. 'How did you happen to come to this place?' I told him that I was on my way back home and had become lost. He pointed me in the right direction and I left."

When Yum's family finally settled in Ampil Krânhanh, a village near Banyan in Kompong Cham province, they found themselves living in a radically different world, one without money, markets, courts, telecommunications, postal service, or religious worship. In their attempt to initiate a "super great leap forward" (*moha lot phloah*) into communism – a leap that would outpace all other socialist revolutions – the Khmer Rouge abolished anything that might encourage "privatism" and undermine the revolutionary society in the making. The Khmer Rouge collectivized economic production, ownership, and consumption, requiring Cambodians like Yum to perform back-breaking labor for long hours, often on starvation rations. "I was so skinny, Leak," Yum told me, "that it hurt to sit down. Sometimes 500 people had to share just five cans of rice. It was pure suffering (*vetonea*), Leak, oh, such misery. Some people planted crops like potatoes and corn near their homes, but they weren't permitted to eat it. Anyone who did would be sent for reeducation, though the head of the cooperative sometimes shared such foods with the 'old people,'" the villagers who had lived in Khmer Rouge zones during the war.

Such inequities illustrate how status hierarchies were inverted during DK, with the poor and the young replacing the rich and the elderly at the apex of society. The urban evacuees were referred to as "new people" (*brâcheachon tmey*) and generally had fewer rights, suffered more, and were more readily killed than the "old people" (*brâcheachon chas*). Nevertheless, both old people and new people suffered greatly under the Khmer Rouge, who radically curtailed freedom of speech and communication, regulated marriage, banned Buddhism, separated family members, and ultimately attempted to control what people thought, said, or did.

Their ultimate goal was to create a society of revolutionaries imbued with a "progressive" consciousness (A. L. Hinton, 2005). Such a person would work relentlessly and unquestioningly to "build and defend" (*kâsang ning kâr pear*) the new social order, thereby propelling the super great leap forward toward utopia. When the economic schemes of the "clear-sighted" and "all-knowing" Party began to fail, however, the Khmer Rouge leadership, already suspicious about perceived plots and *coups*, blamed subversives, not their own unrealistic and problematic plans, for the failures.

In response, Pol Pot and his associates initiated a purge of "hidden enemies burrowing from within," ranging from traitors within the Party ranks to regressive elements within the masses – particularly the new people.

Teeda Mam (1997), who like Yum was a new person from Phnom Penh, recalled that the Khmer Rouge list of enemies

was long. Former soldiers, the police, the CIA, and the KGB. Their crime was fighting in the civil war. The merchants, the capitalists, and the businessmen. Their crime was exploiting the poor. The rich farmers and the landlords. Their crime was exploiting the peasants. The intellectuals, the doctors, the lawyers, the monks, the teachers, and the civil servants. These people thought, and their memories were tainted by the evil Westerners. Students were getting an education to exploit the poor. Former celebrities, the poets. These people carried bad memories of the old, corrupted Cambodia.... The list goes on and on. The rebellious,... the individualists, the people who wore glasses, the literate,... and those with soft hands. These people were corrupted and lived off the blood and sweat of the farmers. Very few of us escaped these categories. (p. 13)

As the purges and the Party Center's paranoia intensified, terror and death became a routine part of everyday life for Cambodians.

To ferret out the hidden enemies, the Khmer Rouge intensively researched backgrounds on the local level. In Ampil Krânhanh, local cadre questioned Yum's husband and several of his brothers, who were also former Lon Nol soldiers, about their former occupations soon after their arrival. Yum recalled how the officials asked them what work her husband had previously done. "When they asked me," Yum said, "I told them that he had driven a pedicab and guarded a house. They then asked, 'If that's the case, then why are his hands, legs, and face in such nice condition?' I replied, 'What can he do if he is nice and clean like this?'" Soon thereafter, the Khmer Rouge began to test Yum's husband to see if he was really from the countryside, as he had claimed. She continued,

First they tested him by seeing if he could use a plow. Then they had him fix a plow and plow a field. The first time, they said, 'If you are really from the countryside, you should be able to use a plow. My husband carefully watched others who were plowing and was able to do it. A while later, [the cadre] tested him again, asking him to build a house. My husband also did this successfully. Later on, they had him train a cow. He tried hard and was able to do this, as well. Leak! Training a cow is really difficult if we're not used to holding a cow. We can't control it. But he tried and tried until he could. Next, they asked him to harvest fruits and vegetables and to gather jackfruit. He and 15 other people had to harvest a hectare of land. He did this, as well. They also asked him to build up small dikes around the rice fields. When he had done this, they sent him to cook for four or five nights. He was then sent to dig earth [for irrigation projects], one cubic meter each morning, afternoon, and evening.

It was around this time that they accused my husband of being a soldier. Someone who knew him informed on him.... The [Khmer Rouge] did research. We had returned to my husband's birth district. They had driven many people from Banyan there. The villagers from Banyan knew my husband. Someone, who hated him – I don't know who – told the [local officials] that my husband had been a soldier. Because my husband had passed so many tests, [the officials] thought he had not been a soldier. So they investigated further and eventually came to believe he was a former [Lon Nol] soldier.

So they called him for questioning. When they asked my husband about this accusation, he denied that he had been a soldier, saying he had guarded a house and had driven a pedicab in his free time. After this, they sent him to plow the rice fields, to dig more dirt, and, later, to transplant rice. But, in April, they decided to execute him.

As the repeated tests of Yum's husband illustrate, the Khmer Rouge were intent on ferreting out hidden enemies among the populace.

Former soldiers remained near the top of the target list. In his 1977 confession, Sreng, the deputy secretary of the northern zone where Ampil Krânhanh is located, recalled how lists of these suspected enemies were compiled on the grassroots level and then passed on to higher administrative levels, often reaching the zone office where decisions were made about who should be executed:

The grassroots area [had] all successfully implemented these Party instructions [of successively smashing officers]. Every sector has implemented them at the levels of general officer, field-grade officer, and junior officer, and then also down to the level of enlisted men (those who were active), who the Zone stated were also to be swept out. There was quite a powerful dynamism with regard to this matter. Each sector drew up list after list, which was proposed to the Zone and sorted out one after the other. Actions to search for these officers have continued constantly right up to the present. . . . They were discovered not because the Zone Committee knew who they were. Rather, they were discovered by the grassroots' inquiries and investigations among the masses. (Heder & Tittemore, 2001, p. 109, n. 425)

This appears to be exactly what happened to Yum's husband. At that time, Yum's husband's youngest brother, Nim, whom the Khmer Rouge did not know was linked to a familial "string" of Lon Nol soldiers, was working at the district security office. One day in 1976, the office received a letter instructing them to execute Yum's husband, two brothers, and two brother-in-laws, all of whom were former soldiers. Yum explained how Nim told them about the letter and how he would bring guns, ammunition, and rice so that all of them could flee that night: "Nim came and said to us, 'Bang [elder brother], tonight at 9 o'clock– they sent a letter instructing me to execute you. . . . Bang, wait here at the house. We won't let them kill us. We'll all run away together [at 9 o'clock]. If we die at some other place, then that's when we'll die.'"

As Yum recounted this painful moment, she began to break down, weeping and speaking in an increasingly fragmented manner, eventually saying that she didn't want to talk anymore about what happened. Even as she said this and I tried to break off the interview, she continued, no longer hearing what I was saying:

When I think of this story I don't want to talk about it at all, about [this story of] being separated from my husband, about an entire family being separated. When they left, it was raining and they were guarding the house. When [the Khmer Rouge] came to kill my husband, I lied and told them, "He went to cut bananas." They searched the house. When [my husband left], he cried as he embraced his children and his wife.... I don't want Leak to ask me about this at all. He knew he was going to die. So much difficulty and suffering arose from this path.... My husband never sinned against his children. He loved his wife and children so much. Starting from the time that they took him, I have raised all five children [by myself] up to the present. I have had such enormous difficulty. He really loved his children. I don't want to go into this matter again, Leak. When I think about it, I start to hurt (*chheu*).... Please don't ask about this matter any more, because my forehead will hurt without fail.

Yum's pain and trauma, so evident in these words, are overwhelming – most of all to her, of course, but also to me as her interlocutor and no doubt to the reader. Such moments not only force us to confront our own suffering and mortality, but also demand an empathetic engagement with the pain and trauma of another human being. Moreover, as the person who had in effect stirred up these powerful memories, it was incumbent on me to help her through her pain.

I had thought abstractly about what I would do if confronted by a situation like this (a handful of people had become mildly upset and even cried during interviews, but Yum's response was much more intense) and discussed strategies with Bros, my Cambodian research assistant, who was present at the interview. Still, the situation was daunting and required an understanding of Cambodian culture to navigate successfully. When my attempts to stop the interview failed – Yum kept on talking between the gasps of her sobs – I tried various culturally appropriate strategies to help her regain her sense of balance, which, as we shall see, is viewed by Cambodians as critical to well-being.

Besides evincing empathy for her suffering (in Cambodia this is crucial because a person who loses composure is vulnerable to losing face for having upset the social equilibrium), for example, I tried to gently redirect the focus away from her husband's death. Each time, Yum momentarily regained her composure only to return to her husband's death amid sobs. Bros, who had also become a friend to Yum during the course of my fieldwork, also showed empathy for her plight and even briefly recounted the pain of his own father's death. At yet another point, he attempted to promote another common Cambodian coping strategy, forgetting, which might be referred to as "repression" in a Western biomedical context but is linked to the Buddhist notion of letting go of one's attachments and thereby regaining one's equilibrium.

Yum [starting to cry again]: When I think of this event, I hurt (*chheu*) immediately. If I need to do something, I can't gather the desire to do it.

Hinton: It's not necessary to think about it any more. I don't want you to have a problem, Aunt.

Bros: Aunt, stop thinking about this. You must take care since doing so leads us to have a greatly troubled heart (*pibak chett*).

Yum [sobbing]: I never think about it. When I do start to think about it, I hurt (*chheu*) at once.

Hinton: Aunt, I want to thank you for thinking about this. I know it's really difficult.

Yum: It's so difficult, Leak.

Bros: We can stop. It's not a problem. Don't speak any more. It will only lead you to difficulty and hurt (*chheu*).

Soon thereafter, Yum's sobs subsided and she asked to be taken home, saying that she had a bad headache. This entire episode had lasted for only about 5 to 10 minutes, though at the time it seemed like an eternity.

I asked Bros, who was driving her back to Banyan, to stay with Yum until she felt better and help her regain her bearings in the flow of village life. By doing so, we were drawing on another important Cambodian coping strategy, social reintegration, which helps a person regain composure, forget about a troubling matter, and improve his or her spirits through social interaction.

When they arrived at Yum's house, Yum's daughter was home and Yum, who had sobbed a bit during the ride home, began to act normally. Neither she nor Bros mentioned the incident on the way home, and Bros said that he doubted she would tell her daughter. He explained, "Cambodians only talk about such sad stories once in a while. . . . If a person starts to get upset and begins to cry [like Yum], the person should stop speaking about the matter that is making them suffer. They should think about something else. If we had continued talking about [Yum's story], her troubled feelings would only have kept increasing."

Again, this more Buddhist coping strategy stands in contrast to long-standing Western therapeutic models, which hold that it is only through talking (or, more recently, by taking appropriate medication) that one may work through one's psychological troubles. Over the next few days, Bros and I kept an eye on Yum to make sure that she was okay. To our relief, she seemed normal. If she had showed signs of continued upset (for example, somatic ailments, social withdrawal, altered affect, persisting "hurt"), we would have needed to encourage her to make offerings to local spirits or to go see a Cambodian "therapist" – a traditional healer, a fortune teller, or a Buddhist monk – each of whom has culturally specific means of helping a person deal with a "troubled heart."

CULTURAL AND RELIGIOUS MEANINGS OF ANGER AND SUFFERING

As this incident suggests, trauma in other cultural worlds cannot be packaged easily in terms of the taken-for-granted folk understandings and biomedical categories that are familiar to us. If we were to say that Yum simply suffers from PTSD, we would invoke a specific set of precipitants (experiencing, witnessing, or confronting a deeply traumatic event that generated intense "fear, helplessness, or horror"), symptoms ("increased arousal" or "outbursts of anger"), folk understandings of what emotion and trauma are (internal states as opposed to an emotion intimately linked to social and moral life), and prescriptions (therapeutic treatment, medication) that are rooted in our own historical and cultural tradition, thereby overlooking culture-specific dimensions of her experience that are crucial both to understanding and figuring out how Cambodians cope with trauma. Such culturally sensitive understanding is critical to successful outcomes with Cambodians (see D. Hinton, Hinton, Um, Chea, & Sak, 2002; D. Hinton, Um, & Ba, 2001a, 2001b, 2001c).

To further illustrate this point, I will explore some of the other dimensions of Yum's response to trauma. Like many other Cambodians who lost family members during DK, Yum continues to bear strong feelings of malice toward the Khmer Rouge. In general, she discussed the Khmer Rouge period in broad terms (versus the painful specificity of our interview), ranging from expressions of strong anger to more Buddhist understandings of suffering and rebirth. Prior to our interview, for example, Yum often invoked words like "hate," "suffering," and "anger" when discussing DK, as illustrated by the following remark: "I hate the Khmer Rouge. I hate them. I don't ever want to hear or see them again. I hate them. I'm getting angry as I think about them." She would often indicate her contempt toward the Khmer Rouge by describing them using a derogatory pronoun, *vea*, which means "he, she, they," or "it" but is frequently used to describe people of a low social status, animals, objects, or those one holds in contempt (*Khmer Dictionary*, 1967, p. 1196; Marston, 1997, pp. 130–131). Another time, when discussing her fear of dying, Yum suddenly invoked Pol Pot: "Those who sin go to [Buddhist] hell; those who do not [sin] will go to [Buddhist] heaven. Pol Pot will be reborn as a slimy form of life that lives in muddy, dirty places." At the same time, when discussing her husband's death, Yum often noted his meritorious behavior, which made his fate seem paradoxical.

Yum's response parallels that of many other Cambodians who still struggle to cope with the legacy of DK. For example, Neari, a woman whose entire family of 11, save herself and one sister, were killed by the Khmer Rouge, continues to bear strong feelings of malice toward the perpetrators who killed their family members. Neari recounted her feelings when she sees Hean, a former student of her father who joined the Khmer Rouge and then killed her father, in part because Neari's father had beat him at school:

When I see Hean, I get angry. But I don't know what to do about it. I'm a woman. I think to myself, "This despicable person killed my father but didn't die himself." When I see him, I become angry in my heart. In one part of my heart I want revenge.... When I recall [what he did], I get hot and angry. I want to kill him. I want to ask him, "What did my father do to you to make you kill him? You were beaten because you were lazy." When I think about him, I get so angry. I have an angry heart. But I have another thought out of laziness. I think to myself, "Don't take revenge upon that despicable one. Let him suffer from his kamma. 'Do good, receive good. Do bad, receive bad.'" ... My heart wants to harm and kill him. But another part of me thinks that this is not necessary. I expect that another person who hates him (*vea*), who is tied in malice with him, will make him croak. They will do this to console themselves [about what Hean did to their family]. So if I don't do it, another person will.

To understand such remarks, and thus to begin to understand Yum's and Neari's response to trauma, one must unpack the local idioms that structure their response – in particular, the ontological resonances that give them power and force. If an ontology is a theory of being, I use the term "ontological resonance" more broadly to refer to the ways in which human actions and local understandings are imbued with motivational salience because of their self-implicating resonances with local ontologies and embodied experience, or modalities of being-in-the-world that are generated as people engage in social practices through time (A. L. Hinton, 2005).

Yum and Neari both foreground their enormous anger, an emotion that links trauma to ontologically resonant notions of heat and balance. When discussing the Khmer Rouge, for example, Yum told me, "As soon as I think of Pol Pot I get hot (*kdav*).... I feel anger (*kheong*) and hatred toward those despicable ones (*vea*) who abused us." Similarly, Neari says that she feels "hot and angry" when she sees Hean and thinks about what he did to her father. The term that Yum and Neari use for anger, *kheong*, is defined in the *Khmer Dictionary* as "to be moved by a pressure" when the "object of one's mind (*arâmma*) is unsatisfied.... This causes choking heat to arise in one's heart (*chett*)" (*Khmer Dictionary*, 1967, p. 123). Anger, which is hypercognized in Khmer, is often described through metaphors of heat: An angry person is described as "hot" (*kdav*), as having a "hot heart" (*kdav chett*), or as being "hot and irritated" (*kdav krâhay*).

Although metaphors of heat are salient in both Euro-American and Cambodian conceptual systems, Cambodian anger is linked to a different ethnophysiology, which has been influenced by the Buddhist, animistic, Ayurvedic, and Chinese medical traditions and is centered around the notion of equilibrium and proper flow, particularly with regard to the "wind" and blood that course through small vessels (*sârsai*) in the body.

In this humoral system, well-being is linked to physiological balance, particularly the balance between hot and cold. The various humors have heating and cooling properties; thus, "phlegm" tends to be associated with disorders linked to overheating and "bile" to those associated with excessive cooling (see Eisenbruch, 1992; D. Hinton et al., 2001a, 2001b; Marcucci, 1986, 1994; Sargent, Marcucci, & Elliston, 1983; White, 1996). "Wind," the central humor in Khmer ethnophysiology, has cooling properties and, through its movement of the blood, directly affects the balance of hot and cold (D. Hinton et al., 2001a, 2001b; Marcucci, 1986). When a person experiences distress, this circulation may become disrupted and impaired, leading to various somatic symptoms and ailments (see Marcucci, 1994). At such times, Cambodians may simply say that they "have pain/hurt" (*chheu*), the term that Yum repeatedly invoked during our interview. To restore physiological balance, Cambodians often use local treatments that remove inner blockages or release excess wind, such as "coining" (firmly scraping the skin with the edge of a coin), pinching or massaging key spots on the body, "cupping" the skin with a heated cup so that wind is suctioned out, or rubbing in a wind-releasing oil. More serious illnesses may necessitate a trip to a Buddhist monk or traditional healer, who have more powerful rituals for restoring bodily health.

As such practices illustrate, equilibrium is crucial to well-being for Cambodians, both in terms of social relations and bodily health, the two being highly interrelated in Cambodian ethnopsychology. Emotions like anger constitute a potential disruption of this balance, signaling a disturbance in the social fabric in which a person is embedded and producing "felt" somatic manifestations, such as pain (*chheu*), discomfort (*min sruol khluon*), dizziness (*vil*), or heat (*kdav*), symptoms for which Cambodians constantly scan (D. Hinton et al., 2001a, 2001b). The "choking heat" of anger thus metaphorically references the felt "pressure" of an animating, yet potentially disruptive, psychosocial process that strongly "moves a person's heart" to act. Yum's invocation of heat and anger, then, indexes a culturally meaningful state of imbalance associated with her trauma, one that is not just an "inner disturbance," but also a signifier of social suffering with its political and moral implications (Kleinman, Das, & Lock, 1997).

On the other hand, Neari references Buddhism, saying that perhaps she should just let Hean "suffer from his kamma." She invokes a Buddhist saying: "'Do good, receive good. Do bad, receive bad.'" Buddhism is also central to Yum's experience and understanding of trauma, providing an explanatory frame for what happened (her frequent invocations of two central Buddhist concepts, suffering [*dukkha, vetonea*] and sin [*bap*]) and for ultimate justice (her assertion that Pol Pot will be reborn as a hideous entity). Buddhist doctrine provides an explicit ontology that explains how violence originates in ignorance and desire. If the consequences of violence are manifest in overt signs, such actions also have long-term consequences. On the one hand, violence may lead others to seek vengeance against you. On the other hand, harming others is considered a Buddhist sin, resulting in a loss of merit and, most likely, diminished status in the next life. A person who kills will likely be reborn as a lowly form of life or perhaps even in one of the Buddhist hells, such as the Lohakumbha hell, where he or she will be repeatedly decapitated and boiled (Reynolds & Reynolds, 1982, p. 75).

Besides providing an etiology of violence and its consequences, Buddhism offers a remedy to avoid this toxic state of being – the middle path. On the local level, Cambodians are enjoined to follow five moral precepts (*seyl bram*), the first of which is the injunction not to kill. Monks preach that one must learn to control and extinguish one's anger, which arises from ignorance and desire and leads to violence and suffering. In Buddhism, the mindful way of dealing with anger and other powerful emotions is to recognize their source and to let them disappear because such emotions, like everything else in the world, are impermanent. Those who continue to act in ignorance will suffer from the consequences of their actions, with their deeds following like a shadow, as one suffers through the countless cycles of birth and rebirth.

If Buddhism provides a sort of ontological justice for victims, it also suggests that their suffering is a cosmic consequence of their own bad actions in the past (e.g., Haing Ngor, 1987, p. 157, 312). Some viewed what was going on as the fulfillment of Buddhist millenarian prophesies, such as well-known Buddhist predictions (*put tumneay*). Many of these foretold of a time when demons or members of the lowest rungs of Khmer society would take over and invert the social order, leading to an assault on Buddhism and wide-spread famine and death (see Ledgerwood, 1990; Smith, 1989). In fact, during DK Cambodians frequently invoked a phrase, "plant a Kapok tree," that seems to have been derived from just such a prophesy.

In Khmer, the term for "kapok tree," *kor*, is a homophone of the word *ko*, which can mean "mute, muffled, and hollow" (Headley, Chhor, Lim, Kheang, & Chun, 1977, p. 113). The phrase "plant a kapok tree" therefore signified that one had to build a wall of silence in order to survive this period of genocidal terror. Thus, Haing Ngor's father warned his son: "From now on, keep your mouth shut. Plant a kapok tree. *Dam doeum kor.* No matter what happens, don't give them any excuse to take you away again. . . . So plant your kapok tree, son. Be patient, be quiet and stay calm. One day, sooner or later, the revolution will be overturned" (Haing

Ngor, 1987, p. 253; see also p. 258, 266, 310). Pin Yathay (1996) explains the Buddhist origin of this saying:

> Puth was a nineteenth-century sage who prophesied that the country would undergo a total reversal of traditional values, that the houses and the streets would be emptied, that the illiterate would condemn the educated, that infidels – *thmils* – would hold absolute power and persecute the priests. But people would be saved if they planted a kapok tree – *kor*, in Cambodian. *Kor* also means "mute." The usual interpretation of this enigmatic message was that only the deaf-mutes would be saved during this period of calamity. Remain deaf and mute. Therein, I now realized, lay the means of survival. Pretend to be deaf and dumb! Say nothing, hear nothing, understand nothing! (p. 63)

On a cosmological level, such prophesies played on Khmer understandings of purity and contamination, which are in part structured in terms of the opposition between the Buddha and demons, dhamma and adhamma, order and disorder, coherence and fragmentation (A. L. Hinton, 2002b; see also Kapferer, 1988). Some Cambodians even came to view the Khmer Rouge as red-eyed demons, who, in Khmer lore, eat the flesh of their victims – a model that was occasionally affirmed (both in rumor and direct observation) by the Khmer Rouge practice of consuming the livers of their victims (A. L. Hinton, 2005).

CONCLUSION

In such ways, then, Cambodians responded to their trauma through a complex set of ontologically resonant local understandings. I want to conclude by stressing five points.

First, we need to take cultural differences into account when examining and treating trauma. As my discussion of Buddhism, Khmer ethnophysiology, and "planting a kapok tree" suggests, these ontologically resonant, local understandings can shape a person's experience of and response to trauma in powerful ways. Moreover, we must remain sensitive to the relationship of culture and healing because treating culturally variable idioms of distress often demands greater understanding of different cultural worlds and approaches to healing.

Second, by learning about such cultural differences, we gain a new perspective on the assumptions and biases of our own folk understandings. For example, in the Cambodian language, Khmer, there is no one term that can be directly glossed as "trauma." To speak of something along the lines of psychological trauma one must speak of suffering (usually in the Buddhist sense) or of a hurt. These concepts may be linked to somatic symptoms, which Cambodians often experience as an imbalance of the humors signified by a headache, sweating, local pain, or dizziness. To regain one's balance, one does not simply look for a biomedical cure since balance is linked to the moral, spiritual, and interpersonal environments beings inhabit, environments that directly influence bodily balance. We need to reconsider the benefits of immediately medicalizing and pathologizing such "symptoms" because these biomedical discourses may obfuscate the cultural, social, moral, and political dimensions of trauma.

Third, and relatedly, we must be careful not to view the traumatized in an overly passive manner. As Allan Young (1995) has so nicely demonstrated, the idea of trauma is a particularly modern one that connotes passivity – it suggests a lasting psychological wound that is done to a person, afflicting him or her with symptoms that need to heal. More broadly, this emphasis on trauma as an affliction the individual passively endures, like a physical wound, is linked to modernity, which has ruptured the local enmeshments of human beings and produced the idea of the individual who has a biological nature. Trauma emerges as a sort of psychobiological malady afflicting a person. Such a perspective fails to fully acknowledge the ways in which this suffering is mediated by social, moral, and political understandings. Despite their trauma, people remain meaning-constructing beings, responding to and acting within their very difficult conditions of life.

Moreover, this notion of a primary "wounding" may direct our attention away from the ways in which past traumas may be amplified by subsequent events. How, for example, are Cambodian or Rwandan victims affected when they are forced to live by perpetrators? Or, how might the wounds of Cambodian refugees be affected by immigration to a radically different cultural world in the United States, one in which they often encounter a range of new difficulties, such as a loss of status, disrupted social networks, living in dangerous neighborhoods, and raising children who are learning a new set of cultural values and may have to serve as their guides at times because of their children's better language skills and familiarity with American ways of life?

Fourth, besides the attempt to heal and to examine the responses to and effects of trauma, we also need to turn our attention to the origin and prevention of the violence that causes trauma in the first place. My own research on the processes involved in genocide (see A. L. Hinton, 2002a, 2002c, 2005) has convinced me of the importance of making such understanding a public health goal. And, finally, as we think about trauma, let us respect different domains of analysis, taking the insights of each as we attempt to find integrative ways of understanding trauma that move among the cultural, psychological, and neurobiological levels of analysis (see Hinton 1999).

I want to end with the words of Ronnie Yimsut. The Khmer Rouge marched his entire family to a killing field and clubbed everyone to death. Despite being struck over a dozen times on his neck and body, Ronnie awoke, dazed, in a blood-filled mass grave containing the bodies of his loved ones and dozens of other victims. He writes, "I still have nightmares about the massacre on that dark December night. It has never completely gone away from my mind, and I am still horrified just thinking about it. Time does not heal such emotional trauma, at least not for me. I have long since learned to live with it. My life must go on" (Yimsut, 1997, p. 124).

ACKNOWLEDGMENTS

I would like to thank Rob Lemelson for his comments and for organizing the conference from which this volume originated. I appreciate Laurence Kirmayer's editorial initiative and Tamara Marshall-Keim's help in copyediting the manuscript. Nicole Cooley, Devon Hinton, and Ladson Hinton also provided extremely helpful suggestions on this paper.

References

Becker, E. (1998). *When the war was over: Cambodia and the Khmer Rouge revolution*. New York: Public Affairs.

Boua, C. (1982). Women in today's Cambodia. *New Left Review, 131,* 45–61.

Chandler, D. P. (1991). *The tragedy of Cambodian history: Politics, war, and revolution since 1945*. New Haven, CT: Yale University Press.

Chandler, D. P. (1999). *Voices from S-21: Terror and history in Pol Pot's secret prison*. Berkeley: University of California Press.

Ebihara, M., & Ledgerwood, J. (2002). Aftermaths of Cambodia: Cambodian villagers. In A. L. Hinton (Ed.), *Annihilating difference: The anthropology of genocide*. Berkeley: University of California Press.

Eisenbruch, M. (1992). The ritual space of patients and traditional healers in Cambodia. *Bulletin de l'Ecole Francaise d'Extreme-Orient, 79*(2), 1–35.

Haing Ngor. (1987). *A Cambodian odyssey*. New York: Warner Brooks.

Headley, R. K., Chhor, K., Lim, L. K., Kheang, L. K., & Chun, C. (1977). *Cambodian–English dictionary*. Washington, DC: Catholic University of America Press.

Heder, S., & Tittemore, B. D. (2001). *Seven candidates for prosecution: Accountability for the crimes of the Khmer Rouge*. Washington, DC: War Crimes Research Office, American University.

Hinton, A. L. (Ed.). (1999). *Biocultural approaches to the emotions*. New York: Cambridge University Press.

Hinton, A. L. (Ed.). (2002a). *Annihilating difference: The anthropology of genocide*. Berkeley: University of California Press.

Hinton, A. L. (2002b). Purity and contamination in the Cambodian genocide. In J. Ledgerwood (Ed.), *Cambodia emerges from the past: Eight essays* (pp. 60–90). DeKalb, IL: Northern Illinois University Press.

Hinton, A. L. (Ed.). (2002c). *Genocide: An anthropological reader*. Malden, MA: Blackwell.

Hinton, A. L. (2005). *Why did they kill? Cambodia in the shadow of genocide*. Berkeley: University of California Press.

Hinton, D., Hinton, S., Um, K., Chea, A., & Sak, S. (2002). The Khmer "weak heart" syndrome: Fear of death from palpitations. *Transcultural Psychiatry, 39,* 323–344.

Hinton, D., Um, K., & Ba, P. (2001a). A unique panic-disorder presentation among Khmer refugees: The sore-neck syndrome. *Culture, Medicine and Psychiatry, 25*(3), 297–316.

Hinton, D., Um, K., & Ba, P. (2001b). Kyol goeu ('wind overload') part I: A cultural syndrome of orthostatic panic among Khmer refugees. *Transcultural Psychiatry, 38,* 403–432.

Hinton, D., Um, K., & Ba, P. (2001c). Kyol goeu ('wind overload') part II: Prevalence, characteristics, and mechanisms of Kyol goeu and near-kyol goeu episodes of Khmer patients attending a psychiatric clinic. *Transcultural Psychiatry, 38,* 433–460.

Kapferer, B. (1988). *Legends of people, myths of state: Violence, intolerance, and political culture in Sri Lanka and Australia.* Washington, DC: Smithsonian Institution Press.

Khmer dictionary [Vochânanukrâm Khmaer]. (1967). Phnom Penh: Buddhist Institute.

Kiernan, B. (1985). *How Pol Pot came to power: A history of communism in Kampuchea, 1930–1975.* London: Verso.

Kiernan, B. (1996). *The Pol Pot regime: Race, power, and genocide in Cambodia under the Khmer Rouge, 1975–79.* New Haven, CT: Yale University Press.

Kleinman, A., Das, V., & Lock, M. M. (Eds.). (1997). *Social suffering.* Berkeley: University of California Press.

Ledgerwood, J. L. (1990). *Changing Khmer conceptions of gender: Woman, stories, and the social order.* Unpublished doctoral dissertation, Cornell University, Ithaca, NY.

Mam, T. B. (1997). Worms from our skin. In K. De Paul (Ed.), *Children of Cambodia's killing fields: Memoirs by survivors* (pp. 11–17). New Haven: Yale University Press.

Marcucci, J. L. (1986). *Khmer refugees in Dallas: Medical decisions in the context of pluralism.* Unpublished doctoral dissertation, Southern Methodist University, Dallas, TX.

Marcucci, J. L. (1994). Sharing the pain: Critical values and behaviors in Khmer culture. In M. M. Ebihara, C. A. Mortland, & J. Ledgerwood (Eds.), *Cambodian culture since 1975: Homeland and exile* (pp. 129–140). Ithaca, NY: Cornell University Press.

Marston, J. (1997). *Cambodia 1991–1994: Hierarchy, neutrality and etiquettes of discourse.* Unpublished doctoral dissertation, University of Washington, Seattle, WA.

Pin Yathay. (1987). *Stay alive, my son.* New York: Touchstone.

Reynolds, F. E., & Reynolds, M. B. (Trans.). (1982). *Three worlds according to King Ruang: A Thai Buddhist cosmology.* Berkeley: University of California Press.

Sargent, C., Marcucci, J., & Elliston, E. (1983). Tiger bones, fire and wine: Maternity care in a Kampuchean refugee community. *Medical Anthropology, 7*(4), 67–79.

Short, P. (2005). *Pol Pot: Anatomy of a nightmare.* New York: Henry Holt.

Smith, F. (1989). *Interpretive accounts of the Khmer Rouge years: Personal experience in Cambodian peasant world view.* Madison, WI: Center for Southeast Asian Studies, University of Wisconsin-Madison.

White, P. M. (1996). *Crossing the river: A study of Khmer women's beliefs and practices during pregnancy, birth and postpartum.* Unpublished doctoral dissertation, University of California, Los Angeles.

Yimsut, R. (1997). The Tonle Sap massacre. In K. De Paul (Ed.), *Children of Cambodia's killing fields: Memoirs by survivors* (pp. 185–194). New Haven: Yale University Press.

Young, A. (1995). *The harmony of illusions: Inventing post-traumatic stress disorder.* Princeton, NJ: Princeton University Press.

21

Trauma in Context: Integrating Biological, Clinical, and Cultural Perspectives

Robert Lemelson, Laurence J. Kirmayer, and Mark Barad

The contributors to this book offer diverse perspectives from which to view trauma and its impacts. In this chapter, we consider how these approaches might work together to deepen our understanding of individual and collective responses to traumatic experience. Our hope is that this will illustrate the value of interdisciplinarity for advancing scientific research, clinical practice, and cultural analysis. We will weave together strands from many of the contributions but begin with a discussion of three further narratives of traumatic experience.

THE DIVERSITY OF TRAUMA RESPONSES

The three case studies we present are drawn from ongoing clinical visual ethnographic research on culture and mental illness in Indonesia by Robert Lemelson (RL).[1] All three individuals suffered trauma during the

[1] The authors thank Dr. Luh Ketut Suryani, Dr. I Gusti Putu Panteri, Dr. Made Nyandra, Dr. Mahar Agusno, and Dra. Ninik Supartini. Thanks also to Wing Ko, Dag Yngvesson, Diyah Larasati, and Yulin Sun for their work and insight on the three cases. RL also thanks I Wayan Sadha for his long friendship and assistance. All participants gave informed consent for their participation in this study. Consent for filming was obtained at the time of the interviews and recorded on film. In this chapter, we have used pseudonyms and changed identifying details of the cases except for Bu Lanny, who is a public speaker, educator, and meditation teacher who regularly presents this autobiographical account to audiences. She presented much the same account at a conference organized by the Foundation for Psychocultural Research (FPR) in Yogyakarta in August 2004. A film with these case histories, *1965 and Its Aftermath*, was presented at the 2nd FPR-UCLA interdisciplinary conference, "Four Dimensions of Childhood: Brain, Mind, Culture, and Time" (February 11–13, 2005), at UCLA.
As a clinically trained ethnographer, RL asked specific questions, modeled on diagnostic interviews, that were designed to uncover core symptoms of trauma-related disorders. However, the saliency of the symptoms varied significantly: Some were volunteered, others were elicited only when explicitly asked about. Both volunteered and elicited symptoms were related to the traumatic events, but some symptoms typically thought of as related to

political upheaval in Indonesia in 1965.[2] All three experienced intense fear or terror witnessing family members being severely beaten, taken away, or killed in front of them. They all have lived in a political climate, from 1965 through the late 1990s, in which their status as relatives of alleged communist party members[3] made them continued targets for harassment, intimidation, violence, and discrimination, often enacted by community members. However, although their exposure to traumatic events was similar in some ways, the long-term outcomes they and their families have experienced are vastly different. These divergent trajectories illustrate the complex interaction of sociocultural, psychological, and neurobiological processes that give rise to individuals' strengths and resiliencies.

PAK NYOMAN'S STORY[4]

Pak Nyoman was born in 1944 in a small rural village in central Bali, Indonesia, about 30 kilometers from the capital, Denpasar. He continues to live in the village that he was born in, in the same extended family compound. Pak Nyoman has been married since the late 1970s to a woman who is a member of his *dadia* (clan). He has been a farmer his whole life, farming a number of hectares in wet rice irrigation.

Pak Nyoman traces his present illness back to 1965, when he witnessed a massacre of a number of his fellow villagers in the bloodbath that engulfed Bali and the rest of Indonesia following the failure of a purported communist coup and the purging and massacre of those accused of being communist party (*Partai Komunis Indonesia* or PKI) members. Following this, 80,000–100,000 Balinese (out of a total population of approximately 2 million) were killed in the period from November 1965 to early 1966. In early 1966, when Pak Nyoman was 21 years old, military and paramilitary

---

trauma were not consciously considered by the interviewees to be connected to the trauma they had experienced.

[2] Some of this history is described in the chapter by Dwyer and Santikarma (this volume). See also Cribb (1990) and Robinson (1998).

[3] Many individuals were accused of communist party affiliations if they belonged to a wide range of progressive or mutual aid organizations, such as the woman's organization Gerwani (*Gerakan Wanita Indonesia*, Indonesian Women's Movement). See Wieringa (2003).

[4] This material on Pak Nyoman is drawn from RL's five home visit interviews between 1996 and 1997 as part of a 12-year follow-up study of 113 cases of acute-onset psychosis, based on hospital admissions at Wangaya Government Hospital in Denpasar, Bali, beginning in 1984. The study was conducted by RL's colleague, Luh Ketut Suryani, MD, PhD (Udayana University, Denpasar). The research was part of a wider World Health Organization (WHO) investigation on the course and outcome of acute psychosis in the developing world. This account is based on Dr. Suryani's original case notes, which included in-patient observation, a formal psychiatric evaluation, and an interview in 1984; her subsequent home interviews in 1984 and 1985; and RL's eight follow-up video-recorded interviews in 2000–2005. This case is explored in much greater depth in Lemelson (in press).

forces of the Indonesian Nationalist Party (*Partai Nasionalist Indonesia*, PNI) entered his village looking for suspected PKI members. A number of the villagers were singled out as PKI members and were marched off to the cemetery. Pak Nyoman followed along with some other village members, at a distance. He felt a sense of great terror and a feeling that someone might hurt or kill him, even though he had not been singled out for execution. He quietly left the group witnessing the execution and climbed a tree near the cemetery. There he witnessed the group being systematically hacked to death with machetes. From that time to 1997 when he disclosed this history to RL, Pak Nyoman had never spoken about the incident with anyone, including members of his village who had also witnessed the massacre. Several of the perpetrators of this massacre were still living in the region – in fact, one was a member of his hamlet.

Pak Nyoman's long-standing problems with social withdrawal and fear started soon after witnessing the PKI massacre. During this experience he was extremely terrified (b.i. *ketakutan terus*[5]) and afterward felt that his life force (b.b. *bayu*) had become very weak. He began to have problems with feeling his heart beating rapidly and felt an "inner pressure" (b.i. *tekanan batin*) weighing down his body. For months afterward he had a difficult time eating and became very thin and withdrawn. His eyes felt like they were deeply sunken. He was jumpy and easily startled and had periods in which he felt his mind go blank. He had difficulty falling asleep and was frequently awakened by nightmares of being chased and of people being butchered.

Pak Nyoman became increasingly afraid of social gatherings and avoided public events and places. He withdrew from the common social activities of his hamlet and stopped participating in community work projects. He often displayed what Balinese term a "quiet" or "closed" demeanor (b.b. *nyebeng*), in contrast to the more socially desirable self-presentation as "friendly and open" (b.b. *mebraya*). He said that he did not feel frightened or anxious when guests came to his house compound but only when he had to go out in the village for social or ritual events.

Around this time, while cutting grass in the field, Pak Nyoman began seeing small, black figures who he understood were spirits known as the *wong samar*, literally the "indistinct people" – a commonly recognized form of potentially dangerous spirit.[6] He described the creatures as wandering

---

[5] b.i. = Bahasa Indonesia, the national language of Indonesia (most Indonesians also speak their own cultural or regional language); b.b. = Bahasa Bali, Balinese, the language spoken in Bali in addition to Bahasa Indonesia.

[6] Balinese recognize several different types of spirits. The *wong samar* are nonancestral spirits that inhabit rivers, graveyards, ravines, and Banyan trees. They are believed to cause illness or emotional or interpersonal problems if not treated with the proper respect or propitiated with special offerings.

over the grass and hiding in stagnant water. At first they made noises that he could not understand, but gradually the noises coalesced into words with clear meaning.

When occupied by these spirits, Pak Nyoman would stay home or avoid social contact by hiding in solitary places, like remote rice fields or the deeply cut canyons that crisscross the Balinese landscape. He knew that the spirits could be found in these quiet places and, at times, it seemed he sought a relationship with the spirits by going to their likely dwelling places.

Pak Nyoman would sometimes leave his home for days at a time. When he returned he explained to his family that he had been taken into the *wong samar* world, where he had been forced to marry a beautiful *wong samar* woman. He believed the *wong samar* sometimes took human form in order to mix with human society and find victims who were vulnerable, such as the very young, the very old, and people who were ill, such as himself.[7]

Pak Nyoman began withdrawing further, finally refusing to leave his room to go to work. At this point, his family members brought him to a traditional healer (*balian*) in a nearby hamlet. According to the *balian*, Pak Nyoman's illness was caused by witchcraft, as a result of the ill wishes of unspecified village members (b.b. *pepasangan*). Pak Nyoman stayed in the *balian's* house compound for a month and received treatment.

Nyoman himself described his illness as "*ngeb*." *Ngeb* is a state of being caused by witnessing something horrific, frightening, or bizarre, such as occurred with the devastating cholera epidemic that swept through Bali in the 1920s. Seeing spirits, such as the *wong samar*, causes another variant of *ngeb*. As a result of these frightening or horrific experiences, sufferers put themselves in a self-imposed exile characterized by "muteness" (b.b. *membisu*) and lack of participation in the social world. Nyoman felt that his *ngeb* began with witnessing the massacre in 1965.

Because of Pak Nyoman's deteriorating condition, and the belief that in addition to sorcery his illness was caused by his weak nerves, the *balian* brought Nyoman to the state mental hospital in Bangli, where he was treated with antipsychotic medications. The voices of the *wong samar* gradually decreased in frequency and prominence, until after about 1 week they had become "hazy and unclear." Nyoman was hospitalized for 3 weeks and then discharged.

---

[7] While it may seem bizarre that Pak Nyoman entered into a marriage with a spirit being, in Bali it is commonly believed that people can take *wong samar* as wives. They are reputed to be affectionate and loyal spouses, whose only desire is to make their husbands happy. However, if the husband does not pay proper attention to their spirit wives, the latter can become angry and bring misfortune and illness. Thus, Pak Nyoman's ideas involving the *wong samar*'s need to be taken care of and given proper respect have a cultural basis.

Pak Nyoman slowly recovered from this episode over the ensuing years. He currently continues farming his paddy and experiencing visits from his spirits. He reports that his fears have diminished, because many of the perpetrators have died (often suddenly, which Pak Nyoman believes is caused by the law of karma). However, during events that are politically charged (such as the recent national elections in 2004), Pak Nyoman often returns to his fearful, withdrawn *ngeb* state. Most recently, his protective *wong samar* spirits have been battling with the "spiritual energy" of a villager who was a prominent perpetrator of the massacres of 1965–66 and who continues to maintain a powerful position in village political organization. He believes that this spiritual energy is pressuring him to rejoin the communist party, which Pak Nyoman believes would open him to further discrimination and attacks at the hands of his fellow villagers. Pak Nyoman wears a uniform of army fatigues under his normal clothes to provide protection against the negative spiritual energy of this feared villager.

JOKO'S STORY[8]

Joko is a 13-year-old boy who lived in a semi-urban area outside of Yogyakarta, Java, before being placed in an orphanage at age 11. Joko had initially been brought to see Dr. Mahar Agusno, a Javanese psychiatrist with whom RL collaborates on mental health research, by one of the nuns who cared for him. She was concerned about Joko's health and behavior and reported that Joko had difficulties doing schoolwork and getting along amicably with peers. He often had nightmares and physical complaints including chest cramps, dizziness, and difficulty breathing. She was also concerned because Joko often talked about committing suicide. She caught him once as he stood on the brink of a well, which he had planned to jump into.

At our first meeting, Joko was waiting in a drab but clean meeting room in the orphanage. Joko is a slight, somewhat gaunt young adolescent, who often has a distant or lost expression on his face. He spoke clearly and

[8] Joko was a patient of Dr. Mahar Agusno, a Javanese psychiatrist, with whom RL has been conducting ongoing research on neuropsychiatric disorders in Indonesia. The patient was referred to Dr. Agusno by the staff of the Catholic orphanage where Joko was placed by his parents. Joko had been experiencing severe psychological and somatic symptoms and appeared suicidal. RL received consent to include him in the study from Joko himself, his parents, his therapist, teachers, social workers, and the director of the orphanage. The video-recorded clinical ethnographic interviews with Joko were conducted by Dr. Agusno. In addition, RL interviewed Joko's family, social workers, and the orphanage staff, as well as children from his home village and other members of his community. The interviews were undertaken with the understanding and agreement of Joko and his family that this material would be used for documentary, educational, and research purposes. The interviews were conducted at different times in 2002–2005.

articulately during the interview, though in a low voice, politely answering questions and describing in some detail the social problems his family had encountered that contributed to his distress: "I came to this home because I had a problem. It was a rather complicated problem, you know. My family was tortured, slandered, terrorized." However, in response to questioning by Dr. Mahar about the specific incidents of the torture he experienced, Joko's face tightened; he bent over in his chair, clenched his fists, and began silently sobbing and rocking back and forth. After some coaxing by Dr. Mahar, Joko began to tell more of his story.

At age 9, Joko witnessed his 17-year-old brother, Paidjo, being tortured by his fellow villagers on two occasions. Paidjo was severely beaten, hit by stones, and forced to walk naked on his hands. Joko has vivid memories of Paidjo screaming and crying out Joko's name. As his brother was screaming his name, Joko himself was dragged away by youngsters who started to beat him as well, but he escaped and sought help. Joko explained his physical illness and mental distress mainly as a result of constantly remembering the scene of his older brother being tortured.

Joko has weekly, sometimes daily, flashbacks of the numerous traumatic events he witnessed when he was in the village. The emotional distress caused by this repetitive recollection has hindered him from carrying out schoolwork and interfered with his daily routine. Joko also reported frequent nightmares of his brother being tortured and killed. Whenever he remembers the face of his brother who had been beaten until his face was almost unrecognizable, Joko reports having severe stomach cramps that are totally debilitating. The sisters at his orphanage report that he often appears lost in daydreams and has difficulty concentrating at school.

Joko has numerous symptoms of autonomic arousal and anxiety. Whenever he remembers the traumatic events, his breathing becomes difficult, his heart pounds, and he has a stabbing pain as if being pricked with needles. He feels his body temperature increase and his palms get sweaty. His fists clench, and he has the desire to punch anything around him. He feels out of breath, dizzy, hot, and then sometimes faints.

Joko has frequent thoughts of suicide and recurrent desires to take revenge, to torture and kill the people who hurt him. He enjoys watching movies that feature revenge as a central motif. He frequently wakes up in the middle of the night with the sense that someone is whispering to him to take revenge. These incidents are coupled with violent and detailed revenge fantasies.

Initially, it was unclear why Joko was in an orphanage because both of Joko's parents are well and live about 10 miles away from the orphanage. In a meeting at the orphanage, the nun explained that, in order for Joko to attend school and be away from the "hostile environment" of his family, it was arranged to have him live in the orphanage away from his parents and older brother. At the orphanage he could get a start on a better life with discipline, supervision, and free education. In a subsequent interview with a social worker from the church, it became clear that Joko's family was viewed as highly dysfunctional with frequent domestic violence and that the family had been pressured to place him in an orphanage for his own safety. The context and meaning for this violence became clearer only as our interviews progressed. Indeed, to understand why the villagers scapegoated and tormented Joko and his family, it is necessary to understand the impact of the events following September 30, 1965 (G-30-S),[9] on Joko's father, Pak Sukiman.

Pak Sukiman is short, thin man, with skin wizened and darkened by many years working in the open sun. He is missing most of his teeth, and because of this his speech at times is difficult to understand. Pak Sukiman grew up in a poor *kampung* outside of Yogyakarta. As a teenager he had to work while going to school to support himself. His schooling did not go smoothly because of his family's extreme poverty. He also said that, as a youngster, he was known as a troublemaker, often getting into fights because he had a hard time controlling his temper.

When he was in his late teens he worked as a salesman at a coffee factory. There he fell in love with a young woman from his village and planned to marry her. However, another young man who was the son of the village headman also wanted her, and as the event of G-30-S unfolded he denounced Pak Sukiman as a prominent PKI member and activist. Pak Sukiman stated that although he socialized with PKI members (not uncommon, because at that time the PKI was the third largest communist party in the world and a legal entity in Indonesia), he was never a member himself. He was arrested and imprisoned for 14 years. When he was released he found out that the young woman he had been in love with years earlier had married the man who had informed on him.[10]

When Pak Sukiman was released from the gulag on Buru Island, he faced numerous difficulties. With his spoiled identity as an alleged ex-PKI member, his choice of occupations was limited. In addition, given his low social status, it was difficult for him to find a spouse. After he was released he had a marriage arranged with Bu Suwarti, a woman 15 years

---

[9] The acronym G-30-S (*Gerakan 30 September*) is used in official New Order history to refer to the alleged coup attempt in 1965.

[10] Pak Sukiman's prison experiences identify him as a "Category B" prisoner, which was defined as a PKI functionary, member, sympathizer, or someone suspected to have played a role in or otherwise approved of the aborted communist coup attempt of 1965. Starting in 1969, Category B prisoners were confined indefinitely on the East Indonesian island of Buru for what in 1974 came to be referred to as "rehabilitation" (Cribb, 1990).

his junior. Their marriage was marked by Pak Sukiman's violent and abusive behavior.

Pak Sukiman clearly recognized the effects that his torture and imprisonment had in aggravating his propensity for violence and lack of emotional control: "That's it . . . that's the problem. It seems that my burden falls into my wife, and that's the problem. It has impacts in our family life because I am an emotional person."

Before their marriage, his wife was not told of Pak Sukiman's status as an accused PKI. She found out about it only after Pak Sukiman was required to attend a reeducation meeting at the village office. She felt despair over their spoiled identity and low status in the community. The discovery of Pak Sukiman's past also evoked memories of the disappearance of her father, associated with the PKI as well, under similar circumstances. In an attempt to improve their lot, the family moved to a neighboring *kampung*, but they continued to have low status because they were among the poorest members, they were the only Christian family, and the villagers soon found out that Pak Sukiman was an ex-PKI member who had been imprisoned on Buru Island. Bu Suwarti became the target of frequent sexual harassment by men in the village. When she went to the village office to report this problem, one of the local leaders told her "not to do anything stupid"; otherwise, the villagers would send her husband back to jail.

Bu Suwarti related that, because of their status as family of a former PKI member (*anak PKI*, literally "children of the communist party"), the villagers often created situations in which her sons Paidjo and Joko would be likely to get into trouble and therefore become the legitimate target of village scorn and oppression. For example, villagers placed a bike in a rice field. An older child asked Paidjo to steal it together with him. When they did it, the villagers caught Paidjo but released the other child. Paidjo was made to walk on his hands for about 200 meters without any clothes on while people whipped and hit him. Village customary law (*adat*) in many parts of Indonesia prescribes severe punishment for thieves or suspected thieves, who are often beaten and tortured, not infrequently to death, by angry village members. Police are usually notified only after the incident occurs and the punishment has been meted out.

By 2005, after finishing elementary school, Joko had returned home from the orphanage. He had dropped out of junior high school due to behavioral problems and was associating with the same group of street children with whom his brother Paidjo had left home to live with. He still reported daily revenge fantasies and seemed unimpressed when his mother tried to dissuade him from enacting them. In a recent interview, Paidjo revealed that he had joined a secretive and strictly observant Muslim organization, which recruits throughout Java and trains youth during month-long retreats in remote locations. He said it has as its highest goal the dedication of one's life to the cause of one's faith.

LANNY'S STORY[11]

Bu Lanny is a 54-year-old, well-educated English teacher in Java, Indonesia. She was born into a socially respected, well-off Chinese-Indonesian family in 1952. Her father, Alex, was a prominent community leader in the Chinese Indonesian community and a successful businessman. Bu Lanny remembers being very close with her father and describes herself as his favorite child. Alex owned several motor vehicles, which was very rare at that time, and liked to show off his little Lanny, having her ride his motorcycles. She described him as "my hero."

For several months after G-30-S, there were frequent riots led by youth brigades, paramilitary forces, and other groups associated with the PNI. Although few in the Chinese merchant community in Klaten were associated with the PKI, during this period more than 200 Chinese homes and businesses were burned (Gathering in the paddies, 1965). Numerous members of the Chinese community were arrested or disappeared. During one of these protests, hundreds of people surrounded Bu Lanny's house throwing stones and axes and shouting Alex's name. Shots were fired into the house, and the family hid in terror behind sandbags to avoid being killed. For Bu Lanny, the most painful memory from this terrifying event was her father's response to the mob violence. During the height of the terror, with the crowd shouting his name in anger, Alex ran away, in just his undershirt. Bu Lanny's last image of her father was of him taking terrified deep breaths, leaning against the wall, alone, having abandoned his family. Alex was picked up several weeks later and brought to a local internment camp near Klaten.

The family was able to visit Alex in prison before he disappeared forever. Bu Lanny recalls seeing him through the iron bars of his prison cell:

> I saw my father. At that time I realized that "This is my hero" ... with short underwear and also with undershirt. And there was ... this bar, you know, and he asked me and the first question was, "How's school?" And I said, "OK, good." ... I didn't want to cry because, you know, since I was small I liked to hear heroic stories and things like that. And he said, "Be good," and then he took off his ring and gave it to me.... That was a very, very maybe big trauma because for many years I had headache if I saw vertical lines ... you know, we were separated by the vertical lines.

Bu Lanny reported that after witnessing her father's brutalization and imprisonment, she began getting severe headaches. She would startle

---

[11] RL met Bu Lanny, who teaches English at a language school in Klaten (Java), through mutual friends. Bu Lanny has written and spoken extensively about her experiences (Anggawati, 2001). RL conducted a series of ethnographic interviews with Bu Lanny, as well as with her mother, her brothers and sisters, other friends and community members, and her sibling's children, in 2002–2005.

easily and could not stand loud noises. She panicked when seeing vertical lines and was also frightened whenever she saw people in official uniforms. She often felt her heart beating rapidly but attributed it to heart disease. She also reported becoming angry easily.

Bu Lanny became very forgetful and had great difficulties remembering people's names. She also reported having episodes of mental "blankness." For example, she was sometimes surprised to find herself riding a motorcycle, not knowing why she was there in the first place. She often forgot her deskmate's name, and during these periods of dissociation she often fell down while riding her bicycle. These symptoms persist to the present day.

The imprisonment and disappearance of Bu Lanny's father caused a social and financial crisis in her family. After her father was imprisoned, her mother was frequently distraught and unable to function. As the eldest still at home, Lanny was expected to shoulder much of the burden for caring for the store and her younger siblings.

Bu Lanny described herself as one who has always played the heroine role, the toughest one in the family, ever since childhood. She played most of the boys' games and wanted to win all the time. She always stood up to any bullies in her community. When someone slapped her brother, she would slap the person back. However, although Bu Lanny described herself as tough and strong, her younger brother Pak Edy told a different story: "My sister was Dad's golden child. She was absolutely at a loss at that time. So ... as soon as Dad was taken away she ... was devastated, you know, she was devastated."

As a result of her experiences in 1965, Bu Lanny saw life as full of hatred and vengeance. She became harsh in her own reactions. She lost control and became enraged easily. She would get upset at people who showed sadness or signs of weakness and was cold and indifferent to peers and friends. She described herself as an "iron fist" (b.i. *tangan besi*) over her younger siblings.

This way of coping helped her to survive but also caused her great suffering, until in 1978 she had a spiritual awakening:

So maybe, maybe hatred made me live. But also, at the same time, it killed me. Spiritually, I was very, very disappointed. I would sit outside and say, "Why? Where is God? Why does he let this happen?" And some priest would come and he would say, "Oh, please don't doubt God's love. Let's pray and ask for forgiveness" and on and on.... And I said, "Bullshit!" You know?... And when I started to really rebel against God, then I had this experience of seeing light. You know, very bright light. And I heard something like, "I am God." So I still remember, I kneeled ... knelt down and I said, "Okay, I now know that you are there," and then I said, "Use me for good things." And I got the promise "From now on, I'm not going to leave you." Then I felt peace in my heart – a feeling I had never had. Wonderful peace.

In 1992, Bu Lanny had another compelling religious experience in which she confronted some of her worst fears.

I consider myself lucky because I came across Buddhism. When I went to this... ten day vipassana course, I didn't know anything about meditation. So I paid attention to whatever the teacher was telling us. He said, "Observe. Whatever comes up will go away. Arising only to pass away." And I had to do that meditation for ten days. After three or four days, there was a big eruption in my mind and I started to see my thoughts very clearly. And it went on and faster and faster, until I panicked, you see, I couldn't control myself. I realized I was going to go crazy. I am being crazy, I said: "Oh, a crazy person has this experience." I was alone. I wanted to see my teacher but I didn't know where he was. So I said, "What am I supposed to do? Whatever rises will pass away." Maybe 20 minutes elapsed. My mind started to calm down. I felt very, very tired. And sweat flowed down like a stream. But suddenly, I understood so many things about what had been hidden deep in my heart. I had been buried in fear. I had feared separation, death. But at that very moment, I was not afraid of death anymore. So calmly, I put everybody in their very last moment. So I imagined facing a bed and on the bed, I put the dead body of everyone I loved, one by one. Ninik, Mahar, Pak Rob, right? Everybody. And at last, my own dead body.

The insight into impermanence and the ability to let go that Lanny learned through meditation have had lasting effects on her life. She became a practicing Buddhist and founded a centre for Buddhist meditation. Through the self-understanding she has achieved, she has become an inspiring figure and teacher of others.

THE MULTIPLE CONTEXTS OF TRAUMA

These three case studies represent some of the diverse ethnic, cultural, and religious strands within the rich tapestry of Indonesian society. These people had markedly different socioeconomic and educational backgrounds, and different resources were available to them for coping with the aftermath of the violence and losses they sustained. Although they shared some similarities in their symptoms and suffering, the divergences are just as striking. Different cultural models and social positions contribute to their unique experiences. Understanding these stories of trauma thus requires that we consider how they are embedded in – and emerge from – multiple contexts: biological processes of learning and memory; embodied experiences of injury, pain, and fear; the narrative trajectories of personal biography; the knowledge and practices of cultural and social systems; and the power and positioning of political struggles enacted on individual, family, community, and national levels.

For some clinicians, a crucial part of each of these stories is captured by the diagnostic construct of PTSD. All three individuals endured similar terrifying experiences. All three had persistent nightmares, avoidance of stimuli associated with the trauma, detachment from others, problems with anger control and irritability, and other common symptoms of the disorder. The PTSD diagnosis focuses on these characteristic symptoms, links them to specific causal events, and legitimates them as expressions of a universal (and in many ways normal and evolutionarily adaptive) response to trauma (see chapters by Konner, Shalev, and Silove, this volume).

This pattern of response to trauma clearly has its roots in the systems that allow humans, like other animals, to learn to avoid dangerous situations in their environments. Such situations occur frequently and sometimes unexpectedly, and the animals that survive best are the ones who best convert the unexpected into the anticipated – that is, the ones that learn to fear. However, although it is very costly to be unafraid of a deadly danger, it is also costly to avoid what is safe. Animals that are too fearful cannot forage, mate, or raise offspring. People who are too fearful cannot think clearly. As a result, it is very important to learn as well to distinguish what is truly dangerous from what is safe, and to extinguish fear of safe situations. The biology of fear suggests that fear and security exist in balance and that PTSD may be due either to an excess of fear or to a failure of the mechanisms of learned safety.

Each person had unique configurations of symptoms. Joko had persistent and overpowering feelings of rage and helplessness, and obsessive revenge fantasies about maiming and killing the villagers who had harassed and tortured his family. Lanny, too, had problems controlling her anger and rage, and she became "an iron fist," who tightly controlled her siblings. Over time, her personal struggle with anger and her understanding of its negative effects on her life led Lanny to confront her strong feelings and transform them into motivations for personal empowerment and growth through her teaching and meditation practice. Pak Nyoman withdrew into a culturally shaped yet, by psychiatric standards, delusional world, where he did not have to face those who had tortured and killed his family members. From the perspective of the psychobiology, we might say that Lanny was able to extinguish her fear successfully, whereas Pak Nyoman could not – but each was also simultaneously using strategies to position her- and himself within a complex social world with its own exigencies and demands.

Clinical diagnosis is intended to lead to specific guidelines for treatment and predictions of the course or prognosis of illness. By its very nature psychiatric diagnosis decontextualizes and essentializes human problems, treating them as disorders that can be understood and treated with approaches that generalize across situations (Gaines, 1992; Kirmayer, 2005; Kleinman, 1988; López & Guarnaccia, 2000). As well, current psychiatric nosology focuses almost exclusively on problems located within the individual and lacks a developed conceptual vocabulary for relational, social, communal, or cultural problems (Alarcón et al., 2002). An individualistic approach to trauma tends to de-emphasize the effects on families, kinship networks, and communities. These collective impacts of trauma are important issues in their own right but, as the contributions to this volume make clear, family, communal, political, and sociocultural contexts profoundly shape both clinical symptomatology and personal experience.

Cultural models orient, explain, and give meaning to traumatic events and their consequences. Although diagnostic categories have utility for treatment providers working within biomedical health care systems, they may not fit the popular cultural models by which people make sense of historical events and subsequent suffering. Of course, psychiatric categories themselves become part of folk knowledge and practice but may be understood and applied in ways that are different from their original technical use. Indeed, as Allan Young's work on the history of PTSD makes clear, popular and professional understandings of psychiatric disorders are in constant circulation and contestation, and influence each other (Young, 1995). As a result, the technical and sociomoral meanings of diagnosis can never been entirely disentangled.

THE TEMPORAL LANDSCAPE OF TRAUMA

Presenting clinical or ethnographic vignettes tends to obscure the way in which stories of trauma evolve over time. All of the stories presented above are condensed from many hours of conversation. Some parts of each person's story were offered spontaneously whereas others emerged only gradually, as trust was established and individuals rethought their experience or were confronted with alternative versions of events provided by others. This form of ethnographic interviewing is similar in some respects to the process of psychotherapy, including exposure therapy, which requires that patients narrate their distress repeatedly.[12] Although aspects of their experience fit the commonly accepted features of PTSD, what they chose to focus on and disclose in the interview setting varied markedly – as did the ways they narrated their experiences to others in everyday life. These varying stories reflect processes of psychological coping or adaptation – creating order, coherence, and value from chaos, meaninglessness, and suffering – but they are also acts of social positioning, locating the person in a specific role, status, or stance vis-à-vis the interviewer and others not present. To understand their subjectivity, we must to return to their accounts to explore what is at stake for their remembering, interpreting, and managing trauma's long-term effects.

[12] In research interviews with refugees in Montreal, we have found that many participants report that narrating their illness experience is helpful and leaves them feeling relieved (Groleau & Kirmayer, 2004).

The temporal structure of the response to trauma is complicated by the dynamics of memory and narrative. Although sometimes symptoms may begin at or soon after a discrete event, often causal attributions are made after the fact. Because memory is fallible and relies on reconstruction, our recollection of the sequence and timing of events on which causal attributions may be based is shaped by the conceptual models we hold. Thus, if one accepts traumatic experience as the cause of symptoms, it is easy to reconstruct one's history with a temporal sequence that supports trauma as a causal explanation. This inevitable process of reconstruction of the past according to present theories of the self has led Allan Young to remark that in the construct of PTSD "time flows backward" from current symptoms to the singular causal event. The issue is not that people fabricate or distort their past history in any conscious way (though, of course, there are many circumstances in which they do) but that the complex, polysemous, and ambiguous elements of one's history are constantly reorganized to single out specific strands that have personal and collective meaning and that suit the current contexts in which one's story is told.

One of the contentious features of PTSD has been the claim that for some individuals exposed to traumatic events, symptoms and memories can emerge after a long period of having no overt difficulties (McNally, 2003). The biobehavioral research on the return of fear with changes in context, time, or internal state, described by Bouton and Waddell in this volume, makes it clear how this might happen. In most cases, in fact, individuals who suffer from PTSD also had an acute stress disorder – that is, they suffered symptoms during and immediately after the event. Indeed, the intensity of response in the acute period, and the presence of dissociative symptoms in particular, may predict the likelihood of later symptoms of PTSD (Cardeña & Croyle, 2005). This link between acute dissociative symptoms and poor outcome after exposure to trauma might occur because such dissociative symptoms are either (1) a marker of a certain type of individual vulnerability based on personality or previous traumatic experiences; (2) an ineffective or problematic avoidant coping strategy that prevents exposure, extinction learning, or mastery; or (3) an indication of difficulties with memory and suggestibility that will encourage misattribution of symptoms (Merckelbach & Jelicic, 2004).

One salient critique of the PTSD construct rests on the appropriateness of the prefix "post" (Scheper-Hughes, 2005). In many circumstances, exposure to trauma may be prolonged and persistent so that the posttraumatic period does not arrive. The consequences of such prolonged exposure to trauma may not be captured by models that explain the effects of briefer exposures to more discrete traumatic events. For individuals who experience repeated traumas within abusive families or communities, for example, the effects of trauma are said to give rise to complex PTSD (see van der Kolk, this volume). More than this, there are many communities in conflict-ridden parts of the world where the social and political conditions responsible for the original trauma continue to exist, along with more pervasive forms of structural violence, so that traumatic stress is ongoing (Farmer, 2003). These scenarios demand a different sort of model than the ones typically studied in animal research on fear conditioning or in clinical studies of prolonged exposure with individuals who have survived single discrete traumas and are now safe.

This persistence and recurrence of trauma over time is an important aspect of all three of our case studies. In contemporary Indonesia, everyday life presents a great number of situations or cues that can reactivate fears acquired during the period of political violence. There are state-orchestrated national memorials, which have included the showing of television documentaries (e.g., Noer's *Pengkhianatan G 30 S/PKI*, 1985), that enshrine an authorized version of collective history and that convey a sense of menace for those associated in any way with the banned PKI. There have been long-standing campaigns on a regency and village level that echo these national themes and emphasize a monolithic view of history in which ex-PKI members and their supporters were the cause of social disruption and therefore are to be held responsible for the atrocities committed by their foes.

Next, because of the historical context of G-30-S, many victims and perpetrators of the violence live in the same communities, often side by side. Living next door to villagers who have tormented one's family and being compelled to behave in a polite and deferential manner is a common fact of life in village Indonesia. Following the events of 1965, many victims had no choice but to interact on a regular basis with the perpetrators of the violence. Although the circumstances varied in different parts of Indonesia, in central Java and Bali the perpetrators were often members of the community, and when the violence ended and the normalization campaign was begun by the central government, many individuals continued living their lives in the shadows of neighbors who had committed the atrocities.[13] This is further compounded by the fact that some of the perpetrators were actually forced to do the killings themselves, as a way of implicating them in the actions and demonstrating their loyalty, often under the threat of their own death if they did not comply.[14] Although not the case with Pak Nyoman, it was the case for others in his village and for a number of other *ngeb* sufferers the first author has encountered in his fieldwork.

How this situation has played out in terms of individual experience is extremely varied. For Joko, ongoing repression and fear were daily

[13] This is quite similar to what Hinton (2004) describes in post–Khmer Rouge Cambodia.
[14] In some cases family members were forced to kill family members, both as a test of their loyalty and because of the desire to do proper funerary arrangements, which they knew would not be done if the person killed was buried in a hidden mass grave.

experiences of life in his village, where violence against him was socially sanctioned because he was an *anak PKI*. This was compounded by the ongoing threat of domestic violence at the hands of his father and older brother, and the privation of life in the institutional setting of the orphanage.

For Bu Lanny these socially contextualized triggers were also ever present in her interactions with members of her community, some of whom had organized the anti-Chinese campaigns, the most recent of which followed the fall of Suharto and the Orde Baru in 1998. However, Lanny also had individual reminders of her past traumatic experiences, in that whenever she saw vertical li   fences she recalled the bars behind which she last saw her   ured and killed.

For Pak Nyoman th   ; traumatization were also social. Perhaps most ii   iat the perpetrators of the massacres in which h   nily were members of his *banjar*, with whom he   a daily level. His continuing uncertainty over t   his status as a possible PKI member may have co   val into a culturally meaningful "delusional" sy   ccount Nyoman appears to be victim and surviv   ed massacre, some members of his community view l   or instigator of the events of 1965 because he was a sy   e communist party. Only in 2004 did his brother say that Nyoman himself had been forgiven by villagers for causing the disorder of 1965.

Although the biology of fear and extinction result in specific temporal dynamics of trauma and recovery, these case studies show how larger contextual factors may supervene. Thus, social and political circumstances determine the temporality of trauma and may not allow the "post" of PTSD to emerge. Instead, there is layer upon layer of acute response to constantly changing threats – which may be real or imagined with equal effect. Throughout, the meaning of trauma depends on its personal, social, cultural, and political context and interpretation.

TRUST AND THE FABRIC OF COMMUNAL LIFE

Many forms of trauma involve interpersonal violence and betrayals that destroy individuals' trust in others. When severe and prolonged, trauma can damage the individuals' capacity to trust others. When violence is arbitrary, incomprehensible, and without sense, it erodes individuals' belief in a just world, where trust makes sense. Rebuilding the capacity for appropriate trust therefore is central to recovery from trauma. In the clinical literature on trauma, trust is usually discussed in terms of personal relationships and disrupted internal relational models of self and other. But trust also has a situated, sociohistorical dimension, rooted in a reliable and responsive social order that acknowledges and does not exploit individuals' vulnerability.

In Joko's case it is clear that basic trust has become difficult, if not impossible, to reestablish, given the ongoing nature of the social stigmatization of Pak Sukiman's identity and that of his family. In addition, the individual and family pathology that may have some of its roots in Pak Sukiman's oppression and imprisonment have undermined family solidarity until the family has disintegrated, with one child ending up on the street and another in an orphanage. The sense of loss and anger that Joko feels toward his family (and perhaps toward some of the professionals who are trying to help him) is displaced by his anger at the villagers and intense fantasies of revenge. Indeed, it is possible that the very intensity of these fantasies serves to deflect his attention from the more intimate betrayals he has endured.[15] Indeed, a common theme in survivors' accounts of Bali during this period is that perpetrators were "doing their duty" in response to superiors' orders, whereas the real anger and desire for revenge is reserved for friends and family members who informed on suspected PKI members and supporters (D. Santikarma, personal communication, October 1, 2005).

In Pak Nyoman's case, there were understandable reasons why he did not tell anyone about witnessing the massacre for over 30 years. Some of the perpetrators were his *banjar* members, with whom he had to interact on a daily basis. His sister was forced into an arranged marriage with one of the key perpetrators of the massacres in his area. In addition, because of his status as an ex-PKI, he was seen as responsible for the massacres, at the same time being a victim and survivor of them. Withdrawing from the community network in which some of the members were perpetuators of his traumatic experience, Pak Nyoman established a trusted social network with the spirit world. However, even in this spirit world there are fears and conflicts, and the issues of G-30-S continue to haunt him in the form of negative spirits who entreat him to rejoin the communist party.

In Bu Lanny's case, the enduring trust between family members was obvious. The family had thrived due to their persistence and independence. However, the family as a unit never regained trust in the community and still felt (as do many ethnic Chinese in Indonesia) that they were outsiders within their own society. It was only with the fall of the New Order regime

---

[15] Jessica Freyd has written of the ways in which the violence of sexual and emotional abuse within families is compounded by a sense of betrayal of trust of one's most important caretakers and protectors (Freyd, 1996). Although Freyd's concern is with the circumstances that promote repression or forgetting of abuse, the likelihood is that individuals do not simply forget these events but work actively to avoid thinking about them to avoid the distressing conclusion that they cannot trust those they love.

in Indonesia in 1998 that Lanny felt it was safe to publish her memoirs of this period.[16]

THE POLITICS OF MEMORY

As the chapters in this volume show, remembering and forgetting, commemorating or denying traumatic events depend on memory systems that inscribe trauma on body and brain, but also on social and political processes that aim to regulate both public and private recollection. These systems may be independent, contradictory, or in active opposition to each other.

Although Joko's thoughts of the abuse he had endured caused him great suffering, his mother encouraged him to actively forget the abuse and its contexts, while still resisting the actions of his tormentors. She spoke to him of her Christian religious beliefs, stressing tolerance and acceptance of suffering, and this seemed to help stave off the intense feelings of desire for revenge that would frequently engulf Joko.

In Pak Nyoman's case, his silence and lack of disclosure about the events he witnessed were supported by a national political culture that, until the fall of Suharto, made remembering 1965 a politically and socially dangerous act (Zurbuchen, 2005). Suppression of these social memories took place at all levels of Indonesian society and was supported by notions regarding the potentially negative effects of discussing these traumatic events on mental health, economic development, and Indonesia's percieved national status on the world stage. This political concern about the dangers of remembering fit with prevalent cultural ideas about the negative effects of expressing and dwelling on negative emotions and events. In anthropology Javanese and Balinese cultures are classic (if at times caricatured or essentialized) examples of cultures that value harmony, smoothness, and containment of negative feelings. These translate into strategies for managing painful memories and regulating the expression of strong emotion (see, for example, Wikan, 1990). Ignoring the political injunction for silence challenges the social order and invites repression. Ignoring the cultural norms for containment challenges the cosmological order and so risks exposing the community to natural disasters.

Bu Lanny dealt with the memory of 1965 in a very different way than either Joko or Nyoman. Lanny's grandmother always told her that her father was not a criminal, that his death was caused by people with base motives like racism and jealousy. Lanny went on to write about her experiences in a self-published memoir and, after the fall of Suharto, spoke

---

[16] Yet even in 2004 it was still felt to be politically very dangerous to discuss these issues in public settings, as Lanny did at a trauma training workshop for Indonesian professionals held in Yogyakarta that year.

publicly about her experience on many occasions. Far from suppressing her memory of the events, she found ways to make active use of it as historical testimony and evidence of her own resiliency, and still more importantly as an experience of basic truths about existence that led her toward becoming a teacher of Buddhist meditation. In this way, she was able to situate her experiences in a framework of meaning that acknowledged but, in some ways, transcended the politics of trauma. In addition, Lanny's actions highlight the redeeming aspects of the will to bear witness that has been seen as crucial to the survivor's recovery.[17] However, it should be noted that although the will to bear witness may be a strong, and perhaps universal, response in some people to forms of violence and trauma, its enactment and realization can take place only when political conditions allow it.[18,19] As well, although much of the trauma literature views silence as an indication of psychological repression or social oppression, silence can also serve as a form of witness with its own psychological, moral, and esthetic value.

Finally, for at least some people, the experience of trauma and subsequent survivorship affords an achieved status that has its own value. At the end of their first interview, Bu Lanny turned to RL and asked, "So, Robert, what trauma did *you* have?" RL apologetically admitted that he had been lucky because he had never experienced any trauma remotely comparable to what she and her family had endured. Lanny began to

---

[17] See, for example, Douglass and Vogler (2003). In many Latin American communities and for refugees from diverse backgrounds, the notion of *testimonio* has played an important role in recovery (e.g., Aron, 1992; Lustig, Weine, Saxe, & Beardslee, 2004). However, bearing witness and giving testimony may be less helpful in cultures where equanimity and containment are highly valued or situations where ongoing oppression or rigid social structures make disclosure dangerous. As well, it is in the nature of some forms of violence that talking about them may aggravate their social impact. For example, in situations where rape is used as a political weapon, women may be put in an untenable position in which speaking about what they have endured undermines the viability of their marriage or whole community.

[18] See also Young (this volume) on the politics of memory and the Shoah.

[19] Lanny's case also illustrates how memories of a traumatic event are distributed across a single family, with aspects of them in contestation or disagreement. For example, Lanny's memory of her father running away and leaving the family had very different meaning or salience for her brother Hari, who stated:

> I know my sister Lanny was disappointed but I was not. I saw my father run away.... Why was it so bad to run? That's not a problem for me. I have told my children that if you are afraid, run. But don't think it is over. If you are strong enough, fight back, seek revenge. I myself would have run like my father.... But it did teach me one thing. Never join a political party.

> Throughout RL's research with this family and others there are numerous examples of seemingly straightforward memories being remembered, reconstructed, retold, and reinterpreted in surprisingly divergent ways by different family members.

laugh and said, "Oh no, you are not lucky. I am the lucky one. I went through these traumas and came out on the other side. You don't have that experience."

CONCLUSION

Taken together, the contributions to this volume suggest that, although the neurobiological processes underlying an acute posttraumatic stress response have universal components, their temporal configuration and interaction is powerfully shaped by developmental, social, and cultural contexts. Does this mean that psychiatric constructs like PTSD have limited explanatory or heuristic value for non-Westerners? This is a crucial question, given the debilitating symptoms found in culturally diverse refugee populations and the fact that many forms of violence are most prevalent in parts of the world where people do not share Western assumptions about the appropriate ways to respond to suffering and adversity. A conservative response would insist that the question is still open: the salience and usefulness of PTSD in diverse social and cultural contexts is an empirical question that can be resolved only by research in the particular contexts in which it is utilized.

Most research on the relationship of trauma to clinical symptomatology and personal experience has occurred in the United States, in a distinctive set of sociohistorical contexts. In particular, the predicament of Vietnam veterans has been central to the development of notions of PTSD and trauma-related pathology. At present, clinical trauma studies in the United States continue to be influenced by the particularities of this veteran population but are also shaped by the dominant modes of interpersonal violence: domestic violence, child abuse, criminal acts, and gang-related violence. Terrorism has become a new focus of concern but is viewed as a traumatic vector that originates in foreign places. On a global basis, the dominant forms of violence causing trauma tend to be more local and collective in nature: interreligious or interethnic conflict, state forms of terror, gendered violence, and the structural violence that besets poor communities everywhere. One can hypothesize that the PTSD diagnostic category would have been significantly different if it had been constructed with these populations in mind, instead of the types of trauma sufferers typically seen in the West.

This raises questions about the applicability of current models of pathology and treatment to other types of traumatic experience occurring in different social, cultural, and political contexts. Many would argue that the response to collective trauma must be collective reconstruction which, as some of the chapters in this volume demonstrate, may be problematic. Although an individual approach to posttraumatic disorders need not preclude this, and may even make it possible by helping individuals whose functioning is impaired, some would argue that the approaches can work at cross-purposes.

There is a wide range of culturally mediated strategies for coping with the dilemmas posed by traumatic events. Explicit talk about traumatic events may be countertherapeutic when talking about the experience is politically dangerous, when other cultural or spiritual coping strategies compete (such as the Buddhist notion of "letting go" or "nonattachment") in order to restore individual and social equilibrium, or when silence itself wields political power and moral authority.

Both clinical and political objections have been raised over the use the PTSD diagnosis for survivors of political violence and torture (Desjarlais, Eisenberg, Good, & Kleinman, 1995). The most consistent concern is that applying a medical label to victims of political repression and torture may pathologize the victim and result in further disempowerment and stigmatization (Bracken, Giller, & Summerfield, 1995; Eisenbruch, 1991; Summerfield, 1999; for counterarguments see Boehnlein & Kinzie, 1995).

As Arthur Kleinman has argued, in order to build bridges between the clinical concerns of subjects and the social contexts in which their experiences and suffering are embedded, we need to focus on "what is at stake" in the lives of individuals and communities (Kleinman, 1999). This type of phenomenological and cultural analysis provides a common ground on which the shared and disparate concerns of anthropologists and psychiatrists can be addressed and potentially integrated. It may point toward unavoidable tensions and trade-offs between the needs of individuals and larger social agendas.

What is at stake for individuals who have suffered trauma is usually much broader than any discrete psychiatric disorder, encompassing social and political dimensions that articulate with individual experience in complex ways. The accounts in this volume illustrate some of the limitations of accounts of trauma produced within the narrow confines of any one discipline. Although the suffering and impairment caused by a discrete traumatic event may be the primary focus for some individuals, in other cases the social, moral, and political dimensions of trauma are paramount, and the crucial questions center on how to make sense of violence and loss and how to rebuild one's life and one's community in the face of stigmatization, discrimination, genocide, or exile. Given this reality, it is striking to find that the psychiatric construct of PTSD continues to guide international treatment programs that are offered to individuals and entire communities who have suffered mass trauma (for critiques see Atlani & Rousseau, 2000; Breslau, 2000).

Trauma may become part of the founding myth and charter of a people. In such cases, keeping trauma alive becomes important for moral and political legitimacy.[20] This social appropriation of trauma to cover a vast array of wrongs creates new niches for sufferers, physicians, and the legal profession. Here we are far from the biology of PTSD, but these social categories and ways of responding to violence and its aftermath feed back into individuals' psychological and physiological responses in what the philosopher Ian Hacking has called "the looping effect" (Hacking, 1995, 1998, 1999). Indeed, these loops between professional diagnostic constructs and everyday understanding occur not only in local systems of health care but also on a global scale.

Stories of trauma can be constructed for different purposes: to guide scientific research; to assign causality, identify responsibility, and apportion blame; to allow individuals to make sense of and get over their fears and suffering; to enable people to live together despite the injuries of the past; or to write a history that informs their identity and warrants the social and moral order. The story that works for one of these purposes may not have the same efficacy for the others. Consequently, there may be no one story that gets it right from biological, clinical, cultural, and political perspectives. We must judge each story in terms of the audience to which it is addressed and the goals it aims to achieve. And yet, stories created for one purpose and told in one context go out into the world to be taken up and used for other ends. We cannot ignore these wider implications of the stories we tell about trauma.

References

Alarcón, R. D., Bell, C. C., Kirmayer, L. J., Lin, K.-H., Ustun, T. B., & Wisner, K. L. (2002). Beyond the funhouse mirrors: Research agenda on culture and psychiatric diagnosis. In D. J. Kupfer, M. B. First, & D. A. Regier (Eds.), *A research agenda for DSM–V* (pp. 219–289). Washington, DC: American Psychiatric Press.

Anggawati, L. (2001). *Di dalam derita manusia membaja*. Klaten: Wisma Sambhodi.

Aron, A. (1992). Testimonio, a bridge between psychotherapy and sociotherapy. *Women & Therapy, 13*(3), 173–189.

Atlani, L., & Rousseau, C. (2000). The politics of culture in humanitarian aid to refugees having experienced sexual violence. *Transcultural Psychiatry, 37*(3), 435–449.

Boehnlein, J. K., & Kinzie, J. D. (1995). Refugee trauma. *Transcultural Psychiatric Research Review, 32*(3), 223–252.

---

[20] For example, Carol Kidron (2005) has described how the experiences of the Holocaust survivors in Israel warrant the very existence of the state. To keep this identity alive, it must be taken on by successive generations. The concept of transmitted PTSD – which conflates the experience of parents or grandparents exposed to the horrors of concentration camps with intrafamilial stressors experienced by their offspring – serves to link the generations in ways that maintain an identity and moral authority for the individual that legitimates the state.

Bracken, P. J., Giller, J. E., & Summerfield, D. (1995). Psychological responses to war and atrocity: The limitations of current concepts. *Social Science & Medicine, 40*(8), 1073–1082.

Breslau, J. (2000). Globalizing disaster trauma: Psychiatry, science, and culture after the Kobe earthquake. *Ethos, 28*(2), 174–197.

Cardeña, E., & Croyle, K. (2005). *Acute reactions to trauma and psychotherapy: A multidisciplinary and international perspective.* Binghamton, NY: Haworth Press.

Cribb, R. (Ed.). 1990. *The Indonesian killings of 1965–1966: Studies from Java and Bali.* Clayton, Victoria, Australia: Centre of Southeast Asian Studies, Monash University.

Desjarlais, R., Eisenberg, L., Good, B., & Kleinman, A. (1995). *World mental health; Problems and priorities in low-income countries.* New York: Oxford University Press.

Douglass, A., & Vogler, T. A. (2003). *Witness and memory: The discourse of trauma.* New York: Routledge.

Eisenbruch, M. (1991). From post-traumatic stress disorder to cultural bereavement: Diagnosis of Southeast Asian refugees. *Social Science & Medicine, 33*(6), 673–680.

Farmer, P. (2003). *Pathologies of power: Health, human rights, and the new war on the poor.* Berkeley: University of California Press.

Freyd, J. J. (1996). *Betrayal trauma: The logic of forgetting childhood abuse.* Cambridge, MA: Harvard University Press.

Gaines, A. D. (1992). From DSM-I to III-R; Voices of self, mastery and the other: A cultural constructivist reading of U.S. psychiatric classification. *Social Science & Medicine, 35*(1), 3–24.

Gathering in the paddies. (1965, November 12). *Time, 86*(12), 17–18.

Groleau, D., & Kirmayer, L. J. (2004). Sociosomatic theory in Vietnamese immigrants' narratives of distress. *Anthropology & Medicine, 11*(2), 117–133.

Hacking, I. (1995). The looping effect of human kinds. In D. Sperber, D. Premack, & A. J. Premack (Eds.), *Causal cognition: A multidisciplinary debate* (pp. 351–383). Oxford, UK: Oxford University Press.

Hacking, I. (1998). *Mad travelers: Reflections on the reality of transient mental ilnesses.* Charlottesville: University Press of Virginia.

Hacking, I. (1999). *The social construction of what?* Cambridge, MA: Harvard University Press.

Hinton, A. (2004). *Why did they kill? Cambodia in the shadow of genocide.* Berkeley: University of California Press.

Kidron, C. A. (2005). Surviving a distant past: A case study of the cultural construction of trauma descendant identity. *Ethos, 31*(4), 513–544.

Kirmayer, L. J. (2005). Culture, context and experience in psychiatric diagnosis. *Psychopathology, 38*(4), 192–196.

Kleinman, A. (1988). *Rethinking psychiatry.* New York: Free Press.

Kleinman, A. (1999). Experience and its moral modes: Culture, human conditions, and disorder. In G. B. Peterson (Ed.), *The Tanner lectures on human values* (Vol. 20, pp. 357–420). Salt Lake City: University of Utah Press.

Lemelson, R. (in press). The spirits, *ngeb* and the social suppression of memory: A complex clinical case from Bali. *Culture, Medicine and Psychiatry.*

López, S., & Guarnaccia, P. J. (2000). Cultural psychopathology: Uncovering the social world of mental illness. *Annual Review of Psychology, 51*, 571–598.

Lustig, S. L., Weine, S. M., Saxe, G. N., & Beardslee, W. R. (2004). Testimonial psychotherapy for adolescent refugees: A case series. *Transcultural Psychiatry, 41*(1), 31–45.

McNally, R. J. (2003). *Remembering trauma.* Cambridge, MA: Belknap Press of Harvard University Press.

Merckelbach, H., & Jelicic, M. (2004). Dissociative symptoms are related to endorsement of vague trauma items. *Comprehensive Psychiatry, 45*(1), 70–75.

Noer, A. C. (Director). (1985). *"Pengkhianatan G 30 S/ PKI"* [film]. Perum Produksi Film Negara.

Robinson, G. (1998). *The dark side of paradise: Political violence in Bali.* Ithaca, NY: Cornell University Press.

Scheper-Hughes, N. (2005). *Getting over: The politics of the impossible in new South Africa.* Unpublished manuscript, University of California, Berkeley.

Summerfield, D. (1999). A critique of seven assumptions behind psychological trauma programmes in war-affected areas. *Social Science & Medicine, 48*(10), 1449–1462.

Wieringa, S. (2003). The birth of the New Order State in Indonesia: Sexual politics and nationalism. *Journal of Women's History, 15*(1), 70–91.

Wikan, U. (1990). *Managing turbulent hearts: A Balinese formula for living.* Chicago: University of Chicago Press.

Young, A. (1995). *The harmony of illusions: Inventing posttraumatic stress disorder.* Princeton, NJ: Princeton University Press.

Zurbuchen, M. S. (2005). *Beginning to remember: The past in the Indonesian present.* Seattle, WA: University of Washington Press.

Epilogue: Trauma and the Vicissitudes of Interdisciplinary Integration

Laurence J. Kirmayer, Robert Lemelson, and Mark Barad

The chapters in this volume emerged from a series of workshops and a conference organized by the Foundation for Psychocultural Research that sought to bring neuroscientists, clinicians, and anthropologists together to address a common object of study and a common set of questions. We assumed that each disciplinary perspective and research program had something to contribute to a comprehensive view of the problem of trauma. We hoped that this encounter would lead to creative exchange – and some significant steps toward the integration of diverse models and levels of explanation.

In modest ways this integration occurred. In some cases, the integration reflected a preexisting connection between two disciplines. For example, the approach to treating PTSD symptoms by exposure, as advocated by Yadin and Foa, is based directly on the procedures and results of extinction learning, which the authors in Section I have begun to explain in terms of neuropsychological, physiological, and molecular mechanisms.

In other cases this effort made tentative new links. For example, the role of narrative in traumatic experience cuts across disciplines. This reflects the central importance of narrativity in human experience.[1] Stories of suffering anchored in bodily experience, overarching cultural models, and ideologies of the person are all grist for the clinical encounter, and the transformation of narratives is a means both of effecting psychological

---

[1] There is a rich tradition in philosophy and psychology that understands the self as a narrative construction; see Bruner (1990), Freeman (1993), Kirby (1991), McAdams, Josselson, and Lieblich, (2006), Schechtman (1996), and Taylor (1989). For a critique that emphasizes non-narrative bases of identity and action, see Strawson (2004).

Even biological research is presented in narrative form, shaped by the narrative conventions of science, presenting evidence and argument in a standard form to create a coherent story that fits (or, less often, challenges) dominant paradigms. Hence, the cultural critique of biology aims to uncover these narrative forms to show how biological research is shaped by cultural values and concerns.

change and of reconnecting the individual to his or her social and cultural contexts. The neurophysiology of fear conditioning and extinction inscribes a rudimentary narrative structure on brain and body that interacts with more elaborate cultural templates to give rise to autobiographical memories and narratives of oneself as victim, survivor, or resilient thriver.

Learning theory and evolutionary biology suggest another way of looking at the pathological nature of trauma in terms of the appropriateness of response. Fear, avoidance, hypervigilance, and autonomic arousal all have adaptive functions when they are appropriately attached to specific stimuli and elicited at the right time and place. Appropriate fear is part of an evolutionarily adaptive system designed to help us recognize, remember, and avoid dangerous situations. Inappropriate fear occurs when this response is attached to events that are not dangerous. This can happen through dysfunction of the fear system; as an inevitable consequence of its normal functioning (through mechanisms of generalization and association); or, independently of the status of the underlying learning systems, when external circumstances change. For animals, inappropriateness can be understood in terms of an imbalance between seeking safety and other basic needs to forage, feed, and reproduce. Clinically, inappropriateness is identified as excessive withdrawal and fear in an environment that is judged by others to be safe. Socially, fear may be inappropriate because it does not fit with cultural styles of coping and self-presentation. Of course, fear may be appropriate but still damaging when it prevents the individual from acting to correct injustices or imbalances of power that give rise to violence. The notion of appropriateness then can be understood in terms of ever larger contexts of experience, requiring different levels of description that correspond to social, cultural, and political discourses.

Finally, there were ways in which the hoped-for integration did not materialize. This reflected the limited state of current knowledge, the lack of representation at the conference of scholars working at some of the intermediate levels of explanation (e.g., cognitive psychology and cognitive neuroscience) needed to bridge the different levels of organization, and the tendency for all of us to stay within the bounds of the disciplines to which we belong. In this epilogue, we consider some of the obstacles to interdisciplinary exchange.

DISCIPLINE BOUND

What lessons can be learned from this encounter among disciplines? First, interdisciplinary discussions are difficult. Each discipline uses markedly different styles of reasoning, rhetoric, and presentation. For example, the anthropologists seemed nonplussed at the inevitability of bullet points, graphs, and tables in the neuroscience presentations, whereas the neuroscientists were frustrated by the uncharted narratives that unfolded as the anthropologists read their papers. More fundamentally, however, the disciplines differ in their assessment of what constitutes an interesting question and what counts as evidence or answer.[2] These differences are so great that some would argue that these disciplines are based on paradigms that occupy different universes of discourse that simply cannot be reconciled. We wondered whether these disciplines involve constructs that are truly incommensurable or whether there was some way to bring them together around a common issue or concern like trauma – a notion basic to the strategy of "triangulation" in mixed-methods research.

There is, of course, a genre of popular scientific writing that makes a shotgun wedding between wildly different paradigms or leaps across levels of explanation in a single bound. Sometimes this is based on noticing analogies or extending metaphors far beyond their original domain. Although such cross-domain metaphors are the very stuff of creativity, scientific and otherwise (Dunbar, 1995, 1997), in less than careful hands they may lead to vague generalities, which offer little new insight or testable hypotheses. Our aim here was something more substantial: a serious encounter and dialogue between neurobehavioral scientists, clinicians, and anthropologists.

This encounter required new ways of listening. It asked researchers, clinicians, and scholars to step outside the boundaries of their disciplines, with their tacit knowledge, technical vocabulary, and styles of argument, to make their assumptions explicit to others and seek points of contact,

---

[2] Even citation styles vary markedly across disciplines. Each shapes its own way of reading, organizing, interpreting, and remembering. With the aim of making this book more accessible and readable, we have adopted one style. Imposing a single style, however, changes the way we read and may subtly privilege certain disciplinary assumptions about knowledge.

For example, the author and date in-text style of the American Psychological Association encourages us to think about knowledge as tied to specific people and studies located in time; this gives them authority and a defining moment, and helps to construct a map of knowledge creation and intellectual positions centred around individuals. The sheer number of names listed when multiple studies are cited creates a numerical sense of the weight of evidence. When the dates are recent, they suggest we are reporting evidence from the cutting edge; when older, they create a sense of the pace of progress.

In the social sciences and humanities, the order of authors' names reflects their relative contribution to the work, whereas the convention in biosciences is to put the laboratory director's name last. This requires that we look at the long list of names to find the "source" of the ideas (this, of course, reflects a hierarchy of power and prestige within the laboratory or academic institution as well). One must be in the know to identify the work as coming from "the Fleming lab" when the first author is a student, postdoctoral fellow, or junior colleague. In contrast, when references are buried in a dense footnote, as is common in history and humanities, we are encouraged to think about knowledge as occurring in a community of contention, with one author commenting on or reinterpreting the same events. Again, the length of the note suggests the depth of scholarship, but no simple numerical count of authors is readily at hand and dates are less conspicuous. Older work may be given a weight comparable to more recent studies.

bridging concepts and models that would situate their own constructs within and across multiple levels of explanation.

The examples of survivors of war, genocide, assault, domestic violence, and other forms of trauma provided specific objects of study that allowed the conversation to begin, but the object constituted by one disciplinary perspective could be contested and destabilized by critiques from another perspective. For example, the construct of PTSD depends on attributions of causality that are shaped by social and psychological processes of mimesis, so that reasons (culturally intelligible explanations) cannot be separated from cause (Young, 1995). The biological research on trauma insists that behind all the biographical details and rhetorical claims that emphasize individual and cultural differences, one can discern a common pattern of fear, avoidance, and stress response. The very notion of trauma as a distinctive sort of event depends on the sense that it is out of the ordinary, but the evolutionary and cross-cultural view advanced by Konner shows the ubiquity of potentially traumatic events and calls into question the clinical assumption that stress and trauma are primarily sources of pathology. This contest of disciplinary perspectives can be clarified and sometimes resolved by exploring the contexts in which specific constructs were used.

DISCIPLINARY CONTEXTS AND COMMITMENTS

As the contributions to this volume make clear, the contexts in which traumatic experiences occur and are later interpreted, constructed, and represented by survivors, researchers, and clinicians vary markedly. To understand these contexts one needs to consider not only theoretical and methodological differences between the disciplines, but also the practical considerations and constraints each discipline places on its practitioners. These commitments and constraints, though central to each discipline's methodology and identity, may present obstacles to interdisciplinary work.

One contextual difference between the disciplines lies in the choice of subjects. In many cases anthropologists have "samples of convenience" that arise from the situated context of their particular fieldwork site. Usually, these are time-limited engagements, with populations that are determined by the anthropologist's personal interests or preferences for particular types of informants and by a host of logistical constraints. Some ethnographic research involves clinical populations and settings, where anthropologists collaborate with psychiatrists or other clinicians. However, because of their interest in social and cultural processes, anthropologists often conduct research that involves other members of the family and community. In contrast, psychiatric research, with its individualistic focus, often does not include sources of data from family members and rarely considers the perspectives of members of the extended social networks of clan or community.

In the basic sciences, the subjects are most often animals, rather than human beings. They are usually studied in laboratory settings to maximize control over all the variables that are not the immediate object of study. Finally, the protocols themselves are very much simplified; for example, in the case of modeling fearful experiences, studies use relatively mild stimuli, both for procedural and ethical reasons, which differ markedly from the life-threatening trauma suffered by the populations of interest to both anthropologists and clinicians.

DISCIPLINARY GOALS AND TASKS

Another fundamental difference is found in the goals of each discipline. On the most obvious level, psychiatric practice is concerned with relieving suffering and treating disease and distress. Increasingly, mental health practitioners treat ethnically and culturally diverse populations, and those who work with survivors of trauma may encounter a broad range of experiences ranging from state terror and torture, to forms of collective trauma involving ethnic and religious violence, to displaced person and war-related trauma, to forms of gendered violence. Working with diverse populations compels one to come up with a practical framework that reduces the apparent diversity of these populations to a smaller set of problems that can be recognized and treated with existing resources and techniques. This tends to push practitioners toward an assumption of universality.

On the other hand, anthropologists make their living identifying new and distinctive modes of being and experience and so put a premium on difference. Anthropologists aim to provide thick descriptions, to invoke as much context as is needed to adequately frame the webs of significance in which their subjects are situated. In terms of trauma, this means they need to look beyond the clinical context with its emphasis on diagnosing and treating suffering individuals. Indeed, only a relatively small number of anthropologists focus on individuals' suffering as their primary concern.[3] Instead, anthropological inquiry aims to locate the individual in relation to larger social and cultural contexts and to document, describe, and understand social processes at the level of local worlds, cultural communities, or more global systems.

In relation to the human experience of trauma, the goal of the basic neuroscientist is to discern what is universal, not only within the species, but

---

[3] However, this has been an important strand in medical anthropology, exemplified by the work of Arthur Kleinman (1988, 1999). A focus on individual experience is more common in psychological anthropology, where a variety of approaches have been brought to bear, most recently with experience-near ethnography (Hollan, 1997).

also to a large extent across different species. Such researchers work with the assumption that one mouse is much the same as another (at least of the same strain) and do everything possible to make that true, for example, by inbreeding so that every mouse in a given strain has exactly the same genetic complement. Moreover, they assume that the brains of mice and men – as mammals separated by evolution less than 100 million years ago and sharing well over 90% of their DNA sequences as well as every identifiable structural component of their brains – function in similar ways.[4] Many neuroscientists do not look for the pathological extremes of individual animal behavior but rather focus on the behavior of the normal animal under relatively physiological conditions, in an attempt to understand the normal function and regulation of the brain.[5]

A key area where anthropologist, psychiatrist, and neuroscientist diverge is in the consideration of context and meaning. The central task of the clinician is to help or heal the individual, and social context usually is considered only as potential aid or hindrance to that endeavor. A central task of the psychological anthropologist is to "think through others" to understand the world from the native's point of view. This involves not merely an exploration of the individual's modes of experience, and how a particular disorder expresses itself in that individual, but rather an understanding of the ways in which the individual is embedded in social and cultural systems of meaning and practice. The neuroscientist does everything possible to control the context in order to throw into relief the effect of the experimental manipulation under study. Indeed, for many neuroscientists the concept of "meaning" is a vague generality that can be replaced by more precise notions of cause and effect in neural systems interacting with an environment.[6]

---

[4] Of course, this is only a working assumption. The mouse brain is largely devoted to olfaction and spatial orientation and this is reflected in its anatomy (Kaas, 2005). There are many species-specific behaviors and capacities, and the similarities in genomes across species only show that even proportionally small changes in the genome may have profound effects on structure and function (Marks, 2002).

[5] There is, of course, an approach within animal and human research that studies pathological conditions both as an objective of interest in itself and as a way to understand normal functioning. Indeed, some of the basic methods of neuroscience research involve creating pathological conditions by lesions of the nervous system, abnormal forms of stimulation (electrical or pharmacological), and genetic manipulations. But caution is required in interpreting these results because one cannot assume that the way the brain functions when damaged directly reveals its usual modes of functioning when intact.

[6] A rapprochement between the meaning-centered constructs of anthropology and this type of neuroscientific explanation can be found in the notion that meaning resides in the relationship between organism and environment (MacKay, 1969). Hence, researchers who examine the way organism–environment interactions shift over time are, in effect, studying the meaning of stimuli or events. However, the higher order meanings that occupy much of human discourse and cognition depend on the self-referential capacities of language and cannot be captured by animal models.

All of these differences raise crucial questions, which cut across disciplinary boundaries. How much of the response to trauma is universal, embedded in the fundamental physiology of the brain by mammalian and human evolution? To what extent can the human capacity for self-reflection and self-control through cognition and social interaction reshape these basic responses? How much context must be considered to get an accurate account of how a particular trauma has affected a person's experience and subjectivity? How much do we need to know about the trauma itself, its local interpretation and meaning, its historical context, and its various impacts on a person's life in order to provide a "good enough" account for any given purpose?

VARIETIES OF REDUCTIONIST EXPERIENCE

Remarkable progress has been made in dissecting the molecular mechanisms of emotion and of memory. Neuroscience has made these gains by adopting a strategy of methodological reductionism: Carefully controlled experimental work on the molecular building blocks of the nervous system has yielded hard facts about our brains and bodies with broad areas of consensus, powerful explanatory theories, and an advancing frontier where elegant methods are available to design experiments that can test hypotheses and resolve disputes. Medical science shares much of this technology and can, through clinical research (including clinical epidemiology, case-control studies, and randomized clinical trials), identify meaningful diagnostic constructs and evidence-based practices. The power, scope, and speed of this progress can lead to impatience with the vagueness, self-criticism, and contradictions of social sciences. Although for some anthropologists reductionism is among the cardinal sins to be avoided at all costs in theory and practice, as a methodological strategy, reductionism can lead to fundamental insights not attainable with other approaches.

It is crucial, however, to distinguish between reductionism as a methodological strategy of decomposing complex systems into simpler components for close study and the more sweeping reductionist claim that no knowledge of higher order levels of organization is necessary to understand a complex system. This latter form of reductionism is much harder to justify. Indeed, the very fact that neuroscientists work at many levels to study molecular mechanisms, cellular function, neural networks, and regional brain function testifies to the need to use multiple levels of description and explanation – each with their own technical methods and language – to explain human behavior.[7] The hierarchical organization of

---

[7] The inadequacy of reductionistic explanations is readily apparent when transposed to other domains. For example, while it is possible (theoretically) to describe an earthquake in terms of the movement of individual atoms this will not yield an adequate explanation of the geological phenomena better understood in terms of plate tectonics (Gold & Stoljar, 1999).

human behavior does not end at the boundaries of the skin. There may be feedback connections or looping effects between biology and culture so that the biological underpinnings of behavior are affected by processes of meaning making and social positioning, both over the time span of a human life and the evolutionary *longue durée*.[8]

The notion of a hierarchy of levels of organization in the biological world (from molecules to cells, neural circuits or systems, brains, persons, social groups, communities, and social and political entities) provides a natural way to locate and coordinate specific discourses and search for correspondences and interactions across levels. In this hierarchy, lower levels are not more basic or fundamental because each new level has new structures and dynamics that emerge owing to its organization (Mainzer, 2004; Morowitz, 2002). Hence, higher levels of organization are not reducible to lower levels, and each requires its own language of description and level of explanation.

To understand behavior and experience, therefore, we need a biology that goes beyond reductionist models to consider the dynamics of complex interacting systems that, in the case of human beings, extend outside the individual to include the social world (Henningsen & Kirmayer, 2000; Wexler, 2006). For example, the predicament of refugees movingly portrayed by David Kinzie and other contributors to this volume typically involves both terror and loss, with the disruption of whole communities (Eisenbruch, 1991). Approaching this solely in terms of animal models of fear seems profoundly reductionistic. So does approaching it exclusively through models of attachment and other aspects of social behavior, as studied by Stephen Suomi and his colleagues in monkeys (Suomi, 2003) and by Michael Meaney and his colleagues in rats (Bagot et al., this volume; Meaney & Syf, 2005). We can come a step closer to the complexity of human experience, however, by considering how systems involved in fear learning (which lead to avoidance) and extinction (which allows reengagement) interact with systems involved in attachment and loss, or with those systems involved in anger and aggression. There will be complex emergent neural and behavioral dynamics when two or more brain systems interact. But the central role of narrativity and self-reflection in human experience is not captured by animal models, which therefore remain insufficient to explain some of the most basic causes and consequences of human suffering.

NARRATIVE, MEANING, AND MECHANISM

Neurobiology suggests a sort of protonarrative for trauma that may influence individuals' accounts of their experiences, but illness narratives draw

---

[8] This possibility follows from current work in developmental systems theory. See Oyama (2000) and Oyama, Griffiths, and Gray (2001).

from the whole span of the person's biography and from the larger social context, which provides cultural and historical depth and resonance to every idiosyncratic detail. The ruptures and intrusions that may characterize the organization of memory and behavior in the wake of trauma can be papered over by cultural templates for what is salient, important, or even intelligible and what can and should be ignored. Equally, narrative templates provided by cultural authorities and institutions, or implicit in discursive practices, may lead individuals to think about and tell their stories in ways that fit the expectations of others. The influence of culture is never complete, but it is powerful enough to create real tensions or to provide substantial resolution and relief.

For clinicians, the models of basic and clinical science provide a way to map human suffering, identifying specific problems for which some remedy can be offered and applied. Clinicians try to relate their patients' idiosyncratic stories to the generic accounts supplied by medical diagnoses, which aim to provide an account in terms of causal mechanisms, but for clinicians who listen closely, there are inevitably aspects of their patients' stories that do not fit any simple causal model. This occurs because any illness experience is embedded in cognitive and social processes of meaning making and adaptation that may provide solutions or may themselves come to constitute additional clinical problems. In recognition of the central role of meaning making in human experience, there is a move in contemporary biomedicine to complement the current emphasis on evidence-based practice with narrative-based attention to the details of a person's life (Greenhalgh, 1999; Greenhalgh & Hurwitz, 1998; Haidet & Paterniti, 2003; Hurwitz, Greenhalgh, & Skultans, 2004).

Illness narratives and medical reasoning are powerfully shaped by prevalent cultural models. Both patients and clinicians from Western societies are strongly influenced by the cultural values of individualism. These tend to situate human problems and their solutions entirely within the heads or the brains of individuals. This emphasis, though appropriate for many problems, and even liberating or empowering at times, gives short shrift to the social embedding of human experience. The social sciences offer ways to understand this embedding both as a developmental process through which the physical and social environment shape the brain and in terms of ongoing interactions among people in families, communities, and social institutions – with each level of organization having its own dynamics and requiring a different language of description and explanation (Turner, 2002; Wexler, 2006).

Within anthropology proper, taking seriously the nosological systems of psychiatry has been a difficult, and at times a disparaged, enterprise. Most attempts in medical and psychological anthropology to examine personal experience and subjectivity in relation to social suffering do not attempt to compare or link the subjects' experience with psychiatric diagnostic categories. When psychiatric diagnoses are mentioned, it is often to insist on their culturally and historically situated nature and to reveal their embedding in hegemonic cultural and professional values.

This anthropological critique has been valuable in exposing many of the historical and cultural assumptions implicit in psychiatric research. Does this mean, though, that these categories have especially limited explanatory or heuristic value? If so, what is the most effective way to mediate between the clinical concern for helping people suffering from the effects of trauma and the theoretical and conceptual effort to "get it right" from cultural or critical perspectives? Is it possible to construct an account of trauma that balances the need for clinical effectiveness, grounded in part on neuroscience research on fear and its extinction, with providing an accurate sociohistorical account? Or does the effort to construct a more comprehensive account stand in the way of more modest, partial explanations that effectively serve our immediate purposes?[9]

The case histories presented in the chapters by Kinzie and Lemelson and colleagues reflect stories collected over extended periods of time. The stories have changed and become more complex, not only as each person's own self-understanding has changed, along with the theories and assumptions of his or her interlocutors, but also as the surrounding social and political climates have shifted. Every story is told to someone in a specific context and for a particular set of purposes. The different stories may converge at times, only to diverge again in response to new exigencies. One conclusion might be that an overarching account cannot be constructed, that the processes identified in these differing accounts and the stories themselves interact in complex ways that shift over time so that there can be no fixed, final and inclusive story.

Many stories of trauma can be told, and the larger questions concern in what setting and for what purposes they are told. The stories themselves are embedded in multiple contexts, and our way of reading them is shaped by particular aims we have in mind, as a clinician (concerned with therapeutic efficacy), as an anthropologist (concerned with generating thick descriptions), as a biologist (concerned with designing experiments to identify clear and unambiguous mechanisms), or even as a people or a nation using traumatic events to establish an authoritative history and collective identity.

---

[9] In clinical work in cultural consultation, anthropologist consultants have sometimes produced accounts that were far too rich and complex to provide an effective guide for clinicians. The clinician is like a gem cutter looking for the fault line where a single tap will expose a new facet. Anthropologists working with our team have had to learn to consider the clinician's obligation to act, with limited time and resources, and simplify and prioritize their case formulation to help identify potentially effective interventions (Kirmayer, Groleau, Guzder, Blake, & Jarvis, 2003).

Each of these stories has its own discursive domain. Problems arise, however, when they are presented as totalizing explanations or interpreted as the whole story. The tendency to reduce the many-stranded complexity of human phenomena to one or another story reflects both our cognitive limitations (the difficulty of thinking in terms of interactions among multiple levels or dimensions) and the power and politics of specific interests that seek to advance an authoritative account.

CONCLUSION: DISCIPLINES UNBOUND

This book is a contribution toward a cultural biology and a biosocial anthropology that is pertinent to clinical concerns. It recognizes that multiple levels of description, or disciplinary languages, are needed to encompass the complexity of the phenomena of trauma and healing. Though we may use the notion of living in different (culturally constituted) worlds to emphasize the divergence, distance, and uncertainty of others' experience, as embedded in culturally different ways of life, in the end we live in one world – a statement not so much of metaphysics or ontology, but of ethics and pragmatics: ethics, because we must find ways to live together, respecting our marked differences; pragmatics, because, from a clinical perspective, what counts is what helps alleviate or make sense of suffering.

The clinical relevance of this interdisciplinary work is threefold. First, it offers a more comprehensive view of the processes at work in the individual response to trauma. This more complete model allows the clinician to consider a wider range of issues that may contribute to individuals' suffering and that may offer strategies and resources for healing and recovery.

Second, the interdisciplinary work challenges the nature of clinical evidence. Increasingly, clinicians are enjoined to base their practices on scientific evidence. But often this amounts to drawing from a literature that is constrained by narrow definitions of problems and highly selected treatments that have been investigated because they fit some preconceived theoretical notion or, still more tendentiously, represent an opportunity for economic profit. The pharmaceutical industry, in particular, is waiting in the wings for evidence that some medication can help with the treatment of trauma-related syndromes because this will allow them to expand the market for their products dramatically. Evidence is not produced in a neutral and value-free process of scientific inquiry but emerges from highly contentious political and economically motivated programs of research that, whatever their ideological underpinnings, always produce partial knowledge with a particular slant.

Beyond this, disciplinary differences reflect not only different methods but also more profound differences in epistemology or assumptions about how to generate knowledge and what counts as evidence or even as an important question and a satisfying answer. Rather than critiquing the benefits and limitations of each discipline, we want simply to acknowledge that each perspective opens up possibilities for inquiry. When multiple disciplines come together around a common object of inquiry, that object is revealed to be more intricate than any one discipline can characterize or contain.

Recognizing the differences in what each discipline finds in a many-facetted construct like trauma can uncover the hidden assumptions of the discipline's terminology and technology. This cross-disciplinary critique may destabilize the construct and suggest a new and more precise conceptual vocabulary. However, this does not imply that one discipline can simply sweep away the misguided conceptualizations of another, to replace them with its own more enlightened or sophisticated account. More likely, it will lead us to appreciate the multiple dimensions of a complex reality, while refining the use of our own disciplinary tools and perspectives.

The interdisciplinarity we advocate extends beyond the sciences to include social, cultural, political, and ethical analyses. The narratives that guide scientific research enjoy great authority in Western discourse but do not provide moral guidance. For that we need other ways of thinking through the stories of trauma to their moral and ethical implications. To see this clearly, consider the following dilemmas.

Research on the memory for traumatic events suggests that some of the vividness conferred on those memories by horror can be blocked by drugs, raising the prospect that disorders like PTSD could be prevented by treating soldiers going into battle, for example, with beta-blockers (which block neurotransmission mediated by noradrenaline) (Baard, 2003). What are the social consequences of reducing the vividness or salience of memories for traumatic events? Might preventing the distress of individual soldiers by blocking their memories of battle rob society of some necessary awareness of the horrors of war and, ultimately, of passionate activists who work to avoid future conflict? Although an ethic of autonomy and human rights might argue that individuals should remain free to follow their own paths, when a society as a whole chooses to forget the consequence may be a moral abyss.

Of course, asking people to carry memories or scars as witness to a terrible past "lest we forget" may be no less oppressive than silencing them before they have had a chance to think about or tell others their stories. Whether societies encourage or suppress individuals' stories of trauma, there is an inherent tension between what may be helpful or damaging for the individual and what serves larger social, cultural, and political values. To think through this dilemma, we need ways of identifying the trade-offs between actions and outcomes at different levels. The notion of social suffering offered by medical anthropology is too imprecise to take us far along this path (Das, 2001; Kleinman, Das, & Lock, 1997).

The research reported in Part I of this volume suggests one way to begin to reframe this problem with more precision. As discussed in the chapters by Bouton and Waddell; Quirk, Milad, Santini, and Lebrón; and Barad and Cain, extinction of fear after a traumatic event does not erase the memory of that event but inhibits or suppresses it with a new memory of safety. In this model, the memory of traumatic events may remain intact, whereas the devastating emotional cost of that memory to the individual can be reduced. The testimony of those who have suffered can then contribute to the historical consciousness and moral life of the community, while the individual who is not driven by excessive pain, anger, or avoidance helps to create an environment of safety.

Recent history shows that the memory of past horrors is not often a bulwark against future violence; rather, it may be used to provoke intense anger and justify hatred toward others. Collective memories of genocide may weld a people together and make individuals more empathic toward other peoples who face a similar fate. But when personal or collective identity is centered on this history, it may also create feelings of being uniquely damaged, marked, and morally elevated and so foster intolerance or even hatred and desire for revenge. Mitigating the intensity of emotional pain that follows from trauma and loss is crucial to allow individuals, communities, and whole societies to find that combination of forgiving and remembering that allows learning from the past and opening toward a more hopeful, tolerant, and compassionate future.[10] To place these processes of reconstructing collective and community life at the center of local and global responses to trauma, we must move beyond the boundaries of academic disciplines and clinical professions to reflect on our predicament with the widest range of conceptual resources at hand. Ultimately, this will allow us to replace the metaphor of trauma with more precise language that captures the specificity of each predicament and points us toward the most humane and effective response.

References

Baard, E. (2003). The guilt-free solder: New science raises the specter of a world without regret. *Village Voice*, January 22. Retrieved June 20, 2006, from http://www.villagevoice.com/news/0304,baard,41331,1.html.

Bruner, J. (1990). *Acts of meaning*. Cambridge, MA: Harvard University Press.

Das, V. (Ed.). (2001). *Remaking a world: Violence, social suffering, and recovery*. Berkeley: University of California Press.

Dunbar, K. (1995). How scientists really reason: Scientific reasoning in real-world laboratories. In R. J. Sternberg & J. Davidson (Eds.), *Insight*. Cambridge, MA: MIT Press.

[10] On memory and forgiveness, see Margalit (2002), Schimmel (2002), and Jankélévitch (2005).

Dunbar, K. (1997). How scientists think: Online creativity and conceptual change in science. In T. B. Ward, S. M. Smith, & S. Vaid (Eds.), *Conceptual structures and processes: Emergence, discovery and change*. Washington, DC: APA Press.

Eisenbruch, M. (1991). From post-traumatic stress disorder to cultural bereavement: Diagnosis of Southeast Asian refugees. *Social Science & Medicine, 33*(6), 673–680.

Freeman, M. (1993). *Rewriting the self: History, memory, narrative*. London: Routledge.

Gold, I., & Stoljar, D. (1999). A neuron doctrine in the philosophy of neuroscience. *Behavioural and Brain Sciences, 22*, 809–830.

Greenhalgh, T. (1999). Narrative based medicine: Narrative based medicine in an evidence based world. *British Medical Journal, 318*(7179), 323–325.

Greenhalgh, T., & Hurwitz, B. (Eds.). (1998). *Narrative based medicine: Dialogue and discourse in clinical practice*. London: BMJ Publishing Group.

Haidet, P., & Paterniti, D. A. (2003). "Building" a history rather than "taking" one: A perspective on information sharing during the medical interview. *Archives of Internal Medicine, 163*(10), 1134–1140.

Henningsen, P., & Kirmayer, L. J. (2000). Mind beyond the net: Implications of cognitive neuroscience for cultural psychiatry. *Transcultural Psychiatry, 37*(4), 467–494.

Hollan, D. (1997). The relevance of person-centered ethnography to cross-cultural psychiatry. *Transcultural Psychiatry, 34*(2), 219–234.

Hurwitz, B., Greenhalgh, T., & Skultans, V. (2004). *Narrative research in health and illness*. Malden, MA: BMJ Books.

Jankélévitch, V. (2005). *Forgiveness*. Chicago: University of Chicago Press.

Kaas, J. H. (2005). From mice to men: The evolution of the large, complex human brain. *Journal of Bioscience, 30*(2), 155–165.

Kirby, A. P. (1991). *Narrative and the self*. Bloomington: Indiana University Press.

Kirmayer, L. J., Groleau, D., Guzder, J., Blake, C., & Jarvis, E. (2003). Cultural consultation: A model of mental health service for multicultural societies. *Canadian Journal of Psychiatry, 48*(2), 145–153.

Kleinman, A. (1988). *The illness narratives*. New York: Basic Books.

Kleinman, A. (1999). Experience and its moral modes: Culture, human conditions, and disorder. In G. B. Peterson (Ed.), *The Tanner lectures on human values* (Vol. 20, pp. 357–420). Salt Lake City: University of Utah Press.

Kleinman, A., Das, V., & Lock, M. M. (Eds.). (1997). *Social suffering*. Berkeley: University of California Press.

MacKay, D. M. (1969). *Information, mechanism and meaning*. Cambridge, MA: MIT Press.

Mainzer, K. (2004). *Thinking in complexity: Tthe computational dynamics of matter, mind, and mankind*. New York: Springer.

Margalit, A. (2002). *The ethics of memory*. Cambridge, MA: Harvard University Press.

Marks, J. (2002). *What it means to be 98% chimpanzee: Apes, people, and their genes*. Berkeley: University of California Press.

McAdams, D. P., Josselson, R., & Lieblich, A. (2006). *Identity and story: Creating self in narrative*. Washington, DC: American Psychological Association.

Meaney, M. J., & Szyf, M. (2005). Maternal care as a model for experience-dependent chromatin plasticity? *Trends in Neuroscience, 28*(9), 456–463.

Morowitz, H. J. (2002). *The emergence of everything: How the world became complex*. New York: Oxford University Press.

Oyama, S. (2000). *Evolution's eye: A systems view of the biology-culture divide*. Durham, NC: Duke University Press.

Oyama, S., Griffiths, P. E., & Gray, R. D. (Eds.). (2001). *Cycles of contingency: Developmental systems and evolution*. Cambridge, MA: MIT Press.

Schechtman, M. (1996). *The constitution of selves*. Ithaca, NY: Cornell University Press.

Schimmel, S. (2002). *Wounds not healed by time: The power of repentance and forgiveness*. New York: Oxford University Press.

Strawson, G. (2004). Against narrativity. *Ratio, 17*(4), 428–452.

Suomi, S. J. (2003). Gene-environment interactions and the neurobiology of social conflict. *Annals of the New York Academy of Sciences,1008*, 132–139.

Taylor, C. (1989). *Sources of the self: The making of modern identity*. Cambridge, MA: Harvard University Press.

Turner, S. P. (2002). *Brains/practices/relativism: Social theory after cognitive science*. Chicago: University of Chicago Press.

Young, A. (1995). Reasons and causes for post-traumatic stress disorder. *Transcultural Psychiatric Research Review, 32*(3), 287–298.

Wexler, B. (2006). Brain and culture: Neurobiology, ideology, and social change. Cambridge, MA: MIT Press.

Glossary

Acetylcholine: A neurotransmitter.

Acoustic startle response: The reflex muscular response to an unexpected stimulus, such as a sudden noise. In rats this unconditioned response can be measured by the force of their jumps.

Adrenal cortex: The portion of the adrenal gland that produces cortisol.

Adrenergic: Depending on the neurotransmitters epinephrine (adrenaline) or norepiphine (noradrenaline).

Adrenocorticotropin hormone (ACTH): A hormone released by the pituitary gland in response to corticotropin-releasing factor (CRF), which stimulates the production of cortisol by the adrenal cortex.

Agonist: A drug that increases the activity of a receptor.

Amygdala: A group of connected nuclei in the anterior temporal lobe, which regulates emotional responses including fear.

Antagonist: A drug that that decreases the activity of a receptor.

Anterior cingulate cortex: A region of the frontal cortex that is near to the midline and to deep, noncortical structures.

Autonomic nervous system (ANS): The part of the vertebrate nervous system that innervates smooth muscles and glands, and regulates unconscious processes such as secretion, digestion, blood pressure, and the speed and power of heart contractions.

Bed nucleus of the stria terminalis (BNST): A nucleus (anatomically identifiable group of brain cells) located in the main output tract of the amygdala.

Benzodiazepines: A class of drugs that act as agonists on GABA$_A$ receptors, used to prevent seizures and reduce anxiety.

Beta-adrenergic receptors: The beta subtypes of the norepinephrine/noradrenaline receptor.

Beta-blocker: An antagonist of the beta subtypes of the norepinephrine receptor.

Brain-derived neurotrophic factor (BDNF): A small peptide that acts as a growth hormone for the developing brain and as a neurotransmitter in the adult brain.

Calcium channel: A molecule in the cell membrane that admits calcium into cells under regulation of a ligand (e.g., a neurotransmitter) or of changes in the electrical potential of the cell.

cAMP-response-element–binding protein (CREB): A transcription factor, that is, a protein that regulates the copying of a gene in the DNA into an RNA, which can then be "translated" into a protein.

Cognitive behavioral therapy (CBT): A structured form of psychotherapy that combines elements of cognitive therapy (which examines explicit assumptions about the individual and the world) and behavior therapy (which involves systematic alterations of behavior, often by exposing anxious people to feared cues in order to generate extinction of the fear response).

Consolidation: The stage during which a new memory becomes permanent.

Conditional mutant: A mutation engineered in a mouse that can be turned on and off by experimental manipulations, such as giving the animal a drug.

Conditioned (or conditional) stimulus: A stimulus, initially neutral (i.e., evokes no response), which can be conditioned to evoke a response by pairing it with an unconditioned stimulus (a stimulus that intrinsically evokes a response).

Corticotropin-releasing factor (CRF): A peptide and neurotransmitter released by cells in the brain. Among other functions, it ultimately stimulates the release of cortisol by the adrenal cortex.

Counterconditioning: Training an animal to associate a conditioned stimulus with a new unconditioned stimulus of the opposite valence to that used in the original conditioning. For example, an animal first trained to fear a cue by pairing with a shock can be counterconditioned by pairing that cue with food.

Cross-fostering: Transferring the offspring of a mother with one characteristic to a mother with a different characteristic for rearing.

Dendrite (dendritic branching): The receptive portion of a neuron, which often has the appearance of branches of a tree.

Depolarization: Neurons are strongly polarized at rest; that is, they are electrically negative compared to the outside of the cell. When stimulated by an excitatory neurotransmitter they become more positive in potential, or "depolarize."

Dopamine: A neurotransmitter.

Downregulation: A decrease in the sensitivity of a receptor to a neurotransmitter, often by a decrease in receptor number at the synapse.

Endogenous opoids: Neurotransmitters produced by neurons, which bind to the same receptors as opium.

Endorphins: A class of endogenous opioids.

Epigenetic mechanisms: Mechanisms that change the expression of genes without changing the DNA sequence itself. This can include methylation of DNA, acetylation of histones, and regulation by the products of other genes.

Epinephrine (adrenaline): A neurotransmitter.

Explicit memory (declarative memory): Memory that is conscious in human beings, or its unconscious homologs in animals, such as spatial memory, and the memory for a specific event in time.

Fornix: The output tract of the hippocampus.

Freezing: A fear response characterized by complete motionlessness except for breathing.

Functional magnetic resonance imaging (fMRI): A brain imaging technique that allows the activity of brain areas to be determined (and not just their structure).

GABA (gamma amino butyric acid): An inhibitory neurotransmitter.

GAD (glutamic acid decarboxylase): An enzyme that converts glutamate into GABA.

Gene expression: The generation of RNA and protein products in a cell. Different genes are expressed in different cell types, and in a given cell over the course of development, or in response to environmental stimuli.

Glucocorticoid receptor (cortisol): A receptor sensitive to cortisol and similar steroid hormones.

Glutamate: The most common excitatory neurotransmitter in the brain.

Handling: Holding, touching, and carrying an adult or infant animal.

Hippocampus: A subcortical structure in the brain that has been experimentally connected to the generation of explicit memories.

Hypothalamic–pituitary–adrenal (HPA) axis: The hierarchical anatomical system that governs the production of cortisol by the adrenal cortex.

Homeostasis: The tendency of a living organism to maintain a constant internal environment.

Hypothalamus: The most basal part of the thalamus, an important source of regulation of peripheral hormones.

Implicit memory: Unconscious memory, including conditioned associations, habits, and complex learned behavioral patterns, such as playing the piano or riding a bicycle.

Infralimbic cortex: A deep and medial portion of the frontal cortex.

Ion channels: Molecules in the cell membrane that form pores through which charged molecules, ions, can pass.

Ionotropic receptors: Receptors that form ion channels, which open or close when they bind neurotransmitters.

Long-term memory: Memory that lasts at least 24 hr. These memories clearly involve stable changes in synaptic structures.

Long-term potentiation (LTP): Lasting change in the response of one neuron to another, generated by a strengthening of the synaptic connection between the two.

Locus coeruleus: A nucleus in the brainstem that contains the cell bodies of neurons that use noradrenaline as a neurotransmitter. The axons of these neurons project throughout the brain.

Medial prefrontal cortex: The parts of the frontal cortex which are near the midline and anterior to the motor strip.

Methylation: The addition of methyl (CH_3) groups to other molecules, such as the base cytosine in DNA.

Morris water maze: A test of spatial learning and memory, in which a mouse or rat learns to find a platform hidden under the surface of a tank of milky water.

NMDA (*N*-methyl D-aspartate) receptor: An ionotropic receptor for glutamate that makes an ion channel for calcium. It has the special characteristic of being a coincidence detector because it requires the coincidence of both glutamate binding and postsynaptic depolarization to open.

Naloxone: A drug that blocks opioid receptors.

Neurotransmitter: One of the chemicals made by neurons and released by one neuron to communicate with another at a synapse, or connection between two cells.

Norepinephrine/noradrenaline: A neurotransmitter and precursor to the hormone epinephrine/adrenaline.

Neuroendocrine stress response: The coordinated nervous and hormonal response to stress.

Neurogenesis: The generation of new neurons.

Neurotransmitter: A molecule released by the axon (or output portion of a neuron), which binds to receptors in the same or other neurons to affect their function.

Noradrenergic system: The system of cells and receptors that use noradrenaline/norepinephrine as neurotransmitters.

Novel object recognition: A test of learning in which the animal demonstrates its memory for a familiar object by spending more time exploring a novel object.

Pavlovian (classical) conditioning: A simple form of learning in which an initially neutral stimulus, the conditioned stimulus (CS), is paired to a stimulus that evokes an intrinsic response, the unconditioned stimulus (US). The CS comes to evoke some of the response that would normally follow the US.

Paroxetine: A serotonin-selective reuptake inhibitor, one of a class of drugs used as antidepressant and antianxiety medications.

Periaqueductal gray: A brain stem area important for the behavioral expression of fear.

Phosphorylation: The addition of a phosphate group to a protein or other molecule. Phosphorylation by a protein kinase often modifies the function of a protein.

Positron emission tomography (PET): A method of brain imaging that localizes brain activity from the decay of radioactive isotopes.

Prepulse inhibition: Reduction of the brain response to a sound after the presentation of a softer sound shortly (tens of milliseconds) before it.

Propranolol: A beta adrenergic receptor antagonist.

Protein kinase: An enzyme that adds a phosphate to a protein.

Reinstatement: The reestablishment of a conditioned fear response after extinction by presenting a noxious stimulus (such as the unconditioned stimulus alone, with no paired conditioned stimulus).

Renewal: The return of conditioned fear after extinction, when the conditioned stimulus is presented in a context different from that of extinction training.

Resting potential: The negative charge of cell relative to its external environment. For a neuron the resting potential is usually around 50 to 70 millivolts.

Serotonin: A neurotransmitter.

Short-term memory: Memory lasting from minutes to a few hours.

Spontaneous recovery: The return of a conditioned response after extinction due to the passage of time alone.

Startle: A reflex muscular response to an unexpected stimulus.

Stress hormone: One of the hormones released by the adrenals – adrenaline or cortisol.

Sympathetic nervous system: The division of the autonomic nervous system that generally prepares the body to respond to stress or emergency and consists largely of adrenergic fibers.

Synaptic plasticity: The capacity of the strength of a synapse to change in response to the electrical activity of the pre- and postsynaptic cells.

Unconditioned stimulus (US): A stimulus that intrinsically elicits a specific response. Footshock is an unconditioned stimulus that elicits fear.

Upregulation: A regulated increase in the activity of a system.

Yohimbine: An antagonist of presynaptic alpha-2 adrenergic receptors. Activity of these receptors mediates autoinhibition of noradrenaline release by the neuron so that yohimbine tends to maintain high levels of noradrenaline activity.

Index